D0911837

Probation, Parole, and Community Corrections in the United States

Stephen G. Gibbons

Western Oregon University

John Dana Rosecrance

University of Nevada, Reno

PEARSON

Boston   New York   San Francisco
Mexico City   Montreal   Toronto   London   Madrid   Munich   Paris
Hong Kong   Singapore   Tokyo   Cape Town   Sydney

Series Editor: *Jennifer Jacobson*
Series Editorial Assistant: *Emma Christensen*
Senior Marketing Manager: *Kelly May*
Editorial-Production Service: *Omegatype Typography, Inc.*
Manufacturing Buyer: *Megan Cochran*
Composition and Prepress Buyer: *Linda Cox*
Cover Administrator: *Kristina Mose-Libon*
Electronic Composition: *Omegatype Typography, Inc.*

For related titles and support materials, visit our online catalog at www.ablongman.com.

Between the time Website information is gathered and published, some sites may have closed. Also, the transcription of URLs can result in typographical errors. The publisher would appreciate notification where these errors occur so that they may be corrected in subsequent editions.

Library of Congress Cataloging-in-Publication Data

Gibbons, Stephen G.
    Probation, parole, and community corrections in the United States / Stephen G. Gibbons, John Rosecrance.
        p. cm.
    Includes bibliographical references and index.
    ISBN 0-205-35946-9
    1. Probation—United States—History.   2. Parole—United States—History   3. Community-based corrections—United States—History.   I. Rosecrance, John.   II. Title.

HV9278.G53 2005
364.6'0973—dc22

                                                                      2004053441

Printed in the United States of America

10 9 8 7 6 5 4 3 2 1   09 08 07 06 05 04

To Will and Sean Gibbons. I cherish every moment with you both.

To the loving memory of my mother, Bernice Hahn Rosecrance, whose constant encouragement guided me into a lifelong love of education.

Contents

Preface

Probation and parole are vital components in the criminal justice system. In recent years they have taken on added significance as community alternatives to an overburdened prison system. Probation and parole courses are popular in criminal justice and sociology departments throughout the United States, serving as valuable training ground for future officers and administrators. As a former correctional practitioner and professor of criminal justice, John Rosecrance appreciates the importance of suitable classroom material. As a current criminal justice professor who is often called on to teach parole and probation, Stephen G. Gibbons is perhaps even more appreciative. Required texts make up the bulk of course reading material. Such texts should be readable, relevant, and theoretical while capturing the authenticity of probation and parole work.

The current text addresses these concerns and should please both professors and students. It features discussions of topical issues, such as intermediate sanctions, offender recidivism, supervision classification, restorative justice, electronic surveillance, house arrest, shock incarceration, and intensive supervision—issues that will dominate probation and parole for the next decade. The book presents an extensive analysis of the factors behind the decision by most contemporary probation and parole agencies to openly advocate restrictive supervision methods and close offender monitoring.

By presenting an authentic description of contemporary practices, the text demystifies the worlds of probation and parole. When students complete the book, they will recognize probation and parole work as an assignment at which they can succeed. Students will get a feel for what it is like to work as a probation or parole officer; they will be exposed to the "guts of the system." In addition, the book introduces theoretical concepts and historical perspectives that help explain the growth and development of probation and parole.

Authors' Perspective

It does not take much to realize that, in many jurisdictions, public, judicial, and academic support for probation and parole is tenuous. This is true for many community corrections programs as well. Budgets are down, caseloads are up, and workers are being laid off. All this despite the increasing numbers of people on probation and parole. It should not be surprising that in many agencies the vitality of the personnel and often of the conventional practices is hardly apparent. It would be accurate to state that times are tough in community corrections. In light of this situation, a bland recitation of current community correctional practices would be inappropriate. The current issues facing probation, parole, and other personnel working in community corrections must be clearly identified and objectively examined. Although at times it is necessary to present evidence critical of correctional practices, such information is presented in an effort to be constructive. Many readers of this book will soon be working in probation, parole, or in the various components of community corrections, and their informed input is needed.

Notwithstanding the problems confronting practitioners, this book is not a gloom-and-doom recital of the woes of community corrections. There are, in fact, many positive developments in the field. In Minnesota, for example, well-run departments that make positive differences in the lives of their clients administer probation. Georgia and Alabama have experienced success in reducing incarceration rates for nonserious felons at least in part because of the development of such probation-run intermediate sanctions as intensive supervision and shock incarceration. Throughout the United States, electronic monitors have been effective in monitoring probationers' and parolees' compliance with release conditions. In New York, state parole offices offer job placement services that have significantly improved the financial circumstances of released prisoners. And in Massachusetts, an intensive probation supervision program, emphasizing a combination of surveillance and treatment, resulted in a significant reduction in recidivism. In addition, in every probation and parole office there are dedicated officers who strive to be objective and fair in dealing with clients. Such workers need to be acknowledged and rewarded. Even though there are many problems facing community corrections, solutions are available if the jurisdictional bureaucracies will recognize and seize them.

At the same time community correctional agencies are faced with perplexing problems of funding and credibility, signs of revitalization have appeared. The serious problems faced by these agencies could lead many to abandon their traditional emphasis on the status quo and to start implementing meaningful change. Hopefully, as a result of the many challenges, community corrections will develop more realistic programs. The potential for such development will be helpful for future clients as well as correctional personnel and the communities they serve.

During this time of scarce financial resources, community corrections agencies may need to turn inward and develop the potential of their own personnel. Staff enrichment is a vital concern of all departments. Every department has an untapped reservoir of talent. Similarly, although restorative justice programs, prisoner reentry initiatives, and intermediate sanctions, such as intensive supervision, house arrest, and electronic surveillance, are promising developments, they will not yet affect the majority of offenders currently under community supervision. Many jurisdictions do not have these programs, or the criteria for offenders inclusion in the programs significantly restrict their usage. Most offenders will continue to receive "regular supervision" from "regular" probation and parole personnel. The needs and concerns of the offenders must not be overlooked in the rush to develop alternatives, no matter how promising. Effective supervision can be provided within the large regular caseloads found in most departments. New strategies in caseload management and classification provide clues to achieving this goal. The issue of employee burnout is a pressing concern because many of the best probation and parole workers either leave the field prematurely or develop overly cynical work attitudes. Organizational unresponsiveness, rather than excessive client contact, seems the most plausible explanation for wholesale employee discontent. Administrators have the potential to provide relatively inexpensive incentives that could effectively reduce staff burnout. Providing services for offenders with special needs, such as the mentally ill, the developmentally delayed, and substance abusers, will continue to be difficult. And, continuing to improve such community-based programs as pretrial release, halfway houses, and diversion will remain important to better serve those eligible for such programs, which ultimately means communities will be safer too. The challenges facing community corrections are great, but none are as great as the challenge to maintain the balance between assisting the offender and controlling him or her.

Acknowledgments

We wish to acknowledge the people who helped us write this book. The book would not have been completed without Jennifer Jacobson and the great staff at Allyn & Bacon. Several students gave assistance, most notably Toby Bottorff, John Fisher, Brian Walker, Toni Dragt, Debbie Hanson, and Ruth Taylor. We would also like to thank Bob Bersson for his encouraging words and editorial assistance on a couple of chapters; Billy, Sean, and Will Gibbons for their patience and support throughout the process; and Sean for his creativity in helping with the artwork in Chapter Eight. We would also like to acknowledge the libraries and staffs at the University of Nevada and Western Oregon University and the numerous reviewers who provided valuable advice: Donald Alsdurf, Kansas Community College; Joseph Arvidsun, Metropolitan State University/Concordia University; Joseph Carrier, Columbia College; Steven Hurwitz, Tiffin University; Howard Kurtz, Oklahoma City University; Deborah L. Laufersweiler-Dwyer, University of Arkansas; and Sudipto Roy, Indiana State University. Finally, Professor Rosecrance would like to acknowledge his loving wife Molly, who has been at his side for nearly 50 years; his children Ann, John, and William; and his sister Kathleen, for their support and confidence. He is also deeply appreciative of his trustworthy assistant and friend, Fred DiPasquale, for encouraging and challenging him, and his friend Susan Forkush, for believing in him and admiring his determination.

This text was developed and nearly completed by Professor Rosecrance until an automobile accident in the Australian Outback halted its progress. The resulting traumatic brain injury prevented Professor Rosecrance from completing the text. Dr. Stephen Gibbons updated and completed the text and Professor Rosecrance wishes to express his gratitude to Dr. Gibbons for his compassion and diligence in undertaking this project. "The individual can make a difference" is a statement Professor Rosecrance often shared with his students during his teaching career. This is truly exemplified by Dr. Stephen Gibbons' commitment to this work.

1

Probation, Parole, and Community Corrections

An Overview

Orientation to the Book

In Texas, there is public outrage when an inmate, convicted of multiple murders and sentenced to three 100-year terms, is paroled after serving only eight years in prison. In New York, similar public indignation is expressed after a nineteen-year-old, first-time (as an adult) offender pleads guilty to a brutal assault on an eighty-five-year-old woman. He is sentenced to prison; however, the imposition of the sentence is suspended, and the defendant is placed on probation for two years under the condition that he performs ninety hours of community service and reports to the probation officer as ordered. This type of disposition and the resulting outcry illustrate two central aspects of probation and parole: (1) They are designed to mitigate punishment, and (2) the public questions their usage.

In response to the public's outcry, policy makers and administrators throughout the United States are attempting to downplay the concept of mitigation and to emphasize instead the punishment and control features of current supervision practice. These administrators recognize a basic political reality: Unless the public's perception of probation and parole practice changes, correctional resources will continue to be shifted elsewhere, either to institutional corrections or to new private-sector alternatives. The question that must be addressed is whether public opinion can be improved by symbolic, short-term programmatic responses or whether fundamental changes in the underlying philosophy of probation and parole practice must be made.

At the core of any discussion of probation and parole "philosophy" is the concept of mitigation. *Webster's New Collegiate Dictionary* defines **mitigation** as the process of making mild, soft, or less severe. This process is the traditional basis of probation and parole. Whereas crime-fighting legislators are free to mandate draconian penalties and tough-sounding judges are encouraged to impose maximum sentences, the correctional system must deal with the realities of overcrowded facilities and the fact that incarceration, in some cases, can be counterproductive. In point of fact, it is not possible or practical for society to lock up all its offenders. In this sense, probation and parole, and other alternatives in the community, are the tools of mitigation—necessary but not appreciated.

Both probation and parole were invented in the nineteenth century, and since that time many criminal justice professionals have argued that these practices should be discontinued. Much of today's public would agree with this sentiment. The complexities of really dealing with offenders who are shaped by various societal and psychological forces do not appeal to the public. Rather, most prefer locking up the criminals and throwing away the key. **John Conrad,** a leading correctional theorist, once suggested that the public would never fully support probation and parole, and continued efforts to curry such support were counterproductive because they detracted correctional officials from discharging their main responsibilities of protecting society and reintegrating offenders into that society.[1] But regardless of whether the public supports probation and parole, both increased dramatically during the 1980s, the 1990s, and into the 2000s. In fact, by year-end 2001, there were more than 3.9 million adults on probation and more than 730,000 on parole.[2]

Parole (or postprison supervision) is the conditional release of incarcerated offenders to community supervision, whether by parole board decision or by mandatory conditional release, after serving a prison term and subject to a return to jail or prison for rule violations or other offenses. At one time thought to be on its way out because of determinate sentencing, parole has made a comeback, as prisons are full to overcrowding. Presently, incarcerated inmates simply must be released to make room for new prisoners. For example, at the present rate of prison commitment the Texas Department of Corrections must release 150 inmates on parole each day to remain in compliance with court-ordered population limits. Nationwide, the parole population increased 38 percent between 1990 (531,407) and 2001 (731,147).[3] Meanwhile, **probation,** which is a sentence to community supervision with conditions (which may include a short term of incarceration), has grown an average of 3.1 percent since 1990, increasing from 2,670,234 to 3,932,751 in 2001 for a total probation population growth rate of 47 percent.[4] Nationwide, 70 percent of all felony and misdemeanor offenses result in sentences of probation. These growth rates are occurring at the same time that cost-conscious county and state officials are cutting back on probation and parole budgets. Supervision caseloads of 300 are common in large jurisdictions. Many probation and parole officials have responded with familiar cries for more money and manpower. Their reasoning, often made without empirical support, is that if caseloads could be reduced, probation and parole could significantly reduce recidivism, or as McGruff the Crime Dog says: "Take a bite out of crime." It is in this context that the new wave of intermediate sanctions (e.g., electronic monitoring, intensive supervision, boot camps, and day reporting centers) have been developed as techniques to foster support for community-based corrections. Although probation and parole continue to be the major components of community corrections, community corrections also include all other sanctions not involving incarceration and in which the offenders serve all or part of their sentences in the community. Many of these other programs are administered by probation and parole departments around the country.

Probation officers and parole agents are traditionally pictured as dedicated workers whose opinions are influential in the sentencing process. In many instances, however, these officers and agents find their decisions structured by more powerful district attorneys and judges. Furthermore, in some jurisdictions, they have little input into the regulations that govern their workplaces. Internal criticism and questioning of department policies by staff have generally been discouraged by most correctional officials, often leading to situations where the administration has lost touch with street-level services. In the past, the administration of probation and parole had been characterized by bureaucratic rigidity and organizational inactivity. In order to be more effective, agencies in the field need to develop a new sense of mission and a new perspective as much as, if not more than, new funding. But before a viable mission can be suggested we need an overview of the policies, the personnel, the practices, and the past history of probation and parole. Based on extensive research efforts, and informed by two decades of work experience in the field by one of the authors, we provide such an overview in this book.

The Challenge

In an ongoing effort to restore public, judicial, and legislative confidence in their ability to adequately supervise offenders in the community, probation, parole, and community corrections officials have advocated and implemented more stringent supervision methods. Control, rather than assistance, is the new watchword. Whereas probation and parole traditionally maintained that rehabilitation and community protection were inseparable goals, community protection has now become the dominant concern. This shift is by no means universal. Often based on "what works" research,[5] some departments and jurisdictions continue to stress offender assistance, maintaining that clients need to be treated as much as they need to be monitored in order to fully protect the community. Such views, however, still seem to be in the minority, as most agencies have shifted to control models. The more punitive approach to offender supervision has changed the face of probation and parole.

Probation is often advertised as a retributive sentence. In the words of one administrator: "Let's call it control and mean it!"[6] The main goal of parole, in most departments, is strict monitoring, whereas offender reintegration is often relegated to a secondary concern. In the past it was not uncommon to hear calls for community corrections officials "to inform legislative bodies that community-based correctional programs are more than a slap on the wrist"[7] wanting to get the message across that offenders supervised in the community are carefully scrutinized by officers skilled in surveillance techniques. New classification schemes, technological gadgetry, and disciplinary programs are being used to make offenders responsible. Many states have instituted widely publicized **intensive supervision programs** with the avowed purpose of keeping probationers in check. **Electronic monitoring** of offenders is a popular supervision strategy because it guarantees around-the-clock surveillance. **Shock incarceration/boot camp** programs featuring physical training and military-type discipline followed by parole or probation supervision are used in more than thirty states and by the federal government.[8]

New programs and tougher supervision of regular caseloads are being proposed not only as safer methods of supervising offenders but also as cost effective alternatives to incarceration. Construction costs of jails and prisons generally range between $50,000 and $100,000 per cell, whereas estimates place the average annual cost of housing an inmate at $28,000 per year.[9] However, the cost of supervising a probationer or parolee for one year typically runs between $300 and $700 for minimum supervision probationers[10] to more than $8,000 for some intensive supervision probation and parole programs.[11] The more stringent supervision practices of probation and parole agencies are increasingly being termed **intermediate sanctions;** they are harsher than traditional supervision but not as restrictive, and much cheaper, than incarceration. But assistance remains necessary. We know treatment works for some offenders under some circumstances. Inmates released from prison often need a variety of services and help to successfully reintegrate into communities. Perhaps ironically, such assistance enhances the safety of communities by making it less likely that some of those assisted will reoffend. The tendency toward harsher control must be tempered by the effectiveness of assistance.

In order to adequately understand the response of probation and parole to contemporary challenges, it is essential to examine their place in the criminal justice system and to analyze the impact of a major shift in correctional philosophy. Although probation and parole remain a form of mitigation, it is a different and harsher form than has traditionally been associated with those services.

The Place of Probation and Parole in the Criminal Justice System

The 1967 President's Commission on Law Enforcement and Administration of Justice defined criminal justice as "the structure, functions, and decision processes of those agencies that deal with the management of crime—the police, courts and corrections."[12] Figure 1.1 graphically illustrates the movement of cases through the criminal justice system. Community corrections programs are found

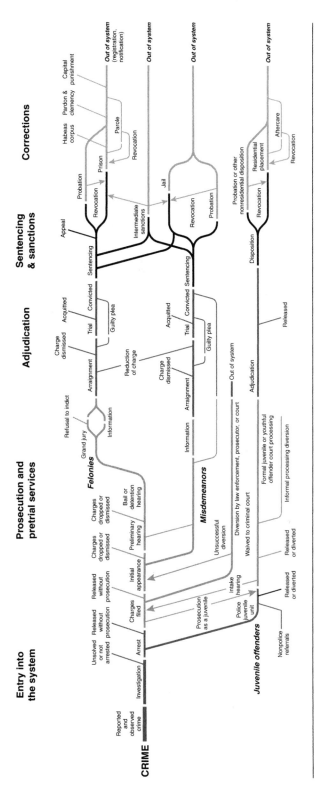

FIGURE 1.1 *What Is the Sequence of Events in the Criminal Justice System?*

Note: This chart gives a simplified view of caseflow through the criminal justice system. Procedures vary among jurisdictions. The weights of the lines are not intended to show actual size of caseloads.

Source: Adapted from *The Challenge of Crime in a Free Society.* President's Commission on Law Enforcement and Administration of Justice, 1967. This revision, a result of the Symposium on the 30th Anniversary of the President's Commission, was prepared by the Bureau of Justice Statistics in 1997.

at various levels of the system. There are diversion and pretrial release programs found at the preadjudication stage. Next, there are community corrections programs that receive their clients after the sentencing decision, with the goal of keeping offenders out of prison. These include restitution, community service, probation, intensive supervised probation, home confinement, and residential community facilities or halfway houses. The case flow continues to include community corrections after incarceration (or in combination with incarceration) with such programs as split sentence probation (some jail time followed by probation), shock probation (some prison time followed by probation), prison furlough programs, work and educational release, and parole programs.

All of these programs have the goal of reducing or eliminating criminal behavior. Therefore, the efforts of those working in community corrections will hopefully lead to offenders leaving the system never to return. However, those supervised in community corrections programs can reenter the system by either committing new offenses or violating their release conditions. It is important to note that judges place defendants on pretrial programs and sentence offenders to various community corrections programs, such as probation, whereas administrative bodies (e.g., parole boards or corrections departments) are in charge of parole.

One of the main tenets of **systems analysis** is that changes in one component have ramifications for the other components. This tenet helps explain the effect that changes in sentencing philosophy have had on contemporary community corrections. The implementation of determinate sentencing, an increased willingness on the parts of judges to impose prison sentences, and the abandonment of rehabilitation as a sentencing goal have directly affected community corrections. Determinate sentencing, where a strict range of penalties are set by legislative statute, has meant, in most jurisdictions, longer prison sentences. This type of sentence, combined with a more punitive judicial stance, has resulted in massive prison crowding and a nationwide prison construction binge. The explosion in the nation's prison population can be seen in Table 1.1. The major shift in sentencing philosophy was ushered in by what **Francis Allen** termed the "decline of the rehabilitative ideal."[13] Because changing attitudes toward rehabilitation have dramatically influenced the course of probation and parole, this demise should be examined in some detail.

The Demise of Rehabilitation

The rehabilitative ideal promised that "criminal offenders can be reformed or their behavior changed in such a way that they can live socially productive lives in their larger community without engaging in more criminal activity than most of their fellow citizens."[14] Although the rehabilitative ideal was espoused by prison reformers of the nineteenth century[15] it was not until the mid-twentieth century that it became a primary goal of sentencing. In 1949, Supreme Court Justice Black, writing the majority opinion in the *Williams v. New York* Supreme Court case, argued, "punishment

TABLE 1.1   *Change in the State and Federal Prison Populations, 1990–2002*

	Annual Increase in the Number of Prisoners		
Years	*Custody*	*Jurisdiction*	*Percentage Change*
1990	60,000	61,555	8.6
1991	49,153	51,640	6.7
1992	58,031	56,941	6.9
1993	58,815	64,992	7.4
1994	80,766	84,258	8.7
1995	88,395	71,172	6.7
1996	49,222	57,494	5.1
1997	48,800	58,785	5.0
1998	47,905	58,420	4.7
1999	36,957	43,796	3.4
2000	25,182	18,191	1.3
2001	14,647	15,521	1.1
2002	37,849	36,623	2.6
Average annual increase, 1995–2002	43,620	45,000	3.6

Source: Allen J. Beck and Paige M. Harrison, *Prisoners in 2000* (Washington, DC: U.S. Department of Justice, 2000) 3; Paige M. Harrison and Allen J. Beck, *Prisoners in 2002* (Washington, DC: U.S. Department of Justice, 2003) 3.

should fit the offender and not merely the crime." He rejected retribution as an appropriate sentencing consideration, stating, "Reformation and rehabilitation of offenders have become important goals of criminal jurisprudence."[16]

The *Williams v. New York* case served to legitimate the presentence investigation report, generally considered an instrument of individualized justice. Individual treatment of offenders was the cornerstone of the rehabilitative model of offender supervision, and probation and parole were thought to be integral components of that model. The rehabilitative ideal and its treatment-oriented approach to offender supervision flourished until the 1970s when both the ideal and its methods were assailed from several fronts.

The rehabilitative ideal found its natural expression in the medical model, whose message was persuasive: Diagnose the individual criminal's problem, develop a treatment plan to fix the problem, and then apply the treatment. The "cured" patient was released to parole officers who would continue the treatment until the offender was "rehabilitated."[17] Many probation and parole officers used this model to guide the "treatment" (supervision) of offenders. Unfortunately, in actual practice, the results of treatment were uncertain or even counterproductive. When individualized treatment failed to deliver cured offenders who stayed out of trouble, disillusionment with rehabilitation set in.

Somewhat surprisingly, among the first to express their disillusionment were inmates, as chronicled in the classic work *Struggle for Justice* by the American Friends Service Committee.[18] The problem, according to the inmates, was that prison officials supported the rehabilitative model because it was an effective means to control inmates. The treatment aspects always came second to control they argued. **John Irwin,** himself a former prisoner, described the discontent that was rampant among California inmates in the early 1970s:

> After prisoners were convinced that treatment programs did not work (by the appearance of persons who had participated fully in treatment programs streaming back to prison with new crimes or violations of parole), hope shaded to cynicism and then turned to bitterness. The disillusioned increasingly shifted their focus from their individual pathologies to their life situation. They realized that under the guise of rehabilitation the correctionalists had gained considerable power over them and were using this power to coerce prisoners into "phony" treatment programs and "chickenshit" prison routines. In addition, they realized that parole boards arbitrarily, whimsically, and discriminatorily were giving many prisoners longer sentences and bringing them back to prison for violations of parole conditions that most prisoners believed to be impossible.[19]

At about the same time that California inmates were voicing their criticism, conservative observers were also attacking the rehabilitation model.[20] The latter group, who had always opposed rehabilitation on philosophical grounds, became more vocal in denouncing the treatment methods used by corrections practitioners. Citing rising crime rates as "proof" that rehabilitation had failed, conservatives pressed their argument that deviant behavior could most effectively be deterred by judicial punishment. **James Q. Wilson** and **Ernest van den Haag,** influential professors, strongly denounced lenient judicial decisions and treatment approaches to community supervision. They published widely read books advocating long prison sentences to keep offenders off the streets and to reinforce the concept that crime does not pay.[21] The conservative critique of rehabilitation was particularly persuasive because fear of crime had become an important political issue. Legislators and politicians vied with one another to draft retributive sentencing statutes. Support for rehabilitation was waning, whereas the sentiment for punishment continued to mount.

A team of academic researchers delivered the final blow to the rehabilitation ideal. In 1975, after examining 231 studies of rehabilitation efforts in a wide variety of settings (ranging from prison to community supervision), Lipton, Martinson, and Wilks[22] reported: "With few and isolated exceptions, the rehabilitative efforts that have been reported so far have had no appreciable effect on recidivism. . . . These data are the best available and give us very little reason to hope that we have in fact found a sure way of reducing recidivism through rehabilitation."[23] The researchers' work, which came to be known as the *Martinson Report*, led to the conclusion that, with respect to rehabilitation, "nothing works!"

The report was widely publicized in the media and seized on by advocates of more stringent correctional methods. Although criticized by some academicians on the grounds of methodological errors, a panel of researchers specifically formed to independently survey rehabilitative techniques supported the *Martinson Report*'s main conclusions. The prestigious panel, funded by the National Academy of Sciences, concluded: "The entire body of research appears to justify only the conclusion that we do not know of any program or method of rehabilitation that could be guaranteed to reduce the criminal activity of released offenders."[24] Therefore, these gloomy predictions concerning the effectiveness of rehabilitation led many criminal justice elites to advocate either abolishing or severely restricting the use of probation and parole. A leading correctional figure, who at that time advocated ending parole, summed up the feelings of many concerning expanding supervision services by entitling his work: "Who Needs a Doorbell Pusher?"[25]

The late 1970s witnessed the temporary decline of community programs such as probation and parole. Support for programs that emphasized rehabilitation was further eroded by the development of the justice model. In his popular book *We Are the Living Proof*,[26] published in 1975, **David Fogel** presented a clearly defined model for fairness and justice in sentencing. In order to remove discretion from the system, Fogel advocated doing away with indeterminate sentencing (legislative statutes would determine sentence length), eliminating or scaling back on parole, and making correctional treatment programs strictly optional and not a requisite of preferential treatment or prison release. A few states actually did away with parole, and the growth of county probation agencies was severely restricted by budget cutbacks. The temporary retrenchment of probation and parole services that followed the demise of the rehabilitation ideal left those agencies unprepared for a sudden influx of clients. Once again, a change in one part of the criminal justice system was to dramatically affect probation and parole.

Community Supervision: An Alternative to Prison

The get-tough rhetoric of the early 1980s resulted in unparalleled prison commitments throughout the United States. Although some researchers attributed prison growth to "public demand,"[27] others have identified criminal justice elites (e.g., judges, district attorneys, attorney generals, and academicians) as the moving forces behind this development.[28] In any case, the nation's prisons soon were filled to overflowing, and many states embarked on a prison construction binge unparalleled in history. It became obvious that the prison population, in some measure, had to be restricted. The front door approach of probation and the back door release via parole were readily available options, and they were implemented. Therefore, the continuing increases in the use of probation, parole, and other programs to supervise offenders in the community did not result from a philosophical concern for more humane treatment but from a pragmatic reaction to the cost of prison crowding.

However, contemporary community corrections agencies generally no longer feel obligated to undertake extensive efforts to rehabilitate their new clients. Instead they have often opted to implement strict monitoring programs that are in line with a conservative correctional climate.

Summary

More punishment-oriented sentencing practices led to prison overcrowding, which eventually stimulated a resurgence in probation and parole and intermediate sanctions as pragmatic forms of mitigation. The supervision techniques used by community corrections agencies were in turn affected by disillusionment with prior rehabilitative programs. In many cases this led to the implementation of control rather than assistance models to make the mitigation process more acceptable.

Although the problems facing today's community corrections agencies seem compelling and unique, prior generations have faced similar situations. There are important lessons to be learned from identifying and describing the important historical developments that influence the creation and growth of probation and parole. A historical review of probation and parole is undertaken in Chapters Two and Three.

Key People and Terms

Francis Allen (6)
John Conrad (2)
Electronic monitoring (4)
David Fogel (9)
Intensive supervision program (4)
Intermediate sanctions (4)
John Irwin (8)

Mitigation (1)
Parole (2)
Probation (2)
Shock incarceration/boot camp (4)
Systems analysis (6)
Ernest van den Haag (8)
James Q. Wilson (8)

Key Legal Case

Williams v. New York

Questions for Discussion and Review

1. Are probation and parole populations increasing or decreasing? Why?

2. How has the practice of probation and parole changed during the past decade? What are the implications of this change for probation and parole officers?

3. How does the prison and jail crowding problem affect probation and parole?

4. How bad are the prison, jail, probation, and parole crowding problems in your state? Are you better off or worse off than other states in your region? How do you rank nationally?

Relevant Internet Sites

American Probation and Parole Association: www.appa-net.org

Bureau of Justice Statistics, for the latest parole and probation statistics click on the corrections tab: www.ojp.usdoj.gov/bjs

Bureau of Justice Assistance, for information on innovative programs: www.ojp.usdoj.gov/BJA

National Criminal Justice Reference Service, to look for U.S. government documents on probation and parole: www.ncjrs.org/corrhome.htm

Notes

1. John P. Conrad, "The Penal Dilemma and Its Emerging Solution," *Crime and Delinquency* 31 (1985): 421.

2. Lauren E. Glaze, *Probation and Parole in the United States, 2001* (Washington, DC: Bureau of Justice Statistics, 2002).

3. Glaze 1.

4. Glaze 1.

5. See, for example, P. Gendreau and D. Andrews, "Tertiary Prevention: What the Meta-Analysis of the Offender Treatment Literature Tells Us about 'What Works,' " *Canadian Journal of Criminology* 32 (1990): 173–184.

6. Walter L. Bardull, "Probation: Call It Control—And Mean It," *Federal Probation Quarterly* 40 (1976): 3–8.

7. Malcolm MacDonald, "Probation and Parole: Sanctions That Work," *Corrections Today* (February, 1986): 6.

8. Camille B. Camp and George M. Camp, *The 2000 Corrections Yearbook: Adult Corrections* (Middletown, CT: Criminal Justice Institute, 2000) 120.

9. Colorado Criminal Justice Reform Coalition, "Cost of Incarceration," Retrieved June 12, 2004, from www.ccjrc.org/pdf/costofincarceration.pdf.

10. North Carolina Department of Correction, "Cost of Supervision, FY 2001–2002," Retrieved June 13, 2004, from www.doc.state.nc.us/DOP/cost/cost2002.htm.

11. Colorado Criminal Justice Reform Coalition 1.

12. President's Commission on Law Enforcement and Administration of Justice, *The Challenge of Crime in a Free Society* (Washington, DC: U.S. Government Printing Office, 1967) 58–59.

13. Francis A. Allen, *The Decline of the Rehabilitative Ideal* (New Haven, CT: Yale University Press, 1981).

14. Lee Sechrest, Susan O. White, and Elizabeth D. Brown, eds., *The Rehabilitation of Criminal Offenders: Problems and Prospects* (Washington, DC: National Academy of Sciences, 1979) 11.

15. David Rothman, *Conscience and Convenience: The Asylum and Its Alternatives in Progressive America* (Boston: Little, Brown, 1980) 117–158.

16. Quoted in Allen 5.

17. Harry E. Allen and Clifford E. Simonsen, *Corrections in America: An Introduction,* 9th ed. (Upper Saddle River, NJ: Prentice Hall, 2001) 61–62.

18. American Friends Service Committee, *Struggle for Justice* (New York: Hill and Wang, 1972).

19. John Irwin, *The Felon* (Englewood Cliffs, NJ: Prentice Hall, 1970) 63.

20. Judith Wilks and Robert Martinson, "Is the Treatment of Criminal Offenders Really Necessary?" *Federal Probation Quarterly* 40 (1976): 3–9.

21. James Q. Wilson, *Thinking about Crime,* (New York: Basic Books, 1975); and Ernest van den Haag, *Punishing Criminals* (New York: Basic Books, 1975).

22. Reported in Robert Martinson, "What Works? Questions and Answers about Prison Reform," *Public Interest* 25 (1974): 22–25.

23. Martinson 25.

24. Lee Sechrest, Susan O. White, and Elizabeth D. Brown, eds., *The Rehabilitation of Criminal Offenders:*

Problems and Prospects (Washington, DC: National Academy of Sciences, 1979) 34.

25. John P. Conrad, "Who Needs a Doorbell Pusher?" *Prison Journal* 59 (1979): 17–26.

26. David Fogel, *We Are the Living Proof: The Justice Model for Corrections* (Cincinnati, OH: W. H. Anderson, 1975).

27. Joan Petersilia, Susan Turner, James Kahan, and Joyce Peterson, *Granting Felons Probation: Public Risks and Alternatives* (Santa Monica, CA: Rand Corporation, 1985).

28. Francis T. Cullen, Gregory Clark, and John F. Wozniak, "Explaining the Get Tough Movement: Can the Public be Blamed?" *Federal Probation Quarterly* 49 (1985): 16–24.

Part I

The Historical Background of Probation and Parole

Probation, which is granted by judges, and parole, which is administered by state agencies, are both used to mitigate judicial sentencing by allowing offenders to serve all or a portion of their sentences in the community. As community-based programs they are alternatives to incarceration: Probation generally is granted in lieu of incarceration and parole is an early release from incarceration. The offender's status in the community is conditional on maintaining law-abiding behavior and following certain release conditions. Both probation and parole developed from historical antecedents that are rooted in English common law. However, the widespread implementation of these concepts was a particularly American development.

In the United States, probation and parole had parallel patterns of growth and usage. These two services grew out of correctional reform movements. Champions of probation and parole offered them as humane and expedient solutions to the problems of incarceration (which ranged from inhumane conditions and counterproductive environments to severe overcrowding). Progressive reformers in the nineteenth and early twentieth centuries viewed probation and parole as integral components of offender rehabilitation. To them, prisons and jails had failed to reform and instead were "schools of crime" that should be avoided except for those few criminals who represented a clear and present danger to the community.

Probation and parole were first seen as possible prison alternatives in the latter part of the nineteenth century. Although a few states had experimented with probation or parole at that time, these services remained a novelty until the twentieth century. Between 1900 and 1920 the progressives were successful in establishing probation and parole as accepted and routine legal procedures. This development was a monumental shift in correctional philosophy that is reflected in the following statistics. In 1900 only six states sanctioned some form of probation, whereas in 1920 all states had juvenile probation and thirty-three states authorized adult probation. Prior to 1900 the overwhelming number of prison inmates served fixed sentences and were released only when their time had been fully served. By 1923 more than 50 percent of all prison releases were to parole.[1]

The progressive reformers were led by correctional "entrepreneurs"[2] who were successful in marshalling public, political, and judicial support for probation and parole. These leaders worked tirelessly to advance the legalization and funding of probation and parole departments. While advocates of the new probation and parole programs promised reform and rehabilitation, the actual implementation of these programs generally fell far short of stated goals. The gap between goals and reality was often so great that it can be questioned whether programs of offender rehabilitation were ever implemented.[3]

Chapter Two reviews the history of probation, and Chapter Three does the same for parole. The history of other forms of community corrections, such as halfway houses and electronic monitoring, as well as other historical material, is included in the text where appropriate.

2

The History of Probation

Early Forms

The concept of probation evolved gradually as an extension of English common law. Colonial America adopted and modified certain English sentencing precedents that, over time, formed the basis for the emergence of a formal probation system. A U.N. monograph on probation concluded the history of this concept should be "principally concerned with England and America" and further that "The origin of probation was not the result of a deliberate creative, legislative or judicial act, but rather the result of gradual growth, and almost unconscious modification of existing legal practices."[4]

The historical forerunners of probation all involved some form of mitigation. English jurists traditionally found ingenious ways to circumvent the severity of legal codes. This was done, in the words of the U.N. report, "to avoid the mechanical application of the harsh and cruel precepts of a rigorous, repressive criminal law."[5] As early as the tenth century, in the reign of the Anglo-Saxon king Athelstane, judges had established a rudimentary system to divert young offenders from receiving the death penalty. A court ruling from that period pronounced

> men should slay none younger than a fifteen winters' man. If his kindred will not take him nor be surety for him, then swear he as the bishop shall teach him, that he will shun all evil, and let him be in bondage for his price. And if after that he steal, let men slay him or hang him, as they did to his elders.[6]

Many of these early mitigation practices involved considerable judicial discretion and often were employed in an unsystematic and arbitrary manner. However, three practices emerged as routine legal alternatives to the immediate enforcement of sentence: (1) benefit of clergy, (2) judicial reprieve, and (3) recognizance. All of these procedures sanctioned suspension of either imposition or execution of sentence and as such were the precursors of probation. These three English practices were transported to the colonies and became integral parts of the American criminal justice system.

Benefit of Clergy

The **benefit of clergy** concept originated in eleventh-century England as a means to end the harsh penalties existing in secular or kings courts. At that time, the standard punishment for felonies was death by hanging. Clerics, such as nuns, priests, abbots, monks, and ordained clerks, were allowed to have their criminal cases transferred to ecclesiastic or bishops courts where the penalties were far less severe. This practice was later modified so that criminal cases were not actually transferred to a church court; instead, benefit of clergy cases were resolved in secular courtrooms. Such benefit was generally tantamount to acquittal because no evidence was presented against the cleric in these cases. Rather, the cleric gave testimony as to his or her version of the case and brought in witnesses who confirmed that story; thus it was not surprising that most cases ended with acquittal.[7]

The advantages of being granted benefit of clergy were so obvious that nonclerics attempted to have their cases disposed of in that manner. Some defendants claimed that although they were not under church orders, they were qualified to be religious clerks by virtue of their literacy.[8] English courts accepted this line of reasoning and by the sixteenth century benefit of clergy was routinely granted to those who could demonstrate their ability to read. In order to prove their reading proficiency, criminals were required to read passages from the Bible. The most commonly read passage was Psalm 51:

> [1]Have mercy upon me, O God, according to thy loving kindness: according unto the multitude of thy tender mercies blot out my transgressions.
> [2]Wash me thoroughly from mine iniquity, and cleanse me from my sin.
> [3]For I acknowledge my transgressions and my sin is ever before me.
> [4]Against thee, thee only, have I sinned, and done this evil in thy sight: that thou mightest be justified when thou speakest, and be clear when thou judgest.
> [5]Behold, I was shapen in iniquity; and in my sin did my mother conceive me.
> [6]Behold, thou desirest truth in the inward parts: and in the hidden parth thou shalt make me to know wisdom.
> [7]Purge me with hyssop, and I shall be clean: wash me, and I shall be whiter than snow.

This psalm became known as the "neck verse" because successful recitation of it saved defendants from the gallows. Some accused criminals, although unable to read, committed the neck verse to memory and were able to convince the court they deserved benefit of clergy.

When benefit of clergy was expanded to include nonclerics, courts took steps to restrict indiscriminate use. For example, convictions for particularly heinous felonies, such as treason, arson, murder, or rape, rendered defendants ineligible for benefit of clergy regardless of their clerical standing or reading ability. In other instances, after being granted benefit of clergy, defendants were branded on their thumbs: *M* for manslaughter or *T* for theft. This was done to ensure that defendants could have benefit of clergy only once for a class of felony.[9]

Benefit of clergy was imported to colonial America; however, the pretense of an ecclesiastic trial was abandoned and offenders were either released outright or branded. The colonials were vigorous in their branding techniques, typically burning the whole hand or imprinting a letter on the defendant's forehead. In 1628, court records reveal that a Virginia resident, after being convicted of manslaughter, was brought before the bench "being asked what hee had to say for himselfe that he ought not to dy demanded his clergy whereupon hee was delyvered to the ordinary."[10] In 1638, the Maryland assembly passed a bill allowing benefit of clergy to be granted for certain felonies, such as manslaughter, forgery, theft, or mayhem.[11] In an interesting development, which demonstrated the importance of tobacco, a Maryland statute of 1737 decreed, "Death as a felon without Benefit of Clergy" for offenders who burglarized a tobacco house.[12] In the Puritan colonies a modified benefit of clergy was routinely granted. A seventeenth-century Plymouth court record indicated that after being convicted of manslaughter, Robert Latham, "desired the benefit of law, viz., a psalve [Psalm] of mercye, which was granted him."[13]

As benefit of clergy was claimed by an increasing number of defendants it lost favor with the courts. In many cases women and noblemen were successful in convincing courts that they too should be granted clergy status. By the latter part of the eighteenth century there was general agreement that it had degenerated into "a clumsy set of rules which operated in favour of all criminals to mitigate in certain cases the severity of the criminal law."[14] Benefit of clergy fell into disuse until it was formally abolished in early nineteenth-century England and America.

Although benefit of clergy was not a direct antecedent of probation it did establish the precedent that certain categories of defendants were entitled to preferential treatment. In addition it advanced the concept that judicial rulings could appropriately mitigate the harshness of legal codes. The judicial implementation of benefit of clergy clearly formed the historic groundwork for the later development of probation.

Judicial Reprieve

It was commonplace by the seventeenth century for English judges to grant sentence reprieves in cases where mitigation seemed warranted. A **judicial reprieve** temporarily halted the execution of judgment and allowed defendants time to apply for a pardon. Judges were predisposed to grant reprieves in cases where the evidence was weak or unclear, reasoning that a royal or legislative pardon was possible. Reprieves were automatically given to pregnant women and those judged insane. When the women gave birth, the insane were cured, or pardons denied, sentences were then imposed. Although reprieves were originally intended as temporary measures, through inaction they often became more or less permanent suspensions. If judges, for what they deemed good cause, decided not to pursue a case, their inactivity allowed defendants to remain at liberty. This laid the groundwork for later claims that courts had the inherent right to indefinitely suspend sentences.

The concept of judicial reprieves was a part of the early American judicial system. The Massachusetts, Maryland, Rhode Island, and Connecticut colonies allowed their courts to issue reprieves.[15] The granting of reprieves was later expanded in nineteenth-century Massachusetts into a practice known as the *filing of cases*. Under this system, judges and prosecutors agreed not to impose immediate sentence on certain convicted defendants; instead the criminal cases were "filed," an act that suspended all further court action. The defendants remained at liberty under specific conditions set by judges and prosecutors. If defendants violated these conditions (usually by being arrested), they were brought back to court and their criminal cases reinstated. However, if defendants followed the agreed conditions, their cases remained "filed" indefinitely. The filing of cases was an early form of court probation that significantly involved the prosecutor's concurrence. The practice of filing was unique to Massachusetts and did not involve active supervision of defendants in the community.

Recognizance

An early English judicial practice that contained components of probation was the use of recognizance. The basis for **recognizance** was the assumption that persons with criminal tendencies could be forced, on pain of incarceration, to abide by certain conditions. Once a judge set the conditions, other community members would monitor compliance. The historian Bradley Chapin stated that there were two types of recognizance in seventeenth-century England, one for the peace and one for good behavior.[16] Judges would often ask for recognizance for the peace to end a threat of violence, asking a person to "swear the peace" against someone from whom he or she feared violence. Recognizance for good behavior was more general and could be applied to any suspicious person, often used for those accused of moral offenses. A bond for the peace or for good behavior usually required the offender to appear in court at a later date to decide if he or she had met the conditions of the bond. If the conditions were not met, the bond was forfeited to the king.

The small inward-looking communities found in colonial America facilitated the use of recognizance. In these isolated settlements it was readily apparent whether individuals were complying with the conditions of their recognizance. Colonial judges routinely used recognizance in cases of drunkenness, swearing, adultery, or simple assault. Use of this procedure involved judges as the arbiters and protectors of community morality. Apparently the recognizance system worked as available court records indicate that cases of forfeited bond were unusual.[17]

Massachusetts's courts were again the leaders in expanding the concept of judicial mitigation. In the famous 1830 *Commonwealth v. Chase* case, Judge Peter Oxenbridge granted recognizance without requiring that a bond be posted. His ruling describes the practice of recognizance prevailing at that time:

> The indictment against Jerusha Chase was found at the January term of this court. . . . She pleaded guilty to the same, and sentence would have been pronounced at that time, but upon the application of her friends, and with the consent of the attorney of the Commonwealth, she was permitted, upon her recognizance for her appearance in this court whenever she should be called for, to go at large. It has sometimes been practiced in this court in cases of peculiar interest, and in the hope that the party would avoid the commission of any offense afterwards, to discharge him on a recognizance of this description. The effect is that no sentence will ever be pronounced against him, if he shall behave himself well afterwards, and avoid any further violation of the law.[18]

Widespread use of recognizance served as both a symbolic and instrumental acceptance of suspended sentence and conditional release to the community. In this sense, it served as an undeveloped forerunner to probation. Therefore, by the middle nineteenth century sufficient precedents existed for the full development of the modern concept of probation. The catalyst for such development was to come from an unlikely source—a Boston bootmaker.

The First Probation Officer

Each profession has a pioneer to whom credit is given for "founding" the field. In probation this honor goes to **John Augustus,** generally considered the "father of probation." Claims to this paternity are disputed. Some have argued that probation first emerged in England, citing the fact that in 1841 an English recorder (judge) Matthew Hill had instituted a system of community supervision not unlike probation.[19] Hill allowed youthful offenders to be diverted from jail by suspending sentence and placing them under the supervision of a guardian. He reasoned, "There would be a better hope of amendment under such guardians than in the gaol of the county."[20] This program was later expanded to include informal police inquiries into the living situations of those released to guardians. Other scholars have contended that an 1836 Massachusetts law, which allowed municipal courts to release minor criminals on their own recognizance under the supervision of sureties, established a de facto probation system.[21]

Although the British jurist Matthew Hill and the Massachusetts legislation certainly did establish community supervision programs, it is our view that the honor of being the "father of probation" rightly belongs to John Augustus. Not only was Augustus the first to use the term *probation* in a correctional context but he was also the original source of practices that today are considered essentials of probation: investigation, selection of clients, maintenance of a case file, contacts with probationers in their environment, and presentation of progress reports to the court. In addition, he was successful in legitimating probation as a treatment process in the eyes of the court, the legal profession, and the public, while also attracting other workers to the field. A bootmaker accomplished all these achievements with no legal or academic background.

The modern history of probation began in a small Boston courtroom with the bailing of a common drunk. John Augustus (whose business was located near the police court) described the first probation case:

> In the month of August, 1841, I was in court one morning, when the door communicating with the lockroom was opened and an officer entered, followed by a ragged and wretched looking man, who took his seat upon the bench allotted to prisoners. I imagined from the man's appearance, that his offense was that of yielding to his appetite for intoxicating drinks, and in a few moments I found that my suspicions were correct, for the clerk read the complaint, in which the man was charged with being a common drunkard. The case was clearly made out, but before sentence had been passed, I conversed with him for a few moments, and found that he was not yet past all hope of reformation. He told me that if he could be saved from the House of Correction, he never again would taste intoxicating liquors; there was such an earnestness in that tone, and a look of firm resolve, that I determined to aid him; I bailed him, by permission of the Court. He was ordered to appear for sentence in three weeks from that time. He signed the pledge and became a sober man; at the expiration of this period of probation, I accompanied him into the courtroom. . . . The Judge expressed himself much pleased with the account we gave of the man, and instead of the usual penalty—imprisonment in the House of correction—he fined him one cent and costs, amounting in all to $3.76, which was immediately paid. The man continued industrious and sober, and without doubt has been by this treatment, saved from a drunkard's grave.[22]

From this rather inauspicious beginning probation spread until today almost four million Americans find themselves "on probation." The remainder of this chapter describes how this was accomplished.

The Expansion of Probation

The Boston judge who witnessed the resurrection of the "wretched looking man" encouraged John Augustus to take care of other problem drinkers who appeared in his court. During the next year Augustus stood bail for almost two dozen defendants charged with drunkenness. After participation in a supervised temperance program, the probationers were returned to court in a sober condition. Both the judges and Augustus were encouraged by these successes and it was agreed that other classes of defendants charged with such offenses as theft, public disturbance, battery, and lewd conduct were to be considered possible candidates for probation. Many of these new probationers were women who had "fallen from grace." In the course of supervising and counseling such women Augustus invariably involved himself with their children. His work with children became well known, and on several occasions court and police officials asked him to supervise wayward youth. In the process of fulfilling such requests Augustus, in effect, became a juvenile probation worker.

From all accounts, Augustus was a tireless worker who, from 1841 on, devoted his entire life to probation services. After three years of probation work his involvement with court duties had become such an all-consuming endeavor that he was forced to give up his bootmaking business. During his seventeen-year tenure as America's first probation officer John Augustus was an unpaid volunteer. In his autobiography Augustus explains his status as an unaffiliated volunteer:

> I devote my time daily; and often a large portion of the night, in the performance of the various labor which fall into my province. I am no agent for any sect, society or association whatever. I receive no salary, neither have I received a dollar for any service as a salary.[23]

After his own business closed Augustus received donations from wealthy Bostonians who supported his work. In addition, the Unitarian Church and the Washington Temperance Society provided funding for many of the treatment programs used by probationers. Augustus, somewhat defensive about private donations, kept painstaking records to prove that he had not profited from probation work. According to his accounting, all contributions were expended in the service of probationers; nothing was put to personal use.[24]

A System Develops

As John Augustus expanded his probation activities he found it necessary to keep accurate records on those he bailed. Toward this end, he developed a case file in which each probationer's legal and personal history was recorded along with periodic progress reports. With an eye to external scrutiny, Augustus developed a method of accountability wherein a roll of his overall efforts was maintained. The roll system was used to advance the conception of probation and offender rehabilitation. Legislative records of an 1848 committee considering a shelter for drunkards (what today would be termed a *detoxification center*) reveal a knowledge of Augustus's work and the detail contained in his roll for 300 men and women whom he had "saved." The roll included the date of conviction, the sentence length, and fines paid.[25]

The first probation officer did not confine his activities to the courtroom; instead he made frequent visits to the residences and workplaces of probationers. These field calls were conducted in a horse carriage. In one year Augustus claimed to have traveled 15,000 miles in order to make more than 1,500 calls on probation business. He wryly remarked in his journal that the horse survived these comings and goings none the worse for wear but three chaises had to be replaced.[26] In many cases those placed on probation had no permanent residence. The volunteer probation officer responded to this problem by setting up a type of halfway house that allowed homeless probationers a temporary abode until more permanent living quarters could be located. The temporary shelter afforded the homeless was in typical Augustus manner—his residence.

John Augustus did not accept all those who desired his services, but instead developed elaborate screening methods. By being selective, Augustus sought to ensure a high rate of success thereby gaining acceptance for his probation system. In the ensuing years advocates of new probation techniques have used similar reasoning. While trying to facilitate the selection process, Augustus developed a presentence investigation format, taking great care to determine whether the convicted he reviewed held promise for probation. In doing this investigation, he looked into their character, age, and social influences. In those cases for which probation was deemed appropriate, Augustus would make sure they went to school or acquired a good job, and he reported to the court whenever they required it.[27] Despite all of this good work, Augustus was not without his detractors. These are discussed next.

Criticisms of Augustus

The pioneering work of John Augustus was not without its critics. Criticisms united around three points: (1) probation was too lenient a disposition, (2) court officials were financially hurt by probation, and (3) Augustus was abrasive and contentious.

Lenient Probation.   Some criminal court observers (not unlike their "get-tough" counterparts today) decried the mitigating component inherent in the concept of probation. These critics assumed that judicial mitigation would be taken the "wrong way" by the criminal community, and in fact would encourage rather than deter illegal activity. Such criticism was referred to by Augustus:

> Those who are opposed to [probation] tell us that it is rather an incentive to crime and, therefore, instead of proving salutary, it is detrimental to the interest of society, and so far from having a tendency to reform the person bailed, it rather presents inducements for them to continue a career of crime; the law is robbed of its terrors, and its punishments, and there is nothing, therefore, to deter them from repeating the offence with which they were previously charged.[28]

Other critics complained that convicted criminals would never be rehabilitated by probation supervision—no matter how well intended. To these critics Augustus used his success with his own clients to reply, pointing out that his ratio of success to failure was three to one and that his own efforts have saved hundreds of people from a life of drunkenness and crime.[29]

Court Officials Hurt by Probation. Police officers, process servers, court clerks, and turnkeys in Massachusetts led the opposition to probation. Their motivation was a simple one—it cost them money. For example, in each probation case police officers and process servers lost a seventy-five-cent fee delivering defendants to jail, the clerk a twenty-five-cent recording fee, and the turnkey forty cents for accepting the offender into jail. The opposition of court officers was generally offset by judicial support for Augustus's efforts.

John Augustus was single-mindedly determined to advance the idea that probation was a necessary tool of rehabilitation. On many occasions he admonished judges, court officials, and the public, "the object of law was to reform criminals and to prevent crime and not to punish maliciously or from a spirit of revenge."[30] From his perspective, reformation often was enhanced by a period of probation supervision.

Augustus was also critical of judicial sentencing, observing that judges sometimes are biased against poor people in their sentencing, and that is one reason he bailed some of the more "pitiable objects" whenever he could.[31] He further took upon himself the responsibility of monitoring judicial fairness, familiarizing himself with prisoners' offenses and conditions, and helping those without much reason to hope because of their poverty and relative powerlessness compared to that of the prosecuting attorney. He, therefore, took it upon himself to ". . . inquire who was imprisoned that should go free."[32]

An Abrasive and Contentious Augustus. Mike Walsh, a Boston reporter, described Augustus in an 1848 newspaper account and found him to be a pretentious conniver, stating that he had "a great itching for notoriety" and believed his arrogance needed to be put in its place. Walsh also implied that Augustus was using probation as a means of making money ("bleeding thousands") and that by bailing women, he was "gratifying other propensities," concluding that unless Augustus changed his ways, Walsh would take it upon himself to "teach him decency."[33]

Apparently John Augustus was able to successfully counter criticisms of both probation and his personality because he continued bailing offenders until his death in 1859. In 1858, Augustus released a record, or roll, indicating that since 1841 he had bailed 1,946 persons: 1,152 males and 794 females. Of the first 1,100 cases bailed to probation, Augustus claimed a fantastic success rate—only one forfeited bail. In retrospect this claim seems suspect and was probably made to enhance acceptance of a fledgling probation system. Notwithstanding this caveat, John Augustus was a true visionary who almost single-handedly developed what has become a taken-for-granted component of the criminal justice system. In the best sense, he was his brother's keeper.

The plaque in Figure 2.1 can be found on the outer wall of the Boston City Hall Annex and commemorates the one-hundred-year anniversary of probation. It is a fitting testimonial to John Augustus. An excerpt from the Boston journal *Raising the Veil* located by Sheldon Glueck and included in his Preface to the 1939 edition of Augustus's autobiography describes a typical day in the life of our

FIGURE 2.1   *John Augustus:*
The Father of Probation

first probation officer.[34] The article describes Augustus as a tireless philanthropist in court every day to bail the less fortunate. It also suggests that he had an affinity for attractive women, pointing out that he did not bail one unfortunate woman because she was "too old and ugly" and that his house was "swarmed" with fair-looking females. But generally, the article is very flattering toward the man, pointing out that many of his charges have been reformed and that there is no doubt that he had done much good.

1860–1900: Slow Growth

By 1860 probation had become part of a common law system in that suspending sentences, bailing on probation, and returning probationers to court for either revocation or dismissal were generally accepted judicial prerogatives.[35] Probation expanded slowly for the next forty years, at first through increased public and judicial acceptance and then through enabling legislation. This sequence first occurred in Massachusetts and then spread to other states. However, until 1878, probation work remained the province of volunteers.

Volunteerism

None of the volunteer probation officers that followed John Augustus were able to match his zeal or dedication. His handpicked successor, John Spear, finding expectations from the bench and community too demanding, gave up probation work after four years. Spear was thus the first (but not the last) probation officer to experience burnout. When the Boston Children's Aid Society was founded in 1863, the pace of probation activity increased. Several agents of the Aid Society became involved, on an informal basis, in bailing probationers—both adults and children. The U.N. report describes the activities of these volunteers as men who carry out the essential mission of probation: investigation of defendants before release, regular reports, and home visits, although all of their efforts were of the "rescue sort." Thus, their investigations were "meager," the probation programs very short, and there really were no treatment plans or close supervision.[36]

The most famous of the Children's Aid Society agents was **Rufus "Uncle" Cook** who also served as chaplain for the Suffolk County Jail. He did keep accurate records, witnessed by the report of his activities for 1870: "I have bailed, during the year, about 450 persons of all ages from sixty down to little children. One hundred and sixty-four of them within the last three months. I judge that 87 percent of these persons, put on probation, have done and are doing well."[37] One of Cook's associates was Miss L. P. Burnham who frequently conducted background checks of probationers, provided supervision for those bailed, and is credited with being the first career woman in probation.[38] Rufus Cook regularly attended the monthly superior court sessions and occasionally accepted felons on probation for six-month periods of supervision. As the volunteer probation officers became a regular part of Boston courts, it was only a matter of time before one of their number would be accorded official status.

Legalization: Massachusetts

Predictably, the step toward official status of the position of probation officer came from the state of Massachusetts. Passage of the 1869 Board of Charities Act authorized "the appearance of some qualified persons who would act as the friend of the child" and "encouraged the policy of putting juvenile offenders on probation." A state Visiting Agency was formed and juvenile probation was a reality. From 1869 until 1879, 4,892 Massachusetts children were placed on juvenile probation.[39]

The first adult probation law, sponsored by Michael J. Flatley, a senator for Suffolk County, was introduced into the Massachusetts Assembly in 1878. With little debate, Chapter 198 was passed, and the mayor of Boston was authorized to hire a probation officer for Suffolk County. The probation bill provided for annual appointment of a "suitable person either from the ranks of the police force or from citizens at large" who would be supervised by the chief of police (probation officers were to remain under police control for the next thirteen years).[40]

The language of the bill clearly indicated that probation was to be a form of mitigation. It specified those eligible for probation as "such persons as may reasonably be expected to be reformed without punishment."[41] No legal restrictions were placed on the type of defendant eligible; therefore, all misdemeanants and felons were probation candidates. The probation bill delineated the duties of a probation officer: "court attendance, the investigation of the cases of persons charged with or convicted of crimes, the making of recommendations to the courts with regard to the advisability of using probation, the submission of periodical reports to the chief of police, visiting probationers and the rendering of such assistance and encouragement [to probationers] as will tend to prevent their again offending."[42] If probationers failed to respond to supervision or committed new offenses, they were to be returned to court so that judges could "proceed to sentence or make such other disposition of the case as may be authorized by law."[43]

The first probation officer appointed under the act was Lieutenant Hemmenway of the Boston Police Department. He left the post after only four months to accept a captaincy with the police force. An ex-chief-of-police Edward Savage was then appointed, and served fourteen years at an annual salary of $1,500. After one year on the job Savage reflected on his new assignment and the complexities of probation work: "Years of police service offer opportunity to learn much of city life; but the last year has brought to my notice, even in the better walks of life, trials, temptations, and struggles new to me. Causes that lead to vice and crime lie hidden beneath the surface that are but little known or understood."[44]

The Massachusetts assembly was favorably impressed with "its very important experiment" and in an 1880 amendment granted all cities and towns the right to appoint their own probation officers.[45] In 1891, the Massachusetts legislature, firmly convinced of probation's merit, mandated that all municipal courts must have probation officers (in 1898 this was broadened to include superior courts) in regular attendance. With this statute, Massachusetts effectively established a statewide department of probation. Significantly, the 1891 statute transferred authority to appoint and supervise probation officers from the mayor to the courts, and further stated that active members of police forces were *not* to be considered for probation posts. The legislators reasoned that probation officers could be more objective if they were separated from mayoral offices and police departments, a distinction that remains today. By the latter part of the nineteenth century, probation in Massachusetts was firmly established both in practice and in statute. The fact that our first probation officers had *police* backgrounds suggests that the newest wave of surveillance-oriented community corrections programs may actually reflect a *return* to probation's roots rather than a radical departure from "traditional" probation practice.

Probation in Other States

Although various forms of juvenile probation were enacted in Michigan in 1873, New York in 1875, and Baltimore in 1894, adult probation developed more slowly. It was not until 1898 that Vermont became the second state to adopt a comprehensive adult probation law. Vermont established probation departments on a county level with each department operating independently, governed only by the framework of the state law. The county-based administrative probation unit was later adopted by a majority of states. In 1899, Rhode Island passed a probation law that was significant for a provision making defendants convicted of certain crimes (for example, murder, rape, and treason) ineligible for probation. Most states have followed Rhode Island's lead by ruling out certain offenses from probation regardless of extenuating factors. In 1900, only three states had full-fledged adult probation systems. In the next twenty-five years this number was to change dramatically as an age of unparalleled correctional reform swept the United States.

1900–1925: Probation Comes of Age

In the first two decades of the twentieth century, probation was an idea whose time had arrived. A score of states passed probation legislation without controversy or spirited debate. Figure 2.2 indicates when the various states first passed probation laws. Probation was wholeheartedly endorsed by a diverse coalition of social workers, psychiatrists, sociologists, newspaper editors, criminologists, legislators, and civic-minded citizens, as well as by judges, district attorneys, and prison directors. A new breed of enterprising practitioners advanced the probation concept and a Supreme Court decision solidified its legal basis. Support for probation reached its zenith in the successful campaign for a federal probation system, which was finally realized by passage of the **Federal Probation Act** in 1925.

Ideological Underpinnings

The implementation of probation systems was considered an integral component in an overall program of correctional reform. This perspective held that progressive reforms would be lightening rods in turning away from outmoded philosophies of revenge and retribution. **Charles Chute,** a probation supporter whose contributions are discussed more thoroughly shortly, described the importance of achieving such a philosophical turn by pointing out that even more important than changing the laws and the system of punishment, there was an even greater need to change the public's attitude toward the offender. Specifically, Chute argued that "primitive emotions" such as hatred, revenge, and fear must be controlled, and the thought that offenders are all equally responsible and cannot be reformed, must all be replaced by a more "rational, altruistic, humane, and . . . a more civilized outlook."[46]

Central to the concept of reform was the assumption that causes of crime could be determined and subsequently corrected. At that time there were two prevailing explanations for criminality. The first explanation maintained that environmental forces caused crime; the second prevailing belief was that psychological abnormalities caused criminality. In both instances individual offenders should

FIGURE 2.2   *States with Juvenile and Adult Probation Laws, 1923*

States	Year Enacted Juvenile	Adult
Alabama	1907	1915
Arizona	1907	1913
Arkansas	1911	1923
California	1903	1903
Colorado	1899	1909
Connecticut	1903	1903
Delaware	1911	1911
Georgia	1904	1907
Idaho	1905	1915
Illinois	1899	1911
Indiana	1903	1907
Kansas	1901	1909
Maine	1905	1905
Maryland	1902	1904
Massachusetts	1878	1878
Michigan	1903	1903
Minnesota	1899	1909
Missouri	1901	1897
Montana	1907	1913
Nebraska	1905	1909
New Jersey	1903	1900
New York	1903	1901
North Carolina	1915	1919
North Dakota	1911	1911
Ohio	1902	1908
Oklahoma	1909	1915
Oregon	1909	1915
Pennsylvania	1903	1909
Rhode Island	1899	1899
Tennnessee	1905	1915
Utah	1903	1923
Vermont	1900	1900
Virginia	1910	1910
Washington	1905	1915
Wisconsin	1901	1909

Source: Adapted from Fred R. Johnson, *Probation for Juveniles and Adults,* pp. 12–13. (New York: Century Co., 1928.)

not be held totally responsible for their behaviors. Environmentalists maintained that members of disorganized or slum-ridden neighborhoods were literally driven to crime by the poverty of their situations. Proponents of psychological explanations held that mental difficulties predisposed one to criminal activity. In either scenario the offenders' criminality was determined by factors over which they themselves had little or no control. Supporters of both explanations agreed that probation officers should be the ones to diagnose the individual's "problem" and initiate programs of rehabilitation.

Advocates of probation were fueled by unbridled optimism that the social sciences would find cures for criminality, cures that could be incorporated into programs of community supervision. Their optimism was part of the positive philosophy that, in large part, had been taken from the writings of Cesare Lombroso, perhaps best known for his notion of a "born criminal." The American Institute of Law translated and popularized Lombroso's work in the early twentieth century. The institute contended that his research was "scientific" validation that the future of criminology is individualizing correctional treatment for each criminal and for each crime.[47] Simply put, this meant the classical dictum that "punishment should fit the crime" would be turned on end, and in the future "punishment would fit the offender." Although the correctional pendulum would shift in the 1970s, for the time being, probation was seen as an ideal tool to achieve that end. And, as an added bonus, the fledgling probation systems provided tangible benefits for key criminal justice figures.

Although probation was typically presented under a banner of reform, there were a variety of philosophical and pragmatic dynamics that helped explain its near universal acceptance. Historian David Rothman believed that it was not just the ideological underpinnings of probation that made it so appealing—promising to change the system *and* make it more effective—but there were also practical reasons wardens, judges, and district attorneys supported the practice. In fact, each group could see some very concrete ways that they would benefit from probation.[48]

Pragmatic Acceptance

For the wardens of the United States, the benefits were a direct result of the population of the nation's prisons at the time. As the twentieth century began, the U.S. prison system was in the throes of a crowding crisis. Recent immigrants from Eastern Europe swelled the inmate population. Immigrant inmates combined with a growing number of urban offenders to seriously strain existing facilities. Although prison construction was moving ahead, it could not keep pace with the number of new commitments. Wardens throughout the United States supported both probation and parole as effective and relatively inexpensive ways to deal with overcrowding.

The vast majority of judges were enthusiastic supporters of probation and generous in their praise of probation officers. Richard Tuthill, a prominent Chicago jurist, called probation "the cord upon which all the pearls of the court were strung."[49] From a practical standpoint, judges had much to gain by probation because it extended their discretion and authority, while leaving their sentencing options intact. It should be made clear that judges were under no obligation to grant probation and were always free to impose sentence within statutory boundaries. Furthermore, there were no ready avenues for appealing a probation sentence. In most jurisdictions it was judges who were to select probation officers and to supervise their work. Presentence reports compiled by probation officers were useful sentencing guides that in no way restricted judicial decision making. However, the existence of probation reports would allow judges to evade responsibility; they could announce that although they did not necessarily agree with a recommendation, their "hands were tied" and therefore were "reluctantly going along" with the probation officer's plan.

The use of probation allowed the judiciary to exert more control over the lives of defendants. Whereas the judge's authority ends with the imposition of a terminal sentence (fine or incarceration), probation allows judicial authority to remain in force for the duration of probation. During the probation period, judges could request periodic reports as to how defendants were complying with the various conditions of release. Judges had always been uneasy about openly granting mitigation, fearing it would be construed as too lenient or a deliberate evasion of legislative intent. By sentencing an offender to probation, judges could grant a measure of mitigation while also appearing firm and legalistic. Judges could sternly admonish defendants that their behavior would be closely monitored by probation officers, and failure to comply with court orders would subject the defendants to the full force of the law.

District attorneys, although not openly agitating for probation, certainly did not oppose its implementation. As traditional advocates of tough sentences, their lack of opposition was viewed as tacit approval for this new sentencing alternative. Because prosecutors generally have considerable influence with state legislators, they could have presented a formidable roadblock to new legislation. While making statements that probation rules must be vigorously enforced, district attorneys did not oppose the basic concept.

The district attorney's acquiescence to probation was significantly enhanced by the specter of crowded courts. Because they were charged with the major responsibility for moving cases through court, the massive increases in criminal cases that greeted the twentieth century made prosecutors receptive to programs that would facilitate the quick resolution of criminal charges. Prosecutors had increasingly turned to plea bargaining as a pragmatic solution to clogged court calendars. Probation offered them a valuable negotiating wedge in this process. District attorneys could now offer the defendants a tangible benefit to pleading guilty—a guaranteed grant of probation (judges invariably went along with plea bargains). From the defendant's perspective, the certainty of an immediate grant of probation was far superior to the risk of future trial and the possibility of incarceration. The prosecutor could satisfy his or her law and order responsibilities, reasoning that during a probationary period the criminal justice system retained jurisdiction over offenders and could always sentence them at a later date to the full term prescribed by law. Probation, by encouraging guilty pleas, made district attorneys' jobs easier, while not seriously compromising their roles as sentencing hard liners.

The **Killits** *Case*

With major players in the criminal justice system backing the concept of probation, many states enacted formal laws making the practice legal. Moreover, by the early twentieth century, courts in states without a formal probation law had been routinely granting probation under the assumption that such power was granted them by common law. Because of this, state legislators in such states felt no compelling reason to enact formal probation laws. However, legislative inattention to probation ended when the U.S. Supreme Court decided the *Killits* case (Ex part U.S. 242-US-2753, 1916).

Judge Killits, a northern Ohio federal judge, had suspended the five-year sentence of a defendant convicted of embezzling $4,700 from a Toledo bank.[50] The defendant did not have a prior record and had agreed to make full restitution to the bank. One of the few opponents of probation, U.S. Attorney General T. Gregory, claiming Judge Killits had exceeded his authority in suspending the sentence, asked the Supreme Court to vacate the decision that had placed the defendant on probation. On December 1, 1916, the Supreme Court held that judges had no "inherent power to suspend sentence permanently or indefinitely."[51] This was quite a blow to the judicial system because 5,000 federal prisoners were under suspended sentences at the time. A strict legal interpretation of this decision meant that those on suspended status should be immediately sentenced to prison. However, this would have placed an unusual strain on the prison system; consequently, the suspendees received presidential pardons from Woodrow Wilson on June 11, 1917.[52]

Ironically, even though the attorney general had won this case, he did not achieve his goal of doing away with probation; in fact just the opposite occurred. The majority opinion written by Chief Justice Edward White, while rejecting the common law argument, indicated that legislative bodies, by statute, could authorize indefinite suspension of sentence. This ruling upheld an earlier New York state court decision (*Forsythe v. Court of Sessions*) that similarly held that courts had the right of suspension, if that had been granted by statute. The *Killits* case guaranteed that in the future probation systems would be governed by legal statute.

The U.N. monograph detailing the history of probation concluded that rather than slowing probation's growth, the *Killits* decision "actually served as a stimulus for the enactment of statutes expressly authorizing the suspension of sentence and probation."[53] The *Killits* case clearly specified that through enabling legislation, state and federal courts could qualify for the right to use suspended sentences. The concept of probation at last had a firm legal basis. In time all states and the federal government enacted laws authorizing suspended sentences as part of probation. At the federal level, the lobbying effort was led by the National Probation Association (NPA) and one of its founders, Charles L. Chute.

A Moral Entrepreneur: Charles Chute

Sociologists use the term *moral entrepreneur* to describe leaders who are able to convince the public and influential groups that a new social movement should be legitimated.[54] Such a term definitely applies to Charles Chute, probation advocate par excellence.

If John Augustus is the father of probation, Charles Lionel Chute ("Charlie" to his friends) should be considered its adolescent guardian. In 1907, Chute helped found the National Probation Association. Using this organization as a base for the next forty years, he led a relentless crusade to advance the probation movement. David Dressler, a criminologist who worked with the probation leader, described Chute as a master organizer, promoter, and public relations man. Dressler credited Chute with convincing many judges to use probation, and he conducted numerous surveys that indicated the need for probation services. But according to Dressler, Chute's greatest contribution to probation was giving the field direction and momentum, making it conscious of itself as a professional field.[55] Perhaps Chute's crowning achievement was his effort on behalf of the federal probation law.

The Federal Probation Law.   Beginning in 1909, thirty-four bills were introduced (many sponsored by the National Probation Association and Charles Chute) to establish a federal probation law. Finally, in 1925 a Federal Probation Act was passed. It succeeded not because of a groundswell of public opinion but from the determined efforts of Chute and his associates, and the retirement of a key congressional committee member. The bill was also seen as a solution to the perplexing problem of what to do with the new "criminals" created by Prohibition.

Some federal judges had opposed a probation law in principle and agreed with the sentiments of Judge Foster Symes of Colorado: "My observation of probation law is that it has been abused and has tended to weaken the enforcement of criminal laws. What we need in this country is not a movement to create new officials with resulting expense, but a movement to make the enforcement of our criminal laws more certain and swift."[56] The federal attorney general's office was generally opposed to probation. A staff assistant called it "maudlin rot and misplaced sympathy for criminals."[57] (Some prosecutors and judges express similar sentiments in the modern era.)

Notwithstanding such opposition, Chute and colleagues at the NPA, by virtue of extensive lobbying for fifteen years, were able to convince most judges and political leaders of the merits of probation. However, Congressman Volstead, Chairman of the House Judiciary Committee, fearing probation might weaken enforcement of liquor prohibition laws, adamantly refused to support a federal probation bill. Volstead was able to keep pending probation legislation bottled up in committee. Only when his term of office expired in 1923 would probation bills be judged on their own merits.

By 1924, many judges had concluded that Prohibition was a judicial headache. One federal judge expressed the dilemma faced by those charged with enforcing an unpopular law by complaining that he was "embarrassed" by the restraints put on him in sentencing as a result of federal statutes and the *Killits* case. Commenting on the numbers of liquor law violators he had to try, from ignorant teenage boys caught near stills to older men who believed they needed a drink to help them feel better, the judge concluded: "I have every type and form of so-called criminals. If we had this probation law, numbers of them could be dealt with intelligently and successfully."[58] Chute, however, took a pragmatic position toward Prohibition by either remaining silent on the issue or by emphasizing to such groups as the Anti-Saloon League that probation authority might even make Prohibition workable.

By 1924 the stage was set for the final legislative struggle. A retired federal probation officer, Victor Evjen, recalled that the probation bill passed the Senate unanimously on May 24, 1924, but it received serious opposition by a few prohibitionists in the House. One prohibitionist, for example, proclaimed that ". . . all the 'wets' were supporting the bill and the bill would permit judges to place all bootleggers on probation!"[59] The National Probation Association lobbied hard for the measure and on March 2, 1925, the bill was brought before the House for the sixth time. Despite continued opposition from the "wets" as well as some of the "drys," the bill passed, 170 to 49. President Coolidge, a former governor of Massachusetts (where probation started!) had no trouble signing the bill two days after it passed. Therefore, forty-seven years after Massachusetts passed the first probation law in the United States, the federal government had a probation law.[60]

The prediction by "wets" that passage of the Federal Probation Act would allow all bootleggers to be placed on probation was perhaps not so far-fetched. Figures regarding the use of probation in the years after the federal bill was passed suggest that most probationers were involved with illegal liquor violations. For example, in 1933, of the 16,907 persons placed on probation, 13,537 were convicted under the National Prohibition Act.[61] This finding led sociologist John Hagan to conclude that probation had become part of a plea bargaining process, used to resolve an increasing and often unwieldy Prohibition caseload. He wrote that the "use of probation as an alternative to imprisonment was apparently an important part of this process [plea bargaining], cooperatively concealing the unenforceability of an otherwise coercive law."[62]

Regardless of the latent functions of the probation movement, in 1925 Charles Chute had a right to be proud! Probation systems were firmly in place in most locales and the concept itself was almost universally applauded. While fine-tuning some probation methods would be needed, there was a perception that hard work and dedication were all that was required. Unfortunately this was not the case.

1925–1965: Growth, Problems, and Professionalism

From the passage of the Federal Probation Act until the middle 1960s, probation as a practice and an idea grew at a relentless pace. More states developed their own probation laws, the use of probation in those states with existing laws increased dramatically, the number of full-time probation officers rose significantly, and the concept of probation as both a reform vehicle and meaningful judicial alternative grew in acceptance. However, serious problems with the implementation of probation systems soon became apparent. These problems often either were overlooked or seemed solvable and the concept of probation itself was rarely questioned. Probation officers attempted to professionalize the field by adopting a social casework methodology.

Support Continues

By 1930 all but a handful of states (Kentucky, Tennessee, Texas, New Mexico, North and South Dakota, Nevada, and Wyoming) had passed probation laws. The major urban areas (including those in states that had not yet enacted probation laws) had large probation departments and growing caseloads. Rural areas were less inclined to have full-scale probation departments, and frequently judges resorted to summary or court probation wherein defendants were released into the community unsupervised, and only brought to the court's attention if and when they committed new offenses. The trend toward probation rather than incarceration is exemplified by the Massachusetts experience. In 1900, 6,000 defendants were placed on probation and approximately 28,000 were incarcerated in state prisons or in local jails. In 1929, this trend had reversed dramatically; 33,000 people were placed on probation, whereas only 19,000 were incarcerated.[63] New probation workers were regularly entering the field. For example, in 1907 there were approximately 500 probation officers in the United States, whereas in 1937 this number had grown to almost 4,000.[64] In 1930, a mimeographed newsletter served to keep probation officers informed of new developments. This newsletter was expanded to a journal form and renamed *Federal Probation Quarterly* in 1937.

Probation continued to be vigorously defended by progressive reformers as well as by district attorneys and judges. In a 1933 article, prominent Harvard sociologist Sheldon Glueck waxed poetic in the praise of probation: "The human race toils and moils, straining and energizing, doing and suffering things multitudinous and unspeakable under the sun, in order that like the aloe-tree it may once in a hundred years produce a flower. In the barren soil of penology, probation gives promise of developing into the flower among the weeds."[65] An Illinois crime survey conducted in 1933 polled district attorneys and judges regarding their opinions of probation. Every judge questioned favored probation, whereas twenty out of twenty-three prosecutors approved it. Another survey of prosecutorial and judicial views of probation in Wisconsin found similar results: virtually unanimous approval.[66] Just prior to World War II, it was safe to "conclude that probation, in its essential element, has become firmly established in the administration of criminal justice in the United States of America. The first phase—when the battle was for the extension of the system and the acceptance of the idea—has passed, and the present-day concern is with the improvement of organization, administration, and coordination."[67] However, this does not mean that there were no other problems to contend with.

Problems Develop

Although the idea of probation as a form of individualized justice was firmly entrenched, the reality of its implementation was a different story. As the concept of probation was put into practice, the rhetoric of reform was subverted by the realities of inadequate budgets and organizational shortcomings. In many cases the result was a failed system that bore little resemblance to its idealized concept. Historian David Rothman stated that committees investigating probation in the 1930s, whether made up of legislators, social workers, district attorneys, blue-ribbon grand jurors, or concerned citizens, all reached similar conclusions: Probation supervision was superficial, routine, and careless, with almost every county and city having its own way of doing things. This haphazard approach included the inadequate training of probation officers.[68]

All too often the practice of probation had become a meaningless bureaucratic routine that did little either to help offenders or to protect the community. In examining the plight of probation during the 1930s certain factors emerge as dominant themes: (1) Expectations for success were unrealistic, (2) probation was fragmented, (3) funding was inadequate, and (4) probation officers lacked professional status.

Unrealistic Expectations.   Sheldon Glueck, while a vigorous advocate of probation, pointed out that "grossly unwarranted claims as to the miracles [probation] can work were and are being made."[69] Glueck stated that sales techniques borrowed from the private sector were often used to "sell" probation to judges and communities, and those strategies often led to disappointment later. Indeed, a "boomerang" effect may occur, he said, in which resentment over cases of failure will be that much more pronounced and expressions of pessimism will be that much greater.[70]

In the same vein, even though probation supporters promised reformation through community supervision, there was never conclusive empirical evidence this could be achieved with large numbers of offenders. Thus, while John Augustus could claim high success rates with a small number of carefully selected defendants, there was no guarantee that similar success could be expected when probation was granted on a wholesale basis and administered by officers who did not possess his dedication. As we shall see, this became particularly significant in the 1970s.

Fragmentation.   The second problem emerging in the 1930s was that the organization of probation was very fragmented. The *Killits* case had forced each state to develop its own unique probation law. There was little uniformity among the states because state legislators and officials with varied backgrounds and interests had written the probation legislation. Furthermore, probation typically was administered on a local or county level. This introduced even more disparity and generally resulted in an uneven distribution of services. Even though some probation departments were run efficiently, persons with dubious backgrounds and uncertain motivation controlled many. Chiefs of probation departments were often political hacks with "contacts" rather than administrative insight. An attorney general's study of probation at this time concluded: "in no state is the administration of probation of the same quality and standard throughout the state," and further "a splendid well-administrated probation department operating right next to a notoriously 'black spot' on the probation map" is common and ". . . even within the limit of a single metropolis a wide variation in probation procedure may be observable."[71]

Inadequate Funding.   The third problem evident in the 1930s was inadequate funding. Even when a probation staff was well trained and dedicated, the quality of service, to a large degree, was dependent on local funding. Typically, probation departments were part of city or county bureaucracies in which they occupied a marginal position. There were no lobbies or special interest groups working for adequate department funding, and probation expenditures were add-ons to the court budget. The result often was an understaffed probation department, ill equipped to handle the rush of new probationers. For example, in Milwaukee, probation officers carried average caseloads of 290, whereas in New York City they ran as high as 500. A Brooklyn chief probation officer estimated that contacts with clients were usually less than ten minutes a year.[72] In many offices there was no support staff and probation officers were expected to type their own case records.

 In an ironic budgetary situation, the funding of probation departments often was not in the best interests of local communities because the locale had to pay for probation whereas the state paid for confinement in prison. Therefore, from a local standpoint, it was cheaper to send offenders to prison than to place them on probation. This often-overlooked budgetary reality distorted the laudable goals of probation. For example, a 1934 Virginia criminal justice commission indicated the state's probation statute "leaves the financing of probation to the local communities. It is not difficult to understand why there has been little use of this form of penal treatment when one realizes that a community may send its lawbreakers to jail or prison at the expense of the state but must itself bear the burden of placing them on probation."[73]

Low Status.   The final problem that emerged for probation during the 1930s was the lack of professional status afforded probation officers. That is, the position and status afforded probation officers within the court system generally was not conducive to effective and independent administration of services. During the 1930s, in most cases, judges had authority to select probation officers of their own choosing. Often positions were given to reward friends, relatives, or political supporters rather than qualified candidates. Even though some states (ten in 1930) chose applicants from a civil service list, judges retained considerable discretion in selecting from the list. Judges, although openly praising probation officers, in private were not overly impressed with skills and techniques of workers who "lacked legal training." The officers were treated as secondary court workers, more like clerks than professional colleagues. It was clear, in most courtrooms, that probation officers were hired to do the judge's bidding.

Probation's Response

Supporters of community supervision were not immune to the problematic aspects of probation administration previously discussed. They responded on the one hand by requesting additional funding and on the other hand by exhorting probation officers to exert greater efforts. They reasoned that if sufficient money could be found to hire more and better-trained probation officers, and if existing officers would diligently apply themselves, the goal of reformation through probation supervision could be attained. Therefore, while admitting its implementation left much to be desired, the appropriateness of the concept was not questioned.

Many probation officers responded to early criticism of their efforts by seeking to develop occupational professionalism. Sanford Bates, chief federal probation officer, at a 1941 convention of probation personnel, commented that probation in the United States will not be content to serve in an advisory capacity to the courts. Bates believed that it would not be long before probation would be organized and administered independently from the courts, and that probation would become completely responsible for the treatment, care, control, and rehabilitation of the convicted offender. In fact, Bates argued, highly educated probation officers would most likely not be satisfied with the same status as a bailiff or some other officer of the court, but rather "[h]is work is important enough to justify the expectation and requirement that it be developed as a profession in its own right."[74]

Frequently the goal of professionalism meant that officers defined their roles as social caseworkers rather than court officers; hereafter they would treat offenders instead of spying on them for the court. Not all probation officers accepted this social work role, but those who did dominated the field until the late 1960s.

Although there were varying definitions of casework, many proponents of this technique borrowed heavily from Freudian interpretations. In so doing officers stressed that probationers must develop insight before they could begin to overcome their problems. Sutherland and Cressey, in their widely used 1947 criminology text, stated that **casework** was the essence of probation supervision because it led to insight by the probationer into the reasons for his or her behavior. It was believed that people with such insight were less likely to continue their criminal activities. The way such insight is achieved, Sutherland and Cressey continued, is through "intensive interviews through which the probation officer not only comes to understand the probationer but the probationer to understand himself." They believed that the probationer would also identify with the probation officer, emulate his or her behavior, and eventually identify with the probation officer, leading to a normal and socially acceptable life.[75] By the late 1950s David Dressler, after examining the growth of social work in probation, concluded, "It has taken a century but at last a great many workers in probation and parole agree that individualization of the offender implicit in a case work treatment is *sine qua non.*"[76]

Casework was based, in good part, on the **medical model,** which assumes the offender is either physically, mentally, or socially "sick."[77] Crime, therefore, is a symptom of a criminal's illness and a cry for help, requiring early and correct diagnosis followed by therapeutic intervention (treatment). In the criminal justice system, the diagnosis came in the form of the presentence investigation, perhaps confirmed and maybe expanded by institutional classification. The sentence specified the treatment, which was made more precise by the institutional staff. The parole board then decided when the "patient" was cured and could be sent back to the community. A basic assumption of this model, therefore, is that the causes of crime are found within the individual and that by doing something to, for, or with her or him, she or he can be rehabilitated.[78] Moreover, the model assumes that a wide variety of treatment alternatives are available in the community and in institutions, and that there are a large number of professional probation and parole officers ready to supervise, service, and support their very manageable caseloads, all of whom are specifically selected by judges and parole boards because they are good candidates for "taking the cure."

The trend to align probation with social casework continued into the 1960s. For example, Lewis Diana, in 1960, while attempting to define probation, found "the bulk of the literature—between 85 and 90 percent—view[s] probation as some form of treatment, more often than not as casework treatment."[79] To those working in probation during the early 1960s it was clear that a social work degree was a valuable asset. For example, John Rosecrance entered probation work in 1958 and remembers distinctly being told that unless he got an MSW (master of social work) his chances for promotion were slim. By 1965 social caseworkers dominated the field and the concept of probation was universally accepted (in 1956 Mississippi became the fiftieth state to pass a probation law). All this was to change rapidly as probation came under severe criticism and casework methods were viewed with increasing skepticism.

1965–1985: Criticism and Response

Much of the criticism of probation that surfaced in the mid-1960s came from sources opposed to the overall concept of rehabilitation (see Chapter One). However, critics for the first time also specifically questioned the effectiveness of probation supervision. Although virtually all studies of probation's effectiveness are subject to methodological weaknesses, several research projects during this period raised serious doubts as to the very nature of probation. The question was raised: Does probation do any good? Implicit in such fundamental reexamination was the issue of whether the use of probation should be severely restricted or even abolished.

The probation world of the late 1960s was shocked by results of the following three studies. First, the California Youth Authority, after a two-year study of caseload size "discontinued the use of smaller caseloads because of an apparent lack of positive results. There was little evidence that caseloads of only thirty-six delinquents did any better after receiving intensive supervision than did caseloads of seventy-two persons."[80]

The second study was the famous San Francisco Project, supervised by sociologists from the University of California, who looked at caseload size and its effect on violation rates in the Federal Department of Probation. The study looked at "regular" caseload sizes of eighty-five, "ideal" caseload sizes of fifty, and "intensive" caseload sizes of twenty-five, randomly assigning clients to the three experimental groups. After two years, the researchers found that the regular caseloads had a violation rate of 22 percent, ideal caseloads had a violation rate of 24 percent, and intensive caseloads had a violation rate of 38 percent. The researchers proposed that the higher violation rates for the intensive groups were the result of probation officers in those groups being able to supervise their clients more closely, thereby noticing more occasions where probationers violated conditions of their probation. Therefore, contrary to what was expected, lower caseloads led to greater failure, not greater success.[81]

The third study that shook up the probation world was the 1967 study of juvenile offenders conducted by McEachern and Taylor who found that those who were placed on unsupervised probation (no contact with a probation officer) had lower recidivism rates than those placed on supervised caseloads.[82] These three studies, coming from conservative, liberal, and academic critics, lambasted probation, indicating that it was no longer seen as the flower of corrections, but simply another weed.

However, not all the criticism in the 1960s came from external sources. Probation officers were also questioning the casework model of supervision. In actual practice, the treatment concept had frequently been implemented in a haphazard, nonspecific manner. For example, Diana, in his study of probation, found that "few probation officers, either in the literature or in the field gave a clear and specific description of what they meant by treatment, casework or otherwise."[83] More than half of the probation officers in his study reported they did *no planning* on any of their cases, and, in general, probation amounted to little more than administrative supervision. When faced with mounting criticism of their work, probation officers, in many cases, were ready to abandon a casework approach. This willingness was enhanced by the fact that probation work was no longer the province of social workers.

This change was because for some time the openings in probation had far exceeded the number of social worker candidates. Graduates of social work schools no longer found probation work attractive. They could command higher salaries in other agencies where the clients generally had more prestige and were more amenable to treatment than probationers. Many MSWs had always found working with involuntary clientele problematic. As the older MSWs from the 1930s and 1940s retired, their ranks were being replaced by graduates with bachelor of arts (BA) degrees from diverse backgrounds. Many of the newly hired probation officers were never comfortable with casework techniques and had no compunction about trying other approaches. In rapid order, the social workers and their treatment model gave way to more traditional court officers willing to implement pragmatic programs. Probation officers became less concerned with professionalism and more concerned with employment security. In many departments, probation work had become a job rather than a "calling."

The probation officers of the 1970s felt less bound by universal or professional standards and, on the whole, were more willing to change their techniques and methodologies to satisfy regional or local demands. In many cases, this meant adopting a reintegration model wherein probation officers operated as community resource brokers (this is discussed further in Chapter Five). In other instances probation officers were willing to "get tough"and adopt control regimens that stressed adherence to court orders rather than insight through treatment. Pragmatic probation officers joined district attorneys and judges (who needed probation for their own purposes) to maintain support for probation in the face of massive criticism. This support, along with three significant conditions and events, were sufficient to keep probation alive, despite calls for its abolition.

1985–Present: Innovation and Reform

As indicated in Chapter One, prison crowding in the 1980s once again made probation the growth field of corrections. New supervision approaches buoyed the optimism of probation supporters who promised that probation can achieve that most difficult of goals—the reduction of offender recidivism. These new supervision approaches, usually termed **intermediate sanctions,** were driven by at least three factors, as discussed in the next section.

Intermediate Sanctions

Three factors and events occurring between 1985 and 1990 combined to develop a consensus in the United States around the need to change the probation system.[84] The consensus centered around the need for midlevel punishments for offenders who were too high risk for regular probation but for whom incarceration seemed unnecessary. The three circumstances or actions leading to this push for change were (1) crowded southern prisons and a poor economy, (2) an in-depth study of felony probation, and (3) the publication of an influential book on sentencing.

Crowded Southern Prisons and a Poor Economy.   Some federal courts ruled that several southern prisons were overcrowded and in violation of the Eighth Amendment's prohibition against cruel and unusual punishment. The courts further mandated that these states either build new prisons or find another way to punish some offenders. The recession of the 1980s prohibited several states, particularly in the South, from building the new prisons because they could not afford to. Therefore, the judicial pressure led these states to develop tough but inexpensive sentences that did not require prison beds. Georgia, for example, developed the first well known **intensive supervision program (ISP)** designed for those offenders who would have otherwise gone to prison if not for the new program. The Georgia program was distinguished by its assignment of twenty-five offenders to a team of two probation officers: a surveillance officer and a probation officer. Also notable was the fact that each probationer was seen five times per week, had to perform community service, paid a fee for supervision, and was required to be employed or enrolled in an educational program.

Georgia conducted an evaluation of this ISP and found it to be very successful on two counts: It saved the state money and it reduced recidivism. Subsequently, the program received some national publicity centered on the findings that ISPs could decrease prison crowding, improve public safety, and rehabilitate offenders, all at a significant savings to the state. In quick order, several states followed Georgia's lead to the point where by 1998 all fifty states reported having some form of ISP program.[85] ISP programs are discussed in more detail in Chapter Ten.

First Significant U.S. Felony Probation Study.   The National Institute of Justice in 1983 awarded a grant to the Rand Corporation to conduct the first in-depth study of felony probation in the United States. The results, published in 1985[86] became the second event to influence the establishment of ISPs throughout the United States. The research showed that serious felons were being granted probation and, because of limited and often decreasing funding, these offenders were not being effectively supervised and consequently public safety was compromised. Specifically, two-thirds of the almost 2,000 felony probationers followed during the study were rearrested within three years; more than half were reconvicted for serious offenses.

The researchers, however, did not call for giving up on probation. Rather, they suggested an alternative, intermediate form of punishment for those too antisocial for traditional probation but not criminal enough for prison. In short, they called for programs very similar to the Georgia ISP—intensive surveillance, substantial community service, and restitution—which would relieve prison crowding *and* improve probation and community safety.

An Influential Book on Sentencing.   In 1990, **Norval Morris and Michael Tonry** published *Between Prison and Probation: Intermediate Punishments in a Rational Sentencing System.*[87] In this book, the authors acknowledged that U.S. judges faced a very difficult choice between prison and probation with hardly anything in between. Morris and Tonry argue for a "rational and principled" sentencing system: rational because it uses a range of sanctions, principled because it fits the punishment to the crime. They further argued that strictly enforced intermediate sanctions better serve victims and the justice system. Therefore, the study gave policy makers the theoretical framework for a system of sanctions that relied on a range of sentencing options including fines, community service, home confinement, intensive supervision probation, electronic monitoring, day reporting centers, shock incarceration, and boot camps. Such a continuum of sanctions, based on the seriousness of the crime and not concerned with any prison crowding issues, would create a rational sentencing system.

Therefore, by 1990 three elements existed that either pushed for or justified the existence of intermediate sanctions: programs that seemed to work, research showing that without the programs communities are at risk, and a theoretical justification for establishing such programs. It should not be surprising that there was a rush by state legislators to implement intermediate sanction programs. Petersilia describes the period from 1985 to 1994 as "the period of ISP implementation and evaluation. Hundreds of programs were started. . . . During this period, virtually every large probation or parole agency developed programs of intensive surveillance, electronic monitoring, house arrest, drug testing and, to a lesser extent, boot camps and day reporting centers."[88] Today, virtually every state and the federal government report having intensive supervision programs and most of these programs have been evaluated. There is a complete discussion of these evaluations in Chapter Ten. For now, it is sufficient to state that these evaluations contributed to some program redesign and, along with the victim's rights movement, influenced the development of community justice or neighborhood probation,[89] as well as the growth of restorative justice programs. Under these justice models, probation officers develop partnerships with other justice agencies and community members, including victims, to improve public safety. Probation and parole officers play an important role in these new paradigms, paradigms that continue to emerge and develop in the first decade of the twenty-first century.

Summary

Although probation has many purposes and varied definitions, historically the main rationale for its use has been the mitigation of punishment. Probation had its origins in the English common law practices, benefit of clergy, judicial reprieve, and recognizance. These practices were imported to colonial America and became forerunners of modern-day probation. The first probation officer was the bootmaker John Augustus who voluntarily bailed on probation and subsequently helped reform a criminal defendant charged with public drunkenness. Augustus expanded his probation work to all categories of defendants and in so doing developed procedures such as presentence reports, supervision classification, and case files that have become the hallmark of probation work. In 1878, Massachusetts became the first state to pass a probation law that officially authorized hiring of probation officers. Early twentieth-century progressives who used probation as the centerpiece in an overall package of correctional reform enhanced expansion of probation significantly. Wardens, district attorneys, and judges who reaped practical benefits from probation supported their reform movements. With passage of the Federal Probation Act in 1925, probation was firmly established as a routine judicial alternative.

Although problems with large-scale implementation of probation became apparent in the 1920s, the optimism of backers was sufficient to forestall basic questions regarding its effectiveness. During the 1930s probation officers embraced both a treatment model and social work techniques to implement it. Social workers dominated the field and strove to develop professional status.

In the middle 1960s, probation, for the first time, was subject to careful scrutiny and because it appeared unable to reduce recidivism was generally found wanting. Probation officers responded to criticism by abandoning the treatment model and social worker methods. The influence of MSWs on the field waned as less professionally oriented officers emerged as leaders. By advancing more punitive supervision methods, probation officers and their supporters were successful in fending off calls for the abandonment or restriction of probation. In the 1980s prison crowding, a recession, and an influential book on sentencing were responsible for renewed interest in probation. Contemporary proponents of probation, like their counterparts in the early twentieth century, are optimistically predicting that such new programs will reduce recidivism. Although there is a growing body of research evidence to support this contention under certain circumstances, the final results remain to be seen.

Key People and Terms

John Augustus (19)
Benefit of clergy (16)
Casework (37)
Charles Chute (27)
Rufus "Uncle" Cook (25)
Federal Probation Act (27)

Intensive supervision program (ISP) (41)
Intermediate sanctions (40)
Judicial reprieve (17)
Medical model (38)
Norval Morris and Michael Tonry (42)
Recognizance (18)

Key Legal Case

The *Killits* case (Ex part U.S. 242-U.S.-2753, 1916)

Questions for Discussion and Review

1. List and describe three early practices that were precursors to probation. How are these practices similar to and how are they dissimilar from probation practice today?

2. Discuss the contributions of John Augustus to the field of probation. How are his practices similar to probation today?

3. Discuss the development of probation from 1900 to 1925. Include a discussion of the *Killits* case and the contributions of Charles Chute to probation.

4. What are some of the issues surrounding the history of probation from 1925 to 1965? From 1965 to 1985?

5. List and discuss the circumstances or actions that led to the push toward intermediate sanctions in the 1990s and beyond?

Relevant Internet Sites

American Probation and Parole Association, for a history of the American Probation and Parole Association; also, their frequently asked questions section includes a question on the history of probation: www.appa-net.org/the_early_years.htm

Timeline of the history of probation: www.henrycty.com/courtservices/history.html

For a history of New York state probation: http://dpca.state.ny.us/nysdpca/pdfs/96annrep.pdf

For a history of Nevada parole and probation: http://ps.state.nv.us/PandP/History.htm

Community Justice Exchange, for information and assistance on community justice programs: www.communityjustice.org

Bureau of Justice Assistance home page, for information on intermediate sanction programs: www.ojp.usdoj.gov/BJA

Notes

1. David J. Rothman, *Incarceration and Its Alternatives in Twentieth Century America* (Washington, DC: U.S. Government Printing Office, 1979) 9.

2. Howard Becker, *Outsiders* (New York: Free Press, 1963) 152.

3. For a full discussion of the gap between reality and practice see David J. Rothman, *Incarceration and Its Alternatives in Twentieth Century America* (Washington, DC: U.S. Government Printing Office, 1979).

4. U.N. Department of Social Affairs, *Probation and Related Matters* (New York: Sales No. IV, 2, E/CN/.5/230, 1950) 15.

5. U.N. Department of Social Affairs 16.

6. L. LeMesurier, *A Handbook of Probation* (London, UK: National Association of Probation Officers, 1935) 19.

7. David Dressler, *Practice and Theory of Probation and Parole* (New York: Columbia University Press, 1962) 17.

8. Dressler 17–18.

9. Bradley Chapin, *Criminal Justice in Colonial America* (Athens: University of Georgia Press, 1983) 48.

10. Chapin 49.

11. Chapin 49.

12. Lawrence Freidman, *A History of American Law* (New York: Simon and Schuster, 1973) 62.

13. Chapin 49.

14. Dressler 18.

15. Chapin 60–61.

16. Chapin 27–28.

17. Chapin 29.

18. Dressler 19.

19. Charles L. Chute, *Crime, Courts and Probation* (New York: Macmillan, 1956) 22–24.

20. Dressler 22.

21. Harry E. Allen, Eric W. Carlson, and Evalyn C. Parks, "The Development of Probation," in *Probation, Parole and Community Corrections,* eds. Robert M. Carter, Daniel Glaser, and Leslie T. Wilkins (New York: Wiley, 1984) 6.

22. John Augustus, *John Augustus, First Probation Officer,* reprint of *The Labors of John Augustus,* Boston, 1852 (New York: National Probation Association, 1939) 4–5.

23. Augustus 4.

24. Augustus 104.

25. Augustus xx.

26. Augustus 24.

27. Augustus xviii.

28. Augustus 99.

29. Augustus 99–100.

30. Augustus 23.

31. Augustus xx.

32. Augustus xxi.

33. Augustus 78–79.

34. Augustus xii–xv.

35. Charles L. Chute, "The Development of Probation in the United States," in *Probation and Criminal Justice,* ed. Sheldon Glueck (New York: Macmillan, 1933) 225–249.

36. U.N. Department of Social Affairs 32.

37. Donald W. Moreland, "John Augustus and His Successors," in *Probation and Parole Progress: Yearbook National Probation Association,* ed. Marjorie Bell (New York: National Probation Association, 1939) 18.

38. Charles Lindner and Margaret R. Savarese, "The Evolution of Probation," *Federal Probation Quarterly* 48 (1984): 5.

39. Moreland 21.

40. Charles L. Chute, "The Development of Probation," in *Probation and Parole Progress: Yearbook National Probation Association,* ed. Marjorie Bell (New York: National Probation Association, 1939) 32.

41. Chute, "The Development of Probation" 32.

42. U.N. Department of Social Affairs 34.

43. U.N. Department of Social Affairs 34.

44. Charles L. Chute, *Crime, Courts and Probation* (New York: Macmillan, 1956) 61.

45. Barbara A. Kay and Clyde B. Vedder, *Probation and Parole* (Springfield, IL: Charles C. Thomas, 1963) 17.

46. Chute, "The Development of Probation" 226.

47. Committee on Translations, "General Introduction" to Cesare Lombroso, *Crime: Its Causes and Remedies* (Boston: Little, Brown, 1911).

48. Rothman, *Incarceration and Its Alternatives* 12–13.

49. Lamar T. Empey, *American Delinquency: Its Meaning and Construction* (Homewood, IL: Dorsey, 1982) 338.

50. Edward J. Latessa and Harry E. Allen, *Corrections in the Community* (Cincinnati: Anderson, 1999) 112.

51. Paul F. Cromwell, George G. Killinger, Hazel B. Kerper, and Charles Walker, *Probation and Parole in the Criminal Justice System* (St. Paul, MN: West Publishing, 1985) 9.

52. Charles H. Z. Meyer, "A Half Century of Federal Probation and Parole," *Journal of Criminal Law, Criminology, and Police Science* 42 (1952): 716.

53. U.N. Department of Social Affairs 24.

54. One of the first researchers to apply the term to a correctional setting was John Hagan in "Symbolic Justice: The Status Politics of the American Probation Movement," *Sociological Focus* 12 (1979): 295–309.

55. David Dressler, *Practice and Theory of Probation and Parole* (New York: Columbia University Press, 1959) 24–25.

56. Victor Evjen, "The Federal Probation System: The Struggle to Achieve It and Its First Twenty-Five Years," *Federal Probation Quarterly* 39 (1975): 5.

57. Evjen 5.

58. John Hagan, "Symbolic Justice: The Status Politics of the American Probation Movement," *Sociological Focus* 12 (1979): 301–302.

59. Evjen 6.

60. Evjen 6.

61. Hagan 304.

62. Hagan 304.

63. David Rothman, *Conscience and Convenience: The Asylum and Its Alternatives in Progressive America* (Boston: Little, Brown, 1980) 111.

64. John A. Wallace, "Probation Administration," in *Handbook of Criminology,* ed. Daniel Glaser (Chicago, IL: Rand McNally, 1974) 949.

65. Sheldon Glueck, "The Significance and Promise of Probation," in *Probation and Criminal Justice,* ed. Sheldon Glueck (New York: Macmillan, 1933) 3.

66. Rothman, *Conscience and Convenience* 103.

67. Kay and Vedder, *Probation and Parole* 27.

68. Rothman, *Conscience and Convenience* 83–84.

69. Glueck, "The Significance and Promise of Probation" 9.

70. Glueck, "The Significance and Promise of Probation" 9–10.

71. U.S. Attorney General, *Survey of Release Procedures, Vol. 2, Probation* (Washington, DC: U.S. Government Printing Office, 1939) 181–182.

72. Rothman, *Conscience and Convenience* 90.

73. Rothman, *Conscience and Convenience* 95.

74. Quoted in Harry Elmer Barnes and Negley K. Teeters, *New Horizons in Criminology* (New York: Prentice Hall, 1944) 392.

75. Edwin Sutherland and Donald Cressey, *Principles of Criminology*, 4th ed. (Philadelphia: Lippincott, 1947) 399–400.

76. Dressler 128.

77. Donal MacNamara, "Medical Model in Corrections: Requiescat in Place," in *Incarceration: The Sociology of Imprisonment*, ed. Fred Montaino (Beverly Hills, CA: Sage, 1978) 153.

78. MacNamara 153.

79. Lewis Diana, "What Is Probation," *Journal of Criminal Law, Criminology and Police Science*, 51 (1960): 96.

80. Empey 379.

81. Empey 379. Although defined as "case failures," the results did hold out the prospect that through intensive supervision community protection could be enhanced.

82. Empey 380.

83. Diana 197.

84. Joan Petersilia, "A Decade of Experimenting with Intermediate Sanctions: What Have We Learned?" NCJRS Research Forum, November, 1998. Washington, DC: National Institute of Justice. Retrieved February 15, 2002, from www.ncjrs.org/txtfiles/172851.txt

85. Petersilia, "A Decade of Experimenting with Intermediate Sanctions."

86. Joan Petersilia, Susan Turner, James Kahan, and Joyce Peterson, *Granting Felons Probation: Public Risks and Alternatives* (Santa Monica, CA: Rand Corporation, 1985).

87. Norval Morris and Michael Tonry, *Between Prison and Probation: Intermediate Punishments in a Rational Sentencing System* (New York: Oxford University Press, 1990).

88. Petersilia, "A Decade of Experimenting with Intermediate Sanctions" 4.

89. Petersilia, "A Decade of Experimenting with Intermediate Sanctions."

3

The History of Parole

Introduction: The Definition of Parole

Parole is defined as the conditional supervised release of inmates from prison after they have served a portion of their imposed sentence. Parole is different from a pardon because inmates are not released outright but remain subject to release conditions and supervision by correctional officials (parole officers). Parole is administered by a state agency, unlike probation, which is solely a judicial responsibility. Parole does not end the defendant's original sentence but extends it into a community setting. The last point is often overlooked and is worth underscoring by considering comments from a past president of the American Prison Association:

> The granting of parole is merely permission to a prisoner to serve a portion of his sentence outside the walls of the prison. He continues to be in custody of the authorities, both legally and actually, and is still under restraint. The sentence is in full force and at any time he does not comply with the conditions upon which he is released, or does not want to conduct himself properly, he may be returned, for his own good and in the public interest.[1]

The "conditional" aspect of parole status can be further illustrated by the strange case of Gary Dotson. Dotson had been freed from an Illinois prison in 1985 after then-governor James R. Thompson commuted his sentence because his accuser, Cathleen Crowell Webb, recanted testimony that had convicted him of rape in 1979. However, Dotson was rearrested on battery and disorderly conduct charges two days after being given a "last chance" parole, and the state Department of Corrections considered the arrest a parole violation, meaning that he would have to complete his original twenty-five to fifty-year sentence. The parole board later revoked his parole, meaning Dotson had to go back to prison for sixteen years, one month, and five days. However, Dotson, in 1989, became the first Illinois prisoner exonerated by DNA testing.[2]

Notwithstanding the possibility of revocation, parole, like probation, serves to mitigate punishment. In this instance, the mitigation is granted by an administrative body (a parole board) and not by a judge (as in the case of probation). Sentenced prisoners are very aware of parole possibilities and in many cases their institutional lives are geared toward making themselves eligible for parole. Parole has always been controversial because those released early from prison have the potential for involving themselves in serious new offenses. When parolees commit heinous crimes while on released status, correctional officials are subject to severe criticism. A prime example of such a scenario occurred when Charles Manson, while on parole, masterminded the string of grisly murders that shocked the nation's sensibilities. Such notorious cases overshadow the fact that most inmates do manage to successfully complete their parole.

Historically, parole developed from two correctional concepts: (1) transportation of criminals and (2) indeterminate sentencing. Both of these concepts originated in England and were modified when implemented in the United States. The moving force for the implementation of parole systems in both England and the United States can be credited to the efforts of nineteenth-century correctional entrepreneurs. Progressives in early twentieth-century America significantly advanced the concept of parole by making it an integral part of their reform agendas. The use of parole experienced a temporary decline in the 1970s as its rehabilitative value was seriously questioned, but recently it has reemerged as an important correctional tool in dealing with prison crowding and the release of convicted felons. The remainder of this chapter elaborates on these historical developments.

Transportation

The concept of **transportation** developed from the medieval practice of banishment. Convicted criminals in the Middle Ages, on occasion, escaped the death penalty by being banished forever from their local communities or villages. Although a form of mitigation (as opposed to death), banishment was a severe sanction because individuals had a difficult time living outside a group setting. **Banishment** established the precedent of "casting out," which was expanded by the English judicial system to include transportation of criminals.

Transportation proved more systematic than banishment in dealing with large numbers of criminal defendants. Offenders could be placed in far-off lands from which it was difficult, if not impossible, to return. The use of transportation provided social and economic benefits in addition to its criminal justice function.

Changing economic conditions in sixteenth-century England brought the twin specters of unemployment and social unrest. During times of economic instability, large numbers of out-of-work men roamed the countryside, frequently engaging in illegal activities. In 1547, England passed its first vagrancy act, one that allowed magistrates to remove "idle persons" from the community and to sentence them to periods of incarceration or forced labor. The vagrancy act was later expanded to become the Transportation Law of 1597. This law authorized deportation of "dangerous rouges" deemed beyond redemption and declared that if these undesirables "shall returne agayne into any part of the realme . . . without any lawful lycene or warrant so to do, that in every such case the offense shall be fellony and the party offending therein suffer death."[3] Most of those deported under the new transportation law were forced to work as galley hands on English ships.

Transportation to America

The opening of the U.S. colonies significantly stimulated the use of transportation. Labor shortages in the colonies were acute and the London, Massachusetts, and Virginia companies petitioned Parliament to authorize transportation of criminals to the new settlements. The trading companies were successful, and in 1617 a privy council ruling granted reprieves and stays of execution to felons deemed fit to work in the colonies. Those transported to America were under sentence of death; for them, service in the colonies was preferable to the hangman's noose. The language of the privy council ruling clarified that transportation was considered a form of mitigation:

> Whereas it hath pleased His Majesties out of his singular clemencie and mercy to take into his princely consideration the wretched estate of divers of his subjects who by the laws of the realme are adjudged to dye for sondry offenses though heynous in themselves, yet not of the highest nature, soe as His Majesty both out of his gracious clemencye, as also for diverse weighty considerations could wishe they might be rather corrected than destroyed.[4]

Mitigation notwithstanding, only those able to work were eligible for transportation. The English government paid the costs of transporting criminals to the colonies (about five pounds) to a shipping contractor. On landing in the colonies, prisoners were auctioned as indentured workers. The length of indenture varied, seven years being the average period. Once the criminals reached America, the English government's responsibility for them ceased. If, however, the transportees managed to return to England, they were subject to execution on detection and apprehension.

In 1619, one hundred "dissolute persons" were offloaded in Virginia and transportation of criminals to America had begun. While no accurate figures as to the number of offenders sent to the U.S. colonies are available (estimates range from 50,000 to 100,000),[5] it is apparent that convicts provided a valuable source of labor and helped build the country. In an effort to ensure that transportees would actually fulfill their indenture, the transportation law was amended in 1656 to specify that pardons were contingent on satisfactory work performance.

Transportation, first used only for felons, was later expanded to include misdemeanants. A 1717 law made transportation virtually mandatory for those convicted of larceny and stealing. The more liberal use of transportation allowed England to rid itself of large numbers of social undesirables and unemployed workers, thus providing much needed labor for the colonies. The economic rationale behind the 1717 enactment was apparent:

> Whereas in many of His Majesty's colonies . . . in America, there is great want of servants . . . be it enacted that any person convicted of any offense for which he is liable to be whipt or barnt on the hand, may be sent to some of His Majesty's colonies in America. Offenders returning before expiration of their term to be liable to death.[6]

Provisions of this bill gave shipping contractors the "property in service" of prisoners for the length of their sentences. When the convicts arrived in America, their service contracts were sold as indentures to American contractors. Although eighteenth-century colonial governments complained vigorously about increased transportation of criminals (convict labor, in good measure, had been supplanted by slave labor), England sent approximately 2,000 criminals per year from 1717 until the Revolutionary War began.

When U.S. shores were closed to transported criminals in 1776, the English turned to Africa as a repository. African penal colonies proved unsuitable because disease, climate, and inhospitable natives wreaked havoc with settlements. Advocates of transportation, undaunted by the African failure, turned to Australia as the location for their next efforts. In 1788, the first shipment of convicts (552 males and 190 females) docked at Botany Bay, Australia, and the largest transportation effort had begun.[7]

Transportation to Australia

Between 1788 and 1852 England transported vast numbers of its convicts to Australia. A. F. Shaw compiled data regarding convict sailings during this period. He found that almost 800 shiploads of convicts were sent to Australia (each ship carried between 200 and 500 inmates).[8] Because the initial number of free settlers was relatively small, the convict population had a dramatic impact on Australian life.[9] Moreover, the method of handling convicts bound for Australia was different from that used for transportation to America. William Parker, in his history of parole, described the new procedures:

> all the expense incurred was met by the government; the criminals transported did not become indentured servants but remained prisoners under the control of the government, which assumed responsibility for their behavior and welfare. The first governor of the penal settlement was given "property in service" for all felons under his supervision. He then assigned the prisoners to free settlers, giving them the "property in service" agreement.[10]

Ticket-of-Leave.   The governor of Australia was given power to pardon inmates whose behavior and work record warranted it. A governor's pardon was accompanied by a grant of land. In the beginning, deserving prisoners received an outright pardon, but later these pardons were contingent on continued good behavior and residence in certain districts. These conditional pardons, called **tickets-of-leave,** were a distinct forerunner of parole. The following is an example of a ticket-of-leave granted to convicts released from the Australian prison system:

> It is His Excellency the governor's pleasure to dispense with the government work of _____ tried at _____ convicted of _____ and to permit _____ to employ _____ (off government stores) in any lawful occupation within the district of _____ for his own advantage during good behavior or until His Excellency's further pleasure be made known.[11]

In 1811, specific procedures were enacted to regulate the granting of tickets-of-leave and prisoners had to serve minimum sentences before being eligible for them. This concept was further defined in 1821 when a severity-of-sentence scale was introduced. For example, prisoners with seven-year sentences were eligible for leave status after serving four years; those with fourteen-year sentences after seven years; and prisoners with life sentences after eight years.

The ticket-of-leave system, therefore, contained many components of modern-day parole. Convicts had their sentences shortened for appropriate prison behavior. Their continued presence in the community was dependent on staying out of trouble and residing in designated districts. If convicts violated these conditions, they could be imprisoned to serve out the balance of their sentences. However, unlike contemporary parole, correctional officials did not supervise the ticketeers.

The end of transportation as an English correctional practice was brought about by complaints from free Australian settlers. In the 1840s gold was discovered in Australia and people flooded there. The labor shortage ceased, and the settlers now resented the convict's presence in Australia. Pardoned inmates and those on ticket-of-leave status were in direct competition with settlers for job openings and gold diggings. When the settlers threatened to revolt if more convicts were sent, wholesale transportation was permanently suspended in 1855. The operation of penal colonies was terminated in 1867, although government-support payments for convict welfare continued until 1890.[12] The ticket-of-leave concept survived the demise of transportation and, with modification, became an important part of English correctional practice. This was accomplished through the work of two correctional entrepreneurs: Alexander Maconochie and Walter Crofton.

Maconochie

Alexander Maconochie, director of an Australian prison colony from 1840 to 1844, is considered by many to be the father of parole. Although he did not originate the ticket-of-leave, he did much to popularize the concept and to stimulate its implementation. Maconochie turned to penology after distinguished service as a naval officer and as the first professor of geography at University College, London. In 1836 he was appointed assistant to the lieutenant governor of Van Diemen's Land (known today as the Australian state of Tasmania). Many of his new duties involved inspection of the large penal colony located in Van Diemen's Land. Maconochie was shocked at the brutal conditions he observed and wrote a scathing report to Parliament detailing the litany of inequities that had become commonplace at the penal colony. The report caused a controversy in Parliament and Maconochie was later dismissed. Undaunted by the firing, he remained in Australia as an advocate for prison reform. By exerting influence on English politicians (some of whom were his former naval colleagues), Maconochie was able to secure an appointment as governor of Norfolk Island, one of Australia's most infamous prison colonies. Although he was only in charge of Norfolk Island for four years, his administration has been heralded as an exemplar of humane and progressive penology.

Norfolk Island

Approximately 1,000 miles from the Australian mainland, Norfolk Island was used as a detention center for prisoners convicted of crimes after their transportation to Australia. Because only recidivists (i.e., prisoners who were convicted of new crimes) were sent to Norfolk, prior administrations felt it necessary to deal harshly with the inmates. Order had been maintained by liberal use of the lash and long periods of solitary confinement. Particularly unruly prisoners were chained to rocks and left exposed to the elements for periods of up to a year. A prisoner's first glimpse of Norfolk Island from the sea revealed the ominous sight of a large gallows dominating the landscape. More than two-thirds of those sent to Norfolk died on the island.[13] Morale among the prison staff, as well as the inmate population, was abysmal and Norfolk was justifiably considered a hellhole.

Maconochie was determined to humanize the Norfolk Prison Colony. Toward that end he dismantled the dreaded gallows, instituted a prisoner's committee, abolished flogging and chaining, did away with rules requiring convicts to be servile toward guards, and ruled out arbitrary punishment for minor infractions. These humanitarian efforts were a radical departure from prevailing policies and drew considerable opposition from traditional prison administrators. Undaunted by stinging criticism from Sydney and London officials, Maconochie forged ahead with his humanizing efforts. He and his wife took daily unescorted walks through the prison grounds and tried to know each convict on a first name basis. Other wardens have been humane and fair, but Maconochie's unique contribution to corrections stemmed from his concept of prisoner release, the mark system.

Mark System

Maconochie firmly believed that the main function of prison was to prepare inmates for their eventual release back into society. Such a philosophy was succinctly described in his autobiography: "The proper object of prison discipline is to prepare men for discharge; the first object of prison discipline should be to reform prisoners."[14] In order to facilitate prisoner release, Maconochie sought to actively involve the inmates themselves in the process. He assumed that prisoners would be strongly motivated to improve their behavior if such improvement would result in a shortened prison sentence. According to Maconochie's statement, his plan would:

> Place the prisoner's fate in his own hands, to give him a form of wages, to impose on him a form of pecuniary fine for his prison offenses, to make him feel the burden and obligation of his own maintenance and to train him, while yet in bondage, to those habits of prudent accumulation which after discharge would best preserve him from again falling.[15]

Maconochie devised a **mark system** whereby prisoners could actually earn their way to freedom. Inmates demonstrating good behavior were rewarded with marks. When prisoners had accumulated sufficient marks, they became eligible for early release; under this plan, inmates were not serving fixed sentences but were progressing toward release at their own pace. A chaplain at the Norfolk Penal Colony described how the mark system operated, explaining that Captain Maconochie treated the prisoners as laborers who could earn marks for their labor, or lose them for misconduct. Each inmate was given ten marks per day for his labor. From this amount the inmates needed to purchase daily food and supplies. Food was sold at three rates; the "coarsest" was three marks, the next four, and the best five. Thus the frugal convict could save seven marks per day, and those who spent the most could save five. However, because extra marks were given for hard or overwork, it was possible to save up to eight or ten marks per day. For each ten marks saved, the convict's term was shortened by a day. However, if a prisoner broke the rules, marks proportionate to the offense were taken away.[16]

As an adjunct to the mark system Maconochie developed a gradation of servitude scheme. At the same time that inmates earned their marks, they moved through progressively less restrictive levels of control. In stage 1 the prisoners were confined to an enclosed prison setting (today this would be called maximum security). Stage 2 allowed inmates to work outside prison walls, returning to their cells each evening. As inmates moved into stage 3 they lived in shelters or huts outside the prison compound (a type of halfway house). When inmates advanced to stage 4, they were released into the community (under certain conditions) on ticket-of-leave status. The release conditions typically required inmates to stay in certain geographical areas, to remain law abiding, and to inform the local police of their residence. Stage 4 was the equivalent of parole—conditional release from a prison sentence. Maconochie released statistics claiming that of the 1,450 prisoners released on tickets-of-leave, only 3 percent had committed new offenses.[17] Although we have no data of our own to refute these statistics, this extremely low recidivism rate should be viewed with some skepticism because it defies correctional logic. It seems likely that Maconochie (like John Augustus) wanted to "sell" the benefits of a new program.

Maconochie continued to come under heavy criticism for his "radical" innovations. In addition, he had incensed English parliamentary leaders by hosting a Queen's birthday celebration where rum was distributed to the inmates.[18] Maconochie staunchly defended his methods but was fired after four years. Prison administrators hoped this would be the end of Maconochie's penal career; however, he vowed to continue his advocacy of the mark system. Maconochie left for England to take his case directly to parliamentary leaders. While he was in England, he accepted a position as warden of Birmingham Borough Prison but was fired after a few months for being "too lenient" with prisoners. Maconochie spoke in favor of the 1853 English Penal Servitude Act that granted legal status to the ticket-of-leave concept. The comprehensive act specified that convicts must serve a certain percentage of their sentence (for example, four years of a ten year sentence) before being eligible for a ticket-of-leave. The following conditions were placed on all ticket-of-leave licensees (holders):

1. The power of revoking or altering the license of a convict will most certainly be exercised in the case of misconduct.
2. If, therefore, he wishes to retain the privilege, which by his good behavior under penal discipline he has obtained, he must prove by his subsequent conduct that he is really worthy of Her Majesty's clemency.
3. To produce a forfeiture of the license, it is by no means necessary that the holder should be convicted of a new offense. If he associates with notoriously bad characters, leads an idle or dissolute life, or has no visible means of obtaining an honest livelihood, etc., it will be assumed that he is about to relapse into crime, and he will be at once apprehended and recommitted to prison under his original sentence.[19]

The act did not specify who should supervise ticket-of-leave holders, an oversight that resulted in no direct supervision at all for released inmates. Although Maconochie's efforts to advance humane treatment of prisoners and implementation of a graduated release program were cut short by failing health (culminating in his death in 1860), he did influence another important correctional leader—Walter Crofton.

Crofton

In 1854, **Sir Walter Crofton** was appointed head of the Irish prison system. Almost immediately he introduced a mark system of graduated release similar in principle to that advocated by Maconochie. Crofton modified Maconochie's plan to include the following stages: (1) solitary labor, (2) public works where marks could be earned, (3) confinement in a minimum-security facility, (4) ticket-of-leave, and (5) release from servitude. Even though Crofton was a disciple of Maconochie, Crofton had different ideas of how ticket-of-leave inmates should be supervised in the community. Maconochie, fearing parole would be used as a form of punishment, was opposed to active supervision, especially by police officials. In contrast, Crofton, believing parole would assist an offender's adjustment, advocated close supervision either by civilians or the police. Under Crofton's scheme, which came to be known as the **Irish Plan,** all ticketeers were given the following instructions:

1. The holder shall preserve this license and produce it when called upon to do so by a magistrate or police officer.
2. He shall abstain from any violation of the law.
3. He shall not habitually associate with notoriously bad characters, such as reported thieves and prostitutes.
4. He shall not lead an idle and dissolute life, without means of obtaining an honest livelihood.

If the license is forfeited or revoked in consequence of a conviction of any felony, he will be liable to undergo a term of penal servitude equal to that portion of his term of _____ years, which remains unexpired when his license was granted, viz., the term of _____ years _____ months.[20]

Each ticket-of-leave man released to Dublin or the County of Dublin had to, within three days of his arrival, report to the Police Office in Dublin. The police would then give him further reporting instructions. Those released convicts who came from the provinces had to report to the local constable for similar instructions. The released convicts also could not change their localities without notifying the constable or police. If they violated the conditions, it was assumed that they were "leading an idle, irregular life and thereby entail a revocation of his license."[21]

The Irish Plan

The release program previously described came to be known as the Irish Plan, and a few more details on the supervision of offenders required by this plan are worth considering. Inmates living in Dublin, after checking in with the police, were placed under the jurisdiction of an Inspector of Released Persons. The inspector was a civilian employee who attempted not only to monitor inmates' behaviors but also to aid them in dealing with their newfound liberty. The inspector's role was virtually identical to that played by modern-day parole officers, and James P. Organ, the first inspector, faced the still-unresolved dilemma of how to be a watchdog and a friend at the same time. Ticketeers who lived in the Irish countryside were supervised exclusively by police officers that made no pretense of providing "assistance."

The Irish Plan was well received by community leaders, judges, police officers, and the convicts themselves. By 1860, it had become a correctional success story. Crofton became a convincing spokesperson for the ticket-of-leave concept as his arguments were backed by several years of practical implementation. His approach to supervised community release directly influenced English and U.S. parole systems.

English Ticket-of-Leave

In 1862, the English ticket-of-leave system, which until that time had not specified the method of supervision, was vilified in Parliament and in the press. Ticket-of-leave holders were implicated in a series of murders and robberies in London. The *London Daily Times* ran several editorials demanding that something be done about released prisoners, and a royal commission was formed to investigate prison release policies. The commission's report strongly urged that a systematic program of supervision for released inmates be instituted and recommended that the Irish Plan be adopted. Subsequently, English ticket-of-leave policies were modified to conform to Crofton's plan. A Prisoner's Aid Society was established and, similar to modern-day parole boards, it supervised all those released on ticket-of-leave status. The society hired agents whose responsibilities were as follows:

1. To visit the local prisoners weekly or oftener, if ordered by the Honorable Secretary and to take his instruction as to dealing with the cases selected for aid.
2. To visit local employers of labor, taking every opportunity of seeing and becoming personally acquainted with foreman and other officials explaining to them the objectives of the Society and endeavoring to secure their cooperation.
3. To see the prisoner at the jail and accompany him to the railway station when needed, and to provide board and lodging for him for a limited time.
4. To visit constantly all persons under the care of the Society so long as they were unemployed and after employment is found.
5. To enter daily in a journal all parties seen and places visited and to submit the journal to the Committee at the monthly meeting.
6. To expend, under the direction of the Honorable Secretary, the money of all ticket-of-leave men under his supervision and to lose no opportunity of procuring suitable employment for them.[22]

Although there were other influences on the development of parole in the United States, when Crofton's ideas became known in that country, they would influence the course of parole development there as well as they did in England.

Origins of Parole in America

Transportation had directly paved the way for development of parole systems in Australia, Ireland, and England. In the United States, although transportation was well known, parole had somewhat different origins. Initially, it developed from commutation laws that lessened a defendant's sentence according to a predetermined formula. Such planned reductions were generally termed *good-time laws* and were attempts to offer inmates some incentives for good behavior in prison. Prison officials assumed the possibility of receiving **good time** made it easier to control inmate behavior because inmates who misbehaved in prison would not qualify for a sentence reduction.

In 1817, New York passed the first statewide good-time law. It specified a formula for rewarding good conduct and diligent work. Several other states in nineteenth-century America passed similar bills. An 1856 Ohio law was typical of these commutation bills. It established a sentence reduction of five days per month providing the inmate was "not guilty of a violation of any of the rules of the prison and labored with diligence and fidelity."[23] Although commutation of sentence was not parole, it did establish the principle that prisoners needed some incentive to change their behaviors, and that reduction of sentence was the best available option. Aside from the influence of transportation and commutation, the major force behind the development of parole in the United States came from the implementation of indeterminate sentencing.

The Indeterminate Sentence

Indeterminate sentencing is a method for linking the probability of committing new offenses with an offender's prison release date. Length of punishment is not based solely on the past offense but also is determined, in large part, by an assessment of the offender's future behavior. Policies of indeterminate sentencing seek to ensure that, within limits, defendants will remain in custody only as long as they remain a danger to others. Such sentences typically are given within certain time frames. For example, a defendant given a sentence of two to ten years must serve at least two years but no more than ten; a parole board sets the release date between these parameters. Under this form of sentencing, much of the responsibility of determining how much time defendants serve in prison passes from judges to correctional officials. The assumption behind indeterminate sentencing is that at the time of sentencing, judges do not know how long it will take an individual defendant to be "reformed" or rehabilitated; therefore, correctional personnel can, over time, observe the defendant's progress in an incarcerated setting and then more accurately determine readiness for release. When defendants are released from custody, they finish out the remainder of their sentences in the community under the supervision of a parole officer.

Acceptance and implementation of the indeterminate sentence was a major watershed in U.S. corrections. Its counterpoint, the determinate sentence, fixes the period of incarceration that can be imposed by the court. This type of sentence is associated with retribution or deserved punishment. Thus, the move to indeterminate sentencing established rehabilitation as the main goal of corrections and signified that parole was a vital component in that process. Indeterminate sentencing is inextricably linked with parole as part of the same reform goal. When indeterminate sentencing was either considered or implemented, there was corresponding growth in parole. Even though parole laws in some states were initially enacted independent of indeterminate sentencing, the widespread acceptance and use of parole was part and parcel of the new sentencing philosophy. Besides the influence of the Irish and English on the parole system in the United States, there were also other Europeans who contributed to its development.

Foreign Origins.   Whereas open-ended sentences were first applied to juveniles based on a New York state law of 1824,[24] the concept of indeterminate sentences for adults had English and European origins. In 1829, Archbishop Whatley of Dublin wrote an article for the *London Review* in which he proposed adoption of indeterminate sentencing. Whatley described his idea in the following manner: "It seems to me entirely reasonable that those who so conduct themselves that it becomes necessary to confine them in houses of correction should not be turned loose upon society again until they give some indication that they are prepared to live without a repetition of their offenses."[25]

In 1835, **Colonel Montesinos** of Spain sanctioned a type of indeterminate sentence for prisoners sent to Valencia Prison. He was opposed to "punishment carried to the length of harshness," and accordingly reduced the sentences of inmates who demonstrated good behavior and hard work. Montesinos wrote: "The moral object of penal establishments should be not so much to inflict punishment as to correct, to receive men idle and ill-intentioned and return them to society, if possible, honest and industrious citizens."[26] Penal observers reported that Valencia was a "model prison" and those released early rarely involved themselves in new offenses.

In 1839, Frederick Hill, inspector of Scottish prisons, while supporting indeterminate sentencing, did so in the name of community safety, rather than individual reformation. In his annual report he wrote that he assumed transportation was going to be abolished and that for some convicts, reduced sentences were possible, but those convicts with no hope of reformation should be confined for the rest of their lives, because it ". . . would not be safe were it intended that they should return again to society."[27]

Also in 1839, the Scottish penologist George Combs, while lecturing in the United States, advanced a correctional proposal that featured indeterminate sentencing and parole. Combs believed that the sentence of a judge should be simply one of finding the person guilty of a crime and then sending him to a penitentiary until he was "liberated." The decision to liberate would come from "inspectors of penitentiaries" who would accept applications for liberation and would then grant them if satisfied that the prisoner had changed his or her mental condition enough to be safely returned to society. Evidence of such a change of mind would come from the demonstration of acquired skills, hard work, and the ability to provide for self-support, control criminal tendencies, and in general be a useful citizen.[28] Comb's proposal, although not implemented at that time, was a blueprint for future development, and would emerge one-hundred years later as the dominant sentencing plan.

Indeterminate sentencing, wherein defendants were sentenced to imprisonment with no fixed terms, was used in Germany as early as 1842. Governor **Georg Obermaier** found its provisions useful in operating the Munich prison. He kept records of inmates released early and claimed that only about 10 percent of them committed new crimes.[29] The low recidivism rate was credited, in good measure, to the work of prison aid societies who supervised released prisoners.

In 1846, M. Bonneville **de Marsangy,** the prosecutor at Versailles, France, delivered a speech on judicial sentencing in which he wholeheartedly supported the concept of indeterminate sentencing. He contended prison officials should have "the right upon the previous judgement of the judicial authority to admit to provisional liberty, after a sufficient period of expiation and on certain conditions the convict who has been completely reformed, reserving the right to return him to prison on the least well-founded complaint."[30] de Marsangy further pointed out that a similar policy existed for the treatment of juvenile offenders in France, and that "when a convict is reformed the imprisonment should terminate, as further detention can do him no good and is a needless burden to the state."[31]

Although the concept of indeterminate sentencing was accepted in England and Europe by the middle nineteenth century, it was not yet well known in the United States. The introduction of indeterminate sentencing to America and its initial implementation were the result mainly of the efforts of two correctional entrepreneurs: Enoch Wines and Zebulon Brockway. From 1860 onward they worked tirelessly to establish indeterminate sentencing and parole in the forefront of correctional reform.

Enoch Wines.   Dr. **Enoch Wines** served for many years as secretary of the New York Prison Association. Using this organization as a forum, he conducted a campaign to reform the nation's prison system. An essential part of this reformation would include the use of indeterminate sentencing and parole. Wines introduced European advocates for tickets-of-leave (better known in the United States as parole) to U.S. correctional leaders. For example, in the 1864 *New York Prison Association Annual Report* he described the work of Maconochie and Crofton with reference to prisoner release while the 1866 *Annual Report* featured a translation of de Marsangy's speech on indeterminate sentencing.[32] After conducting a survey of the New York state prisons in 1867 Wines and Theodore Dwight (chairman of the New York Prison Association) concluded that a new sentencing philosophy was urgently needed, one that would emphasize a program of graduated prison release. Their widely distributed report indicated that in their minds, and coming from some of the best minds in Europe and America, sentencing practices in the United States needed to be changed. Specifically, their belief was that sentences based on time served are wrong in principle and should be replaced by sentences in which reformation is the declared and actual objective of the sentence. Wines and Dwight believed that the Irish system was the best model known because it placed the prisoner's fate in his or her own hands by allowing him or her, through hard work and good conduct, to move through levels of less control, but that idleness and misconduct would result in coercion and restraint.[33]

Dr. Wines was also the prime mover behind the famous 1870 American Prison Association Convention held in Cincinnati. At the convention, correctional leaders from throughout the nation forged a reform program that would alter the course of U.S. corrections. By firmly establishing rehabilitation as the ideal goal of corrections, convention participants laid the groundwork for sweeping changes in U.S. criminal justice. The convention, with Wines's urging, adopted a Declaration of Principles (thirty-seven in number) that became a manifesto for future reform. Following are the principles that most directly apply to parole:[34]

I. Crime is an intentional violation of duties imposed by law, which inflicts an injury upon others. Criminals are persons convicted of crime by competent courts. Punishment is suffering inflicted on the criminal for the wrongdoing done by him, with a special view to secure his reformation.
II. The treatment of criminals by society is for the protection of society. But since such treatment is directed to the criminal rather than to the crime, its great object should be his moral regeneration. Hence the supreme aim of prison discipline is the reformation of criminals, not the infliction of vindictive suffering.
III. The progressive classification of prisoners, based on character and worked on some well-adjusted mark system, should be established in all prisons above the common jail.
IV. Since hope is a more potent agent than fear, it should be made an ever-present force in the minds of prisoners, by a well-devised and skillfully applied system of rewards for good conduct, industry and attention to learning. Rewards, more than punishments, are essential to every good prison system.
V. The prisoner's destiny should be placed, measurably, in his own hands; he must be put into circumstances where he will be able, through his own exertions, to continually better his own condition. A regulated self-interest must be brought into play and made constantly operative.
VIII. Peremptory sentences ought to be replaced by those of indeterminate length. Sentences limited only by satisfactory proof of reformation should be substituted for those measured by mere lapse of time.

After the convention, Wines continued to champion indeterminate sentencing in speeches, lectures, and writings. Although Wines himself never actually implemented a program of indeterminate sentencing, he influenced a young reform-minded warden, Zebulon Brockway, who would become the first American to apply the indeterminate concept to a prison setting.

Brockway and the Elmira Reformatory.   In 1869, **Zebulon Brockway**, then-superintendent of the Detroit House of Correction, experimented with a limited type of indeterminate sentence. His program, which applied only to female prostitutes, specified that these women could be released at any time during a three-year sentence, if and when they demonstrated reformation. Prison officials would determine the point at which reformation was achieved. After attending the 1870 convention in Cincinnati, Brockway was determined to expand indeterminate sentencing and for the next forty years was its ardent champion. In 1871 Brockway drafted an indeterminate sentencing bill for submission to the Michigan legislature. It included establishment of a state parole board with the following mission: "When it appears to said board there is a strong or reasonable probability that any ward possesses a sincere purpose to become a good citizen and the requisite moral power and self-control to live at liberty without violating the law and that such ward will become a fair member of society, then they shall issue to such ward an absolute release."[35] Although correction officials supported the bill, legislators seriously questioned its constitutionality and soundly rejected the proposed legislation.

Undaunted by this setback, Brockway continued to call for the implementation of indeterminate sentencing. His call was answered by the New York State Board of Prisons who tapped him as warden of a new prison at Elmira. New York officials had decided to call the Elmira facility a reformatory and to see that it would be operated by modern penal principles, including indeterminate sentencing.[36] The officials hoped the Elmira Reformatory would become the showplace of the New York prison system. Brockway was asked to draw up a legislative proposal for operation of the reformatory, a proposal that would be approved by the New York state legislature as part of a prison reform bill. Brockway's original proposal called for indeterminate sentencing without reservation (conceivably inmates could remain in custody for their entire lives if they did not change their ways). The proposal was later changed to limit an indeterminate sentence to no more than the maximum term prescribed by law. This change made the proposal more palatable to legislators, and the prison reform bill was enacted in 1877. Besides requiring indeterminate sentencing for all convicted felons, the law also established a "board of managers" with the power to establish rules and regulations for granting parole; maintain authority over released prisoners, with the power to reimprison them if rules of parole are broken; and gave the board the ability to hire people to supervise prisoners released on parole.[37]

Zebulon Brockway himself enumerated the principles that guided the administration of Elmira Reformatory, believing that offenders are reformable and that reformation is the right of every convict, as well as the duty of the state. In addition, reformation means that the emphasis is on the offender, not the offense; for reformation to be effective, the emphasis should not be on rushing offenders out of the prison but on giving them a trade, an education, and changing their attitudes, all of which takes time. Brockway went on to say that reformation is always aided by the prisoner's cooperation and that the most powerful means to gain that cooperation is to lengthen or shorten the term of incarceration, hence calling for a parole system. Finally, he stated that the reformatory process is educational, including instruction and reeducation of attitudes, motivation, and behavior.[38]

In an effort to ensure that inmates would be amenable to treatment and reformation, only defendants between the ages of sixteen and thirty who had never been convicted of felonies were eligible for commitment to Elmira. As we mentioned in our discussion of John Augustus in Chapter Two, limiting eligibility to relatively low risk groups is a common tactic by administrators to "sell" the merits of a new program. In the case of Elmira Reformatory it seemed to work as first reports indicated that parolees from that institution had unusually low recidivism rates and that incarcerated inmates were responding well to treatment. In general, the prison was functioning smoothly and was judged a "success."[39] Of course, the question that remained was whether the inmates' success was directly related to the type of treatment they received or to the method of their selection. Put in prison vernacular, "Light weight boy scouts are going to turn out fine no matter what you do to them." Unfortunately, in many cases, initial high rates of success cannot be maintained when the programs are extended to include other-than-low-risk categories.

For the first years of its existence, Elmira Reformatory stood as a beacon of reform. It was visible proof that a penal institution could be efficiently operated under indeterminate sentencing and that parole release programs could be both productive and comparatively safe. Zebulon Brockway became a popular lecturer and writer. He continued to praise indeterminate sentencing and parole at every opportunity. Other states, attempting to duplicate the success of Brockway, opened a number of reformatories patterned after the Elmira model.

Several states also adopted indeterminate sentencing laws, and even more set up parole systems. In some instances, state legislators were concerned about the constitutionality of indeterminate sentencing. These constitutional concerns were to prove unfounded, and indeterminate sentencing laws were eventually enacted in the majority of states. By 1900, twenty states had parole statutes on their books and eleven of these had indeterminate sentencing; three states had started granting conditional pardons by the governor that provided similar benefits to parole for a few prisoners.[40] Most of the states that passed enabling parole legislation, in contrast to the Elmira institutional model (where prison officials decided who should be granted parole), vested power to grant parole in state boards whose members generally were appointed by the governor. The statewide method proved most acceptable and today individual adult prisons are not authorized to grant parole.

After Elmira Reformatory had been in operation for several years, problems began to surface. Replacement personnel did not share the enthusiasm that original staff members had brought to their work. Pressures to enlarge the prison's capacity forced eligibility requirements to be relaxed, and more serious offenders were committed. This led to an increasing use of solitary confinement, which made the implementation of a rehabilitation plan much more problematic. Also, admitting a higher-risk category of prisoners eventually led to increasing rates of parolee recidivism. The physical condition of the Elmira Reformatory deteriorated and maintenance became a continuing headache. Prisoner complaints were more numerous and adverse editorials appeared in the New York press. Zebulon Brockway was no longer considered a "miracle worker" and in the waning years of his administration was severely criticized for being impractical, inefficient, and overly lenient. By 1900, Elmira Reformatory had become simply another prison with a full complement of problems and a meager supply of solutions. Notwithstanding the realities of long-term prison management, progressive reformers were convinced that such problems could be overcome with renewed dedication. In any case, parole had become an established tool of reformation, and like probation, it was to experience unparalleled growth in the next twenty-five years.

Expansion of Parole: 1900–1925

The growth of parole systems and indeterminate sentencing in the years immediately following 1900 was dramatic. By 1925, forty-four states, the territory of Hawaii, and the federal government had some form of parole, and thirty-seven of those states had indeterminate sentencing policies.[41] The use of parole had been expanded to most categories of criminals, not only young, first-time felons or especially deserving inmates, as had been the policy in the first years of Elmira Reformatory. According to historian David Rothman, ". . . by the Middle 1920s, over 90 percent of discharged inmates in New York, Washington, Colorado, and Indiana went out on parole; in Ohio, Illinois, Michigan, New Jersey, Maine, Kansas, and Massachusetts, the figure was over 80 percent."[42] State legislatures routinely approved new parole laws with little dissent. Typically, the new state laws placed limitations on when inmates were eligible for parole, excluded some offenders, and established a parole board. Edward Lindsey described the laws enacted in Colorado in 1908 and Louisiana in 1916, which were representative. Colorado applied indeterminate sentencing and parole to those sentenced to the state penitentiary for other than a life sentence. The court fixed the minimum and maximum sentence, but the maximum could not be longer than the limit set by Colorado statute. The Colorado act also allowed the governor to parole any convict who completed the minimum sentence, but even in these circumstances, he or she will not be finally discharged until the maximum term has expired.[43]

In Louisiana, the indeterminate sentence applied to those sentenced to the penitentiary except those sentenced to life; those sentenced for less than one year; or those convicted of treason, arson, rape, attempted rape, crimes against nature, bankers misusing funds, notaries public who are defaulters, train wreckers, kidnappers, and dynamiters. The term of imprisonment is fixed by the sentence but had to be within the minimum and maximum set by law. The Louisiana act also created a three member parole board.[44]

Widespread acceptance of the parole concept and a spate of enabling state legislation during this period were stimulated by two factors: (1) the linking of parole with individual justice and (2) the support of criminal justice elites.

Parole and Individualized Justice

Progressive reformers at the turn of the twentieth century embraced parole as the linchpin in a system of **individualized justice.** When inmates were readily eligible for parole, their sentences could be tailored to individual situations. Progressives assumed that the main purpose of incarceration was to reform, and when inmates had undergone the necessary reformation, they would be released on parole. Because the time it took to achieve reformation varied on an individual basis, the length of time in custody would vary accordingly. Reformers further assumed that correctional officials would be able to recognize individual reformation when it had occurred. Parole, in which the defendant "held the key" to his or her own release, was seen as the most logical vehicle for achieving individual justice.

Progressives linked parole with another tool of individual justice, the indeterminate sentence, to forge a united front against determinate or flat-time sentences. Reformers equated fixed sentences with a barbaric past where revenge dominated sentencing policies. Charlton Lewis, in the 1900 National Prison Association *Proceedings,* likened the determinate sentence to organized lynchings and claimed it had originated from the human desire for revenge.[45] In 1907, Roland Molineux, in the progressive journal *Charities and Common,* contended that determinate sentencing laws were "childlessly futile" and compared them to sentencing "the lunatic to three months in the asylum or the victim of smallpox to thirty days in the hospital, at the end of these periods to turn them loose whether sane or insane, cured or still diseased."[46]

Warren Spaulding, a leading progressive and outspoken advocate of indeterminate sentencing and parole, claimed that these policies were absolutely essential because "There is no criminal class. . . . Each criminal is an individual and should be treated as such."[47] Progressives were not above reminding opponents of reform that even though parole systems were designed to mitigate excessive punishment, they could also be used to punish. Because granting parole was discretionary, offenders deemed "incorrigible" or "sociopathic" could be kept in custody for long periods simply by denying their parole petitions. In this manner, professional criminals could be held behind bars for the maximum amount of time. Other inmates whose incorrigibility stemmed from "mental deficiency" or "feeble-mindedness" could also be indefinitely denied their freedom. The latter group was not an insignificant number. Charles Hoffman, a reform-minded judge, claimed, "a great part of the crime wave of which we hear so much, is caused by weak-willed, psychopathic or feeble-minded individuals who are unable to resist the impulses of the moment."[48] It was clear that many progressive reformers supported parole, including some judges. However, did the elites of the criminal justice system also support this new method of prison release? The next section addresses this question.

Support of Criminal Justice Elites

The nation's prison wardens were enthusiastic proponents of indeterminate sentencing and its companion, parole. At the 1900 meeting of the National Prison Association, wardens threw their wholehearted support behind these concepts, indicating "the principle of the indeterminate sentence; that, in the opinion of this body no other penal system yet devised supplies to the offender so many motives and opportunities for reformation, erects so many barriers against crime as an occupation, and affords society so effective protection against the incursions of the habitual criminal."[49] Prison officials assumed they would have considerable input into the decision making of parole, either through service on the boards, or by making notations in the files of inmates that could affect parole decisions (for example "dangerous inmate, many disciplinary infractions, do not release"). Inmates, aware of this possibility, would be willing to "toe the line" to avoid being denied parole. In this way, reformers had given prison wardens a mechanism of control far more effective than the lash, and much more legitimate: They could reward conforming behavior and punish rule breakers. It is not surprising, therefore, that they rushed to endorse parole and indeterminate sentencing.[50]

Judges also generally supported parole as an important weapon in the arsenal of correctional reform. This was evidenced by a series of court rulings that upheld the legality and appropriateness of parole laws. An Ohio judge summed up the sentiments of his colleagues calling parole "a new experiment in the management and discipline of prisoners" that was "prompted by a desire to reform as well as to protect society."[51] The existence of parole also served judges in a very practical way by relieving them of responsibility for the actions of newly released criminals. Because most state laws mandated a minimum and maximum term for criminal offense, judges could legitimately claim that, in the worst-case scenario of a parolee committing a heinous crime, they had imposed the maximum term but the parole board had let the felon out early. Most judges realized that the prison system could not function properly unless there was some way of mitigating unrealistically long sentences. Parole offered this possibility, without sticking judges with the responsibility for its spectacular failures.

District attorneys, on the whole, were also comfortable with parole legislation. Like probation, parole could be used as a valuable bargaining tool. Defendants could be induced to plead guilty if sentences were structured to include the possibility of an early parole date. District attorneys were aware that when notorious criminals came up for release consideration, they could communicate their vigorous opposition to the parole board. Additionally, prosecutors realized that the parole system, properly managed, could actually result in longer sentences for inmates. Studies of prison systems in Minnesota and Illinois revealed that after parole had been instituted inmates, on average, served almost one year longer. One should not be too quick to attribute a direct causal relationship to these findings because a variety of factors are involved, including a more conservative correctional climate. Also, as a result of plea bargaining, some offenders could have received shorter sentences after determinate sentencing.[52]

Opposition

Not all criminal justice participants were happy with parole. Police officials, conservative judges, and hard-line district attorneys still remained skeptical. At their annual convention in 1897, police chiefs expressed their opposition to parole (an opposition that has not changed appreciably over time): "It is the sense of this convention that it is not in the conformity with justice nor with the best interests of our people and society, to parole prisoners committed to the penitentiary. . . ."[53] A Chicago judge defined parole as "giving the dog two free bites instead of one," whereas a New York district attorney indicated that parole was "an overindulgence to the offender."[54] Notwithstanding such views, opponents of parole in the early twentieth century were steamrolled by the force of progressive reform and could do little to halt its dramatic expansion. However, by the late 1920s criticism of parole systems had become more noticeable.

Criticism and Response: 1925–1965

By 1925 most parole systems had been in place for several years and the reality of bureaucratic routine had replaced the ideal of progressive innovation. Ideally, parole boards would be comprised of correctional experts who judged applicants on the basis of objective criteria. In reality, most parole boards were comprised of wardens and part-time managers whose decisions were either arbitrary or based mainly on institutional considerations. Ideally, well-trained specialists would supervise paroled inmates. In reality, parole officers were underqualified and overloaded, resulting in the worst of both worlds—much individual assistance and little community protection.

The Criticism

The realities of parole were not lost on criminal justice elites or the public. According to David Rothman, during this period, "Parole became the whipping boy for the failures of law enforcement agencies to control or reduce crime. Whenever fears of a 'crime wave' swept through the country, or whenever a particularly senseless or tragic crime occurred, parole invariably bore the brunt of attack."[55] As an example, Rothman cites a *Cleveland Plain Dealer* editorial that claimed "Most bandit gangs are made up in large part of paroled men—men who have been turned loose on the public by some board given more to sentimentalism and leniency than to justice. If parole abuse were curbed the keystone of the arch of banditry would fall."[56] Similarly, the *Denver Post,* after reporting the story of a parolee who had killed a police officer, commented, "The number of murders and other crimes of violence committed by paroled criminals shows there is something rotten with the administration of our parole system."[57]

Several commissions and investigatory bodies were formed in the 1920s and 1930s as a result of citizen concern over parole. Two of the most prestigious and influential were the **Wilcox Report,** published in 1929, and the **Wickersham Commission Report,** put out in 1931. Both investigations were severely critical of parole boards and parole supervision. Clair Wilcox's report (submitted to the Pennsylvania Parole Commission) detailed the arbitrary nature of parole board decision making and reported each inmate received an average six minutes of hearing and consultation.[58] The Wickersham Commission, part of the National Commission on Law Observance and Enforcement, complained of the "appointment of incompetent and untrained parole officers," and observed "almost anybody is considered good enough to be a parole officer."[59]

The Response

Parole officials and their supporters responded to such criticism by attempting to shore up parole operations at two key points: the parole board and the supervision of released inmates. Two important changes in the administration and organization of parole systems were undertaken, changes that continue to shape modern-day operations. First, parole boards became centralized units with statewide responsibilities. Individual institutions no longer were empowered to grant parole. Second, an emphasis was placed on community supervision of parolees with a corresponding increase in the number and type of parole conditions established.[60]

A centralized paroling authority significantly changed the composition of parole boards and the criteria used to grant releases. Prison officials no longer were in control of parole boards and behavior in prison was no longer the main criteria of release. Parole boards were often composed of noncorrectional personnel who did not take it for granted that a good prison record meant the inmate would do equally well in a community setting. David Rothman states that before 1925 wardens dominated parole boards. This was so because wardens usually served as one of three members of the boards, the hearings were held on the warden's prison grounds (sometimes in the warden's office), and the inmate's institutional conduct record carried so much weight in the decision making, with wardens having great influence on the content of those records. Later, in the 1920s, however, parole systems became more independent, moving away from the control of wardens, who no longer served on the committees. Also, final decisions were often made in the state capital, and an inmate's prior record became more important than institutional behavior.[61]

The second important change in the organization of parole that occurred during this period regarded supervision. Prior to 1930, parole supervision, in many instances, had been an afterthought. Inmates were released with a warning to "check in with their parole officers" and "sin no more." Supervision of parolees was not given much consideration. For example, in Oregon one parole officer was assigned a caseload of 400 over a territory of 92,000 square miles, whereas in Washington each officer carried more than 500 cases.[62] Under these conditions, not much supervision was expected or accomplished. In 1930, a panel of investigators in New York headed by Alfred Lewisohn recommended sweeping changes in postrelease practices. The report recommended that parole officers be accorded professional status and be assigned caseloads of no more than seventy-five.[63]

Other state commissions recommended similar programs of personnel development. Partly as a result of these recommendations, more parole officers were hired and more attention given to parole supervision. This added concern led to more specific release conditions. Before 1930 conditions were broad admonishments, such as "lead an honest life," "avoid dissolute companions," "conduct yourself as a good citizen," or "respect and obey the law." In response to criticism of parole supervision, release terms became more specific, warning inmates to "stay out of _____ County," "not associate with _____ ," "make restitution of _____ to _____ ," or "not to engage in the business of _____ ."

The Federal Parole System mirrored the changes in state parole administration that occurred in the 1930s. Charles Meyer, a veteran parole officer, described federal developments in a 1952 article published in the *Journal of Criminal Law, Criminology, and Police Science.* In that article, Meyer recalls that the **Federal Parole Act** was passed in 1910 but there were so many lifers in the system at the time that the law was amended in 1913 to make lifers eligible after serving fifteen years. Each penitentiary had its own parole board, with the warden, prison doctor, and superintendent of prisons from Washington, DC, serving as members. The attorney general had final approval of all paroles. In addition, each institution had a parole officer (PO) assigned to supervise released prisoners, and if the parolee did not live too far away from the institution, the PO would make field visits. It was not long, however, before parolees were scattered all over the country, and POs could not make many visits. That is, until 1930 when Congress amended the Federal Probation Act, giving federal POs, who were also under the direction of the attorney general, the added responsibility of supervising federal parolees. This trend toward centralization was aided by Prohibition, which so enlarged the parolee population that an even more centralized system of parole seemed necessary. Thus, in 1930, Congress enacted a law creating a three-member board of parole, under the authority of the attorney general, with complete authority to grant and revoke parole. In addition, the attorney general appointed a parole executive whose office was at the headquarters of the parole board and who gave directions to probation officers in the field.[64]

These two major changes in parole operations during the 1930s (centralization of parole boards and greater emphasis on supervision) were not fundamental overhauls of the system. Parole advocates remained convinced of the system's effectiveness, and rather than call for radical alterations, they opted for fine-tuning. Additionally, parole officers increasingly aligned themselves with the popular treatment model advocated by many correctional elites. For example, in 1949 the National Probation and Parole Association declared the most desirable training for parole officers was the master of social work degree.[65] These changes were sufficient to keep parole virtually intact until the 1960s.

The lack of serious questioning regarding parole's basic purpose did not mean the system had improved measurably. On the contrary, in 1939 an extensive study of parole, *The Attorney General's Survey of Release Procedure,* was highly critical of parole practices, citing many of the same problems that had been revealed by the Wickersham Commission in 1931. In spite of the attorney general's report, by the 1940s and 1950s parole was such an established part of the criminal justice system (in 1944, the last holdout, Mississippi, passed a parole law) that correctional leaders and legislators were unwilling to consider changing its basic organization. However, this reluctance was soon to be overcome.

Abolish Parole? 1965–1980

The opposition to parole that surfaced in the 1960s was part of the general assault on the rehabilitation model (see Chapter One). Parole, viewed as a critical component of the rehabilitative model, was automatically suspect. Particularly open to criticism was the **discretionary release** policy of parole boards and the effectiveness of community supervision as a means of offender rehabilitation. Parole boards were portrayed as arbitrary and subjective, and parole supervision was seen as part of the "nothing works" syndrome. Lawyers were among the first to seriously challenge parole discretion. A 1967 Supreme Court decision, *Morrisey v. Brewer* (which held that parole could not be terminated without a formal hearing) restricted the power of parole boards to revoke parole and in the process changed the nature of parole supervision by making parole officers more accountable for their statements and recommendations. When diverse individuals and groups, such as the liberal American Friends Service Committee, conservative academicians Andrew Von Hirsch and Kathleen Hanrahan, the liberal politician Edward Kennedy, and the centrist administrator Norman Carlson (head of the Federal Prison System), all advocated the abolition of parole, legislators took note. In addition the writings of James Q. Wilson on the need for harsh punishment to deter crime and David Fogel's contention that rehabilitation in prison was unlikely made parole seem less attractive. At the same time, prison riots in California and New York (particularly the Attica prison riot in 1971) where the prisoners demanded that release practices be changed further weakened support for parole.[66]

In the middle 1970s several states and Congress took legislative action to restrict the use of parole. These restrictions usually were incorporated into determinate sentencing bills, which established specific penalties for criminal offenses (only in unusual circumstances could the sentencing judge deviate from prescribed terms). Eventually nine states—California, Colorado, Connecticut, Illinois, Indiana, Maine, Minnesota, New Mexico, North Carolina—and the federal government enacted various types of determinate policies that either limited or removed the parole board's discretion to release inmates in parole. Only three states took action to restrict parole supervision—Maine, Connecticut, and Washington—and only in Maine was supervision completely eliminated.

Actions taken in Illinois to reinstate determinate sentencing and in Indiana to put into effect presumptive sentencing, described by Lawrence Travis and Vincent O'Leary,[67] are representative of legislatively mandated changes in parole practice. Illinois ended discretionary parole release in 1977, except for those convicted and sentenced before the new law was passed. In its place is a system of legislatively determined policies, requiring judges to set sentences within certain limits, although judges do have discretion within those limits. A prisoner review board rules on possible violations of conditions, and if an offender is reincarcerated, the board can grant release at any time to the full term of the original supervised release.

In Indiana, a statute was passed in 1976 abolishing discretionary parole release for all offenders except those sentenced to life imprisonment. The legislature prescribes the term of imprisonment for each category of offense, and the judge must impose that sentence, although the length may be raised or lowered based on aggravating or mitigating factors proved at the sentencing hearing. Good-time credits can be earned by the inmates, and at the end of the sentence, minus time credited for good behavior, the offender is released for one year of supervision. If parole is revoked during that one year, the offender is reincarcerated for the remainder of the sentence, minus good time, although he or she can be paroled at any time before the new release date is met.

After the new sentencing policies took effect, the percentage of inmates released on parole dropped significantly. In 1977, 72 percent of all prison releases were by discretionary parole, only 6 percent were via mandatory release. By 1986, only 43 percent of all releases were via discretionary parole, whereas **mandatory release** accounted for 31 percent of all released prisoners in 1986.[68] Critics continued to condemn parole, while its supporters remained silent. By the late 1970s it appeared to many correctional observers that parole was on its way out.[69] However, as so often in the past, reports of its demise were premature.

Parole—On Its Way Back: 1980–Present

Recent government figures reveal that the average annual increase in parolees between 1980 and 1992 was 10 percent; from 1992 to 2000 the number of adults on parole grew at an average of only 0.7 percent.[70] So it seems the exponential growth in parole numbers may be over (at least for the time being); however, parole is not going away any time soon. Growth in prison populations is the most obvious explanation for this: From 1980 to 1990, the number of state prisoners grew 131.9 percent; from 1990 to 2000 the number of prisoners grew another 74.5 percent.[71] Prison construction cannot keep pace with this population growth, further aggravating the situation. Parole offers a readily available safety valve to compensate for the system's inability to absorb new inmates and the fact remains that 95 percent of all prison inmates will someday be released, 80 percent of these released to parole supervision.[72] Although the prison population boom is the single most important reason for parole's reemergence, other factors are involved: (1) Key criminal justice actors still support it, (2) new release procedures have made it more acceptable, (3) release practices mandate its use, and finally (4) mitigation of sentence severity remains essential.

1. Criminal justice professionals support parole. The reasons that wardens, district attorneys, and judges supported parole in the early twentieth century remain valid today. Wardens continue to believe the availability of parole allows them to manage inmates effectively. District attorneys and judges still assume that the possibility of parole facilitates processing of criminal cases.

2. New release procedures have made parole more acceptable. Parole officials have taken steps to remove unlimited discretion from parole boards and to improve supervision methods. In fact, by 2000 sixteen states abolished discretionary parole and another four had eliminated discretionary release for certain violent offenders; most of the rest of the states had restricted parole by requiring certain standards be met for offenders to be eligible for release.[73] Furthermore, the implementation of salient factor scores and other guidelines that attempt to predict the risk of recidivism have introduced more objectivity into decision making by parole boards. Adoption of new supervision methods based on the principles of differential supervision has allowed caseloads to be managed more effectively. Such changes generally have been well received and serve to bolster support for parole. Many observers share the view of parole expressed by the American Probation and Parole Association: Parole plays a vital role in our criminal justice system, guarding public safety by screening serious offenders before they return to the community, and, since most parole boards now allow victims to attend hearings and make statements concerning release, parole also serves as an important point of contact for victims as a criminal sentence is carried out.[74]

3. Release practices mandate the use of parole. Even though several states and the federal government have done away with parole boards through passage of determinate sentencing laws or adopting of sentencing guidelines, supervision of inmates (released for a variety of reasons) remains a vital parole responsibility. As noted earlier, prison exits that fall into the preceding categories are termed mandatory releases. This concept is defined by the U.S. Department of Justice as releases that do not result from the decisions of a parole board but do involve supervision in the community by a parole agency for a specific period of time.[75]

As noted previously, in 1986, the Bureau of Justice Statistics (BJS) reported that "The percent of mandatory releases from prison increased about fivefold during the past decade, from about 6% in 1977 to over 31% in 1986. By contrast, prisoners released by a parole board decision declined from nearly 72% of all releases in 1977 to about 43% in 1986."[76] More recently, the BJS reported that mandatory releases accounted for 41 percent of releases in 1999, discretionary parole releases decreased to 24 percent, and releases as a result of sentence expiration rose from 13 to 18 percent from 1990 to 1999.[77] The same report states that "Regardless of their method of release, nearly all State prisoners (at least 95%) will be released from prison at some point; nearly 80% will be released to parole supervision."[78] With the prison population growing from 708,393 in 1990 to 1,440,655 in 2002[79] (a 103 percent increase), and with the knowledge that 95 percent of these prisoners will someday be released, parole supervision is not going away any time soon.

4. The mitigation of sentence severity remains essential. In the real world of criminal justice there is a continued need to mitigate judicial sentencing. Legislators and judges, with an eye to the electorate, continue imposing harsh sentences for unpopular offenses. Recently, there has been a spate of sentencing laws increasing maximum penalties for those convicted of drunk driving, drug sales, sex offenses, and child abuse. Moreover, many states have reduced the age that a juvenile may be tried as an adult for certain (usually violent) offenses. Judges, not wanting to appear insensitive to contemporary concerns, in such cases have responded by imposing maximum sentences. However, the prison system cannot handle the current influx of newly sentenced prisoners, and on reflection, there is often no legitimate rationale for keeping so many offenders imprisoned for such long periods. Overcrowding has made prison living conditions deplorable, put an end to many training programs because of space and security considerations, increased the level of prison violence, and put a severe strain on the ability of prison personnel to effectively manage the institutions. Parole offers a convenient way out of this dilemma by mitigating unrealistic sentences. Even in states with determinate sentencing laws there is the realization that parole release is necessary to ensure the safe and sane management of a prison system.[80] Until the ideal of equitable, impartial, and objective criminal sentencing is achieved, the need for mitigation through parole will remain.

Summary

Parole as conditional release from prison traces its origins to the English practice of transportation. Convicts sent to America and Australia escaped the death penalty and were eventually released from custody after working in the colonies. Alexander Maconochie, while head of the Norfolk Island penal colony, popularized the concept of conditional release by implementing a prisonwide ticket-of-leave policy. Sir Walter Crofton, head of the Irish prison system, adopted this release policy, which was essentially a form of parole. Crofton's plan emphasized the importance of community supervision by correctional officials, a policy later incorporated into the English prison system.

In the United States, parole originated from the practice of commuting the sentences of prisoners who demonstrated good behavior. As an essential component in open-ended sentencing, parole was given its major impetus by the acceptance and implementation of indeterminate sentencing. Enoch Wines, a staunch advocate of parole, introduced the ideas of Maconochie and Crofton to U.S. correctional leaders. Zebulon Brockway, first warden of Elmira Reformatory, was also the first American to implement a full-scale program of indeterminate sentencing and parole. When Brockway's program achieved some initial success, several states passed parole and indeterminate sentencing laws. The pace of such legislation quickened when early twentieth-century progressives made parole the cornerstone of their correctional reform program.

When problems surfaced in the 1920s, parole officials responded by centralizing parole decision making in state boards and by increasing community supervision. Although parole was frequently vilified in the press, no significant organizational changes were undertaken until the late 1960s when opponents of parole (with widely different perspectives) were successful in convincing several state legislatures to restrict its usage. However, prison crowding, continued support from criminal justice elites, more effective release methods, mandated prison releases, and the need to counterbalance unrealistic sentences have worked to keep parole in the forefront of U.S. corrections.

Key People and Terms

Banishment (48)
Zebulon Brockway (60)
Sir Walter Crofton (54)
Discretionary release (69)
Federal Parole Act (68)
Good time (56)
Indeterminate sentence (57)
Individualized justice (63)
Irish Plan (55)
Alexander Maconochie (51)
Mark system (53)

Mandatory release (70)
de Marsangy (59)
Colonel Montesinos (58)
Georg Obermaier (58)
Parole (47)
Tickets-of-leave (51)
Transportation (48)
Wickersham Commission Report (66)
Wilcox Report (66)
Enoch Wines (59)

Key Legal Case

Morrissey v. Brewer

Questions for Discussion and Review

1. Discuss transportation and its relationship to parole. How did transportation to America differ from transportation to Australia?

2. What was a ticket-of-leave? How was the ticket-of-leave system similar to, and different from, parole?

3. Discuss the contributions of Alexander Maconochie to the development of parole. What were the five stages in Maconochie's mark system?

4. Discuss Sir Walter Crofton's mark system and how it differed from Maconochie's.

5. What is an indeterminate sentence? Discuss the foreign origins of the indeterminate sentence and how this sentencing structure is related to the development of parole in the United States.

6. Discuss the contributions of Enoch Wines and Zebulon Brockway to the development of parole in the United States.

7. Discuss the expansion of parole from 1900 to 1925. What were the critical elements contributing to this expansion?

8. What were the criticisms leveled against parole from 1925 to 1960? How did parole's supporters respond to these criticisms?

9. Why was parole so often criticized during the 1960s and 1970s? Why is parole probably here to stay?

Relevant Internet Sites

United States Parole Commission: www.usdoj.gov/uspc

History of parole in New York state: http://parole.state.ny.us/history.html

History of parole in Texas: www.tdcj.state.tx.us/parole/parole-history.htm

History of parole in Canada: www.npb-cnlc.gc.ca/infocntr/parolec/phistore.htm

Notes

1. Warren Spaulding, "Keynote Address," *Proceedings* (American Prison Association, 1916) 548.

2. Rob Warden, "The Rape That Wasn't—The First DNA Exoneration in Illinois," Northwestern University School of Law, Center on Wrongful Convictions (2002). Retrieved November 27, 2003, from www.law.northwestern.edu/depts/clinic/wrongful/exonerations/Dotson.htm

3. David Dressler, *Practice and Theory of Probation and Parole* (New York: Columbia University Press, 1962) 57.

4. Gary Cavender, *Parole: A Critical Analysis* (Port Washington, NY: National University Publications, 1982) 7.

5. Dressler 57.

6. Dressler 57–58.

7. Dressler 59.

8. Russel Ward, *The Australian Legend* (Melbourne, Australia: Oxford University Press, 1978).

9. For an excellent overview of the influence of convicts on Australian life see Russel Ward *The Australian Legend* (1978).

10. William Parker, *Parole: Origins, Development, Current Practices and Statutes* (College Park, MD: American Correctional Association, 1972) 16.

11. Parker 17.

12. Dressler 71.

13. Cavender 13.

14. Dressler 63.

15. Edward Lindsey, "Historical Sketch of the Indeterminate Sentence and Parole System," *Journal of Criminal Law and Criminology* 16 (1925): 13.

16. Dressler 68.

17. Dressler 70.

18. Dressler 65.

19. Parker 18.

20. Parker 21.

21. Parker 21.

22. Charles L. Newman, *Sourcebook on Probation, Parole and Pardons* (Springfield, IL: Charles C. Thomas, 1968) 32.

23. Lindsey 10.

24. Dressler 74.

25. Lindsey 14.

26. Lindsey 11.

27. Lindsey 14.

28. Newman 34–35.

29. Paul F. Cromwell, Rolando V. del Carmen, and Leanne F. Alarid, *Community-Based Corrections* (Belmont, CA: Wadsworth, 2002) 163.

30. Lindsey 14.

31. Lindsey 15.

32. Lindsey 15.

33. Lindsey 16–17.

34. Lindsey 20.

35. Lindsey 18.

36. Lindsey 17.

37. Lindsey 22–23.

38. Dressler 75.

39. David J. Rothman, *Incarceration and Its Alternatives in Twentieth Century America* (Washington, DC: U.S. Government Printing Office, 1979) 7.

40. Lindsey 40.

41. Lindsey 69.

42. Rothman 22.

43. Lindsey 55.

44. Lindsey 67.

45. Charlton Lewis, *Proceedings* (New York: National Prison Association, 1900).

46. Roland Molineux, "The Court of Rehabilitation," *Charities and Common* 18 (1907): 739.

47. Warren Spaulding, "The Treatment of Crime," *Journal of Criminal Law and Criminology* 3 (1912–1913): 378, 381.

48. David Rothman, *Conscience and Convenience: The Asylum and Its Alternatives in Progressive America* (Boston: Little, Brown, 1980) 71.

49. Rothman, *Conscience and Convenience* 73.

50. Rothman, *Conscience and Convenience* 74.

51. Rothman, *Conscience and Convenience* 76.

52. Lindsey 76.

53. Rothman, *Conscience and Convenience* 79–80.

54. Rothman, *Conscience and Convenience* 80.

55. Rothman, *Conscience and Convenience* 158.

56. Rothman, *Conscience and Convenience* 160.

57. Rothman, *Conscience and Convenience* 161.

58. Clair Wilcox, *The Parole of Adults from State Penal Institutions in Pennsylvania* (Part II, Report of the Pennsylvania State Parole Commission to the Legislature, Philadelphia, 1927) 62.

59. National Commission of Law Observance and Enforcement (commonly known as the Wickersham Commission), *Penal Institutions, Probation and Parole* (Washington, DC: U.S. Government Printing Office, 1931) 305.

60. Lawrence F. Travis and Vincent O'Leary, "A History of Parole," in *Probation, Parole, and Community Corrections*, eds. Robert M. Carter, Daniel Glaser, and Leslie T. Wilkins (New York: Wiley, 1984) 108.

61. Rothman, *Conscience and Convenience* 183.

62. Rothman, *Conscience and Convenience* 178–179.

63. Rothman, *Conscience and Convenience* 181.

64. Charles H. Z. Meyer, "A Half Century of Federal Probation and Parole," *Journal of Criminal Law, Criminology, and Police Science* 42 (1952): 708.

65. Vincent O'Leary, "Parole Administration," in *Handbook of Criminology*, ed. Daniel Glaser (Chicago: Rand McNally, 1974) 932.

66. For an excellent perspective on the various arguments against parole during the 1970s see American Friends Service Committee, *Struggle for Justice* (New York: Hill and Wang, 1972); Bob Wilson, "Parole Release: Devil or Savior?" *Corrections Magazine* 3 (September, 1977): 48-59; Andrew von Hirsch and Kathleen Hanrahan, *Abolish Parole?* (Washington, DC: U.S. Government Printing Office, 1978); David Fogel, *We Are the Living Proof* (Cincinnati, OH: Anderson, 1975); and John Irwin, *Prisons in Turmoil* (Boston: Little, Brown, 1980).

67. Travis and O'Leary 116.

68. U.S. Department of Justice, *Probation and Parole, 1986* (Washington, DC: U.S. Government Printing Office, 1987).

69. Gary Cavender, *Parole: A Critical Analysis* (Port Washington, NY: National University Publications, and Kennikat Press, 1982) 68–81.

70. Timothy Hughes, Doris James Wilson, and Allen J. Beck, *Trends in State Parole, 1990–2000* (Washington, DC: U.S. Department of Justice 2001).

71. Hughes et al. 2.

72. Hughes et al. 4.

73. Hughes et al. 2.

74. Karen Fuller, "An Editorial in Response to States Considering the Abolition of Parole," undated, American Probation and Parole Association. Retrieved November 29, 2003, from www.appa-net.org/abolition.html

75. U.S. Department of Justice 2.

76. Bureau of Justice Statistics, "Prisoners in 1985," *BJS Bulletin* (Washington, DC: U.S. Department of Justice, 1986) 2.

77. Hughes et al. 4.

78. Hughes et al. 4.

79. Paige M. Harrison and Allen J. Beck, *Prisoners in 2002* (Washington, DC: Bureau of Justice Statistics, 2003) 1.

80. Prison officials from California to Virginia expressed the view that parole release is an essential part of a modern prison system to both authors on several occasions.

Part II

The Mission

Although probation and parole agencies offer a wide variety of services, their missions can be divided into two basic parts: investigation and supervision. Agencies are charged with the dual responsibility of investigating the suitability of probation and parole applicants and then providing community supervision for those granted that consideration. Although there is some overlap between investigation and supervision, the functions stand relatively independent; each involves a unique set of objectives and procedures. For example, there is a different agenda for preparing a one-time investigation report than for undertaking a program of long-term supervision. In addition, organizational dynamics impact investigation officers and parole boards differently than they do personnel providing community supervision. There are sufficient reasons to examine the missions of investigation and supervision in separate chapters.

In Chapter Four the basic working document of probation—the presentence investigation report—is discussed and analyzed. Chapter Five contains a review of the many facets of probation supervision. The subject of Chapter Six is whether to grant parole; a decision that, in most jurisdictions, is made on the basis of an investigation conducted by parole boards with the assistance of correctional officials. Chapter Seven considers the pragmatic and problematic nature of parole supervision.

4

The Presentence Investigation

Overview of the Presentence Investigation

The **presentence investigation (PSI)** is an investigation of a criminal defendant to reveal factors relevant to sentencing. This investigation pertains to the background of the defendant and the nature of the crime committed. When the investigation is written and organized in a prescribed format it becomes a **presentence report.** According to a government study entitled "The Selective Presentence Investigation Report," a presentence report is the basic working document in judicial and correctional administration serving five general functions:

1. To assist the court in rendering an appropriate sentence;
2. To aid the probation department in supervising probationers;
3. To help institutional personnel in developing appropriate classification, release and treatment programs;
4. To assist parole boards in deciding parole applications;
5. To provide information for conducting research.[1]

The PSI is generally requested after a plea of guilty has been entered or a finding of guilty has been secured but before sentence has been pronounced. On occasion, however, PSIs will be done before a conviction has been obtained. Presentence reports are routinely submitted for defendants who apply for pretrial diversion—programs whereby defendants with minor criminal records are allowed to pursue some community program (drug or alcohol counseling) and on completion to have all criminal charges dismissed. In cases other than diversion, "pre-plea" reports are controversial because the defendant's (not having entered a guilty plea) candor and cooperation are questionable. The latter reports are used mainly for plea bargaining in unusual cases.

Although reports can vary considerably from jurisdiction to jurisdiction, their overall content generally follows federal guidelines, consisting of the following five essential (or core) information modules and various subsections:[2]

1. **Offense (Core)**
   Official version
   Defendant's version
   Codefendant information
   Statements of witnesses, complainants, and victims
2. **Prior Record (Core)**
   Juvenile adjudications
   Adult record
3. **Personal and Family Data (Core)**
   Defendant
   Parent and siblings
   Marital
   Education
   Employment
   Health
      Physical
      Mental and emotional
   Military service
   Financial condition
      Assets
      Liabilities
4. **Evaluation (Core)**
   Alternative plans
   Sentencing data
5. **Recommendations (Core)**

Typically, there is a cover sheet attached to the presentence report listing pertinent information.[3] Following is a sample cover sheet.

Presentence Report: Sample Cover Sheet

Name:	Date:
Address:	Docket No.:
	Offense:
Legal Residence:	
Age:	Penalty:
Sex:	
Citizenship:	Plea:
Education:	Verdict:
Marital Status:	Custody:

Dependents: Prosecuting Atty:
Soc. Sec. No.:
                                         Defense Counsel:

FBI No.:
Detainers or Charges Pending:
Codefendants:
Disposition: Date:

Presentence investigators are not expected to determine guilt or innocence but instead should be neutral observers who accurately report the facts and the circumstances surrounding the individual offender in each case. Ideally, probation officers should be objective and unbiased in the conduct of their investigations. Also, because the presentence report is so important to the sentencing process, the report must be accurate, distinguish between verified and unverified information, and distinguish between fact and opinion.[4] The importance of an objective report is given lip service by all departments and no one in probation would openly disagree with the following pronouncement contained in a federal probation presentence manual:

> Each defendant should be investigated without any preconception or prejudgement on the probation officer's part as to the outcome of the defendant's case. The probation officer must be completely objective and impartial in conducting the investigation and in writing the presentence report. He not only reports the tangible facts in the case, but also such subjective elements as the defendant's attitude, feelings, and emotional reactions. He presents them so as to give to the court an accurate, unbiased, and complete picture of the defendant and his prospect for becoming a law-abiding, responsible citizen. Every effort must be made to check the accuracy of information which is likely to be damaging to the defendant or to have a definite bearing on the welfare of the family and the safety of the community.[5]

Because the presentence report is foremost an aid to sentencing, the investigation officer must consider whether probation or incarceration is appropriate. A prominent probation advocate suggests that probation officers consider the following questions:

1. Is the offender dangerous at the present time?
2. Will incarceration help or harm the offender?
3. Is probation an acceptable, constructive substitute for institutionalization in this particular case?
4. Is the individual mentally and emotionally capable of benefiting from probation treatment?
5. Is his or her attitude toward society and probation such as to justify the use of probation in lieu of incarceration?

6. Will society, in the long run, benefit if the defendant is placed on probation? Will the individual benefit?
7. Will granting probation at this time be construed by the offender as leniency or as "beating the rap," and thus be deleterious rather than helpful?[6]

The advice given in the PSI, of course, assumes that the judge has some latitude in sentencing. In many instances such latitude is not the case because determinate or mandatory sentencing now requires a specific judgment (regardless of individual circumstances).

The importance of the PSI has been universally emphasized by a wide variety of practitioners, academicians, and judges. For example, Lawrence Stump, a probation official, called the presentence report, "the very core of the probation process"; Robert Carter, prominent criminologist, wrote of the presentence investigator, "the very success or failure of the philosophy, tradition and practice of probation hinges upon his evaluation and recommendation to the court"; and one judge commented that, "of all the administrative aids to the judge an adequate, comprehensive, and complete presentence investigation is the best guide to intelligent sentencing."[7] The widespread acceptance of the PSI can be seen in Bureau of Justice Statistics estimates that more than one million presentence reports are submitted annually.[8] Moreover, U.S. probation officers wrote presentence investigations for 64 percent of all felons in 1995.[9]

Although much has been written about the PSI, surprisingly little is known about how PSI reports are actually prepared. Especially lacking is an understanding of the organizational dynamics that impact probation officers.[10] In this chapter a comprehensive understanding of the PSI is developed by tracing its historical and judicial basis, analyzing its contemporary usage, delineating its component parts, evaluating its effectiveness, and presenting firsthand evidence of how PSIs are actually conducted. The latter presentation will address two key issues: Do judges "follow" probation officers' recommendations? And what factors do investigators use to arrive at a presentence recommendation?

Historical and Legal Basis

There is a long tradition in English and American jurisprudence that judges should consider a wide variety of information at sentencing and that such information need not have been introduced at earlier stages of the legal proceedings. This practice allows judges to consider unique circumstances about the defendant or the offense and gives him or her the opportunity to individualize criminal sentences within legal limits. Long before there were formal probation reports, sentencing judges considered out-of-court affidavits; personal knowledge of defendants; and the informal statements of arresting officers, victims, and acquaintances of the defendant in arriving at an appropriate disposition. This precedent allowed judges to readily accept the fact that probation officers could provide a systematic source of presentence information.

John Augustus, in an effort to screen out those he deemed unfit for probation, developed an investigation format for judicial consideration. The presentence investigation of criminal cases soon became an explicit part of probation work, evidenced by the first statewide law in Massachusetts:

> It shall be the duty of such officer to inquire into the character and offense of every person arrested for crime in the city or town for which he acts, with a view of ascertaining whether the accused may reasonably be expected to reform without punishment. He shall keep a full record of the results of his investigation.[11]

By the early twentieth century presentence investigations were accepted as a basic probation responsibility. For example, in 1910, Wilfred Bolster, a charter member of the American Institute of Criminal Law and Criminology, wrote: "The duties of the probation officer should begin with an exhaustive investigation into cases of persons under arrest, seeking to obtain all possible information as to previous arrests, family history, environment, employment, present mental attitude of the defendant, and any facts which may have induced or contributed to the offense." He further stated that the results of the investigation should be written, and that the report should be unbiased because it is an essential aid to the judge in sentencing.[12]

These directions for a presentence investigation are significant in that they require the probation officer to obtain all possible information on a wide variety of behavior and facts. The mandate to provide an exhaustive and comprehensive range of data on criminal cases remains an expectation that is difficult, if not impossible, to satisfy. Illinois, in 1911, required presentence investigations in all cases being considered for probation. Emerging social work techniques significantly influenced the content and format of presentence investigations in the early twentieth century.

William Healy, director of a juvenile care facility, and social worker **Mary Richardson** persuasively advanced the concept that criminal offenders could not be fully understood until a social diagnosis of them had been completed. Such a social diagnosis involved a thorough study of the individual, including specific information categories about the environmental and physical aspects of an offender's life. The social classification schemes of Healy and Richardson were directly applied to a court context by New York City's chief probation officer **Edwin Cooley,** and the modern-day presentence format emerged. In a 1925 article, Cooley described the presentence methodology that, by that time, had been accepted and implemented by many probation officials and remains, in its essence, the core of presentence investigations today: "The probation plan of social diagnosis should consider the legal history of the offender, the essential elements of his environment, a study of his developmental history, personality and behavior, his capacities and potentialities, and the etiology of the delinquency."[13]

When probation departments increased in size, many divided their officers into investigation and supervision units. In this division of labor the presentence investigator's responsibility ended when the defendant was sentenced; if probation was granted, the case was transferred to the supervision unit for further attention.

Larger departments standardized their reporting procedures. During the 1920s, California and New York adopted presentence formats that closely resembled currently used schemes (see page 80), and in 1943 the Federal Probation Department standardized its presentence forms to include basic core concepts. Academic leaders such a Frank Tannenbaum, Henry Elmer Barns, and Edwin Sutherland wholeheartedly supported the idea of a presentence investigation. The latter expressed a popular view regarding the type of information that should be developed: "Whatever throws light on the offender's heredity, environment, character, and activities is pertinent to the investigation."[14]

As the PSI became more popular and widely used, surprisingly there was no questioning the relevance of the information it contained. It was taken for granted that a sentencing judge had a right to know intimate details of an offender's life. There was a basic assumption that sentencing decisions would be enhanced if the defendant's personality and life situation were open to scrutiny. Although universally acclaimed, the decision to request a PSI, in most jurisdictions, remained a matter of judicial discretion. In many areas, PSIs were not undertaken because of insufficient staff or judicial custom. However, in the 1940s the use of PSIs was stimulated by two landmark legal developments.

In 1946, the Supreme Court adopted **Rule 32(c)** of the Federal Rules of Criminal Procedure, specifying that the probation department submit a presentence report in every case, unless the court directed otherwise. This rule has since been amended (with regard to presentence disclosure) but not materially changed, and is both symbolic and instrumental in the acceptance of the PSI. Three years later the PSI was further legitimated by a Supreme Court decision in the case of *Williams v. New York* (337 U.S. 21, 1949). This decision was significant for several reasons: It established the PSI as an essential aid to modern sentencing, it approved the inclusion of hearsay evidence into the presentence report, it recommended individualizing sentences, and it demonstrated a presentence report was a consequential document—in this case a matter of life and death as a jury convicted Williams of murder committed during a burglary. The jury recommended a life sentence but the judge, after considering the presentence report, imposed the death penalty. The PSI reported that Williams had confessed to or was a suspect in thirty other burglaries in the vicinity of the crime. The report also indicated he had a "morbid sexuality" and was a "menace to society." Williams appealed the death sentence, stating that the procedure violated the due process of law in that he was not able to confront and cross-examine the witnesses against him. The Supreme Court rejected the appeal and in Justice Black's majority opinion wrote:

> Under the practice of individualizing punishments, investigational techniques have been given an important role. Probation workers making reports of their investigations have not been trained to prosecute but to aid offenders. Their reports have been given a high value by conscientious judges who want to sentence persons on the best available information rather than on guesswork and inadequate information. To deprive sentencing judges of this kind of information would undermine modern penological procedural policies that have been cautiously adopted throughout the nation

after careful consideration and experimentation. We must recognize that most of the information now relied upon by judges to guide them in the intelligent imposition of sentences would be unavailable if information were restricted to that given in open court by witnesses subject to cross-examination. And the modern probation report draws on information concerning every aspect of a defendant's life. The type and extent of this information make totally impractical if not impossible open court testimony with cross-examination. Such a procedure could endlessly delay criminal administration in a retrial of collateral issues. . . .

. . . Appellant was found guilty after a fairly conducted trial. His sentence followed a hearing conducted by the judge. Upon the judge's inquiry as to why sentence should not be imposed, the defendant made statements. His counsel made extended arguments. The case went to the highest court in the state, and that court had power to reverse for abuse of discretion or legal error in the imposition of the sentence. That court affirmed. We hold that appellant was not denied due process of law.[15]

Williams was eventually executed. The dissenting opinion of Justice Murphy in the *Williams* case is also worth considering because he also supported *liberal* use of presentence reports:

Due process of law includes at least the idea that a person accused of crime shall be accorded a fair hearing through all the stages of the proceedings against him. I agree with the Court as to the value and humaneness of liberal use of probation reports as developed by modern penologists, but, in a capital case, against the unanimous recommendation of a jury, where the report would concededly not have been admissible at the trial, and was not subject to examination by the defendant, I am forced to conclude that the high commands of due process were not obeyed.[16]

After Rule 32(c) was put into effect and the *Williams* decision became known, courts throughout the country routinely ordered PSIs in most felony matters, regardless of whether probation was considered. Typically, judges requested PSIs in misdemeanor cases only if probation was a distinct possibility (a practice that remains the norm). However, as misdemeanor probation became more popular so too did the number of presentence investigations. The added requests for PSIs increased the need for probation investigators, and most departments established special units to handle report writing duties.

The *Williams* case opened a long debate over the confidentiality of presentence reports, an issue that only lately has been resolved. Although seemingly contrary to U.S. standards of judicial fairness, the *Williams* decision was interpreted as meaning that full disclosure of presentence reports was not required under due process provisions. In this case, the Supreme Court held that adherence to trial-like procedures such as cross-examination and confronting detractors would interfere with the collection of valuable presentence information. The decision implied that the importance of a complete PSI superseded the defendant's right to see and refute contents of the report. For the next twenty years, lower courts regularly held that the presentence report was a confidential court document. This position stimulated a lively debate between proponents and opponents of presentence disclosure. Probation officer William Zastrow succinctly delineated the pros and cons of this issue:

Arguments against Disclosure

1. Confidential sources will "dry up," depriving the court of information both useful and necessary in the sentencing process.
2. The sentencing process would be delayed, sentence hearings would be protracted, and the probation officer would be required to testify at such hearings and reveal sources of information.
3. Revealing information to the defendant would damage the working relationship between the defendant and the probation officer and might, in certain instances, hurt the defendant emotionally.
4. Informants might be subject to retribution at the hands of the defendant or the disclosed information might prove embarrassing to both the defendant and the informant.
5. Disclosure would result in fewer probation grants.

Arguments for Disclosure

1. Revealing the presentence report helps the defendant better understand the reason for the court's disposition of the case and may well be the first step in rehabilitation.
2. At the trial level, the defendant and attorney have available to them the evidence that will be presented and consequently an overview of the entire trial process. Nondisclosure of the presentence report excludes the defendant from the sentencing process.
3. Disclosure gives the defendant an opportunity to refute damaging information that may be based solely on hearsay. Or the defendant may clarify statements that are inaccurate or are exaggerated.[17]

The issue of accuracy was particularly relevant as several "horror stories" revealed what could happen when investigators' statements were misleading or erroneous. In one instance, for example, the presentence investigator wrote that the defendant "had a knife" when he committed a burglary even though the "weapon" was a small pocketknife the defendant normally carried, and which was not used during the crime. This offhand remark haunted the defendant who was later turned down for release by a parole board, which characterized the offense as "armed robbery."[18]

The classic example of an unsubstantiated presentence accusation occurred in *Weston v. U.S.* The defendant was convicted of receiving, concealing, and facilitating the transportation of heroin. Before requesting a PSI, the judge indicated he was inclined to impose a minimum five-year sentence. However, after reading the confidential presentence report (never shown to the defendant or her attorney), which contained a statement that the FBI *felt* the defendant was a major supplier of heroin, the judge imposed a twenty-year sentence. The FBI allegation proved to be completely erroneous; in reality the defendant had been, as originally portrayed, a small-time mule (illegal courier) and not a major dealer.[19] In *Tucker v. U.S.*, the original sentence was drastically reduced after it was ascertained the presentence investigator had claimed the defendant had a long criminal record when, in fact, all prior charges had been dismissed. Justice William O. Douglas, in a 1966 dissenting opinion on federal policy upholding the confidentiality of PSIs, raised the issue of report accuracy and argued forcefully for full disclosure. Justice Douglas recognized the importance of judges having access to the "fullest possible information" but also stated that fairness would require that the defendant also be aware of the facts, which may be very damaging to him or her. Douglas then listed the possible problems with PSIs, including inaccuracies, exaggerations of the defendant's previous offenses, an incomplete investigation, and "countervailing factors not disclosed by the probation report." Recognizing that trial judges may identify these problems and make appropriate judgments, Douglas nonetheless wondered how a judge might know whether to ask the defendant for a statement concerning facts revealed in the PSI. He concluded his dissent by stating, ". . . Whatever should be the rule for the federal courts, it ought not to be one which permits a judge to impose sentence on the basis of which the defendant may be unaware and to which he has not been afforded an opportunity to reply."[20]

In the early 1970s, proponents of disclosure began to gain the upper hand. States such as California and Minnesota required full disclosure of presentence reports and their sentencing proceedings were not hampered. When other jurisdictions opted for disclosure, the anticipated problems with sources of information did not arise. The conclusions of Zastrow after his jurisdiction had required presentence report disclosure for five years were typical:

1. Release of the presentence report to the defense attorney has not resulted in the problems first anticipated.
2. Sources of information have not dried up. In many instances a more helpful and cooperative attitude on the part of the defendant and counsel have been observed.
3. There is less *sparring* between the client and officer at the outset of probation. The probationer is aware that the courts have knowledge of many of the facets of his or her life including problems, strengths, weaknesses, and potential.
4. The probation officer becomes a better and more objective investigator, carefully screening fact from hearsay.
5. Presentence summaries are less judgmental and more analytical.[21]

Zastrow concluded that the PSI is a central working document in the judicial and correctional process, and that fairness should require its release to the defendant and his or her attorney.

In 1975, overturning prior rulings upholding confidentiality, the Supreme Court amended federal Rule 32(c) by requiring disclosure (subject to certain exceptions) of the presentence report. The exceptions included sensitive mental health reports and information that might jeopardize the informant (used mainly in gang-related cases). When judges invoke exceptions they must summarize for the defense the substance of what is being held confidential. The *Gardner v. Florida* decision in 1977 further strengthened the case for disclosure.

A Florida jury had convicted Gardner of first-degree murder. The defendant had killed his wife after a day-long drinking spree. After the murder he fell asleep and on waking called his mother-in-law and summoned the police. The jury found that mitigating circumstances outweighed those of aggravation and recommended a life sentence. The trial judge found the crime "especially heinous" and imposed the death penalty. Part of the judge's reasoning was based on information in the presentence report, information that was not revealed to the defendant or his attorney. In deciding the case, the justice made frequent references to the *Williams* case, finally concluding: "Since that sentence was written almost thirty years ago, this court has acknowledged its obligation to re-examine procedures against evolving standards of procedural fairness in a civilized society."[22] After considering the disadvantage of not being able to refute confidential allegations in the presentence report, the Supreme Court overturned the trial judge's sentence (subsequently Gardner was sentenced to life).

The effect of Rule 32(c) as amended in the *Gardner* case has been to move most jurisdictions, albeit slowly, toward full disclosure of presentence reports. Although such disclosure generally remains discretionary (in eighteen states it is mandatory), it is rare that defendants and their attorneys are not allowed to see presentence reports. After working in a PSI unit for many years, John Rosecrance fully concurs with a statement of the American Bar Association on Standards Relating to Sentencing:

> Fundamental fairness to the defendant requires that the substance of all derogatory information which adversely affects his interests and which has not otherwise been disclosed in open court should be called to the attention of the defendant, his attorney, and others who are acting on his behalf.[23]

Historically and legally, presentence reports are an integral part of sentencing in America. The material and emphasis contained within the presentence report affects a vast number of criminal defendants. It is important to further examine the makeup of PSIs and the process by which these reports are currently being compiled and used.

The Component Parts

The PSI is divided into various components, which, taken as a whole, present a comprehensive picture of the offense and the offender. Although the number and labeling of information categories may vary, the core concepts of a PSI listed on pages 80 to 81 remain the same.

Generally speaking, the evaluation section is the place where probation officers are allowed to include their subjective assessment of the defendant and his or her situation. The instructions in Figure 4.1, put together by the Washington State Department of Corrections, provide an excellent example of how to prepare a PSI investigation.

(text continues on page 92)

FIGURE 4.1   *Presentence Investigation*

The left side of page 1 and all of page 2 of the Presentence and Intake Report are to be completed and utilized as face sheets for the Presentence Report.

Official Version of the Offense

Briefly describe who did what to whom, when, where, and how. The description should be a summary of Law Enforcement Incident Reports and investigative work by the Community Corrections Officer. It is not to contain evaluative remarks by the officer. Identify sources of information. Include extent of injury and property loss, as applicable.

Provide narrative information concerning charging, prenegotiation, and plea/trial outcome. Describe charges dismissed in prenegotiations. Identify custody status.

Defendant's Version of Offense

Summarize the defendant's explanation of his or her involvement in the offense, mitigating factors, and describe his or her attitude toward the offense. Do not include evaluative statements, interjections, and conclusions. Written statements provided by the offender would not be quoted, unless a phrase or a brief statement is particularly poignant, but must be discussed with the offender.

Victim's Statement

Summary of witness(es), victim(s), and/or codefendant's statement. State "none" if not made available.

Personal History

Criminal History

Juvenile: When dealing with young offenders (under age twenty-three), explore contacts and the quality of those contacts with the legal system. Include date, place of arrest, charge, and disposition of criminal charges. Information concerning noncriminal contact the offender had with a law enforcement agency should be briefly summarized. Sources for both official/verified and unofficial/unverified contacts must be identified.

Adult: Include record checks from the FBI, local and state law enforcement agencies, and other communities and counties in which the offender has lived. Dispositions are to be noted. "$3,500 bail" or "bail forfeited" are not dispositions. Do not include incidents in which the offender was a victim or information that indicates the offender was a suspect in an investigation but no arrest occurred. The following information is to be provided:

1. Felony arrests and convictions in chronological order, mentioning date of arrest, arresting agency, charge, and disposition. If available, in a separate paragraph, include a *brief* descriptions of offense and, if relevant, comments by offender.
2. Parole release date(s), parole status, etc.
3. Outstanding warrants/detainers, pending charges including arrests after presented offense, status of prosecution, and case number(s).

(continued)

FIGURE 4.1   *Continued*

Misdemeanor arrests and convictions are to be summarized by giving the first and last arrest data, the number of times arrested on various charges, and the range of dispositions. (For instance: According to the FBI, between 1/6/76 and 5/7/79, Mr. B. was arrested 12 times for Drunk in Public in California, Idaho, and Oregon. Dispositions range from a $20 fine to 100 days in jail.) If the officer is not able to determine whether a charge was a felony or a misdemeanor, it can be included in the chronological listing of arrests. If a misdemeanor conviction is of particular relevance to the present offense it should be briefly described. Traffic offenses are to be dealt with as other misdemeanor arrests, unless the current conviction is for Vehicular Homicide. In this instance, serious traffic and felony traffic convictions are to be included in the chronological list.

Family Background

List the following questions and respond to them as appropriate:

1. Essentially normal upbringing: yes/no
2. Family residentially mobile: yes/no
3. Reared in financially stable household: yes/no
4. Exposed to mental or physical abuse as a child: yes/no
5. Exposed to mental or physical abuse as an adult: yes/no
6. Parents abused alcohol or drugs: yes/no
7. History of mental illness in family: yes/no

Comment briefly on relevant factors.

Education and Training

Academic: List last school of attendance and address, highest grade completed, date of last attendance, notation if defendant has adequate reading and writing skills, and attendance record if defendant has been enrolled during the past five years.

Vocational: List last school of attendance, date of last attendance, area of study, and vocational certificates received and data, if applicable.

Marital History

Describe present marriage, including cohabital and common-law relationships, date of marriage, support or lack of it for the defendant from spouse and children, marital problems as they may affect the offender's success or failure if placed under supervision. Indicate number of previous marriages and relevant information about all of the offender's children. Indicate reasons for previous marriage failures only if they have bearing on the offense.

Military Service

Include only relevant information, such as date of entry, branch of service, date and type of discharge, disciplinary actions, or commendations.

FIGURE 4.1 *Continued*

Employment History

Describe current employment, including name of employer, length of time on job, type of work, special skills, income, and performance. Summarize previous history, include verification.

Financial History

Financial status is discussed here, as is ability to pay restitution and attorney fees. Include information concerning debts, support obligations, etc. Include community service eligibility (e.g., offenders willingness to do the work); financial history, which might indicate the utility of ordering work instead of financial payments; and availability of work sites in the immediate community. (See Dir-270.) Include a statement that if the offender is placed on community supervision he or she will be expected to pay $15 per month in supervision fees.

Substance Use or Abuse

Discuss the extent of alcohol or drug use, treatment programs entered, completed, failed, reason for failure, offender's willingness to submit to treatment, and impact of use/abuse on offender.

Mental Health History

Describe mental/emotional health problems relevant to sentencing (sexual adjustment, psychopathy, retardation, hospitalization, psychotropic medication, attempted suicide, etc.). Community service—Might the above adversely affect involvement.

Medical History

Discuss only a history of serious and/or disabling diseases or accidents, and their present affects on offender's employment, social relationships, health problems, etc. relevant to sentencing. Community service—Might the above adversely affect involvement.

Recommendation

Evaluation and Plan

Evaluate defendants degree of risk to the community and ability to comply with conditions of supervision (probation). Describe and evaluate defendant's plan. List *special conditions* needed to enhance successful completion of supervision.

Make a specific recommendation for the appropriate disposition.

Do not explain why you are not recommending another type of sentence. Only justify your actual recommendation.

Not all jurisdictions require that a recommendation be submitted. Some judges do not want officers' subjective conclusions to influence their sentencing decisions, preferring instead to rely on information contained in the body of the report. However, most judges want and even require a recommendation. There is still some debate on this issue and some, for example, Yona Cohn, a correctional practitioner and criminologist, argue that the recommendation should be abolished. Although her conclusion is a minority one, it does represent the views of those opposed to probation officers including a presentence recommendation and is based on the fact that the PSI writer may have access to data that contradict the proposed recommendation. What is the writer to do with such information? To include it may confuse the court and risk having the recommendation accepted. Not to include it may be dishonest and misleading. Cohn, therefore, recommends replacing the recommendation with predictions of how the offender would do under alternative sanctions, for example, probation or incarceration. In other words, based on knowledge of the offender, the PSI writer would predict the effects of the possible sanctions on the offender. The judge would then be free to make a decision based on those predictions.[24]

Although most departments have designated officers who specialize in doing PSIs, others maintain that the officer who does the report should be held accountable for supervision of the probationer because he or she already knows the offender and has a good idea what the needs and issues of the client are. There are pros and cons to the specialization argument as well. For example, the specialization created by establishing PSI units, usually occurring in larger departments, can lead to greater efficiency. Such specialization can also save training time and money, and result in improved reports and recommendations because the writers become more skilled. These improvements can in turn lead to better relations with the courts, who appreciate the efficiency and improvements. However, workload distribution can be a problem in this system. Court cases do not necessarily come in a steady stream—caseloads often rise and fall with the season or the economy, for example. Therefore, when they are high, the PSI writers may need help from the "regular" POs, who then may neglect their own caseloads to get the added work done. When the caseload is low, the PSI writers may not have much to do. It is also possible that PSI specialists may not be as satisfied with the PO's work because their interaction with the probationer is limited to the investigation, depriving him or her of the supervision process where results—positive or negative—are readily seen.[25]

Current Usage

In order to illustrate the use of PSIs, three actual reports are presented. Names and other identifying data have been removed to protect the defendants. The first two documents contain a full complement of information elements and, as such, are considered long-form reports. The long form traditionally is used for serious felony matters. Many PSI units, in an effort to save time, have developed a more concise format in which several categories (especially those related to social history) are summarized. These shorter documents are appropriately termed short-form reports and are

(text continues on page 113)

FIGURE 4.2   *Example 1 of a Presentence Report*

```
                    OREGON DEPARTMENT OF CORRECTIONS
                      PRESENTENCE INVESTIGATION

  PSI NO: 531032-01
  DATE:   10/26/
  SID NO:

  NAME: Offender XYZ
  TRUE:
   AKA: John Doe                        PSI TEXT TRANSFER INFO:
   AKA:                                 TRANSFER DATE:
   AKA:                                 WORD PROCESSOR:  WP

  ADDRESS: 123 Main Street
           Anytown, Oregon


  DOB:
  DOB2:
  SEX:     MALE
  RACE:    WHITE
  HGT:     6ft 00in
  WGT:     200
  HAIR:    Brown
  HAIR:    Black
  EYES:    Green          OTHER NUMBERS            SCARS-MARKS-TATTOOS
    NO:                                            SC R KNEE   SC R ANKL
  SS NO2:
  FBI NO:
  DR LIC:

  CUSTODY STATUS: OWN RECOG

  DETAINERS OR    NONE KNOWN.
  OTHER CHARGES:

  CONCERNED       DEPARTMENT OF CORRECTIONS
  AGENCIES:

  SUBMITTED BY:                          BRANCH: LINN

                        CURRENT CONVICTIONS

  SET # CNTY   JUDGE              DIST ATTORNEY      DEFENSE COUNSEL    A/R
   1    LINN   RICK MCCORMICK     ANI YARDUMIAN      TOM REUTER         APP

                          ORS           SENTENCE SG   COURT        DA
   ORS    PAR AT PV M4 MIN ABBREV  CS CH  RANGE   STS NUMBER      NUMBER
  163.405             0  SODO I    10 H  061 - 65  IN        PV  94102241PV
  166.270             0  XCON WEAP 06 D  013 - 014 IN            95071764
```

PSI: 531032-01   PAGE: 1

(continued)

FIGURE 4.2 *Continued*

```
                    OREGON DEPARTMENT OF CORRECTIONS
                  SENTENCING GUIDELINES HISTORY SCALE


ADULT CRIMINAL HISTORY RECORD            JUVENILE CRIMINAL HISTORY RECORD

A. Adult Person Felonies -        001   E. Juvenile Person Felonies -000

B. Adult Non-person Felonies -    000   F. Juvenile Non-Per Felony - 000

C. Adult Person Misdemeanor  -    000

D. Adult Non-person Misdemeanor - 002

Computer Calculated Criminal History Scale Selection:     D

Court Stipulated Criminal History Scale Selection:

Criminal History Scale Selection:                         D
```

FIGURE 4.2   *Continued*

OREGON DEPARTMENT OF CORRECTIONS
PRESENTENCE INVESTIGATION

ITM	DATE	CRIME	DISPOSITION	INCR VIOL

Juvenile Adjudications:

None known or admitted.

Adult Adjudications:

1. 02-04-   DUII   Albany Office
                (M - 1 - N/P)

    02-06-   Linn County District Court Docket No.
                               $255.00 fine

2. 02-27-   DUII   Linn County Sheriff's Department
                (M - 2 - N/P)

    07-12-   Linn County District Court Docket No.
                               - one year probation, $370.00 fine

3. 10-19-   Sodomy I   Linn County Sheriff's Department
                (F - 1 - P/P)

    05-12-   Linn County Circuit Court Docket No.   1 -
                               14 years probation, $139.00 money judgment

CRIMINAL HISTORY: (AMPLIFIED)

Entry Number 3 is in regards to an incident which occurred in   but was brought to the attention of the Linn County Sheriff's Department in October,   . Reports indicated that the defendant's wife was working at her job for Burlington Northern Railroad in Klamath Falls and was away from home. She had been working away from home for quite a period of time and the defendant was heavily involved in using "crank". The defendant stated that during the time she was away, he decided that his stepdaughter was sexually attracted to him. He exposed his penis to her and requested that she touch it with her hands. She did this. The defendant also stated that on at least two occasions, he fondled her vagina and breasts with his hands and also on at least two occasions, he had her place her lips on his penis. He also placed his lips on her vagina. When asked if he had had any sexual intercourse with the victim or if he had done anything else besides what he stated, the defendant denied having done anything else.

The defendant advised Detective Thurman that his wife,   found out about the incident because his conscience was bothering him a great deal. About a week after having had sexual contact with the victim, he confessed to his wife what he had done. At that point, they decided to obtain counseling to keep him from breaking up the family and possibly prevent any further reoccurrence of what he had done to the victim. He also stated that he did not recall specifically how many sexual contacts he had had with the victim stating that the contacts continued for approximately one week during that time period and that it occurred on several occasions. He denied threatening the victim stating that she agreed to have sex with him. As indicated, the victim was his stepdaughter,

NAME: SID: **PAGE:**   2

FIGURE 4.2 *Continued*

OREGON DEPARTMENT OF CORRECTIONS
PRESENTENCE INVESTIGATION

SUPERVISION SUMMARY:

The defendant's probation file reflects that he is progressing in a satisfactory manner. In a recent report received from Psy.D. it was learned that the defendant has been presen— -- --- ---quired group meetings and has done the homework and has participated fully in group process. Furthermore it is noted that the defendant has been given permission by   and his probation officer to have visitation with his two sons. His ----- ordered financial obligations are paid in full. The only area of concern appears to be in the area of his work crew but apparently this has been straightened out.

PENDING CHARGES:

None known.

LEGAL SUMMARY:

Date of Finding or Plea of Guilty: - Sodomy in the First Degree (Probation Violation) - Admitted Allegation Number 1 and 2 that he was in possession of firearm on October 26,

                    - Felon in Possession of a Firearm - Entered a plea of Guilty on October 26,

Plea Negotiations/
Stipulations:

Unknown.

Sentencing Date: December   at 9:00 a.m. before the Honorable Rick McCormick.

SCOPE OF CRIME:

Linn County Circuit Court Case No.   , Count I - Sodomy in the First Degree:

See Amplified Criminal History Entry Number 3.

Linn County Circuit Court Case No.   , Felon in Possession of a Firearm:

According to available Albany City Police Incident No. 95-0
           witnessed the defendant and one Mr W   speak for a few minutes when they walked to the rear of the defendant's vehicle. Mr. ᄯ   told Officer Corder that the defendant opened the trunk to his vehicle and removed a rifle later identified as a Marlin 30.30 lever action with scope. Mr.

PAGE: 3

FIGURE 4.2 *Continued*

OREGON DEPARTMENT OF CORRECTIONS
PRESENTENCE INVESTIGATION

☒ further indicated that the defendant had "presented" the rifle to Mr. W

Mr.   indicated that Mr.   examined the rifle for approximately ten minutes when he (Mr.   n) walked over toward the defendant and Mr.   Mr.   stated that he stood next to Mr. and the defendant and commented on how nice the rifle was. At this point, Mr.   left and entered his office. Still observing the defendant and   he observed Mr.   "shoulder" the rifle. He then observed Mr. W handing the defendant some money from his wallet. At this point, the defendant closed the trunk to his vehicle.

Upon contact with Mr W   it was learned that on July 2,   , he came back to the office from work. Mr W   told Officer Corder that after he pulled into the parking lot and parked, the defendant pulled into the parking lot. Mr. W   stated that the defendant was driving a dark green Ford Maverick and admitted that the defendant had sold him the weapon in question.

On July 25,   , the defendant was indicted by the Linn County Grand Jury for Felon in Possession of a Firearm.

PROBATION VIOLATION INFORMATION:

Case No.   - Sodomy in the First Degree - Admitted to allegations Number 1 and 2 that he violated the law: to wit; defendant was in possession of a firearm. Sentencing set for December   ,   at 9:00 a.m. before the Honorable Rick McCormick.

DEFENDANT'S STATEMENT:

The defendant chose not to make a statement.

ACCOMPLICES/CO-DEFENDANTS:

Not applicable.

VICTIM'S STATEMENT/DAMAGES:

Not applicable.

SOCIAL PROFILE:

The defendant was born on August 30,   in Grants Pass, Oregon to   and   . The defendant's parents are divorced, however, both have remarried. The defendant indicates having three siblings and three step-siblings. He graduated from South Albany High School in ' . No further education and/or training has been achieved by the defendant. He married his present wife,   in Klamath Falls, Oregon in August, . One child has been born between the defendant and his wife;

PAGE: 4

(continued)

FIGURE 4.2   *Continued*

OREGON DEPARTMENT OF CORRECTIONS
PRESENTENCE INVESTIGATION

DOB: 06-26- . Although not officially adopted by the defendant, two other
children were brought into the marriage by   At the present
time, the defendant is under court order not to live with his family nor to
associate with the children as   was the victim in Case No.
9   The defendant has never served in the United States Military. At
the present time, the defendant is working part-time
                          Prior to this time, the defendant and his wife owned
                    which was a construction company they began in
December,   . This company is no longer is business. From 19: through
19   and from 19   through 19 , the defendant was employed with
                    Company.   The defendant continues to reside in his camp
trailer at the home of   It is also
noted that the defendant has been allowed to have brief supervised contact
with the two boys.

SUBSTANCE ABUSE:

    Alcohol: The defendant indicated that he began consuming alcohol at the
age of 16 or 17.   At the present time, the defendant is involved with
Serenity Lane on an outpatient basis. This has been the case since he was
granted probation in Case No.   However, no information has been
received from Serenity Lane to verify this information.

    Drugs: The defendant stated that he began using illegal drugs at the
age of 16 or 17 and he used "pot and speed". Again, the defendant is
involved with Serenity Lane regarding his drug addiction. No response has
been received from Serenity Lane to verify this information.

    Regarding Case No.   statements made by the defendant suggest
that drugs were an influencing factor in the commission of this offense.

    Regarding Case No.   there is no indication that alcohol and/or
drugs played a role in the commission of this offense.

PHYSICAL/MENTAL HEALTH:

    Physical: The defendant stated that he continues to be in good physical
health and denies suffering from any physically disabling conditions. In
19 , the defendant severed his tendons in his right knee and broke his right
leg and ankle.

    Mental: The defendant denies suffering from any form of mental
disorder.

    In a letter recently received from William   it was
revealed that the defendant "appears to be addressing the issues relating to
his sexual abuse of his daughter. We are beginning to see the deterioration
of some of the more sophisticated forms of denial utilized by   to
protect himself from the responsibility for his behavior. He appears to be
doing some solid work in the areas of understanding his internal motivation
to a greater degree, recognizing and describing his cycle of abuse, the role
that substances and his emotional condition has played in his abuse, and
learning lifestyle changes which he must execute in order to keep from

NAME: **SID:**   **PAGE:**   5

FIGURE 4.2 *Continued*

OREGON DEPARTMENT OF CORRECTIONS
PRESENTENCE INVESTIGATION

triggering himself into an acting out posture." Furthermore, it was the opinion of Mr.   that   is progressing at an average rate for someone with his personality within his treatment context. He needs to continue to work in the curriculum we have provided for him and to continue to control his own motivations for making the choices that he makes in his life, thinking errors which excuse him from irresponsible behavior, his sexual fantasies structure, and his relationship with his wife."

GUIDELINES APPLICATION:

Linn County Circuit Court Case No.   Sodomy in the First Degree (Probation Violation):

According to Sentencing Guidelines, the Crime Seriousness for Sodomy in the First Degree is 10. The Criminal History Scale is H*. The Presumptive Sentence is 61 to 65 months incarceration followed by 175 to 179 months post-prison supervision.

Subcategory Rationale:

Sodomy in the First Degree shall be ranked at Crime Category 10 if one or more of the following factors are included in the commission of the offense.

    A.   The offender used or threatened to use a weapon;

    B.   The offender caused or threatened to cause serious physical injury;

    C.   The victim was under the age of 12; or

    D.   The victim was incapable of consent by reason of mental defect, mental incapacitation or physical helplessness.

Aggravating Factors:

    B.   The offender knew or had reason to know of the victim's particular vulnerability, such as the extreme youth, age, disability or ill health of the victim, which increased the harm or threat of harm caused by the criminal conduct. The victim was his stepdaughter, age 8 years old at the time the offense occurred.

Mitigating Factors:

    H.   The offender's criminal history indicates that the offender lived conviction-free within the community for a significant period of time preceding his or her current crime of conviction.

Linn County Circuit Court Case No.   . Felon in Possession of a Firearm:

According to Sentencing Guidelines, the Crime Seriousness for Felon in Possession of a Firearm is 6. The Criminal History Scale is D*. The

                                                        PAGE: 6

(continued)

FIGURE 4.2 *Continued*

OREGON DEPARTMENT OF CORRECTIONS
PRESENTENCE INVESTIGATION

Presumptive Sentence is 13 to 14 months incarceration followed by 24 months post-prison supervision.

Subcategory Rationale:

    Not applicable.

Aggravating Factors:

    None.

Mitigating Factors:

    None.

RATIONALE/RECOMMENDATION:

    Before the Court is a 36 year old defendant who has pled Guilty to Felon in Possession of a Firearm and has admitted to violating his probation (Sodomy in the First Degree) through the commission of this offense. In May, , the defendant was given a 14 year probationary term for Sodomy in the First Degree in which his stepdaughter was the victim. Reports received from his therapist indicate that he is doing satisfactorily with his Sex Offender Program. Furthermore, the defendant's probation file reflects that he is in compliance with most of the conditions of his probation. However, the defendant had prior knowledge that he was not to be in possession of a firearm and yet took upon himself to attempt to sell a firearm knowing full well that it was against the conditions of his probation and against the law. Therefore, the following is being recommended:

    Linn County Circuit Court Case No.   Sodomy in the First Degree - Probation Violation: It is respectfully recommended that the defendant be continued on probation under the same terms and conditions as previously imposed.

    Linn County Circuit Court Case No.   Felon in Possession of a Firearm: It is respectfully recommended that the defendant be sentenced to thirteen (13) months incarceration to be followed by 24 months post-prison supervision.

    It is also recommended that the weapon in this case be destroyed.

_____   _____
Adult Parole/Probation Officer   Unit Supervisor

Dated: _____   Dated: _____

: December 18,
MB:blm

NAME: **SID:**   **PAGE:**   7

FIGURE 4.3 *Example 2 of a Presentence Report*

DISTRICT COURT, __DENVER__ COUNTY, __DENVER___, COLORADO
Case No. 86CR1628 Div/Ct. Rm. Ten.

PRESENTENCE REPORT Application for Probation.

THE PEOPLE OF THE STATE OF COLORADO v. _____
                                                                    Defendant

JUDGE: JOHN BROOKS, JR.

NAME:	HEARING DATE: November 17, ____
nee:	
ALIAS:	PRESENTENCE Eight days
	INCARCERATION: good time = 8 days
ADDRESS: 2690 West Water Avenue	
Denver, CO 80219	AGE: 26
	DOB: 1/6/___
TELEPHONE NO.:	SEX: Female
MARITAL	SOCIAL SECURITY NO.:
STATUS: Married	
	HEALTH: See report.
DEPENDENTS: Two children	
OFFENSE: Unlawful distribution, mfg.,	
dispensing, sale, and possession of	EDUCATION: Eighth grade – Verified.
controlled substance (C3F).	GED – Not Verified
PLEA OR	OCCUPATION: See report.
CONVICTION: Guilty plea to Felony Four.	
DATE OF PLEA	FINANCIAL:
OR CONVICTION: Sept. 15, _____	
DISTRICT	DEFENSE
ATTORNEY: NORMAN S. EARLY, JR.	COUNSEL: JIM CASTLE

POSSIBLE PENALTY:
    C.R.S. 12-22-311 and 18-18-105 POSSESSION OF A CONTROLLED SUBSTANCE,
    Class Four Felony, two to eight years, $ 2,000.00 to $ 500,000.00, or both.

Defendant does not meet Community Corrections Board criteria; (8)

Presentence Confinement Dates:
    Date of arrest: January 24, _____
    Date of bond: January 31, _____

(continued)

FIGURE 4.3   *Continued*

PRESENT OFFENSE:

On January 16,   , Detectives Vasquez and Mumford and agents from the DEA Task Force were watching a vehicle being driven by   . She and another party were suspected of setting up a methamphetamine laboratory and she was followed at least twice to the home of   at 2895 West Amherst. An informant had also reported being in the Amherst residence and detecting a strong odor of what the informant knew was a methamphetamine laboratory. In addition, the informant heard a police scanner in the residence and from the description of the radio traffic, it was felt that the police channel being used by the surveillance detectives was being monitored. The informant overheard   tell someone that the "narcs" were on the way and that they were "cleaning up" (moving the dope). Detectives quit using the police radio channel and set up surveillance at the Amherst address. Immediately they saw a truck with several occupants leaving the address and the vehicle was stopped at Winona Court and Jewell, Denver.   was the driver and   and   were passengers with   in the back.   threw a small pouch onto the street and the cont4ents were later found negative for controlled substance.

                 said her identification was in a small suitcase in the back of the truck and permitted officers to retrieve it. The case was opened and it contained   's identification as well as several bags which contained 7,.32 grams of methamphetamine. A loaded revolver was recovered from the rear of the truck as well as other paraphernalia, and a Radio Shack brand police scanner was inside the truck.   signed a Consent to Search form for 2895 West Amherst Avenue, Denver. Officers noted the strong odor associated with the manufacture of methamphetamine. Papers to   were found as well as a baggie containing 125.3 grams of cannabis.   told police that there had been a methamphetamine laboratory in her home within the prior week, that the dope in her case belonged to   and that he and   were giving her an eighth ounce of that dope. She was released at that point and arrested January 24,   on the warrant that was issued.

Defendant's Statement:

A statement received from the defendant is attached to the Court's report with a copy in the Probation Department file.

CRIMINAL HISTORY:

According to information defendant provides, she was picked up once for shoplifting and lectured and released concerning the matter. No other information concerning any juvenile record is available. Known criminal record is as follows:

May 11,   Lakewood. Possession of Marijuana – disposition not noted.

FIGURE 4.3 *Continued*

May 27,	Denver. Disturbance and Unlawful Threat to Injure Person or Damage Property – disposition not noted.
June 24,	Denver. Investigation Possession of Illegal Firearm and Investigation Narcotics Use – both dropped.
	At the time of the June 24, arrest, she also was held on a Bench Warrant and fined $50.00 for Contempt of Court as a result of her yelling at the judge.
August 6,	Denver. Hold Fugitive Detail – released to Lakewood. Defendant was Charged with Dispensing Dangerous Drugs, Jefferson County Court, Information 79F2464 - dismissed due to her plea in a federal case.
September 13,	Denver. Probable Cause Warrant (Theft) – dropped; Hold for Lakewood – released on bond.
December 21,	Denver. United States Marshal. Obstruction of Justice, Aiding and Abetting. These charges were dismissed and defendant entered a guilty Plea March 17, to Possession of Schedule III Controlled Substance (amphetamines), United States District court case 80CR11. On April 14, , a one-year sentence was suspended and she was granted probation for five years. She was ordered to participate in a drug aftercare program, to reside 120 days in a community treatment facility, and to participate in an education program for her GED. She was extremely hostile when she reported to the probation officer after Court and was admitted to the New Horizons treatment facility. She left there without permission April 22, and did not return. She later admitted using marijuana while at the facility and staying high on other drugs. She surrendered and May 23, , her federal probation was revoked with an eleven month sentence being imposed. She was received at the Federal Correctional Institution at Fort Worth May 16, , referred to Empathy House in Boulder November 12, and released at expiration of the sentence January 13, .
January 21,	Denver. Hold for Lakewood.
December 8,	Denver. Held again for Lakewood.
January 16,	Denver. Defendant charged, along with her husband and , with Unlawful Distribution, Manufacturing, Dispensing, Sale, and Possession of Controlled Substance (cocaine and methamphetamine) Information 84CR469. The case was dismissed as to the defendant on February 13, .
	At the time of the above arrest, defendant also was held for Failure to Appear.

(continued)

FIGURE 4.3 *Continued*

April 25,	Denver. Hold for Commerce City – released to Adams County.
	According to the defendant, she was released and her former husband was charged with Disturbance.
February 20,	Denver. Shoplifting – guilty, $50.00 fine.
June 15,	Denver. Shoplifting – disposition not noted. She states she was fined.
January 16,	Denver. Defendant was picked up for the present matter and released; she was, however, held for failure to appear and two Bench Warrants Wherein three fines totaling $513.00 were imposed.
January 24,	Denver. Probably Cause Warrant – the present offense.
May 7,	Denver. Probable Cause Warrant (Possession of Controlled Substance) - dropped.

SOCIAL HISTORY:

was born in Denver January 6,   , to   ,
who divorced when defendant was less than one year of age. Defendant stayed with grandparents to age nine and then lived with the mother, who had remarried. She returned to the
grandparents' home about two years later as she did not get along with the stepfather, and moved
out on her own at age fourteen or so. A prior presentence report indicates that she was raised in
an environment where there was tension, no warmth or affection. The mother is married to
                        , and they live in Colorado Springs. He is a heavy equipment mechanic
and she is a flagger for the Highway Department. The father is remarried with two more
children, he lives at 6491 Newport in Commerce City and is a tow truck driver.

Defendant was withdrawn from Jefferson County Senior High School December 13,   in
grade ten. Her grades had been average to below-average, school behavior was poor and she had
been suspended a number of times for fighting, smoking, and selling marijuana. During a
Evaluation at Denver General Hospital, defendant claimed her natural father had paid her to be truant
from school, to say bad things about the mother, and to sell marijuana at school. She had also
made the accusation that he had sexually assaulted her. She was discharged from Denver
General Hospital to Jefferson County Social Services Child Protection Team. A CHINS Petition
apparently was filed and she was under supervision for one year.

A prior report indicates that defendant lived with   from age fourteen to
seventeen. She states that she and   married in   , and their daughter,
Leona, was born October 30,   . The couple separated and divorced in   . She and
                    Married that year. He was convicted in Adams County of Distribution of
Controlled Substance and on February 14,   , and was sentenced to the Department of

FIGURE 4.3 *Continued*

Corrections for four years. Defendant advises that he now is in community placement and working for a paving company. Her younger daughter, Amanda, was born March 16,

Three friends provide references in defendant's behalf. They write that she is a unique person, is well liked, and is a good mother and friend. She is described as respectable, honest, and caring and that she maintains a clean, orderly, relaxed home for her children. A friend of ten years adds that   has grown up a lot since this happened and knows now how much she needs her children and they need her.

RESIDENCE:

For about four months, defendant has been living with the children at 2690 West Water, a home her mother has been buying.

EMPLOYMENT AND FINANCIAL CONDITIONS:

Defendant states she has been working on a part-time basis shagging cars for   .
She indicates she earns $100.00 or less weekly. She claims no other work experience outside her home.

She advises that her husband earns about $350.00 per week, they have no outstanding bills, and make her mother's house payment of $564.00 per month.

ADDITIONAL INFORMATION:

Defendant denies alcohol abuse and says she began using drugs as a teenager primarily using speed. She has reported the intravenous use of heroin, of amphetamines, and use of valium, Tylenol, codeine, dilaudid, qualudes, and percodin. She had been taken to Denver General Hospital on November 23,   by her mother due to her bizarre behavior and the diagnosis was multiple drug abuser. She was evaluated at ARTS and started outpatient therapy which she says lasts about three to six months. Defendant informs that she was drug free from   to   , and that after her husband was sentenced to the penitentiary, she started seeing someone else and began using drugs again. She believes she started using speed again because she was depressed but denies drug use since becoming pregnant with her baby.

SUMMARY:

                    is twenty-six years of age, married, and has two children who are ages eight months and five years. She completed an approximate ninth grade education and claims receipt of a GED while serving a federal sentence. She and her children have been living at 2690 West Water and claims no employment experience outside the home except during recent months working as a shagger in a car lot.

She has been arrested on several occasions, but the present matter constitutes her first known felony conviction. She was afforded probation in the Federal Court in April of   following

(continued)

FIGURE 4.3 *Continued*

a plea to a misdemeanor count, violated probation in a matter of days, and was sentenced to an eleven month term. She has a long history of drug use and in   , her husband was sentenced

to the Department of Corrections following a drug conviction. She states that he now is in community placement and is employed.

Respectfully submitted,

Mary Gray
Probation Officer

November 12,

RECOMMMENDATION:

The instant report describes a 26 year-old female with a long history of drug involvement. After being afforded a misdemeanor plea in Federal Court for a narcotics offense, she was granted probation, violated probation, and was ultimately sentenced to a Federal Institution in Texas.

In the present offense, the defendant admitted to police that she had a drug laboratory in her home. A quantity of narcotics was found in her home and in her personal property, which suggests an active role in the drug culture.

The overall circumstances of her background and this offense warrant a Department of Corrections sentence. In lieu of ordering her confined in the Department of Corrections at the present time, it is recommended the Court continue the case for a period of two weeks, and order that she be interviewed by the Intensive Supervision Program personnel to determine the appropriateness of granting her probation to that unit.

JOHN L. YURKO
Chief Probation Officer

By: _____

Dennis A. Maes
Division Supervisor

DISPOSITION: _____

_____

JUDGE: _____   DATE: _____

FIGURE 4.4 *Example 3 of a Presentence Report*

DALLAS COUNTY ADULT PROBATION DEPARTMENT
PRE-SENTENCE REPORT

CAUSE NUMBER:	OFFENSE:	PROBATION DATE:	BOND ____	PRESIDING JUDGE:
F86 -P	Theft $750.	5-16-	JAIL __X__	Thomas B. Thorpe

PROSECUTOR:	DEFENSE ATTORNEY:	APPOINTED:__X__ RETAINED: ____ PUBLIC DEFENDER ____	DETAINERS/CHARGES PENDING:
HODGSON	JOE BELLINO		

PERSONAL DATA

NAME:	LAST	FIRST Raymond	MIDDLE Eugene	ALIAS NAMES None

RACE B	SEX M	DATE OF BIRTH 3-26-	AGE 22	PLACE OF BIRTH Dallas, Texas	ID MARKS none

HT. 5'7"	WT. 150	EYES Dk. Brown	HAIR black	COMPLEXION dark	MARITAL STATUS single	DEPENDANTS 2

FBI # 0463361X8	DPS # 2963382	DSO # 0362342	DRIVERS LICENSE # 12264___	SOC. SEC.NO.

CURRENT ADDRESS: . Southerland Ave. Dallas, Texas 75203	MAPSCO # 55Q	PHONE # unknown

EDUCATION: ACADEMIC AND/OR VOCATIONAL **MILITARY SERVICE: ___ YES _x_ NO**
Cedar Hill High School, completed 11the grade
Cedar Hill, Texas

PRESENT EMPLOYER/ADDRESS: Unemployed	MAPSCO # N/A	PHONE # N/A

SUPERVISOR N/A	SALARY N/A	DATE EMPLOYED: N/A

TOTAL MONTHLY INCOME FROM ALL SOURCES: None reported.	TOTAL MONTHLY LIABILITIES: None reported.

NEAREST RELATIVE NOT LIVING WITH DEFENDANT: Barbara (mother)	ADDRESS/ZIP Lancaster, Texas	PHONE # (214)227

CHARACTER REFERENCE: None provided	ADDRESS/ZIP	PHONE #

(continued)

FIGURE 4.4   *Continued*

COURT DATA

PRIOR CRIMINAL REDORD: (JUVENILE, ADULT MISDEMEANOR AND FELONY)

DATE	LOCATION/AGENCY	OFFENSE	DISPOSITION
PER JI55			
5-4- (file date)	F81-	Burg. Bldg.	NBIL
1-19- (file date)	MB8640023	DWLSH	Jail/$492.00

OFFICIAL VERSION OF PRESENT OFFENSE: (BRIEF)

On April 10,   , at about 7:14 a.m., a theft occurred on Service number 197801-T from complainant Montgomery Ward's #1947, located at 100 North Town Mall Shopping Center, Dallas, Dallas County, Texas. Suspect Raymond Eugene   , an employee, took three (3) Minolta cameras, total value $1,199.97, from the store without effective consent of complainant or its agent, Witness Ray Strauss, who was the manager on duty at the time of the offense. The cameras were released back to the complainant.

DEFENDANT'S VERSION OF PRESENT OFFENSE: (BRIEF)

"I was staying with Michelle and her mother. They was paying me $5.00 an hour and by the time they take out taxes, I was bringing home $100.00 a week. I was giving Michelle's mom $40.00 a week. By the time I finished this and the children, I'm broke. I stole the cameras because I thought this was the quickest thing to pawn."

CO-DEFENDANT(S):	VICTIM IMPACT STATEMENT ATTACHED: _____ YES _____ NO

RESTITUTION RECIPIENTS

1) NAME: Montgomery Ward #1947	2) NAME: General Fund
ADDRESS: 100 North Town Mall, S.C.	ADDRESS:
CITY: Dallas, Texas ZIP: 75224	CITY: ZIP:
PHONE: (214) 888-0141	PHONE;
AMOUNT: $900.00	AMOUNT: $250.00
REMARKS: See chrono dated 5-15-	REMARKS: Ct. Appt. Attorney
3) NAME:	4) NAME;
ADDRESS:	ADDRESS:
CITY: ZIP:	CITY: ZIP:
PHONE:	PHONE;
AMOUNT:	AMOUNT:
REMARKS:	REMARKS:

TOTAL RESTITUTION AMOUNT: $1150.00	**SUPERVISING OFFICER:** R-8
MONTHLY PAYMENTS: $ 48.00	
PROBATION FEE ASSESSED: $ 40.00	**SUPERVISION LEVEL:** MAX

INTERVIEWED BY: B. L. Clayton

FIGURE 4.4 *Continued*

PROBLEM AREAS: (CHECK THOSE THAT APPLY AND EXPLAIN IN THE EVALUATION/PROGNOSIS)

_____ **DRUGS**	_____ **FINANCIAL**
_____ **ALCOHOL**	_____ **EDUCATION**
_____ **MENTAL/EMOTIONAL**	_____ **RESIDENTIAL**
_____ **EMPLOYMENT**	_____ **MARITAL/FAMILY**
_____ **PHYSICAL HEALTH**	_____ **OTHER**

EVALUATION/PROGNOSIS

Raymond Eugene   is a 22 year old unemployed black male appearing in court on a charge of Theft/$750. The following is an account of events leading to the theft:

> "I was staying with Michelle and her mother. They were paying me $5.00 an hour
> and by the time they take out taxes, I was bringing home $100.00 a week. I was
> giving Michelle's mom $40.00 a week. By the time I finished this and the
> children, I'm broke. I stole the cameras because I thought this was the
> quickest thing to pawn."

TCIC reflected the following:

Charges	Convictions	Offense
1	0	Burglary
1	0	Theft/Larceny (present case)
1	0	Weapon offenses

JI55 revealed the following:
F81-33666   Burglary of a Building – NBIL
MB8640023   DWLS – PGBC

On May 9,   , subject was given one day
jail time and $492.00.

The following information was provided by the defendant in a pre-sentence interview conducted at the Old Dallas County Jail (6MN2) on Tuesday, May 13,   :

Raymond Eugene   , the oldest of four children to Johnny   and Barbara   , was born in Dallas, Texas on March 22,   . He had a "close" relationship with all family members and denied incidences of physical or sexual abuse. Mr.   was reared by his step-father, TeDella   , until age 18 at which time he left home. It was also about this time that he first met his father, only to have no more than two subsequent contacts.

The defendant has fathered two children with a third child to be born about August,   . Five year old   has been residing with his mother, Sharon, and three year old   with her mother, Ramona. Donna   is expected to give birth in August,   . The defendant has not consistently contributed toward his children's care. He reported no plan to provide for his soon-to-be born child in that the mother,   , will be marrying this summer. Mr.   is now reported to be dating Patricia   , with whom he has been residing at the Century Valley Apartments,   , Dallas, Texas.

(continued)

FIGURE 4.4 *Continued*

EVALUATION/PROGNOSIS (continued)

The defendant attended public schools in Dallas, Texas and completed the 11th grade at Cedar Hill High School after which he enlisted in the Job Corp in San Marcus, Texas. He was "kicked out" after four and one-half months due to an altercation having been experienced with another resident.

Mr. _____ employment history has appeared to have been unstable. Even though he reportedly worked about three years laying tiles at $5.00 per hour for Henry Roofing and Company, this employment was terminated when he enlisted in the Job Corp. The defendant was fired after six months employment with Co-Ho Construction when he refused to follow directions from his supervisor. Subsequent employment has been with "Tree Trimming Tree Service" via contracts with the State Highway Department and with Montgomery Ward from where he was fired after two months part-time employment.

The defendant was reported to be in good physical health. Medical treatment, when necessary, has been secured from Parkland Hospital.

There was no reported history of out-patient or in-patient treatment for psychological or emotional disorders.

Mr. _____ last used marijuana about three or four months ago at which time he decided to discontinue usage. He stated, "I didn't see anything in it. Then, too, it was a waste of my money." Reference alcohol consumption, the defendant stated, "I don't drink just to be drinking, only when I'm around the fellows." There have been no alcohol or drug-related arrests.

RECOMMENDATION

Based upon available information, a two-year grant of probation with restitution of

$900.00 to the victim seems an appropriate disposition.

FIGURE 4.4 *Continued*

PROBATION EVALUATION SCORE SHEET

Complete and attach to Pre-Sentence Report. If a person does not qualify in any item, enter a zero for that item in the score column.

DATE: _____

NAME: _____ CAUSE NO: _____ OFFENSE: _____

		WEIGHT	SCORE
A. PRIOR CRIMINAL HISTORY:			
1.	No prior arrest (other than present offense)	5	_____
2.	No arrest in past 5 years (other than present offense)	4	_____
3.	No felony convictions, felony probation or misdemeanor probation	4	_____
4.	No use of underworld slang or terminology	4	_____
5.	Present offense not for checks, burglary, robbery, theft, or DWI	3	_____
6.	No aliases or tattoos	3	_____
7.	No more than 2 prior arrests	4	_____
8.	Has not been to a juvenile training school	3	_____
9.	Has not had prior jail commitments (sentenced to jail)	3	_____
10.	No assaultiveness in prior criminal history	3	_____
11.	First arrest did not occur prior to age 20	2	_____
	TOTAL: PRIOR CRIMINAL HISTORY	38	_____
B. NARCOTICS, DRUGS, AND ALCOHOL:			
1.	No history of opiate addiction	10	_____
2.	No history of other type of illegal drug usage	3	_____
3.	No history of alcohol involvement in this or prior arrests	4	_____
	TOTAL: NARCOTICS, DRUGS, AND ALCOHOL	17	_____
C. EMOTIONAL AND PHYSICAL:			
1.	No history of psychological disorders	3	_____
2.	No sex offense attributed to personality or emotional disorders	3	_____
3.	Sexual adjustment appears normal	2	_____
4.	Favorable physical condition (health)	2	_____
5.	Favorable physical appearance	1	_____
6.	Delinquent behavior not attributed to associates	4	_____
7.	Has favorable attitude toward probation and future	2	_____
	TOTAL EMOTIONAL AND PHYSICAL	17	_____
D. EMPLOYMENT AND EDUCATION:			
1.	Employed at present (if housewife or full-time student, give credit	3	_____
2.	Has held present job six months or more	3	_____
3.	Has a vocational skill	2	_____
4.	Attending school in addition to work	2	_____
5.	Veteran with Honorable Discharge	1	_____
6.	Completed high school or has GED	2	_____
7.	Has a good work history	2	_____
8.	If children involved, has suitable care arranged during work hrs.	2	_____
	TOTAL EMPLOYMENT AND EDUCATION	17	_____
E. FAMILY TIES			
1.	No immediate family criminal record	4	_____
2.	Lives with spouse or family	2	_____
3.	Parents neither separated nor divorced	2	_____
4.	Supports dependent or self, if single	2	_____
5.	Marital stability – no divorces or separations (give credit if single)	1	_____
	TOTAL FAMILY TIES	11	_____
	TOTAL ALL ABOVE SECTIONS:		_____
F. INTANGIBLE FACTORS (May add or subtract up to total of 10 points) + or -			_____
	ACTUAL RATING:		_____

INITIAL SUPERVISION CLASSIFICATION SCALE:

0 5 10 15 20 25 30 35 40 45 50 55 60 65 70 75 80 85 90 95 100
       MAX SUPERVISION   MED SUPERVISION   MIN SUPERVISION

(continued)

FIGURE 4.4   *Continued*

NAME: _____ , Raymond Eugene _____   SEX: ___M___ .

EDUCATIONAL LEVEL: 11TH grade completed _____   AGE: ___22___ .

TIME AT CURRENT RESIDENCE: ___YEARS _3_MONTHS ___RENT ___ OWN

NUMBER OF LEGAL DEPENDANTS: _2_ AGES: _5 Years AND 3 Years_____ .

OCCUPATION: _____ SKILLED_____ UNSKILLED_ X _.

EMPLOYER: __ unemployed_____ LENGTH OF EMPLOYMENT _____

IF LESS THAN 12 MONTHS – PREVIOUS EMPLOYMENT:

___ Montgomery Ward (2 months)_____ .

_____ .

MONTHLY INCOME:		**MONTHLY LIABILITIES**		
			Monthly	Balance
1) Salary/Wages (Individual)	$ 0 .			
2) Total Family:	$ 0 .	1) Rent/Mortgage	$ 0 .	$_____
3) Other (AFDC, Child Support, Etc.)	$ 0 .	2) Car Pmt/Transp.	$ 0 .	$_____
4) Unreported (Tips, Cash, Etc.)	$ 0 .	3) Utilities (Phone, Water, Electricity, Gas)	$ 0 .	$_____
TOTAL:	$ 0 .	4) Food/Meals Out	$ 0 .	$_____
		5) Child Support	$ 0 .	$_____
MONTHLY:		6) Loans/Credit Cards	$ 0 .	$_____
INCOME $ 0 ,		7) Restitution	$ 0 .	$_____
LIABILITIES $ 0 .		8) Other Expenses	$ 0 .	$_____
DISPOSABLE		(itemize on back)		
INCOME $ 0 .		TOTAL:	$ 0 .	$_____

RECOMMENDED SUPERVISION FEE: $ 40.00 .

designed for use in misdemeanor matters, minor felony cases, or requests for pre-trial diversion. The third example involves a routine theft case wherein a short form was used, augmented by a hand written evaluation sheet and financial profile. In this case a risk assessment form is also included. Not all presentence reports are as comprehensive or inclusive as these three. Some reports, unfortunately, are very sketchy and provide judges with little information on which to base a decision.

Evaluation

Although many have hailed the PSI as an invaluable aid to sentencing and others as vitally important to the probation movement, its actual usefulness can be seriously questioned. After doing hundreds of PSIs, interviewing countless probation and court personnel in several jurisdictions, and researching the subject in scores of academic and practitioner journals, the authors conclude that, on balance, the effectiveness of presentence reports should be considered as an unfulfilled promise. The PSI's potential is unquestionably significant. Properly conducted and presented it could be the linchpin of an objective and independent probation service. All too often, however, the PSI becomes a predictable exercise in bureaucratic busy-work. In many situations, probation investigation units have been co-opted by powerful district attorneys or judges and no longer are able to produce independent reports of high quality and objectivity. Often in these instances, investigators structure the PSI to satisfy pragmatic considerations, and the report's real impact is symbolic rather than real.

Although all practitioners or academicians do not share the authors' assessment of the PSI, others have come to similar conclusions. For example, Abraham Bloomberg, after firsthand observation of courts in the Midwest, concluded

> The presentence investigation document is often cynically employed to validate judicial behavior or is otherwise used to reinforce administrative behavior already taken. The circumstances under which probation reports are prepared casts serious doubts on their validity and integrity. . . . The importance of the presentence investigation as a decision-making tool for the judge is overrated.[26]

While studying probation offices in the Southwest, Richard Lawrence found that "many officers do question the objective, impartiality and value of the presentence report in the sentencing decision."[27] Michael Norman and Robert Wadman found that judges, prosecutors, and probation officers believed that inaccurate and unverified information was a great area of weakness in PSIs.[28]

From a different perspective, Anthony Walsh, a criminal justice researcher with years of probation service, contends that presentence reports are generally objective documents that play a crucial role in the sentencing decision.[29] Edward Latessa, a criminal justice professor who has done several studies of probation, also believes that the PSI is a valuable resource that is typically presented in an appropriate manner.[30] Some judges would agree with the latter sentiments because they rely heavily on PSIs to structure their sentencing decisions. Information contained in the PSI is used not only for the decision to grant probation but also for setting terms of imprisonment (especially in those states that have presumptive guidelines where the judges must look for mitigating or aggravating circumstances before sentencing). There is no question that some PSI writers conduct professional, objective investigations. But these "shining examples" should not blind us from the overall picture. Even though opinions are divided about the influence of PSIs, this does not mean that research findings (however controversial) should be withheld from texts pending future consensus. With this in mind, the following evaluation is presented. Hopefully, it will encourage dialogue and lead to better report writing.

In order to evaluate the PSI's effectiveness, it is essential to first examine the probation officers' position in the court system and how this affects their information gathering, report writing, and decision making. The following analysis is based largely on research data collected from observing and interviewing probation investigators in California, Louisiana, New York, and Nevada.[31] While not all the data are directly applicable to every jurisdiction, similar practices do exist throughout the United States.

Status of Probation Officers

The probation officers' relationship to the court is that of a paid employee, and their status in relation to judges and other attorneys is a subordinate one. The work of C. Everett Hughes provides a useful perspective for understanding the relationship between the status of probation officers and their presentence duties. According to Hughes, occupational duties within institutions often serve to maintain status relationships as those in higher positions pass on lesser duties to subordinates.[32] Other researchers have demonstrated that while judges may give lip service to the significance and worth of PSIs, they often remain suspicious of the probation officers' lack of training and the hearsay nature of the reports. For example, Samuel Walker maintains that in highly visible cases, judges tend to disregard the probation reports entirely.[33] Thus, the judiciary, by delegating the collection of routine information to probation officers, reaffirms its authority and legitimacy. In this context the responsibility for compiling presentence reports can be considered a "dirty work" assignment that is devalued by the judiciary.[34]

In many jurisdictions throughout the United States, crowded court calendars, determinate sentencing guidelines and increasingly conservative sentencing philosophies have made it problematic for judges to thoroughly consider individual offender characteristics. Thus, judges, working in tandem with district attorneys, often emphasize the legal variables of the offense and the criminal record at sentencing.[35] Judges expect probation officers to help speed cases through court by submitting noncontroversial reports that provide a facade of information accompanied by bottom-line recommendations that do not significantly deviate from a consideration of offense and prior record. Probation officers generally respond to such judicial expectations by emphasizing similar variables in their presentence reports. This does not mean that probation officers are completely passive; individual styles and personal philosophies do influence their reports. However, unusual approaches are usually reserved for a few special cases. The vast majority of *normal* cases are handled in a manner that follows relatively uniform patterns.

In most presentence investigations, the variables of the present offense and prior criminal record are the factors that determine the probation officer's final sentencing recommendation. This is true regardless of the sentencing structure in which the PSI is written. The influence of these variables is so dominant that other considerations have minimal influence on probation recommendations. The chief rationale of probation officers for this approach is "that's the way judges want it." There are other methods of investigation; for instance, some officers do attempt to consider factors contained in the defendant's social history and to interject personal opinions or philosophies. However, all probation officers seek to develop credibility with the court. Such reputation building is similar to that reported by Richard McCleary in his study of parole officers.[36] In order to develop rapport with the court, probation officers must submit reports that facilitate a smooth workflow. Probation officers assume that in the great majority of cases this can be accomplished by emphasizing offense and criminal record.

Once the officers have established reputations as *producers*, they have *earned* the right to some degree of discretion in their reporting. One investigation officer succinctly described this process: "When you've paid your dues, you're allowed some slack." Such discretion is limited to a minority of cases. In these *deviant* cases probation officers frequently allow social variables to influence their recommendations. For example, in one report, an experienced officer recommended probation for a convicted felon with a long prior record because the defendant's father agreed to pay for an intensive drug treatment program. In another case, a probation officer decided that a first-time shoplifter had a "very bad attitude" and, therefore, recommended a stiff jail sentence rather than probation. Although variations from normal procedure are interesting and important, they should not detract from an investigation process that is used in the majority of cases.

Based on the research data reported by Rosecrance,[37] the following patterns occur with sufficient regularity to be considered *typical*. Probation officers, after considering offense and criminal record, place defendants into categories that represented the eventual court recommendation. This typing process occurs early in the course of presentence inquiry, and the balance of the investigation is used to reaffirm the private typings that are later to become official designations. In order to clarify the decision-making processes used by probation officers, the three stages in a presentence investigation are categorized as (1) typing the defendant, (2) compiling further information, and (3) filing the report.

Typing the Defendant

A presentence investigation is initiated when the court orders the probation department to prepare a report on a criminal defendant. Usually the initial court referral contains such information as police reports, charges against the defendant, court proceedings, plea bargaining agreements (if any), offenses to which the defendant has pled or been found guilty, and the defendant's prior criminal record.

Probation officers consider such information as relatively unambiguous and part of the "official" record. The comment of a presentence investigator reflects the probation officer's perspective of the court referral:

> I consider the information in the court referral hard data. It tells me what I need to know about a case, without a lot of *bullshit*. I mean the guy has pled guilty to a certain offense—he can't get out of that. He has such and such a prior record—there's no changing that. So much of the stuff we put in these reports is subjective and open to interpretation. It's good to have some solid information.[38]

Armed with information contained in the court referral, probation officers begin typing those defendants assigned for presentence investigation. Defendants are placed into general types based on possible sentence recommendations. A probation officer's statement is indicative that typing begins early in a presentence investigation:

> Bottom line, it's the sentence recommendation that's important. That's what the judges and everybody wants to see. I start thinking about the recommendation as soon as I pick up the court referral. Why wait? The basic facts aren't going to change. Oh, I know some POs will tell you they weigh all the facts before coming up with a recommendation. But that's propaganda—we all start thinking recommendation right from the get-go.[39]

At this stage in the investigation the factors known to probation officers are, in the main, legally relevant variables. The defendant's unique characteristics and special circumstances generally are unknown at this time. Although probation officers may be cognizant of the offender's age, sex, and race, how these variables relate to the case is not yet apparent.

These initial typings are private definitions[40] based on the officer's experience and knowledge of the court system. On occasion, when officers are not sure of a particular typing, they will informally discuss the case with their colleagues or supervisors. Until the report is complete their typing remains a private designation. The probation officers' **typing of defendants** is done, in most cases, by considering the known and relatively irrefutable variables of offense and prior record. Probation officers are convinced that judges and district attorneys are most concerned with that part of their reports. The following comment (or versions thereof) has been heard on many occasions: "Judges read the offense section, glance at the prior record and then flip to the back and see what we recommend."[41]

Officers indicated that during informal discussions judges made it clear that in the majority of cases offense and prior record determined sentences. In some cases judges consider other variables, but the officers indicated that this occurred in *unusual* cases with *special* circumstances. One such case, for example, involved granting probation to a woman who was a victim of domestic violence who killed her husband.

PSI writers are also in regular contact with prosecuting attorneys and frequently discuss their investigations with them. In addition, district attorneys seem to have no problem calling a probation administrator to complain about what they consider an inappropriate sentencing recommendation. Investigators unanimously agreed that prosecutors usually viewed a defendant's social history as "immaterial" and wanted the PSI to stick to the legal facts. Samuel Walker, in his critique of the court system, termed such informal networks *courtroom work groups.* He observed that personnel who appeared regularly in court developed an "informal understanding of how routine cases should be handled."[42]

Probation officers use offense and prior record to place defendants into dispositional types (based on recommendation). In describing these types the actual terms used by probation officers themselves in the typing process are used. The following typology, therefore, is community (rather than researcher) designated.[43]

Dispositional Types
1. Deal case
2. Diversion case
3. Joint case
4. Probation case with some jail time
5. Straight probation case

Within each of these types, probation officers also assign the severity of punishment by labeling the case as either lightweight or heavy duty.

In a **lightweight case** the defendant will be given some measure of leniency because the offense was a minor one, the offender had no prior criminal record, or the criminal activity (regardless of the penal code violation) was relatively minor. However, **heavy-duty cases** will receive more severe penalties because the offense, the offender, or the circumstances of the offense are seen as particularly serious. Diversion and straight probation types generally are considered lightweight, whereas the majority of joint cases are usually heavy duty. Cases involving personal violence are almost always designated heavy duty. Most misdemeanor cases where the defendant has no or a relatively minor prior criminal record are termed lightweight. However, if the defendant has an extensive criminal record, even misdemeanor cases can call for stiff penalties, and therefore such cases are considered heavy duty. Certain felony cases can be thought of as lightweight if there was no violence, the victim's loss was minimal, or the defendant had no prior convictions. On occasion, even an offense such as armed robbery can be considered lightweight. The following example (taken from an actual report) is one such instance: A first-time offender with a simulated gun held up a convenience store and returned to the scene, gave back the money, and asked the store employees to call the police.

The typings are general guides, and specifics, such as terms and conditions of probation or diversion, or length of incarceration, are worked out later. Each type has a set of criteria placing it in its category. For example, **deal cases** involve those situations where a plea bargain exists. In California, and in most jurisdictions, many plea bargains specify the sentence that should follow the guilty plea. Probation officers rarely recommend sentences contrary to those specified in plea-bargaining agreements. Although probation officers are technically free to recommend a sentence different from that contained in the plea bargain (at which time *if* the judge agrees, the guilty plea will be withdrawn and criminal proceedings reinstated), they have learned that such action is unrealistic and often counterproductive to their own interests because judges almost always uphold the sentencing agreements. The following observation represents the probation officers' view of plea-bargaining deals:

> It's stupid to try and bust a deal. What's the percentage? Who needs the hassle? The judge always honors the deal—after all, he was part of it. Everyone, including the defendant, has already agreed. It's all nice and neat, all wrapped up. We are supposed to rubber stamp the package—and we do. Everyone is better off that way.[44]

Diversion cases usually involve relatively minor offenses committed by those with no prior record and are considered *a snap* by probation officers. In the vast majority of cases, those referred for diversion have already been screened by the district attorney's office and the probation investigator merely agrees that they are eligible, and, therefore, should be granted diversionary relief (and eventual dismissal of charges). In rare cases there may be an oversight and it is discovered that the defendant is ineligible (based on prior criminal convictions) for diversion. The probation officer then informs the court and normal criminal proceedings are resumed. In either situation there is not much decision making by probation officers about what disposition to recommend. Reports in diversion cases are usually submitted in an abbreviated format on a short form. Diversion cases are discussed further in Chapter Eleven.

The last three typings generally refer to cases where the sentencing recommendations are ambiguous and some decision making by probation officers is required: send the offender to prison, or place him or her on probation. Those categorized as **joint cases** (prison cases) are denied probation and instead the investigator recommends an appropriate prison sentence. In certain instances the nature of the offense (e.g., rape, murder, or arson) renders defendants legally ineligible for probation. In other situations defendants' prior records (especially felony convictions) make it impossible for them to be granted probation.[45] In many cases the length of prison sentences has been set by legal statute and can only be marginally increased or decreased (depending on the aggravating or mitigating circumstances of the case). In California, for example, the majority of defendants sentenced to prison receive terms between the minimum and maximum set by law. The length of time varies with offense. Those cases that fall outside the middle term usually do so because of something about the crime or conviction (e.g., using a weapon) or because the criminal record is either serious or very light. Those originally typed as joint cases are treated as qualitatively different from other probation applications. Concerns with rehabilitation or the defendants' life situations are no longer important and proper punishment becomes the main point of the investigation. This perspective was described by a probation officer-respondent: "Once I know so and so is a heavy-duty joint case I don't think in terms of rehabilitation or social planning. It becomes a matter of how long to salt the sucker away, and that's covered by the code."[46]

For those typed as probation cases, the issue for the investigator is whether to recommend some time in jail as a condition of probation. This decision is made based on whether the case is lightweight or heavy duty. A **straight probation case** is usually reserved for those convicted of relatively less serious offenses or for those without a prior criminal record (i.e., first timers). Also, some probation officers candidly admitted that, all things being equal, middle-class defendants are more likely to get straight probation than other social categories. The split sentence or shock probation (**probation case with some jail time**) has become popular and is a consideration in most misdemeanor and felony matters (especially when the defendant has a prior criminal record). There is a perception that drug offenders should receive a jail sentence as part of probation to deter them from future drug use. Once a probation officer has decided "some jail time is in order" the final recommendation includes that condition. Although the actual amount of jail time frequently is determined late, the probation officer's perception that a jail sentence should be imposed remains constant. The following comment typifies these sentiments and also illustrates the imprecise nature of recommending a period of time in custody:

> It's not hard to figure out who needs some jail. The referral sheet can tell you that. What's hard to know is exactly how much time. Ninety days or six months—who knows what's fair? We put down some number but it is usually an arbitrary figure. No one has come up with a chart that correlates sentencing equity with jail time.[47]

Compiling Further Information

Once an initial typing is made, the next stage in the investigation involves collecting further information about the defendant. Most of the facts and figures collected at this stage do not involve legal issues, such as offense and prior convictions. The defendant is interviewed and his or her social history is outlined. Probation officers often contact sources known to the offender, such as school officials, victims, doctors, counselors, and relatives, to learn more about the defendant's individual circumstances and to verify statements made during the initial interview. Attempting to verify information is often a tiresome task because former employers, ex-spouses, and neighbors are often uncooperative. This feature of the presentence investigation involves considerable time and effort and is often neglected in the crush of work, especially because this information gathering is done primarily to legitimate earlier probation officer typings or to satisfy judicial requirements. A presentence investigator describes this process:

> Interviewing these defendants and working up a social history takes time. In most cases it's really unnecessary since I've already decided what I am going to do. We all know that a recommendation is governed by the offense and prior record. All the rest is just stuffing to fill out the court report, to make the judge look like he's got all the facts.[48]

Presentence interviews with defendants are a required part of the investigation and are often routine discussions described by a probation officer as "anticlimactic."

These interviews are usually conducted in settings familiar to probation officers (e.g., jail interviewing rooms or probation department offices). Because probation officers and defendants normally do not trust each other, it is difficult for them to be candid and open. Probation officers are concerned that they might be conned or manipulated because they assume that defendants "will say anything to save themselves." However, defendants are trying to picture themselves in a favorable light and are wary of revealing any information that might be used against them.

The interview process is one in which, in most cases, the probation officers act as interrogators and defendants as respondents. Because presentence investigators select the questions, they control the course of the interview and can draw out the kind of responses that serve to validate their original defendant typings. One probationer described his presentence interview in the following way:

> I knew what the P.O. wanted me to say. She had me pegged as a nice middle-class kid who had fallen in with a bad crowd. So that's how I came off. I was contrite, a real boy scout who had learned his lesson. What an acting job! I figured if I didn't act up I'd get probation.[49]

A veteran probation officer related how she conducted presentence interviews:

> I'm always in charge during the interviews. I know what questions to ask in order to fill out my report. The defendants respond just about the way I expect them to. They hardly ever surprise me.[50]

Occasionally, potential probationers refuse to go along with structured presentence interviews. Some offenders either attempt to control the interview or are openly hostile to probation officers. Reminders such as "I don't think you really appreciate the seriousness of your situation" or "I'm the one who asks the questions here" sometimes work to discourage uncooperative defendants, but some are openly hostile toward the court process and demonstrate an open disregard for possible sanctions.

Most veteran probation officers have interviewed some defendants who simply do not seem to care what happens to them. For example, a defendant once informed an investigation officer "I don't care what you motherf_____s try and do to me. I'm going to do what I f_____g please. Take your probation and stick it." Another defendant told her probation officer: "I'm going to shoot up every chance I get. I need my fix more than I need probation." Probation officers label such confrontational defendants and those unwilling to "play the probation game" as dangerous or irrational.[51]

In these situations the investigator's initial typing frequently is no longer valid, and probation will either be denied or be stringently structured. However, the majority of interviews progress in a predictable manner as probation officers collect information that will be included in the section of the report termed "defendant's statement."

Although some defendants submit written comments, most of their statements are actually formulated by the probation officer. The defendant's statement, in a sociological sense, can be considered an "account,"[52] and probation officers at times attempt to shape the defendant's account to fit their own preconceived offender typing. Many probation officers believe the reported defendant's attitude toward the offense and toward his or her future potential for leading a law-abiding life are the most important parts of the statement. In most presentence investigations the defendant's subjective attitudes are identified and interpreted by the probation investigator and then included in the report. Using this procedure probation officers look for and are able to report attitudes that "logically fit" with their final sentencing recommendation.[53]

For example, defendants who have been typed as joint cases typically are depicted as having socially unacceptable attitudes about their criminal actions and unrealistic or negative attitudes about future possibilities for living upright lives. However, those who have been typed as probation cases are described as having such acceptable attitudes as politeness and contriteness about their present offenses and optimism about their abilities to lead crime-free lives. A presentence investigator described the structuring of accounts about defendant attitudes in the following manner:

> When POs talk about the defendant's attitude we really mean how that attitude relates to the case. Naturally I'm not going to write about what a wonderful attitude the guy has—how sincere he seems—and then recommend sending him to the joint. That wouldn't make sense. The judges want consistency. If a guy has a [crummy] attitude but is going to get probation anyway, there's no percentage in playing up his attitude problem.[54]

The presentence interview, in most cases, is the only contact the investigating officer has with the defendant. The briefness of this contact and the lack of postreport interaction often lead to a very legalistic perspective by the PO. PSI writers want to "get the case through court" and do not really want to concern themselves with any special supervision problems offenders may pose later. Also, these one-time-only interviews rarely lead to probation officers becoming emotionally involved with the cases. In fact, the individual aspects of the defendant's personality are generally not uncovered during a half-hour presentence interview. For many POs one of the benefits of working in presentence units is the fact that they do not have to get emotionally close to the offenders. An investigation officer related such an opinion: "I really like the one-shot-only part of this job. I don't have time to get caught up with the clients. I can deal with facts and not worry about individual personalities."[55]

The probation officer has a wide discretion in the type of collateral information (from sources other than the defendant or the official record) that is collected. Although a defendant's social history must be included in the presentence report, the details of that history are left to individual investigators. There are few established guidelines for this section of the report, except in cases where a psychiatric or psychological report needs to be submitted because there is strong evidence that the offender is mentally disturbed. However, there are informal guidelines that suggest, for example, that in misdemeanor cases reports should be shorter and more concise than in felony cases. Officers in the Rosecrance study indicated that reports for municipal court (all misdemeanor cases) should range from four to six pages in length, whereas superior court reports (felony cases) were expected to be six to nine pages long. In controversial cases (only the most experienced officers are assigned these) presentence reports are expected to be longer and include considerable social data. Reports in these cases are as long as thirty pages.

Although probation officers learn what general types of information to include through experience and feedback from judges and supervisors, they are allowed considerable leeway in deciding exactly what to put in their reports (outside of the offense and prior record sections). Because investigators decide what collateral sources are relevant to the case, they tend to include information that will reflect favorably on their sentencing recommendation. In this context, the observation of a probation officer is understandable: "I pick from the mass of possible sources just which ones to put in the report. Do you think I'm going to pick people who make my recommendation look weak? No way!"[56]

Filing the Report

The final stage in the investigation includes writing the report, getting it approved by a probation supervisor, and appearing in court. All three of these activities reinforce the importance that prior record and offense have on sentencing recommendations. When they actually write the report, probation officers determine what to include in the report and how to express their remarks. For the first time in the process, presentence officers receive formal feedback from their superiors and other officials. Presentence reports are read by three groups important to the probation officers (1) probation supervisors, (2) district attorneys, and (3) judges.

Although in some cases presentence investigators consider the arguments of the defendant's counsel, probation officers generally are not influenced by the recommendations of defense attorneys. However, probation officers often identify with prosecutors because theoretically both groups have a common goal—the protection of the community. This common purpose is contrasted with the assumed goal of the defense attorneys—to get their clients off scot-free. Many probation officers believe that natural barriers such as different goals and differing perspectives make it difficult to develop rapport with defense attorneys. This sentiment is so prevalent that the public defender's office is often referred to as "enemy territory."[57]

Investigating officers assume that their supervisors, prosecutors, and judges all emphasize the legally relevant variables of offense and prior criminal record when considering an appropriate sentencing recommendation. These types of considerations act to reaffirm the probation officer's initial private typing. A probation investigator described such a process:

> After I've talked to the defendants I think maybe some of them deserve to get special consideration. But then I remember who's going to look at the reports. My

supervisor, the D.A., the judge; they don't care about all the personal details. When all is said and done, what's really important to them is the offense and the defendant's prior record. I know that stuff from the start. It makes me wonder why [we end up doing such] long reports.[58]

Probation officers assume that their credibility as presentence investigators will be improved if their sentencing recommendations are approved by probation supervisors, district attorneys, and judges. However, officers whose recommendations are consistently "out of line" are subject to censure, transfer, or finding themselves engaged in "running battles"[59] with court officials. During this final step in the investigation, probation officers must figure out how to make sure their reports will get through court without "undue personal hassle." Most investigation officers have learned that presentence recommendations based on a consideration of prior record and offense can achieve that goal.

Although keeping their jobs is an important factor in deciding how to complete a presentence investigation, other issues are involved. For example, many probation officers agree with the retributive philosophy of punishment and therefore believe using current offense/criminal history to determine the recommendations is valid. Other officers believe that their discretion had been *short circuited* by determinate sentencing guidelines, reducing them to "merely going through the motions" when conducting their investigations. Still other officers believe that using legal variables to structure recommendations is an acceptable shortcut that partially offsets large case assignments. One probation officer stated: "If the department wants us to keep pumping out presentence reports we can't consider social factors—we just don't have time."[60] Although there are varied dynamics impacting on probation offices, there seems little doubt that in many jurisdictions the social history once considered the "heart and soul" of presentence probation reports[61] has been largely diminished.

Maintaining the Myth—Is It Worth It?

Given the importance of offense and prior record in sentencing considerations, the relevance of current presentence investigation practices is in doubt. Continuing to collect a mass of social data of uncertain relevance seems ineffective and wasteful. However, an analysis of courtroom culture suggests that the presentence investigation helps maintain judicial mythology as well as probation officer legitimacy.[62] Judges generally are not interested in considering individual variables in detail, nor do they normally have the time. Therefore, the presence of a presentence investigation perpetuates the myth of individualized sentences. Including a presentence report in the court file affords the appearance of individualization without significantly influencing sentencing practices.

Even in states where determinate sentencing has in principle replaced individualized justice, the judicial system feels obligated to maintain the appearance of individualization. Rosecrance argues that it is clear that a major reason for maintaining such a practice is to make it easier for criminal defendants to accept their sentences.[63] The presentence report allows defendants to feel their case has at least received a considered decision. One judge candidly admitted the "real purpose" of the presentence investigation was to convince defendants they were not getting "the fast shuffle." He went on to say that if defendants were sentenced without such investigations many would complain and file "endless appeals" over what seemed, to them, a hasty sentencing decision. Even though judges typically only consider offense and prior record when they make a sentencing decision, they want defendants to believe their cases are being judged on an individual basis. The presentence investigation makes this assumption possible. Furthermore, some judges use the PSI as an excuse for a particular type of sentence, perhaps denying responsibility for the sentence by stating that their "hands were tied" by the probation officer's recommendation. Judges using this excuse are thus "off the hook" for handing out an unpopular sentence.

The presentence report contributes significantly to the legitimacy of probation. Several issues support the probation officers' stake in continuing their roles in these investigations. As noted in Chapter Two, probation has historically been connected to the concept of individualized treatment. In principle, the presentence report is ideally suited to reporting on the individual circumstances of defendants. However, from a historical perspective, this ideal has always been more symbolic than substantive.[64] Furthermore, if the legitimacy of the presentence report is questioned, so then is the entire purpose of probation. Regardless of its usefulness, it is doubtful that probation officials would consider the lessening or elimination of presentence reports. For one thing, the number of workers assigned to presentence investigations is substantial, and their numbers represent an obvious source of bureaucratic power. Second, conducting presentence investigations allows probation officers to remain visible with the court and the public. The media often report on controversial probation cases, and presentence writers generally have more contact and association with judges than others in the probation department.

Probation officers, as secondary court workers, are assigned the mundane tasks of collecting largely irrelevant offender data. Investigation officers have learned that emphasizing offense and prior record in their reports will enhance relationships with judges and district attorneys, as well as improve their occupational standing within probation departments. Thus, the presentence investigation serves to maintain the courts' claim of individualized concern while preserving the probation officer role, even if it is a subordinate one, in the court system.

Although the myth of individualization serves various functions it also raises serious questions. For instance, in an era of severe budget restrictions, should scarce resources be used to compile predictable presentence reports of questionable value? Also, if social variables are only considered in a few cases, should courts continue to routinely require presentence reports in all felony matters (as is the practice in most areas)?

One development to watch in the area of presentence report writing is the increasing number of privately commissioned presentence reports.[65] Such reports, often written by private investigators, caseworkers, or former probation officers, are often ordered by defense attorneys to overcome the biases reported in the official PSI. These reports also are not without criticism. They are expensive—they average about $250 and can run to $2,000 or more, depending on the amount of detail contained in the report—so only relatively well off defendants can afford them. There are also ethical issues involved in their use. For example, the need to make a profit and satisfy clients must not get in the way of a fair and accurate report. Any actual or implied guarantee of the final recommendation must be avoided.[66]

Summary

The PSI has a firm historical and legal basis. From the beginnings of probation an investigation of applicants was considered appropriate and essential. In *Williams v. New York* (1949) the Supreme Court affirmed the importance of a PSI, held that inclusion of hearsay was permissible, and ruled that the presentence report could be held confidential. Subsequently, the fairness of withholding presentence reports from defendants and their counsel was seriously questioned, and most jurisdictions have moved toward full disclosure of the PSI (stimulated in part by *Gardner v. Florida*, 1977). In the 1920s a standard presentence format emerged. Today, most probation departments include subsections from the core concepts of offense, prior criminal record, social history, evaluation, and recommendation. In less serious cases a short form with condensed categories has been developed.

Although the PSI had the potential to be a significant part of the court process, we contend (based on Rosecrance's research in California probation departments) that it has become, in many cases, bureaucratic posturing rather than objective reporting. The probation officers' position in the court is an inferior one, and they are subordinate to prosecutors and judges. Following judicial and prosecutorial cues, probation departments have chosen to deemphasize the defendant's social history and instead concentrate on the offense committed and the offender's prior criminal record. In conducting PSIs, probation investigators weigh these two factors and place defendants into types that reflect eventual sentencing recommendations. Although other data, such as defendant's attitude and social history, subsequently are collected and included in the presentence report, investigators structure this information to legitimate their initial typing. On the one hand, the usefulness of current PSIs can be questioned; on the other hand, their use fosters the myth of individualized justice, a myth that helps sustain judicial authority and probation legitimacy.

Key People and Terms

Edwin Cooley (83)
Deal case (117)
Diversion case (118)
William Healy (83)
Heavy-duty case (117)
Joint case (118)
Lightweight case (117)

Presentence investigation (PSI) (79)
Presentence report (79)
Probation with some jail time (119)
Mary Richardson (83)
Rule 32(c) (84)
Straight probation case (119)
Typing of defendants (116)

Key Legal Cases

Gardner v. Florida
Tucker v. U.S.

Weston v. U.S.
Williams v. New York

Questions for Discussion and Review

1. What are the five general functions of a presentence investigation (PSI) report? What are the five core information modules contained within a PSI?

2. What information should probation officers consider when compiling a PSI?

3. Discuss the significance to presentence investigations of federal Rule 32(c) and the case of *Williams v. New York.*

4. What are the arguments for and against the disclosure of information contained in the PSI?

5. Discuss the component parts of a PSI.

6. Discuss whether the PSI is a useful document or has become unnecessary to the sentencing process.

7. Explain how the status of a probation officer affects the information contained in a PSI.

8. List and discuss the five dispositional types in which probation officers place defendants for whom they are writing presentence investigations.

9. What is involved in compiling further information for the PSI? How important is this stage to the overall sentencing process?

10. Discuss the three activities involved in filing the PSI report. What is the significance of these activities?

11. What, ultimately, is the purpose of PSIs? Will PSIs remain a part of the sentencing process? Why or why not?

Relevant Internet Sites

U.S. federal court rule, covers the presentence investigation and the sentencing process: www.uscourts.gov/rules/supct1101/CRStyle2.pdf

U.S. Probation Office for the Western District of North Carolina, a guide to the PSI process: www.ncwd.net/probation/psida.html

Justice Policy Institute, provides a history of the PSI process: www.cjcj.org/jpi/psireport.html

Description of the presentence investigation, the report that it generates, and steps offenders ought to take to ensure its accuracy: www.prisonerlife.com/s_writings17.cfm

Notes

1. Administrative Office of the U.S. Courts, "The Selective Presentence Investigation Report," in *Probation, Parole and Community Corrections*, 3rd ed., eds. Robert Carter, Daniel Glaser, and Leslie Wilkins (New York: Wiley, 1984) 22.

2. Administrative Office of the U.S. Courts 22.

3. Administrative Office of the U.S. Courts 29.

4. U.S. Probation and Pretrial Services, "Probation Officers," *Court and Community* (Washington, DC: Administrative Office of the U.S. Courts, 2003): 1.

5. Administrative Office of the U.S. Courts, "The Presentence Investigation Report," in *Probation, Parole and Community Corrections*, 2nd ed., eds. Robert Carter and Leslie Wilkins (New York: Wiley, 1976) 177.

6. David Dressler, *Practice and Theory of Probation and Parole* (New York: Columbia University Press, 1969) 107–108.

7. For a summary of the favorable comments about the presentence investigation see John Rosecrance, "Maintaining the Myth of Individualized Justice: Probation Presentence Reports," *Justice Quarterly* 5 (September, 1988); and Lawrence Stump "Court Investigations and Reports," *Federal Probation* 21 (June, 1957): 9–17.

8. Ann L. Pastore and Kathleen Maguire, eds., *Sourcebook of Criminal Justice Statistics, 1999* (Albany, NY: Hindelang Criminal Justice Research Center, 2001).

9. Thomas P. Bonczar, *Characteristics of Adults on Probation, 1995* (Washington, DC: U.S. Department of Justice, 1997).

10. Neal Shover, *A Sociology of American Corrections* (Homewood, IL: Dorsey, 1979).

11. Quoted in Charles L. Chute, *Crime, Courts and Probation* (New York: Macmillan, 1965) 137.

12. Wilfred Bolster, "Adult Probation, Parole and Suspended Sentence," *Journal of Criminal Law and Criminology* 1 (1910): 440.

13. Quoted in Robert Carter, *Presentence Report Handbook* (Washington, DC: National Institute of Law Enforcement and Criminal Justice, 1978) 4.

14. Quoted in David Rothman, *Conscience and Convenience: The Asylum and Its Alternatives in Progressive America* (Boston: Little, Brown, 1980) 61.

15. Both the majority and the dissenting opinions in the *Williams* case were taken from Leonard Orland, *Justice, Punishment, Treatment: The Correctional Process* (New York: Macmillan, 1973) 20–23.

16. Orland 20–23.

17. William Zastrow, "Disclosure of the Presentence Investigation Report," *Federal Probation* 36 (March, 1971): 20–22.

18. Stephen Fennell and William Hall, "Due Process at Sentencing: An Empirical and Legal Analysis of the Disclosure of Presentence Reports in Federal Courts," *Harvard Law Review* 93 (June, 1980): 1629.

19. Fennell and Hall 1628–1629.

20. Quoted in Zastrow 21.

21. Zastrow 22.

22. *Gardner v. Florida*, 97 Sup. Ct. 1197 (1977): 1204.

23. Quoted in Zastrow 22.

24. Yona Cohn, "Recommended: No Recommendation," *Federal Probation* 48 (September, 1984): 71.

25. James Dahl, Jerry Banks, Eric Carlson, Julius Debro, Kenneth Kirkpatrick, and Laurel Vernon, *Improved Probation Strategies* (Washington, DC: National Institute of Justice, 1979) 48–49.

26. Abraham Bloomberg, *Criminal Justice Issues and Ironies*, 2nd ed. (New York: New Viewpoints, 1979) 283, 285.

27. Richard Lawrence, "Professionals or Judicial Civil Servants?" *Federal Probation* 48 (December, 1984): 16.

28. Michael D. Norman and Robert C. Wadman, "Utah Presentence Investigation Reports: User Group Perceptions of Quality and Effectiveness," *Federal Probation* 64, 1 (2000): 9.

29. Anthony Walsh, "The Role of the Probation Officer in the Sentencing Process," *Criminal Justice and Behavior* 12 (September, 1985): 288–303.

30. Private conversation with John Rosecrance at the Academy of Criminal Justice Sciences Annual Convention, San Francisco, CA (April, 1988).

31. Some of this research was reported by John Rosecrance, "A Typology of Presentence Probation Investigations," *International Journal of Offender Therapy and Comparative Criminology* 31 (September, 1987): 163–177.

32. Everett Hughes, *Men and Their Work* (New York: Free Press, 1958).

33. Samuel Walker, *Sense and Nonsense about Crime* (Monterey, CA: Brooks/Cole, 1985); see his "Wedding Cake" analogy, pp. 16–24.

34. For a full explanation of the context of "dirty work" and how it applies to a probation context, see John Hagan, "The Social and Legal Construction of Criminal Justice: A Study of the Pre-Sentencing Process," *Social Problems* 22 (1975): 620–637.

35. Norman and Wadman 7–12.

36. Richard McCleary, *Dangerous Men: The Sociology of Parole* (Beverly Hills, CA: Sage, 1978).

37. John Rosecrance, "Maintaining the Myth of Individualized Justice: Probation Presentence Reports," in *The Administration and Management of Criminal Justice Organizations,* eds. Stan Stojkovic, John Klofas, and David Kalinich (Prospect Heights, IL: Waveland, 1999) 355–373.

38. Rosecrance, "Maintaining the Myth" 360.

39. Rosecrance, "Maintaining the Myth" 360–361.

40. For an excellent discussion of typing and private definitions in a criminal justice context see Robert Prus and John Stratton, "Parole Revocation Decision-Making: Private Typings and Official Designations," *Federal Probation* 40 (March, 1976): 48–53.

41. Rosecrance, "Maintaining the Myth" 361.

42. Walker 31–36.

43. For a discussion of fieldwork techniques see Robert Emerson, "Ethnography and Understanding Members' Worlds," in *Contemporary Field Research,* ed. Robert Emerson (Boston: Little, Brown, 1981) 19–35.

44. Rosecrance, "Maintaining the Myth" 362.

45. David Neubauer, *Criminal Justice in Middle America* (Morristown, NJ: General Learning, 1974) 240.

46. Rosecrance, "Maintaining the Myth" 363.

47. Rosecrance, "Maintaining the Myth" 363–364.

48. Rosecrance, "Maintaining the Myth" 364.

49. Rosecrance, "Maintaining the Myth" 364.

50. Rosecrance, "Maintaining the Myth" 364.

51. See McCleary, *Dangerous Men: The Sociology of Parole.*

52. For a full discussion of the sociological concept of "accounts" see Marvin Scott and Stanford Lyman, "Accounts," *American Sociological Review* 33 (1968): 46–62.

53. For an appreciation of why probation officers "fit" information to justify their recommendations, see James R. Davis, "Academic and Practical Aspects of Probation: A Comparison," *Federal Probation* 47 (1983): 7–10.

54. Rosecrance, "Maintaining the Myth" 365.

55. Rosecrance, "Maintaining the Myth" 366.

56. Rosecrance, "Maintaining the Myth" 366.

57. John Rosecrance, "The Probation Officers' Search for Credibility: Ball Park Recommendations," *Crime and Delinquency* 31 (October, 1985): 546.

58. Rosecrance, "Maintaining the Myth" 367.

59. Neal Shover, "Experts and Diagnosis in Correctional Agencies," *Crime and Delinquency* 20 (October, 1974): 357.

60. Rosecrance, "Maintaining the Myth" 367.

61. Walter Reckless, *The Crime Problem* (New York: Appleton, 1967) 673.

62. An excellent analysis of probation officer legitimacy is found in John Hagan, John Hewitt, and Duane Alwin, "Ceremonial Justice: Crime and Punishment in a Loosely Coupled System," *Social Forces* 58 (1979): 506–525.

63. Rosecrance, "Maintaining the Myth" 370.

64. This same point is made several times in Rothman, *Conscience and Convenience.*

65. David A. Fruchtman and Robert T. Sigler, "Private Pre-Sentence Investigation: Procedures and Issues," *Journal of Offender Rehabilitation* 29, 3–4 (1999): 157–170.

66. Fruchtman and Sigler 166.

5

The Decision to Grant Probation and the Supervision Process

Granting Probation

In a typical sentencing hearing in a California courtroom, the defendant, who earlier pled guilty to possession of cocaine, nervously awaits the start of court proceedings that include the all-important sentence hearing. Even though a prior plea-bargaining agreement stipulating probation instead of prison was recommended by the probation officer in the presentence report, the defendant's attorney warned the defendant that today's judge, known for harsh sentences, is not strictly bound by the deal. After court is called to order, the defendant waits while several other cases are disposed of, noting with apprehension the person led away in handcuffs after being sentenced to prison. Finally, the defendant's name is called and he walks to the center of the courtroom, noticing the judge and prosecutor shuffling papers until they come to his case.

Many of the judicial formalities had been handled at an earlier stage of the criminal process. Three weeks ago the judge carefully explained the possible penalties and the rights the defendant was waiving by entering a guilty plea. The Supreme Court case *Boykin v. Alabama* had established the legal criteria for acceptance of guilty pleas by ruling it was an error "for the trial judge to accept petitioner's guilty plea without an affirmative showing that it was intelligent and voluntary."[1] This decision was taken to mean that, prior to accepting a guilty plea, judges must determine that defendants understood

1. The nature of the charge or charges to which a plea is offered;
2. The mandatory minimum penalty, if any, the maximum possible penalty, and the effect of any special parole term for each offense to which a plea is offered; and

129

3. That he has the right to plead not guilty, and that if he pleads guilty he will be waiving the right to be tried by a jury, the assistance of counsel at trial, the right to cross examine witnesses against him and the right not to be compelled to incriminate himself.[2]

Because all this had transpired at the time this defendant's guilty plea was entered on the record, the sentencing hearing proceeded smoothly.

When the judge asks the defendant if he has anything further to say, the defendant replies in a barely audible voice, "No." The district attorney looks sternly but approves the recommendation contained in the probation report; as of course does the defendant's attorney who adds that her client has learned a valuable lesson from his recent brush with the law. The judge makes a few comments about the drug menace plaguing our society and then states he is going to follow the pre-sentence recommendation and grant probation. The judge then gives a brief lecture admonishing the defendant to never appear in the judge's court again or else (the *else* punctuated by an ominous stare). The judge quickly orders the defendant to see the bailiff, and the next case is called. The defendant's attorney shakes the defendant's hand, gives him a knowing wink and returns to her other clients.

In this scenario, the decision to grant probation instead of prison was influenced by legal and social factors. From a legal perspective, because the defendant pled guilty to possession of a controlled substance, he could be granted probation. In many jurisdictions defendants convicted of drug sales, by law, must be sentenced to prison (regardless of their individual circumstances). If the defendant had been found with larger quantities of drugs, he could have been charged with possession for sale, conviction of which, in some jurisdictions, mandates a prison term. From a social standpoint the prison systems in most areas are so crowded that drug offenders convicted of possession (unless large quantities are involved) simply are not being sentenced to prison. This practice has changed in some states where available prison space has increased or because of ever-hardening sentiments toward drug offenses. If the current crackdown on drugs intensifies, simple possession cases could result in prison sentences (regardless of overcrowded conditions).

Meanwhile, a uniformed court officer motions the defendant to a side table and tells him to read and sign probation orders. The defendant glances at a long sheet of legal-size paper with several conditions listed. After pausing for a short time, to appear as if reading the formal and stilted words, he signs all three copies of the orders. The bailiff gives the defendant a copy, tells him to check with the probation department in a week, and dismisses the case with a nod. "That's it!" The defendant breathes a sigh of incredible relief as he walks from the courtroom. When he is finally out of the court chambers, he raises his hand in the air and jauntily walks toward the outside saying over and over to himself, "I'm free, I'm free."

Although the defendant's euphoria is understandable, his freedom remains conditional on compliance with the conditions of probation. The orders he signed, perhaps without fully comprehending them, will now be interpreted and enforced by a probation officer. The defendant will soon learn that being on probation carries with it certain responsibilities, and failure to fulfill them is grounds for return to court to receive the "or else" that the judge warned him against. The next phase of the correctional process—probation supervision—is about to begin.

Probation supervision lacks the strong drama of a presentence investigation or a courtroom appearance. It is played out over long periods of time in small offices far from the spotlight, often with ambiguous guidelines. Neither the defendant nor his or her probation officer is precisely certain how the court-ordered period of probation will develop. And yet, the maintenance of that supervision period is the crucial mission of probation. The remainder of this chapter explains this mission; it also includes a brief discussion of pretrial services. Before examining the PO's crucial role in the supervision process, a brief look at how probationers feel about supervision is warranted.

Probationers' Views of Supervision

Discretion in the supervision process exists to the extent that each officer is a separate department unto him or herself. This means that probation can involve very different experiences, depending on who is assigned to supervise a particular case. Because probationers generally have no voice in choosing their probation officers, they feel powerless over certain aspects of their own supervision. The following verbatim comment of an ex-probationer is representative of what some have called PO bingo:

> I was on probation for three years, and had four POs. Each one was different. The first one wanted me to come into the office every week—no matter what. He told me I'd better not miss or I'd be seeing the judge. He kept tabs to make sure I attended AA meetings, even though I told him it was a waste of time. The next lady didn't want to see me in the office at all. She gave me forms to check off and mail in; and never made a fuss about AA; I don't think she really cared.
>
> I got transferred to a young snot-nosed PO who came on like he wanted to be my buddy. He gave the revolutionary shake and always tried to assure me he was cool—you know, not a cop type. Well I never trusted him and besides he forced me to go to some stupid group therapy. What a bunch of crap! A bunch of whining losers, all trying to impress each other by spilling their dirty guts. This PO wanted me to tell him all my problems, the deep secrets that "inhibited insight." Never liked that dude. Finally I got transferred to some guy who made it plain he was a busy man. After one face-to-face, which took about two minutes, he told me to phone him *only* if I moved or got busted. Otherwise he could care less. Well I coasted with him for a year and I guess my probation is over now—you know expired. It seems like I should've gotten a piece of paper or some commendation. I tell you the whole probation trip was weird. (personal communication with John Rosecrance)

In one of the few studies of probationers' reactions to supervision, Indiana University of Pennsylvania professor John Gibbs found that loss of autonomy was an important consideration. The following three comments reflect such concern:

> When I come down here with a gut feeling, I'd like to blow this building off the face of the earth. I don't need nobody checking on my personal life. I don't like the fact that when you're on probation you have no civil rights—you are a convicted criminal. You can do nothing about this. This man controls your life. If he wants to bust you today, and take you to court and jail your ass, he's going to find a way to do it.

> I don't ask her where she goes. As long as I'm not getting arrested and I'm going to work, and I attend AA then I don't see why they have to go into your personal life. As long as you're not getting arrested, and you're showing up when you're suppose to or whatever what else you have to do, as long as you're doing that I don't see why they have to know where you go at night or what you do.

> Yeah, and I don't think that's the way probation gotta be, cause it's gonna screw you up, man, she was too strict. It's gonna screw you up, something like that. Definitely, it's gotta, you know? People on probation are on probation because say, some sort or rebellion against authority or something like that, you know? And then your probation officer is gonna be like that, authority again, be strict, with you again, you understand what I'm saying? So that's not cool, that isn't the way probation should be.[3]

It is clear from these quotes that the probation officers' role in supervision is often characterized by ambiguity. Such uncertainty stems from what has been termed a *dilemma*, one that is not easily resolved.

The Probation Officer's Dilemma: Its Effect on Supervision

The **probation officer's dilemma** stems directly from the dual functions of supervision. David Dressler labels these functions (in a manner supported by most probation advocates and practitioners) as twofold: "protecting the community and helping individuals under care," noting that each "is inextricably bound up with the other" because the most effective community protection is often helping the offender change so that he or she no longer commits offenses.[4]

The dual purposes of supervision are clearly spelled out for federal probation officers in Title 18 Section 3603 of the U.S. Penal Code, which states that probation officers shall "keep informed concerning the conduct and condition of a person under supervision and shall report his or her conduct and condition to the sentencing court . . ." while at the same time "use all suitable methods, consistent with the conditions specified by the court, to aid a person under supervision and to bring about improvements in his or her conduct and condition."[5]

Although public protection through offender rehabilitation is a laudable goal, in actual practice it is very difficult (some say impossible) to achieve. The problem with this goal lies in the assumption that it is possible to provide individual assistance while closely monitoring offender behavior. The question of whether probation officers can maintain surveillance at the same time they are helping (or treating) probationers has never really been resolved. To put this issue in the perspective of line probation officers (those who actually manage a caseload of offenders), "it's tough to be a cop and a social worker at the same time." Richard Gray, a federal probation officer, described the role conflict by pointing out that the social work perspective sees probation and parole work as a helping profession. From this point of view, the profession has little need for law enforcement because the duty to report violations and make arrests weakens the client–helper relationship and may make it of little use. However, Gray writes that every PO has had law enforcement officers call him or her a soft-hearted do-gooder who just undoes what the police have worked so hard to do.[6]

Criminologists Clear and Cole suggest the difficulty of managing both guidance and authority in a supervision setting is because of the mixed message the officer is sending. On the one hand, the PO is trying to get the client's trust and confidence so he or she might change some behaviors that lead to crime. On the other hand, both know that the officer can arrest the client any time he or she steps out of line, resulting in the mixed message "Let me help you—or else!"[7]

In an effort to solve the control/assistance dilemma, some officers choose to emphasize one of these polar positions. For example, officers who opt for control develop a supervision style that stresses strict adherence to court orders and the liberal use of authority, either to force compliance or to rescind probation. Those who choose assistance demonstrate an overriding concern for the offender's needs and adjustment, often overlooking full compliance with probation orders. Other officers, unable to decide on control or assistance, vacillate between the two positions in an inconsistent manner, described by David Duffee as "wrapping his client in a hello hug, brushing him with his gun as he does . . . helping an offender find a job one day and issuing a technical violation the next."[8] There are some officers, frustrated by the supervision dichotomy, who decide merely to "go through the motions" and in so doing unenthusiastically fulfill minimum job responsibilities. However, some officers are able to successfully resolve these role conflicts by exercising control with some offenders and emphasizing assistance with others. Although these various supervision styles are composites, and as such necessarily exaggerated, they were drawn from characteristics commonly observed in probation officers. Such composites have been usefully organized into categories and typologies to help understand a wide range of probation officer behaviors. Such typologies are examined in detail in Chapter Nine.

The development of individual styles is made possible by the lack of standards about what constitutes supervision and the prevalent assumption that good probation work involves individualization. Cromwell, del Carmen, and Alarid argue persuasively that probation supervision should be a mix of active treatment (for example, encouragement and guidance) within what they call a "broad frame-work of control."[9] In an attempt to exert some control over officer discretion, the federal probation system requires a six-month case review of all supervision plans and progress.

There is virtually no case law on probation supervision. Furthermore, there are no statutory rules specifying how much supervision can be imposed. Consequently, probation officers have wide discretion regarding the supervision of probationers assigned to their care. After conducting a comprehensive study of probation practices, researchers for the Center for Research in Law and Justice concluded that there are three distinctly different dimensions of supervision. Officers differ in the extent to which they

1. Mobilize resources on behalf of the probationers. This was particularly important regarding social services and treatment resources, and the use of coercion to gain participation.
2. Require probationers to report, including the frequency with which they report and whether the reporting needs to be in person or by mail.
3. Tolerate violations. Even in those departments with written policies regarding revocation, there is a great deal of leeway allowed.[10]

Administrative Attempts to Address the PO's Dilemma

The probation officer's dilemma has been the subject of considerable study, causing some departments to undertake efforts (albeit occasionally abortive) to resolve the dichotomy of control or assistance. One of the first to call attention to the problematic nature of probation supervision was Lloyd Ohlin in his 1956 book *The Sociology of Corrections*. In 1965, Arthur Miles wrote an article entitled "The Reality of the Probation Officer's Dilemma" that appeared in *Federal Probation*. This phenomenon has since been discussed in many academic and practitioner journals. Recent journal articles and personal discussions with probation officers clearly indicate the control/assistance quandary has not been resolved; in spite of administrative efforts to resolve the PO's dilemma, it has remained amazingly resilient and persistent.

A frequently cited reason for the supervision dilemma is lack of a clear-cut mission. This line of reasoning holds that absence of a definitive mandate for supervision invariably opens the door for role conflict and excessive discretion. In an effort to develop clear supervision goals, many (but not all) agencies in the 1970s abandoned the traditional model of probation supervision as a counseling process and replaced it with a community-brokerage system where probation officers would no longer be faced with a supervision dichotomy but instead would act as referral agents. In order to understand the significance of this shift, readers should have some familiarity with the type of treatment modalities that were (are) part of the counseling process. It is worth noting that even today probation officers are still using some of these modalities or therapies.

Treatment Modalities

Three of the most popular treatment approaches are reality therapy, transactional analysis, and guided group interaction. All of them are based to some degree on the medical model (see Chapter One), which assumes that offenders are *sick* or maladjusted and need to be treated. The following discussion is a brief (perhaps oversimplified) synopsis of these approaches as they are applied in correctional contexts. (*Note:* For a comprehensive picture of these treatment modalities readers are referred to *Understanding, Assessing and Counseling the Criminal Justice Client* by Anthony Walsh.[11])

Reality Therapy. **William Glasser,** a psychiatrist who broke with traditional Freudian treatment approaches, developed **reality therapy.** Glasser rejected the psychoanalytic concept that insight will motivate individuals to give up maladaptive behavior as "wishful thinking."[12] He contended the process of gaining insight in therapy is needlessly long and often unnecessary. Instead, he argued, a much quicker and more effective approach would be to encourage individuals to deal with the reality of their current situations. Once this had been achieved, clients could then begin to alter their maladaptive behavior patterns (which in many cases involved criminality).

Glasser suggested that people have two basic needs: to be loved and to be respected. Accordingly, those individuals who do not have these needs fulfilled will fail to correctly recognize reality and, therefore, will act irresponsibly. The therapist's role is to convince clients they must fulfill their needs in an appropriate manner. This is accomplished by helping them to acknowledge responsibility for their actions. Having accomplished this, clients can fulfill their needs within the framework of reality. Glasser defined reality therapy as a method that "leads all patients toward reality, toward grappling successfully with the tangible and intangible aspects of the real world."[13] Such an approach deemphasizes the client's past behavior as irrelevant to the present reality. Instead therapists stress coping with the here and now as the crucial element in the treatment process. Thus, a probation officer using reality therapy might tell a client

> It doesn't matter that your parents were criminals and treated you badly, or that you didn't finish high school, or even that you have been to prison. That's past history. It's your present behavior, right now, that bothers me! It's your refusal to report regularly that has gotten you into trouble and may land you back in prison. Take responsibility for that, don't make excuses and we might get you out of this yet. Now tell me, do *you* want to make *your* probation work?

Counselors using reality therapy are advised to take an active role in the treatment process. Ideally, they should be willing to know and experience the reality of the client's life. Thus, probation officers using reality therapy should immerse themselves in the lives of their clients: Visit them at home, see them at their employment, talk with their significant others, and understand their frustrations;

in other words, get involved. All this involvement is directed toward the goal of reeducation to a realistic and law-abiding life. Glasser has identified the process that such reeducation follows:

1. The counselor must be involved with the client, developing a relationship involving caring and respect. The counselor must act as a good model for the client to follow.
2. The emphasis is on the client's behavior. A counselor must reject unrealistic and irresponsible behavior of the client but accept the client, maintaining the relationship with him or her. If behaviors change, then attitudes change as well.
3. Help the individual make a judgment about his or her behavior as responsible or irresponsible. In this manner, each person examines his or her own behavior in a nonthreatening environment to determine how the behavior is contributing to success or failure.
4. Focusing on the client's behavior and present life, interests, hopes, fears, values, and ideas of right and wrong, the counselor teaches the client better ways to realize his or her needs.
5. The counselor and client talk about new plans, expanding the client's interests, trying to make him or her aware of life outside of present problems.
6. The counselor never sympathizes with or accepts excuses from the client. If a person fails in his or her pursuit of planned behaviors, excuses are not needed; rather a new plan has to be developed.
7. Hold the client to responsible behavior through love and discipline.[14]

Transactional Analysis.   The psychiatrist **Eric Berne** developed **transactional analysis (TA)** as an understandable, sophisticated theory about people's thinking, feelings, and behavior, describing what happens when people interact.[15] TA acknowledges the importance of early childhood development as the "script" that influences later behavior. If early childhood input was inappropriate, the adult may engage in misbehavior to the point of criminality. This approach involves the special use of five terms: scripts, games, parent, adult, and child.

Scripts refer to the "memory tapes" that all people carry with them. The most important of these tapes was recorded during childhood and involves defining the meaning of life for them, whether they are OK and will have a good life, or whether they are not OK and will somehow fail. Moreover, people can feel OK or not OK about others as well, resulting in four main positions: "I'm OK, you're OK"; "I'm OK, you're not OK"; "I'm not OK, you're OK"; and finally, "I'm not OK, you're not OK." When children receive messages of love they are OK. If, however, they receive negative messages they are not OK. Such evaluations of "OKness" persist throughout life.[16]

From a TA perspective, *games* refers to interactions that involve manipulation and insincerity. Game players seek "strokes" or reinforcers of their own points of view. Probationers often attempt to game play with their POs in order to justify behavior or to gain some advantage. This form of game playing is often referred to as a *con job.* The PO, using TA, attempts to move clients away from games into an honest dialogue (which is often difficult to do).

The terms *parent, child,* and *adult* in transactional terms refer to ego states or behavior patterns that borrow heavily from Freud's concepts of the id, ego, and super ego. Most people move in and out of these states in the course of their everyday lives. The parent state involves controlling, critical, and moralizing behavior. A person exhibiting a child state appears as happy-go-lucky, vivacious, and irresponsible. The adult manifests objective, rational, and realistic behavior. One of these ego states usually dominates an individual's personality. However, those individuals who rarely change their ego state (called constants) are not necessarily well adjusted. For example, a constant adult ego state lacks spontaneity and tends not to be fun loving; a constant child cannot be relied on and never seems to grow up; whereas a constant parent is difficult to be around because of all the control he or she exhibits.

TA counselors help clients analyze their transactions with others so they can be aware of their ego states. When clients can relate their behaviors to a particular ego state, they can take action to alter the state and change their behaviors. Thus, if drug abusers can see their behavior as emanating from a child state they can shift to an adult mode and "kick the habit." It is obviously not so easy, but that is the theory. Ideally, clients should learn to keep a balance between their ego states and know when to use them in appropriate situations. Thus, while decorating a Christmas tree, the child would be an appropriate state to assume. However, when disciplining a young person, it is often necessary to adopt a parent state, and an adult ego state is best suited for behavior at work. Therefore, if probationers can learn their ego states, they can maneuver through life in a responsible manner and avoid situations that might lead them to criminality.

Guided Group Interaction.   **Guided group interaction** was developed, in large part, to deal with the trauma of combat in World War II. It was seen as a method for effectively dealing with large numbers of shell shocked or psychologically disturbed soldiers, those who today we would say suffered from posttraumatic stress syndrome. The shortage of trained counselors and time constraints led military personnel to attempt counseling in groups. One of the pioneers in applying guided group interaction to a correctional setting was **Lloyd McCorkle.** In 1949, he initiated the Highfields Project in New Jersey to use group encounter techniques with young probationers.[17]

Guided group interaction is concerned with using peer group dynamics. It is based on the assumption that a group can influence an individual's behavior and thinking, and by proper manipulation of this influence, offenders can be led to prosocial behavior. If groups are organized correctly, their members will become close to each other, and individuals will develop a stake in conforming to the group's noncriminal norms. In theory, groups become small subcultures and members conform to the group's value system (which is geared around law-abiding behavior).

A leader guides and directs conversations among group members and puts guided group interaction into motion. The leader's role is to develop mutual trust among participants and then to introduce searching questions that force group members into authentic reactions. Such reactions lead other group members to respond, suggesting ways others can change maladaptive behavior. Leaders are trained to identify and handle abusive confrontational behavior, and those behaviors engaged in for the purposes of gaining power. However, if the group is functioning properly, leaders must avoid overprotecting some members of the group—the group members must be encouraged to take most problems to the group where they will be worked out.[18]

The experiences of either running (serving as a group leader for) several probation groups or observing other correctional groups in action have convinced us that guided group interaction depends on the leader's skill and capability. All too often, unless the group leader is particularly able to probe and draw out individual members, these *counseling* efforts become gripe sessions dominated by a few vocal participants. In addition, dealing with disruptive or withdrawn clients, who often have been coerced into attendance, can cause problems. Those considering using group counseling should be aware that positive group dynamics do not evolve naturally; they must be carefully nurtured by patient group leaders. Some probation/parole departments simply assume that officers (often without proper training) are qualified to *run* groups. This is simply not the case!

All three of these treatment approaches can be useful in dealing with *certain* groups of offenders. However, each has its drawbacks, and applying them to large numbers of correctional clients may not be successful. Moreover, empirical evidence that any of these three approaches significantly reduces recidivism is slim. In the 1970s and to this day, correctional critics seized upon this lack of evidence as sufficient reason to try different techniques, especially those approaches that deemphasize treatment. Counseling was seen as overly lenient and too closely aligned with the assistance end of the supervision dichotomy. A popular perspective held that it was time for a change, and that probation's mission should be community control rather than individual treatment. Implementation of a brokerage system was an important step in that change process.

The Brokerage System.   The **brokerage system** defined probation's mission in narrow terms by shifting a large part of the responsibility for servicing offender needs to other community agencies. The brokerage model also envisioned that a team of officers would supervise probationers. In 1973, the National Advisory Commission on Criminal Justice Standards and Goals emphatically recommended that "The probation officer's role should shift from that of primarily counseling and surveillance to that of managing community resources."[19] The probation officer thus becomes a community resource manager. In that role, the PO needs to know what the needs of the clients are and what resources are available to meet those needs; the PO refers clients to available resources and ensures the service is delivered and that the client participates. Under this model, if a needed service does not exist, the PO attempts, or at least encourages, its development. There is not much importance placed on the quality of the relationship between the PO and clients. Instead, the relationship between the PO and the service agencies is emphasized.

The probation officer as community broker was based on the assumption that reintegration of offenders was the main goal of probation. However, in the minds of many, reintegration was synonymous with rehabilitation. With the general demise of the rehabilitative model, the concept of reintegration gradually lost favor until, according to the editor of a publication on intermediate sanctions, "the term has fallen from common usage."[20] Additionally, the team concept was never popular with supervision officers who preferred to maintain individual control of "their" cases. Adding to the problems of implementing a brokerage model in many jurisdictions was the lack of community services available to probationers. In most communities, there simply were not sufficient agencies to handle the varied needs of offenders. Many public and private agencies, already burdened with their regular clientele, were unable or unwilling to deal with an influx of probationers with multiple problems.

In order to overcome community resistance, some states implemented a contract system where charitable agencies were paid to supervise probationers. The most famous of these contracts was in Florida where the Salvation Army was authorized to provide probation services to misdemeanants.[21] Although some probation contracts have been satisfied, legal issues concerning the appropriateness of outside agencies providing supervision, along with the fact that most private agencies do not want to accept serious felons as clients, have worked to keep the number of probation contracts relatively small. By the early 1980s, it was obvious that a community brokerage model was not going to be the dominant probation paradigm. In effect, probation officers were stuck with their supervision clients.

Reacting to perceived demands that probation become tougher, several departments attempted to resolve the supervision dichotomy by opting to implement systems based on control. From this perspective, probation officers would become risk-control managers[22] and no longer would be overly burdened with satisfying offender needs. Probation's mission, therefore, would become clearly one of public safety. However, different types of people can act better in one probation officer role than another. Not all probation officers are compatible with a tough role.

Although the probation-as-control mandate seems to resolve the supervision dichotomy, in actual practice it does not work that way. Many supervision officers are simply unable or unwilling to abandon concern for offender needs. They continue to see their charges as individuals and respond to them accordingly. Supervision officers must deal with flesh and blood people. Rigid control, however laudatory in theory, is difficult to implement in a community setting. The variety of behavior exhibited by probationers is too wide ranging to simply fit into a control model. In an insightful study of one of the nation's toughest probation systems, Charles Lindquist and John Whitehead found that supervision officers (who were often ex-prison guards) ranked "Opportunity to assist offenders" as an important and satisfying component of their work. The researchers concluded, "Control-oriented strategies may not be as punitive as some might have intended them to be."[23] While noting the increase in control-oriented models, Franklin Marshall, a probation officer, and Gennaro Vito, a college professor, concluded, "that the helping versus surveillance dichotomy is likely to remain with us for some time."[24] This is especially true given the recent meta-analytic work of Don Andrews, Paul Gendreau, and their colleagues on the effectiveness of treatment.[25] These researchers found that treatment, given under the right circumstances and to the right offenders, can be very effective in reducing recidivism.

In short, considering the persistence of the PO's dilemma, a realistic approach may be to accept the inevitability of this dichotomy. Perhaps it would be beneficial to POs and their clients to admit that the control/assistance dilemma is a given. In the end, developing realistic supervision programs appears more fruitful than attempting to resolve the seemingly unsolvable. One of the cornerstones of any program of supervision involves the conditions of supervision, a topic to which we now turn.

Probation Conditions

The most basic duty of probation supervision is to monitor offender compliance with court ordered conditions of probation. Because of this, judges play important roles in supervision because they decide what conditions to impose and what penalties to invoke for violation of those conditions. In this way the court retains influence over all probationers. During the entire supervision period, defendants are aware that if they violate their probation orders they will come back before the judge. At that time, the judge can rescind (revoke) the original grant of probation. The decision to grant probation, therefore, is not irrevocable; rather it is conditional on the defendant abiding by certain conditions. Probation conditions can be divided into two broad categories: (1) general and (2) special. General conditions, which apply to all probationers, include such requirements as reporting to the probation department when instructed, not violating any laws, notifying the probation office of an address change, cooperating with probation officers, and not associating with known criminals.

Special conditions are matched with individual circumstances and can require offenders to make restitution; submit to random drug testing; attend drug, alcohol, or mental health counseling; serve jail sentences; pay fines; or submit payments to defray the costs of probation. Although judges have wide discretion as to what conditions to set, the conditions must be reasonable and have a relationship to future criminality or to a program of rehabilitation. Therefore, an appellate court, ruling that it had no bearing on criminality, declared a probation order requiring church attendance unconstitutional. In another case, a judge's order that an offender not become pregnant without being married was ruled invalid on appeal because it was deemed pregnancy had no relationship to her prior robbery conviction. Appellate courts have also rejected conditions requiring blood donations, ordering a vasectomy, and banishment from a town.[26] However, appellate courts have upheld orders that a defendant convicted of bookmaking not be allowed to have a phone in his home, that a child molester avoid contact with children under sixteen years of age, and that a convicted drug offender submit to drug testing. Figures 5.1 and 5.2 are examples of currently used forms that will further familiarize the reader with commonly used probation orders.

It is surprising that because probation orders frame the supervision process (and in so doing significantly affect the offender's life) so little consideration is given to them, either before or at the time of sentencing. Probationers and their attorneys rarely question the list of conditions that effectively strip defendants of many due process rights (for example, most probation orders contain a condition specifying that the defendant must allow the search of his person, property, or place of residence without a warrant) for the term (length) of probation. Judges, when granting probation, routinely impose a set of general conditions that are not applicable or desirable to specific cases. In some states (such as Illinois) general conditions are mandated by statute. Presentence investigators matter-of-factly recommend that general probation conditions be imposed in all cases, and then *augment* them with specific ones geared to the offender (such as restitution or time in jail). This casual approach to setting probation orders leaves the supervision officer in the position of enforcing conditions that are so general and nonspecific that they are unenforceable, or they are not applicable. That is, because offenders vary as to severity of offense, amount of harm, prior record, and their personalities and behaviors, some standard conditions simply are not appropriate for all offenders.

In fact, various researchers have pointed out that the wholesale use of general probation conditions can undermine the supervision process. In some instances, POs overlook inappropriate conditions, and in so doing lose face with their charges. In other situations the supervision officer is made to look absurd by enforcing restrictive conditions better suited to juvenile offenders (such as not moving, changing employment, leaving the county, or marrying without approval of a probation officer). Taking this into consideration, the American Probation and Parole Association advocates the use of only one general condition: that the defendant remains law abiding. Other conditions would be added on a case-by-case basis and on the recommendation of the presentence investigator.

The American Bar Association Standards Committee has also considered this issue and concludes that because probation is a penal sentence its orders (1) should be limited and specific, (2) should be proportionate to the seriousness of the crime, (3) should be imposed in a regularized due process setting, (4) should be based on evidence presented in court, and (5) should not be determined by rehabilitative goals of sentencing.[27] Despite these efforts to restrict the use of catchall conditions, there are few indications that judges are about to change the accepted practice of imposing a set of general conditions on all defendants. The practice seems so ingrained that it will undoubtedly continue for the foreseeable future, with POs continuing to

(text continues on page 145)

FIGURE 5.1 *Example 1 of Probation Orders*

STATE OF NEVADA
DEPARTMENT OF PAROLE AND PROBATION
CARSON CITY. NEVADA 89710

PROBATION AGREEMENT AND RULES

THE STATE OF NEVADA.

Plaintiff,

vs.

Defendant

Criminal Case No...

ORDER ADMITTING DEFENDANT TO PROBATION AND FIXING THE TERMS THEREOF

DEFENDANT is guilty of the Crime of ....

...., a Felony or Gross Misdemeanor.

DEFENDANT is sentenced to a term of imprisonment in the ....

for .... years. Execution of that sentence is suspended and the DEFENDANT is hereby admitted to probation for ....
years under the following conditions:

1. REPORTING/RELEASE: Upon release by the Court you are to report directly and in person to the Department of Parole and Probation. You are required to submit a true and correct written monthly report to your supervising probation officer each month on forms supplied by the Probation Department. In addition. you shall report as directed by your probation officer.

2. RESIDENCE: You shall not change your place of residence. employment, nor leave the community without first obtaining permission from your probation officer in each instance.

3. INTOXICANTS: You shall not drink or partake of any alcoholic beverages whatsoever/to excess (.10 blood alcohol or above, as determined by any medically recognized valid test. shall be sufficient proof of excess).

4. CONTROLLED SUBSTANCES: You shall not use. purchase. possess. give. sell or administer any controlled substance. nor any dangerous drugs. unless first prescribed by a licensed physician. You shall submit to drug testing as required by your probation officer.

5. WEAPONS: You shall not possess or have under your control any type of weapon.

6. ASSOCIATES: You will not associate with people who have criminal records.

7. COOPERATION: You shall at all times cooperate with your probation officer and your behavior and attitude shall justify the opportunity granted to you by this probation.

8. LAWS AND CONDUCT: You shall comply with all municipal. county. state and federal laws. ordinances and orders and conduct yourself as a good citizen. You shall comply with convicted person registration requirements where applicable.

9. OUT–OF–STATE TRAVEL: You shall not leave the state without first obtaining written permission. in each instance, from your probation officer.

10. EMPLOYMENT/PROGRAM: You shall seek and maintain employment. or maintain a program as approved by the Probation Department.

11. SPECIAL CONDITIONS OF PROBATION: ....

....

....

....

....

The Court reserves the right to modify these terms of Probation at any time and as permitted by law. DATED this ....

day of ...., 19........ in the .... Judicial District Court of the State of Nevada,

in and for the County of ....

....
District Judge

AGREEMENT BY PROBATIONER

I do hereby waive extradition to the State of Nevada from any State in the Union and I also agree that I will not contest any effort to return me to the State of Nevada. I have read. or have had read to me. the foregoing conditions of my probation, and fully understand them and I agree to abide by and strictly follow them and I fully understand the penalties involved should I in any manner violate the foregoing conditions. I have received a copy of this document and NRS 176.225.

....
Probationer   Date

APPROVED..
Probation Officer   Date

FIGURE 5.2 *Example 2 of Probation Orders*

IN THE COUNTY COURT OF PLATTE COUNTY, NEBRASKA

THE STATE OF NEBRASKA,   )
)
      Plaintiff,)   Case No. _____
)
  -vs-   )   ORDER OF PROBATION
)   (Misdemeanor)
)
)
      Defendant.)

NOW on _____, __, this matter came on for sentencing. The defendant was adjudged guilty of _____

on _____, __. The defendant appeared personally [ ] with [ ] without counsel. The _____ County Attorney appeared for the State of Nebraska. The Court asked the defendant if there was any reason sentence should not be announced, to which the defendant replied in the negative.

The Court being fully advised in the premises, herewith ORDERS THAT THE DEFENDANT be sentenced to PROBATION for a term of: _____ days; _____ months; _____ year/s under the following terms and conditions: THE DEFENDANT SHALL:

1. Not violate the laws of the State of Nebraska or any other state or the ordinances of any municipality.

2. Work faithfully at suitable employment, or attend school regularly.

3. Report to the Probation Officer as directed by the Probation Officer and submit a written report as directed by the Probation Officer.

4. Seek the advice and counsel of your Probation Officer in your school or work program, and not change your residence or employment nor leave the State of Nebraska without the written permission of your Probation Officer.

5. Permit the Probation Officer to visit probationer at home or elsewhere and answer any inquiries of your Probation Officer.

6. Abstain from the excessive use of alcoholic beverages and not use or possess any controlled substance, except by prescription.

7. Remain or reside within the following place or locality, to wit: _____ and shall not leave _____ County or the State of Nebraska without written permission of the Probation Officer.

8. FINE: Pay a fine of $ _____; Court Costs of $ _____; [ ] Forthwith [ ] Given _____ days to pay fine and costs. RESTITUTION $ _____ to be paid to: [ ] County Attorney, [ ] County Court, [ ] Forthwith [ ] Given _____ days to pay restitution. Payments shall be completed no later than thirty (30) days prior to the date of discharge.

(continued)

FIGURE 5.2 *Continued*

9. Satisfy other conditions of which you are notified in writing by your Probation Officer which are reasonably related to reconstructing your behavior.

SPECIAL CONDITIONS:

[ ] 10. JAIL: Be and hereby is sentenced to the _____ county jail for _____ hours, _____ days, _____ months; sentence shall be served as follows: [ ] served on consecutive days commencing _____ ____ [ ] served on weekends as follows: _____

[ ] 11. Perform public **service work** under the direction of your Probation Officer for a period of _____ hours and submit proof of same to Probation Officer.

[ ] 12. Attend & successfully complete an **Alcohol/Drug Education Course** at your own expense.

[ ] 13. Attend & successfully complete a **Defensive Driving Course** at your own expense.

[ ] 14. Attend & successfully complete a **Money Management Course** at your own expense.

[ ] 15. Not drink any alcoholic liquor, including beer for the period of probation, and shall submit to a chemical test of blood, breath or urine upon reasonable suspicion of alcohol/drug consumption. Said chemical test shall be at the defendant's expense and failure to submit to said test will constitute a violation of probation.

[ ] 16. Not enter any place where alcohol is primarily served or sold for the period of probation without written permission of your Probation Officer.

[ ] 17. OTHER CONDITIONS: _____

_____

IT IS SO ORDERED, ADJUDGED, AND DECREED.

BY THE COURT:

_____
County Judge

The undersigned defendant acknowledges receipt of a copy of the above order of probation, certifies that he/she has read and understands the same and agrees to abide by the conditions thereof.

_____
Defendant/ Probationer

Address: _____

_____

Phone: _____

make sure their charges comply with the conditions of their probation, including periodically reporting to the PO, and dutifully keeping detailed records of this compliance. It is to this reporting and record keeping that we now turn.

Reporting and Recording Keeping

Central to the supervision process is reporting by offenders and the recording of these contacts by probation officers. From the officer's perspective, maintaining contact with probationers and updating case files is the "stuff" of supervision. The supervision process begins when a probationer is assigned to his or her probation officer.

Assignment Methods

Methods for assigning offenders to individual officers vary throughout the United States;[28] however, they are based on either randomness or categorization. Random models assign offenders to officers on the basis of geographical areas or of case flows. In the geographic area system, a PO will be assigned to all offenders living within designated street boundaries or in a particular area of a county. A case flow model (often called the numbers game) is an attempt to balance the total number of cases assigned to each PO; new cases are distributed to maintain an even caseload count, and, ideally, all officers are responsible for exactly the same number of probationers. In both random methods there is no effort to select or match up probation cases, and officers receive a wide range of assignments and cases.

Categorization models place offenders into groups based on considerations such as type of offense, age, gender, or potential for violence, and then attempt to match these groupings with a corresponding set of POs who specialize in supervising a particular group of offenders. Examples of specialized caseloads that might be assigned to specific groups of officers are drunken driving cases, drug offenders, young offenders, sex offenders, violent offenders, and emotionally disturbed offenders. This approach assumes that dealing exclusively with particular kinds of offenders allows probation officers to more efficiently supervise them. Officers under this model become specialists rather than generalists and may receive education or training to further enhance their specialization. A variation of the classification model assigns cases to officers on the basis of a predictive scale that evaluates possible recidivists. Persons with a low risk for getting into further trouble (for example, first-time petty offenders) would be categorized together as would moderate and high-risk probationers.

Although probation observers contend that assignment by categorization is more efficient, many departments use random methods.[29] Often this is done because supervision officers at the same job level resent what they believe are easy cases (for example drunk drivers) being assigned to a favored few officers. The establishment of elite or special units often breeds office disharmony. Some departments use both methods, assigning most cases on a random basis but establishing a special category for low-risk clients, often called a bank or write-in caseload. Once the case is assigned to a probation officer, the next step is the initial interview.

Initial Interview

Regardless of whether an agency uses a random approach or a categorical approach to case assignment, after an offender receives word of his or her PO, the next step in the probationary process is the **initial interview.** This generally occurs in the probation office when the defendant meets his or her PO for the first time. The initial visit to a probation office can be both a maddening and traumatic experience, especially for those new to probation. Waiting areas in probation lobbies can be austere settings controlled by bureaucratic receptionists. Old magazines strewn around often add to a disheveled, haphazard appearance. Typically, probationers are obligated to sign in at the desk and then are told to "sit down and wait your turn." Idly passing time in a probation office is a disheartening experience. The other waiting probationers are often confused and uncertain as to what awaits them. Because of this "waiting game," by the time officers meet their new clients they often find them impatient and strained. The authors urge students and POs to go "undercover" to probation offices and observe the waiting room. Such an experience may sensitize you to the dehumanizing aspects of probation supervision.

The initial interview can be crucial in framing the supervision process. Although officers are often busy, they should prepare themselves for these first interviews by becoming thoroughly familiar with the case and by developing a preliminary supervision plan. First impressions are important for most relationships and this meeting will determine whether the PO and client will have a positive or negative relationship. Therefore, honesty and openness should characterize this first meeting, letting the client know the purpose of the interview, the kind of information about which you will ask, what it will be used for, and who will have the right to use it.[30]

In addition, during the first interview the all-important reporting schedule should be clearly explained. Many of the problems incurred during later supervision stem from the offender's failure to report regularly. Most probation officers require frequent reporting during the early stages of supervision and then gradually reduce contacts as defendants demonstrate they are following their release conditions. In some jurisdictions, at the first interview, a risk (of further criminal activity) and needs (of the offender) form is completed. Based on the result of these scoring guides defendants are supervised with different levels of watchfulness, ranging from reduced to intensive. Subjective factors can be introduced to "override" the objective scale results. The risk and needs chart, first used in Wisconsin in 1966,[31] is becoming widely accepted. Many probation departments use forms similar to those shown in Figure 5.3. A further discussion of client classification is undertaken in Chapter Ten.

FIGURE 5.3   *Offender Risk and Needs Assessment Forms*

Offender Risk and Needs Assessment

Client Name Last	OID Number
First Middle	

Date of Review (Day, Month, Year)	Agent Last Name	Agent Number	Conviction Offense(s)

SCORE

Number of address changes during last 12 months client was in community	0	None
	2	One
	3	Two or more
Age at first conviction (or juvenile adjudication)	0	24 or older
	2	20–23
	4	19 or younger
Number of prior probation/parole adjudicated violations (adult or juvenile)	0	None
	4	One or more
Number of prior felony convictions (or juvenile adjudications)	0	None
	2	One
	4	Two or more

Convictions or juvenile adjudications for:
(select applicable and add for score—do not exceed a total of 5—include current offense)

Burglary, theft, auto theft or robbery	2	
Worthless checks or forgery	3	
	0	N/A
Percentage of time employed during last 12 months client was in community	0	60%
	1	40%–59%
	2	Under 40%
	0	N/A

Alcohol usage problems (last 12 months in community)

No interference with functioning	0
Some interference with functioning	2
Serious interference with functioning	4

Other drug usage problems (last 12 months in community)

No interference with functioning	0
Some interference with functioning	1
Serious interference with functioning	2

Attitude:

Motivated to change; receptive to assistance	0
Dependent or unwilling to accept responsibility	3
Negative; rationalizes/justifies behavior or not motivated to change	5

Number of prior supervised periods of probation/parole (adult or juvenile)	0	None
	4	One or more

Conviction or juvenile adjudication of any crime against a person (felony, gross misdemeanor or misdemeanor) within the last five years . . . .

	15	Yes
	0	No
	Total	

(continued)

FIGURE 5.3 *Continued*

OFFENDER NEED ASSESSMENT

Client's Name _____ Officer _____

Select the appropriate answer and enter the associated weight in the score column. Total all scores to arrive at the need assessment score.

Score

1. ACADEMIC/VOCATIONAL SKILLS:
   a. High school or above skill level . . . . 0 [ ]
   b. Has vocational training; additional not needed . . . . 1 [ ]
   c. Has some skills; additional needed . . . . 2 [ ]
   d. No skills; training needed . . . . 3 [ ]
2. EMPLOYMENT:
   a. Satisfactory employment for 1 year or longer. . . . . 0 [ ]
   b. Employed; no difficulties reported; or homemaker, student, retired or disabled
      and unable to work . . . . 2 [ ]
   c. Part-time, seasonal, unstable employment or needs additional employment;
      unemployed, but has a skill. . . . . 3 [ ]
   d. Unemployed & virtually unemployable; needs training . . . . 5 [ ]
3. FINANCIAL STATUS:
   a. Longstanding pattern of self-sufficiency . . . . 0 [ ]
   b. No current difficulties . . . . 1 [ ]
   c. Situational or minor difficulties. . . . . 2 [ ]
   d. Severe difficulties . . . . 4 [ ]
4. LIVING ARRANGEMENTS (Within last six months):
   a. Stable and supportive relationships with family or others in living group 0
   b. Client lives alone or independently within another household. 1
   c. Client experiencing occasional, moderate interpersonal problems within living group . . . 2
   d. Client experiencing frequent and serious interpersonal problems within living group . . . 4 [ ]
5. EMOTIONAL STABILITY:
   a. No symptoms of instability 0
   b. Symptoms limit, but do not prohibit adequate functioning 3
   c. Symptoms prohibit adequate functioning . . . . 5 [ ]
6. ALCOHOL USAGE (Current):
   a. No interference with functioning 0
   b. Occasional abuse; some disruption of functioning 3
   c. Frequent abuse; serious disruption; needs treatment . . . . 6 [ ]
7. OTHER SUBSTANCE USAGE (Current):
   a. No interference with functioning . . . . 0 [ ]
   b. Occasional substance abuse; some disruption of functioning; may need treatment 3
   c. Frequent substance abuse; serious disruption; needs treatment . . . . 5 [ ]
8. MENTAL ABILITY:
   a. Able to function independently 0
   b. Some need for assistance; potential for adequate adjustment; mild retardation. 2
   c. Deficiencies suggest limited ability to function independently; moderate retardation . . . . 3 [ ]

9. HEALTH:
   a. Sound physical health; seldom ill 0
   b. Handicap or illness interferes with functioning on a recurring basis 1
   c. Serious handicap or chronic illness; needs frequent medical care . . . . 3 [ ]
10. SEXUAL BEHAVIOR:
    a. No apparent dysfunction. 0
    b. Real or perceived situational or minor problems 2
    c. Real or perceived chronic or severe problems . . . . 3 [ ]
11. OFFICER'S IMPRESSION OF CLIENT NEEDS:
    a. None 0
    b. Low 1
    c. Moderate. 2
    d. High . . . . 4 [ ]

TOTAL SCORES 1 THROUGH 11

Maintaining a Case File

One of the essential parts of an officer's job involves maintaining a record of what transpires during the supervision process. Keeping case records current is a continuing responsibility that many POs find unrewarding. However, record keeping serves an accountability function that allows third parties to monitor the supervision process. Each contact with offenders should be reported and logged in the defendant's file. This is usually accomplished through a series of chronological entries commonly called **chronos.** Each chrono should include the purpose, nature and circumstances of the contact, and action taken. If the contact involves a problem or need the client has, these should be listed, as well as what action was taken to address the problem or need. An evaluation of earlier problems or needs should also be noted as well as any change in the supervision plan made as a result of the contact.[32]

Keeping chronos up to date typically involves the officer entering the information into a computer using a word processing program or some software specifically designed for this application. To ensure that case files are current, supervisory personnel inspect or threaten to inspect case records. These supervisory checks can uncover discrepancies that reflect unfavorably on the officer. In one probation office, an officer was demoted for reporting monthly contacts with a client who had died nine months earlier. To facilitate record keeping and to reinforce court orders, many probation departments have defendants fill out a monthly report that is incorporated into their case file. Figure 5.4 is used in Nevada, is filled out each month, and is then brought to the officer. In several jurisdictions low-risk probationers are allowed to mail in their monthly reports on forms similar to that used by the Georgia State Probation Department shown in Figure 5.5 (p. 152). Another aid to case file maintenance is an activity sheet on which the PO records case contacts. The form used by Nebraska state probation officers is shown in Figure 5.6 (p. 153) and is an example of such a system.

Continuing Supervision

Ideally officers develop a supervision plan and implement it in such a way that offenders are encouraged to improve their situations and to lead law-abiding lives. Supervision plans need to be periodically revised to reflect ongoing developments. Figure 5.7 (p. 154–157) shows an example of supervision planning, including chronos of visits, developed by the Federal Probation Department.

A part of supervision that is often considered very important involves visiting the clients in their homes, or perhaps where they work or attend school. These are called field visits, or field contacts, and are the next topic of discussion.

Field Contacts

Field contacts are thought by many to be the very essence of probation work. Practitioner manuals and academic texts alike extol the virtues of contacting offenders in their natural environments. Such contacts can be particularly helpful if the officer is middle class and has no idea how lower-class clients live. Probation lore

(text continues on page 153)

FIGURE 5.4 *Monthly Report Form*

DISTRICT OFFICES
100 CALIFORNIA AVENUE
RENO, NEVADA 89509
MAIL ROOM
LAS VEGAS, NEVADA 89158
STATE BUILDING
850 ELM
ELKO, NEVADA 89801
106 E. ADAMS, ROOM 206
CARSON CITY, NEVADA 89710
977 W. WILLIAMS
FALLON, NEVADA 89406

STATE OF NEVADA
DEPARTMENT OF PAROLE AND PROBATION
Carson City, Nevada 89710
Telephone 885-5040

PAROLE/PROBATION MONTHLY SUPERVISION REPORT FOR...

Name..Phone Number.............................

1. Address.., ...
   Number and Street   City and State
   Mailing Address..., ...
                                                           City and State

2. Did you move during the month?...............If yes, did you notify police agency? ....

3. I live with...Relationship..............................

4. Did you change employment   If so,
   during reporting period? ....why? ....

   Current Employer..Phone No. ....

   Address..My job is..

   My parole/probation status is
   known at my employment by (Give name and title) ....

   Monthly   Monthly take-   Expenditures for   Other
   wage $ ....home pay $ ....month were $ ....Income $......................

   Working days absent............................Reason..

5. Do you have a bank account?............Checking: balance $......................Savings: balance $ ....

   Name of bank and/or credit union..

6. List all motor vehicle(s) owned or operated:
   ..../..................../..................../.................../...................../.:................../......................
   ..../..................../..................../.................../...................../...................../......................
   ..../..................../..................../.................../...................../...................../......................
       Year   Make   Model   Color   License No.   Owner   Insured by

7. Were you arrested or questioned by police officers during the month?.............If yes, explain in detail......................
   ....
   ....
   ....
   ....

8. Problems regarding family, home, employment, etc.—explain..
   ....
   ....
   ....

9. Did you consult a physician during the month? ....Reason..

   Was medication prescribed?.............. Name of medication..

10. If you have been ordered to pay restitution, fine, and/or attorney fees, complete the following: Are you current on your
    obligation, if not explain why..
    ....
    ....

MY SUPERVISING OFFICER IS......................................   **READ AND COMPLETE REVERSE SIDE**

150

FIGURE 5.4 *Continued*

FOLLOWING ARE GENERAL RULES TO GUIDE YOU IN COMPLYING WITH THE RULES AND REGULATIONS OF YOUR PAROLE OR PROBATION AGREEMENT

1. I have complied with all municipal, county, state and federal laws, ordinances, and orders and conducted myself as a good citizen.

2. I will consult my Parole and Probation Officer for verbal/written permission to:
   a. Buy an automobile or any other motor vehicle.
   b. Borrow money or go into debt.
   c. Change residence, employment, and/or program.
   d. Leave the Community or the State.
   e. Marry.

3. Whenever problems arise or I do not understand what is expected of me, I will consult my supervising officer for assistance and will be guided by his advice.

4. I will not associate, correspond or communicate in any way with persons who are on parole or probation nor anyone who has been convicted of a crime.

5. I DO NOT possess, own, or have under my control any type of weapon.

6. I have not used, purchased, possessed, given, sold, or administered any illegal, narcotic, or dangerous drugs.

I HAVE THIS MONTH READ AND UNDERSTAND THE ABOVE, AND THE INFORMATION I HAVE SUBMITTED IN THIS REPORT IS TRUE TO THE BEST OF MY KNOWLEDGE AND BELIEF.

....
Signature

....
Date

Countersigned by:

....
Sponsor/Volunteer Officer

Report approved by:

....
Parole and Probation Officer

COMMENTS:

FIGURE 5.5   *Mail-In Monthly Report Form*

-9-   Georgia State Probation

MONTHLY SUPERVISION REPORT

_____
Date

RETURN IMMEDIATELY TO PROBATION OFFICER	
	Print your name

Dear Sir:

I submit my report for the month of _____

Present Address_____
                   STREET AND NUMBER   CITY   STATE

Employer_____Type Work _____

Employer's Address_____
                   STREET AND NUMBER   CITY   STATE

Days Worked_____ Amount Earned_____

If Unemployed, Give Reason_____

_____

_____

When and where will you go back to work _____

_____

_____

I am familiar with all the conditions of my probation and have fully complied with them:

           Yes   No

Remarks: _____

_____

_____

_____

_____
Your Signature

P-48

THIS FLAP IS GUMMED READY TO SEAL.
NO ENVELOPE IS NECESSARY
FILL OUT COMPLETELY – FOLD – SEAL – STAMP – MAIL

FIGURE 5.6 *Activity Sheet to Record Case Contacts*

Name _____

Contact Codes:
- (S) School visit
- (H) Home visit
- (O) Office visit
- (T) Telephone
- (J) Job visit
- (W) Written report
- (OT) Collateral contact
- (MA) Missed appointment

Date	Contact	Description of Activity

holds that "real" probation work occurs during field visits to the client's home or place of employment. POs are continually encouraged to get out from behind their desks and out into the field. Officers who do not take such advice often feel guilty about not partaking in the "true" meaning of supervision. A major reason for the inability to make field calls is the amount of administrative work and bureaucratic record keeping that is involved in managing a caseload. With large numbers of clients (often in excess of 150) officers do not have time to actively pursue field contacts or home visits. Probation departments must support officers with more than rhetoric if field contacts are to become a routine part of supervision. However, although it is generally helpful to see different aspects of an offender's life, in some situations, the effectiveness of field visits has been exaggerated.

On the one hand, field visits are important if the officer suspects that the offender is violating probation conditions. On the other hand, routine field calls in cases where defendants are in full compliance can be construed as spying and can actually be counterproductive to the supervision process. Rosecrance, in his tenure as a supervision officer, made hundreds of home visits that, at times, were productive, but no more so than meetings in more traditional settings, such as the

(text continues on page 158)

FIGURE 5.7 *Supervision Plan Including Chronos of Visits*

PROB 42

CLASSIFICATION AND INITIAL SUPERVISION PLAN

Name: David _____   **Type of Case:** Probation _____

Period of Supervision: _____   **RPS 80 Score:** Automatic Assignment _____
or SFS Score: _____

Special Conditions: Mr.   has a $150 restitution obligation

Supervision Level: Low Activity

Supervision Problems:

Employment: Mr.   has limited skills and his employment experience consists of 6 months as a janitor. He has been unemployed since his arrest.

Family: He has significant unresolved problems with his parents, in particular with his disabled father upon whom he is still dependent.

Supervision Objectives:

Obtain vocational training and related job placement. Improve family relationship and/or establish independent residence.

Supervision Plan (include third party risk assessment): Prior to sentencing, Mr.   has been referred to the Springfield Regional Skills Center for an interview and aptitude testing. He has been accepted in an 18-week building maintenance program where he will receive training in basic carpentry, plumbing, and electrical work. He will be instructed to begin making restitution after he begins working.

Mr.   has reluctantly agreed to attend one counseling session with his parents at the Family Service Agency within 2 weeks. Continued attendance will be discussed with Mr.   and his parents after the first session. If Mr.   resists counseling and poor family relationships appear to adversely affect his stability, consideration will be given to his establishing an independent residence contingent upon financial ability. Mr.   's parents will be encouraged to contact this office if serious problems develop in the home.

Once the referral to the Family Service Agency has been resolved with Mr.   and his parents, personal contact will be reduced to one per quarter. Collateral contact will be maintained with the Skills Center and Family Service Agency to monitor his progress.

Third Party Risk problems: None foreseen at this time.

_____   _____
Probation Officer/Date   **Supervisory Approval/Date**

FIGURE 5.7 *Continued*

CHRONOLOGICAL RECORD   **Page 1**

8/25
P-OV

Mr.   and his parents were interviewed after he was placed on probation this date. Conditions of probation were explained and discussed with   and signed. He was given a copy of the conditions. Mr.   stated he recently was accepted at the Skills Center for their training program for building maintenance. He appears to be enthusiastic about this training and employment in this trade. We also discussed his $150 restitution obligation. We provided him with specific written instructions regarding payments which are to be made to the clerk of the court. He understood these directions and added that he will begin making payments as soon as he begins making money. Family difficulties were discussed with Mr.   ; and his parents and they were referred to the Family Service Agency for an evaluation. They agreed to go there within the next 2 weeks to discuss possible counseling. We also discussed his difficulties with negative peer associations in the past and he indicated that his experience in the present case has taught him a lesson and he intends to disassociate himself from these people in the future. Mr.   does not represent a "third party risk" — Supervisor Jones concurs.   mjk

8/30
C-T

Memo forwarded to our Clerk's Office apprising them of Mr.   s $150 restitution and giving them the name of the victim,   and his address in Westfield, Connecticut. Also advised them that Mr.   has been given appropriate payment instructions.
                                                                                                mjk

9/7
C-T

Mr. Greene, Skills Center (692–1234). Counselor verified that Mr.   has enrolled in their building maintenance program. The probationer has been attending classes regularly since starting on August 30   . Initially he appears to be applying himself to training and the counselor feels that he will be a very good student.   mjk

9/8
C-T

Family Service Agency, Mr. Rogers (684–1000) contacted. Had first meeting with   and his parents last night. The family has agreed to a contract with the Family Service Agency to see Mr. Rogers two times a month on alternating Wednesday evenings for a total of 2 months.   mjk

9/15
P-HV

Probationer and parents seen. Mr.   reports attending class at the Skills Center regularly. He stated that he likes the program and feels he is accomplishing a great deal. The parents are more satisfied with his adjustment and this seems to be related to his progress in school. They report that he seems to have shut himself off from former negative peer associations. The family stated they had attended two counseling sessions at the Family Service Agency and that these sessions have been helpful. They also noted that the problems have lessened on their own. They will attend 1 more month, but feel that if things continue to be stable they will drop the counseling program.   mjk

10/13
P-HV

Mr.   and family seen. No changes since last contact. Still going to Skills Center and feels he is progressing toward completion of the program. Family is still in counseling, but plan to drop after completion of four meetings with the counselor. The family situation seems much improved. The probationer will establish his own residence once employed. The family seems closer and there appears no rush for his change of residence at this time.   mjk

10/27
C-T

Mr. Greene at Skills Center. Reported that Mr.   had progressed well and is halfway through the program. He has only missed 1 day of the training since enrolled, due to illness.   mjk

10/28
C-T

Mr. Rogers, Family Service Agency. The probationer, parents, and counselor have agreed to terminate counseling due to resolution of family problems.   mjk

11/16
T

The probationer states his relationship with his parents is very good now, but he still wants to move out on his own. He feels that he should because of his age and because of his desire to be responsible for himself. The probation officer agreed with this and intends to promote this plan in the future. The probationer feels that his parents would like to see him stay on

(continued)

FIGURE 5.7 *Continued*

CHRONOLOGICAL RECORD

at the house, but he intends to move as soon as he is employed and can support himself. He has a new girlfriend. She resides at her parents' home located at 552 South Lebanon Street, telephone   Mr.   states that he sees her a lot and spends most of his free time with her.   mjk

12/15/.
C-T

Mr. Greene at the Skills Center.   will complete training on December 17,   He has already had several referrals for placement through the Center's job referral office. Mr. Greene feels that the probationer may soon be employed after his graduation from the building maintenance program. He described the probationer as having been an excellent student. mjk

12/16
P-HV

            reported that he had several good job leads. He stated he will interview tomorrow at the Serene Development Company as an apartment maintenance man. This company operates several large complexes in this area. The parents were seen briefly and they seemed very satisfied with the subject's progress toward gaining employment.   mjk

12/23/
r

Telephoned probation officer to notify that he landed a job with the Serene Company. He will work at their West Terrace Apartments maintaining 200 units. They will provide him an apartment at a reduced rate in order for him to live on the premises. The starting gross salary is $ a month. He starts the job after Christmas, but may move into his apartment sooner than that. Told him to provide us with appropriate documentation relative to his income and rent.   mjk

12/27/
r

Mr.   reported that he just moved into his apartment at 444 Terrace Drive, Number 210. He can be reached during the day at !   0. He starts the job January 2.   mjk

1/10/
T

Mr.   likes his work. The manager of the apartment refers maintenance problems to him and then he works on his own to complete them. He pays $200 a month rent on an apartment which normally rents for $450 a month furnished. Mr. states the apartment manager, James   , is aware of his probation status. Advised Mr.   to report to my office first week in March and reminded him to bring salary and rent verification. Also, we directed him to make a restitution payment of at least $25 to the Clerk's Office and continue with such payments on a biweekly basis.   mjk

2/2/
C-T

With mother. Parents pleased over the probationer's adjustment. They like his new girlfriend and the mother feels that they may be getting serious in their relationship. They visit regularly with the probationer and have not seen any old friends around him.   mjk

2/21/
C-T

     Received notice from Clerk's Office that   made $50 restitution payment on 2/18   Probationer now has $100 restitution balance. Probation office is encouraged by this relatively large initial payment. At this point we anticipate no problems with probationer satisfying this restitution obligation within the near future.   mjk

FIGURE 5.7 *Continued*

PROB 43

CASE REVIEW

Name: _____   **Type of Case:** __Probation_____

Period Covered: _____ _____ to _____ _____

Special Conditions: Restitution — $150 — Balance owed — $100

Previous Supervision Level: Low Activity

Number of Contacts: Personal _____4_____ **Collateral** _____6_____ **Tel. w/Subj.** _____3_____

Supervision Problems and (Revised) Objectives:

Mr. ¯ has no supervision problems at this time. He is now working full time after completing training at the Skills Center. He has obtained housing away from his parents' home and the family relationships have improved after the completion of the family counseling sessions. We will continue to verify the aforementioned progress.

Supervision Plan: (Include Review of Third-Party Risk)

Verify his stability with quarterly personal contacts and periodic collateral contacts with parents and employer. Continue to log subsequent restitution payments. No risk to third-party at this time.

Supervision Level (Revised): Low Activity

_____   _____

Probation Officer/Date   *Supervisory Approval/Date* probation office, courthouse, or jail. Regardless of the use of field visits, they sometimes result in the PO discovering violations or even illegal activity, which often means a return visit to the sentencing court.

Returning to Court

There are three major reasons to bring probationers back before the judge: (1) to terminate probation supervision early as a result of commendable behavior, (2) to hold defendants in violation of their probation but continue them in probation, or (3) to revoke probation and impose terminal sentences for serious breaches of release conditions. Typically, these actions are initiated by POs and acted on by the court. Judges depend on supervision officers to inform them of changes in a defendant's situation (especially violations of probation) through reports submitted to the court. Each of these actions has significant impact for both defendants and probation officers. The defendant's life is obviously altered by such court activity, whereas the officer's job performance is often gauged by the quality of his or her court reports. There are few tangible measurements of supervision progress, and court reports offer some (albeit inconclusive) basis for evaluating an officer's effectiveness. Some of these reports indicate that the probationer is doing so well that it is recommended that the probation be terminated.

Early Termination

Policies on early termination vary considerably; some jurisdictions make extensive use of this practice, whereas others use it not at all. Some courts require defendants to complete one-half of their probation period before being eligible for early termination, whereas others have no such limitation. Most courts probably do not make sufficient use of early termination, and countless numbers of offenders, who no longer benefit from supervision, remain on the probation rolls. After a brief period on probation, many defendants can be safely and quickly removed from the system. Wholesale terminating of those who represent only minimal risks to the community would allow probation departments to concentrate on more problematic offenders. From the defendant's perspective, early termination is a reward for good behavior and an important indication that the system is not always stacked against the individual.

Even though early termination seems like a win–win situation (for both offenders and the court system), there are two major roadblocks to its widespread implementation: (1) the get-tough movement and (2) supervision officer unwillingness. Courts and probation departments do not want to appear soft on crime by letting offenders off early. Such reasoning holds that if probation is really a sentence, then offenders should serve all of it. Supervision officers do not want to give up their easy cases, those they can count on to stay out of trouble, in order to receive a new batch of problem cases. One PO explained:

Why should I terminate those cases I've worked so well with in order to get a bunch of new cases to start working on? If you terminate them early you lose your winners—that's not a good deal. Besides, it doesn't hurt those guys to stay on probation, I never hassle them, and my case count stays up.

A second reason probationers return to court is because they have violated a condition of their probation.

Violations and Revocations

Violations of probation fall into two categories: (1) technical violations and (2) new offenses. Technical violations are actions, which, although not involving commission of a crime, are contrary to the orders of probation. New offenses are those violations of law committed after the granting of probation. **Revocation** of probation means that, for cause, probation is rescinded. In the latter case the type of sentence that accompanied the original probation now becomes very important. There generally are two possible sentences that involve probation grants: (1) suspended sentence and (2) imposition of judgment suspended. In the first option, at the time probation is first granted, the judge does not impose a specific sentence, reserving the right to do so at a later date. Should probation subsequently be revoked, judges have the right to impose sentence as though probation had never been granted. The second option allows judges to impose a definite sentence (for example three years in prison) and suspend carrying it out during the period of probation. In these cases, in the event of revocation the defendant begins serving the previously imposed sentence.

Violations and revocations of probation represent failures in the supervision process. Perhaps because failures are unpleasant to consider, there has been a lack of research into probation violations. However, these failures can become very public when active probationers commit sensational new crimes. In the ensuing hue and cry probation supervision is invariably openly criticized. Even though some individual departments have undertaken studies of how their officers deal with supervision problems (in order to profit from mistakes), there is little definitive data about factors such as when probation violations should be reported, what the grounds are for revocation of probation, or even when precisely is probation violated. Furthermore, it is often difficult to determine what percentage of probationers "fail" because many violations are not reported or the statistics on revocation include both probation and parole. We do know that the statistics vary. For example, an Oregon Department of Corrections report stated that 80 percent of all prison admissions in 1991 were revoked community supervision cases, whereas a 1993 North Carolina study reported that 13 percent of prison admissions were probation or parole violations.[33] An analysis of a probation agency conducted by the National Institute of Corrections (NIC) revealed what types of violations led to revocations and what the typical responses were. Many observers believe new criminal behavior is a frequent reason for violation. The NIC study, however, found that new criminal behavior accounted for only 16 percent of petitions to revoke, whereas failed drug tests, failure to participate in treatment, and failure to report accounted for almost 60 percent of all violations. This study also found that 60 percent of petitions to revoke led to sanctions involving incarceration.[34]

Data such as these can lead to understanding and better policy decisions. With a more detailed view of the violations, the resources used to deal with the violations, and who the violators typically are, the system can be more responsive. Rules will be clearer, POs will have a better idea of when and under what circumstances they should use their discretion and revoke a probationer who has violated the probation conditions (or not!), probationers will view the system as less arbitrary, and the community will be safer. Although individual agencies or jurisdictions may write such rules, three court decisions have established the grounds for probation revocation hearings.

Court Rulings

Although discretion is still the watchword in supervision, the three court decisions that have established ground rules for probation revocation hearings are *Mempa v. Rhay, Morrissey v. Brewer,* and *Gagnon v. Scarpelli.* The decisions in these cases reflected the concern for due process rights that surfaced so dramatically in the 1960s and early 1970s. Rulings in these instances established the defendant's right to have a full hearing before probation could be revoked, and at that hearing the defendant's rights to refute testimony and be represented by counsel were to be protected. The *Mempa* ruling in 1967 (*Mempa v. Rhay,* 389 U.S. 128) was important for its precedent-setting opinion that probation revocations were an extension of the sentencing process, and as such they should be governed by some measure of due process. On June 17, 1959, Jerry Mempa was convicted of "joy riding" in Washington state. He was placed on probation for two years, with the condition that he spend thirty days in jail, although the imposition of sentence was deferred. About four months later, the Spokane County prosecutor moved to have Mempa's probation revoked on the grounds that he had been involved in a burglary. Seventeen-year-old Mempa was accompanied to the hearing by his stepfather, was not represented by counsel, and was not asked if he wished to have counsel appointed for him.

At the hearing, Mempa was asked if he had been involved in the alleged burglary and he answered that he had been. His probation officer testified without cross-examination that his information told him that Mempa had been involved in the burglary and had previously denied participation in it. Without asking Mempa if he had anything to say or any evidence to supply, the court revoked his probation and sentenced him to ten years in the penitentiary.

The Supreme Court noted that the sentencing judge and prosecutor are required by statute to provide the Washington State Board of Prison Terms and Paroles a recommendation for the length of sentence, as well as other information about the crime and the character of the offender. The Court further noted that to the extent that the board gives these recommendations weight in determining the final sentence, the need for aid of counsel in bringing together the facts of the case, introducing evidence of mitigating factors, and generally assisting the defendant in the presentation of his or her case regarding the eventual sentence is clear. Noting that certain legal rights, such as the right to appeal, might be lost at this stage if counsel is not present, the Court ruled that "... a lawyer must be afforded at this proceeding whether it be labeled a revocation of probation or a deferred sentencing."[35]

One of the significant features of *Mempa* was that it was the first time the Supreme Court had ruled in favor of the rights of a probationer. However, lower courts interpreted *Mempa v. Rhay* in a variety of ways. Some took it to mean that counsel was only required in revocation hearings involving deferred sentences and was not applicable in cases where sentence had already been imposed and suspended. Other courts extended right to counsel to all revocation hearings, and some jurisdictions even applied the ruling to parole hearings. Much of the confusion raised by *Mempa v. Rhay* was clarified by the *Morrissey* and *Gagnon* decisions.

In 1972, the Supreme Court in *Morrissey v. Brewer* established procedural safeguards to protect parolees during revocation proceedings. The Court considered revocation to be a two-step process: (1) a preliminary hearing to ascertain if there were sufficient grounds to proceed and (2) a more comprehensive revocation hearing for the purposes of rendering a final decision. During the revocation hearing, parolees were entitled to some (but not all) due process rights, which were enumerated as (1) written notice of the alleged violation, (2) disclosure of evidence pertinent to the case, (3) right to confront and cross-examine witnesses, (4) right to present independent evidence, (5) a hearing before a "neutral and detached body," and (6) a final written statement as to the reasons for the action being taken.

One year later due process rights provided in *Morrissey* were applied directly to probation revocations in *Gagnon v. Scarpelli* (411 U.S. 778). In the latter case Gerald Scarpelli, in 1965, pled guilty to armed robbery. A Wisconsin court sentenced him to fifteen years in prison, suspended that sentence, and placed him on probation for seven years. The probationer was allowed to reside in Chicago and, under the Interstate Compact Agreement, was supervised by the Cook County Probation Department. One month after arriving in Illinois, Scarpelli was arrested and charged with burglary. He was returned to Wisconsin where, without a hearing, probation was summarily revoked and he was ordered to begin serving his fifteen-year prison sentence. After three years in prison, Scarpelli petitioned for a writ of habeas corpus to affect his immediate release. Although the petitioner was subsequently released on parole, his original case went forward because the probation revocation was an obvious factor in his parole status. A district court ruled that revocation of probation without a hearing and counsel present was, in fact, a denial of due process. The Wisconsin attorney general appealed the decision and, in 1973, the U.S. Supreme Court held that "Probation revocation, like parole revocation, is not a stage of a criminal prosecution, but does result in loss of liberty. Accordingly, we hold that a probationer, like a parolee, is entitled to a preliminary hearing and a final revocation hearing in the condition specified in *Morrissey v. Brewer.*"[36]

The *Gagnon* decision affirmed that other due process rights accorded to parolees under *Morrissey v. Brewer* should be applied to probationers. The court did not rule that all probationers had an absolute right to counsel but certainly was leaning toward that direction by indicating:

> Counsel should be provided in cases where, after being informed of his right to request counsel the probationer or parolee makes such a request based on a timely or colorable claim:
>
> 1. That he has not committed the alleged violation of the conditions upon which he is at liberty; or
> 2. That, even if the violation is a matter of public record or is uncontested, there are substantial reasons which justified or mitigated the violation and make revocation inappropriate and that the reasons are complex or otherwise difficult to develop or present.[37]

Lower courts and probation officials have interpreted *Gagnon* as requiring hearings in all revocations, and in virtually every jurisdiction such a policy is followed. In subsequent court decisions the procedures governing revocations were clarified in the following manner: Probation may not be revoked if an indigent probationer failed to pay fines or make restitution if a reasonable effort to pay has been made; probation cannot be revoked because of an inability to pay child support even though those payments are part of the probation conditions; judges are not generally obligated to consider alternatives to incarceration before they revoke probation and place an offender in jail or prison;[38] an accumulation of a few minor violations was not necessarily grounds for revocation; hearsay evidence that had been judged "reliable" was not subject to cross-examination; probationers could not claim their Fifth Amendment rights against self-incrimination during revocation proceedings; and evidence justifying revocation did not have to meet the standard of "beyond a reasonable doubt," but rather a "preponderance of evidence" was sufficient.[39] Thus, *Mempa, Gagnon,* and other court rulings have provided procedural safeguards in probation violation proceedings. These procedures are generally followed by sentencing courts, but only after the decision to bring violations before the court and revoke probation are made by a supervision officer.

The Decision to Revoke

The decision to institute revocation proceedings is a crucial one because it involves exchanging informal supervision pressure for formal legal sanction. The PO usually initiates revocation proceedings and presents most of the evidence; in this capacity officers act as quasi prosecutors. Whereas the PSI is governed by specific guidelines, there are few prescriptions for the violation report. On the one hand, supervision officers are told that defendants should, at all times, remain in compliance with their probation conditions and further that instances of noncompliance should be promptly reported to the court. On the other hand, POs are warned that enough evidence to sustain formal revocation proceedings must verify all violations. In actual practice, violations are not always objective in nature, and discretion must be employed regarding what to report and when to report it. The NIC report of revocations found that agencies varied in their approach to revocation. For example, in some agencies young offenders were more likely to be revoked than older offenders, whereas in other agencies drug use was the most important violation problem. In one agency in the NIC study, failing a drug test and failing to participate in treatment accounted for 47 percent of the violations, whereas a new felony or misdemeanor accounted for only 16 percent of motions to revoke.[40]

The decision to file a violation report is often governed by what has been called the "norm of seriousness."[41] This norm allows POs to exercise the option of not reporting all violations to the court. Many probation agencies have developed internal mechanisms for processing less serious violations. Rather than routinely scheduling formal hearings, probation departments implement their own sanctions, such as increasing the defendant's reporting schedule; stepping up surveillance; requiring attendance at counseling programs; or filing an incident report in the case record, to be used against the probationer if and when it becomes necessary to institute formal revocation proceedings. Boundaries for the norm of seriousness vary considerably (even within the same department) and this variance introduces some inconsistency and unfairness into the supervision process. Some jurisdictions have taken steps to correct this situation by establishing violation severity scales. These jurisdictions develop explicit categories of "serious" and "less serious" violations. Also, some severity scales list specific violations, whereas others suggest categories.[42] Figure 5.8 is an example of a severity rating scale used in one of the agencies studied by the NIC. The last three columns on the right indicate the number of times the offender has violated that particular condition, with H referring to a high-severity rating and L a low one.

Although technical violations, other than absconding, are often difficult to substantiate during revocation proceedings, courts have revoked probation for failure to comply with orders to pay fines, make restitution or pay child support, attend counseling, report regularly, cease participating in political demonstrations, live in certain areas, and cooperate with probation officers. In one case, a convicted child molester's probation was revoked when he failed to comply with probation orders that he put signs on his house and car warning that he was a menace to young children.

There is no disagreement that new offenses should be reported to the court in a timely manner; however, there is considerable controversy about what effect the new criminal case should have on the existing probation. Some contend that merely being involved in a new offense is sufficient to justify revocation. Others have argued persuasively that a new offense should not affect the existing probation.[43] This perspective holds that guilt in the new case must be proved before revocation is warranted. The National Advisory Commission on Criminal Justice Standards and Goals followed that line of reasoning, believing that probation should not be revoked because someone has committed a new crime until that person has been tried and convicted of the new crime. Once a probationer has been convicted of a new crime, the ". . . criteria and procedures governing initial sentencing decisions should govern resentencing decisions."[44] An actual violation report with the accompanying warrant request appear in Figures 5.9 and 5.10.

(text continues on page 169)

FIGURE 5.8 *Severity Rating Scale*

Severity Rating	Violation	1	2	3
High	New offense (excluding traffic violations)	H	H	H
High	Possessing weapons	H	H	H
High	Denying access to residence and searches	H	H	H
High	Absconding	H	H	H
High	Positive drug test	H	H	H
High	Positive alcohol test	H	H	H
High	Failure to register as sex offender	H	H	H
Low	Associating with felons, gangs, etc.	L	H	H
Low	Possessing contraband	L	H	H
Low	Travel violations	L	H	H
Low	Failure to participate in treatment	L	H	H
Low	Failure to submit to urinalysis or blood alcohol test	L	H	H
Low	Failure to take Antabuse	L	H	H
Low	Failure to remit paycheck (intensive probation supervision)	L	H	H
Low	Failure to maintain employment	L	L	H
Low	Failure to pay restitution/other fees	L	L	H
Low	Failure to participate in education program	L	L	H
Low	Failure to participate in community service	L	L	H
Low	Changing residence without notice or permission	L	L	H
Low	Failure to report	L	L	H
Low	Violating curfew/approved schedule	L	L	H
Low	Making false statements	L	L	H
Low	Failure to follow orders	L	L	H
Low	Violating jail rules	L	L	H
Low	Failure to notify sheriff of change of address (sex offender)	L	L	L
Low	Being financially irresponsible	L	L	L

FIGURE 5.9 *Probation Violation Report*

NEVADA DEPARTMENT OF PAROLE AND PROBATION
PROBATION VIOLATION REPORT
<u>_____</u>

```
TO THE HONORABLE                      DATE:  AUGUST 1,
SECOND JUDICIAL DISTRICT, DEPT. II

NAME:          , Victoria Sue CRIM. CASE NO.:  C83-9876
DOB:   APRIL 4,                    FILE NO.:  R83/84-1313
                                         F  XX  GM
  I.    ALLEGED VIOLATION
 II.    DETAILS OF VIOLATION        CRIME:  COUNT II:  SALE OF A
III.    RECOMMENDATION                      CONTROLLED SUBSTANCE
 IV.    WHEREABOUTS AND                     (HEROIN)
        AVAILABILITY
                       DATE PROB. GRANTED:  JULY 13, .
                               SENTENCE:  8 YEARS NEVADA STATE PRIS
                                                (SUSPENDED)
                                  TERM:  FIVE (5) YEARS PROBATION
                            EXPIRATION:  JULY 13,
```

```
  I.     ALLEGED VIOLATION:

         RULE  5:  NARCOTICS
         RULE  6:  WEAPONS
         RULE 10:  LAWS AND CONDUCT
         RULE 12:  EMPLOYMENT
         RULE 13:  RESTITUTION
         RULE 14:  SPECIAL CONDITION - (2) YOU SHALL ENTER AND
                   COMPLETE AN OUT-PATIENT DRUG COUNSELING
                   PROGRAM APPROVED BY THE DEPARTMENT OF PAROLE
                   AND PROBATION.

 Ia.  .  DETAILS OF ARREST:

         On July 30,     , Ms. Victoria          was arrested by
         officers of the Washoe County Sheriff's Department for
         Sales Of Controlled Substance (Cocaine) and Ex-Felon In
         Possession Of A Firearm.  She was booked at the Washoe
         County Jail without incident.  All evidence remains under
         the control of the Washoe County Sheriff's Department.
         Bail is set at $15,000 and a Probation 'Hold' was placed
         on July 30,     .  She is scheduled to appear in Depart-
         ment II for Arraignment on August 13,

 II.     DETAILS OF VIOLATION:

         RULE 5 - NARCOTICS; RULE 6 - WEAPONS; RULE 10 - LAWS
         AND CONDUCT:  Ms. '          was arrested for Sale Of Con-
         trolled Substance on July 30,     , for having allegedly
         sold approximately one-half ounce of cocaine, street
         value of $800, to an undercover Washoe County Narcotics
         Officer.
```

(continued)

FIGURE 5.9 *Continued*

OBATION VIOLATION REPORT   Date:_____
ıme)
3/84-1313 CC#C83-9876

I.   DETAILS OF VIOLATION - continued:

When placed under arrest she had in her purse a .38 caliber,
chrome, Smith and Wesson Revolver, Serial #V89706. The
weapon was registered to her father, John D.
1145 Fourth Street, Reno, Nevada.

In addition, a urine sample submitted by Ms.   on
April 10,   , proved to be positive for cocaine and
morphine. The sample was analyzed by Washoe County Criminal
istics Laboratory on April 17,

On May 30,   , during an office visit fresh drug track
needle marks were observed on both arms of the subject by
this officer and Unit Supervisor John Stokes. Ms.
stated that she had injected drugs two weeks prior, but
would not divulge which drug.

Ms.   has failed to pay monthly supervision fees of $12.00
per month to defray the cost of her supervision as mandated
by Nevada Revised Statutes. She is currently five (5) months
for a total of $60.00 in arrears. It should be noted that
Ms.   paid supervision fees totalling $108.00 during
the first nine (9) months on supervision. Her last fee
payment was made on March 13,

RULE 12 - EMPLOYMENT: Except for approximately three weeks
in July   , when she was employed as a bar maid at Tony's
Bar and Grill, the subject has been unemployed. On February
5,   , March 15,   , and May 1,   , the Department's
Job Developer referred Ms.   to the Pancake House,
the Lyon's Den and the Yellow House Restaurant, respectively,
for employment interviews, however in each instance she
failed to show for the interview. Despite admonishments
to seek employment and assistance offered by the Department's
Job Developer Ms.   has failed to obtain employment.

RULE 13 - RESTITUTION: On July 13,   , Ms.
agreed to pay $20.00 per month toward her Court Ordered
restitution. Thus far she has paid $100.00; the last pay-
ment of $25.00 was made on January 5,   . Currently she
is $400.00 in arrears.

FIGURE 5.9 *Continued*

PROBATION VIOLATION REPORT   Date:_____
(Name)
R83/84-1313 CC#C83-9876

II.   DETAILS OF VIOLATION - continued:

        RULE 14 - SPECIAL CONDITION - (2) YOU SHALL ENTER AND
        COMPLETE AN OUT-PATIENT DRUG COUNSELING PROGRAM APPROVED
        BY THE DEPARTMENT OF PAROLE AND PROBATION: On July 15,
             the subject was referred to the Washoe County Drug
        Treatment Program. She failed to appear for the first
        three scheduled interviews, however was finally interviewed
        and placed in a weekly thearpy group. She was discharged
        from that program on August 30,   , for lack of atten-
        dance and non-participation when present. She was referred
        to the Evergreen Drug Program on September 2,   , and
        again was terminated on February 3,   for lack of
        attendance and non-participation. On March 3,   a third
        referral was made to the Northern Area Substance Abuse
        Program, however Ms.   has never attended that
        program.

III.   RECOMMENDATION:

        It is recommended that a Bench Warrant be issued for Ms.
             arrest and that her probation be revoked.

IV.   WHEREABOUTS AND AVAILABILITY:

        Ms.   is currently incarcerated in the Washoe County
        Jail.

                        Respectfully submitted,

                        _____
                        J. SMITH,
                        PAROLE AND PROBATION OFFICER II
                        DISTRICT II, RENO, NEVADA

APPROVED: Reviewed,

_____   _____
CARLOS C. CONCHA,   CAMILLE CARACAPPA,
UNIT SUPERVISOR   SUB-UNIT SUPERVISOR
CPR SUPERVISION UNIT   CPR SUPERVISION UNIT
DISTRICT II, RENO, NEVADA   DISTRICT II, RENO, NEVADA
DEPARTMENT OF PAROLE & PROBATION

                        -10-
JS:bjp
110585

FIGURE 5.10 *Violation Report Warrant Request Form*

P & P Form No. 3A

STATE OF NEVADA

DEPARTMENT OF PAROLE AND PROBATION

WARRANT APPLICATION

Date _____ _____

TO ___ The Honorable Douglas R. Jones
Second Judicial District Court
Department Ten, Reno, Nevada

CASE OF _____ Victoria Sue _____ Case No. _____ R83/84-1313

Criminal Case No. C83-9876

Birthdate ___ October 26, ___ Race _____
Sentence ___ Eight Years Nevada State Prison, Suspended
Five Years Probation _____ County ___ Washoe

Original offense ___ SALE OF A CONTROLLED SUBSTANCE, HEROIN

Sentence began ___ July 13, _____ Released _____

Sentence expires ___ July 13, _____ Violation date ___ August 1, ___

Charges: Violation of the following rules:

Rule 5 — Narcotics
Rule 6 — Weapons
Rule 10 — Laws and Conduct
Rule 12 — Employment
Rule 13 — Restitution
Rule 14 — Special Condition #2

RECOMMENDATION: THAT A BENCH WARRANT BE ISSUED AND SUBJECT BE RETURNED TO COURT FOR A PROBATION REVOCATION HEARING.

Attachment: VIOLATION REPORT   WARRANT APPROVED BY:

District to which sent ___ II _____

J. Smith

XXXXXXXXXXXXXX
Carlos C. Concha
Supervision Unit II

It is important to point out that not all violations of probation conditions result in revocation. In some cases, the judge adjusts or modifies the conditions and sends the offender back to the community. A brief discussion of this alternative follows.

Modification

On occasion, judges will severely admonish defendants who have violated the conditions of their probation, warning them that future violations will most certainly result in revocation, and then continue them on probation. In other situations, the court will order a modification of existing conditions to include more stringent or restrictive provisions. For example, defendants can be ordered to attend various counseling programs, pay additional fines, stop associating with certain individuals, or serve time in the county jail. Defendants generally welcome such modifications because, in this manner, their probation remains intact and they escape the full force of the criminal sentence. In certain cases the defendant's term of probation is extended. Often this is done to allow probationers more time to pay off restitution or fines. When the main issue of a hearing is the commission of a new offense, probation typically is revoked only if the new offense is of equal or greater severity than the probation offense. For example, if a defendant is on probation for armed robbery and he or she is involved in a petty theft, probation will generally not be revoked. However, if an offender is on probation for burglary and she or he is found guilty of another burglary, probation would most assuredly be revoked.

When defendants are unavailable for court appearances (usually because absconding) the term of probation is tolled. **Tolling probation** means probation is temporarily suspended, and remains so until the defendant appears in, or is brought to, court. In this way, the term of probation does not expire and the court retains jurisdiction. Typically, when defendants have absconded, there is a warrant issued for their arrest. According to the Illinois Code of Corrections: "The issuance of such warrant or summons shall toll the sentence of probation or of conditional discharge until the final determination of the charge, and the term of probation or conditional discharge shall not run so long as the offender has not answered the summons or warrant."[45]

Summary

Supervision of those placed on probation is often an ambiguous mission that encourages the use of discretion and the development of individual methodologies. The dilemma of whether to emphasize control or assistance in dealing with probationers, in spite of individual and administrative efforts to alleviate its salience, remains largely unresolved. Many scholars have argued that the inability to resolve the dilemma is due to a lack of a clear cut mission. Some agencies attempted to achieve resolution by abandoning probation as counseling and adopting the brokerage approach to supervision. Regardless, probation is a form of conditional release, and officers are expected to make certain that defendants live up to their release conditions. In many jurisdictions, general and special conditions are imposed on offenders, increasing the problematic aspects of monitoring individual compliance. The supervision process involves defendants reporting at regular intervals and officers maintaining a record of contacts in case files. Initial interviews with probationers are often crucial in establishing rapport and developing cooperative relationships. Field visits to the defendant's home or place of employment are recommended, but many officers are unable to do this because of large caseloads or other responsibilities. Supervision planning, frequently updated, is an essential probation officer task.

Although early termination, as a reward for good behavior, is available, the combination of POs being unwilling to give up their easy cases and courts not wanting to appear overly lenient restricts its general use. When defendants are not complying with conditions of probation, it is the supervision officer's responsibility to notify the court and to justify the allegations of noncompliance. Based on Supreme Court rulings, revocation hearings must be formal and defendants are entitled to some due process rights during these proceedings, namely, the rights to cross-examine witnesses, introduce independent evidence, and have counsel present. Even though departmental and judicial guidelines structure revocation hearings, the decision when to file a violation report remains a judgment call of the probation officer.

Key People and Terms

Eric Berne (136)
Brokerage system (138)
Chronos (149)
Field contacts (149)
William Glasser (135)
Guided group interaction (137)
Initial interview (146)

Lloyd McCorkle (137)
Probation officer's dilemma (132)
Reality therapy (135)
Revocation (159)
Tolling probation (169)
Transactional analysis (TA) (136)

Key Legal Cases

Boykin v. Alabama
Gagnon v. Scarpelli

Mempa v. Rhay
Morrissey v. Brewer

Questions for Discussion and Review

1. What is the probation officer's dilemma? What are the reasons the dilemma exists? Discuss how POs and their supervisors have addressed the dilemma.

2. Discuss the three treatment modalities examined in this chapter: reality therapy, transactional analysis, and guided group interaction.

3. What is the brokerage system and how does it differ from traditional methods of probation service delivery?

4. What is the difference between general and special conditions of probation? Give an example of each.

5. What are the two different methods for assigning officers to their caseloads? What are some advantages and disadvantages of each method?

6. What is the initial interview? Discuss its importance to the supervision process.

7. What are the three reasons probationers may be brought back before the sentencing judge? Discuss each with respect to probationers and probation officers.

8. Discuss *Mempa v. Rhay, Morrissey v. Brewer,* and *Gagnon v. Scarpelli* in terms of the facts of each case and their effects on probation supervision and the rights of probationers.

9. What is the "norm of seriousness" and how does it influence the decision to revoke probation? What are some other considerations and influences on POs when making the decision to revoke?

Relevant Internet Sites

American Probation and Parole Association, for information on supervision, casework, and treatment programs: www.appa-net.org

Center for Community Corrections web site, for information on probation programs: www.communitycorrectionsworks.org

National Institute of Corrections, for publications, training, and technical assistance in all areas of corrections: www.nicic.org

National Criminal Justice Reference Service, an excellent source of information on probation programs: www.ncjrs.org

Notes

1. *Boykin v. Alabama,* 395 U.S. 298, 89 Sup. Ct. 1709 (1969).

2. *North Carolina v. Alford,* 400 U.S. 25, 91 Sup. Ct. 160 (1970).

3. John J. Gibbs, "Inside Supervision: A Thematic Analysis of Interviews with Probationers," *Federal Probation* 46 (December, 1982): 45.

4. David Dressler, *Practice and Theory of Probation and Parole* (New York: Columbia University Press, 1969) 159.

5. Probation and Pretrial Services Division, *Supervision of Federal Offenders* (Washington, DC: Administrative Office of the U.S. Courts, 1991) 2.

6. Richard Gray, "Probation: An Exploration in Meaning," *Federal Probation* 50 (December, 1988): 26.

7. Todd Clear and George Cole, *American Corrections,* 6th ed. (Belmont, CA: Wadsworth, 2003) 197–198.

8. David Duffee, "Models of Probation Supervision," in *Probation and Justice: Reconsideration of Mission,* eds. Patrick McAnany, Doug Thomson, and David Fogel (Cambridge, MA: Oelgeschlager, Gunn and Hain, 1984) 187.

9. Paul F. Cromwell, Rolando V. del Carmen, and Leanne F. Alarid, *Community-Based Corrections,* 5th ed. (Belmont, CA: Wadsworth, 2002) 117.

10. Patrick McAnany and Doug Thomson, *Equitable Responses to Probation Violations* (Chicago: Center for Research in Law and Justice, University of Illinois at Chicago Circle, 1982) 28.

11. Anthony Walsh, *Understanding, Assessing and Counseling the Criminal Justice Client* (Monterey, CA: Brooks/Cole, 1998).

12. William Glasser, *Reality Therapy* (New York: Harper and Row, 1975) 53.

13. Glasser 6.

14. David Lester, "Group and Milieu Therapy," in *Correctional Counseling and Rehabilitation,* eds. Patricia Van Voorhis, Michael Braswell, and David Lester, (Cincinnati, OH: Anderson, 2000) 201–212.

15. "A Compilation of Core Concepts," ed. Claude Steiner, August, 2000, Berkeley, CA. Retrieved

December 7, 2003, from www.emotional-literacy.com/core.htm

16. "A Compilation of Core Concepts" 1.

17. Lloyd McCorkle, Albert Elias, and Lowell Bixby, *The Highfields Story* (New York: Henry Holt, 1958).

18. Lester 208–209.

19. National Advisory Commission on Criminal Justice Standards and Goals, *Corrections* (Washington, DC: Department of Justice, 1973) 334.

20. Belinda McCarthy, "Introduction," in *Intermediate Punishments: Intensive Supervision, Home Confinement and Electronic Surveillance*, ed. Belinda McCarthy (Monsey, NY: Willow Tree, 1987) 3.

21. Charles Lindquist, "The Private Sector in Probation: Contracting Private Services from Community Organizations," *Federal Probation* 45 (1980): 58–64.

22. The original proponents of a "risk control" model were Todd Clear and Vincent O'Leary, *Controlling the Offender in the Community* (Lexington, MA: D. C. Heath, 1983).

23. Charles Lindquist and John T. Whitehead, "Correctional Officers as Parole Officers: An Examination of a Community Sanction," *Criminal Justice and Behavior* 13 (1986): 216.

24. Franklin H. Marshall and Gennaro Vito, "Not Without the Tools: The Task of Probation in the Eighties," *Federal Probation* 46 (December, 1982): 39.

25. See, for example, Don Andrews, Ivan Zinger, Robert D. Hóge, James Bonta, Paul Gendreau, and Francis T. Cullen, "Does Correctional Treatment Work? A Psychologically Informed Meta-Analysis," *Criminology* 28, 3 (1990): 369–404; and Paul Gendreau, Tracy Little, and Claire Goggin, "Meta-Analysis of the Predictors of Adult Offender Recidivism: What Works!" *Criminology* 34, 4 (1996): 575–608.

26. Cromwell, del Carmen, and Alarid 75–81.

27. McAnany and Thomson 16.

28. See the article by James B. Eaglin and Patricia A. Lombard, "Statistical Risk Prediction as an Aid to Probation Caseload Classification," in *Probation, Parole and Community Corrections*, eds. Robert Carter, Daniel Glaser, and Leslie Wilkens (New York: Wiley, 1984) 78–88.

29. See Edward E. Rhine, William R. Smith, and Ronald W. Jackson, *Paroling Authorities: Recent History and Current Practice* (Laurel, MD: American Correctional Association, 1991) 112.

30. Walsh 42–43.

31. S. Christopher Baird, Richard Heinz, and Brian Bemus, "The Wisconsin Case Classification/Staff Deployment Project: A Two-Year Follow-Up Report," in *Classification: American Correctional Association Monograph* (College Park, MD: American Correctional Association, 1982).

32. Paul F. Cromwell, George G. Killinger, Hazel B. Kerper, and Charls Walker, *Probation and Parole in the Criminal Justice System*, 2nd ed. (St. Paul, MN: West, 1985) 231.

33. Peggy B. Burke, *Policy-Driven Responses to Probation and Parole Violations* (Washington, DC: National Institute of Corrections, 1997) 1.

34. Burke 11–13.

35. Excerpts from the Supreme Court ruling were taken from Leonard Orland, *Justice, Punishment, Treatment: The Correctional Process* (New York: Macmillan, 1973) 70–73.

36. Dean J. Champion, *Corrections in the United States: A Contemporary Perspective*, 3rd ed. (Upper Saddle River, NJ: Prentice Hall, 2001) 447–448.

37. Christopher E. Smith, *Law and Contemporary Corrections* (Belmont, CA: Wadsworth, 2000) 247.

38. Champion 448–449.

39. James Inciardi, *Criminal Justice* (San Diego, CA: Harcourt, Brace, Jovanovich, 1987) 643.

40. Burke 11–13.

41. McAnany and Thompson 36.

42. Burke 13.

43. Stevens H. Clarke, "What Is the Purpose of Probation and Why Do We Revoke It?" *Crime and Delinquency* 25 (October, 1979): 421.

44. National Advisory Commission on Criminal Justice Standards and Goals 159.

45. Cromwell et al., *Probation and Parole in the Criminal Justice System* 79.

6

Parole Selection

Introduction: From Prison to Parole

Prison life varies considerably depending on the type of institution, the area of the country, the kind of prison management, and the length of sentence (see Focus Box 6.1). However, two factors seem to be present in most prison experiences: (1) rules and (2) violence. An indoctrination speech given by a Texas corrections captain is an example of the omnipresent influence of prison rules:

> You are in the custody of the Texas Department of Corrections. Stand where I can see you! [Pause] That book I just gave you is the most important thing you'll ever receive here. It lists all the rules and regulations. You're responsible for knowing them. If you can't read, we'll have someone read it to you as many times as you need. . . . Now, if you need education—and we all do—we've got it right here. You can learn a skill in here, you can earn good time. . . . The best way to do time is to do your own time. Do your own time! Nobody else can do it for you. If you listen to some inmates inside, you'll have trouble for sure. You get in trouble, and you'll be right here with me for a longer time; I guarantee it. Now, you have family and friends waiting on you—don't let them down. Don't let yourself down. Do your own time, and you'll be fine. The rules are for your own protection and health. . . . There is a reason for each and every rule. They are to help you, to keep you whole.[1]

A California inmate describes the violence that dominates many prisons:

> At San Quentin there is a terribly hostile atmosphere. You have to adapt yourself. Everyone puts up a front that they are strong. If you are weak people know that you won't fight back and you will be used. You will be forced into homosexual relations and be forced to buy dope. When you first arrive you are tested. We call that "getting your face." The first month I was here I had to physically defend myself. I didn't want to fight—I just wanted to do my number, but I had to fight in order to show that I couldn't be pushed around, and once I had shown that, I was left pretty much alone. There is a real strong protection racket here: if you let yourself

173

be pushed around and don't defend yourself, you can get forced to pay for your own protection.[2]

Adapting to prison rules and coping with violence unfortunately are not skills that prepare inmates for release into the community. For example, a newly paroled convict told John Rosecrance:

> I know how to make my bed real neat, how to wash and shave in ten minutes, how to eat in seven, how to carve a shiv from a spoon, and how to make body armor from cardboard boxes, but on the street that counts for nothing. Parole is great but how am I supposed to make a living? (personal communication, undated)

Although parole continues to undergo changes, as it comes under closer legislative and judicial scrutiny, it remains a vital link in the correctional process. Parole decision makers recently have been caught in a maelstrom of conflicting pressures as attitudes toward criminals have become increasingly punitive at the same time the prison population has grown at staggering rates. In the process, decisions to grant parole, which in the best of circumstances are difficult, have become even more complex. But nevertheless, hundreds of thousands of such decisions are rendered each year. In Chapter Six we examine how they are made.

Release from Prison

It is axiomatic that inmates get out of prison (at least 95 percent of them are eventually released). The real question is how long do they stay in. In the recent past, the general answer has been longer and longer. In 1984, the average released prisoner had served 23.4 months, including credit for jail time. Figure 6.1 compares the national prison release figures for 1990 and 1999. By 1990 the total time served had grown to 28 months and in 1999 the total time served was 34 months. Figure 6.2 shows release patterns for all states in 1993, 1996, and 1999 for violent offenders. Although the mean maximum sentence has gone down from 108 months to 103 months, the mean time served has gone up from 46 months to 53 months. This is in large part a result of the continuing shift to determinant sentencing and because twenty-nine states and the District of Columbia adopted the federal **truth-in-sentencing** standard requiring that Part I violent offenders (those convicted of murder, nonnegligent manslaughter, rape, robbery, or aggravated assault) must serve not less than 85 percent of their sentence in prison before becoming eligible for release. States adopting this standard are eligible for truth-in-sentencing funds under the Violent Offender Incarcerations and Truth-in-Sentencing (VOITIS) incentive grant program established by the 1994 Federal Crime Act.

Even with truth-in-sentencing, time served in prison is obviously not the same as time sentenced to prison. Sentences can be reduced for a variety of reasons: time served in jail awaiting sentence, good time, meritorious good time

FIGURE 6.1 Sentence Length and Time Served for First Releases from State Prison, 1990 and 1999

	Mean Sentence Length[a]		Mean Time Served In—				Total Time Served[c]		Percent of Sentence Served[d]	
			Jail[b]		Prison					
	1990	1999	1990	1999	1990	1999	1990	1999	1990	1999
All offenses	69 mo	65 mo	6 mo	5 mo	22 mo	29 mo	28 mo	34 mo	38.0%	48.7%
Violent offenses										
Murder[e]	99 mo	87 mo	7 mo	6 mo	39 mo	45 mo	46 mo	51 mo	43.8%	55.0%
Manslaughter	209	192	9	10	83	96	92	106	43.1	53.1
Rape	88	102	5	6	31	49	37	56	41.0	52.5
Other sexual assault	128	124	7	6	55	73	62	79	45.5	58.3
Robbery	77	76	5	6	30	42	36	47	43.8	57.0
Assault	104	97	7	6	41	48	48	55	42.8	51.6
	64	62	6	6	23	33	30	39	43.9	58.7
Property offenses	65 mo	58 mo	6 mo	5 mo	18 mo	25 mo	24 mo	29 mo	34.4%	45.6%
Burglary	79	73	6	5	22	31	29	36	33.9	44.3
Larceny/theft	52	45	6	4	14	19	20	24	35.5	46.9
Motor vehicle theft	56	44	7	5	13	20	20	25	33.1	52.5
Fraud	56	49	6	4	14	19	20	23	33.2	41.7
Drug offenses	57 mo	59 mo	6 mo	5 mo	14 mo	22 mo	20 mo	27 mo	32.9%	42.8%
Possession	61	56	6	5	12	20	18	25	29.0	42.4
Trafficking	60	64	6	5	16	24	22	29	34.8	42.0
Public-order offenses	40 mo	42 mo	5 mo	4 mo	14 mo	19 mo	18 mo	23 mo	42.6%	51.1%

Note: Based on prisoners with a sentence of more than one year who were released for the first time on the current sentence. Excludes prisoners released from prison by escape, death, transfer, appeal, or detainer.

[a]Maximum sentence length for the most serious offense. Excludes sentences of life, life without parole, life plus additional years, and death.

[b]Time served in jail and credited toward the current sentence.

[c]Based on time served in jail and in prison. Detail may not add to total because of rounding.

[d]Based on total sentence length (not shown) for all consecutive sentences.

[e]Includes nonnegligent manslaughter.

Source: Timothy A. Hughes, Doris James Wilson, and Allen J. Beck, *Trends in State Parole, 1990–2000* (Washington, DC: U.S. Department of Justice, 2001) 5.

FIGURE 6.2   *Time Served, Maximum Sentence, and Percent of Sentence Served for Part 1 Violent Offenders, by State, 1993, 1996, and 1999*

	Mean Maximum Sentence[a]			Mean Time Served			Percent of Sentence Served[b]		
	1993	1996	1999	1993	1996	1999	1993	1996	1999
All states	108 mo	99 mo	103 mo	46 mo	50 mo	53 mo	46%	52%	56%
Truth-in-sentencing states[c]	89 mo	88 mo	93 mo	41 mo	46 mo	50 mo	50%	54%	58%
Arizona	69	71	60	43	48	49	62	68	81
California	58	63	60	33	36	37	57	57	61
Connecticut	71	74	80	38	49	64	54	65	80
Delaware	—	—	—	42	42	46	—	—	—
Florida	74	84	91	31	45	53	42	54	58
Georgia	150	134	117	63	67	76	42	50	65
Illinois	91	99	107	40	45	48	44	45	45
Iowa	192	135	146	39	48	58	20	36	40
Kansas	—	—	—	29	33	41	—	—	—
Louisiana	104	98	96	67	68	45	64	69	48
Maine	—	—	—	43	44	39	—	—	—
Michigan	43	50	52	46	53	59	/	/	/
Minnesota	50	56	60	34	37	39	68	67	65
Mississippi	106	118	128	45	58	57	43	49	44
Missouri	96	98	99	74	78	85	77	80	86
New Jersey	121	108	120	47	46	53	39	43	44
New Mexico	70	67	77	38	37	57	54	56	74
New York	94	96	98	50	53	66	53	56	68
North Carolina	136	121	120	33	44	52	24	36	44
North Dakota	47	60	38	31	47	29	66	78	76
Ohio	237	226	165	61	71	64	26	32	39
Oregon	111	65	62	43	37	42	39	58	67
Pennsylvania	117	119	140	54	61	80	46	51	57
South Carolina	100	90	104	44	44	46	44	48	44
Tennessee	130	121	131	48	58	65	37	48	50
Utah	121	90	100	43	36	35	36	40	36
Virginia	107	97	113	41	50	62	38	51	55
Washington	41	47	49	31	34	38	76	72	78
Wisconsin	84	82	80	41	43	51	49	52	64
Other states[d]	129 mo	113 mo	104 mo	53 mo	54 mo	55 mo	42%	48%	54%
Alabama	—	—	—	—	—	—	—	—	—
Alaska	115	124	88	65	71	63	57	57	72
Arkansas	131	109	157	35	37	56	27	34	36
Colorado	98	89	96	39	40	50	40	45	52
Hawaii	138	124	125	64	57	59	47	46	47
Idaho	104	90	98	59	80	36	57	89	37
Indiana	108	111	102	54	56	46	50	51	45

FIGURE 6.2 *Continued*

	Mean Maximum Sentence[a]			Mean Time Served			Percent of Sentence Served[b]		
	1993	1996	1999	1993	1996	1999	1993	1996	1999
Other states[d] continued									
Kentucky	242	156	196	77	71	/	32	45	/
Maryland	118	106	99	63	59	57	53	56	58
Massachusetts	123	110	98	51	61	61	42	55	63
Montana	89	119	—	61	54	60	69	46	—
Nebraska	118	123	140	55	49	61	47	40	44
Nevada	—	86	107	—	34	41	—	40	39
New Hampshire	98	89	100	36	39	48	37	44	48
Oklahoma	104	110	111	34	42	47	33	38	42
Rhode Island	80	80	68	44	50	46	55	63	67
South Dakota	101	78	72	36	37	29	35	48	40
Texas	157	123	97	48	57	59	31	46	61
Vermont	100	113	121	29	56	54	29	50	45
West Virginia	171	108	139	76	50	62	44	46	45
Wyoming	140	123	137	69	69	55	49	56	40

Note: Data were obtained from the Violent Offender Incarceration and Truth-in-Sentencing (VOITIS) Incentive Grant Program. Includes only offenders with a sentence of more than one year released for the first time on the current sentence. Excludes persons releeased from prison by escape, death, transfer, appeal or detainer. Part 1 violent crimes include murder/nonnegligent manslaughter, rape, robbery, and aggravated assault.

—Not reported.

/Not calculated.

[a]Excludes sentences of life or death.

[b]Based on states that reported both mean maximum sentence and mean time served.

[c]States met the federal 85 percent requirement for VOITIS grants in fiscal year 2000 based on 1999 data. Excludes the District of Columbia.

[d]Requirement for percent of sentence served may vary by state and be type of offender.

Source: Timothy A. Hughes, Doris James Wilson, and Allen J. Beck, *Trends in State Parole, 1990–2000* (Washington, DC: U.S. Department of Justice, 2001) 6.

(participation in prison programs), and parole release. A Pennsylvania judge put this into perspective when she told John Rosecrance that it frequently was necessary to significantly increase a sentence to ensure that a "fair" amount of time was actually served. For instance, in a rape case she wanted the offender to serve five years. After calculating the offender's good time and estimating when a favorable parole decision would be made, she sentenced him to twenty years (in hopes he would serve five).

There are three major ways to be released from prison: (1) discretionary parole, (2) mandatory release, and (3) completion of the maximum sentence, known as a max out. Pardons, commutations, or new trials are other possible avenues of release, but such occurrences are relatively rare. **Discretionary parole** is granted by parole boards but has become less and less common. By year-end 2000, twenty-eight states had abolished discretionary parole and most of the rest of the states had restricted parole by establishing standards offenders must meet to be eligible for release.[3] However, those inmates who are released in states with discretionary parole must serve a minimum of time before they are first eligible for parole consideration. Eligibility is determined by computing the minimum sentence minus good time credit (often given automatically for staying out of serious trouble) and meritorious good time. **Meritorious good time** is gained by participating in various programs such as vocational training, work details, counseling, medical experiments, or educational classes. Some states also allow sentence reduction for inmates performing well in unsupervised or minimum custody situations. For example, a defendant given a four- to ten-year sentence could be eligible for parole in two years and three months. In this case, the original four-year minimum was reduced by six months of jail time while awaiting sentence and fifteen months of good time. The following illustrates these calculations:

Minimum Term: 4 years = 48 months

Jail time	6 months
Prison time served	27 months
Good time (1 for 3)	9 months
Meritorious good time	6 months
Total	48 months

Eligibility for parole release, of course, does not mean that release will be granted; this decision remains at the discretion of a parole board. Although it is difficult to be definitive, prison officials estimate that 50 percent of those applying are granted parole at their first hearing.[4]

Mandatory release occurs when the unserved portion of the maximum term equals the inmate's earned good time; however, if the defendant served jail time this is included. This method of release is prevalent in states with determinate sentencing. For example, if an offender was sentenced to a flat three-year sentence (without having served any appreciable time in jail) and good time credits equaled one year, he or she would be released after two years in prison. The remaining year would be completed in the community under parole supervision. Eligibility for mandatory release is set by statute, and parole boards have no input into the release date, except for keeping a record of time served and credits earned. However, correctional officials have considerable influence in determining what constitutes good time. In some states a combination of good time and meritorious good time allows inmates to reduce more than half their original sentence. Other states allow inmates to serve up to a year of their sentence in halfway houses, restitution centers, or work release programs. Some states, faced with severe overcrowding, have summarily advanced parole eligibility for all prisoners in their systems.

In some respects, mandatory release is a misnomer because before prisoners are actually freed they must agree to follow release conditions and be supervised by parole officers for the remainder of their sentences. Inmates who do not agree to release conditions are denied release. Although almost every inmate is eager to agree to any conditions, this was not the case for Theodore Streleski. Three times he refused to accept a release condition barring him from visiting the Stanford University campus where, as a graduate student, he had bludgeoned his doctoral advisor to death. California officials refused to allow his mandatory release and Streleski served his entire seven-year twenty-day sentence in Vacaville State Prison.[5]

Max out occurs when inmates have completed their maximum term—there simply is no more time to serve. This happens when prisoners have not earned good time (or at least not enough to warrant community supervision) or they have been returned to prison for violation of parole or mandatory release. When inmates have received a max out they are no longer subject to correctional supervision or control. This was the case when Theodore Streleski was released in 1986.

Today some states have opted to enact legislation that requires that defendants serve a mandatory minimum time of incarceration before becoming eligible for parole. For example, defendant number one receives a five- to ten-year sentence and at the time of sentencing the judge states on the record that the defendant must serve five years before becoming eligible for parole. Defendant number two, however, receives five to ten years with no stipulation and is eligible for parole (in some states) after serving one-third of the maximum term (approximately three years). These statutes have removed the initial time of the parole decision from the parole board. In New Jersey, nearly one-half of all defendants imprisoned receive a stipulated initial parole minimum release date. The discretion of the parole board in these cases is severely limited. The New Jersey system is no longer unique. Several other states have implemented or are considering this sentencing approach.

Prison release statistics, appearing in Figure 6.3 (see also Chapter Three), show that, over time, the percentage of those whose sentence expired has remained relatively stable, whereas mandatory releases have increased significantly and discretionary releases increased from 1980 to 1992, then decreased from 1992 to 1999. In the early 1990s, mandatory release replaced discretionary parole as the most common form of prison release. In 1980, over 50 percent of all prison releases were a result of discretionary parole; about 20 percent were mandatory releases. By 1995, mandatory releases had replaced discretionary parole as the most common form of release, and by 1999, 40 percent of all releases were mandatory with just a little over 20 percent discretionary. However, states still employ parole boards to decide who is going to be released from prison and when and under what conditions that release is to take place.

FIGURE 6.3 *Method of Release from State Prison, for Selected Years, 1980–1999*

Year	All Releases[a]	Discretionary Parole	Mandatory Parole	Other Conditional	Expiration of Sentence
1980	143,543	78,602	26,735	9,363	20,460
1985	206,988	88,069	62,851	15,371	34,489
1990	405,374	159,731	116,857	62,851	51,288
1992	430,198	170,095	126,836	60,800	48,971
1995	455,140	147,139	177,402	46,195	66,017
1999	542,950	128,708	223,342	66,337	98,218

Note: Based on prisoners with a sentence of more than one year who were released from state prison. Counts are for December 31 for each year.

[a]Includes releases to probation, commutations, and other unspecified releases and excludes escapees, AWOLs, and transfers.

Source: Timothy A. Hughes, Doris James Wilson, and Allen J. Beck, *Trends in State Parole, 1990–2000* (Washington, DC: U.S. Department of Justice, 2001) 4.

Parole Boards

Despite the changes is the method of release, moving away from discretionary release and toward mandatory release, almost all states and the federal government maintain parole boards to aid the release decisions. Unlike probation, parole is centrally administered on a state or federal level. Consequently, there are fifty-two parole boards in the United States, one for each state, the federal system, and the District of Columbia. There are two basic models for administering parole decisions: independent and consolidated. The **independent parole board** is a separate department from a state's department of corrections responsible for making its own decisions. It is a distinct entity, with its own staff and hierarchy of command. In many states, independent boards are physically located within buildings that also house the state department of corrections. Several states use a system in which the parole board is responsible for deciding who should be granted parole, whereas community supervision is provided by the department of corrections. The **consolidated parole board** is an agency within a larger department of corrections. Staff personnel and working guidelines are provided by the state board of corrections. Figure 6.4 illustrates the characteristics of state paroling authorities.

The designation of an independent board refers to organizational structure rather than insulation from outside influence. Many parole board members are appointed by the governor and serve at his or her pleasure. Even the Federal Parole Commission is not immune from executive pressure. Stephen Gettinger documented the politicization of federal parole as Reagan administration officials

FIGURE 6.4   *Characteristics of State Paroling Authorities*

State	Governor Appoint	Legal Confirmation	Chair Salary	Members Salary	Term Years	Number on Board	F-Full or P-Part Time
Alabama	X		$ 71,235	$ 71,235	5	5	P
Alaska	X	X	$150 diem	$150 diem	5	5	P
Arizona	X	X	$ 57,499	$ 54,499	5	5	F
Arkansas	X	X	$ 76,592	$ 68,529		5 F, 2 P	F
California	X	X	$103,317	$ 99,693	7	6	F
Colorado	X	X	$ 83,439	$ 77,928	6	7	F
Connecticut	X	X		$110 diem	4	15, 3 full	F/P
Delaware	X	X	$ 55,000	$110 diem	4	5, 1 full	F/P
Florida	X	X	$ 83,273	$83	6	3	F
Georgia	X	X	$111,509	$111,509	7	7	F
Hawaii	X	X	$ 77,966	$29.99 phr.	4	3, 1 full	F/P
Idaho	X	X	NA	$150 diem	3	5	P
Illinois	X	X	$ 78,831	$ 70,620	6	15	F
Indiana	X		$ 65,000	$ 53,500	4	5	F
Iowa	X	X	$ 75,000	$ 75,000	4	5, 2 full	F/P
Kansas	X	X	$ 99,831	$ 97,366	4	4	F
Kentucky	X	X	$ 65,000	$ 45,000	4	8	F
Louisiana	X	X	$ 46,904	$ 39,312	–11	7	F
Maine			$55 diem	$55 diem			
Maryland	X	X	$ 90,000	$ 85,000	6	8	F
Massachusetts	X		$ 89,632	$ 72,352	5	7	F
Michigan	Director of Corrections		$ 88,550	$ 80,500	4	10	F
Minnesota	Director of Corrections		NA	$ 44,119 to $ 66,712			
Missouri	X	X	$ 77,988	$ 71,988	6	7	F
Montana	X	X	$50 diem	Same	4	5	P
Nebraska	X	X	$ 62,241	$ 56,824	6	5	F
Nevada	X		$ 86,522	$ 68,709	4	13, 7 full	F/P

(continued)

FIGURE 6.4 *Continued*

State	Governor Appoint	Legal Confir-mation	Chair Salary	Members Salary	Term Years	Number on Board	F-Full or P-Part Time
New Hampshire	X		$100 pd	$100 diem	5	7	P
New Jersey	X	X	$117,928	$104,000	6	15	F
New Mexico	X	X	$75 diem	$75 diem	6	9	P
New York	X	X	$120,800	$101,600	6	19	F
North Carolina	X		$ 83,000	$ 75,000	4	3	F
North Dakota	X	X	$75 diem	$75 diem		6	P
Ohio	Director of Corrections		$54,432 to $75,321	$49,363 to $68,275	life	9	F
Oklahoma	1		$ 30,800	$ 30,800	4	5	P
Oregon	X	X	$ 72,576	$ 73,576	4	3	F
Pennsylvania	X	X			6	9	F
Rhode Island	X	X	$ 85,000	$ 18,500	3(12)	7, 1 full	P
South Dakota	2	X	$75 diem	$75 diem	4	6	P
Tennessee	X		$ 82,008	$ 63,984	6	7	F
Texas	X	X	$ 85,800	$ 83,200	6	18	F
Utah	X	X	$ 86,736	$ 83,186	5	5	F
Vermont	X	X	$ 13,000	$80 diem	3	5	P
Virginia	X	X	$104,000	$ 87,000	–11	3	F
Washington	X	X	$ 79,600	$ 45,420	5	3	F
West Virginia	X	X	$ 45,000	$ 45,000	6	5	F
Wisconsin	X	X	$ 68,000	$49,654 to $60,234	2(10)	7	F
Wyoming	X	X	$125 diem	$125 diem	6	7	P
National Board of Canada	X		203,100CN	$112,600CN	–5	43 F, 46 P	F/P
U.S. Parole Commission	President	X	$130,000	$121,000	6	5	F
Puerto Rico	X	X	$ 75,000	$ 60,000		5	F

Source: Parole Board Survey 2001, Association of Paroling Authorities, International, 2002, California, Missouri. Retrieved March 26, 2003, from www.apaintl.org/Pub-ParoleBoardSurvey2001.html

jockeyed to control the commission through firings, transfers, and intimidation of appointees left over from the Carter administration.[6]

The power of parole boards has been severely reduced (and in some cases eliminated) by **determinate sentencing.** Under this sentencing structure, the boards, although still independent, have lost authority over most prison releases. In a study of parole in Illinois, Minnesota, and Connecticut, criminal justice researchers John Hepburn and Lynne Goodstein concluded that determinate sentencing has "transferred power from independent paroling agencies to each state's Department of Corrections."[7] Determinate sentencing has also increased discretionary power of prosecutors to plea bargain because they can offer sentences to less serious crimes that, although still determinate, carry a lesser penalty than those originally charged.

The following descriptions demonstrate three varieties of parole boards that currently exist in the United States.

The Alaska Board of Parole is a five-member, part-time body appointed by the governor to five-year overlapping terms. Its small staff is headquartered in Juneau, with an office in Anchorage. The board conducts hearings at facilities around the state and is responsible for release and revocation decision making, setting supplemental conditions for mandatory releases, executive clemency functions, as well as commutation release reviews—the emergency mechanism that responds to population crises. During calendar year 1999, the board held 590 hearings in support of those functions. During 2000, the board held 595 hearings. Field supervision of parolees comes under the jurisdiction of the State Department of Corrections.[8]

The Missouri Board of Probation and Parole has seven full-time members appointed by the governor, with the advice and consent of the senate. It is an autonomous body administratively located within the Department of Corrections. The board makes decisions about parole release and revocation and is responsible for all probation and parole services for adult felons and misdemeanants, including field supervision. The board also investigates and reports to the governor on all applications for pardons, commutations of sentence, reprieves or restorations of citizenship. During 2002, the board conducted 8,300 parole hearings.[9]

The Texas Board of Pardons and Paroles is an independent body consisting of eighteen full-time members appointed by the governor, with the advice and consent of the senate, to overlapping six-year terms. The board is the administrative head of the agency and is legislatively empowered to provide its rules and policies. The board is separate from the Texas Department of Criminal Justice (TDCJ) whose Parole Division carries out the directions of the board but is not governed by the board. The board has responsibility for making release and revocation decisions, setting conditions of parole, and for managing field supervision of parolees. In addition, it is responsible for supervision of releasees of the Department of Corrections who are released to discretionary mandatory supervision and makes recommendations to the governor on matters of clemency. During fiscal year 2001, the board completed 64,235 reviews to determine parole actions (e.g., release, revocation, reinstatement). At the end of fiscal year 2001, the board had 80,744 releasees under its jurisdiction, of whom 80,602 were on active supervision. The board is headquartered in Austin with eight regional offices and twenty-three hearings offices throughout the state.[10]

Besides being organized differently, states also differ in requirements for appointment to parole boards.

Qualification for Membership on Parole Boards

The preceding discussion makes it clear that the makeup and composition of contemporary parole boards varies widely. In some states, such as Alabama, Alaska, Montana, and Oklahoma, members serve only part-time and spend most of their time in the community. Other states employ correctional professionals who specialize in parole decision making and often are insulated from community influence. There are also differences in how people become parole board members. In most states, parole board membership is a result of appointment by the governor and is determined by political patronage, although in some states members are selected from civil service lists. In a few states, members are appointed by the director of corrections or the state attorney general.[11] Qualifications for membership in several states specify that parole board candidates have a criminal justice or social science background. However, several states have *no* statutory qualifications for appointment to parole boards.

In many instances, states want to retain their regional character and therefore resist efforts to establish uniform standards. States have begun to choose their parole members as representatives of ethnic groups or geographical region rather than as individual experts. Some regions manifest a distrust of "professionals" and believe that private citizens should have more input into the criminal justice system. Recently, the Florida Parole Commission included a career state government bureaucrat, a retired police executive, and an adult and juvenile corrections professional; the chair of the South Carolina Board of Paroles and Pardons is a former state legislator, social worker, and community activist; the Oregon board consisted of two attorneys and a former probation and parole officer; and a host of states have ministers and retired schoolteachers sitting on their parole boards. A member of the Idaho Parole Commission told John Rosecrance that citizens feared that parole specialists would "identify too much with the correction bureaucracy and come to think their job is to parole people, rather than to balance the interests of the individual inmate and those of the community" (undated personal communication).

The trend toward selecting board members from the ranks of private citizens whose experience is unrelated to corrections is not universal. For example, New York state requires that each board member have a four-year college or graduate degree along with at least five years of experience in either criminology, criminal justice, law enforcement, sociology, law, social work, corrections, psychology, psychiatry, or medicine.[12]

Iowa law, however, states that the members of the Board of Parole must be of good character and judicious background, must include a member of a minority group, and may include a person ordained or designated a regular leader of a religious community and who is knowledgeable in correctional procedures and issues. In addition, the Iowa Board of Parole must meet at least two of the following three requirements:

1. It must contain one member who is a disinterested layperson;
2. It must contain one member who is an attorney licensed to practice law in this state and who is knowledgeable in correctional procedures and issues;
3. It must contain one member who is a person holding at least a master's degree in social work or counseling and guidance and who is knowledgeable in correctional procedures and issues.[13]

Missouri requires that members be persons of recognized integrity and honor, who are known to possess education and ability in decision making through career experience; not more than four of the seven-member board may be from the same political party.[14] It is doubtful that any parole board member can meet the standard set by the American Correctional Association (which perhaps should be seen as *goals*), summarized as follows:

1. Personality. Members must be of such integrity, intelligence, and good judgment as to command respect and public confidence. They must be forthright, courageous, and independent. They should be appointed without reference to creed, color, or political affiliation.
2. Education. Board members should have educational backgrounds broad enough to provide them with a knowledge of those professionals most closely related to parole administration. Specifically, academic training in a field such as criminology, education, psychiatry, psychology, law, social work, and sociology is desirable.
3. Experiences. They must have an intimate knowledge of common situations and problems confronting offenders.
4. Other. They should not be officers of a political party or seek to hold elective office while members of the board.[15]

Parole board members that the authors have known are, for the most part, conscientious and diligent in fulfilling their responsibilities. Their decisions are generally considered and thoughtful; they are doing their best to complete a difficult and complex task. Although arguments continue whether board members need correctional experience, or if insulation from community pressure is a good thing, parole boards continue to function according to established procedures, and thousands of men and women each year are released early from prison sentences.

Parole Board Procedures

According to the New York state provisions for parole hearings, which are typical of procedures followed in most states, at least one month before a sentence expires, one or more members of the parole board must interview inmates serving indeterminate sentences and decide whether they should be paroled at the end of the minimum term of their sentences. If parole is not granted, New York inmates will be informed in writing of the reasons for the denial within two weeks of the original hearing. The board will also set a date for reconsideration of parole, which cannot be more than twenty-four months from the first hearing. If an inmate is released, a copy of the conditions of parole is provided.[16]

Parole board members hold release hearings at individual prisons (but in some situations prisoners are brought to a central location). The members have access to the defendant's file which is prepared by prison officials or parole officers assigned to the prison. Inmate files contain an extensive amount of information: police reports, records of court activity, the PSI report, results of psychological and physiological tests, mental health records, institutional reports concerning participation in self-improvement or treatment programs, disciplinary reports, and an overall summary of the inmate's adjustment. In addition, the file contains letters of recommendation, an inmate's release plan, correspondence from sponsors, and a calculation of the earliest possible release date.

In a growing number of jurisdictions scoring devices or scales to rate the seriousness of an offense, prior criminal activities, or readiness for release are compiled and included in the inmate's file. Such devices are often used as part of what the NIC calls "structured decision making" for paroling authorities.[17] There are many variations to the structure used, such as sentencing guidelines, caseload classification schemes, risk prediction instruments, and parole guidelines. The NIC identified seven characteristics of structured decision making:

- Explicitly stated goals for decision-making practices (e.g., just deserts, rehabilitation, risk management, etc.);
- Explicit, written policy covering topics such as release, offender eligibility for parole, setting terms, conditions of parole release, or supervision levels;
- Explicit decision-making tools (e.g., rating sheets, risk prediction devices);
- Revocation policy;
- Explicit rules for overriding policy;
- Tracking systems to document compliance with policy; and
- A mechanism for systematic revision of policy.[18]

Although there is a growing emphasis placed on predictive devices, parole officials invariably assert that such instruments are only guidelines and that members make the final release decisions.

After meeting and talking with inmates for a brief period (usually about ten minutes), the parole board members discuss the case in private and decide whether to release, and if so, when. If parole is recommended, there is usually a time lag of approximately one month before actual release is completed. Some parole agencies use this period to conduct on-site investigations of an inmate's proposed living situation. In cases where there is something significantly amiss, the inmate's release can be delayed. When parole is denied, a new hearing date (usually within two years) is set, and the inmate is promptly notified of the decision. Although this process is usually set by statute or bureaucratic rules, it does not mean that problems do not arise or that release decisions made by parole board members are made for different reasons for different offenders. There are various criteria for release, and sometimes these variations can cause problems.

Criteria for Release

Many parole boards have been severely criticized over the criteria they use to make release decisions. Public and correctional officials alike have expressed the view that decisions often seem a matter of whim or impulse.[19] In other instances, parole board members are accused of heeding the views of powerful interest groups or making judgments based on expediency (for example the availability of prison space). In 1951 criminologist **Lloyd Ohlin** clearly delineated the issues involved in parole decision making. More than fifty years later they remain relevant and topical concerns.[20]

Ohlin argued that there are three major problem areas that need to be considered in careful parole decisions. The first involves the purpose of imprisonment. The parole decision made will vary greatly depending on whether punishment, rehabilitation, incapacitation, or deterrence is thought to be the major objective of imprisonment. Belief in one or the other of these philosophies of punishment may delay or expedite an inmate's release from prison. The second major problem area Ohlin identified is the protection of society and the individual. Here, the paroling authority must assess an inmate's risk of reoffending, a very difficult task because there are often several intangible variables to be considered, including past history, social support, adequacy of parole supervision, and factors that contribute to crime generally. The third major problem area identified by Ohlin is determining the offender's readiness for parole. This is also a very difficult state to predict for it must be determined based on the individual's institutional behavior, which may not be a good predictor of behavior in the community. An important factor here is the placement in the community. Will the offender be placed back in his or her old neighborhood? Or will there be a fresh start? What are the chances for employment? If treatment is necessary, is it available? Have the reasons for the criminal behavior been replaced or at least considered? For the offender to make a successful adjustment, the parole board must have information on all of these issues.

In 1966 parole board members throughout the United States were surveyed regarding the criteria they deemed most important in making release decisions. The criteria included a member's estimate of the chances the prisoner would commit a serious crime if released (92.8 percent of those polled reported this was one of five most important); their judgment that the prisoner would benefit from further institutional programs or would at least be a better risk if confined longer (87.1 percent included this); their judgment that the prisoner would become a worse risk if confined longer (71.9 percent); the probability that the prisoner would be a misdemeanant and a burden to his or her parole officer (35.3 percent); their feelings about how the decision would affect the feelings or welfare of the prisoner's relatives or dependents (33.8 percent); and what they thought the reaction of the judge might be if the prisoner was released (20.9 percent included this item as important).[21] A study of New York state parole board decision making revealed that members considered an assortment of criteria, including poor behavior at the parole hearing, poor attitude toward authority, selling narcotics, poor parole plan, breaking rules in prison, poor family attitude, and adverse attitudes toward other officials.[22]

A handbook for new parole board members published by the National Institute of Corrections lists several goals or purposes of parole decisions. These include rehabilitation, just deserts, incapacitation, deterrence, orderly institutional operation, public reaction, and the intent of the sentencing judge.[23] It is obviously impossible for parole boards to meet all of these criteria, especially when some of them contradict each other. It is important to remember that each parole board member brings his or her own goals and values to the decision-making process. Consequently, each case may be decided by different criteria, depending on the circumstances surrounding the case and the board members deciding it. It should not be a surprise, therefore, that some have criticized parole decision making as inconsistent, arbitrary, and even capricious. As noted previously, such criticism has resulted in many paroling authorities attempting to structure decision-making criteria by developing guidelines and rating scales, ranging from an unweighted list of factors or items that need to be considered to a specific decision matrix specifying the range for each inmate's term of imprisonment. An example of such a rating scale is presented in Figure 6.5. For those states that use such a scale, the relative weight given each variable will, of course, vary from state to state.

Even in those states that use a rating scale such as the one depicted in Figure 6.5, parole hearings for notorious inmates are gauged by special criteria. When their decisions are subjected to media glare or the scrutiny of community leaders, parole board members err on the side of denial. For example, Sirhan Sirhan (the murderer of Robert Kennedy) has been routinely denied parole even though he has been imprisoned far longer than other murderers, is reportedly a model prisoner, and by most criteria is eligible for release. In the same manner, members of the infamous Charles Manson family were routinely denied parole, although seeming to meet all standards for release. Crimes that particularly offend the public's sensibilities are put into special categories by parole board members. The "special treatment" given some inmates by parole boards contributes to the overall view of the boards by the inmates as arbitrary, capricious, and generally not well liked. These beliefs, plus other aspects of the inmate subculture, contribute to the convicts' perspectives toward parole boards.

FIGURE 6.5 *Parole Readiness Assessment*

Name _____   Date _____

Institution_____

1. Seriousness of Crime ____
   2 Not of serious nature
   0 Serious crime
   0 Habitual or multiple crimes

2. Time Served ____
   2 Has served enough time
   1 Has served minimum time
   0 Has not served long enough

3. Criminal Violence ____
   3 No violence
   0 "Aggravated" crime
   0 Violent crime
   0 Propensity toward crime

4. Recidivism ____
   4 Good risk
   3 Fair risk
   2 Could go either way
   1 Poor risk
   0 Will need a lot of help to make it work

5. Mental/Physical Health ____
   3 Excellent
   2 Good   Retarded ____
   1 Fair   Psychotic ____
   0 Poor

6. Parole Plan ____
   3 Strong parole plan
   2 Has not gotten job or residence
   1 Has skills but no parole plan
   0 No skills, no plan, no interest

7. Institutional Behavior ____
   2 Good instit. behavior
   1 Discipline reports of minor nature
     or none in past six to nine months
   0 Poor record

8. Substance Abuse ____
   3 None
   2 Little or long ago
   1 Some or questionable
   0 Much

9. Attitude ____
   3 High/positive motivation
   2 Cooperative
   1 Lackadaisical
   0 Negative/hostile

10. Community ____
   3 Much community support
   2 Community noncommittal
   1 No community support
   0 Community antagonistic
     to offender return

11. Past Criminal Record ____
   3 No or minor past record
   2 Past record marginal
   1 Other felonies
   0 Lengthy past record

12. Programming ____
   3 Has taken advantage
     of vocational/social/
     educational opportunities
   2 Has made good use of time
   1 Cooperated but showed little initiative

Boards Decision:
   Pass _____
   Continue _____
   Parole _____
   Detainer _____
   Parole to _____

The Convicts' Perspectives

The convicts' views of parole boards have generally been unfavorable. They see it as an arbitrary body whose main purpose is social control. In jurisdictions with discretionary release, convicts invariably are unsure how to prepare themselves for parole hearings or how to behave during their interviews. This ambiguity colors their entire prison experience, which often becomes an exercise in how to con the parole board. Malcolm Braly, ex-convict and best-selling author, states that from the time he entered the prison and throughout his time inside, he was waiting to appear before the California Adult Authority (A.A.). Most inmates appear before the A.A. once a year, and if they are denied, they immediately begin waiting for their next appearance, always hoping to "get a date," telling them when they will be released and can start their lives over again.

Braly emphasized that no one knew exactly how long they had to serve—his sentence was one year to life, giving the A.A. "a lot of time to play with." But he also said that most knew about how much time they had, and no conversation was more interesting than one involving trying to figure out how to predict what the Adult Authority was looking for, debating which programs to participate in, determining how much public pressure there was, and discussing which members of the A.A. were liberal and which were conservative. Braly thought that the inmates knew within a few months how much time they would do, and even if they knew they did not have a chance at parole during a particular hearing, it would not stop them from dreaming that they would be set free. He said it drove him crazy that these people could release him from prison on the basis of a whim, and there was nothing the guard force could do about it. But he also knew it was very difficult to make a favorable impression. The board had seen it all, and they knew the inmates would say anything to get out, which, Braly admits, is the truth.[24]

Another author-inmate, Walter Burckhard, reflects about his upcoming parole board appearance.

> This time, I thought, I'll tell no lies. This time I'll ease into the armchair, rest my forearms on the chair arms, set my left ankle on my right knee and not budge an inch, except for maybe a thought-out poignant gesture of emphasis, a gentle gesture. What a gentle man is he, they will say.
>
> I should lie, my destiny is in the hands of men who know all motives but their own, but I won't. I haven't prepared any speeches, so I can't. I'll trust in the immediate. I knew a man who would silently begin his orations months beforehand. I'd come to his cell and he'd be staring at the wall, dark circles under his eyes, his lips moving as he invented both sides of the argument. Every time they would ask questions he hadn't thought of.[25]

The traumatic aspect of appearing before a parole board, when your freedom is on the line, can be seen in the following excerpt from a conversation (taped by a parole officer) with an anonymous inmate who was so nervous before his parole hearing that he vomited and became disoriented:

Then they came to the door and told me to come in and . . . I walked over, I sat down and said my hellos more or less and I was still feeling upset over being sick and my mind really wasn't working at all. The first question that guy asked me took me a long time to answer. . . . He asked me what I was trying to prove to the world and [of] all the questions that ran through my mind the night before and all that day that wasn't one of them that I thought about. . . . I was nervous and shaky and my hands were twitching.

I wanted to look around the room and see who else was there. You know, I just couldn't move my head. I couldn't take my eyes off this guy because I was afraid he was going to throw . . . a question under the table I wasn't ready for and I wanted to be ready for it. I waited for the other two guys to start firing you know saying you should have done this or you shouldn't have done that or why didn't you do that and they never said a word, not once. I got uptight because nobody yelled at me. No one yelled and no one said you should have done this or you should have done that. Nobody got on my case. It upset me.[26]

Convicts hold varied assumptions about the factors used by parole board members to reach a decision. Many of these assumptions develop from the fact that most parole decisions are made in private, with the inmate out of the room. This practice, although meant to protect the confidentiality of parole board members' actions, does not help the inmate understand his or her fate any better. Moreover, research by West-Smith and her colleagues suggests that inmates believe that good institutional behavior, completion of programs, and a good parole plan will result in a release decision by the parole board. However, this research found that parole boards first look at the inmate's offense and incarceration history, and also determine whether the time served is adequate punishment for the crime, when they make a release decision. This different understanding of how parole decisions are made can lead to confused and angry inmates if they are denied parole even though they have done everything they think they need to do to make parole.[27]

It is, therefore, understandable that a denial of parole often triggers bitter resentment against a system that is seen as being stacked against individual inmates. The following comment reflects such resentment and was made by an inmate whose parole hearing went sour when one parole board member started talking about a recent crime committed by a parolee in another part of the state:

he starts talking about that guy who was passing checks in L.A. and blew some bull out when the bust came down. He's talkin' like he thinks I'm goin' out, get a checkbook and a gun, and blow some bull out. What kind of shit is that? Man, I just gave up! I can talk about my beef, but how in hell can I defend myself on somebody else's beef? . . . Yeah, they'll probably deny me on what somebody else did—but let some poor motherfucker go up there talkin' about he oughta get out 'cause everybody else with a beef like his is gettin' out—you'll see how fast he gets to be an individual case, they'll give him a good goddamn individual screwing right quick."[28]

Some inmates have thoughtfully examined the parole process and in so doing have enumerated what they perceive as flaws in decision making. The observations of ex-inmate Ed Tromanhauser fall into that category; he has three gripes about parole decision making.

- The first gripe deals with the weight given an inmate's past record. Inmates who are continually denied parole for their "past record" are frustrated because there is nothing they can do to change this, leading to feelings of helplessness and anger. There is no way to "rehabilitate" one's past record.
- Closely related is the gripe that both the parole board and the inmate know that turning an inmate down for parole does not increase his probability of success; that he will have an even lower probability of success if *not* paroled, having spent additional years in the negative prison environment.
- The third gripe is that parole boards are too easily influenced by outside sources: letters by police officers or prosecutors, newspaper editorials and letters to the editor opposing parole for someone, and pressure from victims.[29]

Inmates frequently complain that procedures governing parole hearings are not administered in a fair and equitable manner. The issue of how hearings should be conducted and who should be present at those hearings traditionally has been left to individual states. For example, five state boards do not allow face-to-face hearings, twenty-one allow the media to be present at hearings, but thirty-three do not allow videocameras.[30] Thirty-five states allow victims to attend parole hearings.[31] In some instances, concerns about the conduct of hearings have escalated into legal suits.

In 1970 the case of *Menechino v. Oswald* reached the U.S. Court of Appeals. Inmate Menechino claimed that his due process rights, guaranteed by the Fourteenth Amendment, had been abridged by absence of counsel at his parole release hearing. The court held that parole hearings were not adversarial proceedings because rehabilitation was the major concern, and further that parole decision making necessarily involved a wide range of considerations not involving the facts of the case, such as the inmate's mental health, moral attitude, and emotional balance, as well as the extent of community resources available. The court was clear that due process rights did not cover initial parole hearings, wondering if it is even required that parole boards hold hearings to decide whether a prisoner should be released on parole. The court also differentiated between a parole hearing and a revocation hearing, noting that a board's decision regarding release on parole is an aspect of prison discipline, not an adversarial proceeding. Therefore, despite the dissenting opinion pointing out the "gravity of the consequences" of a parole hearing leading to the belief that a prisoner in a parole release hearing should be allowed to be represented by an attorney, the majority of the court ruled that representation by counsel at a parole hearing was not required.[32]

This decision, and general prisoner discontent with parole board decision-making practices, was in part instrumental in the move toward determinant sentencing and away from parole. In the 1970s, many prisoners' rights groups strongly opposed indeterminate sentencing, and during the Attica prison riots, inmates prominently displayed a banner proclaiming ABOLISH PAROLE.

The issue of how much discretion individual states should have in determining procedures for parole-granting hearings was argued before the Supreme Court in *Greenholtz v. Inmates of Nebraska,* 1979. This landmark decision, which defined the nature and substance of parole hearings, should be closely examined.

The Greenholtz *Case*

In *Greenholtz v. Inmates of Nebraska Penal and Correctional Complex,* the Supreme Court finally decided the question of whether due process applied to parole release decisions, and if so, how much process inmates were due. Their answer was yes, but not by much. By a five to four vote the court found that in specific instances (depending on the language of the state's parole law) due process did apply to parole release, but that process is limited to (1) an opportunity to be heard and (2) in case of denial, information about why the inmate fell short of qualifying. Although this decision significantly impacted parole, it did so in an unusual way.

The Supreme Court had always been reluctant to interfere with correctional practices, preferring to leave such matters in the hands of practitioner "experts." Therefore, when it broke its traditional silence, correctional practices invariably were altered. This was certainly the case in earlier decisions, especially *Morrissey v. Brewer, Gagnon v. Scarpelli,* and *Wolff v. McDonnel.* The *Morrissey* and *Gagnon* rulings changed the nature of supervision practices by requiring that formal hearings be held before parole and probation could be revoked, whereas *Wolff* changed the prison discipline process by mandating that officials substantiate "flagrant and serious misconduct" before an inmate's good-time credits could be taken away.[33]

All three of these rulings applied substantial due process guarantees to correctional procedures in which an individual's liberty was in question. The decisions served to limit correctional discretion by creating formal procedures at which the offender could expect a fair hearing, and from which an appeal was possible. In *Greenholtz,* the Court broke from this pattern by affirming the status quo and allowing parole release procedures to continue unchanged. Individual states interpreted the decision to mean that it was possible for them to structure parole release hearings as they saw fit. The decision ended the possibility of challenging parole hearings on constitutional grounds and, in essence, left the inmate at the mercy of state parole laws and release proceedings. The *Greenholtz* decision did not follow up on *Morrissey v. Brewer* rulings reducing institutional discretion; instead, it defined the parole hearing as an informal process governed by subjective interpretation.

On the one hand, the *Greenholtz* Court paid lip service to the goal of inmate rehabilitation. On the other hand, it did not consider that inmates who believe the parole process is blatantly unfair are problematic candidates for rehabilitation. From reading the Court's ruling, it is clear that the majority felt that adversarial proceedings are somehow antithetical to inmate rehabilitation. This perspective assumes that as long as the goal of rehabilitation is foremost, correctional officials need not be restrained by concern for due process. However, overlooking individual rights in the name of correctional rehabilitation has, in the past, proven counterproductive and even dangerous.[34] There is little reason to believe that parole release is exempt from similar concerns. The *Greenholtz* ruling, in a strange line of reasoning, raised the possibility that if states were burdened with excessive procedural demands, they might discontinue their "experiment" with parole. There was no evidence that any state had even contemplated taking such a step. Also, parole is an institutionalized correctional practice, not a tentative experiment.

The prisoners did achieve a moral victory of sorts because the court ruled that parole release hearings must have some procedural safeguards. However, the safeguards listed as essential and sufficient are so basic and implicit that parole boards (including Nebraska) already provided such guarantees and did not have to alter existing procedures to be in full compliance with *Greenholtz*. Even those minimal due process rights, according to the *Greenholtz* Court, applied only if state codes included a specific type of language that made the possibility of parole more likely (for example, including the term "shall receive parole unless" followed by certain conditions). Lacking such precise language, release hearings are not governed by due process restraints; they are discretionary hearings.

The *Greenholtz* decision was further expressed by the court in 1987 in *Montana Board of Pardons v. Allen*. In *Allen*, the court ruled that the language of the Montana statute, "the board *shall* release on Parole . . . ," created the expectation that parole would be granted "when" certain criteria were met.[35] This semantic requirement is not merely an academic point because subsequent lower court decisions, reviewing the parole statutes of Arkansas, Nevada, Ohio, and Oklahoma, concluded that because these codes lacked a "shall/unless" provision, inmates were not entitled to constitutional protection at parole release hearings.[36] Justice Marshall, in a strong dissenting opinion, questioned the decision's basic fairness and lack of concern for the "most elementary due process protection."[37] To fully understand the ruling and its impact it is necessary to scrutinize the facts and circumstances of the case.

In 1972 several inmates of the Nebraska Penal and Correctional Complex, claiming several improprieties in the hearing process, filed a class action suit in federal court against John D. Greenholtz, chairman of the parole board. Nebraska State Parole Board policies held that

> Whenever the Board of Parole considers the release of a committed offender who is eligible for release on parole, it shall order his release unless it is of the opinion that his release should be deferred because:
>
> (a) There is considerable risk that he will not conform to the conditions of parole;
> (b) His release would depreciate the seriousness of his crime or promote disrespect for law;
> (c) His release would have a substantially adverse effect on institutional discipline; or
> (d) His continued correctional treatment, medical care, or vocational or other training in the facility will substantially enhance his capacity to lead a law-abiding life when released at a later date.[38]

The inmates specifically claimed that parole release procedures violated their Fourteenth Amendment right to due process by

- failing to inform the inmates of the criteria which they must meet to obtain a parole or work release;
- failing to inform the inmates in advance of the date and time of their hearing before the Parole Board;
- failing to permit the inmates to present evidence or call witnesses in their own behalf;
- failing to confront the inmates with the evidence presented that opposed their release on parole or work release;
- failing to give the inmates the right to cross-examine witnesses who appeared before the Parole Board in opposition to the inmate's release on parole or work release;
- failing to maintain a complete and permanent record of all proceedings held in considering release of inmates on parole or work release;
- failing to permit full representation of inmates by legal counsel in the proceedings before the Parole Board and failing to provide such counsel to indigent inmates;
- failing to provide inmates denied parole or work release with specific written reasons for the denial; and
- failing to inform inmates of the evidence relied on to deny the parole or work release.[39]

Both the district and the appeal courts agreed with the inmates' contention that due process should be applied to parole release hearings. The Nebraska attorney general appealed the appellate ruling to the Supreme Court, who accepted the case. The inmates' argument rested on two assumptions: (1) that parole release hearings were essentially the same as revocation hearings and, therefore, should be accorded similar constitutional protection and (2) the language of Nebraska's statute creates a legitimate expectation of parole, thus invoking due process protection.

The Supreme Court, in its 1979 decision, reflected the inmates' first argument, stating that parole release and parole revocation are very different: One is a conditional liberty one desires, the other is being deprived of liberty one already has. Thus, the parolees in *Morrissey* and the probationers in *Gagnon* were already free and could lead "normal" lives. The inmates in *Nebraska,* however, are confined and therefore ". . . subject to all of the necessary restraints that inhere in a prison."[40]

The Court indicated there was a second important distinction between revocation and release: namely, that revocation involved factual decision making, whereas the parole release decision is more subtle and depends on several factors, including facts but also some purely subjective evaluations by the board members based on their experiences. Therefore, unlike a revocation decision, which is determined by facts, in a parole release decision there is no set of facts that, if shown, require a decision favorable to the individual. Parole decisions are discretionary, the Court ruled, and primarily involve deciding what a man is and what he may become rather than simply what he has done.[41]

The Court agreed with the inmates that "the word 'shall' binds the Board of Parole to release an inmate unless any one of the four specifically designated reasons [for denial] are found."[42] After this agreement, the issue became how many procedural safeguards should be required. The Court laid the groundwork for a narrow interpretation of due process by stating that our system encourages experimentation, believing that if parole hearings are burdened by unnecessary procedures, states may stop the "experiment." Just because rehabilitation has not reached the expectations of the past does not mean states should stop trying to rehabilitate convicted persons to be useful, law-abiding citizens. Encouraging adversarial relations between an inmate and the state does not contribute to the goals of rehabilitation.[43]

The *Greenholtz* Court then eliminated two important procedures mandated by the Appellate Court namely, "the requirement that a formal hearing be held for every inmate, and the requirement that every adverse parole decision include a statement of the evidence relied upon by the Board."[44] When these safeguards were stricken, Nebraska release procedures were in accord with minimum due process and need not be altered because, in the Court's final statement, "The Constitution does not require more."[45]

The end result of this case was that parole boards throughout the United States could continue with their release procedures unfettered with constitutional concerns. According to many legal scholars, the *Greenholtz* decision followed a pattern of deferential treatment of states' rights and a narrowing of due process safeguards. Susan Herman, writing in the *New York University Law Review,* stated: "Identical depravations of freedom are treated differently, depending on how the state characterizes the deprivation; the meaning of due process varies from state to state."[46] While the states retain their discretion, it is doubtful the parole process has been enhanced by the *Greenholtz* decision. Fred Cohen, editor of the *Criminal Law Bulletin,* for example, stated: "*Greenholtz* . . . invites states to deal with eligible inmates as numbers and case files and to continue the uncertainty and 'having been hustled' feeling expressed by many inmates."[47]

Although *Greenholtz* effectively removed judicial pressure to change release procedures, several states have chosen to grant certain privileges during parole hearings. For example, twenty-one states allow the use of counsel, and inmates are allowed to present witnesses in nineteen states.[48] Most states also have laws or rules regarding how much time an inmate must serve before being eligible for parole. For example, some require the completion of the minimum sentence before being eligible; others require an inmate complete a portion of his or her sentence—for example, one-third—before becoming eligible for parole consideration. Other states have independently undertaken efforts to structure the parole-granting decision. Such efforts generally involve either the use of predictive scales or the implementation of sentencing guidelines. In either case the elusive goal is equitable treatment for similarly situated offenders. Both are part of a general trend in corrections to structure release decisions, a topic to which we now turn.

Structuring Release Decisions

Salient Factor Scores

The idea of devising predictive scales to aid parole decision makers is an old one. In 1923, Sam Warner, after examining the records of Massachusetts inmates, developed a list of criteria used by parole board members in their decisions to grant parole. He demonstrated that many of the criteria, for example, sexual indulgence, use of tobacco, or sweetheart's character, had little or no effect on parole success or failure. Warner suggested that a limited number of variables were real-life determinants of parole behavior and that these variables could be placed into a predictive scale.[49] In 1928, Burgess related offense variables with offender characteristics and assigned numerical values to those factors that proved predictive. The end result was a scoring table that purported to predict an offender's chance of parole success.[50] These first efforts were later refined, and in 1973, Gottfredson, Wilkins, and Hoffman developed a sophisticated scoring device called the **salient factor score** for use as an assessment of an applicant's probable success on parole.[51] The federal government implemented the salient factor score in conjunction with offense severity to develop a parole decision-making matrix. Subsequently, several other state parole boards adopted versions of the federal guidelines.

The federal parole system used a printed guideline table called a matrix to rate parole applicants. The applicant's salient factor score (a combination of six predictive variables) was placed on a horizontal axis, and the offender's crime severity rating (based on the offense for which the defendant was sentenced) was ranged on a vertical axis. To determine length of sentence, the scorer plots the intersection of the two axes and arrives at a range of months to be served. In this manner, an offender with a "good" salient factor who committed a "moderate" offense, such as embezzlement of less than $40,000, would serve up to ten months. However, an offender with a "poor" salient factor score, convicted of the same crime of embezzlement, should serve between twenty-four and thirty-two months. An offender with a "poor" salient factor rating, who committed a serious offense such as robbery, would receive between sixty and seventy-two months. The point scale used to arrive at a salient factor score is listed in Figure 6.6. The federal matrix used for determining length of sentence can be seen in Figure 6.7.

Many states followed the federal system's lead by also adopting parole guidelines. The Michigan Parole Board, for example, uses a parole guideline score sheet that classifies prisoners' probability of parole into three categories: high, average, and low. The board places prisoners within these categories by looking at each prisoner's current offense, prior criminal history, conduct in prison, assaultive and property risk, age, programs successfully completed while in prison, and past or present mental health. In most cases, the parole board is not required to interview prisoners classified as high probability of parole success before granting them parole. The board is also not required to interview those placed in the

FIGURE 6.6 *Salient Factor Score (SFS 98)*

SALIENT FACTOR SCORE (SFS 98)

Item A.   PRIOR CONVICTIONS/ADJUDICATIONS *(ADULT OR JUVENILE)*......................

None = 3; One = 2; Two or three = 1; Four or more = 0

Item B.   PRIOR COMMITMENT(S) OF MORE THAN 30 DAYS *(ADULT/JUVENILE)* ....

None = 2; One or two=1; Three or more = 0

Item C.   AGE AT CURRENT OFFENSE/PRIOR COMMITMENTS................................

26 years or more	Three or fewer prior commitments	= 3
	Four prior commitments	= 2
	Five or more commitments	= 1
22-25 years	Three or fewer prior commitments	= 2
	Four prior commitments	= 1
	Five or more commitments	= 0
20-21 years	Three or fewer prior commitments	= 1
	Four prior commitments	= 0
19 years or less	Any number of prior commitments	= 0

Item D.   RECENT COMMITMENT FREE PERIOD *(THREE YEARS)* ....

No prior commitment of more than 30 days (adult or juvenile) or released to the community from last such commitment at least 3 years prior to the commencement of the current offense =1; Otherwise = 0

Item E.   PROBATION/PAROLE/CONFINEMENT/ESCAPE STATUS VIOLATOR THIS TIME ....

Neither on probation, parole, confinement, or escape status at the time of the current offense; nor committed as a probation, parole, confinement, or escape status violator this time =1; Otherwise = 0

Item F.   OLDER OFFENDERS ....

If the offender was 41 years of age or more at the commencement of the current offense (and the total score from Items A - F above is 9 or less) = 1; Otherwise = 0

TOTAL SCORE ....

Source: U.S. Parole Commission, *Rules and Procedures Manual.* Retrieved March 1, 2001, from www.usdoj.gov/uspc/rules_procedures/rulesmanual.htm

FIGURE 6.7 *Guidelines for Decision Making* (guidelines for decision making customary total time to be served before release [including jail time])

Offense Characteristics	Offender Characteristics: Parole Prognosis Guideline Range (Salient Factor Score 1998)			
Severity of Offense Behavior	Very Good (10–8)	Good (7–6)	Fair (5–4)	Poor (3–0)
Category One	≤4 months	≤8 months	8–12 months	12–16 months
Category Two	≤6 months	≤10 months	12–16 months	16–22 months
Category Three	≤10 months	12–16 months	18–24 months	24–32 months
Category Four	12–18 months	20–26 months	26–34 months	34–44 months
Category Five	24–36 months	36–48 months	48–60 months	60–72 months
Category Six	40–52 months	52–64 months	64–78 months	78–100 months
Category Seven	52–80 months	64–92 months	78–110 months	100–148 months
Category Eight[a]	100+ months	120+ months	150+ months	180+ months

[a]*Note:* For Category Eight, no upper limits are specified due to the extreme variability of the cases within this category. For decisions exceeding the lower limit of the applicable guideline category *by more than 48 months,* the Commission will specify the pertinent case factors upon which it relied in reaching its decision, which may include the absence of any factors mitigating the offense.

Source: U.S. Parole Commission, *Rules and Procedures Manual.* Retrieved March 1, 2001, from www.usdoj.gov/uspc/rules_procedures/rulesmanual.htm

low range of parole success before denying them parole. The board must interview all other prisoners.[52]

The Texas Board of Pardons and Paroles uses parole guidelines combining a risk assessment instrument and an offense severity scale to guide their parole decisions. The risk assessment instrument includes static and dynamic factors. Static factors are those that cannot change, such as age of first admission to a juvenile or adult correctional facility, prior incarcerations, employment history, and the current commitment offense. Dynamic factors are variables that can or do change, such as offender's age, gang affiliation, education, vocational training, and current prison custody level. Risk assessment scores are combined with an offense severity rating for the sentenced offense of record to determine a parole candidate's guidelines level.[53]

Even though predictive scales and other parole guidelines have been available for many years, some parole boards were reluctant to formally implement them. For example, Colorado did not approve the use of an empirically based matrix that was structured from the board's past decision making.[54] One reason for this refusal comes from the parole board members' views of themselves as individual decision makers who consider each case on its own merits. Scoring instruments are seen as dehumanizing, coldly removing the human factor from parole release decisions. Additionally, parole board members believe that overreliance on scales could cause them to release notorious inmates whose premature presence in the community would cause public indignation.

Adding to concerns of board members is the fact that criminal justice researchers have seriously questioned whether scoring devices can, in fact, accurately predict future criminal activity. In a National Institute of Justice research note, distinguished scholars Norval Morris and Marc Miller enumerated the problematic aspects of predicting violent and dangerous criminal behavior.[55] Some academicians have argued that parole guidelines, which place considerable weight on the offender's prior criminal record, are discriminatory because minority group members, based on historical patterns of selective arrest and enforcement, are likely to have police records.[56]

Arguments for the use of empirical scoring devices center on both practical and ethical issues. Because parole board members throughout the United States are faced with numerous applications, they simply do not have the time to thoroughly consider individual cases. Using scoring tools significantly simplifies processing an inmate's parole application. Parole guidelines have been advocated on the basis that they will reduce discretion while increasing equity and fairness. Scoring devices, by making implicit the standards used for parole release, allow applicants to understand the reasons for those decisions. If they are properly used, parole guidelines should ensure that similar offenders will be treated similarly. Peter Hoffman, the former head of the U.S. Parole Commission, indicated that by adopting written guidelines parole boards could escape criticism of unfettered discretion, decision inconsistency, and disparity.[57] Also, in his 1994 study of the effectiveness of the salient factor score (SFS), Hoffman concluded that the SFS was still accurate after seventeen years of use, that it is "able to separate prisoners into categories having significantly different probabilities of recidivism."[58] The National Advisory Commission on Criminal Justice Standards and Goals stated

> The absence of written criteria by which decisions are made constitutes a major failing in virtually every parole jurisdiction. . . . Parole boards must free themselves from total concern with case-by-case decision-making and attend to articulation of the actual policies that govern the decision-making process.[59]

Another development in the battle against disparity has been the implementation of sentencing guidelines.

Sentencing Guidelines

Rather than waiting for parole boards to make comparable dissimilar sentences for similarly situated offenders, as is done with salient factor scores, many jurisdictions have attacked the problem at the point of sentencing. From this perspective, guidelines should be followed by judges, not parole boards. Sentencing guidelines, in some instances, take release decisions away from parole boards completely (except in cases of inmates sentenced before the guidelines went into effect). In 1983, Florida implemented sentencing guidelines with the intended goal of eliminating "unwarranted variation in the sentencing process by reducing the subjectivity in interpreting specific offense- and offender-related criteria and in defining their relative importance in the sentencing decision." The Florida guidelines also attempted to reduce sentencing variations that were not based on "the instant offense as well as the nature and length of the offender's criminal history."[60] By relying on these factors, David Griswold concluded: "Florida's guidelines are most consistent with incapacitation which calls for isolating other members of society until their risk of future criminality is diminished." However, after examining the effects of Florida's policy, Griswold found that discretion and disparity had not been eliminated. Variables that were not included in the sentencing guidelines, such as whether there was a negotiated plea or a probation violation, significantly increased "unwarranted sentencing disparity."[61]

The federal government overhauled its sentencing policies in 1984, instituting **sentencing guidelines.** Led by Senator Edward Kennedy, the Comprehensive Crime Control Act was enacted. The reform bill established determinant sentencing in that the sentence imposed by the judge is the actual sentence an offender will serve, minus good-time credit. After November 1, 1987, parole boards no longer make release decisions on newly sentenced cases. A sentencing commission, consisting of seven voting members appointed by the president and confirmed by the Senate, establishes sentencing guidelines that serve to structure judicial discretion. The sentencing commission establishes the criteria to be used in sentencing decisions. The guidelines set an offense level from one to forty-three for every crime, with low levels for minor crimes and high levels for serious crimes. Prior record is then factored in. A person with a clean record receives zero points and points are added for each offense of record. The judge looks on a grid for the point where the offense level intersects the criminal history and a period of time in custody is determined. Aggravating and mitigating circumstances can then increase or decrease the final sentence and the inmate is not released until the sentence is completed, minus any good time earned (a maximum of fifty-four days of good time can be earned per year in the federal system).[62] The federal sentencing guidelines grid is depicted in Figure 6.8.

In early 1988, sentencing guidelines were challenged in several U.S. district courts on constitutional grounds, but in 1989 the Supreme Court ruled in *Mistretta v. United States* (488 U.S. 361) that the statute is constitutional. Today, besides the federal system, about one-third of the states use sentencing guidelines, although each jurisdiction uses its own version. There have been calls to change the laws in

FIGURE 6.8   *2002 Federal Sentencing Guidelines*

Sentencing Table (in months of imprisonment)
Criminal History Category (Criminal History Points)

	Offense Level	I (0 or 1)	II (2 or 3)	III (4, 5, 6)	IV (7, 8, 9)	V (10, 11, 12)	VI (13 or more)
	1	0–6	0–6	0–6	0–6	0–6	0–6
	2	0–6	0–6	0–6	0–6	0–6	1–7
	3	0–6	0–6	0–6	0–6	2–8	3–9
	4	0–6	0–6	0–6	2–8	4–10	6–12
Zone A	5	0–6	0–6	1–7	4–10	6–12	9–15
	6	0–6	1–7	2–8	6–12	9–15	12–18
	7	0–6	2–8	4–10	8–14	12–18	15–21
	8	0–6	4–10	6–12	10–16	15–21	18–24
	9	4–10	6–12	8–14	12–18	18–24	21–27
Zone B	10	6–12	8–14	10–16	15–21	21–27	24–30
	11	8–14	10–16	12–18	18–24	24–30	27–33
Zone C	12	10–16	12–18	15–21	21–27	27–33	30–37
Zone D	13	12–18	15–21	18–24	24–30	30–37	33–41
	14	15–21	18–24	21–27	27–33	33–41	37–46
	15	18–24	21–27	24–30	30–37	37–46	41–51
	16	21–27	24–30	27–33	33–41	41–51	46–57
	17	24–30	27–33	30–37	37–46	46–57	51–63
	18	27–33	30–37	33–41	41–51	51–63	57–71
	19	30–37	33–41	37–46	46–57	57–71	63–78
	20	33–41	37–46	41–51	51–63	63–78	70–87
	21	37–46	41–51	46–57	57–71	70–87	77–96
	22	41–51	46–57	51–63	63–78	77–96	84–105
	23	46–57	51–63	57–71	70–87	84–105	92–115
	24	51–63	57–71	63–78	77–96	92–115	100–125
	25	57–71	63–78	70–87	84–105	100–125	110–137
	26	63–78	70–87	78–97	92–115	110–137	120–150
	27	70–87	78–97	87–108	100–125	120–150	130–162
	28	78–97	87–108	97–121	110–137	130–162	140–175
	29	87–108	97–121	108–135	121–151	140–175	151–188
	30	97–121	108–135	121–151	135–168	151–788	168–210

FIGURE 6.8 *Continued*

	Offense Level	I (0 or 1)	II (2 or 3)	III (4, 5, 6)	IV (7, 8, 9)	V (10, 11, 12)	VI (13 or more)
Zone D	31	108–135	121–151	135–168	151–188	168–210	188–235
(continued)	32	121–151	135–168	151–188	168–210	188–235	210–262
	33	135–168	151–188	168–210	188–235	210–262	235–293
	34	151–188	168–210	188–235	210–262	235–293	262–327
	35	168–210	188–235	210–262	235–293	262–327	292–365
	36	188–235	210–262	235–293	262–327	292–365	324–405
	37	210–262	235–293	262–327	292–365	324–405	360–life
	38	235–293	262–327	292–365	324–405	360–life	360–life
	39	262–327	292–365	324–405	360–life	360–life	360–life
	40	292–365	324–405	360–life	360–life	360–life	360–life
	41	324–405	360–life	360–life	360–life	360–life	360–life
	42	360–life	360–life	360–life	360–life	360–life	360–life
	43	life	life	life	life	life	life

Sentencing Table (In months of imprisonment)
Criminal History Category (Criminal History Points)

Commentary to Sentencing Table
Application Notes:
  1. The offense level (1–43) forms the vertical axis of the sentencing table. The criminal history category (I–VI) forms the horizontal axis of the table. The intersection of the offense level and criminal history category displays the guideline range in months of imprisonment. "Life" means life imprisonment. For example, the guideline range applicable to a defendant with an offense level of 15 and a criminal history category of III is 24–30 months of imprisonment.
  2. In rare cases, a total offense level of less than 1 or more than 43 may result from application of the guidelines. A total offense level of less than 1 is to be treated as an offense level of 1. An offense level of more than 43 is to be treated as an offense level of 43.

Source: U.S. Sentencing Commission, *Guidelines Manual.* Retrieved November 2002, from www.ussc.gov/2002guid/5a.htm

order to continue some form of discretionary parole release, and these efforts have been vigorously opposed by congressional leaders. Most of the criticism of guidelines centers around the need for more judicial discretion and the dramatic increase in costs of corrections attributed to the implementation of the guidelines. Regarding the first criticism, The Coalition for Federal Sentencing Reform bemoans the fact that judges have no flexibility in sentencing: ". . . the federal guidelines are not simply guidelines, as the name suggests: they are mandatory. Judges are required to follow them, no matter how inappropriate the result. The loss of flexibility makes it impossible to tailor the punishment to fit the crime and the criminal."[63] The coalition also points out that the federal guidelines, and by inference the state guidelines, are one reason for the tremendous growth in corrections in the past fifteen years. For example, the number of federal prisoners quadrupled between 1980 and 1996, from 24,000 to 106,000. The increase has meant that taxpayers have had to pay for fifty new federal prisons during that time, which has led to a commensurate fourfold increase in the budget. Additionally, it costs approximately $22,000 to $25,000 per year to incarcerate each of these inmates. The cost of incarcerating the nonviolent, low-level drug offenders alone costs about $1.7 billion annually.[64] Nonetheless, in their history of federal sentencing guidelines, the coalition concludes: "The general experience has been that guidelines represent an improvement over unfettered judicial discretion, but that they must be well structured and carefully conceived in order to succeed."[65]

Summary

There are several ways inmates can be released from prison. About 40 percent achieve mandatory release: They complete their sentence minus good-time credits and must be released. About 20 percent are released early through discretionary parole. Most of the rest complete their maximum sentence and then must be released (max out). Discretionary release is controlled by state parole boards whose members are often appointed by governors. These boards vary considerably in composition. Some states use part-time members with little or no correctional experience, whereas others employ full-time correctional specialists. The criteria used by parole members to make release decisions also varies but is focused on the meaning of imprisonment, the protection of society, and readiness for release.

Inmates who apply for early release typically receive hearings before parole boards. These hearings frequently are traumatic experiences for inmates who are uncertain how to prepare themselves for release as well as how to impress parole board members. Prisoners express frequent complaints that parole procedures are unfair and that board decisions are arbitrary. Inmate complaints about parole policies have been the focus of several lawsuits. One of these suits, *Greenholtz v. Inmates of Nebraska Penal and Correctional Complex* reached the Supreme Court. In the *Greenholtz* case, the Court ruled that parole release hearings were governed by due process safeguards, limited to an opportunity to be heard and a brief indication why inmates did not qualify for release. The Court specifically held that parole release was qualitatively different from parole revocation; therefore, *Morrissey v. Brewer* guarantees were not applicable to release hearings. The Court's ruling left undisturbed the right of states to exercise wide discretion in establishing parole release policies.

Many states and the federal government have developed and implemented predictive devices, such as salient factor scores, and combined them with offense severity ratings to structure parole board decision making. In a continuing effort to curb judicial disparity and move toward equal treatment for similarly situated offenders, some jurisdictions have implemented sentencing guidelines that restrict or eliminate discretionary parole. The federal system, effective November 1, 1987, did away with parole release (for prisoners sentenced after that date) and empowered a sentencing commission with structuring specific guidelines for judicial sentencing.

Key People and Terms

Consolidated parole board (180)
Determinate sentencing (183)
Discretionary parole (178)
Independent parole board (180)
Mandatory release (178)
Max out (179)

Meritorious good time (178)
Lloyd Ohlin (187)
Salient factor score (197)
Sentencing guidelines (201)
Truth-in-sentencing (174)

Key Legal Cases

Gagnon v. Scarpelli
*Greenholtz v. Inmates of Nebraska Penal
    and Correctional Complex*
Menechino v. Oswald

Mistretta v. United States
Montana Board of Pardons v. Allen
Morrissey v. Brewer
Wolff v. McDonnel

Questions for Discussion and Review

1. Compare and contrast the three major ways prisoners are released from prison.

2. Discuss the difference between independent and consolidated parole boards.

3. What are some of the different ways parole board members are selected in the states? How will these different methods affect the decision-making process?

4. What is structured decision making?

5. List and discuss the three main problem areas Ohlin identified as evident in parole decision making.

6. Summarize convicts' perspectives on parole release decisions.

7. Discuss the significance of the *Greenholtz* case on due process rights for inmates at parole hearings.

8. Discuss the significance of salient factor scores in release decisions.

9. What are sentencing guidelines and how have they affected the sentencing and release process?

Relevant Internet Sites

Directory of State Parole Boards: www.crimelynx.com/stateparole.html

Association of Paroling Authorities International: www.apaintl.org

U.S. Sentencing Commission: www.ussc.gov/index.htm

Coalition for Federal Sentencing Reform: www.sentencing.org

EXERCISE • *The Decision to Grant Parole*

Different states have different sentencing structures. Those with indeterminate sentencing structures have parole boards making release decisions. The individual's sentence may determine when he or she is eligible for release, but the paroling authority decides if and when an offender is actually released. In the following case, imagine you are a member of a parole board with the task of determining whether to release this offender and, if so, under what conditions. In making your decision, you may want to consider the likelihood of recidivism, the offender's institutional behavior, the release plan developed, and the potential impact on the victim.

Offender Jones: Jones is serving a five- to fifteen-year sentence for forcible rape. While he and his then-wife were high on cocaine, she refused his sexual advances and he brutally raped her. He has served the minimum of four and a half years necessary to be eligible for his first parole hearing. He has no prior convictions or arrests and has been a model prisoner, completing an education program and a sex offender treatment program while in prison. He also has attended Narcotics Anonymous (NA) meetings once a week for the past year, missing only a few meetings, and has no disciplinary write-ups. While he was in prison, his grandmother died, leaving him her house in his hometown, a town of about 40,000, which is also the town where the offense was committed. He has been offered his old job back, working for his father's construction firm building homes. His release plan includes moving into his grandmother's house, working for his father, paying court-ordered child support, seeking further sex-offender treatment in the community, attending NA meetings, and completing an anger management course. His victim and their two children remain in the home they all shared at the time of the crime. She has not had any contact with him during his incarceration and has not let him see his children. In her victim statement, she says that she is fearful of his reaction when he gets out, afraid that he might seek her out for revenge. In his release plan he states that he feels "very bad" about what he did, feels no animosity toward his ex-wife, and wants desperately to see his children again. A parole officer would supervise him if this inmate were released.

Notes

1. Quoted in John J. DiIulio, *Governing Prisons: A Comparative Study of Correctional Management* (New York: Free Press, 1987) 109.

2. Erik Olin Wright, "The Meaning of Prison in the Lives of Prisoners," in *Criminal Justice: Allies and Adversaries*, eds. John R. Snortum and Ilana Hadar (Pacific Palisades, CA: Palisades Publishers, 1978) 186.

3. Timothy A. Hughes, Doris James Wilson, and Allen J. Beck, *Trends in State Parole, 1990–2000* (Washington, DC: U.S. Department of Justice, 2001) 2–3.

4. John Rosecrance interviewed prison officials in six states and it was the consensus that about half of the parole applicants were granted release at their

first hearing. Those interviewed agreed that this figure was lower than it had been in previous years.

5. Steve Geissinger, "On Release Day from Prison, Killer Feels No Remorse for Crime," *Reno Gazette Journal* (October 17, 1986): A1.

6. Stephen Gettinger, "The Power Struggle over Federal Parole," *Corrections Magazine* 8 (1982): 41–43.

7. John R. Hepburn and Lynne Goldstein, "Organizational Imperatives and Sentencing Reform Implementation: The Impact of Prison Practices and Priorities on the Attainment of the Objective of Determinate Sentencing," *Crime and Delinquency* 32 (July, 1986): 339–365.

8. Alaska Board of Parole, *Statistical Report, 1996–2000.* Retrieved April 2003, from www.correct.state.ak.us/corrections/Parole/default.htm

9. Missouri Department of Corrections, "Probation and Parole: General Information." Retrieved April 2003, from www.corrections.state.mo.us/division/prob/prob.htm

10. Texas Board of Pardons and Paroles, *Fiscal Year 2001 Annual Report.* Retrieved April 2003, from www.tdcj.state.tx.us/bpp/publications/2001TBPP.pdf

11. The Association of Paroling Authorities, International, *Parole Board Survey 2001.* Retrieved April 2003, from www.apaintl.org/PubParoleBoardSurvey2001.html

12. New York State Executive Law, *State Division of Parole, Article 12-B,* p. 259-b.2.

13. Iowa Board of Parole, *2002 Annual Report.* Retrieved April 2003, from www.bop.state.ia.us/2002Report.pdf

14. Missouri Revised Statutes, *Chapter 217, Section 217.665,* August 28, 2002.

15. American Correctional Association, *Manual of Correctional Standards* (College Park, MD: American Correctional Association, June, 1980).

16. New York State Executive Law, *State Division of Parole, Article 12-B,* EL-9, p. 259 I.

17. Peggy McGarry, *Handbook for New Parole Board Members,* 2nd ed. (Washington, DC: National Institute of Corrections, 1989) 36–40.

18. McGarry 37–38.

19. For an example of parole board decisions by whim, see William Hart, "Oklahoma's 'Down Home' Parole Board," *Corrections Magazine* 4 (September, 1978): 55–60.

20. Lloyd Ohlin, *Selection for Parole* (New York: Russell Sage, 1951) 30–35.

21. National Parole Institutes, *Selection for Parole* (New York: National Council on Crime and Delinquency, 1966).

22. Keith O. Hawkins, "Parole Selection: The American Experience" (diss., University of Cambridge, 1971).

23. McGarry 32–35.

24. Malcolm Braly, *False Starts: A Memoir of San Quentin and Other Prisons* (Boston: Little, Brown, 1976) 251–253.

25. Quoted in Robert J. Minton, *Inside: Prison American Style* (New York: Random House, 1971) 174.

26. David T. Stanley, *Prisoners among Us* (Washington, DC: Brookings Institute, 1976) 41–42.

27. Mary West-Smith, Mark R. Pogrebin, and Eric D. Poole, "Denial of Parole: An Inmate Perspective," *Federal Probation* 64, 2 (2000): 3–10.

28. Minton 179.

29. Quoted in Leonard Orland, *Justice, Punishment, Treatment: The Correctional Practice* (New York: Macmillan, 1973) 464.

30. Association of Paroling Authorities International, *Parole Board Survey, 2001.* Retrieved May 2003, from www.apaintl.org/Pub-ParoleBoardSurvey2001.html

31. Joan Petersilia, "When Prisoners Return to Community: Political, Economic and Social Consequences," *Sentencing and Corrections: Issues for the Twenty-First Century* (Washington, DC: U.S. Department of Justice, November, 2000).

32. James Inciardi, *Criminal Justice* (San Diego, CA: Harcourt, Brace Jovanovich, 1987) 653.

33. Quoted in Debora A. DeLeo, "*Greenholtz v. Inmates of the Nebraska Penal and Correctional Complex,*" *New York Law School Review* 25 (1980): 1032.

34. David Rothman, *Conscience and Convenience: The Asylum and Its Alternatives in Progressive America* (Boston: Little, Brown, 1980).

35. McGarry 43.

36. Fred Cohen, "Corrections—Law Developments," *Criminal Law Bulletin* 17 (1981): 347.

37. DeLeo 1040.

38. *Greenholtz v. Inmates of Nebraska Penal and Correctional Complex,* 442 U.S. 1, 60 Sup. Ct. 2100 (1979): 2106.

39. Quoted in Ralph E. Lewis "Constitutional Law—Due Process in Parole Release Hearings," *Kansas Law Review* 28 (1980): 635.

40. *Greenholtz v. Inmates of Nebraska Penal and Correctional Complex* 2100, 2105.

41. *Greenholtz v. Inmates of Nebraska Penal and Correctional Complex* 2100, 2105.

42. *Greenholtz v. Inmates of Nebraska Penal and Correctional Complex* 2100, 2106.

43. *Greenholtz v. Inmates of Nebraska Penal and Correctional Complex* 2100, 2107.

44. *Greenholtz v. Inmates of Nebraska Penal and Correctional Complex* 2100, 2107.

45. *Greenholtz v. Inmates of Nebraska Penal and Correctional Complex* 2100, 2108.

46. Susan N. Herman, "The New Liberty: The Procedural Due Process Rights of Prisoners and Others under the Berger Court," *New York University Law Review* 59 (1984): 574–575.

47. Cohen 348.

48. Edward J. Latessa and Harry E. Allen, *Corrections in the Community* (Cincinnati, OH: Anderson, 1999) 220.

49. Sam B. Warner, "Factors Determining Parole from the Massachusetts Reformatory," *Journal of Criminal Law and Criminology* 14 (1923): 172–207.

50. Ernest W. Burgess, *The Working of the Indeterminate Sentence Law in the Parole System in Illinois* (Springfield: Illinois Parole Board, 1928).

51. Don M. Gottfredson, Leslie Wilkins, and Peter Hoffman, *Guidelines for Parole and Sentencing* (Lexington, MA: D. C. Heath, 1978).

52. Thomas H. McTavish, *Performance Audit of the Intake to Parole Process* (Lansing, MI: Office of Auditor General, 1998). Retrieved June 3, 2003, from www.state.mi.us/audgen/comprpt/docs/r4712198.pdf

53. Texas Administrative Code, *Standard Parole Guidelines*. Retrieved June 3, 2003, from http://info.sos.state.tx.us/pub/plsql/readtac$ext.TacPage?sl=R&app=9&p_dir=&p_rloc=&p_tloc=&p_ploc=&pg=1&p_tac=&ti=37&pt=5&ch=145&rl=2

54. Mark Pogrebin, Eric Poole, and Robert Regoli, "Parole Decision Making in Colorado," *Journal of Criminal Justice* 14 (1986): 147–155.

55. Norval Morris and Marc Miller "Predictions of Dangerousness in the Criminal Law," *Research in Brief* (Washington, DC: National Institute of Justice, March, 1987).

56. John L. Lombardi, "Objective Parole Criteria: More Harm Than Good," *Corrections Today* 48 (February, 1986): 86–87.

57. Peter B. Hoffman, "Screening for Risk: A Revised Salient Factor Score," *Journal of Criminal Justice* 11 (1983): 539–547.

58. Peter B. Hoffman, "Twenty Years of Operational Use of a Risk Prediction Instrument: The United States Parole Commission's Salient Factor Score," *Journal of Criminal Justice* 22 (1994): 477–494.

59. National Advisory Commission on Criminal Justice Standards and Goals, *Corrections* (Washington, DC: U.S. Department of Justice, 1973) 397–398.

60. David B. Griswold, "Deviation from Sentencing Guidelines: The Issues of Unwarranted Disparity," *Journal of Criminal Justice* 215 (1987): 318.

61. Griswold 317.

62. "Federal Sentencing Guidelines,"*NIJ Reports No. 205* (Washington, DC: National Institute of Justice, September/October, 1987).

63. Coalition for Federal Sentencing Reform, "The Case for Reform," February 1997. Retrieved June 13, 2003, from www.sentencing.org/reform.html

64. Coalition for Federal Sentencing Reform, "The Case for Reform."

65. Coalition for Federal Sentencing Reform, "History of the Guidelines," revised February 1997. Retrieved June 4, 2003, from www.sentencing.org/hist.html

7

Parole Supervision

A Problematic Process

The Challenge of Supervision

Although considerable attention has been focused on the parole selection process, relatively little concern is given the supervision of inmates once they are actually paroled. Discretionary parole release has been the center of endless controversy; at the same time discretionary practices of parole officers have received far less scrutiny. Notwithstanding a lack of public awareness, postrelease supervision is an essential responsibility of parole agencies. Unfortunately, parole supervision is often a problematic process for both parole officer and parolee.

Released inmates face serious problems in adjusting to community life after leaving a highly structured institutional environment. Adding to their reintegration difficulty is the fact that parole involves continued monitoring and control. Further, parole success requires cooperation with the agent of that control—the parole officer. From the inmate's perspective parole officers are representative of an all-powerful bureaucracy, often uncaring and unfeeling, but always dangerous. The following observations are typical of such perspectives. Shortly after release from prison Malcolm Braly wrote:

> My parole officer, a former cop, had no interest in me. I signed papers, received the balance of my release money, and was told, "Good luck."
> "Where should I live?" I asked.
> "Get yourself a room in a cheap hotel. You've got a job waiting. When you get paid you can look for something permanent. Look, you and I aren't going to be any trouble to each other if you just remember one thing, get your report in every month by the fifth."[1]

Chuck Terry describes his relationships with his parole officers as varied:

> Some were more understanding than others. Urinalysis tests were the center attraction of all our encounters. . . . Immediately after I was paroled, I tested positive

for heroin eight weeks in a row. Because I was working at the time, and my parole officer (PO) did not believe I was doing felonies to support my habit, she encouraged me to get on a methadone maintenance program. . . . A few years later, upon finishing another stretch in prison, on my first day out, I was assigned a PO who told me he did not think I was fit to live in the free world. [He said] "Terry, you belong in San Quentin, and I will do everything within my power to send you there." The guy hounded me to urinate in bottles three and four times a week to see if I was using heroin. Each time I reported to his office, he examined my arms with a magnifying glass in the hopes of finding needle marks.[2]

Willy, a narcotic addict, graphically described his parole officer as

A hope-to-die asshole. Man, he's so square—one of those educated fools. Got book learnin' up the ass, but he doesn't know a fuckin' thing about life or people. He's one of those guys that lived in a neat white house with a picket fence and pretty lawn and went to Sunday School everyday until he was sixteen. Him and his wife both teach Sunday School. . . . He acts like his job is some kind of missionary work among the heathen parolees. . . . He wants everyone to be like him. People are different. I know that, and I'm just an illiterate dope fiend. I'll show you what an asshole he is. If he knew I was driving a car he'd throw me in jail and write a report to the parole board. He'd feel bad but to him it would be his responsibility. Can't he understand that being without a car in LA is like being in Death Valley without water? It'd take me four hours to ride a bus to work.[3]

Parole officers charged with supervising released convicts are themselves faced with a variety of complex social and legal problems. They are caught in the assistance/control dilemma as they attempt to rehabilitate offenders while protecting society. Moreover, the issue of how to adequately protect the public from the actions of parolees has become the subject of liability suits against parole personnel. Difficulty in working with offenders is compounded by the fact that parole officers often see released convicts as losers without much going for them. The following observations, reported to John Rosecrance, reflect a common perspective:

These guys come out of the joint with two strikes against them. Before being committed they were foul-ups and joint time didn't improve the situation. Too frequently we're dealing with piss-poor protoplasm. No skills, no job, no money, no training, and no prospects. What can I do for them? I try to place them in some crummy job and hope for the best. But too often they drift back to their old tricks and wham-bang, it's revocation time—the old revolving door scenario.[4]

Another PO explained to Rosecrance that social distance and lack of empathy structured relationships with parolees:

I've read a lot of stuff about POs not "relating" to clients and not understanding them. Perhaps, but that's not such a bad thing. We're supposed to be models, not friends. Most of my caseloads are poor and come from a lower-class background. These girls don't expect me to be one of them, they wouldn't respect me if I were.

I'm a middle-class woman with a college degree, not a junkie with three illegitimate kids. If I'm going to enforce parole orders I can't over-identify with my parolees.[5]

The problematic nature of parole supervision is reflected in alarming **recidivism** figures. A Bureau of Justice Statistics special report on parole published in 2001 stated that 58 percent of parole discharges in 1999 failed to successfully complete supervision.[6] The recidivism rates were even higher for those who were re-releases (79 percent), under age twenty-five (64 percent), and male (71 percent). These rates are very similar to historical recidivism rates. In the largest recidivism study ever conducted in the United States, tracking released prisoners in fifteen states, 67 percent of the former inmates released in 1994 committed at least one serious crime within the next three years.[7] A Rand report showed that 76 percent of parolees surveyed in California committed new offenses within three years of their release; in Texas it was 60 percent reporting offenses within three years, whereas in Michigan the percentage committing new offenses was 53 percent. According to Rand researchers, the 286 surveyed inmates in California "may have committed over ten-thousand crimes in the three year period of their return to the streets.[8] Illinois officials kept track of 537 inmates released on parole and found that almost half (48 percent) were arrested in the first twenty months of freedom.[9] The federal government closely monitored a group of young parolees (ages eighteen to twenty-two) for six years and found that 69 percent were rearrested and 49 percent returned to prison.[10]

Joan Petersilia, examining these recidivism figures, concluded that the United States's "experiment with building lots more prisons as a deterrent to crime has not worked."[11] Others suggest that parole is at fault, concluding: "The evidence that parole supervision is effective in reducing (or even delaying) recidivism among released offenders is weak and contradictory; fundamentally questioning the utility of post-institutional community supervision as a deterrence mechanism.[12] After thoroughly examining parole supervision David Stanley contended: "The alternative is plain: abolish supervision of the releasee.[13] **Andrew von Hirsch** and Kathleen Hanrahan maintain: "Instead of routinely imposing supervision on ex-prisoners, supervision should be eliminated entirely—or if retained, should be reduced substantially in scope. . . ."[14]

Several states, including Maine, California, Indiana, Connecticut, Washington, Colorado, and Florida, heeded such suggestions and abolished parole supervision in the 1970s and 1980s. However, since then California, Connecticut, Colorado, and Florida have reinstituted parole, leaving fifteen states with parole. In addition, twenty-one states have parole boards with limited release powers and most of those states that abolished discretionary release have some term of "post-prison supervision" for their releasees. In short, it does not appear that the abolition movement will spread to other jurisdictions; on the contrary, in 2002 the number of people on parole stood at an all-time high of more than 753,000.[15] The current pressures for releasing large numbers of inmates into the community to make room for newly sentenced prisoners ensures that parole supervision will not be abandoned, regardless of its deterrent value. A parole board member of a large state candidly admitted to John Rosecrance that although parole supervision "wasn't much good, it was something" and "[a]t least these new parolees have some tail on them. The public isn't going to stand for parole without somebody watching over the parolees."[16]

Although recidivism rates seem high, they do not necessarily correlate with supervision "failures." A new arrest does not mean the offender's parole status will automatically be revoked. Raw arrest data include a multitude of minor law violations that may not represent a serious threat to the community. For example, an individual on parole for armed robbery would not be sent back to prison if he or she was involved in petty theft or disturbing the peace. In point of fact, a large number of parolees in most jurisdictions are not returned to prison. For example, from 1990 to 1999 the average percentage of successful parolees for all fifty states ranged from 42 to 49 percent, without any distinct trend.[17] Furthermore, most of those returned to prison eventually make it in the community, although not always as model citizens.

Moreover, there have been some reported supervision successes. Massachusetts, Mississippi, North Carolina, and North Dakota all had parole success rates ranging from 79 to 83 percent in 1999.[18] In some states, specific programs contributed to parole success. In Wisconsin parolee recidivism was lowered through special supervision techniques; in Massachusetts prison prerelease programs helped reduce the criminal activity of parolees; in California the issuance of unemployment payments to parolees acted to reduce recidivism; and in Alabama use of close supervision combined with restitution has produced promising recidivism figures.[19] Particularly noteworthy is the rehabilitation potential demonstrated by programs that combine intensive supervision with rehabilitative programming. Such programs are discussed in some detail in Chapter Ten. At this time, although successful programs are generally limited to special offender categories, they do provide some optimism that parole supervision can be more than routine "checking in."

Notwithstanding the problematic nature of watching over released inmates in community settings, more than 750,000 people are currently under parole supervision, a number that will likely continue to increase in the next decade. Unfortunately, so will the number of civil suits brought against parole personnel for alleged negligence. Parole supervision, an often-neglected aspect of the correctional system, remains an integral part of the mitigation of punishment. It is important to thoughtfully examine what some criminologists have termed the *other parole*.[20] The parolees' first problems involve coping with a world that has changed considerably during their incarceration.

Reentry

Inmates spend much of the time in prison contemplating their eventual release. Freedom from incarceration is so eagerly anticipated that actual release is often anticlimactic, and the inmate's immediate situation, far different from the idealized version, can be disillusioning. In the 1970s, the California Department of Corrections anticipated such problems and issued each released inmate the following warning:

> You are going to get out. "The free world! The streets! The ever-loving bricks!" What do you expect? "The sky to split? Heavenly music to waft in four directions? Wide Open Arms to Greet Every Entrance?"
>> It Aint
>> Like That!!
>> It Aint
>> Like That
>> At All!!!
> The world has been rocking on all the time you've been in.
> Usually, few people actually know that you have been away.
>> No one is going to do all your planning for you. Chances are pretty good that you'll have to start from scratch in building a social life—any life.
>> Loneliness is one of the greatest problems facing a parolee. It may help if you give this a little thought before you jump out there. It won't be easy. Don't expect to swim in milk and honey.[21]

Malcolm Braly contrasts the dream and the reality of prison release, imagining that his first night out of prison would involve a good room and then a big steak at a fancy restaurant where he would end up spending the night with the waitress, listening to jazz music, and making love. The reality: He was too shy to speak to anyone so he went to a jazz club and stared at himself in the mirror until he left.[22]

Chuck Terry describes his last reentry in the following way:

> Walking into a supermarket was like entering Disneyland. All those things—lights, products, lines of people—anything you wanted, right there at your fingertips. And, I'm supposed to pay? Compared to the caged-in prison canteen, this place was wide open. Eating in restaurants was awkward. So many choices. I quickly learned that, unlike in the prison chow hall, making efforts to trade for food was taboo. "Excuse me, would you like to trade those green beans for these mashed potatoes?" After being looked at like I was from Mars and politely being told no, I realized that it's not OK to ask strangers in line at the college admissions office if they want a drink of my soda.[23]

Most parole agencies are aware of the difficulties faced by **reentry** of prisoners to society. Many state officials inform all their parole officers of the inmates' readjustment problems, pointing out that the approach and techniques to supervise parolees are complex and varied. Many need assistance to readjust to community life because of serious personal issues or inadequacies. Others need help simply because they have been released from a highly structured prison life to the freedom of the community. Moreover, some may experience mild anxiety, whereas others may react with severe anger, hostility, or depression. No matter what the new parolee might say, there will be some effect from his release from prison, and it is up to the parole officer to anticipate these effects and assist with the adjustment.[21]

Released inmates often find the pace of life on the streets faster and more confusing than that of which they have become accustomed. A new parolee said that in prison work details there are two speeds: slow and slower. He found it difficult to meet employer demands that he increase his work output. **John Irwin's** field notes of contacts with recently paroled convicts reflect similar initial disorientation:

> I mean, I was shook baby. Things were moving too fast, everybody rushing somewhere. And they all seemed so cold, they had this up tight look.

> The first thing I noticed was how fast everything moves outside. In prison everybody even walks slow. Outside everyone's in a hurry.

> The first time I started across the street, I remember, I was watching a car coming and couldn't judge his speed very good. I couldn't tell if he was going to hit me or not. It was weird.

> On about the second day I'm out I get this trolley and start fumbling in my pocket for money. There're a lot of people behind me trying to get on, but I can't figure out how much to put in the box. You know what, man, I don't know how to find out how much to put in the box. The driver's getting salty and I don't want to ask him cause I'm embarrassed, so you know what I do? I back off the fucking thing and walk fifteen blocks.[24]

Parolees face relationships with family members and acquaintances that have been severely strained by incarceration. An inmate described this phenomenon as "broken pieces," coming home to "suspicions and stares." His old girlfriend was married and ignored him when she saw him in the grocery store. His parents were worried about setting him off, always watching for "tell-tale signs." At his old hangout, most of his old friends were long gone, and those who were there acted suspicious; they did not have much in common anyway. He did get along with ex-cons he met on the street, swapping stories from the joint.[25]

Released prisoners must immediately face a host of practical problems such as finding employment, getting a car, obtaining a driver's license, taking care of unpaid warrants, purchasing a new wardrobe, finding a place to live, or resuming child support payments. The varied number of immediate responsibilities and significant decisions can leave parolees feeling overwhelmed. The major adaptations that parolees must cope with in their first months of release would test the mettle of the most normal and adjusted among us. One group of researchers who conducted a comprehensive investigation of parole reentry likened the experience to a class of normal human role changes known as "status passages," when, for example, a person returns to civilian life after serving in the military, or when someone gets married, or loses a loved one. However, these researchers also realized that the magnitude of the adaptations necessary for parolees exceeded those faced in more normal, or usual, status transitions. For example

- The parolee can use few, if any, of the behavior patterns that were useful and appropriate in prison.
- The role changes involved in most status passages affect some, but not all, parts of an individual's social life, leaving room for some stability in the person's life. However, the parolee role affects all aspects of a person's life in some way, so problems in one area may affect all others, making the social experience difficult to manage.
- The reentry process usually occurs with low social support and very limited resources, both of which are often needed to manage crises.
- The parolee moves into reentry under conditions in which it is easy to lose the newfound freedom and be sent back to prison. This feeling of jeopardy lasts throughout the period of parole because until discharge, a parolee can be revoked and sent back to prison for misbehavior much less serious than that which would cause the incarceration of "normal" men and women.[26]

John Irwin argues that the ex-convict's efforts to make it are often upset by "a barrage of disorganizing events which occur in the first days or weeks on the outside." These events, according to Irwin, include moving from a world with one set of meanings, to another with an entirely different set of meanings; being faced with numerous demands for which the parolee is unprepared; and extreme loneliness. As a result, many parolees "careen and ricochet" through the first few weeks of their release, when, in desperation, they do something that will land them back in prison, or perhaps they simply retreat to their former deviant world. Even those who do not have their plans ruined and do not go back to prison after a short stay in the community experience often-painful strains and have their sense of self altered.[27]

In addition to the many problems previously listed, released felons often face **civil disabilities** as well: legal restrictions on rights and opportunities resulting from past criminal convictions. Depending on the jurisdiction, these restrictions may include the right to vote, to hold public office, to obtain some occupational licenses, or to be employed in certain occupations.[28] A 1998 study estimated that 3.9 million Americans were either currently or permanently unable to vote because of a felony conviction. Of these, 36 percent were African American males, a figure that represents 13 percent of all African American men.[29] Refusing to allow large numbers of minorities the right to vote alienates them from the democratic process and probably makes them less willing to participate in other community activities. This is important because many believe that the most effective tool for preventing crime is active community collaboration and commitment,[30] and therefore policies and laws restricting civic participation also limit commitment and collaboration, and may in the long run lead to more criminal activity.

An estimated 630,000 offenders were released from prison during 2001, and it is estimated that 160,000 of those were violent.[31] In an attempt to facilitate the reentry process, many states and the federal government have made prerelease and reentry programs a high priority. For example, Congress passed the Public

Safety Ex-offender Self Sufficiency Act of 2002, which seeks to help offenders by providing housing and numerous services throughout the United States. In October 2002, the Department of Justice reported that their Serious and Violent Offender Reentry Initiative had awarded $100 million to forty-nine states, the District of Columbia, and the Virgin Islands to support reentry efforts.[32] These efforts begin while the offenders are incarcerated and professionals work with the offenders through the transition process to help lower recidivism and improve public safety. Two examples of these programs are the Maryland Reentry Partnership Initiative and the Richland County (Ohio) Reentry Court.

The Maryland Reentry Partnership Initiative is a pilot program that tries to provide a complete array of services for released offenders to make certain their transition from prison to the community will be successful. The partners in this initiative include the Baltimore Mayor's Office on Criminal Justice (MOCJ) and the Maryland Division of Correction, the Maryland Division of Parole and Probation, the Baltimore Police Department, the Baltimore City Health Department, and five other public and private city organizations or associations in Baltimore City. The initiative requires the partners to create interagency systems to help prepare inmates for successful reentry to the community. Partners develop a comprehensive plan for each offender that supports his or her needs and provides a variety of state, local, and community social and medical services.[33]

The Richland County (Ohio) Reentry Court is a model that also offers a comprehensive approach to managing offenders from court, to incarceration, and back into the community. In this case, the court develops a reentry plan that identifies what the offender must do to improve his or her eligibility for release and assists with his or her success in the community once released. The reentry plan accelerates offender processing into prison, placing the offender in an institution near Richland County, where programming outlined in the reentry plan is begun. Coordination among the institution, the court, and the parole system continues throughout the process, all working to plan for the release of the offender to the community. The core issues of the reentry plan continue on release when collaborations grow to include law enforcement, treatment providers, and citizen organizations. Once in the community, the offender must report to a joint court/parole authority for a formal progress review every month for a year.[34]

These programs and all others funded by this Department of Justice program can be reviewed by visiting the web site of the **Serious and Violent Offender Reentry Initiative** (www.ojp.usdoj.gov/reentry).

In 1997, only about 12 percent of released prisoners participated in a release program, a number that had remained unchanged since 1991.[35] Generally, inmates who are within three to six months of their actual release date, and who have compiled a satisfactory prison record, are eligible for placement in a reentry program. These reentry efforts help ex-offenders with such services as employment training and substance abuse and mental health treatment. The programs require close coordination among institutional corrections, law enforcement, community corrections, and many other community-based service providers.

A vital aspect of prison-to-community reintegration (for most released convicts) involves parole supervision. This supervision begins immediately on release from prison and continues (barring termination) until the sentence has expired. The term of supervision is clearly spelled out by the New York State Parole Board:

> Persons paroled and conditionally released from an institution under the jurisdiction of a department for correctional services shall, while on parole or conditional release, be in the legal custody of the division of parole until expiration of the maximum term or period of sentence, or expiration of the period of supervision, or return to such institution, as the case may be.[36]

It is worth underscoring the fact that the parolee's freedom is conditional. He or she must abide by a series of parole orders.

Parole Orders

All inmates on parole status or mandatory release (also called supervised or conditional release) must agree to and sign a **parole order,** which is a set of general conditions, as well as any special individual conditions. The parole conditions of New York state (see Figure 7.1) are typical of states with discretionary parole. New York state defines special conditions of parole in a commonly accepted way by stating that the Board of Parole, or a parole officer, can add conditions that apply specifically to an offender or his or her situation. These special conditions might include imposing a curfew, prohibiting drinking alcoholic beverages, not associating with certain people, or staying away from specific areas or types of areas, and these conditions must be obeyed just like general conditions. In New York, if the board imposes a special condition, only the board can remove it; if a parole officer imposes the special condition, then the PO can remove it.[37] Minnesota, a state without discretionary parole, also requires that inmates who are released early sign and abide by release orders (which are synonymous with parole orders). A sample of these orders is shown in Figure 7.2. California shortened and condensed its general parole orders in 1985 and then added a list of possible special conditions in 2001. Figure 7.3 (pp. 221–222) shows the parole order format currently in use in that state.

The rationale behind the widespread use of parole orders is difficult to pinpoint. It is unclear whether they are designed to punish released inmates by imposing restrictions on their liberty or whether they are imposed to deter future criminality by attempting to structure specific behavior patterns. After analyzing the use of parole orders Deborah Star and John Berecochea found that parolees were rarely returned to prison for violation of parole conditions (except for commission of a new offense) calling into question the need for large numbers of release conditions. They concluded: "In sum, the evidence from this study clearly supports the need for the rationalization of the conditions of parole, but the available evidence provides no clear support for any of several possible goals served

(text continues on page 223)

FIGURE 7.1 *New York State Conditions of Parole*

1. I will proceed directly to the area to which I have been released and, within twenty-four hours of my release, make my arrival report to that office of the Division of Parole unless other instructions are designated on my release agreement.
2. I will make office and/or written reports as directed.
3. I will not leave the State of New York or any other state to which I am released or transferred, or any area defined in writing by my Parole Officer without permission.
4. I will permit my Parole Officer to visit me at my residence and/or place of employment and I will permit the search and inspection of my person, residence, and property. I will discuss any proposed changes in my residence, employment, or program status with my Parole Officer. I understand that I have an immediate and continuing duty to notify my Parole Officer of any changes in my residence, employment, or program status when circumstances beyond my control make prior discussion impossible.
5. I will reply promptly, fully, and truthfully to any inquiry of, or communication by, my Parole Officer or other representative of the Division of Parole.
6. I will notify my Parole Officer immediately any time I am in contact with, or arrested by, any law enforcement agency. I understand that I have a continuing duty to notify my Parole Officer of such contact or arrest.
7. I will not be in the company of, or fraternize with, any person I know to have a criminal record or whom I know to have been adjudicated a Youthful Offender, except for accidental encounters in public places, work, school, or in any other instance without the permission of my Parole Officer.
8. I will not behave in such manner as to violate the provisions of any law to which I am subject which provides for a penalty of imprisonment, nor will my behavior threaten the safety or well-being of myself or others.
9. I will not own, possess, or purchase any shotgun, rifle, or firearm of any type without the written permission of my Parole Officer. In addition, I will not own, possess, or purchase any dangerous instrument or deadly weapon as defined in the Penal Law or any dangerous knife, dirk, razor, stiletto, or imitation pistol. In addition, I will not own, possess, or purchase any instrument readily capable of causing injury without a satisfactory explanation for ownership, possession, or purchase.
10. In the event that I leave the jurisdiction of the State of New York, I hereby waive my right to resist extradition to the State of New York from any state in the Union and from any territory or country outside the United States. This waiver shall be in full force and effect until I am discharged from Parole or Conditional Release. I fully understand that I have the right under the Constitution of the United States and under law to contest an effort to extradite me from another state and return me to New York, and I freely and knowingly waive this right as a condition of my Parole or Conditional Release.
11. I will not use or possess any drug paraphernalia or use or possess any controlled substance without proper medical authorization.
12. I will follow my special conditions as specified by the Board of Parole, my Parole Officer, or other representative.
13. I will fully comply with the instructions of my Parole Officer and obey such special additional written conditions as he/she, a member of the Board of Parole, or an authorized representative of the Division of Parole, may impose.

Source: New York State Division of Parole, "New York State Parole Handbook."

FIGURE 7.2 *Minnesota Release Order*

STATE OF MINNESOTA
DEPARTMENT OF CORRECTIONS
450 NORTH SYNDICATE STREET
ST. PAUL, MINNESOTA 55104

Office of
Adult Release

ORDER IMPOSING RULES OF SUPERVISED RELEASE

WHEREAS, _____ presently confined in the

Minnesota Correctional Facility-_____ has reached his/her
scheduled release date.

Signed in quadruplicate this _____ day of _____, 19____ .

CERTIFIED

By_____
Institution Records Officer

NOW, THEREFORE, be it known that the Commissioner of Corrections, under the authority vested in him/her by law, sets out the rules and conditions to be followed by _____ on supervised release and does authorize an agent to supervise per those rules and conditions. Upon release he/she shall be and remain in the legal custody and under the control of the Commissioner of Corrections, subject to the rules and conditions set forth in the rules of release contained on this document.

A request to modify or restructure the standard or special condition of release contained in this document may be submitted in writing by the releasee to the supervising agent or district supervisor.

The Executive Officer of Adult Release shall have the final authority to grant or deny modification or restructure of the conditions of release, and any modification shall be in writing.

RULES OF SUPERVISED RELEASE

1. Within 24 hours of release, excluding weekends and holidays, the supervised releasee will report at the destination specified, either by telephone or personal visit as directed by the supervising agent who is:

Name:_____ Telephone No.:_____

Address:_____

If a releasee fails to make his first appointment with the supervising agent and fails to call and explain this failure, or fails to report to a residential program, a fugitive warrant shall immediately be issued. Upon apprehension, the presumption shall be to return the releasee to a Minnesota correctional facility to serve to the expiration of the sentence or a period of six months, whichever occurs first. Departure from this guideline can occur only when this failure was beyond the control of the releasee and/or other substantial and compelling reasons exist to mitigate the failure.

2. The supervised releasee will at all times follow the instructions of the supervising agent and keep that agent informed of residence and activities. The supervised releasee will advise agent within 24 hours if arrested.

3. The supervised releasee will maintain monthly contact with the supervising agent in the manner prescribed by that agent unless otherwise directed by that agent.

4. The supervised releasee shall submit such reports as may be required by the supervising agent and shall respond promptly to any communication regarding supervised release.

(continued)

FIGURE 7.2 *Continued*

5.   The supervised releasee will follow the supervising agent's instructions with respect to use of intoxicants and will not possess or use narcotics or other drugs, preparations, or substances as defined by Minnesota Statutes, Chapter 152, except those prescribed for the supervised releasee by a physician.

6.   Possession of pistols (handguns) is regulated by Minnesota Statutes, Sections 624.713-642.718 and possession of firearms by persons convicted of a felony is prohibited by the Federal Gun Control Act; therefore, the supervised releasee may not purchase or otherwise obtain or have in possession any type of firearm or dangerous weapon as defined by Minnesota Statutes 609.02, Subdivision 6.

7.   Conviction of any misdemeanor, gross misdemeanor, or felony punishable by confinement, repeated convictions of traffic offenses other than parking, or involvement, in any activity defined as criminal by any state or federal law constitutes a violation of supervised release and may result in its revocation. Acknowledgement in the form of a confession under oath in open court before a judge may be considered a conviction for the purpose of this condition. A finding of probable cause by a court of competent jurisdiction or a grand jury indictment shall be considered grounds to hold the releasee in custody unless and until the defendant is found not guilty.

8.   Supervised releasee will not leave the state without written permission from the supervising agent and then only under such terms and conditions as may be prescribed in writing.

9.   SPECIAL CONDITIONS

I hereby do waive extradition to the State of Minnesota from any jurisdiction in or outside the United States where I may be found and also agree that I will not contest any effort by any jurisdiction to return me to the State of Minnesota.

I hereby certify that the rules of supervised release have been read and explained to me, and that I have received a copy thereof this _____ day of _____, 19_____.

_____
Supervised Releasee

Rules read by _____
Institution or Field Agent

Date released: _____   Cash received: $ _____

Balance: $ _____   Expiration date: _____

Dist: 1. Central Office, 2. Institution, 3. Supervised Release, 4. Agent

CR-00186-01

FIGURE 7.3 *California General Parole Order with Special Conditions*

STATE OF CALIFORNIA   DEPARTMENT OF CORRECTIONS
NOTICE AND CONDITIONS OF PAROLE
CDC 1515 (REV 05/01)

You will be released on parole effective _____for a period of _____ **3 YEARS** _____ . This parole
is subject to the following notice and conditions. Should you violate conditions of this parole, you are subject to arrest, suspension, and/or revocation of your
parole.

You waive extradition to the State of California from any state or territory of the United States or from the District of Columbia. You will not contest any effort
to return you to the State of California.

When the Board of Prison Terms determines, based upon psychiatric reasons, that you pose a danger to yourself or others, the Board may, if necessary for
psychiatric treatment, order your placement in a community treatment facility or state prison or may revoke your parole and order your return to prison.

You and your residence and any property under your control may be searched without a warrant by an agent of the Department of Corrections or any law
enforcement officer.

If another jurisdiction has lodged a detainer against you, you may be released to the custody of that jurisdiction. Should you be released from their custody prior to
the expiration of your California parole, or should the detainer not be exercised, you are to immediately contact the nearest Department of Corrections'
Parole and Community Services Division Office for instructions concerning reporting to a parole agent.

You have been informed and have received in writing the procedure for obtaining a Certificate of Rehabilitation (4852.21 PC).

CONDITIONS OF PAROLE

1. SPECIAL CONDITIONS MUST: a) Relate to the crime for which you were convicted, b) Relate to conduct which is itself criminal, c) Prohibit conduct
which may be related to future criminality. You are subject to the following special conditions:

 1. **You will participate in antinarcotic testing in accordance with instructions from a parole agent.**
 2. **You will totally abstain from the use of any alcoholic beverages or liquor.**
 3. **You will participate in the psychiatric treatment program approved for you by P&CSD.**
 4. **You will not have contact with minors without prior approval of P&CSD.**
 5. **You will not contact _____, in any manner without the approval of P&CSD.**
 6. **You are prohibited from possessing, utilizing or having access to pagers, scanners, police radios or mobile phone equipment,
    unless you can demonstrate that they are related to legitimate employment needs.**
 7. **You will not wear, possess, have access to or display gang attire, insignias or paraphernalia.**
 8. **You will not associate with gang members without prior approval from P&CSD.**
 9. **You are prohibited from residing within one-quarter mile of any school that contains grades Kindergarten through six.**
 10. **You shall not engage in gang participation as defined in CA. Code of Regulation Title 15, Section 2513(e).**
 11. **Not to enter the United States Illegally.**
 12. **You will successfully complete a batterer's program as directed by P&CSD.**
 13. **You will successfully complete a domestic violence/anger management program as directed by P&CSD.**
 14. **You shall participate in a drug treatment program at the direction of your parole agent.**
 15. **You are prohibited from residing in a "single family dwelling" with any person also required to register pursuant to PC Section
    290, unless they are legally related to you by blood, marriage or adoption, "single family dwelling" shall not include a residential
    facility that serves six or fewer persons.**
 16. **You are not to use any name other than _____.**
 17. **You will successfully complete parenting counsels classes.**

Reasons for the imposition of special conditions of Parole:_____

 **1) History of drug use/abuse 2) History of alcohol abuse 3) Related to commitment offense 4) History of psychiatric problems
 5) Nature of commitment offense 6) Nature of criminal history 7) History of violence or threats of violence 8) Request of _____
 9) Due to nature of commitment offense 10) Due to gang membership or affiliation 11) BPT imposed due to validated gang
 member 12) Illegal alien status 13) PC 3053.2 14) History of anger management problems 15) Pursuant to PC 3053.2 16) Prop 36
 Mandated.**

_____ I acknowledge my special conditions of parole.
Parolee's Initials   SIGNATURE OF UNIT SUPERVISOR   DATE SIGNED

(continued)

FIGURE 7.3 *Continued*

2. RELEASE, REPORTING, RESIDENCE, AND TRAVEL: Unless other arrangements are approved in writing, you will report to your parole agent on the first working day following your release. Any change of residence shall be reported to your parole agent in advance. You will inform your parole agent within 72 hours of any change of employment location, employer, or termination of employment. .

3. PAROLE AGENT INSTRUCTIONS: You shall comply with all instructions of your parole agent and will not travel more than 50 miles from your residence without his/her prior approval. You will not be absent from your county of residence for a period of more than 48 hours and not leave the State of California without prior written approval of your parole agent.

4. CRIMINAL CONDUCT: You shall not engage in conduct prohibited by law (state, federal, county or municipal). You shall immediately inform your parole agent if you are arrested for a felony or misdemeanor crime. Conduct prohibited by law may result in parole revocation even though no criminal conviction occurs.

5. WEAPONS: You shall not own, use, have access to, or have under your control: (a) any type of firearm or instrument or device which a reasonable person would believe to be capable of being used as a firearm or any ammunition which could be used in a firearm: (b) any weapon defined in state or federal statutes or listed in California Penal Code Section 12020 or any instrument or device which a reasonable person would believe to be capable of being used as a weapon as defined in Penal Code Section 12020; (c)any knife with a blade longer than two inches, except kitchen knives which must be kept in your residence and knives related to your employment which may be used and carried only in connection with your employment; or (d) a crossbow of any kind.

6. You shall sign the parole agreement containing the conditions of parole specified in the Board of Prison Terms (BPT) Rules Section 2512 and any special conditions imposed as specified in BPT Rules Section 2513. Penal Code Section 3060.5 provides that the BPT shall revoke any prisoner/parolee who refuses to sign the Notice and Conditions of Parole. You have the right to appeal the special conditions of parole. Special conditions imposed by the Parole and Community Services Division may be appealed pursuant to California Code of Regulations (CCR), Section 3084 and 3085. Special Conditions of parole imposed by the BPT may be appealed pursuant to CCR, Section 2050.

I have read or have had read to me and understand the conditions of parole as the apply to me.

CDC NUMBER	PAROLEE'S NAME (Print or Type)	PAROLEE'S SIGNATURE	DATE SIGNED

TO BE COMPLETED BY STAFF:

Does the inmate/parolee have a qualifying disability requiring effective communication?   [ ] YES   [ ] NO

If yes, cite the source document and/or _____

What type of accommodation/assistance was provided to achieve effective communication to the best of the inmate's/parolee's ability?_____

STAFF NAME (Print or Type)	STAFF SIGNATURE	DATE SIGNED

by the conditions of parole.[38] Star and Berecochea found themselves in full agreement with this statement of the American Bar Association: "Lost in the past history of parole condition development appears to have been any underlying theoretical foundation or purpose of the use of conditions."

Although the overall goals of parole orders may be vague, parolees and parole officers must deal with orders as written, and technical violations, although not always sufficient for revocation, significantly affect the supervision process. Before release, parolees must sign their orders, acknowledging they understand and agree to the release conditions. This signed agreement sets the stage for possible revocation should parolees fail to abide by their parole orders. The most basic of parole requirements is reporting to a parole officer on a regular basis. The initial contact takes place shortly after the parolee is released from prison.

Reporting

New parolees generally are required to contact the parole office nearest their residence within forty-eight hours of release. On arrival, they meet with their assigned PO and the supervision process begins. Parolees already have preconceived notions about parole supervision, drawn mainly from other inmates. Frequently, these conceptions are negative because returned inmates whose parole was revoked have shaped them. Supervision officers need to be aware of these negative images and dispel them as soon as possible.[39] For this and other reasons, (e.g., the parolees may be suspicious of the officer), **initial interviews** are crucial in establishing groundwork for future supervision because it establishes the rapport between the PO and the parolee and sets the stage for supervision.

New York officials have written a *Parole Handbook* to advise new parolees. The handbook emphasizes the importance of the initial interview, pointing out that it is a good opportunity for the parolee and his or her parole officer to establish a positive relationship with each other and for the parolee to understand what the PO expects of him or her. The handbook also suggests that issues such as employment and residence should be brought up, and any fears or concerns the parolee may have concerning living in the community should be addressed.[40]

The initial interview covers two important phases: explaining release conditions (often referred to as "housekeeping chores") and establishing a reporting schedule. The PO thoroughly reviews the inmate's parole conditions, noting any special conditions, and the manner in which they are to be fulfilled. For example, if parolees are required to participate in psychological treatment or alcoholic counseling, they are referred to such programs. Some parolees are informed they will be regularly tested for drugs, whereas others (convicted of sex offenses or drug sales) are told they must register their addresses with local police departments. In many jurisdictions, the PO gives the parolee a check for financial assistance, often called gate money. California awards each parolee $200, half of which is given at the time of release, the other half is handed over by the PO at the initial interview.

At these initial interviews parolees are warned against owning or possessing firearms. Travel restrictions, usually requiring that the parolees receive permission for travel outside a designated area (county or city boundaries), should be fully explained at this time. Additionally, employment requirements (such as the necessity of maintaining employment or not changing jobs without prior approval) should be clarified. During the first interview parolees are advised that violations of release conditions can result in revocation proceedings and are informed of their appeal rights should such action be taken.

The second major component of the initial interview involves establishing a reporting schedule. Frequency of contacts, which include office visits and field calls (typically at the parolee's home and place of employment), are determined by supervision levels assigned to individual parolees. Many states determine the supervision level by employing a risk/needs test, whereas others assign new parolees to relatively intensive supervision and then reduce its intensity as time passes (providing the parolee's adjustment is not problematic). Pennsylvania uses the former method, and Figure 7.4 shows the risk/needs assessment used to determine the supervision level. Based on the parolee's overall score, he or she is placed in one of the following categories (with decreasing frequency of contact with parole officers): intensive, close, regular, or reduced supervision. A prerelease officer working in the institution where the inmate was incarcerated generally compiles the initial assessment score.

Georgia, however, assigns virtually all parolees to a high level of supervision and then reduces the level downward as certain criteria are met. By the same token, supervision can be increased if conditions warrant. The Georgia classification scheme is clearly outlined in Figure 7.5 from *Field Operations Supervision Policies and Procedures.*

Virtually all states require that parolees submit a monthly report form, either in person or by mail. During the initial interview such forms are given to parolees and the method for submitting them is carefully explained. The Wisconsin monthly report is typical of such forms and can be seen in Figure 7.6 (p. 228).

The PO's demeanor during the initial interview often sets the tone for further interaction. This is where a spirit of cooperation or coercion is established. For example, an officer who appears friendly will often get more cooperation than one who comes off as dictatorial.

Parole supervision obviously is an intrusive process; just how deeply the parolee's life is penetrated remains largely a matter of discretion. Although there are formal parole orders and written department policies, there is a limiting factor to all parole work; namely, it is impossible to fully monitor parolee behavior and therefore rigid compliance with parole conditions can never be assured. This basic fact inevitably leads to discretionary decision making by supervision officers. To quote one parole officer: "If I enforced every parole condition, three-quarters of my cases would be violated. You have to allow parolees some slack. The trick is to know how much to give and when to give it" (John Rosecrance, personal communication). These types of decisions generally are made during the first few months of supervision when officers begin working with their charges. It should

(text continues on page 227)

FIGURE 7.4   *Risk/Needs Assessment for Parolee Supervision*

COMMONWEALTH OF PENNSYLVANIA
BOARD OF PROBATION AND PAROLE
PBPP 20 (1-85)

INITIAL CLIENT ASSESSMENT

CLIENT NAME (Last, First, Middle Initial)	PAROLE NO.	AGENT NAME	OFFICE	DATE

RISK ASSESSMENT

1. Age at First Conviction: (or juvenile adjudication)
- 24 or older 0
- 20-23 2
- 19 or Younger 4

2. Number of Prior Probation/Parole Revocations: (adult or juvenile)
- None 0
- One or more 4

3. Number of Prior Felony Convictions: (or juvenile adjudications)
- None 0
- One 2
- Two or more 4

4. Convictions or Juvenile Adjudications for:
(Select applicable and add for score. Do not exceed a total of 5. Include current offense.)
- Burglary, theft, auto theft, or robbery 2
- Worthless checks or forgery 3

5. Number of Prior Periods of Probation/Parole Supervision:
(Adult or Juvenile)
- None 0
- One or more 4

6. Conviction or Juvenile Adjudication for Assaultive Offense within Last Five Years: (An offense which involves the use of a weapon, physical force or the threat of force.)
- Yes 15
- No 0

7. Number of Address Changes in Last 12 Months:
(Prior to incarceration for parolees)
- None 0
- One 2
- Two or more 3

8. Percentage of Time Employed in Last 12 Months:
(Prior to incarceration for parolees)
- 60% or more 0
- 40%-59% 1
- Under 40% 2
- Not applicable 0

9. Alcohol Usage Problems: (Prior to incarceration for parolees)
- No interference with functioning 0
- Occasional abuse; some disruption of functioning 2
- Frequent abuse; serious disruption; needs treatment 4

10. Other Drug Usage Problems: (Prior to incarceration for parolees)
- No interference with functioning 0
- Occasional abuse; some disruption of functioning 1
- Frequent abuse; serious disruption; needs treatment 2

11. Attitude:
- Motivated to change; receptive to assistance 0
- Dependent or unwilling to accept responsibility 3
- Rationalizes behavior; negative; not motivated to change 5

TOTAL

INITIAL ASSESSMENT SCALES

Risk Scale		Needs Scale
0-5	Reduced Supervision	– 8-10
6-18	Regular Supervision	-1-10
19-30	Close Supervision	11-25
31 & above	Intensive Supervision	26 & above

SCORING AND OVERRIDE

Score Based Supervision Level ...... Intensive ☐   Regular ..... ☐
Close ...... ☐   Reduced..... ☐

Score Override .... No ...... ☐   Yes .... ☐

FINAL GRADE OF SUPERVISION .... Intensive ..... ☐   Regular ..... ☐

Override Explanation: Close ...... ☐   Reduced..... ☐

NEEDS ASSESSMENT

1. Academic/Vocational Skills
- High school or above skill level .... – 1
- Adequate skills; able to handle everyday requirements 0
- Low skill level causing minor adjustment problems ...... + 2
- Minimal skill level causing serious adjustment problems ...... + 4

2. Employment
- Satisfactory employment for one year or longer .... – 1
- Secure employment; no difficulties reported; or homemaker, student or retired 0
- Unsatisfactory employment; or unemployed but has adequate job skills .... + 3
- Unemployed and virtually unemployable; needs training .... + 6

3. Financial Management
- Long-standing pattern of self-sufficiency; e.g., good credit rating – 1
- No current difficulties 0
- Situational or minor difficulties .... + 3
- Severe difficulties; may include garnishment, bad checks or bankruptcy .... + 5

4. Marital/Family Relationships
- Relationships and support exceptionally strong .... – 1
- Relatively stable relationships 0
- Some disorganization or stress but potential for improvement .... + 3
- Major disorganization or stress .... + 5

5. Companions
- Good support and influence .... – 1
- No adverse relationships 0
- Associations with occasionally negative results .... + 2
- Associations almost completely negative .... + 4

6. Emotional Stability
- Exceptionally well adjusted; accepts responsibility for actions ... – 2
- No symptoms of emotional instability; appropriate emotional responses 0
- Symptoms limit but do not prohibit adequate functioning; e.g., excessive anxiety .... + 4
- Symptoms prohibit adequate functioning; e.g. lashes out or retreats into self .... + 7

7. Alcohol Usage
- No interference with functioning 0
- Occasional abuse; some disruption of functioning .... + 3
- Frequent abuse; serious disruption; needs treatment .... + 6

8. Other Drug Usage
- No interference with functioning 0
- Occasional substance abuse; some disruption of functioning ... + 3
- Frequent substance abuse; serious disruption; needs treatment ... + 5

9. Mental Ability
- Able to function independently 0
- Some need for assistance; potential for adequate adjustment; mild retardation .... + 3
- Deficiencies severely limit independent functioning; moderate retardation .... + 6

10. Health
- Sound physical health; seldom ill 0
- Handicap or illness interferes with functioning on a recurring basis + 1
- Serious handicap or chronic illness; needs frequent medical care . + 2

11. Sexual Behavior
- No apparent dysfunction 0
- Real or perceived situational or minor problems .... + 3
- Real or perceived chronic or severe problems .... + 5

12. Recreation/Hobby
- Constructive 0
- Some constructive activities .... + 1
- No constructive leisure-time activities or hobbies .... + 2

13. Agent's Impression of Client's Needs
- Minimum .... – 1
- Low 0
- Medium .... + 3
- Maximum .... + 5

TOTAL

FIGURE 7.5   *Classification of Supervision and Supervision Contacts*

I. Levels of Supervision

All newly released parolees are to be assigned Maximum supervision unless otherwise stated on the field notebook sheet. Maximum supervision shall continue for a minimum of 6 months. Prior to a reduction in the level of supervision, a thorough review of the case file should be conducted to ensure that there are no unfulfilled Special Conditions, conditions prohibiting a reduction, or any other information which may preclude a reduction in the level of supervision.

A. *Maximum*

Maximum supervision shall consist of no less than 3 personal filed contacts per month. One contact should be made with the parolee and/or his family at the parolee's residence: one contact should be made with the parolee and/or his employer at place of employment; and the third contact should be made with the parolee wherever the officer deems appropriate. In cases where a home contact is not feasible, officers are to substitute an employment contact. Monthly Arrest Record Checks are to be conducted on all parolees under Maximum supervision. Monthly Supervision Reports are to be submitted by the parolee.

B. *Medium Supervision*

Medium supervision shall consist of no less than 2 personal field contacts per month. One contact should be made with the parolee and/or employer at place of employment. The second contact should be made with the parolee either at home or work. Monthly Arrest Record Checks shall be conducted on all parolees under Medium supervision. Monthly Supervision Reports are to be submitted by the parolee.

C. *Minimum*

Minimum supervision shall consist of not less than 1 personal field contact per month, alternating between the parolee's residence and employment. Monthly Arrest Record Checks shall be conducted on all parolees under Minimum supervision and Monthly Supervision Reports are to be submitted by the parolee.

II. Reduction in Levels of Supervision

A. *Medium*

The following criteria must be met by all parolees before a reduction to Medium supervision:

1. Six months on Parole/Conditional Release.
2. Currently employed full time for 3 consecutive months.
3. Six consecutive months without a delinquent report resulting in disciplinary action.
4. No unauthorized/unjustified employment/residence changes.
5. Stable home life.
6. No current arrearages in supervision fee/court ordered payments.
7. In compliance with Special Conditions.

B. *Minimum*

The following criteria must be met by all parolees before a reduction to Minimum supervision:

1. Twelve consecutive months under Medium supervision.
2. Currently employed full-time for 6 consecutive months.

FIGURE 7.5 *Continued*

3. No delinquent report in past 12 months resulting in disciplinary action.
4. No unauthorized/unjustified employment/residence changes.
5. Stable home life.
6. No current arrearages in supervision fee/court ordered payments.
7. In compliance with Special Conditions.

Deviations from the above criteria for reduction in levels of supervision may include parolees who are confined to mental institutions or convalescent centers; or parolees who are confined to their homes due to physical or mental handicaps or illnesses.

III. Increase in Levels of Supervision

During the parole period, there will develop reasons to increase levels of supervision. All increases in supervision, whether the parolee's former level of supervision was Medium or Minimum, shall be made to the highest level (Maximum).

Future reductions in supervision should be made after the parolee once again attains the criteria established under Medium or Minimum supervision, excluding criterion number 1: (Medium—6 months on Parole/Conditional Release; Minimum—12 consecutive months under Medium supervision.)

Officers are encouraged to use increases in levels of supervision as a supervision tool when a parolee's progress changes or other developments occur which negatively affect the parolee's stability. The point to keep in mind is that higher levels of supervision should be reserved for those parolees who: (1) may pose a greater risk to the community, and (2) for those parolees who have not been on parole long enough to assess their potential for lower levels of supervision. Therefore, officers are to use their discretion in increasing levels of supervision when parolees become unemployed, are arrested for minor offenses, violate numerous technical conditions of parole such as frequently changing residence and/or employment without permission, associating with persons of bad reputation, failing to follow instructions, etc. Additionally, parolees who continuously fall behind on their supervision fee and court ordered payments should be increased to Maximum supervision.

be noted that POs do not have unregulated discretion. Organizational imperatives and bureaucratic dynamics often serve to structure the use of discretion. This issue is discussed thoroughly in Chapter Nine.

Working a Caseload

Parole officers must face dealing with parolees as well as detailing and explaining their actions. The latter is accomplished through compiling and maintaining a case file on each of their parolees. Rationalizing case activity takes considerable effort but is necessary to satisfy departmental requirements. Keeping case or chronological

FIGURE 7.6   *Wisconsin Monthly Report Form*

WIS DEPT OF HEALTH AND SOCIAL SERVICES
DIVISION OF CORRECTIONS
DOC-8 (Rev. 11/74)   **MONTHLY REPORT**

Name _____ Today's Date _____

Address _____ Apt. # _____ City _____ Zip Code _____

Telephone _____ (If no telephone, give number where you can be reached)

Employer _____ Employer's Address _____

What kind of work do you do? _____

How much are you paid per hour? _____ How often are you paid? _____

Working hours? _____ Days missed since last report? _____ Why? _____

Other money received? _____ Amount? _____ From where? _____
                        (Yes or No)   (Welfare, Social Security, etc.)

IF YOU ARE ATTENDING SCHOOL:

Name of school _____

Days missed since last report? _____ Why? _____

SINCE YOUR LAST REPORT, DID YOU:

Change your address   ☐ Yes ☐ No   Change employment   ☐ Yes ☐ No

Buy on credit or borrow money ☐ Yes ☐ No   Buy or change automobile*   ☐ Yes ☐ No

Have any police contacts   ☐ Yes ☐ No   *If "YES", fill out a new permission form C-56
    (Traffic and other)   with your agent.

If you answered "YES" to any of the boxes above, explain here:

_____

_____

_____

_____

Other comments: _____

_____

_____

I hereby declare that the above is a true and accurate account of my activities since my last report and further understand that any false or misinformation can be sufficient reason for the revocation of my supervision.

                    Sign Your Name Here _____

records also allows parole officers to avoid criticism if their parolees become involved in criminal activity. When the PO has visible "proof" (case or "chrono" entries) that appropriate precautions and warnings were given, he or she is not responsible if parolees fail. Some officers believe that protecting one's position is an integral part of casework.

A time-honored method for positioning oneself against future criticism is the development of a **supervision plan.** Such plans (which in some states are mandatory) specify what parolees should do to overcome problems (unemployment, alcoholism, drug abuse, or marital) that might interfere with law-abiding reintegration. Parole officers can structure these plans to cover almost any contingency. Therefore, in the event of recidivism it will appear that the parolee took this course of action in spite of supervision efforts to the contrary. In such an instance, POs are rarely, if ever, blamed when parole is revoked and the client is returned to prison. Because virtually all parolees are potential recidivists, maintaining up-to-date files is crucial to parole work.

All contacts with parole subjects should be noted in the case file. According to California parole officials, recording is evidence of

    a. Agent performance and credit for tasks accomplished
    b. Parolee/collateral/witness statements
    c. Proof of instructions for agent of record and other agents if case is reassigned
    d. Actual visits to document parolee's physical presence
    e. Resource phone numbers
    f. Statistical research[41]

A contact sheet used by California POs illustrates how this is accomplished and can be found in Figure 7.7. A chronological record (chrono) used by Minnesota POs to record contacts is another popular format. This is illustrated in Figure 7.8. Most states now use an electronic medium to perform these tasks. The forms remain very similar and are filled in and stored via a computer.

On occasion, parolees request permission to relocate to other states. If they have suitable reasons for moving, such as employment or family residence, their requests are generally granted. Parolees must sign a waiver of extradition agreement indicating they will not contest return to the original jurisdiction in cases of possible or actual parole violation. In these cases, parole supervision is transferred to the state where the parolee moves under an Interstate Compact Agreement, a topic to which we now turn.

Interstate Compact

The **Interstate Compact Agreement** was drafted in 1934, and all fifty states, the District of Columbia, Puerto Rico, and the Virgin Islands have agreed to its provisions. This is one area where states have shown remarkable willingness to cooperate, and

(text continues on page 233)

FIGURE 7.7   *Parolee Contact Sheet*

Parolee: Tiev, Carl
CDC Number: C-00000
Agent of Record: Darwin

	Residence	Employment	Office	Telephone	Jail	Collateral	Case Review	Other	
Type of Contact				X					3-27, 0900, S called office regarding remainder of release funds. Advised that check has arrived. Darwin 5.
			X						3-27, 1530, S in to pick up check. Said is in route to job interview. Will advise me of results. Very talkative. Darwin 8.
	X								4-2, 1800, Contact w/S and wife. Started work at J&J Electronics yesterday. Wife still working. Discussed progress with personal stress management. He is cognizant of personal triggers when financial pressures build. Is attempting improved financial management. Referred him to nonprofit credit counseling. Darwin 20.
				X					4-7, 1330, S called office regarding changing next office visit due to work schedule. Visit changed to 4-10 at 1830. Darwin 5.
			X						4-10, 1845, S in for office visit. Discussed progress with work and credit counseling. Has not contacted credit agency. Advised him to do that ASAP. Wife still working. Somewhat nervous. Darwin 20
				X					4-11, 1010, S called office to inform that he had made appointment with credit agency for 4-18. Darwin 5.

FIGURE 7.8   *Parolee Chronological Record*

HENNEPIN COUNTY
PAROLE FIELD SERVICES
Chrono Record

NAME: _____   NO.: _____

AKA: _____

OFFENSE: _____   EXPIRATION: _____

Rec'd: _____   DATE PAROLED: _____

Agent: _____

SPECIAL CONDITIONS:

DATE OF REPORT	TYPE OF REPORT	CAR ACTION	ACTION DATE

RESIDENCE: (Address, Telephone)

_____

_____

_____

_____

_____

SIGNIFICANT ADDRESSES

_____

_____

_____

_____

_____

	EMPLOYMENT			
DATE STARTED	EMPLOYER AND ADDRESS	POSITION	WAGE	DATE TERM.

(continued)

FIGURE 7.8 *Continued*

DATE	TREATMENT (Referrals and involved Agencies

DATE	OTHER RELEVANT INFORMATION (Arrests, complaints, etc.)

historically, the agreement works well. The general provisions of the agreement, which have been validated by court decisions,[42] are that

1. Any state may be a receiving state and will supervise a parolee or probationer from any other state (the sending state) if the parolee or probationer is a resident of the receiving state and has employment there;
2. The receiving state will supervise the sending state's parolee using the same standards used for its own parolees;
3. The sending state may revoke parole or probation at any time during the term of the parole or probation and retake the parolee or probationer at its discretion and with a minimum of procedure.[43]

To be considered a resident of the receiving state, the parolee or probationer must have resided in that state for more than a year before he or she went to the sending state and must have resided in the sending state for less than six months immediately before the commission of the crime of conviction. If these conditions of residence are fulfilled, the receiving state must accept him or her, as long as his or her family resides in the state and the person is able to find employment there. In all cases the receiving state has the opportunity, before the parolee or probationer is sent there, to investigate the home and the prospective employment. If residence or employment is deficient, the client may nevertheless be sent from one state to another if the receiving state agrees.[44]

Since 1997, thirty-five states have enacted legislation to amend the 1937 Interstate Compact. Many compact administrators (each state has one) believed the compact was outdated and overwhelmed. The new compact remains substantially the same. The main differences are that it legally empowers "compact authorities to effectively conduct business on behalf of the compact states, and it sets forth a structure that will keep compact activity at a visible point within state government."[45]

An application for Compact Services and the Report of Sending State forms used by Michigan demonstrate how a request for an interstate agreement is initiated and can be seen in Figures 7.9 and 7.10. Once supervision is accepted, periodic progress reports are submitted using a form similar to that used by Minnesota, shown in Figure 7.11 (p. 236). Regardless of whether the supervision is conducted in a new state or the original state of jurisdiction, one of the parole officer's basic functions is to anticipate trouble and to take steps to correct a problematic situation, or at least document efforts in that regard. In order to do this effectively, given large and diverse caseloads, categorization, or typing, of parolees is inevitable.

Typing the Client

Richard McCleary, in his classic study of Illinois parole officers, indicates that trouble "... relates directly to control. If a PO can control his clients in an efficient manner he eliminates trouble."[46] One way to do this, according to McCleary, is to

(text continues on page 237)

FIGURE 7.9 *Application for Compact Services*

MICHIGAN DEPARTMENT OF CORRECTIONS
INTERSTATE COMPACT—Application for Compact Services & Agreement to Return   CFR-166

SENDING STATE:___MICHIGAN_____   RECEIVING STATE:_____

I, _____, hereby apply for supervision as a parolee or probationer pursuant to the Interstate
Compact for the Supervision of Parolees and Probationers. I understand that the very fact that supervision
will be in another state makes it likely that there will be certain differences between the supervision I would receive in this state
and the supervision which I will receive in any state to which I am asking to go. However, I urge the authorities to whom this
application is made, and all other judicial and administrative authorities, to recognize that supervision in
another state, if granted as requested in this application, will be a benefit to me and will improve my opportunities to
make a good adjustment. In order to get the advantages of supervision under the Interstate Compact for the Supervision
of Parolees and Probationers, I do hereby accept such differences in the course and character of supervision as may be
provided, and I do state that I consider the benefits of supervision under the Compact to be worth any adjustments in
my situation which may be occasioned.

In view of the above, I hereby apply for permission to be supervised on (parole) (probation) in _____
for the following reasons: (RECEIVING STATE)

In consideration of being granted permission to reside in the State of _____, I hereby agree:
                                                                     (RECEIVING STATE)

1.   That I will make my home with/at _____, until a change

      of residence is duly authorized by the proper authorities of the State of _____.
                                                                          (RECEIVING STATE)

2.   That I will comply with the conditions of (probation)   (parole)   as fixed by both the state of Michigan and the

      state of _____.
                    (REICEIVING STATE)

3.   That I will, when duly instructed by proper authorities of the State of Michigan, return at any time to the State of
      Michigan.

4.   That I herby do waive extradition to the State of Michigan from any jurisdiction in or outside the United States where I
      may be found and also agree that I will not contest any effort by any jurisdiction to return me to the State of Michigan.

5.   Failure to comply with the above will be deemed to be in violation of the terms and conditions of (probation) (parole)
      for which I may be returned to the State of Michigan.

I (have read the above) (have had the above read and explained to me), and understand its meaning and agree thereto.

Date: _____   Signature: _____

Witness: _____

DISTRIBUTION: White, Green, Canary—CO; Pink—PPA; Goldenrod—Parolee/Probationer

FIGURE 7.10 *Interstate Compact Report of Sending State*

MICHIGAN DEPARTMENT OF CORRECTIONS

REPORT OF SENDING STATE UPON PAROLEE OR PROBATIONER BEING SENT TO ANOTHER JURISDICTION   CFO-152   8/79

PAROLE AND PROBATION FORM II

TO _____ _____   DATE _____

PAROLE _____ PROBATION _____ (check one)

Re: _____ _____ _____
              Name   No.

The above mentioned (will depart) (has departed) from _____ _____

by _____ on _____, and was instructed
              (method of transportation)   (date)

to report (in person) (by letter) to:

Enclosed please find: (check appropriate items)
1. (   ) Copies of classification material
2. (   ) Photographs
3. (   ) Fingerprints
4. (   ) Certificate of Parole
5. (   ) Probation or Parole Agreement
6. (   ) Waiver of Extradition Form (Form III)
7. (   ) Other material described below

Please acknowledge receipt of this material and send arrival report as soon as possible.

Interstate Compact Administrator for Michigan

By: _____

FIGURE 7.11   *Interstate Compact Progress Report*

HENNEPIN COUNTY
PAROLE FIELD SERVICES
1800 CHICAGO AVENUE SOUTH
MINNEAPOLIS, MINNESOTA 55404

INTER-STATE COMPACT REPORT

REPORT TO	FROM	
SUBJECT	NUMBER	DATE

PROGRESS REPORT
CONTINUANCE

This case was reviewed on _____. Continuance is being recommended because:

☐ 1. Financial obligation, or other special conditions have not been met.
☐ 2. Adjustment on probation does not warrant consideration.
☐ 3. Adjustment satisfactory but in relation to offense too little time has elapsed to warrant discharge.
☐ 4. New charges pending, ☐ supplemental report shall be forthcoming.
☐ 5. Court policy requires extended term on probation.

REPORTING INFORMATION

ADDRESS

TELEPHONE	LIVING WITH
EMPLOYER/SCHOOL	JOB/COURSE
INCOME	DATE STARTED

PERSONAL INFORMATION

OFFENSE

SENTENCE	EXPIRATION

SPECIAL CONDITIONS

OFFENSE INFORMATION

COMMENTS

HENNEPIN COUNTY PAROLE OFFICER	SUPERVISOR

HC 18009

place clients into various categories, or types, based on the potential for trouble. At one end of this continuum are "dangerous men" and at the other are "paper men." POs expect a lot of trouble from dangerous men and almost none from paper men. But according to McCleary, for POs the term **dangerous men** does not refer to the parolees' violence, like it sounds, but rather to how rationally or predictably the parolee responds to the threats of punishment or promises of reward the PO uses to control a client. If the parolee does not react rationally to threats or promises, the PO knows he or she cannot be effectively controlled.[47] A PO in McCleary's study gave an example of a dangerous man:

> I'll tell you why he's dangerous. With most clients, a friendly warning is enough to straighten a problem out. Sometimes you have to go through the motions of writing an official warning. But that doesn't even faze him. I don't understand clients like that. They're not living in the real world. They go out of their way to make trouble. They've got chips on their shoulders.[48]

The term **paper man** refers to clients who are easy to control, those you do not have to worry about. The term comes from the phrase "on paper," as in "that's how many men I've got on paper." One PO related to McCleary that he only had about a dozen clients he worried about, spending ". . . a lot of time with my men the first week they're out of the joint. If they look like they're doing OK, I don't bother them anymore. I only see most of my men two or three times a year but they're still on paper."[49]

McCleary observed that dangerous men and paper men are treated very differently. Many POs watch dangerous men carefully and as soon as possible find plausible reasons to file a violation of parole. Paper men, however, are allowed wide latitude; they are contacted infrequently (regardless of department regulations) and their parole is rarely revoked (unless they commit a serious law violation).

Drawing on his work experience in this field, John Rosecrance agrees that POs do type their clients, and based on these typings, treat them accordingly. However, not all categorizations follow McCleary's schema. For example, one parole officer based his categorizations strictly on the parolee's prior record, labeling the parolee long rap sheet, medium rap sheet, short sheet, and no sheet. The PO carefully monitored the first two categories and paid almost no attention to the last two.

The typing process generally occurs during the first few months of supervision. POs frequently "test" their parolees to see if their statements can be corroborated by independent sources, such as family members, employees, or police. Some POs attempt various tactics to ascertain how parolees will react. A frequent ploy used by many supervision officers (including your second author) is to be verbally aggressive toward new parolees, in effect "reading them the riot act." Supposedly, such initial tirades make clients more agreeable, especially when the officer gradually relents or backs off from a rigid initial stance. McCleary described a similar situation in which a PO lambasted a new parolee with the following statement: "I've got your number, Ike. If you want to start a new life with me, I'll let you. But if you want to buy trouble from me, mister, that's cool too. I know all about you and I'll be watching." The new parolee appeared frightened by these remarks; the PO explained his actions by saying that he wanted to know how far he could push the parolee. Although he did not really have any bad information about "Ike," the tactic was used to see how he would react. If he had laughed, the PO would expect trouble; because he acted scared, the PO knew he would be a "good parolee."[50]

Whereas POs are typing their charges, a similar process occurs with parolees. Such a process involves the use of subtle suggestions and verbal ploys by parolees to probe for an understanding of how the supervision process is to be played out. John Irwin describes this as "running tests" on the PO, that is, the parolee reveals information about himself or herself to see how the PO reacts. For example, the parolee may mention that he intends to move in with his girlfriend. The PO's reaction to this statement helps the parolee know where he stands with the PO and what their relationship will be like.[51]

After the first few months of supervision both PO and parolee generally have completed the "reading process" and can anticipate each other's reactions. Because violations of parole conditions are inevitable with at least some parolees, the next stage in the supervision process involves managing these violations. In order to understand parole violations it is essential to study the landmark court decision that established procedures for violation and revocation hearings.

Morrissey v. Brewer

In 1972 the Supreme Court decided whether due process should be granted prior to revoking parole. Their answer, in the *Morrissey v. Brewer* case, was a resounding yes! Because this case has had a major impact on parole supervision, it is worth considering in some detail.[52]

In 1967 Morrissey pled guilty and was convicted of false drawing of checks. He was paroled from the Iowa State Penitentiary in 1968, but seven months later he was arrested for violating the conditions of his parole. His parole officer reported that Morrissey bought a car under an assumed name, operated it without permission, gave false statements to the police about his address and insurance company after a minor accident, obtained credit under an assumed name, and failed to report his place of residence to his parole officer. The PO's report continued by stating that he had interviewed Morrissey; that Morrissey could not explain why he had not contacted the parole officer; and that Morrissey admitted that he bought the car, obtained credit under an assumed name, and had been involved in the accident. Morrissey's parole was revoked and he was sent back to prison. Morrissey challenged that revocation. His attorneys argued that his revocation was a violation of the due process clause of the Fourteenth Amendment.

The Court ruled that the liberty of a parolee contains many of the same values of unconditional liberty and therefore inflicts a "grievous loss" on the parolee and sometimes on others. The Court also stated that there are two processes due in a parole revocation: (1) the arrest of the parolee and the preliminary hearing, and (2) the revocation hearing. The Court believed that the preliminary hearing required "some minimal inquiry be conducted at or reasonably near the place of the alleged parole violation or arrest and as promptly as convenient after arrest." The purpose of this inquiry is to determine whether there is probable cause or reasonable grounds to believe that the arrestee committed the acts that could lead to his parole revocation. The Court also ruled that "there must also be an opportunity for a hearing, if it is desired by the parolee, prior to the final decision on revocation by the parole authority." The Court ruled that the following requirements of due process must be met in parole revocation proceedings:

1. Written notice of the claimed violations of parole;
2. Disclosure to the parolee of evidence against him or her;
3. Opportunity to be heard in person and to present witnesses and documentary evidence;
4. The right to confront and cross-examine adverse witnesses (unless the hearing officer specifically finds good cause for not allowing confrontation);
5. A "neutral and detached" hearing body, such as a traditional parole board, members of which need not be judicial officers or lawyers; and
6. A written statement by the fact finders as to the evidence relied on and reasons for revoking parole.

The *Morrissey* decision required POs to protect the constitutional rights of their parolees in a similar manner that the *Miranda* decision required police officers to inform suspects of their rights. This requirement formalized the revocation process and forced POs to carefully document violations and required a change in supervision tactics for many POs. Rather than being free to detain their parolees while "investigating" possible violations in order to get their attention, after *Morrissey* POs would have to go through up to six steps before they would get to a hearing on a revocation.[53]

The *Morrissey v. Brewer, Mempa v. Rhay,* and *Gagnon v. Scarpelli* (see Chapter Five) cases established the ground rules for both parole and probation revocations. *Mempa v. Rhay* made it clear that parole and probation could not be revoked without a formal hearing. *Gagnon v. Scarpelli* had the effect of requiring that counsel be made available to those facing revocation proceedings. *Morrissey v. Brewer* established a two-step process for revocation. The first step involves a preliminary hearing where evidence against the parolee or probationer is present. If the hearing officer decides that evidence is sufficiently damaging, a revocation hearing is set. The second stage requires a full hearing before a parole board or judge (in case of probation). At that time, the parolee or probationer has a right to refute the allegations by presenting witnesses and documentation as well as by cross-examining accusers. However, the revocation hearing is not a trial; consequently, a presumption of guilt is sufficient for revocation. Now that the reader is familiar with the

Morrissey v. Brewer case, it is possible to examine violations and revocations and how they are conducted in the real world of parole.

Revocation

In 1999, more than 197,000 parole violators were returned to state prisons, up from 131,502 in 1990.[54] Parole violators accounted for 35 percent of all prison admissions in 1999, up from 17 percent in 1980. In some states, the number of parole violators as a percentage of new prison admissions is more than 50 percent. In California, for example, 67 percent of all new prison admissions in 1999 were parole violators; in Utah the number was 55 percent; and in Louisiana 53 percent of new prison admissions were parole violators.[55]

Box 7.1 describes the revocation and is based on the New York State Division of Parole's *Report on Violation Procedures*. The process involves an initiation of the violation proceedings, a preliminary violation hearing, a filing of a violation of parole report, and a final revocation hearing.

In some supervision cases, even though there have been no new law violations, the parolee's community adjustment deteriorates to the point where formal proceedings must be initiated. Usually, in these cases informal efforts to correct the situation through either warnings or admonishments have been unsuccessful. Parolees, fearing such hearings, often abscond by leaving the jurisdiction without approval. When this occurs, an arrest warrant is issued and the term of parole is stayed or tolled (parole does not resume until the parolee is located). Tolling protects against expiration of parole and loss of jurisdiction for those who have fled from parole supervision. The case in Box 7.2, from Georgia parole files, is a classic example of this scenario.

Parole **revocation** does not necessarily mean that the parolee will be returned to prison. Frequently, in cases of technical violations or minor offenses, parolees will be ordered to serve time in local facilities rather than being reincarcerated in prison. In many jurisdictions this means brief jail sentences, whereas in others special facilities have been developed for this purpose. For example, Nevada places minor parole violators in minimum-security centers where they can keep their jobs, whereas New York uses a community-based treatment center called a "transition facility." In such cases (revocation without prison recommitment), after a brief jolt in a local detention center, parolees are reinstated on parole and released into the community. This type of disposition is becoming commonplace as prison crowding makes it impractical to return all parole violators to prison. The availability of such an option increases the range of penalties and mitigates the "all or nothing" atmosphere that has characterized many revocation hearings.

Although the *Morrissey* decision introduced considerable formality into the revocation process, supervision discretion has not been eliminated. Just as in probation supervision, the parole officers must initiate revocation proceedings. Except

(text continues on page 245)

BOX 7.1 • *The Revocation Process*

Initiation of Parole Violation Proceedings

Executive law provides that, where a parole officer has reasonable cause to believe that a person under his or her supervision has violated one or more of the conditions of parole in an important respect or has lapsed into criminal ways or company, he or she must report such facts to a member of the Board of Parole or someone designated by the Board of Parole. Under present rules and regulations, the parole officer must report these facts to a senior parole officer and may obtain a warrant for retaking and temporary detention. After a warrant is issued and the individual is either apprehended pursuant to that warrant or that warrant is lodged at his or her place of detention, a notice of violation is given to the alleged parole violator within no more than three days after the execution of the warrant.

Preliminary Violation Hearing

Executive law requires a preliminary hearing within fifteen days after execution of the warrant. It provides that the hearing officer not have any prior supervisory involvement with the alleged parole violator. In the great majority of cases, preliminary hearings are conducted by persons designated as preliminary hearing officers. This is a separate title within the Division of Parole. The preliminary hearing officers are specially trained in the conduct of hearings and are under the direct supervision of the supervising hearing officer of the Division of Parole.

The alleged parole violator may be represented by counsel at the preliminary hearing under certain conditions. It is division policy to admit an attorney if he or she is present and to grant an adjournment to obtain an attorney where it is clear that the alleged violator cannot adequately speak for himself or herself under the circumstances presented.

The alleged parole violator at a preliminary hearing is afforded the opportunity to confront his or her accuser, cross-examine the witnesses presented by the parole officer, and offer evidence on his or her own behalf. Once sufficient evidence of violation of parole has been found with regard to one or more of the charges, the preliminary hearing officer will take no further evidence regarding any other charges that may have been brought against the alleged violator. If probable cause is found, at the conclusion of the preliminary hearing, the preliminary hearing officer will send to the violator or his or her attorney a written statement of the finding of fact. If no probable cause is found, the alleged parole violator will be released from custody and returned to parole supervision.

The Declaration of Delinquency

If probable cause is found at the preliminary hearing, or if the necessity for a preliminary hearing has been obviated by the releasee's conviction for a new crime while under his or her present parole or conditional release supervision, the parole officer must thereafter prepare and forward to his or her senior parole officer a violation of parole report. This violation of parole report contains not only the specific charges being brought against the alleged parole violator but also the names of all witnesses who will be called to prove those allegations (except where the disclosure of names of witnesses may create a danger to their safety) and a listing of any other evidence to be relied on by the division. After a review of the violation of parole report, the senior parole officer will then send the violation of parole report, along with his or her analysis and recommendation to a member of the Board of Parole for review. The board member, after reviewing the documents, may cancel delinquency, declare the alleged parole violator delinquent, or issue a final

(continued)

BOX 7.1 • *Continued*

declaration of delinquency for a violator who has received a new indeterminate sentence. This normally occurs within thirty days of the finding of probable cause or the waiver of a preliminary hearing. Although the alleged violator has the primary responsibility for obtaining counsel, the Division of Parole frequently provides notification of requests for counsel to those agencies that provide legal aid to indigents and has made special arrangements for the assignment of counsel in several locations.

At the hearing, the charges are read to the alleged violator and he or she is asked to enter a plea of guilty, not guilty, guilty with an explanation, or stand mute. He or she is given an opportunity to hear the evidence and to cross-examine each witness. Witnesses, if any, may also be called on his or her behalf. All testimony is taken under oath.

Final Revocation Hearing

Once a board member has declared an alleged parole violator delinquent and ordered a final hearing, the Division of Parole will then provide a final revocation hearing within no more than ninety days after the probable cause determination. Written notice of that hearing, along with a copy of the violation of parole report, are served on the alleged parole violator and his or her attorney no later than fourteen days prior to the actual hearing.

All testimony is on the record, which is transcribed by a hearing reporter within two weeks after the hearing. The strict rules of evidence as they apply at criminal trials do not apply at parole revocation hearings. Relevant hearsay testimony and any other evidence relevant to the charges subject to the alleged violator's right to confrontation are admissible. If the hearing officer, after hearing all the evidence, is not satisfied that there is a preponderance of evidence to support a violation of parole in an important respect, he or she must dismiss the violation, cancel delinquency, and restore the parolee or conditional releasee to supervision. If, however, he or she is satisfied that there is a violation of parole in an important respect, he or she must then report in writing to a member of the board his or her finding of fact and recommendation. The decision notice contains a detailed analysis of the finding of fact and recommendations of the hearing officer. A board member reviews the recommendations and either affirms or modifies the recommendation in writing. Although the executive law does not so require, where a board member modifies the hearing officer's recommendation, reasons for that modification are often included in the board-signed decision notice. Copies of the notice are sent to the alleged parole violator and his or her attorney.

Summary

The parole revocation proceedings of the division constitute a formidable process. It ensures the due process rights of alleged parole violators by including several points in the proceedings where the alleged violator is able to prove his or her innocence. Moreover, the process entails internal checks and balances on whether it is appropriate to revoke parole in individual cases.

BOX 7.2 • *Tolling Parole*

State Board of Pardons and Paroles
Atlanta, Georgia

DELINQUENT REPORT

Date __March 7,__

TO:
(X) Parole Board
( ) Compact Administrator

FROM: Robert C. Smith
Parole Supervisor

__14, Albany (G) 341-4392__
DISTRICT

NAME: __John Jones__   NUMBER: __EF-123456__   STATUS: __Parolee__

Convicted of __Burglary__ in __Dougherty__ County.

Parole Date: __January 11,__   Expiration Date: __January 11,__

Type of Report:
(X) Delinquency   ( ) Arrest   ( ) Conviction   ( ) Follow up

Circumstances of delinquency (include extenuating factors)

Subject failed to report on February 3, and on February 6, , this officer attempted to contact subject at his employment. Mr. Chastain, subject's supervisor, stated that subject walked off the job on January 28, ... after having been reprimanded for failing to follow orders. Mr. Chastain stated that he asked subject to help dig a ditch for some pipe. Mr. Chastain stated subject told him "I ain't going to dig no damn ditch". Mr. Chastain said he told subject to either follow orders or turn in his equipment. According to Mr. Chastain, subject then cursed him and walked off the job site. He added that subject's progress on the job had been poor and he probably would have had to fire subject anyway.

Later that same day, this officer attempted to contact subject at his residence. Subject's mother said subject had moved in with some woman two weeks ago and she had not seen him in two or three days. Mrs. Jones stated that she would have subject contact me as soon as she saw him again.

On February 9, subject reported to the office and stated that he had obtained a job with Coats and Clark on February 7, This officer reprimanded subject for changing his residence without permission and quitting his job. This officer

Arrest Data:
Date: _____ City: _____ County: _____
Charges: _____

( ) Bond Set. Amount: $_____ ( ) Can post bond ( ) Cannot post bond
( ) Presently held in _____
( ) Absconded on _____
(X) Warrant is requested *to Dougherty County*

Conviction Data: Court of Record ( ) Yes   ( ) No
Name under which convicted: _____
Offense: _____
Official Court Name: _____ City: _____
County: _____ Date: _____
Specific Sentence Received: _____

Supervisors Recommendations
(X) Revocation   ( ) Continue under supervision

Summary of progress under Supervision:

Subject was paroled on January 11, , reported for his initial contact on January 12, and was thoroughly briefed on the Parole Conditions. He began the period residing with his mother, Mabel Jones at 215 Slappy Drive, Albany, and working for Chastain's Paving Company. Since that time subject has quit one job, been fired from two others, moved on numerous occasions without permission, used alcohol excessively and always failed to notify this officer of any changes. He has been issued a Letter of Reprimand and there has been an Administrative Hearing for subject, all to no avail. This officer sees no option but revocation with reconsideration in six months.

Copies (3 to Parole Board, 3 to Compact Administrator   PFO-16
and 1 to Offender's File)

(continued)

BOX 7.2 • *Continued*

instructed subject to return to his mother's residence. Subject displayed a negative attitude throughout the interview and denied cursing his previous employer. He stated he quit the job because he did not like the work. Subject agreed to move back to his residence of record with his mother.

On February 10,   , this officer contacted Mr. Bill Reed, subject's supervisor and verified that subject was in fact employed by Coats and Clark since February 7,   Mr. Reed stated subject was progressing satisfactorily. Also, on this date, this officer completed a record's check on subject's girlfriend, Jan Short and learned that she is currently on Probation for Possession of Marijuana (misdemeanor).

On February 20,   , Mr. Reed contacted this officer and advised that subject had not reported to work for the past two days and if subject was not back on the job by February 22,   he would be forced to fire subject. On this same date, this officer attempted to contact subject at his residence. Mrs. Jones advised that she had not seen subject since February 18,   and that he was probably at the residence of his girlfriend, Jan   . 224 Oak Street. She also stated that subject had been drinking heavily for the past few weeks.

This officer then went to the residence of Jan   Subject answered the door and was obviously intoxicated. This officer instructed subject to return immediately to his residence of record, sober up and report to the office on February 21,   . Subject was too drunk to reprimand at this point and after muttering a few obscenities, subject stated he would report if he felt like it. Just as this officer was leaving, Ms.   came to the door and she, too, was obviously intoxicated. She ordered this officer off her property and to stop harrassing subject.

Upon returning to the office, this officer spoke with Chief Parole Officer William Smith. Due to subject's numerous violations, it was determined that subject should receive a stern Letter of Reprimand from Chief Smith for violating Conditions #2, #3, #4, #6, #7, #10, #12 and #13.

On February 21,   subject reported to the office and this officer gave subject his copy of the Letter of Reprimand. The letter was read and discussed and subject advised he would report to Coats and Clarks immediately. This officer later verified that subject went back to work and moved back to his residence of record on February 22,

Subject again failed to report during the first of March,   and on March 6,   this officer contact Mr. Reed and learned that subject had been fired on March 2,   for reporting to work in an intoxicated condition. Later this date, this writer went to subject's residence and learned from his mother that subject had not been home since March 1,   She advised that subject was probably at the residence of Jan   This officer went to Ms.   residence, found subject again intoxicated and instructed him to report on March 7,

Upon returning to the office, this officer discussed subject's case with Chief Parole Officer Smith and it was decided to hold an Administrative Hearing the following morning when subject reported. This officer fully appraised Chief Smith of all violations and gave him copies of the field sheets for his preparations.

Subject reported on March 7,   and the Administrative Hearing was held by Chief Smith. Chief Smith severely reprimanded subject for violation of Conditions #2, #3, #4, #6, #7, #10, #12 and #13. Also, Chief Smith instructed subject to attend Alcohol Counseling which was arranged by this officer. Subject appeared remorseful and indicated he now had a job at Lance Industries. This officer later verified subject's employment and that he was back at his residence of record.

On March 23,   ', this officer contacted Mr. Bert Hardy, subject's supervisor, who stated that subject had been fired on March 13,   for excessive absenteeism and drinking on the job. This officer also contacted subject's mother who stated that subject had not been home since March 10,   was not attending Alcohol Counseling and was again staying with Jan   This officer verified through Alcohol Counseling Center that subject had not attended any sessions.

Subject failed to report during the first of April, _   and attempts to locate subject have been futile. Based on the following violations, this officer requests a Board warrant for subject's arrest.

Condition #2: By failing to report during April,

Condition #3: By changing his residence without permission during March,

Condition #4: By failing to maintain full-time employment and work diligently since his release on parole on January 11,

Condition #6: By using alcoholic beverages to excess on numerous occasions since his release;

BOX 7.2 • *Continued*

Page 3

Condition #7:   By associating with persons of bad reputation on numerous occasions; namely, Jan

Condition #10:   By being away from his residence after 12:00 midnight on numerous occasions;

Condition #12:   By failing to carry out instructions issued to him by Chief Parole Officer Smith in a Letter of Reprimand dated February 21, regarding Conditions #2,#3,#4,#6,#7,#10,#12 and #13;

By failing to carry out instructions issued to him by Chief Parole Officer Smith to attend Alcohol Counseling;

Condition #13:   By failing to notify of changes in his residence and employment on several occasions since his release.

---

in obvious cases, such as the commission of a serious new offense, there are no precise guidelines governing when to inform the parole board or department of corrections of possible violations. Supervision POs can "bank" or stockpile numerous minor violations without taking any formal action. Even in situations where parolees commit new offenses, there is still some degree of discretion. POs who are "loyal" to their clients can still seek to avoid revocation unless the new offense is a particularly serious one. McCleary has devised a scale to measure such discretion.[56] The scale begins with what McCleary calls an absolutely hopeless situation (examples are murder and rape), where the PO has no discretion whatsoever; moves to marginally hopeless situations (e.g., burglary, simple robbery), where the PO has relatively little freedom; to marginally promising (e.g., narcotics possession), where the PO has a relatively great deal of freedom; and finally to absolutely promising (misdemeanors and "victimless" felonies), where discretion is greatest and the parolee normally will not be returned to prison.

Although supervising parolees is often a frustrating and problematic process, not all cases end in revocation, and there are tangible rewards associated with the job. The many supervision successes, those who can adjust to community life, are visible proof that you are "doing something right." One veteran PO showed off a scrapbook in which he kept correspondence of parolees who had made good. In the scrapbook there were letters, newspaper clippings, wedding and birth announcements, graduation notices, and business cards that attested to significant events in the lives of his former clients. While displaying the scrapbook, he beamed with pride, and the rewards of supervising parolees were obvious. New York parole officers writing in their annual report chronicled similar rewards:

> For David Blum, a rewarding experience started . . . when a parolee who had a long sentence and a history of drug abuse went on methadone maintenance and began working at a filing place. . . . He soon got a break and was hired as a property man in a printing firm. The parolee got married, had a child and received an

early discharge after five years on parole. When he finished parole . . . he was making [very good money]. Recently Tom Brancato met on the street one of the first parolees he had ever supervised about seventeen years ago. The ex-parolee proudly introduced his wife and children. An ex-parolee whom Ed Deutsch had supervised opened his business and then called the Parole Office to see if he could help out by employing someone currently under supervision. A parolee was hired through this effort. Diane Stella went the extra mile with a parolee to help insure his readjustment rather than reincarcerating him. He successfully completed supervision and invited Officer Stella to his son's christening.[59]

It is important to remember that parole supervision, although challenging and often frustrating, may also be full of rewards. It is a calling that combines protecting the community and helping individuals adjust to life outside prison. Although these two roles may contradict each other at times (see Chapter Nine), when they do come together and the results are success, the parolee is doing well, the community is safer, and the PO feels good about his or her job.

Summary

Parole supervision is a problematic process for both the PO and parolee. Released inmates face serious problems adjusting to life outside an institutional setting. Frequently, they find their new freedom confusing and stressful, as the realities of everyday life do not match overly optimistic prison expectations. POs are saddled with the dual responsibility of aiding offender reintegration as well as enforcing release conditions. Although general and special parole orders clearly specify acceptable parolee behavior, in actual practice the orders are impossible to rigidly enforce. Supervision officers have considerable discretion regarding which parole conditions to emphasize and how to ensure compliance with them. Parolees are required to report regularly (according to a supervision classification) to the parole office and can expect field visits from POs at their residence and employment. An Interstate Compact Agreement provides for supervision in the event parolees move to another state.

An essential part of parole supervision involves record keeping as POs document contacts with parolees. Proper maintenance of case files allows POs to insulate themselves from criticism in the event parolees fail. Most POs informally categorize parolees and then devote more time to their troublesome types. The *Morrissey v. Brewer* decision established a formal two-step procedure for violation and revocation matters, consisting of a preliminary or probable cause hearing and a final revocation hearing. Parolees are accorded considerable due process rights (a formal statement of charges, the ability to confront witnesses) at these hearings. Even though violations and problems inevitably color the supervision process, most parolees eventually "make it" in the community. POs are rewarded when their parolees succeed on supervision and go on to lead productive lives.

Key People and Terms

Civil disabilities (215)
Dangerous men (237)
Initial interviews (223)
Interstate Compact Agreement (229)
John Irwin (214)
Richard McCleary (233)
Paper men (237)
Parole order (217)

Joan Petersilia (211)
Recidivism (211)
Reentry (213)
Revocation (240)
Serious and Violent Offender Reentry
    Initiative (216)
Supervision plan (229)
Andrew von Hirsch (211)

Key Legal Cases

Gagnon v. Scarpelli
Mempa v. Rhay

Morrissey v. Brewer

Questions for Discussion and Review

1. List and discuss the problems faced by released offenders.

2. What are the characteristics of successful reentry programs?

3. Give examples of typical parole conditions. What is the difference between general and special conditions of parole?

4. What is the significance of the initial interview to the supervision process?

5. What is a "chrono"? Why might it be important when working a caseload?

6. What are the general provisions of the Interstate Compact Agreement?

7. What is the difference between dangerous men and paper men?

8. Discuss the significance of the *Morrissey v. Brewer* case.

9. Discuss the role of discretion in the revocation process.

Relevant Internet Sites

U.S. Parole Commission: www.usdoj.gov/uspc

U.S. Department of Justice Serious and Violent Offender Reentry Initiative: www.ojp.usdoj.gov/reentry

New York State Division of Parole, including the state's parole handbook, a listing of release programs, and program services: http://parole.state.ny.us

American Probation and Parole Association: www.appa-net.org

National Institute of Corrections web site on the Interstate Compact Agreement: www.nicic.org/services/special/compact-adult/default.htm

EXERCISE • *Revocation of Parole*

An important part of parole supervision is deciding whether to revoke a parolee for violating the conditions of his or her release. This decision generally falls on the paroling authority of the state, although the parole officer usually starts the process. Read the following case and decide if the parolee described should be revoked and sent back to prison. Make your decision based on the likelihood of further violations, public safety, and the seriousness of the violation.

Smith was convicted of murder in the killing of a man in a barroom fight. A former combat veteran who had difficulty coping with civilian life, he was homeless at the time of the crime, living under a bridge, and drinking a lot. Even though the victim had shot at him first, Smith shot back, killing the man. He was convicted of murder and sentenced to life under an indeterminate sentence, although he would be eligible for parole after serving nine years. While he was in prison, Smith completed an alcohol and drug treatment program, an anger management program, regularly attended Alcoholics Anonymous (AA) meetings, received a college degree through the prison education program, and, although he had a few disciplinary write-ups, was generally considered a good inmate. He was paroled after serving twelve years, and the day he moved into his transition housing (a flop house hotel in a large city), he attended an AA meeting. At this meeting he was befriended by a married couple who helped him find a job and introduced him to the woman who would become his wife one year later. He continued to attend AA meetings and remained sober. Shortly before his wedding, he landed a job as an alcohol and drug counselor at a local treatment facility. After the wedding he and his wife bought an older house that they began remodeling. Smith seemed to be following his parole orders to the letter. However, a little more than three years after his release his wife called his parole officer, obviously upset over an argument she had had with Smith, and reported that he had guns in the house. The PO went to the home and found a small collection of antique, muzzle-loading firearms, some of which were inoperable. Smith explained that the collection was just a hobby and for display, that he had never fired any of them, and that he didn't even have the gunpowder or musket balls needed to load and shoot them. The PO arrested Smith for felon in possession of a firearm and violation of his parole conditions, remanding him to the parole board for a revocation hearing. If revoked, Smith would spend the rest of his life in prison without possibility of parole.

Notes

1. Malcolm Braly, *False Starts: A Memoir of San Quentin and Other Prisons* (Boston: Little, Brown, 1976) 201–202.

2. Charles M. Terry, "From C-Block to Academia: You Can't Get There from Here," in *Convict Criminology*, eds. Jeffrey Ian Ross and Stephen C. Richards (Belmont, CA: Wadsworth, 2003) 95–119.

3. Todd Clear and George Cole, *American Corrections* (Monterey, CA: Brooks/Cole, 1986) 421.

4. Personal communication with John Rosecrance.

5. Personal communication with John Rosecrance.

6. Timothy Hughes, Doris James Wilson, and Allen J. Beck, *Trends in State Parole, 1990–2000* (Washington, DC: U.S. Department of Justice, October, 2001).

7. Patrick A. Langan, and David J. Levin, *Recidivism of Prisoners Released in 1994* (Washington, DC: Bureau of Justice Statistics).

8. *Corrections Digest* 17 (September 10, 1986): 1–2.

9. *Corrections Digest* 16 (December 4, 1985): 1, 4.

10. Bureau of Justice Statistics, Special Report, *Recidivism of Young Parolees* (Washington, DC: U.S. Department of Justice, May, 1987).

11. Quoted in Fox Butterfield, "Study Shows Building Prisons Did Not Prevent Repeat Crimes," June 3, 2002, *New York Times on the Web*. Retrieved January 5, 2003, from www.nytimes.com

12. Timothy J. Flanagan, "Questioning the 'Other' Parole," in *Probation, Parole and Community Corrections,* ed. Lawrence Travis (Prospect Heights, IL: Waveland, 1985) 179.

13. David Stanley, *Prisoners among Us* (Washington, DC: Brookings Institute, 1976) 190.

14. Andrew von Hirsh and Kathleen Hanrahan, *Abolish Parole* (Washington, DC: U.S. Department of Justice, September, 1978) 38.

15. Lauren E. Glaze, *Probation and Parole in the United States, 2002* (Washington, DC: U.S. Department of Justice, 2003).

16. Personal communication with John Rosecrance.

17. Hughes et al. 11.

18. Hughes et al. 10.

19. S. Christopher Baird, Richard Heinz, and Brian Bemus, "The Wisconsin Case Classification/ Staff Development," in *Classification: American Correctional Association Monograph* (College Park, MD: American Correctional Association, 1982); Daniel P. LeClair, "Community Reintegration of Prison Releases," in *Probation, Parole and Community Corrections,* 3rd ed., eds. Robert Carter, Daniel Glaser, and Leslie Wilkins (New York: Wiley, 1984) 342–349; David Rauma and Richard Beck, "Remuneration and Recidivism: The Long Term Impact of Unemployment Compensation on Ex-Offenders," *Journal of Quantitative Criminology* 3 (November, 1987): 3–27.

20. Flanagan 167–183.

21. John Irwin, *The Felon* (Englewood Cliffs, NJ: Prentice Hall, 1970) 109.

22. Braly 264.

23. Terry 105.

24. Irwin 114–116.

25. Personal communication with John Rosecrance.

26. Elliot Studt, "Reintegration from the Parolees' Perspective" in *Reintegration of the Offender in the Community* (Washington, DC: U.S. Department of Justice, June, 1973) 44–45.

27. Irwin 113

28. Christopher E. Smith, *Law and Contemporary Corrections* (Belmont, CA: Wadsworth, 2000) 254.

29. Joan Petersilia, "Prisoners Returning to Communities: Political, Economic, and Social Consequences," *Sentencing and Corrections: Issues for the Twenty-First Century* (Washington, DC: National Institute of Justice, 2000) 7.

30. Petersilia 7.

31. Vanessa St. Gerard, "New Effort to Reintegrate Offenders," *Corrections Today* (October, 2001): 29.

32. St. Gerard 29.

33. Mayor's Office of Criminal Justice, "Maryland Reentry Partnership Initiative." Retrieved May 21, 2002, from www.ci.baltimore.md.us/government/ mocj/reentry.html

34. Serious and Violent Offender Reentry Initiative, "Richland County Reentry Court (Phase 1: Prepare and Protect)" undated web page. Retrieved May 21, 2002, from www.ojp.usdoj.gov/reentry/ cia/oh.html#3

35. Joan Petersilia, "Prisoner Reentry: Public Safety and Reintegration Challenges," *The Prison Journal* 81 (2001): 360–375.

36. New York State Executive Law, "State Division of Parole, Article 12-B El-9" (1978) p. 259-I.

37. New York State Division of Parole, "New York State Parole Handbook," January, 1998. Retrieved June 24, 2004, from http://parole.state.ny.us/ parolehandbook.html#section%20three

38. Deborah Star and John E. Berecochea, "Rationalizing the Conditions of Parole," in *Probation, Parole and Community Corrections,* 3rd ed., eds. Robert Carter, Daniel Glaser, and Leslie Wilkins (New York: Wiley, 1984) 302.

39. Irwin 149.

40. New York State Division of Parole 20.

40. California Department of Corrections, *Family of Forms* (Sacramento: California Department of Corrections, undated): 22-A.

41. The Interstate Compact Agreement has been approved by several state court cases, most notably in *Ex parte Tanner,* Cal, 2d 670, 128 P. 2d (1942). The Supreme Court has consistently declined to rule on the constitutionality of the issue, leaving favorable court decisions intact.

42. "Original Compact, 1937," Interstate Commission for Adult Offender Supervision, December 1, 2003, Lexington, KY. Retrieved December 16, 2003, from www.adultcompact.org/Resources%20&%20 Information.htm

43. "Original Compact."

44. National Institute of Corrections, *Context for Amending the Parole and Probation Interstate Compact,* August, 1999, U.S. Department of Justice. Retrieved February 13, 2003, from www.nicic.org/services/ special/compact-adult/background.htm#rules

45. Richard McCleary, *Dangerous Men: The Sociology of Parole* (Beverly Hills: Sage, 1978) 111.

46. McCleary 112.

47. McCleary 112

48. McCleary 127.

49. McCleary 110.

50. Irwin 151.

51. All information on the *Morrissey v. Brewer* case is taken from Smith 242–245; Dean J. Champion, *Corrections in the United States: A Contemporary Perspective*, 3rd ed. (Upper Saddle River, NJ: Prentice Hall, 2001) 446–447; and Leonard Orland, *Justice,*

Punishment, Treatment: The Correctional Process (New York: Macmillan, 1973) 519–523.

52. McCleary 138.

53. Hughes et al. 13.

54. Hughes et al. 13.

55. McCleary 84.

56. New York State Division of Parole, *1984–1985 Annual Report* (Albany, NY: New York State Division of Parole, 1986) 8.

The Administration
and Implementation of
Community Corrections

The chapters in Part III focus on the administration of community corrections, the environment in which POs work, new and innovative programs in the field, and other community corrections programs and populations with special needs supervised by community corrections staff.

Chapter Eight provides the reader with an understanding of the administrative functions of community corrections offices and an appreciation of how administrative techniques can actually invigorate the workplace. Community corrections agencies are not directed by faceless robots or computer driven terminals; instead, they are managed by real people with a full range of weaknesses and strengths. Administrators of these agencies must respond to a wide array of pressures and influences in the course of their work. Some administrators are able to successfully adapt to the complex correctional environment, whereas others fall victim to bureaucratic inertia. In the years ahead, additional demands will be placed on probation and parole administrators as prison crowding dramatically increases the demand for community supervision while at the same time adequate funding becomes more difficult to achieve.

In Chapter Nine, the working environment of POs is examined and typologies are presented to help explain their behaviors. The correctional challenges will ultimately rest on the staff working on the correctional front line. POs who investigate clients, supervise those released, and initiate proceedings against those who do not live up to release conditions, determine the success of probation and parole. These line officers have varied perspectives that significantly influence their work. Whereas some POs see themselves as strict enforcers of legal codes, others believe their job is to assist the misunderstood. Line officers develop strategies and maintain postures they believe will enhance their careers. As POs become socialized into the work setting, they learn informal practices that often are in conflict with organizational directives. Unfortunately, some of the best POs are turned off by organizational directives that are the opposite of their personal and professional philosophies. This conflict frequently leads to burnout, cynicism, or resignation from their jobs.

Chapter Ten discusses new programs in community corrections. Both administration and line staff in many jurisdictions are currently involved in new programs that attempt to place community corrections in the mainstream of correctional innovations. Intensive supervision, home confinement, electronic surveillance, differential supervision, day reporting centers, and restorative justice programs have proliferated throughout the community corrections world. These innovations are, in large part, a response to a growing perception that traditional probation and parole is missing something and is either in need of a massive overhaul or at least some major reworking. At the same time that new programs have their ardent supporters, others question whether such efforts represent organic change or merely public posturing.

Chapter Eleven covers other programs and populations of clients managed by community corrections departments. The programs include pretrial release, diversion programs, and halfway houses. Because of the growth of corrections, societal changes, and changes in sentencing practices, there are also several groups of offenders with special needs. These include the mentally ill, sex offenders, those with developmental disabilities, and substance abuse offenders.

8

Administration

In addition to understanding the nature and quality of a POs daily job and role in the agency, one must also understand the administration that oversees POs. Personnel practices in the field stress promotion from the ranks, and administrators are almost always former POs. Therefore, it is important that people considering careers in probation and parole educate themselves about the workings of management and administration. All too often in college, aspiring probation officers learn about dealing with offenders but not about supervising other probation officers. This chapter provides probation and parole students with some understanding of administration and encourages further examination of this important and relevant subject. For instance, additional courses in business management or the sociology of occupations are valuable assets to all probation and parole personnel.

Political Background

Issues of Centralization and Administration

The administration of probation and parole is fragmented. There are a bewildering number of agencies (more than 2,000) organized in various ways. Probation agencies are operated by local, county, state, and federal governments. They are administrated within the executive or judicial branches of government. Parole, although a function of the executive branch in every state and the District of Columbia, is supplemented by a local system under the judicial branch in seven states. Thirty states have combined probation and parole services within the same agency.

Two important issues have evolved from the fragmentation of probation services: (1) whether services in each state should be centralized and (2) whether these services should be administered by the judiciary or the executive branch of government. (The vast majority of parole agencies have decided these issues in favor of centralization in the executive branch.) The primary arguments for centralization include

1. The ability of a state-administered system to develop and implement uniform policies and procedures, meaning that all clients in a state could receive the same level of services.

2. Greater efficiency in the management of resources.
3. State-administered systems have the resources to conduct research and develop innovative programs and demonstration projects.[1]

However, there are also numerous arguments against centralization:

1. The ability of local systems to acquire support from local citizens and agencies.
2. Flexibility of smaller local programs to experiment with new procedures and methods.
3. Familiarity of staff members with the local community.[2]

The other half of the issue—which branch of government should be responsible for probation—also has valid arguments for both sides. The main arguments for judicial control are

1. Probation responsiveness to court direction.
2. Automatic feedback to the court regarding the effectiveness of probation.
3. The majority of work for probation agencies comes from the courts.

The arguments for executive control of agencies include

1. Better coordination of programs because other agencies that carry out court orders are in the executive branch.
2. Better allocation of staff.
3. More access to the budget process and establishment of priorities.[3]

Not surprisingly, states that favor centralized administration seem to favor the executive branch, whereas those with local administration favor judicial control.

Strong arguments can be made for all sides; there is no single best way to organize probation for every state. Each alternative has strengths and weaknesses that must be investigated in order to decide the most appropriate organization for each individual state.[4]

Issues of Combination and Administration

Another debated organizational issue is whether probation and parole should be combined into one agency. On the one hand, a combined unit can take advantage of the efficient hiring, training, and staff development practices best maintained by large departments. Additionally, many of the same services, such as investigation and supervision, are provided by both probation and parole, and a combined unit would avoid duplication of effort. On the other hand, probation and parole have differences that make the merging of such units problematic. Parole boards have goals and agendas (such as helping to control the prison population) that are not shared by judges, and attempting to satisfy each of these entities requires separate perspectives. Also, probationers are less criminally involved than parolees and do not share severe reentry problems. In a similar vein, techniques that are effective with first-time offenders will be useless in dealing with convicted felons who have considerable experience with the criminal justice system. Such differences in clientele, some would argue, call for maintaining separate agencies.[5] As with the issues of locating probation administration, there is no definitive answer to the question of whether a combined probation/parole agency is the "best" solution. Organizational fragmentation not only makes for heated debate but it also has worked against the growth of a national community corrections movement and, in some measure, has rendered probation/parole politically impotent.

Issues of Organizational Diversity

There are many reasons for such powerlessness, but perhaps the most important culprit is the diversity inherent in contemporary community corrections agencies. Organizational diversity of the administration of community corrections makes it difficult for each individual agency and its staff to see the common bonds that unite an occupational field. For instance, a probation office that is controlled by a municipal judge is far different from a statewide probation/parole department run by a correctional administrator. Officers who have split caseloads (comprised of both parolees and probationers) do not share work perspective with specialists, such as parole job counselors or probation officers who deal exclusively with drug offenders. Probation and parole offices that are widely scattered around a state often operate in relative isolation from one another. Such diversity means that when criticism does arise, a national or even regional response is not forthcoming. Community corrections administrators generally must stand up to local criticism without the support of national organizations or correctional leaders. This often means that community corrections developments are shaped by local politics and community pressures.

Allan Breed indicated that without national probation/parole leadership, local concerns "tend to result in fragmentation where we badly need consistency and coordination, vacillation around policy and principles where we need understood positions, calls for reactions to emergencies rather than a provocative stance, and frustration on the part of staff and chaos in terms of organization instead of efficient organizations."[6] Therefore, diversity often leads to muted support for probation.

These problems are worsened by the fact that probation administrators are often competing with other local officials for public support and funding. These other officials—sheriffs, district attorneys, and judges—are often elected and frequently seek reelection. Probation administrators, however, are usually appointed by county commissioners or the judiciary; have no recognizable constituency; and are, therefore, in a relatively weak position to compete for public or monetary support with other criminal justice or social service agencies. In those states where probation is run by the state government, correctional institutions usually attract more money and political interest.[7]

Even though parole has a less diverse organizational structure than probation, local and regional concerns also enter here and work against the emergence of national leadership or outspoken public support. Board members and parole administrators are generally appointed by governors; work under the governor's authority; and are, therefore, restricted by his or her decisions. For example, during the parole abolition movement of the 1970s, only a handful of parole administrators were willing to oppose these efforts. Until probation and parole and other community corrections officials develop a national base, they will remain fragmented and relatively unable to influence events.

An example of the inability to "make things happen" is found in the legal arena. The laws, guidelines, and rules under which probation and parole agencies must function are, for the most part, determined by judges, attorneys, and legislators. Probation and parole leaders do not have a ready forum to influence legal opinion. Rarely do probation and parole officials sit down at bar meetings, sentencing counsels, or ways and means committees to help construct regulations that directly affect their work. Until community corrections officials become activists and work toward their own vision of what is in the best interest of the field, they will remain "the butler in the grand mansion of the law."[8]

An example of this inability to influence policies that directly affect their own services can be seen in events surrounding the implementation of federal sentencing guidelines. The guidelines mandated profound changes in federal probation and parole. They signaled an end to parole and an increased role for the probation officer at sentencing (under the guidelines federal probation officers supervise inmates given mandatory releases). Probation and parole officials had virtually no input into the legislative package that established the guidelines. Even though probation officers doing presentence reports are responsible for placing defendants into appropriate sentencing categories, they were not consulted about establishing criteria for the categories. In addition, probation officials had little input into developing procedures for implementing the guidelines. Donald L. Chamlee, chief federal probation officer at the time, when questioned about the new sentencing policies indicated: "there's going to be a lot of confusion and a lot of chaos." Only days before the guidelines were to go into effect, not withstanding their acknowledged "central role" Chamlee admitted that officers had received no training in the system.[9]

Bureaucratic Theory

Perhaps one of the reasons probation and parole agencies have historically been so powerless is that they find themselves enmeshed in the bureaucracy of the criminal justice system without a full understanding of their place in that bureaucracy or the effects it has on their behavior. The pervasive influence of bureaucracies in Western society has been a central theme of twentieth-century social science. In the field of criminal justice, William Chambliss and Robert Siedman identified **bureaucracy** as "the single most important variable in determining the actual day to day function of the legal system."[10] Most probation and parole departments have already undergone a process of bureaucratization whereby authority, based on formal rules and discipline, was imposed on an informal organization where authority depended on technical expertise.[11]

Robert Townsend, organizational theorist, commented on the historical background of contemporary bureaucracies:

> For the last 200 years we've been using the Catholic Church and Caesar's legions as our patterns for creating organizations. And until the last forty or fifty years it made sense. The average churchgoer, soldier, and factory worker was uneducated and dependent on orders from above.[12]

Max Weber, working in the early twentieth century, identified five major principles that characterized bureaucratic organizations. Harry More, in his influential book on correctional administration, delineated these principles:

1. *Organizational tasks are distributed among various positions as official duties.* Specialization, expertise, and technical qualifications are the hallmarks of bureaucracy.
2. *Positions are organized into a hierarchical authority structure—a pyramid shape.* Each official in the pyramid is responsible to the superior above him or her for personal and subordinates' decisions and actions. This principle tends to limit the degree of freedom that an official is willing to allow subordinates. The hierarchical authority structure implies that persons occupying positions high on the pyramid are superior, more intelligent, and more capable than persons in the lower echelons of the organization.
3. *Officials are expected to assume an impersonal attitude in contacts with clients and other officials.* Clients are treated as cases; officials are expected to disregard all personal considerations and to maintain complete objectivity. The social distance between hierarchical levels and between officials and their clients is intended to foster such formality.
4. *A formally established system of rules and regulations governs official decisions and actions.* Regulations ensure the uniformity of operations and, together with the authority structure, allow for the coordination of various activities. They provide continuity and promote stability. The more rules and regulations an agency has, the less thinking and creativity it requires of its employees. In any given situation, all that is required is an ability to find the general rule in the organizational handbook and apply it to the particular case.
5. *Employment by the organization constitutes a career for officials.* Employment is based on the technical qualifications of candidates. Officials are appointed to positions, not elected, and are thus dependent for promotions on superiors in the organization rather than on a body of constituents. Career advancement is usually made on the basis of seniority and merit.[13]

These principles, according to Weber, were a means to achieve rational decision making and organizational efficiency. Correctional organizations, in many cases, have adopted a traditional bureaucratic hierarchy based on levels of authority. Figure 8.1 reflects a pattern found in many probation and parole departments. The first four levels, in descending order of authority, comprise the administration. Line staff, or the parole and probation agents working on the front lines with offenders, are not considered part of administration.[14]

Although such an organization in general makes for efficient correctional operations, in the real world of running a probation or parole office, it is often difficult to remain "impersonal" when dealing with unruly clients or uncooperative co-workers, or to write rules covering every possible circumstance or problem that might arise. Moreover, such bureaucratic organizations often lead to conservative and habitual behavior by those working in the agency, and unless more adaptable and flexible practices are introduced, community corrections agencies will be unable to cope with an ever-changing society.

These new practices must involve a change not only in the formal organization, the bureaucracy, but in the informal organization as well.[15] The new organi-

FIGURE 8.1 *Levels of Authority in a Traditional Probation or Parole Agency*

zation will be flatter and less hierarchical, with visionary leaders allowing empowered workers to do their jobs. The informal organization, or culture, is the shared norms, attitudes, values, and beliefs the line staff and other workers develop over the course of actually doing their jobs. Because of their experiences on the job interacting with clients and fellow workers, parole and probation agents naturally develop some norms and means of "getting the job done" that may not exactly fit the formal bureaucratic structure. If the formal organization is flatter, with leadership empowering others to use their discretion to make decisions, the norms and attitudes of the informal organization, of course, will reflect that structure, and the entire culture of the agency will be dynamic and more effective.

The American Probation and Parole Association, in an issue paper on organizational response to change, indicated that the changes community corrections agencies must make will be qualitative, hard to envision, and difficult to put into practice. These new organizations will have to abandon the Weberian model, which centers on numbers of clients and procedures, and move to organizations that are "learning based, outcome-driven and customer oriented."[16]

There will be more on what this new organization will look like and how administrators can help create it later in the chapter. First we discuss in more detail the social background affecting the administration of parole and probation agencies: the informal norms that develop and how they influence a department, how and why employees are motivated to do their jobs, and how managers might influence both depending on their approach to their work.

Social Background

Informal Norms

One of the major features of the social background of a probation or parole agency is the informal norms that develop around doing the work. Informal norms are the unofficial rules guiding the daily operations of a department and its personnel. **Richard McCleary**, in his study of an Illinois parole system,[17] demonstrates that informal norms often violate bureaucratic hierarchy. Although the organization of the office he studied resembles the classic Weberian model (presented in the previous section), relationships among personnel cannot be analyzed solely in terms of authority. Power is not distributed in a straight line from the top to the bottom as is depicted on an organizational chart. In other words, although parole officers may lack authority on paper, they are often more powerful than management officers because line officers actually carry out the work of parole; without their cooperation the administration would be unable to manage the department.

According to McCleary, the various organizational units are constrained to work in harmony at maintaining the status quo. It is in the best interest of all concerned to reinforce department stability so that jobs are maintained and careers advanced. Therefore, in most circumstances, the administration allows branch offices to operate independently as long as the office "delivers" by maintaining workloads in a noncontroversial manner. For their part, branch managers see to it that administration policies are nominally adhered to by line staff. The working POs are given considerable discretion in carrying out department policy and often interpret organizational regulations to fit their own ideas of how to control a caseload. In this manner, all three units maintain the symbolic authority structure, whereas in reality they are relatively free to operate independently of one another.

In the course of affairs McCleary maintains that particularly skillful parole officers and supervisors develop reputations that allow them to get around organizational rules and operate independently, often without negative consequences. The development of these individual power bases was not envisioned by Weber's traditional bureaucratic interpretation discussed in the previous section. Several other researchers have found probation and parole departments operating independently of centralized organizational authority. For example, after studying Federal Probation Department policies regarding frequency of client contacts, the comptroller general of the United States concluded, "Although Administration Office guidelines determine contact rates for probationers and parolees, many districts have established their own rates."[18] Earl Beshears, after examining North Carolina parole centers observed: "If the central staff were to formulate and distribute new procedures, it is likely that after initial compliance each center would gradually evolve its own procedures [and in the end] local staff would subvert organizational policies to meet its own perceived needs."[19]

Motivational Factors

Employee motivation also often prevents entrenchment of a bureaucratic organizational structure. One of the best known theories to address this issue is **A. H. Maslow's** hierarchy of needs. His research revealed that people work for a variety of reasons, not exclusively for money. He identified five human needs ranging from basic physical sustenance, such as food and shelter; to safety needs, such as avoidance of harm; to social needs, such as the need for love and affection; to esteem needs, such as self-respect and recognition; and finally to self-realization needs, such as creativity and self-expression. Maslow also discussed satisfiers organizations can provide to employees to allow the employees opportunities to fulfill the various needs. For example, physical needs are satisfied with pleasant working conditions and adequate pay, whereas esteem needs are satisfied through such organizational features as merit awards and providing challenging work to perform. Self-realization needs are gained through such activities as making decisions affecting work and having creative work to perform.[20]

It is also important to note that the lower-level needs are for the most part satisfied externally with such things as salary and tenure, whereas higher-level needs are satisfied internally. Furthermore, only when elementary needs are satisfied can individuals achieve more symbolic rewards such as esteem and self-realization. In order to motivate workers and prevent frustration, organizations should allow for the needs to be fulfilled from lower to higher, for as one level of needs is satisfied it no longer motivates. This principal does not hold true for the higher needs, however, for Maslow believed that once a higher level need is reached—esteem or self-realization—workers will stay very motivated and have an upbeat attitude toward the organization.[21]

Besides needs, other researchers have looked at incentives in organizations and how they affect motivation. Incentives can be material (wages and salaries, benefits, gifts) or intangible (offices, honors, fun, sense of solidarity, successful accomplishments, enacting a law or policy).[22] For many managers and workers in community corrections, a job with tenure and a living wage, good fringe benefits, and valued intangible incentives such as providing an important social service and an esprit d'corps in the workplace may all be sources of motivation.

Organizations providing the opportunities to satisfy the full range of human needs and the proper tangible and intangible incentives will succeed in sufficiently motivating their employees. This suggests that certain management approaches will be more successful than others.

Management Approaches

Management styles, to a large degree, are framed by organizational structure. For example, rigid, hierarchical organizations often lead to managers who are controlling, have a need for power, and follow rules and regulations to the letter. However, new leadership patterns can evolve, and changes in organizational philosophy follow. In order to place management style into a meaningful framework, **Douglas McGregor** advanced the X and Y theories of employee motivation. **Theory X** maintains that

1. Work, if not downright distasteful, is an onerous chore to be performed in order to survive.
2. The average human being has an inherent dislike of work and will avoid it if possible.
3. Because of this human characteristic to dislike work, most people must be coerced, controlled, directed, or threatened with punishment to make them put forth adequate effort toward the achievement of organizational objectives.
4. The average human being prefers to be directed, wishes to avoid responsibility, has relatively little ambition, and wants security above all.[23]

Theory X is closely linked with a traditional bureaucratic hierarchy commonly referred to as a *chain of command.* In this system, employee questioning and individual input into policy decisions is discouraged. Instead, decisions are handed down from above and the rest of the organization is expected to comply. McGregor challenged the effectiveness of theory X in contemporary management, and advanced theory Y as a better way to motivate workers. **Theory Y** maintains that

1. The expenditure of physical and mental effort in work is as normal as play or rest. The average human being does not inherently dislike work. Depending on controllable conditions, work may be a source of satisfaction

(and will be voluntarily performed) or a source of punishment (and will be avoided if possible).

2. External control and threat of punishment are not the only means for bringing about effort toward organizational objectives. People will exercise self-direction in the service of objectives to which they are committed.

3. Commitment to objectives is a function of rewards associated with achievement. The most significant of such rewards (e.g., satisfaction of ego and self-actualization needs) can be direct products of efforts extended to achieve organizational objectives.

4. The average person, under proper conditions, learns not only to accept but also to seek responsibility. Avoidance of responsibility, lack of ambition, and emphasis on security are general consequences of experience, not inherent human characteristics.

5. The capacity to exercise a relatively high degree of imagination, ingenuity, and creativity in the solution of organizational problems is widely, not narrowly, distributed in the population.

6. Under the conditions of modern industrial life, the intellectual potentialities of the average human being are incompletely utilized.[24]

Theory Y attempts to structure organizations around humanistic concerns rather than around a depersonalized, authoritarian system. It replaces a model of authority based on coercion and fear with one based on collaboration and reason. Theories X and Y are, of course, polar concepts and most correctional organizations exhibit characteristics of both management styles. There are indications that theory Y management produces a relatively harmonious work staff with reduced instances of disciplinary action. Although theory Y seems to have many advantages, probation and parole administrators (often socialized in a theory X system) have a difficult time implementing humanistic employee goals. What often happens is new programs begin by applying McGregor theory Y, but after rules and procedures are standardized, or as crises or problems emerge, administrators resort to previously learned authoritarian patterns.

However, even though probation and parole officials may have a difficult time applying humanistic management practices, there are indications they will be forced toward that side of the X–Y equation. In order to deal with the challenges of the coming years, such as increased caseloads and lower budgets, administrators are going to need the full cooperation of their staff. Researchers and writers on this theme have made it clear that in order to achieve a high degree of staff involvement, organizations need clearly defined and realistic goals and some form of participatory or democratic management.

This suggests that in order to be effective, probation and parole administrators need to be not only managers but leaders as well. Alvin Cohn distinguished between the two concepts, borrowing from the work of J. H. Zenger.[25] To Cohn, managers are involved in activities such as planning, budgeting, coordinating, and dealing with staffing issues. Leaders, however, are good communicators who express themselves persuasively, even passionately. Leaders involve other people, provide positive feedback, and engender trust, and because of this, staff members know they are *empowered* because they are trusted and treated as competent. Manager leaders understand that they are responsible for the achievement of organizational goals but that these goals are also realistic and attainable. This gives the staff the confidence to be creative and move on to bigger goals. Leaders also model appropriate behavior, particularly regarding the values and norms of the group. This results in high levels of trust and task accomplishment by group members. Leaders are also able to define problems and work toward reasonable solutions of those problems. They carefully determine what needs to be done and in what priority. And finally, Cohn argues that leaders connect their group to the outside world, recognizing that colleagues need to be apprised of developments and issues in the external environment to be effective and creative in their work.

Cohn concludes that a successful organization endeavors to have manager–leaders who are intelligent and experienced *practitioners* who define the core values and purpose of the organization. Such manager–leaders turn these values and purposes into plans that co-workers accept and attempt to put into practice, motivated to maintain an organization that reflects their own values. To Cohn, **leadership** is a continuous move toward organizational prosperity; it generates an environment that encourages creativity; it produces a manager with vision, direction, and one who thinks about the future so as to anticipate the changes that are likely to—and should—occur.[26]

However, it is important to point out that there is no one best leadership style and that any style may be effective or ineffective depending on the situation.[27] Although concern for people, productivity, and positive theory Y assumptions about human nature may be important for effective managers, these same managers may have to engage in an assortment of behaviors as they face a variety of problems in the workplace, perhaps making these styles of management inappropriate. There may be times when the best way for a manager to show concern for people and production is to "direct, control, and closely supervise."[28] This may be particularly true when dealing with new employees who are insecure and do not yet have the skills to perform their jobs.

Such a flexible leadership style may be very important for staff morale (see the previous discussion on theory Y). Letting co-workers know that you care through your actions and empowering them and allowing them to participate in organizational goal setting gives colleagues a sense of ownership and direction. They see that their day-to-day work is related to the goals and objectives of the agency, clearly demonstrating that their work is worthwhile.

Being an effective leader and allowing workers to participate in organizational goal setting not only has a positive effect on staff morale but it also can reduce job-related stress. Over time, extreme stress can lead to health and emotional problems, alienation from work, and burnout.[29] In early research on probation and parole officer burnout, John Whitehead clearly demonstrates that participation in decision making and organizational responsiveness can mitigate job-related stress.[30] More recently, Slate and his colleagues, after reviewing the literature on stress and burnout, concluded that cooperation in the workplace, decentralization in decision making, the creation of a team environment, and the use of participatory management are all important means of reducing probation and parole officer stress and burnout.[31]

Once one understands the political background, bureaucratic theory, and social background of administration, he or she can comprehend how probation and parole departments are administered in the real world of corrections. This will be accomplished by presenting two case studies involving organizational issues.

Organizations in Operation

The first case study describes four incidents of whistle-blowing. In these instances organizational unresponsiveness precipitated drastic and eventually self-defeating actions by probation officers. The material for the whistle-blowing accounts was taken from an actual study by John Rosecrance of probation departments in California.[32] The second case study is devoted to an organization that saw the need to change and did so in an appropriate manner. Not only did the organization establish clear-cut goals but it also actively worked to implement them.

Whistle-Blowing in Probation Departments

Whistle-blowing, or revealing wrongdoing within an organization to the public or to those in positions of authority, would fit in well with many of the principles of management discussed in the previous section. However, after several years of correctional research, John Rosecrance concluded that the organizational climate prevailing in many probation departments does not facilitate communication from the line staff to management. Specifically, internal criticisms of the organization by probation officers typically are viewed as "troublemaking." Divergent perspectives were discouraged or punished by probation administrators. However, most probation officers were able to adapt and fit into such an organizational milieu.[33] But some officers were unwilling to support organizational philosophies and found adjusting to department policies problematic. Frequently, these officers actively sought to redress grievances within the department and to bring about organizational change. In some instances, when their efforts were thwarted, they felt obligated to take their complaints to sources outside the department, and, in so doing, they became whistle-blowers. Rosecrance studied four incidents of whistle-blowing in probation departments and found that these incidents were not viewed by management as cases of "participation and involvement" or "openness and informality" as would be the case with successful organizations. Rather, the organizations, like many other public and private organizations, viewed these cases as threats to the organization itself and the whistle-blowers as troublemakers.

Using observational and interview data, Rosecrance describes the process whereby probation officers move from voicing their opposition about policies within department channels to sharing their grievances with influential parties outside the agency. The study portrays the organizational response and aftermath of these actions. The whistle-blowers all subsequently left probation work. An analysis of the findings helps explain the unwillingness of many probation officers to propose departmental changes. This unwillingness is exemplified by the observations of a veteran probation officer who had adapted to an organizational climate that was unresponsive to internal reform:

> The administration doesn't really know what's going on in probation work. They issue directives that cannot be applied or can even be dangerous. You know, probationers can be real threats to public safety. I tried to set them straight a couple of times but they didn't even consider my suggestions. So why even try? Forget them, I just keep my head down and hope for the best.

Whether these insights can be generalized to probation departments outside California or to other criminal justice agencies must be ascertained by further investigation. However, it would appear that the reactions of probation officers are not unique and that organizations that discourage internal questioning are courting disaster. For example, testimony before investigation committees has revealed that top officials at the National Aeronautics and Space Administration (NASA) were unaware of reservations and concerns about the *Challenger* launch held by middle-management personnel. If NASA management had encouraged a culture of openness and communication, perhaps that disaster could have been avoided.

Rosecrance was able to contact and interview not only the whistle-blowers but also other probation workers in their departments, as well as probation supervisors and administrators. The departments were located in medium-size California counties. Their organizational structures (typical of other probation departments in the state) consisted of a chief and assistant chief probation officer who were hired and fired by the county boards of supervisors. The rest of the staff (covered by civil service) consisted of three levels: (1) district supervisors who were responsible for all probation services within certain geographical areas; (2) supervisors who oversaw specific functions, for example juvenile intake, adult court report writing, or supervision of felony probation; and (3) line staff with assigned caseloads.

The actual whistle-blowing events involved the following actions: (1) informing the county board of supervisors that grossly unfair promotion policies existed in the probation department; (2) testifying before a grand jury that the chief probation officer was incompetent and that the department was being run inefficiently; (3) stating in open court that probation officers were being told they must recommend specific sentences for defendants—even if they disagreed with those recommendations; and (4) reporting to the local media that the probation department's policy on own recognizance (OR) releases was too liberal and that dangerous criminals were being released from custody. These events should be considered whistle-blowing rather than chronic complaining because the officers took their concerns (generally considered legitimate by other staff members) to influential sources outside the probation department.

After analyzing data from more than fifty in-depth interviews with probation personnel and from observation over a twenty-year correctional career, Rosecrance concluded that the whistle-blowing process typically involved the following five stages: (1) internal criticism (within the department) of questionable activity, (2) state of intransigency (an inability to compromise), (3) external disclosure, (4) organization reaction, and (5) aftermath. Each of these stages is discussed. The verbatim quotes used reflect widely held opinions or statements of fact.

1. *Internal Criticism.* The beginning stage in the whistle-blowing process involved a period of in-house questioning. For some time before actually voicing their criticism, the probation officers had observed what in their opinion was questionable activity. The officers' initial criticisms were directed to their immediate supervisor. One officer indicated

> For years I'd seen POs being promoted whose only qualifications seemed to be their ability to play up to the chief. So I went to my supervisor and asked for a clarification of exactly what criteria were being used for promotion. He tried to put me off with some double talk.

When supervisors seemed unable or were unwilling to explain satisfactorily why the questionable practice continued to exist, the probation officers were faced with another dilemma. In order to press their criticisms further, they had to bypass the hierarchical chain of command. The whistle-blowers were hesitant to take that step. The following quote is typical of that hesitancy:

> Geez, I'd always been taught not to go over your boss' head. If you played by the rules you would come out okay—don't squeal and all that. But it didn't go that way in this situation.

As their determination that something must be done overcame their reluctance to proceed further, the probation officers implemented different strategies. Two took their criticism to the next person in the organizational hierarchy (the district head), whereas the other two went directly to the administration head. Eventually, all of the whistle-blowers voiced some of their criticisms directly to the chief probation officer.

The responses of the probation administration to such criticism were (from the probation officer's standpoint) insufficient. The officers received no assurances that the questionable activity would be altered or corrected. One dissident officer observed

> They really stonewalled me. The administration heard my complaints but they never really said what they planned to do about them. I got the distinct impression they weren't going to do anything. And I was right.

In addition to verbal remarks to supervisors and administrators, two of the whistle-blowers carried on an active memo writing campaign. They wrote more than ten separate memos to department personnel indicating their suggestions or displeasure with department practices. The departmental response to these written communications seemed to be continued inaction. A chronic memo writer remarked

> I spent half my time writing memos. I kept copies of all of them. Man, what a pile. But it didn't do any good. The administration just ignored them. Probably filed all my carefully crafted messages in circular file 13—the wastebasket.

2. *State of Intransigency.* As the dissident probation officers continued to question administration about the "questionable" activity, both sides developed an uncompromising position. From the administration standpoint, the probation officers had pressed their case to the point of becoming disloyal and disruptive. An administrator related

> [This PO] kept on jabbing at the department. At first we listened to his bitching about the OR [own recognizance] policy, and even tried to explain to him why we couldn't change at that particular time. But he wouldn't listen and was unwilling to even consider that there might be bigger issues involved. What did he expect us to do—revamp the whole program because he didn't like it? I finally stopped talking to [that PO] and just waited for him to take the next step.

From the probation officers' perspective, the administration's inaction meant that the questionable activity would continue indefinitely. One of the whistle-blowers recalled

> It finally hit me—once and for all—probation policies weren't going to change—not ever. It was really frustrating, the chief and his flunkies weren't even listening to me. They had written me off as a malcontent whiner. There was no way the OR program was going to be improved.

With the hardening of their respective positions, officers and administration reached a virtual stalemate. Compromise no longer seemed possible. Frustration on both sides escalated, and the hostility between the parties became more visible. A whistle-blowing officer describes this increasing hostility:

> My supervisors hated to see me coming; the chief didn't want to hear *any* of my suggestions. They had it in for me personally—anything I did was labeled as chronic complaining. You could cut the tension with a knife. It was an impossible situation—it couldn't continue.

An administrator described the situation:

> When [that PO] kept on fighting us on the issue of promotion, things kinda got out of hand. He really wasn't complaining about the policies anymore but about us—

the administration. [That PO] just couldn't get it through his thick head that he was a PO and we were his superiors.

3. *External Disclosure.* When probation officers reached the conclusion that further internal criticism was useless, they decided to take action. The probation officers in Rosecrance's study reported that events had left them feeling "backed into a corner." They described their thoughts in the following way: "I knew it was up to me," "It was time to put up or shut up," "I just couldn't allow things to continue," and "They left me no alternative; I had to take some direct action." The dissident officers had reached a level of frustration that forced them to "do something."

The whistle-blowers' decision to take their complaints outside the probation department was not so much a well-conceived plan to bring about positive change as a reaction to a personally intolerable situation. In deciding to "go public," they did not consider thoroughly whether their actions would be effective. Their relative lack of concern about results is evidenced in the following observations:

> I knew going to the Grand Jury probably wouldn't change much. But I really felt better after I did it.

> I wasn't naïve—spilling my guts in court wasn't going to make the judge ream out the chief, though I sure as hell slept better afterwards.

> The administration forced my hand. Going to the papers was not all that effective. But boy, it felt good to see [that administrator] squirm the next day.

> The Board of Supervisors was unlikely to deal with the problem. I realized that. However, testifying was a personal watershed—I finally stood up for what I believed.

4. *Organization Reaction.* After blowing the whistle, one probation officer recalled that he "waited for the other shoe to drop." Although the probation administration responded to the whistle-blowing incidents in varied time sequences and with differing degrees of aggressiveness, their common goal was to isolate the dissident officers. The observation of a probation supervisor is representative of the strategies employed by the various departments:

> We did not want to make a martyr out of [that PO]. It was decided not to fire the SOB but instead to cut him off from the other POs by giving him a chicken shit job. We transferred him to the juvenile hall—way out in the boon docks. Out there he didn't see anybody but some smart-aleck kids. We put out the word that this jerk was persona non grata. After that he could complain all he wanted but nobody would listen to him.

Other administrators referred to their reactions as "fire control," "cutting our losses," or "shipping him off to Siberia."

Instead of dismissing the whistle-blowers, probation officials transferred them to unfavorable positions where they no longer would have a viable work-related forum for expressing opinions critical of the administration. Typically, the new jobs were assignments in which the officers did not have the opportunity to appear in court or to handle controversial cases. One officer was placed in charge of a large write-in or bank caseload that called for relatively little contact with probationers and almost no court report writing. Another officer was transferred to a remote rural office and was given a small caseload of minor offenders; whereas the other two whistle-blowers were assigned essentially clerical functions. The transferred officers were no longer in the mainstream of probation work, and they reported feeling "shafted" by the administration. One of the whistle-blowers commented

> I wish they would have fired me. I could have fought that through civil service and would have had the chance to really blast them out of the water. But instead they sent me to the boonies—that was a really low blow. I was a good officer who got rewarded with a do-nothing assignment. I knew something would happen to me— but I never expected anything like that.

5. *Aftermath.* The whistle-blowing probation officers attempted to have their transfers rescinded by taking such actions as filing a union grievance, complaining to outside sources, and asking other officers to join them in questioning certain probation practices. None of these actions were successful; the union grievance was denied when a labor relations board ruled the transfers were made "in the best interests" of the department. Outside parties were unwilling to question seriously the authority of an administrator to transfer workers within the department, and other officers did not join the dissidents in actively protesting either the transfers or other department policies. A union representative stated: "No one on the labor board wanted to touch the issue of department transfers—to rule for the workers would have opened a can of worms." A judge indicated that he really liked [that PO's] work but was not willing to "question an administrator on what was an internal matter." Several probation officers related the following (or versions thereof): "I know [that PO] got blindsided by the chief. But what could I possibly have done to change the transfer? And what the hell, there was no sense in anyone else getting into trouble."

The dissident probation officers were particularly disheartened by the responses of other parties to their actions and to their subsequent difficulties. The following observation is typical of their disillusionment:

> I don't know what I expected. Guess I thought I'd get some support. Well, when nobody seemed interested in speaking out—even a little bit—it really bummed me out. It may sound corny but somehow I pictured myself doing something "heroic." But the way it came out, it looked like a stupid move by an overwrought PO. After that, I knew my days in the old probation department were numbered.

The probation officers reported feeling burned out by their whistle-blowing experiences. Eventually (within periods ranging from three months to two years), all of the officers quit their jobs; two found employment with social service agencies, one started a small business, and the other became a real estate salesperson.

Although the remaining probation officers in the various departments were glad to see the dissident officers leave, the consequences of engaging in organizational dissent were not lost on them. Officers were impressed with the department's success in deflecting criticism and became wary of questioning departmental practices. The reflections of a probation officer who witnessed whistle-blowing in his department is representative of this perspective:

> It was really more pleasant in the department after [that PO] quit. He was a good PO and all that but his mere presence signaled agitation and bad vibes. There's no doubt that his example was a deterrent to others contemplating some action against the administration. No one wanted to be transferred to some crappy job and be branded disloyal. It sure made me think twice before I would criticize the department. Why do it? You could lose too much.

Although each case of whistle-blowing was slightly different, they all pointed to similar problems within many organizations. Although bureaucracies are bound by formal rules, and most of these rules allow subordinates to participate in decision making, air their grievances, and suggest ways to improve the organization based on those grievances, in the real world of organizational politics such open, two-way communication is often threatening to those in positions of authority, who as a result do what they think is necessary to maintain the status quo. This often means that good workers are lost and the potential for upward communication is stifled. Both results were certainly the case in these whistle-blowing incidents.

Restructuring a Probation Department

The whistle-blowing incidents could be seen as examples of organizational dysfunction. Fortunately, not all probation and parole organizations follow that pattern. The next section is an account of a probation department that set out to implement change and did the right things to bring it about. In this situation, organizational planning and responsiveness to staff concerns were able to overcome bureaucratic inertia and resistance to change. In order to improve its supervision capabilities (spread thin by an increased workload), the Orange County Probation Department decided to institute a differential supervision program called **Case Management Classification (CMC)** (see Chapter Ten for a more thorough discussion of CMC). Through a risk and needs assessment, the system attempts to identify the proper level of supervision for probationers. Ideally, this knowledge would allow officers to budget their time in an efficient manner, concentrating the bulk of their efforts on those who need the most supervision. In implementing the new system, the administration set clear-cut goals and diligently worked to include staff input. Following is a summary of an account written for the journal *Crime and Delinquency*[34] by Chief Probation Officer Michael Schumacher and Supervising

Probation Officer Diane Fish that demonstrates why this example remains an exemplar of positive organizational change.

The Orange County Probation Department supervises about 15,500 people, 11,500 adults and 4,000 juveniles. The department also operates four juvenile detention or treatment facilities. Department staff includes deputized officers in administration, management, and line positions. Support staff includes those with expertise in research, program planning, and administrative and fiscal issues.

The first ingredient for successful reorganization of the probation system was the strong support of the county government and the administration of the department. The county probation department studied the existing probation system, comparing it to the proposed system to determine the amount of change required. An important decision was then made—to completely replace the old system with the new rather than merely "laying it on top of" the old system. It was thought that doing the latter would create unnecessary work for the staff and, perhaps more importantly, allow them to fall back on the old system too easily.

It was important to unequivocally establish that the new system would be *the* method for doing business and would not simply disappear if it was resisted. This was done by showing staff how the parts of the new system fit together and what was similar and dissimilar to the old system. It was also emphasized that this system is not another fad that is here today and gone tomorrow, that the system adapts well to change, and that it would benefit the officers in their day-to-day work.

Because of the quite natural unease and discomfort with change, the managers identified clear goals the new system would accomplish. In very specific and measurable terms, they expressed their intent to improve the service of the department and to reduce recidivism through more effective supervision.

Once the commitment and goals were well understood by all, it was necessary to decide the level of resources needed to put the change into operation. The resources included time spent by management and line staff, research, consultant fees, and material expense. The department discovered that a written plan outlining the goals, timelines, and roles necessary for completion of the changeover was essential. Budgetary issues were also significant. Additional staff time to work on the project, new equipment, revised forms, developing and printing training materials, and paying for training and consultants all had to be accounted for in the new budget.

Although input and recommendations came from all areas of probation, there was clear definition of authority and responsibilities for implementing the new system. It is inevitable that there will be some conflict when so much organizational change takes place. Therefore, if the process for resolving these conflicts is not well established, the entire effort might collapse.

Supervisors on the line must also be completely aware of the new process so they can encourage and reinforce their staff. All of the changes required of staff were not minor. This could mean, for some, that client needs become a low priority relative to the system needs. To overcome this possibility, the county decided that they first needed to design what they believed was the "optimum client service" and then design everything else that would provide support services.

It is probably at the line level—the POs—that this system has the most dramatic effect. To these staff, the system arrives all too suddenly, requiring new case planning based on risk/needs assessments, the use of CMC in certain cases (but not all), differential supervision replacing old ways of doing business, time studies that must be finished, and a new record keeping system that must be learned. Although none of these changes is huge by itself, cumulatively they become major because each is new, must be remembered, and is piled on to existing jobs. Even though in the long run the new process may save time, learning the system to begin with is very time consuming and can cause problems among the line staff.

In order to make this transition easier, the changes were taught to the staff on two levels. First, all staff were educated as to why the decision to change to the new system was made. Second, as many staff members as possible were involved in planning and implementing the new system. Further, all staff were given the opportunity to provide input during the planning stages.

Staff was also told of the potential payoffs inherent in the new system in the form of more equitable distribution of work and greater recognition of job performance. To the working PO, being able to do what they were hired to do better, safer, and more efficiently is the bottom line. Also, the increased efficiency may avoid budget cuts or even justify new positions, resulting in improved job security. Other payoffs may be in the form of better management, and perhaps work relief stemming from computer-generated forms or templates rather than manual calculations and handwritten reports. It is crucial that staff be consistently and continually involved in the project development. Such involvement will, ultimately, make the project "theirs," allowing staff to feel some ownership and even pride in their accomplishments and new-found expertise. The ability of all to have an impact on decision making can go far in reducing resistance to change.

This case demonstrates that an enlightened administration can achieve significant systemwide change. Administrators, instead of merely dictating policy, attempted to involve all probation personnel in the new program. This approach dealt realistically with officer resistance and facilitated program goals. In the process, line officers became convinced that the new system was worthwhile and, therefore, they worked to help implement it.

Summary

The organization and administration of probation and parole services are critical functions. Challenges facing contemporary administrations are heightened by the specter of increased workloads and reduced budgets. Although there are frequent calls for improved delivery of services, the current organizational structure of many probation and parole departments make any significant change problematic.

The scope of such problems can be understood by considering organizational environments. Probation and parole administration is widely diversified and a national power base or supportive constituencies have not emerged. Many agencies are organized along traditional bureaucratic principles as enumerated by Max Weber. Even though clear-cut hierarchal authority structures may appear on organizational charts, in actual practice informal norms and employee needs have often circumvented traditional patterns. Some forward-thinking administrators have moved toward more humanistic management practices (such as those embodied in theory Y).

Administrators who are most able to orchestrate meaningful change do so by clearly defining goals and then encouraging staff involvement in decision making related to the implementation of those goals. Case studies were presented to demonstrate that organizational responsiveness is a vital component in the effective management of probation and parole and can be achieved. Simply put, when managers respond to employee concerns, change is possible; when they do not respond, change is problematic.

Key People and Terms

Bureaucracy (257)
Case Management Classification (CMC) (270)
Leadership (263)
A. H. Maslow (260)
Richard McCleary (259)

Douglas McGregor (261)
Theory X (261)
Theory Y (261)
Max Weber (257)
Whistle-blowing (264)

Questions for Discussion and Review

1. Review the arguments for and against whether probation and parole services should be centralized.

2. Should probation and parole services be located in the executive or judicial branch of government? Justify your answer.

3. Why is it difficult for probation and parole agencies to develop a national response to criticism or emerging issues?

4. What are the five major principles that characterize bureaucratic organizations?

5. Discuss how informal norms affect the authority structure of a probation and parole bureaucracy.

6. Compare and contrast theory X and theory Y of management.

7. What is the difference between a manager and a leader?

8. What are some steps a manager can take to avoid PO stress and burnout?

9. What is whistle-blowing and what are its potential effects on an organization?

10. What types of resistance can managers anticipate when trying to change an organization? How can such resistance be overcome?

Relevant Internet Sites

American Probation and Parole Association's issue paper on organizational response to change: www.appa-net.org/about%20appa/organiza.htm

National Institute of Corrections, which provides a variety of services as well as policy and program development assistance to local, state,

and federal corrections agencies and professionals: www.nicic.org

National Association of Probation Executives, a professional organization representing the chief executive officers of local, county, and state probation agencies: www.napehome.org

Notes

1. Todd Clear and George Cole, *American Corrections,* 6th ed. (Belmont, CA: Wadsworth/Thomson, 2003) 189.

2. Clear and Cole 190.

3. Clear and Cole 190.

4. Clear and Cole 190; Harry Allen, Eric Carlson, and Evalyn Parks, *Critical Issues in Probation* (Washington, DC: U.S. Department of Justice, September, 1979).

5. Clear and Cole 190.

6. Quoted in Timothy L. Fitzharris, "The Federal Role in Probation Reform," in *Probation and Justice: Reconsideration of Mission,* eds. Patrick McAnany and Doug Thomson (Cambridge, MA: Oelgeschlager, Gunn and Hain, 1984) 391.

7. Fitzharris 4.

8. Patrick McAnany and Doug Thomson, *Equitable Responses to Probation Violations* (Chicago: Center for Research in Law and Justice, 1982) 64.

9. *Criminal Justice Newsletter* 18 (November 2, 1987) 4.

10. William Chambliss and R. Seidman, *Law, Order, and Power* (Reading, MA: Addison-Wesley, 1971) 468.

11. John Rosecrance, "Getting Rid of the Prima Donnas: The Bureaucratization of a Probation Department," *Criminal Justice and Behavior* 14 (June, 1978): 139.

12. Robert Townsend, *Up the Organization* (New York: Knopf, 1970) 8.

13. Harry W. More, *Criminal Justice Management* (St. Paul, MN: West, 1977) 287–289.

14. William Archambeault and Betty Archambeault, *Correctional Supervisory Management: Principles of Organization, Policy and Law* (Englewood Cliffs, NJ: Prentice Hall, 1982) 53.

15. Stan Stojkovic and Mary Ann Farkas, *Correctional Leadership* (Belmont, CA: Wadsworth, 2003) 32.

16. "Organizational Response to Change," undated issue paper, Lexington, KY: American Probation and Parole Association. Retrieved July 7, 2003, from www.appa-net.org/about%20appa/organiza.htm

17. Richard McCleary, "How Structural Variables Constrain the Parole Officer's Use of Discretionary Power," *Social Problems* 23 (1975): 209.

18. Comptroller General of the United States, *State and County Probation: Systems in Crisis* (Washington, DC: U.S. Government Printing Office, May, 1976) 14.

19. Earl D. Beshears, "Translating Policy to Procedure: Participatory Management in Corrections," *Federal Probation* 42 (September, 1978) 51.

20. A. H. Maslow, *Motivation and Personality,* 2nd ed. (New York: Harper & Row, 1970).

21. Kenneth J. Peak, *Justice Administration: Police, Courts, and Corrections Management* (Upper Saddle River, NJ: Prentice Hall, 2001) 45.

22. Hal G. Rainey, *Understanding and Managing Public Organizations,* 2nd ed. (San Francisco: Jossey-Bass, 1997) 210–211.

23. Peak 45–47.

24. Peak 47.

25. Alvin W. Cohn, "The Failure of Correctional Management: Rhetoric versus the Reality of Leadership," *Federal Probation* 62 (June, 1998): 26–31.

26. Cohn 31.

27. Paul Hersey, Kenneth Blanchard, and Dewey Johnson, *Management of Organizational Behavior: Utilizing Human Resources* (Upper Saddle River, NJ: Prentice Hall, 1996) 141.

28. Hersey et al. 142.

29. Risdon N. Slate, W. Wesley Johnson, and Terry L. Wells, "Probation Officer Stress: Is There an Organizational Solution?" *Federal Probation* 64 (June, 2000): 56–59.

30. John Whitehead, "Probation Officer Job Burnout: A Test of Two Theories," *Journal of Criminal Justice* 15 (1986): 1–16.

31. Slate et al. 58.

32. John Rosecrance, "Whistleblowing in Probation Departments," *Journal of Criminal Justice* 16 (l988).

33. Rosecrance, "Getting Rid of the Prima Donnas" 138–155.

34. Michael A. Schumacher, "Implementation of a Client Classification and Case Management System: A Practitioner's View," *Crime and Delinquency* 31 (July, 1985): 445–455.

9

Probation and Parole Officers

On the Front Line

In probation and parole, the officers are the personnel who have direct contact with offenders. Policy may originate with administration, but it is the officers who carry it out as they perform essential agency functions. Line officers investigate applicants for probation and parole, supervise those who are released into the community, and initiate sanctions or violation/revocation proceedings against those who do not fulfill release conditions. In the course of their duties, such officers interact one-on-one with correctional clients in a wide variety of settings. As the front line of probation and parole, probation and parole officers are often called "the troops." Although the importance of these officers has been acknowledged, there is little definitive data about what such officers actually do, what affects their work, how much influence they wield, or how their careers develop.

Notwithstanding the war analogy, interactions between officers and offenders are characterized by superficial cooperation. In many situations, each party needs help from the other to achieve personal goals. For example, POs need to maintain a smooth running caseload to impress their superiors, whereas offenders want to avoid trouble and get early releases. Investigators need information from applicants to complete a balanced report, whereas offenders want to appear reasonable and forthcoming to receive favorable recommendations. The ambiguous authority wielded by the officers inhibits development of full cooperation between the two parties. Both parties are aware that POs can take actions that severely impact the offender's liberty, but often both are also uncertain under precisely what circumstances negative sanctions are appropriate.

At times, it may seem that officers are independent operators, free to do what they want, to interpret organizational policy anyway they see fit. However, they also work in bureaucratic organizations that have powerful techniques for controlling independence and enforcing their policies. Friction between officers and organizational structure is a reality of probation and parole. POs have a variety of backgrounds, personal philosophies, and role orientations, factors that inevitably affect their work. Relating the various types of officers to actual job performance is a useful method for understanding parole and probation officers.

POs are traditionally thought to have considerable influence with courts and parole boards. Judges and parole board members are seen as following (almost without question) the recommendations of line officers. There is some research, however, that reveals that such influences may be exaggerated. Like most workers, older employees and supervisors socialize line officers on the job. In many cases, this socialization process follows discernable patterns. Officers, in varying degrees, are concerned with career advancement, and their actions are constrained in predictable ways to achieve this goal. Because of a variety of factors (e.g., excessive client demands, low prestige, or organizational insensitivity), line officers frequently are unable to find job satisfaction. For many workers this inability results in self-defeating burnout, excessive cynicism, or their leaving the field.

In order to portray line officers in a realistic manner, this chapter addresses the following issues: (1) How do probation and parole officers implement organizational policy? (2) What are the tasks that probation and parole officers perform? (3) What types of probation and parole officers can be identified? (4) How much discretion do officers have? (5) How much influence does the typical PO have in the criminal justice world? (6) What attracts recruits to probation or parole work? (7) What are the career stages of a probation or parole officer? (8) Why do POs burn out?

Agents of the Agency: Street-Level Bureaucrats

Probation and parole officers are charged with implementing the purposes of probation and parole. A leading probation administrator succinctly indicated, "probation officers represent the profession."[1] Through their direct contacts with offenders, POs become real-life representatives of probation and parole. From the correctional clients' perspective, the individual PO *is* the agency.

The truly awesome responsibility given to officers, in part, results from the prevailing case management system and from an attempt by administration to shield itself from criticism. The vast majority of correctional clients are assigned to caseloads or investigation rosters maintained by individual POs. Such procedures inevitably lead to a one-on-one relationship between offender and officer. Most offenders assume they are more or less permanently attached to their assigned officers, and it is those officers who will decide the course of their probation or parole.

In her classic study of parole supervision, **Elliot Studt** argues that parole officers play a critical role in accomplishing the goals of the agency. It is their activities, after all, that ensure that the agency will contribute to protecting the community and assisting the clients in their reentry into the community. Similarly, for the parolee, the PO sets the tone for his or her entire parole experience. This is so because the POs definition of acceptable and unacceptable behavior affects the parole experience the client will have. In fact, for the client, the PO becomes ". . . a major 'critical condition' under which he 'does his parole.'"[2]

Studt further indicates the parole agency's organization of work by caseload increases the agents' responsibilities, demanding exceptional effort on the part of the PO to perceive and respond to every conceivable type of situation. In a case-work assignment model of organization, the PO becomes the agency for each client. The PO makes decisions affecting the individual's life, interpreting and applying the rules, gathering information that he or she deems important or relevant, and providing or arranging for services that he or she thinks the parolee needs. The implied role in this model requires an amount of competence that is "super-human" and suggests an incredibly high standard for success.[3] The client cannot help but perceive this role, therefore, affecting his or her behavior as well.

The behavior of correctional clients, regardless of department policy, remains unpredictable, and "successful" probation and parole outcomes, by any standards, are elusive. As a result, administrators often take measures to insulate themselves from the unpredictability of offender behavior, and potential criticism, by passing responsibility and accountability to line staff—the probation and parole officers. When they do this, however, they have necessarily passed ever greater discretion to the lower levels of the agency.[4]

Todd Clear and Kenneth Gallagher, in a review of classification practices, maintain that probation and parole work is characterized by uncertainty because procedures for effectively controlling offender behavior are unknown and, "the boundary decisions of release and revocation are made by other agencies (courts or parole boards)." Therefore, some "administrators are tempted to retain fuzzy and ambiguous goals with internally contradictory policy as a way to defend against the unpredictability of the work."[5] In these situations, street-level officers are given wide latitude in interpreting unclear policy goals, as long as controversy is avoided (often measured by the absence of external criticism).

Such latitude means that probation and parole officers share common experiences with other public service bureaucrats, who **Michael Lipsky** has described as "**street-level bureaucrats.**" The intriguing concept is used to identify "public service workers who interact directly with citizens in the course of their jobs and who have substantial discretion in the execution of their work."[6] This concept refers to most "law enforcement personnel, social workers, judges, public lawyers and other court officers, health workers and many other public employees who grant access to government programs and provide services within them."[7]

Therefore, street-level bureaucrats have a substantial affect on people's lives, for example, they may

- Socialize citizens as to what to expect from government services and how they fit into that service.
- Determine the eligibility of citizens for government benefits—or sanctions.
- Oversee the treatment or service citizens receive.

One of the common characteristics of street-level bureaucrats is that they must deal with personal and often immediate reactions to their decisions. Clients may respond angrily to what they perceive as an unjust decision, or they may be appreciative, thrilled, morose, or submissive in reaction to a bureaucrat's decision. Being treated as a number from someone representing a large bureaucracy is one thing, but it is quite another to be treated that way by someone with whom one has a relationship, someone from whom one expects an open and considerate ear. Thus, ". . . the reality of the work of street-level bureaucrats could hardly be farther from the bureaucratic ideal of impersonal detachment and decision-making. On the contrary, in street-level bureaucracies the objects of critical decisions—*people*—actually change as a result of the decisions."[8]

This phenomenon of dealing with clients in an immediate way is, therefore, policy in action, rather than in the abstract. According to Lipsky, street-level bureaucrats function as policy makers in two ways:

- They exercise wide discretion in decisions about with whom they interact.
- Then, when added together, their individual actions add up to agency behavior.

Therefore, the policy-making roles of street-level bureaucrats stem from the two interrelated aspects of their positions: relatively high degrees of discretion and relative autonomy from organizational authority.[9]

In probation and parole work the issue of officer discretion is a key one in determining what role POs play in policy making. There is consensus that POs must have some discretion in their work. How much discretion is appropriate, however, remains an unresolved issue. On the one hand, some argue that controlling officer discretion is an essential first step in effective management.[10] On the other hand, as discussed in Chapter Eight, there are structural variables existing in most probation and parole agencies that effectively inhibit discretion. Although many researchers contend that POs have considerable autonomy, organizational realities often restrict the independence of staff. Before addressing the issues of how much discretion and autonomy officers really possess, it is appropriate to review their work responsibilities and to identify types of POs carrying out those responsibilities.

The Tasks of Probation and Parole Officers

In 1990, the Oregon Department of Public Safety Standards and Training developed a job task analysis for a parole and probation officer. Figure 9.1 depicts the results of this analysis. As can be seen from the figure, all of the major tasks of a line officer in probation and parole can be categorized as (1) investigation, (2) surveillance, (3) assistance, or (4) paperwork. Although not a major task per se, attendance at periodic staff meetings is another responsibility of the line officer. Investigation requires line officers to present an account of the offender's situation; the format—the Presentence Investigation Report (see Chapter Four)—for doing this is relatively clear-cut. Paperwork tasks require officers to keep case records, fill out forms, and document a variety of activities. Even though paperwork is abhorred and often neglected in the crush of other activities, the staffers' responsibility is comparatively clear. Surveillance, defined as "that activity of the officer which utilizes watchfulness, checking and verification of certain behavior without contributing to a helping relationship,"[11] is a more ambiguous task. Generally, there are no precise guidelines that specify when to use surveillance or how much is appropriate. Surveillance, as an activity to detect behavior that is *potentially* dangerous to society, is often conducted in an atmosphere of uncertainty with POs unsure of what is an accurate "sign" of future criminality.

Recently, some agencies have attempted to make surveillance (especially in intensive supervision programs—see Chapter Ten) a more specific task by clearly defining what is expected of such activity. For instance, Georgia's Intensive Probation Supervision Program requires line officers to have five face-to-face contacts with offenders each week, to enforce mandatory curfews, to conduct unannounced drug and alcohol testing, and to do weekly criminal record checks.[12]

Perhaps the most ambiguous task of line officers is that of assisting offenders. Not much is known about what constitutes assistance, and even less about the effects of such efforts on offenders. Officers define assistance as helping offenders with community adjustment. This can mean everything from job referrals to discussions of psychosexual problems. Studt suggests that helping activities are even more difficult than surveillance activities to identify, largely based on to two assumptions:[13]

1. Some value will occur when there is *any* contact between a parolee and the PO; and
2. Because adjusting to parole involves the total life of the parolee, the PO can and should help in some way whenever there is a problem in the life of a parolee on the POs caseload.

Taken together, these two assumptions lead to an image of the PO as helper, implying a range of problem-solving skills that no one person can sincerely claim. Also, these assumptions suggest that all parolee problems can be solved at the individual level, that all it takes is an ingenious and skillful PO and some motivation on the part of the client to solve the various problems. This assumption is made despite the fact that many of the most significant problems faced by parolees are a result of structural factors out of the control of either the PO or the parolee (high unemployment rate, for example).

The lack of clarity in the helping assignment leads many, if not most, POs to develop a very personalized approach toward helping clients, often based on a combination of current therapeutic technologies, personal experience, and personal beliefs and values. Such a personalized approach allows the PO to respond to almost every type of human problem or crisis, inside the agency, or with his or her clients.[14] It also means that he or she assumes the "superhuman" role that is ultimately impossible to maintain.

FIGURE 9.1 *Job Task Analysis Profile of Oregon Parole and Probation Officer*

OREGON ADULT PAROLE AND PROBATION OFFICER . . . supervises adult offenders in the community

Conduct Offender/ Related Contacts	A-1 Make Home Visits	A-2 Make Jail Visits	A-3 Make Office Visits	A-4 Make Field Contact	A-5 Monitor and Collect Special Condition Verification	A-6 Make/ Receive Collateral Contacts
Conduct Investigations and Report	B-1 Prepare Presentence Investigation Report	B-2 Conduct Violation Investigation	B-3 Conduct Search and Seizure Procedure	B-4 Prepare Revocation Recommendation	B-5 Prepare Notice of Violation Report	B-6 Prepare Program Modification Report
Assess, Counsel, and Refer	C-1 Review Supervision Conditions	C-2 Assess, Counsel and Refer to Mental Health Agencies	C-3 Assess, Counsel, and Refer for Substance Abuse Treatment	C-4 Assess, Counsel, and Refer to Employment Services	C-5 Assess, Counsel, and Refer for Community Service Work	C-6 Schedule Polygraph
Maintain Offender Files	D-1 Conduct Intake	D-2 Open the Offender File	D-3 Prepare Risk Assessment	D-4 Prepare Supervision Plan	D-5 Prepare Needs Assessment	D-6 Maintain Chronological Entries
Arrest and Transport	E-1 Make Decision to Arrest	E-2 Set-up the Arrest	E-3 Make the Arrest			
Participate in Court Proceedings and Hearings Process	F-1 Discuss Offender Release with Release Officer	F-2 Review Case with DA	F-3 Gather Selected Information from Offender File	F-4 Testify in Court or at Grand Jury	F-5 Escort Offender to Jail	F-6 Prepare for and Participate in Morrisey Hearings
Prepare Noninvestiga- tive Reports	G-1 Prepare Monthly Statistical Reports	G-2 Prepare Progress Reports	G-3 Prepare Parole Analyst Report	G-4 File Incident Report		
Maintain Public Relations	H-1 Network	H-2 Participate on Panels	H-3 Supervise/ Train Volunteers, Practicums, and Interns	H-4 Participate in Charitable Projects and Events	H-5 Make Presentations to Schools and Community Organizations	
Continue Professional Development	I-1 Review Department of Corrections Policies, Procedures, and Rules	I-2 Attend Training (Mandatory, Volunteer)	I-3 Orient New Employees	I-4 Obtain Specialized Training	I-5 Review Interoffice Memos, Post Orders, and Letters of Agreement	I-6 Maintain ILDS Certification
Maintain Equipment and Records	J-1 Maintain Safety Equipment	J-2 Schedule Car Maintenance/ Complete Logs	J-3 Maintain Search Kit			

Source: Oregon Department of Public Safety Standards and Training, Monmouth, Oregon (March, 1990).

A-7 Maintain Field Book	A-8 Supervise P.S.R.B. Clients	A-9 Test for Alcohol/ Drugs	A-10 Monitor Electronic Surveillance	A-11 Serve as Duty Officer			
B-7 Prepare Unusual Incident Report	B-8 Prepare Transfer Request/ Conduct Investigation	B-9 Investigate and Prepare Prerelease/ Pre Parole Plan	B-10 Prepare Interstate Compact Request/ Conduct Investigation	B-11 Prepare Special Information Report	B-12 Prepare Pretrial Investigation Report	B-13 Prepare Early Terminiation Report	B-14 Prepare Postsentence Investigation Report
C-7 Arrange for Subsidy	C-8 Deal with Financial Needs	C-9 Asses, Counsel, and Refer for Sex Offender Treatment	C-10 Assess, Counsel, and Refer to Support Groups	C-11 Assess, Counsel, and Refer to Social Services Agencies			
D-7 File Offender Information	D-8 Run DMV/ LEDS Printouts	D-9 Update EPR, as Needed	D-10 Issue Travel Permits	D-11 Prepare Closing Summary Report			

I-7 Conduct Meetings	I-8 Upgrade Certification	I-9 Review Appelate Court Decisions	I-10 Review Meeting Minutes	I-11 Review Circulated Professional Materials	I-12 Review Department of Corrections Publications

Despite this ambiguity, Daniel Glaser has offered one of the best delineations of assistance, stating that it involves:

1. *Material aid,* defined as the officer's taking action necessary to procure employment, money, clothing, or other economic aid for a parolee;
2. *Referral,* defined as directing the probationer or parolee to other agencies that may assist him or her; and
3. *Mediation,* in which the PO works with persons or agencies with whom the client is having difficulty and attempts to help resolve the problem.[15]

Given that we know that the major tasks of probation and parole involve investigation, surveillance, assistance, and paperwork, a logical next step is to ask how much time do POs spend engaged in these various tasks. Several time studies have been done to ascertain how probation officers use their time. Allen and his associates reviewed seven time studies, covering the activities of federal, state, and county probation officers and discovered that POs spend about one-third of their working time doing presentence investigations; between two-fifths and one-half of their working time supervising clients; and the rest of their time doing other activities, such as administrative tasks. In short, between one-half and two-fifths of their time was spent doing "paperwork" or "noncase related" activities in their offices.[16]

John Rosecrance conducted an informal poll of officers (both in probation and parole) from Illinois, Florida, Louisiana, Nevada, Mississippi, California, Michigan, and Washington. The officers assigned to regular (not intensive) caseloads or to investigation units were asked how they allocated their work time. Following are the results (expressed as an overall average expenditure of time): office contacts with offenders—30 percent; paperwork in the office—45 percent; staff meetings and administrative functions—8 percent; fieldwork—17 percent. It should be noted that a few officers reported they rarely, if ever, made field calls.

It appears that staffs do not agree on precisely what their role in correctional work should be. Dale Hardman, in an article entitled, "The Function of the Probation Officer," observed, "I suspect that if you should ask a hundred probation officers how they perceive their roles, you would be astonished at the diversity of opinion."[17] In another article, the chief probation officer of Riverside County, California, Thomas Callahan commented: "The lack of consensus among line officers and other criminal justice professionals on the goals of the probation and parole system is truly amazing. Ask one hundred probation officers to define probation, and you will get one hundred different answers."[18]

All of these varied conceptions of correctional goals and individual philosophies affect the way POs perform their duties. Because each PO is free to follow his or her own personal style to do the work necessary to get the job done, each pays attention to those aspects of life and the job that seem significant to him or her. This is not unique to probation and parole work, and it should not be surprising. In fact, several researchers have identified variations in job orientations and, on that basis, have categorized POs into types. These typologies are useful in understanding the motivation and work performance of line officers.

Types of Line Officers

The pioneers in developing typologies of line officers were Lloyd Ohlin, Herman Piven, and Donnell Pappenfort.[19] Subsequent researchers either modified or expanded on their work. Ohlin and his associates noted three distinct types of job performance of parole officers and related them to corresponding concepts of parole work:[20]

1. The **punitive officer** is the guardian of middle-class morality and attempts to coerce the offender into conforming by means of threats and punishment. The emphasis here is on control, protecting the community, and an underlying suspicion of those under supervision.
2. The **protective officer** fluctuates between protecting the offender and protecting the community. The tools used are direct assistance, lecturing, and praise and blame. Such a PO is recognized by ambivalent emotional involvement with the offender and others in the community, shifting back and forth and taking sides with one against the other.
3. The **welfare officer** has the goal of improving the welfare of the client, achieved by helping the client with individual adjustment. This type of PO believes that the only way to protect the community lies in this individual adjustment because conformity through punishment will only be temporary and in the long run may make a successful adjustment more difficult.

Daniel Glaser later identified a fourth type, the **passive officer.** This type of officer was not deeply committed to either control or assistance and treated the job as requiring very little, yet offering a pretty good paycheck. Glaser also changed the term *protective* (in the Ohlin typology) to *paternal* to better reflect the "many persons in corrections whose abilities derive mainly from experience, dedication, and a warm personality rather than from formal training."[21] The resulting four-fold officer typology was related to the basic variables of assistance and control. For example, the combination of high assistance and high control characterizes the protective agent. However, low control and high assistance is the hallmark of a welfare worker type. Punitive agents exhibit high control and low assistance, while passive agents demonstrate low assistance and low control. John Irwin, after conducting research with parolees, concluded that a fifth type should be added to Glaser's schema, namely, a "detective" who is primarily concerned with uncovering violations.[22]

Paul Takagi, in a study of California parole officers, developed a slightly different typology based on relationships between officers and parole agencies:[23]

1. The *rebels* use up most of their energies fighting the agency and its rules. These POs believe that the organizational rules and procedures are silly and get in the way of their best efforts, and they criticize supervisors for incompetence and a lack of knowledge.

2. The *accommodator* also experiences a lot of frustrations and conflicts but mostly regarding the provision of services to clients. This type of PO is committed to the profession and to the ideology of treatment, trying to work within the framework of the existing administration and organization.

3. The *noncommitted* are "bodies filling positions in the organization." The work of the noncommitted is guided by task objectives, ignoring the goals of the organization. These POs are not oriented toward the needs of the client or the needs of the supervisor. Such a PO is very familiar with the routines of the job and can be depended on to do the minimum, that is, eight hours of work for eight hours of pay.

4. Finally, there is the *conformist*, who is not in conflict with agency rules and procedures. This PO works within the framework of the administrative structure to accomplish objectives as well as strives to meet the officially stated goals of the organization.

Richard Dembo thoroughly examined the backgrounds of New York parole officers and analyzed differences in handling cases (especially the use of technical violations to substantiate parole revocation). By correlating officers' backgrounds with their processing of parole violations, Dembo found two distinct groups:

1. An urban, liberal, probationer-oriented group, favoring an informal approach short of revocation; and

2. A rural, conservative group that was officer oriented and used social order rationalizations favoring revocation.

Dembo concluded that the experience of living in a cosmopolitan culture sensitizes officers to "the antisocial products of indigenous slums." However, living for an extended time in the predominantly white, Protestant, rural culture does not arouse concern for or involvement with antisocial persons, making it much more favorable toward a punitive orientation.[24]

Carl Klockars developed a particularly authentic typology of supervision officers. Drawing on his research with probation officers, he also delineated four types of officers, based on their orientation to casework, that is, "probation is casework" at one end of the continuum, and "probation is not casework" at the other.[25] Klockars's four types are:

1. *The law enforcers* are at the probation-is-not-casework end of the continuum and stress the legal authority and surveillance aspects of the job. These officers emphasize helping the offender comply with court orders; authority; decision-making power; public safety; and, often, police work.

2. *The time servers* are officers who find no law-enforcing or casework vocation in probation. Rather, they see their jobs as having certain requirements they must fulfill before they can retire. They rarely try to improve their skills, will

avoid training if possible, and do not belong to professional organizations. They follow rules and do their jobs methodically but minimally.

3. *The therapeutic agents* are at the probation-is-casework end of the continuum. The officers in this role want to introduce the probationer to a new way of life by motivating him or her to make changes by giving support and guidance and by providing an opportunity to work through their feelings of indecision.

4. *The synthetic officers* recognize both the treatment and law enforcement parts of the PO's role, attempting to satisfy both. To accomplish this, these officers must combine the paternal, authoritarian, and judgmental with the therapeutic, and thus may solve the classic problem of probation and parole, the PO's dilemma (see Chapter Five).

Louis Tomaino, in an attempt to delineate job orientation, developed a widely used concept, termed the *five faces of probation,* also based on the dual functions of assistance and control. According to Tomaino, "probation officers manifest certain strategies, approaches, or styles of 'probationing' which reflect their degrees of concern for meeting the stated goals of help and protection. Each of these styles 'shows its face' to the probationer and starts the interaction which leads to five differential outcomes in probation officer–probationer relationships." The "faces" are shown in Figure 9.2 and have the following meanings:

1. The PO's 1/1 face says to his probationer: "I'm sure you understand these conditions of probation. It's up to you to stick to them. No one can do it for you. If you need me be sure to contact me."

2. The PO's 5/5 face suggests to probationers that "you and I will work together in keeping these probation rules. I know how you must be feeling and thinking, and if you stick with me, you can make it."

3. The PO's 9/1 face says to the probationer: "I expect you to keep these probationary conditions. I'll do what I can to help you, but you will have to 'toe the mark' and there is no room for error."

4. The PO's 1/9 face says to the probationer: "I hope that you will understand the need for these probationary conditions. I will support you in every way I can and help you make your own decisions in a way that you will find contentment and not feel threatened by me."

5. The POs 9/9 face projects credibility and says to the probationer, "let's put our heads together and take a look at what needs to be done now; we may be able to go about doing it and determine the best way of finishing a realistic probation program."[26]

Virtually all typologies have been developed from studies of supervision officers (both probation and parole) rather than from investigation personnel. Because the priorities and responsibilities of probation investigators are often different from

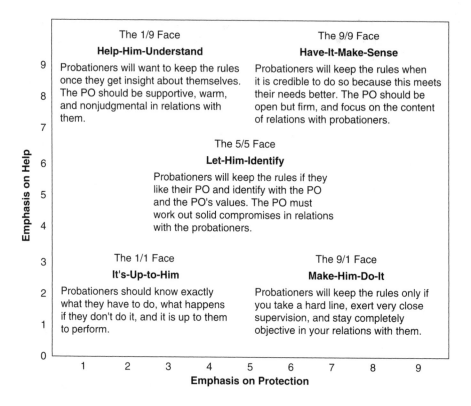

FIGURE 9.2 *Tomaino's "Faces" of Probation Officers*

Source: Louis Tomaino, "The Five Faces of Probation," *Federal Probation* 39 (December, 1975): 38–40.

those of supervision officers, the prevailing typologies are not directly applicable to presentence investigation writers. Typologies of supervision workers are oriented around the continuing dilemma of whether to emphasize control or assistance in relationships with offenders. These typologies invariably depict one type of officer as a problematic figure whose vacillation leads to inconsistent behavior—helping an offender one day and issuing a technical violation the next.[27]

The dichotomy of control or assistance is not a central issue for investigation officers. Their contacts with defendants are brief, usually consisting of one face-to-face interview. Most investigators are interested in presenting plausible reports to the court and rarely concern themselves with the extent or nature of their relationships with applicants. Typically, their overarching goal is to "shepherd the case through court," and they prefer to leave the job of "salvaging offenders" to supervision officers. Although there are, of course, similarities between the concerns of supervision and investigation officers (for example, protecting the community, avoiding controversies, and advancing careers), sufficient differences exist to warrant developing separate typologies.

Considering these facts, John Rosecrance developed a typology of presentence investigators.[28] The typology, based on interviews with investigators and professional experience, was constructed by identifying the types of officers that probation workers recognize and by exploring the criteria they use in placing themselves and other officers into various categories. The concept of role is defined as "a unique combination of certain customary ways of responding to recurrent situations—this unique combination being known and expected by others who deal with persons in this role, as well as by persons who occupy the role."[29] Thus, the resulting schema is a community- (officers themselves) rather than a researcher-designated typology.[30] A short discussion of each type follows.

- *Team player.* The hallmark of the team player category is adherence to department policies, acquiescence to supervisors, and avoidance of controversy. This type of officer closely follows guidelines contained in department manuals.
- *Mossback.* The distinguishing feature of the mossback type is a passive, routine job performance. Mossbacks demonstrate a superficial commitment to their jobs by fulfilling minimum requirements and following department regulations. However, they rarely do more than is necessary and would be characterized by Klockars as "time servers."
- *Hardliner.* The overarching goal of the hardliner is to protect society from its criminal offenders. These officers see themselves as bastions of order in an overly permissive world. They believe that laws must be enforced with continual vigilance, and when offenders flaunt them with impunity, the very fabric of society is threatened.
- *Maverick.* The main characteristic of the maverick type is a search for individual justice. These officers try to consider independently each case and to recommend an appropriate course of action. They attempt to evaluate every case on its own merits. Mavericks conceive of themselves as objective judicial advisors and not advocates of a particular point of view.
- *Bleeding heart liberal.* The unifying characteristic of the bleeding heart liberal type is a common perspective that the criminal justice system is unfair. Liberals contend that the system is so weighted against the defendant that it is incumbent on them to "even up the odds." They frequently view those charged with crimes as "unwitting pawns" in an inequitable social system, and see themselves as champions of the underdog.

In 1987 Arthur Spica, a deputy chief probation officer in Cook County, Illinois, developed a chart to reflect "how the probation officer works with the collected data and how this data affects the style of the presentence report." He believes that collected data "falls into two distinct areas: quantitative data, demographic in nature with a statistical direction (e.g., arrest reports, probation records, juvenile adjudications, etc.), and qualitative data, sociological in nature with a stress toward the clinical (e.g., alcohol adjustment, social history, substance abuse, etc.)."[31] A description of each of Spica's investigation styles follows.[32]

- *The practical style* is characterized by a low emphasis on both qualitative and quantitative data. It is a comfortable, nonthreatening style, with a focus on completing the job. New officers often use this style because they have not committed themselves to any one philosophy and usually do not have a high level of job sophistication. However, long-time officers can take refuge in this style because they can then do the job without making any real commitment.
- *The actuarial style* is distinguished by a high emphasis on quantitative data and low emphasis on qualitative data. As such, it is an "insurance table" style, using probabilities and percentages to make predictions of success or failure. This style has a built in danger of "computerized thinking" containing less of the human element and relying more on group norm predictions. The positive aspect of this style is that there are valid and reliable data to use to predict success or failure, but it is hard to really identify particular cases because of the use of general population data.
- *The social work style* emphasizes qualitative data with very little emphasis on quantitative data. It is the clinical approach to the criminal justice process and focuses on analytical behavior. This style uses interviewing techniques that lead to an approach that is offender oriented. The positive feature of this style is that it uses clinical diagnoses drawn from solid psychological theory; its drawback is that the interpretation of clinical data is often very subjective.
- *The integrative style* emphasizes both qualitative and quantitative data. Officers using this style are very selective of available data from both the qualitative and quantitative areas when they write the presentence report. Spica argues that this style should be the preferred style of any presentence writer because it best uses all data. The officer can draw from his or her academic and philosophical backgrounds and still use the "gut-level" responses based on past experiences.

Although typologies of line officers are useful, individual characteristics are not the only factors influencing work performance. Typologies generally assume that line officers have considerable discretion in the performance of their duties. This assumption should be tempered by the recognition that organization structure and bureaucratic imperatives inhibit individual autonomy. Line officers, in point of fact, do not have unregulated job discretion; their work performance is often guided by practical considerations. Herman Piven first addressed this theme when he acknowledged that parole officers "had to conform to the predominant expectations of their agency, regardless of their initial orientation or training."[33] Robert Martinson and Judith Wilks indicated the discretion of line officers was constrained by the complex limits set by operations manuals, by district officer supervision, and by career concerns.[34] James Davis, a New York City probation officer, concluded: "The immediate goals of probation are adherence to guidelines in manuals, obedience to orders, listening to supervisors and higher officials even though they are disagreeable, and processing cases on time."[35] Obviously, there is some disagreement as to how much discretion exists for parole and probation officers and, therefore, the issue of officer discretion is worth considering in more detail.

How Much Discretion?

Although researchers are initially impressed with the apparent freewheeling use of discretion by line officers, many of those who observe probation and parole over time discern parameters within which officers are forced to operate. In an early work on this subject, Paul Takagi and James Robinson examined the responses and recommendations of both parole officers and their supervisors to ten hypothetical case histories of parolees. They found a significant "congruence between an agent's recommendation and his perception of the district supervisor's orientation." This led the authors to conclude that definitions of parole violations are to some extent governed by style of administrative influence, supervisory practices, and officer orientation.[36] In a later analysis of this study, Takagi concluded parole failure or success is partially a product of the social organization of the district office.[37]

Robert Prus and John Stratton, while analyzing parole revocation practices, came to essentially the same conclusion, and then asked: "Do lowered revocation rates reflect improved supervision and effective parolee rehabilitation programs or do they reflect coping behavior on the part of agents to maintain their jobs and the system in which they operate?"[38]

Shover and Einstadter consistently maintained that organizational forces play a crucial role in decisions to revoke probation and parole.[39] In his classic study of a Cook County parole office, Richard McCleary demonstrated how structural variables inhibit officer discretion. He found: "A PO's case decision, or his interaction with a parolee is determined not only by the PO's personality, but also by organizational contexts and the costs of alternative decisions. In short, the PO often does what he *has* to do, not what he *wants* to do."[40] McCleary stresses that POs strive to develop professional reputations that will allow them to maximize their freedom within the organization. This is done by consistently "delivering" recommendations and reports that are in tune with prevailing organizational policy. Once an officer has established a "solid" reputation within the department, he or she is allowed more freedom and discretion. Accordingly, the "selective PO underrepresents some clients and overrepresents others regardless of the leeway he possesses in the situation." McCleary noted a case in which a PO testified as a character witness for a client charged with a new offense; the PO later told him:

> I don't do that often. If I testify for a client, the judges know the client is all right. I've a good rep with the judges because I'm selective. But if I testified for every one

of my clients who got into a little scrape, the judges wouldn't trust me anymore. They'd think I'd turned into a goddamn social worker. You can't save everybody. If you try, you end up not being able to save anybody.[41]

McCleary concludes that although reputation building "has definite short-term benefits for the organization and for some POs, its long-range effect is to corrupt the goals of the organization."[42]

When analyzing the work of presentence probation report writers Rosecrance found a similar situation in that these investigators used elaborate strategies to advance personal careers or individual points of view. In order to implement these strategies, investigators engaged in maneuvering to enhance their reputations. By cooperating with organizational requirements, investigators were able to promote their particular positions at opportune times. On the surface, these maneuverings seem to aid both individual workers and the probation department: Investigators gained a measure of freedom and the department gained a more or less standardized work output. However, in some cases presentence recommendations were framed more by the pragmatism of the investigating officer than by consideration of the facts and circumstances. In the long run, the overall objectivity of presentence reports and the independence of investigators were called into question. Such questioning raises the issue of how much influence probation and parole officers have in the criminal court system.

How Much Influence?

Although POs generally take it for granted that they can significantly influence judges and parole boards, in reality, their ability to do so is limited. Their limited influence, in large part, stems from a lower status in the criminal court system. No matter how much POs are lauded in public by judges and parole board members, in private those same persons downgrade probation personnel for their lack of legal training. In addition, probation and parole officials have almost no input into legal rulings or sentencing guidelines that directly impact their work. These circumstances leave POs with relatively little influence in the court system. However, this perspective is not shared by most probation and parole observers and remains controversial. At the same time, aspiring POs should be made aware of what they may be facing in the real world of probation and parole.

In order to address the issue of PO influence, it is useful to examine the presentence process. A common assumption (shared by most line officers and some researchers) is that judges follow the recommendations of probation officers. For example, while studying the issue of probation officer autonomy, Anthony Walsh found that: "probation officers do not perceive themselves to be second guessing judges. They view themselves as writing independent reports and professional assessments of unique offenders with unique needs and characteristics." After examining sentencing data he concluded: "The findings of this study strongly suggest that probation officers play an important role, perhaps the major role, in the determination of sentencing outcomes."[43]

However, after examining other sentencing outcomes Rodney Kingsworth and Louis Rizzo came to a very different conclusion. They found that plea bargaining had greatly reduced the influence of probation officers, whose recommendations had been rendered "largely superfluous." They contend that "previous research into sentencing decisions has been limited by its exclusive concern with the probation officer–judge relationship, and that the failure to place this relationship within the broader context of the court system has led to serious misinterpretation of the role of these participants in the sentencing process."[44] Kingsworth and Rizzo concluded that the probation officer's function at sentencing is to rubber stamp a done deal.

Similarly, John Rosecrance's research of presentence investigation units supports the latter conclusion, noting that (1) the presentence reports are structured for an audience, namely the probation administration, the prosecuting attorney, and the judge, and (2) the probation officer uses the reports to establish and maintain credibility with that audience. This is done by providing reports that meet the approval, or at least do not antagonize, the audience, and are therefore "reasonable" in their eyes. Through a process of socialization and winnowing, only probation officers willing to write such recommendations remain on the presentence unit. They are rewarded for their compliance, accept the prevailing sentencing parameters established by the court, and generally require little management. This process gives more weight to the prosecuting attorney's sentencing recommendations, and supervisors, who want to avoid controversy, support those recommendations that they feel best reflect the views of the judge or prosecutor. Therefore, "[a]lthough probation officers and criminologists talk of judges 'following' recommendations, it would be more accurate to report that probation investigators, and their supervisors, have correctly responded to judicial and prosecutorial cues."[45]

Thus, it would seem that the traditional belief that probation officers wield a great deal of influence and exercise a lot of discretion is at least somewhat exaggerated. Both PO discretion and influence operate within parameters set by those in authority. Therefore, the idea that these variables might be one of the attractions to the profession might be overstated. However, we do have a good idea of what does attract new recruits to the career, and these attractions are discussed in the next section.

The Attractions of a Probation or Parole Career

Although there is no consensus about how much discretion or influence POs wield, there is general agreement about what attracts them to the job: social concern and financial security. Many officers are attracted to this work by the opportunity to bring about positive changes in the lives of their clients. Most POs come to the field with a sincere desire to "help others." Typically, this desire is not focused or structured by any theoretical framework. Novice employees learn about probation and parole work on the job. Even though conventional wisdom maintains that officers quickly lose their optimism when faced with correctional realities, a significant number of seasoned employees retain their enthusiasm and interest throughout their careers. Mary Donnellan and Harvey Moore, for example, after interviewing hundreds of Florida probation and parole officers, concluded that most workers retain a desire to help others and are optimistic about their ability to do so.[46] Marilyn Sanchez found that veteran probation officers saw themselves as "instruments of change" and remained vitally interested in assisting their correctional clients.[47]

Another important attraction to this field is secure employment with an adequate wage. To some, a probation or parole job represents a way to support oneself and one's family while pursuing advanced degrees or until a better job becomes available. Todd Clear writes that, ". . . in most organizations probation is seen as an early-career position which most people eventually leave to take other jobs."[48] This tendency is often attributed to the fact probation and parole work generally is not accorded the status of a profession. However, for many officers probation and parole work does represent a career, if not a profession. Such officers have varied work backgrounds and enter the field seeking job security. Typically, they are not "right out of college." David Stanley found the vast majority of parole officers had worked at several jobs (such as teacher, social worker, police officer, prison guard, or municipal worker) before entering parole work.[49] Neal Shover observed that many workers had wide-ranging experience in other fields and began working in probation or parole after age thirty. He concluded that correctional work (which he termed *preprofessional*) was filled with those who "because of a growing family and advancing age are eagerly seeking permanent employment."[50]

Elliot Studt found that, for many, a career in corrections was not a first career choice. Oftentimes, a job in probation and parole was the best job available at some critical time in one's work life. The job provided an opportunity to exploit varied experiences without needing to take the time to complete specialized professional training.[51] Studt describes the histories of several parole agents:

- One graduated from law school; later became an accountant for a stock broker; then, during an economic recession, took a job in the sheriff's office; and later became a parole agent, from which he will retire.
- Another majored in psychology in college, was an interviewer for a research institute, spent some time teaching, worked for public welfare as an investigator, and in his late thirties became a parole agent.
- Three of the POs in her sample retired from highly responsible military careers, then worked in correctional jobs while taking additional college courses in order to qualify for a second career in parole.
- An African American agent started in college to become a doctor, switched to a mathematics major, and finally graduated with a degree in social science after a period of military service. He then worked for four years as a bus dri-

ver while organizing a citywide campaign against racial discrimination in the local transportation system, became a public welfare worker, and finally moved to parole.[52]

Although officers are initially attracted to probation or parole for reasons of social responsibility and employment security, once on the job, they find benefits that keep them working in the field. Studt found that these benefits included

1. Enjoyment of the power they exercised in people's lives;
2. Their freedom from direct supervision in the field; and
3. The drama and variety of the human situations to which they were exposed.[53]

These sentiments were echoed by Harold Duffie, the former chief probation officer for Maricopa County, Arizona. When he was asked what attracted workers to probation, he replied: "It's challenging always dealing with different kinds of problems. Probation allows officers a great deal of freedom in their work environment."[54] In a study of an Alabama program that stresses community surveillance, line officers reported the opportunity to assist offenders was the major source of satisfaction, followed by autonomy and job variety.[55]

The lack of direct supervision is seen as a distinct plus to probation and parole work. Most line officers have some flexibility in their working schedules. Officers can leave their agencies without being held directly responsible for their comings and goings. In the process they can attend to personal business, such as morning dental appointments, midafternoon haircuts or permanents, banking transactions, parent–teacher conferences, clothes-cleaner drop offs—all the details of modern life that those who work nine-to-five schedules often find difficult to accomplish. In addition, POs who are able to work faster and more efficiently than other workers can, on occasion, take time off from work to pursue other interests. POs are expected to manage their own assignments; they are not expected to volunteer for additional work. In the ebb and flow of work routines, most line officers are able to find some free time. Although such practices may be the norm, most administrators and public officials do not condone them. In his study of parole officers, McCleary found that nearly all POs have sidelines of some kind. "Some are full-time students, some have businesses, and some have other jobs. In all cases, POs cite as one of the most desirable aspects of their job the flexible schedule and free time which allows them to have a substantial sideline."[56] These various characteristics of the job attract certain types of people, and we describe them in the next section, along with the career paths followed by some.

Career Stages in Probation and Parole

As noted previously, there are characteristics of working in probation and parole that make it attractive to some people, even though it is not always the first occupational choice of those who end up there. Therefore, it is reasonable to assume that the profession might attract certain types of people. Demographic data can provide clues to the type of people currently pursuing careers in probation and parole. Even though there is no comprehensive profile of the "average" PO, there are some statistics available of PO's traits. For example, more than half (57 percent) are women,[57] a relatively new development since, in the mid-1980s, John Whitehead reported that 62.6 percent of the POs in his survey were male.[58] As might be predicted, 77 percent of POs in 1999 were white, and 75 percent possessed bachelor's degrees.[59] More than 80 percent of jurisdictions now require at least a bachelor's degree for their parole officers, and the majority require the same for probation officers.[60]

Given the type of people who become POs, we can now review some of the career paths they follow. Neal Shover, for example, found that new POs begin their careers without any reliable techniques for interpreting, and therefore reacting to, the behavior of their clients. Rather, they learn their jobs by observing and imitating the practices and jargon of seasoned POs.[61]

Interacting with correctional clients is often problematic. No matter how humanistic or dedicated the individual worker, dealing with offenders is often troubling and difficult. Correctional clients have a multitude of problems, and environmental factors (unemployment, prior associations, poverty, familial background) can swamp the PO's effort, no matter how well intentioned. Because working with offenders in a community setting has its special problems, students can definitely benefit from participation in volunteer or internship programs; such programs allow them to "get their feet wet" without making a full commitment. There are some people who, because of their temperaments and personalities, will never be happy in probation and parole work. The sooner they discover this, the better. Too many POs find themselves stuck in jobs for which they are not suited. The consequence can mean years of lackluster and unenthusiastic work performance.

Career progression, therefore, generally is accompanied by the development of coping strategies for dealing with correctional clients. All line officers must resolve the fact that some offenders cannot be reached and disappointments in working with them are inevitable; the trick is to avoid becoming overly cynical and case hardened. Line officers must realize that a particularly bad experience with a client does not abrogate their responsibilities to other offenders. This may be difficult because when the occasional client "makes a fool of him" its very likely that fellow workers will use ridicule as part of a "toughening-up" education.[62] Therefore, the next phase of a POs career often follows quickly, according to Studt: The PO becomes somewhat harsher and more punitive than many of his or her fellow workers. For example, there may be friendly competition during coffee breaks or social gatherings over who can tell the most demeaning stories about their clients or how smart and tough one has been in detecting violations and imposing sanctions.

Many POs then move on to a third stage, which Studt calls "mellowing,"[63] where the PO once again begins to see clients as human beings in need of help; as people who should have a second chance when they make mistakes. These POs are often viewed as very competent and some continue their careers to a very satisfactory and fulfilling conclusion, whereas a few of the rest are promoted to management positions.

Probation and parole have a tradition of promoting "from the ranks." These promotions progressively move POs away from the client contact that originally attracted them to the field and from the POs with whom they formerly worked. Moreover, most new supervisors have very little training or education in management or administration, which could make life difficult for them and former colleagues who have become their subordinates. The dissatisfaction felt by the subordinates may contribute to a fourth career stage: disillusionment. After years of supervising difficult clients, dealing with crises, coping with "incompetent" and out of touch management, and working long hours unrewarded by advancement, it is not surprising that some POs become disenchanted and cynical about their work. Some then look for opportunities to change careers. Others stay on the job and maintain the stage of permanent disillusionment. This stage is often referred to as burnout and we now turn to this increasingly important and relevant topic.

Burnout

The phenomenon of employee burnout has received increasing attention, even to the point of being called the "disease of modern life."[64] Job **burnout** was defined by pioneer researcher Christina Maslach as a "syndrome of emotional exhaustion and cynicism that occurs frequently among individuals who do 'people work' of some kind." She expanded this definition by characterizing it as "the gradual loss of caring about people they work with. Over time they find that they simply cannot sustain the kind of personal care and commitment called for in the personal encounters that are the essence of the job."[65] This definition identifies client contact as the primary source of burnout. However, another early researcher in this area, G. Cherniss, suggested that organizational factors (such as lack of decision making or role conflict) were the major causes of burnout, stemming from "a process that begins with excessive and prolonged levels of job stress. This stress produces strain in the worker (feelings of tension, irritability and fatigue). The process is completed when the workers defensively cope with the job by psychologically detaching themselves from the job and becoming apathetic, cynical and rigid."[66]

JoAnn Thacker pointed out that one common technique employed by "burned-out" corrections employees is "going by the book" rather than addressing the unique and individual features of a client's situation. This allows the PO to avoid the stress created by making difficult and sometimes painful decisions if instead he or she can say "I'm sorry, but it's not my fault—those are in the rules around here, and I have to follow them." Thacker also found that burnout leads to physical decline, and that "exhaustion, insomnia, ulcers, migraine headaches and other stress-related complaints, such as neck and backaches, were found to be widespread"[67] among burned-out corrections workers.

Will Manning, director of a community-based facility, describes the tell-tale signs of burnout:

- The staff member who is usually talkative at staff meetings suddenly becomes reticent.
- The person appears disenchanted, bored, and confused.
- The person appears edgy, quick to become infuriated, and frustrated at what would ordinarily be considered irrelevant and inconsequential.
- The person becomes paranoid with respect to his or her colleagues.[68]

Several researchers have observed definite signs of burnout in probation and parole departments throughout the United States. In one such study, it was found that burnout was most pronounced in officers with six months to three years experience. However, newly hired and veteran officers had very low rates of burnout.[69] This finding supports Studt's notion of coping strategies wherein POs eventually learn to integrate disappointment into their work styles (referred to previously as "mellowing").

John Whitehead, using the responses of probation officers to job satisfaction questions, tested the causation theories of Maslach (excessive client contact) and Cherniss (organizational unresponsiveness). This study was a landmark one in probation and parole research because it presented empirical data to test theoretical propositions. All too often, this type of rigorous investigation has been lacking in criminal justice research. Whitehead's study should be thoroughly read by administrators because it clearly demonstrated that excessive client contact, in itself, had little to do with probation officer burnout. Instead, he found support for the Cherniss theory. A critical factor in probation officer burnout was "the individual worker's assessment of the level of demands placed on him or her by the employing agency,"[70] and role conflict, role ambiguity, and lack of officer participation in decision making were the biggest reasons POs became burned out. He contended that organizational responsiveness to probation officer concerns could diffuse potential burnout.

Paul Brown, in his study of correctional practices, came to the same conclusion as Whitehead, calling probation officer burnout "an organizational disease with an organizational cure." He proposed several steps the administration could take to reduce line officer burnout, such as offering sabbatical leaves, sharing decision making, and sponsoring training seminars. Brown concluded "individual stress-reducing techniques will have minimal effect on reducing organizationally-induced stress and burnout."[71] In a dissertation on probation officer burnout, T. M. McCabe agreed that ". . . organizational behavior and changing management styles is a necessity for the reduction of burnout in the probation office"[72] and that new ways of coping must be developed in order to have a healthy and productive work place.

Slate and his colleagues also state that organizational factors were much more important than client contact in causing stress.[73] These factors included excessive bureaucracy, lack of communication, lack of support from superiors, lack of promotional opportunities, lack of support from the court, and failure to recognize work accomplishments. Therefore, to do something about stress and burnout requires more than stress management training for POs. Rather than teaching POs to exercise, meditate, or watch their diet to relieve stress, probation and parole managers should focus on organizational and management factors they can change. In a 2000 article, Burrell suggests several steps managers might take to reduce burnout, including fostering participatory decision making; increasing the flow of communication; providing proper resources; delegating authority and responsibility; establishing a clear mission and roles for all employees; and managing with fairness, trust, and dignity.[74]

Summary

Probation and parole officers, who interact directly with offenders, implement department policy through their delivery of correctional services. They generally have some discretion in making decisions that immediately impact offenders. In this regard, they fit Lipsky's category of street-level bureaucrats. The tasks of line officers are wide ranging and encompass investigation, assistance, surveillance, and record keeping. Line officers, especially those with large caseloads, spend much of their time in the office managing paperwork. The individual orientations of line officers influence their job performance. Several typologies of officers have been developed to delineate these variations.

Although line officers have considerable discretion, there are organizational variables that require adherence to certain standards. Those who deviate too far from work norms are sanctioned, and officers soon learn to keep their decision making within certain, often informal, parameters. The influence of POs within the court system is restricted by the dominance of judges and district attorneys.

Individuals are drawn to probation and parole work by a desire to help others and by the financial security of regular employment. Generally, new recruits have other work experience and do not enter the field directly from college. As POs progress through early stages of their careers, they frequently manifest disillusionment because correctional clients are often unresponsive. Most line officers get over these disappointments and recover their initial enthusiasm that positive change is possible. However, some officers do not "mellow out" and instead burn out. These officers demonstrate excessive cynicism and rigid adherence to department policy while psychologically distancing themselves from their work. Several studies have shown that organizational responsiveness can mitigate excessive job stress and defuse potential burnout.

Key People and Terms

Burnout (297)
Michael Lipsky (279)
Passive officer (285)
Protective officer (285)

Punitive officer (285)
Street-level bureaucrats (279)
Elliot Studt (278)
Welfare officer (285)

Questions for Discussion and Review

1. Describe how POs implement the policies of their agencies.

2. Are probation and parole officers street-level bureaucrats? Explain.

3. List and discuss the major tasks of a line officer in probation and parole.

4. Discuss the various typologies of probation and parole officers. Which typology do you think is best? Why?

5. What are the five types of presentence investigation officers discussed in the chapter? Why is this typology different than those for supervision officers?

6. How much influence does the organization have on parole officer discretion? Give examples to reinforce your arguments.

7. How much influence do probation officers have in the sentencing process?

8. What attracts people to a career in probation and parole? What are the typical career stages of a probation or parole officer?

9. What is employee burnout? What are some telltale signs of probation or parole officer burnout?

Relevant Internet Sites

American Probation and Parole Association, the professional organization for probation and parole officers in the United States: www.appa-net.org

Federal Probation, a journal of correctional philosophy and practice published by the U.S. courts: www.uscourts.gov/fpcontents.html

A brief discussion of the tasks of federal probation officers: www.uscourts.gov/misc/ccprob.pdf

Bureau of Labor Statistics, an excellent web site for probation officers, including a description of the nature of the work, working conditions, job outlook, earnings, and more: www.bls.gov/oco/ocos265.htm

California Probation Parole and Correctional Association: www.cppca.org

Notes

1. Henry C. Duffie, "Probation—The Best-Kept Secret Around," *Corrections Today* 49 (August, 1987): 127.

2. Elliot Studt, *People in the Parole Action System: Their Tasks and Dilemmas* (Los Angeles, CA: UCLA Institute of Government and Public Affairs, 1971) 45.

3. Elliot Studt, *Surveillance and Service in Parole* (Los Angeles, CA: UCLA Institute of Government and Public Affairs, 1972) 54–55.

4. Paul Takagi, "The Role of the Inmate in the Prerelease Process," in *Probation, Parole and Community Corrections,* eds. Robert Carter, Daniel Glaser, and Leslie Wilkins (New York: Wiley, 1970) 206–214.

5. Todd Clear and Kenneth Gallagher, "Probation and Parole Supervision: A Review of Current Classification Practices," *Crime and Delinquency* 31 (1988): 439.

6. Michael Lipsky, *Street-Level Bureaucracy* (New York: Sage, 1986) 3.

7. Lipsky 3.

8. Lipsky 4.

9. Lipsky 9.

10. Todd Clear, "Three Dilemmas in Community Supervision," in *Probation, Parole and Community Corrections,* eds. Robert Carter, Daniel Glaser, and Leslie Wilkins, 3rd ed. (New York: Wiley, 1984) 219.

11. Studt, *Surveillance and Service in Parole* 70.

12. Billie S. Erwin, "Turning Up the Heat on Probationers in Georgia," *Federal Probation* 50 (June, 1986): 17.

13. Studt, *Surveillance and Service in Parole* 97–99.

14. Studt, *Surveillance and Service in Parole* 99.

15. Daniel Glaser, *The Effectiveness of a Prison and a Parole System* (Indianapolis, IN: Bobbs Merrill, 1964) 434.

16. Harry Allen, Eric Carlson, and Evalyn Parks, *Critical Issues in Probation* (Washington, DC: U.S. Department of Justice, 1979) 81–82.

17. Dale G. Hardman, "The Function of the Probation Officer," *Federal Probation* 24 (September, 1960): 3.

18. Thomas Callahan, "Probation and Parole: Meeting the Future Head-On," *Corrections Today* 48 (June, 1986): 180.

19. Lloyd Ohlin, Herman Piven, and Donnell Pappenfort, "Major Dilemmas of the Social Worker in Probation and Parole," *National Probation and Parole Association Journal* 11 (1956) 213.

20. Ohlin et al. 213.

21. Glaser 431.

22. John Irwin, *The Felon* (Englewood Cliffs, NJ: Prentice Hall, 1970) 168–170.

23. Quoted in Irwin 165.

24. Richard Dembo, "Orientation and Activities of the Parole Officer," *Criminology* 10 (1972): 212.

25. Carl Klockars, "A Theory of Probation Supervision," *Journal of Criminal Law, Criminology and Police Science* 63 (1972): 550–552.

26. Louis Tomaino, "The Five Faces of Probation," *Federal Probation* 39 (December, 1975): 38–40.

27. David E. Duffee, "Models of Probation Supervision," in *Probation and Justice: Reconsideration of Mission,* eds. Patrick McAnay, Doug Thomson, and David Fogel (Cambridge, MA: Oelgeschlager, Gunn and Hain 1984) 187.

28. John Rosecrance, "A Typology of Presentence Investigators," *International Journal of Offender Therapy and Comparative Criminology* 31 (1987): 163–177.

29. Dale Van Landingham, Merlin Taber, and Ruta Dimantis, "How Adult Probation Officers View Their Job Responsibilities," *Crime and Delinquency* 12 (1966): 98.

30. Joseph P. Spradley, *You Owe Yourself a Drunk: An Ethnography of Urban Nomads* (Boston: Little, Brown, 1970).

31. Arthur R. Spica, "Presentence Reports: The Key to Probation Strategy," *Corrections Today* 49 (August, 1987): 195–196.

32. Spica 195–196.

33. Quoted in Glaser 432.

34. Robert Martinson and Judith Wilks, "Save Parole Supervision," *Federal Probation* 41 (September, 1977): 23–26.

35. James Davis, "Academic and Practical Aspects of Probation: A Comparison," *Federal Probation* 47 (December, 1983): 10.

36. Paul Takagi and James Robinson, "The Parole Violator: An Organizational Reject," *Journal of Research in Crime and Delinquency* 6 (1969): 78–86.

37. Takagi, Paul, "The Role of the Inmate in the Prerelease Process," in *Probation, Parole and Community Corrections,* eds. Robert Carter, Daniel Glaser, and Leslie Wilkins (New York: Wiley, 1970).

38. Robert Prus and John Stratton, "Parole Revocation Decisionmaking: Private Typings and Official Designation," *Federal Probation* 40 (March, 1976): 53.

39. Neal Shover and Werner Einstadter, *Analyzing American Corrections* (Belmont, CA: Wadsworth, 1988) 130–135.

40. Richard McCleary, "How Structural Variables Constrain the Parole Officers' Use of Discretionary Power," *Social Problems* 23 (1975): 210.

41. McCleary 221.

42. McCleary 204.

43. Anthony Walsh, "The Role of the Probation Officer in the Sentencing Process: Independent Professional or Judicial Hack?" *Criminal Justice and Behavior* 12 (1985): 301.

44. Rodney Kingsworth and Louis Rizzo, "Decision-Making in the Criminal Courts: Continuities and Discontinuities," *Criminology* 17 (1979): 12–13.

45. John Rosecrance, "The Probation Officers' Search for Credibility: Ball Park Recommendations," *Crime and Delinquency* 31 (1985): 539–554.

46. Mary C. Donnellan and Harvey Moore, "Rehabilitation and Protection: The Goals and Orientations of Probation and Parole Workers," *Offender Rehabilitation* 3 (1979): 207–218.

47. Marilyn Sanchez, "Probation Officers Do Make a Difference, "*Federal Probation* 46 (March, 1982): 77–81.

48. Todd Clear, "Managerial Issues in Community Corrections," *Probation, Parole, and Community Corrections: A Reader,* ed. Lawrence Travis (Prospect Heights, IL: Waveland, 1985) 40.

49. David Stanley, *Prisoners among Us* (Washington, DC: Brookings Institute, 1976) 92.

50. Neal Shover, "Experts and Diagnosis in Correctional Agencies," *Crime and Delinquency* 20 (1974): 350.

51. Studt, *Surveillance and Service in Parole* 46.

52. Studt, *Surveillance and Service in Parole* 46.

53. Studt, *Surveillance and Service in Parole* 45.

54. Duffie 127.

55. Charles Lindquist and John Whitehead, "Correctional Officers as Parole Officers: An Examination of a Community Supervision Sanction," *Criminal Justice and Behavior* 13 (1986): 197–222.

56. Richard McCleary, *Dangerous Men: The Sociology of Parole* (Beverly Hills, CA: Sage, 1978) 76.

57. Camille Camp and George Camp, *The Corrections Yearbook, 1999* (Middletown, CT: Criminal Justice Institute, Inc., 1999) 206.

58. John Whitehead, "Job Burnout in Probation and Parole: Its Extent and Intervention Implications," *Criminal Justice and Behavior* 12 (1985): 98–99.

59. Camp and Camp 206.

60. Edward J. Latessa and Harry E. Allen, *Corrections in the Community* (Cincinnati, OH: Anderson, 1999) 275.

61. Shover 347.

62. Studt, *Surveillance and Service in Parole* 59.

63. Studt, *Surveillance and Service in Parole* 59.

64. Paul Brown, "Probation Officer Burnout: An Organizational Disease/An Organizational Cure, Part I," *Federal Probation* 50 (March, 1986): 4.

65. Quoted in Whitehead, "Job Burnout in Probation and Parole" 95.

66. Quoted in John Whitehead, "Probation Officer Job Burnout: A Test of Two Theories," *Journal of Criminal Justice* 15 (1985): 2.

67. JoAnn Thacker, "Reducing Burnout," *Corrections Today* 41 (November–December, 1979): 50.

68. Will Manning, "An Underlying Cause of Burnout," *Corrections Today* 45 (February, 1983): 20.

69. Whitehead, "Job Burnout in Probation and Parole" 91.

70. Whitehead, "Probation Officer Job Burnout" 13.

71. Paul Brown, "Probation Officer Burnout: An Organizational Disease/An Organizational Cure, Part II," *Federal Probation* 51 (September, 1987): 260.

72. Quoted in Brown, "Probation Officer Burnout: Part II" 17.

73. Risdon N. Slate, W. Wesley Johnson, and Terry L. Wells, "Probation Officer Stress: Is There an Organizational Solution," *Federal Probation* 64 (June, 2000): 57–58.

74. William D. Burrell, "How to Prevent PPO Stress and Burnout," *Community Corrections Report* 8 (November–December, 2000): 1ff.

10

Innovative Programs and Intermediate Sanctions

The Movement toward Intermediate Sanctions and the Need for Innovation

The prevailing themes in contemporary criminal justice are deserved punishment and community protection. Ensuring that criminal offenders receive their just deserts through appropriate punishment has become a major task of correctional agencies. In order to protect the community, incarceration increasingly is seen as an equitable response to criminal activity. The themes of punishment and community protection have been brought to the forefront by perceptions that offender rehabilitation, although a laudable goal, is not practical or even possible.

Probation and parole agencies have been directly impacted by punitive philosophies and get-tough sentencing practices. Initially, they bore the brunt of criticism and loss of public confidence for policies deemed too lenient. Ironically, the rush to incarcerate soon resulted in jail and prison crowding. This situation then prompted a search for alternatives to mitigate sentencing severity. These alternatives generally incorporated some form of community corrections and resulted in significant increases in clientele. In many instances, the new referrals were felons, a type of client that in the past had not routinely been granted probation. In order to regain public confidence, and to deal with expanding and changing caseloads, community corrections agencies have developed a host of new programs. Although the granting of probation or parole still involves mitigation, these programs are typically control oriented, emphasizing surveillance and compliance with release conditions, and are, therefore, more stringent than past practices. In addition, restorative justice programs, another innovation, involve an entirely new approach to justice, bringing the victim and community into the process while maintaining the goal of holding offenders accountable and restoring the victim and the community as fully as possible. We discuss both intermediate sanctions and restorative justice programs in this chapter.

However before we do, it must be pointed out that establishing new procedures and setting policy does not guarantee that change will actually occur. It takes concerted effort and continuing commitment by both administration and line officers to ensure that program goals are not subverted in the implementation of those programs. For new programs to be successful, administration must set realistic goals and line officers must put aside resistance to change. Both of these requisites are difficult to achieve. Many administrators, in the rush to put forth new programs that satisfy agency critics, claim more for these programs than they can possibly deliver in a realistic manner. In the words of Sheldon Glueck they have "oversold" programs with excessively optimistic projections that (in an all too familiar pattern) will eventually lead to wholesale disillusionment.[1] Line officers, in many cases, do not willingly relinquish their traditional discretion and individual styles, even in the wake of new policy edicts.

James Byrne described the response of Massachusetts's line officers to a significant change in department policy regarding supervision practices as "bending granite."[2] In a survey of criminal justice practitioner's perceptions of intensive supervision programs (ISPs), Bayens, Manske, and Smykla found that many practitioners had broad and often contradictory views concerning the purposes of ISPs and how the public views such programs.[3] These researchers concluded that all participants in ISPs must be in agreement as to the goals of the program and how important it is to conduct risk and needs assessments of participating offenders.

Although problematic, new programs that consider alternative sentencing policies are going to structure the efforts of probation and parole administrators and line officers for the foreseeable future. It is essential to understand what these programs are and how they work. We discuss the intermediate sanctions of intensive supervision, home confinement, shock incarceration, differential supervision, and day reporting centers. We also discuss restorative justice programs and the challenges of innovation in this chapter. First, intermediate sanctions.

Intermediate Sanctions

New probation and parole programs increasingly are seen as a form of **intermediate sanctions,** which is defined by Belinda McCarthy[4] as "those sanctions that exist somewhere between incarceration and probation on the continuum of criminal penalties." Joan Petersilia, a leading criminal justice researcher, indicates: "Policy makers and managers across the country are looking for 'intermediate' or 'middle-range' sentencing options that are tougher than traditional probation but less stringent—and less expensive—than imprisonment. These options reflect the realization that prisons (and jails) are overcrowded, largely because some states have sentenced all kinds of offenders, from first-time welfare cheats to repeat robbers, to prison without considering the different risks they present to the community."[5] A Delaware Commission on prison alternatives describes the requirements of intermediate sanctions:

The programs must be tough and affordable, and exert enough control over offenders so that public safety is assured. . . . We must find intermediate-level sentencing options whereby nondangerous offenders can be sentenced to the community, thereby saving expensive prison beds.[6]

Community corrections administrators have developed several new types of programs to fit the requirements of intermediate sanctions. These programs fall into five main categories: (1) intensive supervision, (2) home confinement (with or without electronic surveillance), (3) shock incarceration, (4) differential supervision, and (5) day reporting centers. Although these programs are not entirely new, the current emphasis on client control sets them apart from prior efforts. Whether the new programs represent true innovations, or are merely pandering to the latest correctional panacea remains to be seen.

Intensive Supervision

Beginning in the early 1980s, **intensive supervision programs** in probation and parole became a national phenomenon. According to Rand Researchers, at least forty states were operating ISPs by 1987, and all fifty states had some type of ISP for adult offenders by 1990.[7]

The basic assumption behind intensive supervision is that for certain offenders placed on probation or parole (usually the high-risk variety), a high degree of intrusiveness is desirable. Because intrusiveness takes considerable time, all ISPs involve small or greatly reduced caseloads (the national average is twenty-five cases per officer). It is assumed that line officers will become intimately familiar with their limited caseloads. Such familiarity allows supervision officers to react quickly to emerging developments, thereby enabling them to prevent criminal activity.

Intensive supervision type programs were tried to a limited extent in the 1960s and 1970s. At that time, they consistently failed to reduce recidivism, leading many researchers to conclude there was "no evidence" that smaller caseloads would result in more effective supervision.[8] However, current ISPs have a significantly different focus than their earlier counterparts. Whereas the first ISP efforts emphasized assistance and reintegration, the programs that developed in the 1980s stressed surveillance and compliance with official orders. After examining the failures of prior ISPs, John Conrad indicated a strong advocacy of these more control-oriented efforts. He believed the programs' strengths lie in the punitive nature of the experience of surveillance, and the fact that "We are no longer deceiving ourselves and attempting to deceive probationers [and parolees] about the therapeutic benefits of the relationship between the officer and the offender. The officer's hot breath may be on the offender's neck; if the offender doesn't like it, he knows what the consequences will be if he strays too far from surveillance."[9]

The early emphasis on client control was related to the fact that ISPs were designed, in most cases, to divert offenders from prison. According to Edward

Latessa,[10] early ISP efforts had been directed toward offenders who normally would have received regular supervision. Today's ISP candidates, however, are typically offenders classified as too serious for regular probation but whose behavior and prior record is not so serious that they can *only* be controlled in a prison setting.[11] Eligibility for ISP is generally based, to some degree, on use of a risk assessment scoring device. Diversion from prison has obvious financial benefits as well as serving to relieve prison overcrowding. These diversion efforts, however, must be compatible with contemporary get-tough policies.

Judges and parole boards are only willing to place offenders on intensive programs if they can do so without seeming to be "soft on crime." Considering the type of client (those in danger of being sentenced to prison) and prevailing sentiments favoring harsh punishments, the avowed program goal of "turning up the heat"[12] on ISP clients is understandable. Because of their surveillance components, most ISPs incorporate stringent supervision practices whose objectives are to control offenders in various ways. Although ISPs vary between and among jurisdictions, they all turn up the "heat" on clients in similar ways. This usually includes numerous contacts between probation officers, other community members, and offenders; making sure the convicted offender is more accountable for his or her crime by requiring restitution and community service; ensuring the offender is financially responsible by having him or her pay supervision fees; requiring random drug testing; and minimizing opportunities for new criminal behavior through, for example, mandatory curfews, home confinement, and electronic surveillance.[13]

A specific example of the conditions of ISPs comes from Georgia, the first state to reintroduce the concept back in 1982. A National Institute of Justice research brief described the supervision standards that have earned the program its reputation as the "toughest probation" in the United States.[14] These standards include

- Five face-to-face contacts per week;
- One-hundred-thirty-two hours of mandatory community service;
- Mandatory curfew;
- Weekly check of local arrest records;
- Automatic notification of arrest elsewhere via the State Crime Information Network listing; and
- Routine and unannounced alcohol and drug testing.

Two officials enforce these supervision standards: a probation officer who provides counseling and has legal authority over the case, and a surveillance officer (usually drawn from the ranks of law enforcement) who monitors the offender's compliance with court orders. Such teams normally manage a caseload of twenty-five; their 12.5:1 client–staff ratio differs significantly from the statewide rate of at least 120:1.

As previously noted, all fifty states have implemented some type of ISP and by doing so these jurisdictions hope to achieve several goals, including reducing prison overcrowding, giving judges more sentencing options, decreasing the cost of corrections, and reducing recidivism.[15] The question then becomes, have ISPs met these goals?

Evaluation of ISPs.   Some researchers do not believe that ISPs have achieved the first goal of decreasing prison overcrowding. Petersilia and Turner's study in California, for example, estimated that at least 10 percent of those entering prison had their probation or parole revoked.[16] Because ISP offenders have more rules and are required to have greater contact with their probation officers, it makes sense that they are also more likely to get caught violating one or more of the rules, and then get sent to prison. Furthermore, Tonry found that some judges sent eligible probationers to prison because they thought correctional staff would then place them in an ISP, which did not always happen.[17]

The second goal, providing more sentencing options, has in practice been achieved. With ISPs, it is clear that judges have one more option when sentencing offenders. Also, corrections officials and parole boards have another release option. However, ISPs may affect sentencing policy in a negative way as well. For example, Von Hirsch, Wasik, and Greene argued that some judges use ISPs as a net widening tool, which means that some offenders who otherwise would be sentenced to regular probation are instead unnecessarily subjected to the stricter conditions and surveillance of an ISP, simply because it is available.[18]

Whether ISPs have accomplished the third goal, decreasing the cost of corrections, depends on the questions asked. For example, if one asks if ISPs save money compared to regular probation, the answer is no. Gendreau and his colleagues reported on a Rand Corporation study that found that in several locations ISPs were about half again more expensive than regular probation. However, if the question is whether ISPs save money compared to prison, the answer is a qualified yes. Gendreau and colleagues, for example, also cite a study conducted by the American Probation and Parole Association that found the following costs associated with three correctional options: regular probation—$2 to $5 per day; ISP—$7 to $15 per day; prison—$35 to $65 per day. So, prison is anywhere from five to nine times more expensive than ISPs.[19]

It would seem that ISP's are more expensive than regular probation, but less expensive than prison. However, there are other factors to consider when evaluating the cost of programs. For example, even though ISPs save money compared to sending an offender to prison, the savings may not be as great as reported simply because of the high violation rates for ISP offenders, eventually sending many of these probationers to prison. The increased initial cost of ISP (compared to regular probation), and the additional cost of prison if the offender is eventually institutionalized anyway, must be added to the overall cost of the program. One study of a Minnesota ISP found that the savings gained from using ISP instead of prison were offset by the increased cost of intensive probation; the money saved at sentencing was offset by the amount it cost in the end.[20]

The problem of **net widening** is also a factor that may increase costs. Judges may sentence to ISP those who would otherwise be on regular probation simply because the ISP is available. Because ISP is about three times more expensive than regular probation, such net widening significantly increases the costs of corrections. Finally, some have argued that ISPs cost more because they contribute to a decrease in public safety.[21] Such a decrease can be the result of more crimes committed by those on ISPs who, if they were imprisoned, would not be able to commit the crimes, or because ISPs take resources away from regular probation so that regular probationers are monitored less strictly, maybe decreasing public safety.

The fourth and perhaps most important goal of ISPs is to reduce recidivism. With some notable exceptions, most researchers agree that this goal has not been met. This is so even though the Georgia program, probably the best-known ISP, reported that the first 1,000 clients committed less than twenty-five serious offenses.[22] However, later researchers drew different conclusions, stating that most of the Georgia ISP clients had not been diverted from prison, that the comparison group did not match the ISP group, and the low recidivism rates were the result of the low-risk offenders chosen for the program, not from the program itself.[23] More generally, Gendreau and colleagues report on a meta-analysis of the intermediate sanction literature that found that ISPs ". . . inevitably result in about the same or slightly higher recidivism rates than comparable regular probation programs . . ."[24] However, these same authors also propose that, among all the poor results, four studies of ISPs deserved more attention. The four are the Pearson evaluation of a New Jersey ISP,[25] the Byrne and Kelly evaluation of a Massachusetts ISP,[26] the Petersilia and Turner study of three ISP programs in California,[27] and Paparozzi and Gendreau's study of a New Jersey ISP.[28]

The Pearson study was important because it reported that ISPs reduce recidivism, supporting Andrews's risk principle that the higher risk offenders should benefit most from interventions that positively reinforce behavior.[29] This program appeared to work because it offered more treatment than regular probation and it selected highly qualified staff from a large pool of applicants. The study was also important because it indicated that, under certain conditions, ISPs could work, whereas no data indicate that offenders benefit from more punishment.[30]

The Byrne and Kelly evaluation of a Massachusetts ISP was notable because the authors found a relationship between the quality of a probation officer's supervision and recidivism. In this study, both ISP and regular probationers had recidivism rates 12 to 33 percent lower when the probation officer provided high-quality compared to low-quality supervision. In their conclusions, Byrne and Kelly believed that these findings provided strong support for funding employment, education, and substance abuse programs, rather than more surveillance equipment.

Petersilia and Turner found the recidivism rates between ISP and control group probationers were not significantly different. However, at two of their ISP sites, those probationers who participated in employment, counseling, or restitution programs had significantly lower recidivism rates.

Papparozzi and Gendreau's study reported recidivism rates 21 to 29 percent lower among ISP offenders compared to a matched sample of regular probationers. Papparozzi and Gendreau also reported that probation officers who had high support for the program had clients with lower recidivism rates and that those officers whose supervision approach was balanced between "law enforcement" and "social work" had lower recidivism rates than those officers whose approach was tilted toward one approach or the other. Along the same lines, those POs who preferred the law enforcement approach to their job had technical violation rates 43 percent higher than other officers.

Other evaluations have revealed a similar relationship between client's participation in treatment and services and lower recidivism rates.[31] In the Rand study of fourteen ISPs, Petersilia and Turner found that, in the California and Texas sites, ". . . higher levels of program participation were associated with 10 to 20 percent reduction in recidivism."[32] These several studies, therefore, offer hope for those who believe ISPs remain a viable probation and parole option. With this research and the research on the "principles of effective intervention" conducted by Andrews and his colleagues[33] in mind, a prototypical ISP was developed by the American Probation and Parole Association (APPA).[34] The next section reviews the components of this prototype and summarizes its evaluation.

The Prototypical ISP.   The prototypical ISP developed by and for the APPA rested on the foundation of intensive services addressing offenders' needs and a balanced approach to supervision. This ISP contained the following parts: a high-risk, high-need population of offenders; small caseloads; numerous contacts, regular case review, a positive reenforcement system, and offender control and accountability; a range of correctional interventions that met principles of effectiveness; offender involvement in the community; ISP officers who served as advocates and facilitators; an objectives-based management system; and reliable evaluation of the program.[35]

In their final report to the National Institute of Justice, Latessa and his colleagues argued that "a complete ideological and behavioral shift" was necessary to successfully develop the prototypical program.[36] For example, although surveillance remains important in the prototypical ISP, instead of simply "watching and catching" clients, POs in the prototypical ISP are to monitor the social environments of offenders as well as their progress in treatment or education programs. POs are to have frequent but "substantive" contact with clients to assist them and help them solve problems. Also, in contrast to the exclusive reliance on negative sanctions for failure to follow rules, POs in this program use positive reinforcement to encourage changing behavior. They also served as role models and counselors for the clients to encourage prosocial behavior and reduce the risk of recidivism. The officers become advocates for offenders in the community, developing resources and assisting with reintegration, while maintaining a range of sanctions to hold offenders accountable and, if necessary, remove them from the community.

The prototypical ISPs were developed at two sites in the United States, one in the Midwest and one in the Northeast. A thorough evaluation was conducted at both sites comparing the performance (measured by success on probation) of offenders randomly assigned to either regular probation or ISPs. The evaluations were consistent with other ISP evaluations in a couple of ways. First, there were no significant differences between groups regarding the percentage of offenders with new arrests. Although this finding may be disappointing to those who advocate for ISPs, as Petersilia and Turner have pointed out it is more likely that crimes and violations will be discovered among the ISP group because of the increased level of supervision. "Thus, it may be that an ISP offender is committing the same number or fewer crimes than someone on routine supervision, who has a lower probability of being arrested for them."[37]

ISP clients also had greater improvements in their employment and in dealing with substance abuse problems, and these improvements were related to having fewer arrests and to successful termination of supervision. Byrne and Kelly noted similar results in their evaluation of a Massachusetts ISP and on that basis strongly supported crime control through treatment.[38]

The question is this: Do these results lead to the conclusion that ISPs should be continued as a community corrections option? After all, the prototypical model, as with ISPs before it, did not really reduce recidivism, and because it costs more than regular probation, why continue its use? Latessa and colleagues offer two compelling reasons for continuing its use. First, the model provides a method for handling high-risk and high-need offenders in the community. Regardless of whether ISPs exist, high-risk and high-need offenders will continue to be sentenced to probation and released from prisons on parole. Probation and parole officers need as many tools as possible to help them supervise such clients and, thereby, help ensure public safety.

Second, as noted previously, ISPs give the courts an important intermediate sentencing option. We know that intermediate punishments are necessary—the options of either probation or prison simply do not work for all offenders. And, as Andrews and Bonta point out, offenders should be sentenced to programs that match their level of risk, not only because they deserve a certain level of punishment but also because public safety demands it and because it is more cost efficient.[39] That is, if we can continue to improve and refine ISPs to the point where more and more of those offenders who will truly benefit from such programs are sentenced or released to them, recidivism rates and costs will go down, and public safety will be enhanced.

Intensive supervision, although perhaps the most visible, is not the only intermediate sanction being tried by community corrections agencies. Home confinement, as part of a close supervision regimen, is an idea that is also being tried.

Home Confinement[a]

The house arrest or home confinement (HC) concept literally exploded on the correctional scene. Although statewide home confinement programs did not begin until 1983, they have rapidly become an accepted part of national crime control policies. The use of electronic monitoring (EM) in conjunction with home confinement has stimulated the development of a host of programs throughout the United States. The merging of high-tech with strict surveillance has proven compelling in many jurisdictions. Whereas at first most home confinement programs targeted prison-bound candidates, an increasing number are being structured to relieve jail overcrowding by accepting misdemeanor offenders (such as drunk drivers and minor drug offenders) and pretrial defendants. Home confinement programs are typically under the control of probation and parole agencies; however, private companies or law enforcement agencies operate some, especially those using electronic monitoring.

Home confinement and electronic monitoring are often used synonymously, resulting in a confusing terminology. In actuality, criminal justice professionals agree that there are at least three levels of **home confinement,**[40] all of which may be used either pretrial or postconviction. The first is the **curfew,** which obliges the client to remain in his or her residence during a specific time period, often at night. The second type of home confinement is home detention. With **home detention,** judges sentence offenders to stay in their homes or dwellings for the length of their sentence. However, most offenders do not exclusively remain in their homes. Rather, they may go to work, attend educational or training classes, participate in a community service program, see a physician for a medical condition, go to church or an approved religious service, or attend mandated treatment programs.[41] The third type of home confinement, true house arrest, is the harshest. With **house arrest,** an offender is incarcerated in his or her home; with few exceptions—such as a medical emergency—the offender must remain in his or her residence day and night. In all three types of home confinement, electronic monitoring equipment may be used to determine if the offender is where he or she is supposed to be—home, work, treatment, and so on. In actuality, electronic equipment is used in relatively few cases. For example, the Florida Department of Corrections reported that of the 14,423 offenders in their Community Control program (Florida's descriptive term for home confinement) in August of 2002, only 1,544 were on electronic monitoring.[42] We discuss home confinement both with and without electronic monitoring.

Home Confinement without Electronic Monitoring. The data cited previously from Florida point out that, although electronic monitoring programs have received

[a]Criminal justice professionals now prefer the term *home confinement* to house arrest. However, both terms are somewhat misleading because most offenders under such sentences (by whatever name) spend fifty or more hours each week out of the home, working, attending treatment, going to school, engaged in community service, or participating in some other approved activity.

the most publicity, home confinement programs without electronic components service the most clients. Most states and the federal judiciary currently use home confinement in some form. Florida, California, Oklahoma, Oregon, and Georgia all have substantial home confinement programs. Florida's program, entitled Community Control, is the largest and most comprehensive. It is described by the Florida Department of Corrections as "a form of intensive supervised house arrest in the community, including surveillance on weekends and holidays, administered by officers with limited caseloads."[43] The freedom of community controlees is restricted to the community, the home, or a noninstitutional residential placement, such as a halfway house or treatment facility. In addition, special conditions are imposed and enforced, and the violation of any condition may result in revocation and the imposition of any sentence the court might have imposed prior to placing the offender on community control.

Three types of offenders are eligible for the Florida program: (1) those convicted of nonviolent felonies (assigned by judges at time of sentencing), (2) active probationers who have committed technical or misdemeanor violations, and (3) parolees charged with technical or misdemeanor violations. Once offenders are placed in the Community Control program, probation or parole officials develop an individualized home confinement plan. The plan includes specific restraints and conditions, community service requirements, and various self-improvement programs in which the offender must participate. The plan is signed by the offender and his or her officer and filed in the case record. The maximum term of home confinement is two years, but it can be terminated early by court or parole decree.

Community control officers are selected from existing staff, presumably by choosing those who are comfortable with a surveillance role. According to Leonard Flynn, Florida's director of probation and parole when the program began, "Experienced probation and parole officers with law enforcement backgrounds and knowledge, as well as those in accord with philosophical concepts of the program were initially selected as community officers."[44] While making their field visits, community officers are in touch with law enforcement via radio communication. On occasion, the community officers report crimes in progress or notify police of suspicious activity. To deal with potentially dangerous surprise visits, teams of two or three officers have been organized. Such teams make calls after normal working hours as well as during weekends and holidays. Community officers are required to have seven contacts per week (including two face-to-face interviews) for each of their cases.

A study done by Florida's Bureau of Research and Data Analysis compared a group of community controlees with a group of felony probationers.[45] The two groups were similar in age and gender, but the community controlees had more prior prison experiences and supervision terms than the felony probationers. This might lead to the prediction that the community controlees would have more revocations because of new crimes. However, this was not the case. Whereas the community controlees did have 20 percent higher revocation rates because of technical violations, their revocation rates for new offenses were very similar to that of the felony probationers: 15.8 percent versus 15.3 percent.[46]

Oklahoma operates a house arrest program for offenders currently serving prison sentences. As such, it serves as a "back door" release mechanism to relieve prison overcrowding. The legislation authorizing the program, passed in 1984, allows the Department of Correction to grant early release into house arrest to no more than 15 percent of the prison population. An offender must have served 15 percent of his or her maximum sentence before being eligible for the program and be within twenty-seven months of discharge if a nonviolent offender, eleven months of discharge for violent offenders. Sex offenders and murderers are not eligible for the program.[47] A correctional case manager and a community correctional officer supervise offenders released to house confinement. The released offenders are subject to a maximum of three random field contacts per week, regular meetings with a community correctional officer, routine and random drug testing, and supervision and restitution fees. In an evaluation following the first year of program operation, 2,404 offenders were released into the program and 67 percent completed the program successfully.[48] Only 5 percent failed because they committed new crimes.

Despite the generally successful nonelectronic house arrest programs in Florida, Oklahoma, and elsewhere, most jurisdictions are being drawn to home confinement programs emphasizing electronic components.

Such programs captured the imagination of both public and criminal justice officials. The basic rationale for this acceptance is that electronic monitoring promises to make house arrest a highly intrusive and restrictive sentencing option. The notion that offenders will be under twenty-four-hour electronic watch is more reassuring than having compliance monitored by surprise visits from correctional personnel. Electronic monitoring represents an important new strategy of social control, one that involves an increasing number of probation and parole officers.

Home Confinement with Electronic Monitoring. Dr. Ralph Schwitzgebel first advocated the use of electronic devices to keep track of subjects in the community in 1964. He later developed a portable tracking device and experimented with mental patients and parolees.[49] At that time little interest was shown in electronic monitoring (EM), and Schwitzgebel's project never advanced beyond the experimental stage. The first formal use of electronic monitoring by a criminal justice agency occurred in 1983. Jack Love, an Albuquerque, New Mexico, district court judge, using the "Spiderman" comic strip as an inspiration, initiated a house arrest program augmented by electronic monitoring. Thus, the imaginative mind of a sentencing judge launched an idea that has changed control concepts and brought corrections into the high-tech age.[50]

It is difficult to keep pace with the growing electronic movement. However, we do know that it has grown, and grown rapidly. Researcher Renzema reported that, in 1986, seven states had EM programs monitoring ninety-five offenders; by 1988, there were thirty-two states monitoring 2,277 offenders, and in 1990, he estimated that 12,000 offenders were being monitored electronically.[51] In 1993 there were 30,000 to 50,000 offenders monitored electronically,[52] and by 1998 it was estimated that 75,000 offenders were monitored electronically.[53]

Annesley Schmidt, a research analyst with the U.S. Department of Justice, defined **electronic monitors** as "devices that use telemetry technology to monitor an offender's presence in a particular place where he/she is required to remain."[54] Although the technology for implementing electronic monitors for house arrest programs is frequently updated, current systems can be placed into two broad categories: those that require a telephone to operate and those that do not. Within these categories there are active monitors, which are continuously signaling devices that constantly monitor the offender's presence (or absence), and passive monitors, which are programmed contact devices that randomly phone the offender to verify compliance with house arrest conditions. Those monitors that do not require a telephone to operate rely on radio signals. The officer monitoring the offender has a handheld receiving device that allows him or her to drive by the house or place of work and determine whether the person being monitored is where he or she is supposed to be. In addition, some states have initiated a geo-positioning system (GPS) to monitor some high-risk offenders.

Many of the newly implemented electronic monitoring systems are essentially jail diversion programs. Frequently, they target drunk drivers or minor misdemeanants and rule out violent offenders. These low-risk programs are operating in locations such as Palm Beach County, Florida; San Diego County, California; and Clackamas County, Oregon. An early electronic monitoring program developed in Kenton County, Kentucky, is typical of these programs. According to J. Robert Lilly, it was started with the avowed purpose of relieving crowding in the county jail.[55] It also accepted relatively minor offenders into the program, offenders with convictions for such crimes as criminal mischief, driving under the influence of alcohol, escape/work release, operating on a suspended license, and possession of LSD.[56] Not surprisingly, the recidivism rate for these types of offenders was low (5.7 percent). In a study of Kenton County's program, Lilly, Richard Ball, and Jennifer Wright found that because of its small size (thirty-five participants) the program did not significantly reduce jail overcrowding.[57] However, it was generally considered a success by local judges and probation officials because 1,250 days were served outside of jail through offender participation in the program. One of the judges in Kenton County observed: "Any time you can save a bed day in jail you have done something positive for the criminal justice system."[58]

In a seven-year study of offenders convicted of driving under the influence or driving with a suspended license, 97 percent of the offenders successfully completed the electronically monitored phase of their probation.[59] However, once these same offenders were no longer under EM, they had a much higher violation rate: Almost one-third of the offenders committed a new offense or a technical violation and about one-fourth failed to successfully complete probation once the electronic monitors were removed.

Judges, in some cases, use electronic monitoring devices in conjunction with house arrest when sentencing prominent offenders. In two cases, for example, slumlords were forced to live in their run-down buildings. In Los Angeles, a Beverly Hills neurosurgeon was fitted with an "electronic leash" (the first of its kind) and ordered to stay inside one of his own apartments for thirty days. Sylvia Smith, a county probation officer, indicated the judge wanted to make sure the landlord would stay put and make the needed repairs. According to a building inspector, the apartment complex "has health violations and unsanitary conditions, extreme amounts of rodent droppings and cockroaches, deteriorated sinks, faulty wiring and other problems." An ankle bracelet attached to the neurosurgeon's ankle emitted a signal if he strayed more than 150 feet from the building.[60] In Brooklyn, a civil court judge imposed house arrest on a seventy-seven-year-old landlord charged with almost 400 building code violations. Electronic monitoring used to enforce the curfew was the first such sentence in that jurisdiction.[61] Both of the landlords were also placed on probation; house arrest had been a condition of their supervision.

Not all electronic monitoring programs are earmarked for minor offenders. Some jurisdictions strictly target prison-bound offenders for such programs. Florida is the leader in using electronic technology in this manner. After operating a successful pilot program in the Tampa jurisdiction, Florida expanded electronic monitoring on a statewide basis as an extension of their already-established home confinement program, Community Control. Appropriately, the new program of electronic surveillance was called Community Control II. Florida officials state that this program is to be a judicially approved enhancement to Community Control. All twenty judicial circuits in Florida use radio frequency electronic monitoring. This system "electronically tethers an offender to their home during specified periods of the day or night with violations noted and investigated."[62] In addition, eighteen judicial courts in Florida use a global positioning satellite (GPS) system to continuously track some offender movements in the community, with uniquely defined inclusion and exclusion zones for each offender. Violations of this system are sent immediately to a PO for investigation and resolution.[63] All participants must agree to the supervision conditions outlined in Figure 10.1.

In 1988, there were 836 electronic monitoring units in use throughout Florida.[64] In June of 2002, there were 838 offenders tracked by some kind of electronic monitoring in Florida.[65] Two hundred seventy-nine of these were tethered to a radio frequency monitor, and 559 were being tracked by a GPS system. In the following excerpt from a state employee manual, the use and installation of the electronic monitoring device is described as well as instructions regarding what actions to take in case of violations.

Electronic Monitoring Equipment

A. All the equipment in Community Control II shall be under the control of the Office Supervisor and/or designee.
B. When not in use, the boxes and transmitters shall be in the custody and control of the Office Supervisor or designee and shall be kept in a locked area with accessibility limited to the Office Supervisor and/or the designee.
C. The transmitter and box shall be checked out by the Office Supervisor or designee to a Community Control Officer for placement with an offender.

(text continues on page 318)

FIGURE 10.1   *Electronic Monitoring Participant Agreement*

FLORIDA DEPARTMENT OF CORRECTIONS
COMMUNITY CONTROL II DIVERSION AGREEMENT

I, the undersigned offender agree to participate in the Community Control II Program in lieu of serving a sentence in the Florida State Prison. I agree with the following rules and conditions of said program:

1. I agree to abide by the House Arrest restrictions and to comply with the Court's order in every respect.

2. I agree to remain at my residence at all times required by the Court Order, to wit: I must stay at my residence at all times except for the days that I work, when I will be allowed to leave my residence as scheduled between myself and my Community Control Officer. The only exceptions to my leaving the residence are in case of emergency and at any other time authorized in advance by my Community Control Officer. If I have to leave my residence on an emergency, I will first try to get the permission of my Community Control Officer, but, in any event, I will report to my Community Control Officer as soon as possible after the emergency is over. I understand that I will be required to furnish documentation and verify any emergency departure from my schedule.

3. The residence to which I am confined is:

   _____ and my telephone number
   is _____.

4. I know that my house arrest restrictions will be enforced by the use of computer technology. To ensure compliance with my participation in Community Control II, I will be monitored by a security/correctional, non-removable ankle bracelet which I agree to wear 24 hours a day during the entire period of Community Control II. I understand that my location will be monitored electronically way by monitoring facilities operated by the Florida Department of Corrections. The house arrest may also be monitored by telephone calls and personal visits to my home by the Community Control Officer.

5. I know that it will be necessary for the monitoring device to be attached to my home telephone and that it will be necessary for installation to be done by the Department of Corrections' personnel. It will also be necessary during the period of Community Control II for persons to maintain or inspect the installation of this device and I agree to allow authorized persons in my home to install and maintain the monitoring device.

6. I understand that the equipment used to monitor me is expensive and I will use my best efforts to take care of this equipment and to avoid any damage whatsoever. However, in the event that damage is caused to the equipment in any way whatsoever, I agree to reimburse the Department of Corrections for the damage that may be caused.

7. I understand that the purpose of this monitoring equipment is to alert my Community Control Officer if I should violate the restrictions established above. I agree that the loss of receiving signal or the receipt of a tamper signal by the monitoring device at the Department of Corrections, shall constitute prima facie evidence that I have violated my restrictions and I further agree that the computer printout at the Department of Corrections may be used as evidence in a Court of law to prove said violation.

8. Any expense of phone calls that may be incurred to monitor the electronic device shall be at my expense.

9. I acknowledge that all of these rules have been explained to me and that my non-compliance with any of these restrictions or rules may result in a violation of Community Control II.

FIGURE 10.1 *Continued*

10. I agree not to venture more than 150 feet from the monitor located in my
     residence other than at approved times.

11. I agree to release and to hold harmless the Department of Corrections and its
     personnel from any liability whatsoever arising from my use of the Community
     Control II equipment and system. This release and hold-harmless is given by me
     without reservation or limitation of any kind.

_____   _____
        Offender   Date

_____   _____
        Attorney   Date

_____   _____
       CC II Officer   Date

The Community Control officer will return the transmitter and box upon termination of use by an offender. The Community Control officer shall not directly transfer a transmitter or box from one offender to another.

Installation Process

A. The anklet will be attached to the offender in the Probation and Parole office.
B. The Community Control officer shall then make arrangements to meet with the offender, within one (1) working day, to install the receiver unit on the offender's home telephone.
C. Upon installation of the receiver unit, the Community Control officer shall call the Probation and Parole Office to verify that the system has been tested and is operational.
D. The Community Control officer shall inspect each anklet for signs of tampering at least once a week and shall inspect the receiver unit in the offender residence at least once per month.
E. All Community Control officers shall be responsible for checking the computer for violations or irregularities.

Violations

A. If the computer sends a violation message, a Community Control officer will attempt to verify the violation as soon as the officer receives the message.
B. During normal office hours, the computer print-out will be monitored *at a minimum* when the office opens, midmorning, upon return from lunch, mid-afternoon, and before leaving the office for the day. After hours, on weekends and holidays, the print-out will be monitored when staff arrive, again before they leave the office, and during reasonable intervals in between those times.
C. If a violation is indicated by the computer, the officer monitoring the computer shall immediately attempt to verify the violation by telephone and should document the incident. The supervising officer should be alerted ASAP.

   When appropriate a Community Control officer will immediately investigate by making a home visit to verify the offender's whereabouts. The Community Control officer assigned to the case shall then follow-up with violation procedures.
D. Reporting Violations—Whenever an officer determines an offender has been away from their residence during an unauthorized time, a violation report will be submitted to the Court within two (2) working days. The Community Control officer shall coordinate with local law enforcement to expedite the early apprehension of Community Control II violators, per current DC Policy and Procedures and the Manual of Procedures regarding arrest practices.

   Unauthorized absences from residence and/or new criminal activity shall be reported to the Court in the customary manner with a recommendation for revocation and commitment to Florida state prison as appropriate.[66]

Electronic Monitoring: Unresolved Issues.   Although most of the legal issues have been resolved—the courts have rejected arguments that EM is an unreasonable search and seizure, that EM violates offenders' rights to privacy, or that it violates the equal protection and due process clauses of the Constitution—there remain unresolved philosophical and practical issues with electronic monitoring programs. Presently, the strict eligibility standards discriminate against certain groups by favoring middle-class offenders who are most likely to qualify for the program.[67] The homeless, a rapidly growing segment of our population, are automatically ruled out. Indigent offenders are disadvantaged because most programs require that offenders have a phone and pay supervision fees. However, officials in Utah and Florida, after analyzing this issue, conclude, "house arrest, with or without electronic monitoring, will withstand constitutional challenges as long as it is imposed to protect society or rehabilitate the offender, and the conditions set fourth are clear, reasonable and constitutional."[68]

Home curfews enforced by an ever-watchful electronic eye have led some to question whether we are moving toward the oppressive society described by George Orwell in his book *1984.* The continuously beeping electronic leash in use today, particularly those using a global positioning system, even though they are for willing offenders, theoretically could some day be adapted for general use as a massive form of social control. Proponents of house arrest counter this argument by stating that an electronic bracelet is surely less intrusive and far more humane than a prison sentence.

Enos, Holman, and Carroll point out four ethical concerns of EM: proportionality, intrusiveness, dignity, and third parties.[69] Proportionality refers to the relationship between the offense and the punishment: Does the punishment fit the crime? Consistent with the mitigation theme of this book, the question arises whether EM actually does mitigate punishment, or is it indeed a harsher punishment than what would have been the case if EM were not available? Enos and colleagues cite recent cases ". . . in which an offender who might previously have been only fined is placed on house arrest and electronic monitoring."[70]

Another proportionality issue is whether EM is being used in a discriminatory manner. That is, are certain types of people more or less likely to receive this form of treatment? Clearly, the large number of homeless in the United States is not eligible for "home confinement." But those who cannot afford telephones are excluded as well. The other side of this question is whether certain people, particularly the poor and members of ethnic minorities, are *more* likely to receive EM rather than a less stringent and less intrusive form of surveillance. As Enos and colleagues put it ". . . It is our view that attention needs to be given to the sentencing of offenders to electronic monitoring, house arrest, and other community-based programs to ensure fairness in regard to race, economic status, and other factors."[71]

The second issue Enos and colleagues point out involves how much intrusiveness is ethical when punishing someone for a crime. The argument on intrusiveness is similar to the argument on proportionality: We should not assume that community-based sanctions are less harsh than prison. In fact, Petersilia points out that surveys of offenders in five states have discovered that those surveyed judged some community-based sanctions, such as intensive supervision programs, as more punitive than prison.[72] Therefore, officials need to be aware of the "pains" that community-based sanctions may impose.

Intrusiveness has another side to it as well. We also must ask whether EM is more intrusive than traditional methods of monitoring compliance with the conditions of probation or parole, such as home visits. It may not be. In fact, Enos and colleagues believe that EM alone may not be more intrusive than traditional methods of control, but officials need to ask whether there are any reasons to think the program is "humiliating or intrusive to the offender"[73] and whether it meets the Fourth Amendment's guarantees for a right to privacy and against unreasonable searches and seizures.

The third ethical issue relevant to EM is dignity.[74] That is, we know that among other things, punishment is meant to produce shame in the offender; it is not, however, necessary to take away his or her personal dignity in the process. Shame is a normal part of punishment. Among other things, it is meant to create a feeling of remorse that then may lead the offender to change his or her behavior so as not to experience the same shame and degradation again. But shame used to humiliate and degrade offenders, to make them feel inferior and teach them that they are inherently bad, strips them of their dignity and most likely does nothing to help prevent future criminality; in fact, such punishment may encourage criminality.[75]

The fourth ethical issue identified by Enos and colleagues revolves around the impact that home confinement and EM has on the offender's family or housemates. Although it may be less intrusive than traditional methods of control, such as home and workplace visits, it is also likely that EM and home confinement do have an impact on the offender's family and housemates, an impact that has hardly been studied.[76] (See Box 10.1.) This impact on other members of the household should be considered before EM or other methods of control are used. We must also consider the fact that EM and home confinement programs actually may benefit the household. Because they are in their homes and not in jail, the offenders may be able to work and help with household expenses, as well as maintain and perhaps strengthen their relationships with family members.

Besides these ethical problems, there are also some practical and technological problems associated with EM. For example, Charles Friel and James Vaughn report that start-up and operational costs often are greater than anticipated and in most cases turn out to be "less cost beneficial to probation administrators than to administrators of overcrowded institutions."[77] Also, offenders need to learn how to use the devices, and they may make mistakes during that learning process; FM radio transmitters can disrupt some signals; computers malfunction or "crash"; and, in some instances, the electronic monitoring devices malfunction and give out erroneous signals. Power outages or surges, low-flying aircraft, large metal objects such as refrigerators, large amounts of iron and steel in the home, or improperly insulated telephone lines can cause inaccurate readings.[78] Crimes can still be committed by offenders wearing the devices; devices that rely on cell phone technology are subject to "dead spots" familiar to all cell phone users. Ultimately, the technology is only as

BOX 10.1 • *House Arrest Is No Easy Out for Criminal Offenders*

By Cathy Keen

Contrary to public perception, home becomes a prison and the entire family is punished when criminal offenders are sentenced to house arrest, a new University of Florida [UF] study finds.

Offenders say the guilt of having to see family members suffer and not be able to help them makes home confinement—a popular alternative to a jail sentence—worse than prison, said Sylvia Ansay, a UF graduate student in sociology who did the research for her doctoral dissertation.

"The public sees people out and about instead of in prison and may see this as an easy thing," Ansay said. "But for family members that I interviewed, it's not a bit easy. It was clear that in some households all members were virtually on community control.

"The meaning of such family rituals as attending weddings and funerals, celebrating birthdays, enjoying the holidays or caring for elders are necessarily discounted, devalued and even penalized," Ansay said. "Little wonder that family members frequently voice their belief that they, too, are being punished."

If a wife's car breaks down at midnight, a child misses a school bus or a disabled grandmother needs a prescription, the family member in home confinement feels totally helpless, she said.

Having to sit by while family members shift roles and do double duty causes a great deal of guilt and stress for the offender, Ansay said. "One public defender said that if it were his son or daughter, he would advise them to take prison time and get it over,'" she said. "Many offenders expressed the same sentiment, that if they had to do it again, they would rather go to prison."

Community-based programs, such as house arrest and electronic monitoring, have become a mainstay in criminal punishment, increasingly replacing jail or prison time, Ansay said. Community control, Florida's version of home confinement and intensive supervision, is one of the nation's most ambitious programs, said Ansay, whose study tracked twenty-six offenders and their families from one circuit court district during the last year.

Although most offenders appreciate being with their families while serving their sentences, the stress of continuing family obligations frequently breaks down the roles and rituals that hold the family together, Ansay said.

"This research is of major significance because it takes a rare look at the everyday experience for families of having a member of the household on house arrest," said Jaber F. Gubrium, a UF sociology professor who supervised Ansay's research.

Ansay said one man could no longer routinely take his daily walk to visit his elderly mother to make sure she had taken her medication.

The same man also was forbidden to bring his young son to a neighborhood park to play. And the women he lived with had to pick up the slack, doing errands they used to share together and feeling lonely going to places they once went to together, Ansay said.

"When he got sentenced to eighteen months, his mom got sentenced to eighteen months, his son got sentenced to eighteen months, and so did I," the man's girlfriend said.

Another offender, in a difficult pregnancy, had to depend upon her mother, sister and aunt to drive her thirty miles to the probation office every week, as well as to doctor's appointments. "It took all day, sometimes, with waiting and all," her sister said. "I felt I was being punished for the crimes she did."

(continued)

BOX 10.1 • *Continued*

Considering the needs of the family is important because if the family is successful in the program, the offender is successful, Ansay said.

"We need to reexamine family support and see it from two sides," she said. "It's more than other members helping someone comply with official rules. There are family rules, too, the things within the family that people do for each other to make family work."

Source: Center for Precollegiate Education and Training, University of Florida, retrieved May 29, 2002, from www.cpet.ufl.edu/sciexpl/beh26.htm

good as the people who use it—if the POs monitoring the equipment do not use it in the way it was designed to be used, it will not be effective.

The volunteer nature of participation can be questioned when the offender is forced to choose between home lock-up and prison confinement. It could be argued that such a decision is not really a "choice." House arrest may be challenged under the equal protection provision guaranteed by the Fourteenth Amendment.

Although ISP and house arrest are the most popular probation and parole innovations, another method of impressing offenders short of long-term incarceration has been developed. Based on the principle that a short jolt of punishment can be a powerful deterrent, shock incarceration has been rediscovered.

Shock Incarceration

Shock incarceration is a program where the sentencing judge sentences an offender to a brief time in prison or jail after which the offender is placed on probation or parole. The probationary period may be part of the original sentence or it may be granted to inmates after they petition the court to suspend their incarceration sentence. Goals of shock incarceration include attempts to (1) impress offenders with the hardship and psychological problems of incarceration, (2) provide an opportunity to better evaluate the needs of offenders, and (3) make individuals aware of the seriousness of their crimes without resorting to long periods of incarceration. Although shock incarceration has been used both on the county and state level for some time, the programs typically involve young, first-time offenders who are placed into **boot camps** under rigid military-type discipline.

The precedent for shock incarceration was established in 1920 when California enacted a law permitting judges to combine incarceration and probation. In 1965, the Ohio legislature passed a statute that allowed judges to resentence imprisoned offenders to probation. The purposes of the program were to

1. Impress offenders with the seriousness of their actions without a long prison sentence;
2. Release offenders found by the institutions to be more amenable to community-based treatment than was realized by the courts at the time of sentencing;

3. Serve as a just compromise between punishment and leniency in appropriate cases;
4. Provide community-based treatment for offenders while still imposing deterrent sentences where public policy demanded it; and
5. Protect the briefly incarcerated offender against absorption into the inmate culture.[79]

Since this landmark program, many jurisdictions have implemented various forms of shock incarceration called "probation and jail," "split sentences," or "shock probation." County judges throughout the United States have exercised the right to include a period of time in jail as part of a probation grant. In California, the combination of jail and probation became such a popular option that it eventually comprised about half of all sentences involving probation.[80] The Ohio shock probation system served as a model for programs of this type. Ohio regulations stipulated that participants could serve no more than 130 days in prison before being granted probation and further that acceptance into the program could come only *after* the offender had been sentenced to prison. Convictions for certain kinds of crimes (for example, rape, murder, possession of major drugs, armed robbery) render offenders ineligible for the program. Following Ohio's example, Idaho, Indiana, Kentucky, and Tennessee initiated shock programs. After examining several shock incarceration programs, Gennaro Vito concluded the deterrent value of these efforts was negligible.[81] However, Vito did believe that shock programs could serve some useful purpose. He concluded: "Although it is not particularly defensible as a deterrent, shock probation has the potential to become a way to reduce institutional overcrowding which is consistent with the objective of reintegration and public safety."[82]

The recent innovations in shock incarceration include a physical training component during the period of incarceration. In these programs shock participants no longer serve their time of incarceration in standard jails, but instead they perform rigorous physical exercise in outside compounds under the watchful eyes of hardened drill instructors. Proponents of these programs argue that a short stint in a demanding boot camp will combine rehabilitation and deterrence.

One of the first programs of this kind was developed by the Oklahoma prison and called regimented inmate discipline (RID). Young, first-time (as an adult) offenders are targeted for participation in hopes of curbing their criminal activity without the negative effects of prison confinement. Although participants may have lengthy juvenile records, most do not have experience in adult jails or prisons. One of the program's organizers indicated "Everyone knows if you dump kids like this into the general prison system they're going to become victims of the homosexuals and thugs. They're going to be punks all their lives. And if they're long-time incarcerates they finally become the thugs."[83] RID participants are subjected to tough physical conditioning with little time for idleness, strict and uniform dress codes, intensive vocational training, mandatory counseling, severe restrictions on personal property, and structured leisure and recreational activities. Almost 2,000 youths completed RID boot camp between 1984 and 1988, and Oklahoma officials claimed an 85 percent success rate in that only 15 percent of the graduates were incarcerated in the twelve months after their release to probation in the community.

In 1985, Georgia initiated a similar program to Oklahoma's RID, called shock alternative incarceration (SAI). The program is open to sentenced prisoners seventeen to twenty-five years of age who have been convicted of a felony, have no previous incarceration in an adult prison, and have no physical or psychological limitations that rule out strenuous physical activity. Those accepted into SAI are separated from the general population and put through a program of physical exercise and discipline modeled after basic training in the Marine Corps. After completing the ninety-day training period, the inmates are transferred to intensive supervision probation. Records of early SAI graduates revealed that less than 10 percent had committed new crimes since their release from prison.

Following the lead of Oklahoma and Florida, boot camp type incarceration programs spread rapidly. By the year 2000, thirty states, the District of Columbia, and the U.S. Bureau of Prisons were all operating boot camps.[84] These programs attempt to combine diversion with efforts to affect behavioral change in young offenders. Several more states have such programs on the drawing board. Figure 10.2 is a flowchart of Louisiana's IMPACT program. The flowchart illustrates a common progression through shock incarceration. Figure 10.3 outlines the daily schedule for offenders sentenced to Minnesota's Willow River Challenge Incarceration Program.

Evaluations of Shock Incarceration Programs.   Keeping in mind that boot camps vary from state to state—length of stay, admission criteria, the emphases in the program itself (discipline and self control or treatment and rehabilitation), age and gender of participants, size of the program—the primary goals of boot camps are very similar to other intermediate sanctions: reduce recidivism, reduce the cost of prisons, and reduce prison crowding. However, another important goal of boot camp programs comes from the belief that military-style training will help improve the self-esteem and attitudes of the participants. Many corrections officials and lawmakers have experienced military boot camps and view them as a good way to learn discipline and self-respect.

Evaluations of boot camps have focused on all of these goals and the results are mixed. For recidivism, a study of the Louisiana IMPACT program found recidivism rates of 7 to 14 percent for boot camp participants versus 12 to 23 percent of the boot camp dropouts or those who failed to complete the program.[85] A New York program reported recidivism rates of 23 percent for its graduates.[86] MacKenzie and her colleagues' study of programs in eight states predictably found mixed results.[87] In five of the states, there was no reduction in recidivism. In the other three states, boot camp graduates had lower rates of recidivism than nonparticipants. These three programs were characterized by longer program duration, participants who were selected from offenders who otherwise would be going to prison, a greater emphasis on rehabilitation and postrelease supervision, and their voluntary nature. The researchers concluded that any or all of these features could

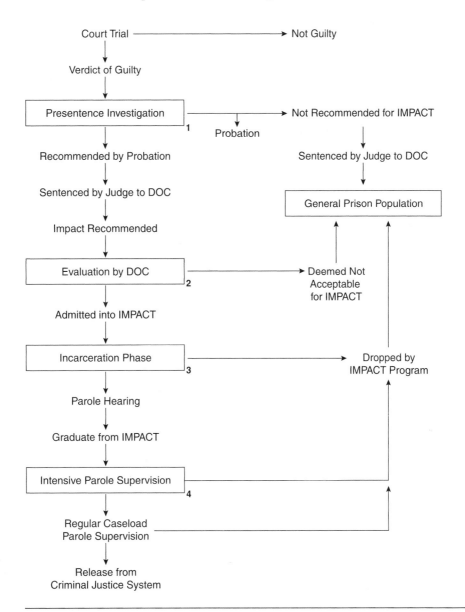

FIGURE 10.2 *Flowchart for Entrance into the IMPACT Program*

have affected the recidivism rate, even if there were no boot camps. Consequently, they concluded that the boot camps alone do not seem to reduce recidivism.

Whether boot camps reduce prison crowding, thereby reducing costs, seems to depend on the selection of program participants. The study by MacKenzie and

FIGURE 10.3 *Minnesota Correctional Facility—Willow River/Moose Lake: Willow River Challenge Incarceration Program Daily Schedule*

Time	Event
5:30	Wake Up/Roll Call
5:35–5:45	Physical Training Preparation
5:45–6:35	Physical Training
6:35–7:00	Personal Cleanup
7:00–7:30	Breakfast Meal
7:30–7:45	Morning Flag Ritual
7:45–8:25	Barracks Maintenance/Offender Inspection
8:25–8:30	Program Readiness Preparation
8:30–9:55	Cognitive Skills Training/Barracks Inspection
10:00–11:55	Education Programming or Work Assignment
11:55–12:00	Roll Call
12:00–12:30	Lunch Meal
12:35–3:15	Work Assignment
3:15–3:30	Physical Training Preparation
3:30–4:30	Physical Training
4:30–4:55	Personal Cleanup
4:55–5:00	Roll Call
5:00–5:30	Evening Meal
5:30–6:00/6:15	Evening Flag Ritual/KP/Administration Building Cleanup/Program Readiness Preparation
6:00–7:00	Lecture or Acupuncture Treatment
7:00–8:00	Chemical Dependency Programming
8:00–9:00	Squad Meeting
9:00–9:25	Individual Offender Programming and Journal/Correspondence and Study Time
9:25–9:30	Personal Cleanup
9:30	Roll Call
9:35	Lights Out

Source: Cindie A. Unger, "Planning and Designing Boot Camp Facilities," *Correctional Boot Camps: A Tough Intermediate Sanction,* eds. Doris L. MacKenzie and Eugene I. Hebert (Washington, DC: U.S. Department of Justice, 1996) 248.

colleagues found that those programs that had the department of corrections select participants were more likely to decrease prison populations than those that had the judiciary select program participants. This seems to make sense because a department of corrections will more likely ensure that prison-bound offenders will be chosen for the program. Programs that limit eligibility to relatively minor first-time offenders who might otherwise receive probation, and then intensely supervises the graduates from the program, are more likely to increase correctional costs than decrease them.[88]

Research does show that boot camp participants show improvements in self-esteem, although the improvement was short lived.[89] Another study found that participants showed improvement in attitudes: Boot camp participants were more positive and optimistic than their counterparts in prison.[90]

Although intensive supervision, house arrest, and shock incarceration are important innovations, the combined participants in these programs represent only a small percentage of the total offenders on probation and parole. Perhaps the most sweeping innovation in the field is implementation of differential supervision, often referred to as classification. More probation and parole staff and their clients will be affected by this development than any other.

Differential Supervision

The use of differential supervision is hardly a new or radical idea. It is based on the common sense assumption that not all offenders need the same level of supervision. Supervision officers have always developed methods to prioritize their time and have tried to concentrate their efforts on those clients needing the most attention. In most cases, however, their efforts were done on an informal basis using knowledge and skills developed from personal experience. Christopher Baird and a group of researchers studying supervision methods found that "most experienced probation and parole agents utilize an intuitive system of classifying offenders into differential treatment or surveillance modes, usually based on their judgments of client needs and their perception of the client's potential for continued unlawful behavior." However, such an "untested, highly individualized approach does not provide information necessary to rationally deploy staff and other resources."[91]

The innovative aspect of the **differential supervision** programs is the introduction of an objective and tested scale to place offenders into appropriate supervision categories. In 1975, Wisconsin developed such a scale, calling it a risk/needs assessment. The scale measures the offender's needs and the risk of recidivism. Taken together, these factors point out the proper level of supervision and the type of case management strategy to be employed. This development was monumental for probation and parole agencies because, for the first time, there was a quantifiable method for determining supervision levels. The Wisconsin assessment scale was incorporated into a supervision system known as **Client Management Classification (CMC).** Subsequently, components of this system were implemented in more than one hundred jurisdictions throughout the United States (see

Chapter Eight for a discussion of how Orange County, California, accomplished this). Today, 25 percent of probation and parole agencies in the United States use this system of classification.[92] Malcolm MacDonald, past president of the American Probation and Parole Association, commented that classification scales revolutionized parole and probation in the United States. MacDonald believes that classification scales make communities safer because the highest risk clients are placed in the maximum category and supervised more closely. The system also helps administrators allocate their resources more rationally.[93]

The first step in the CMC process is administering a forty-five-minute risk and needs questionnaire. The questionnaire is then scored, which takes about fifteen minutes. Based on the results of this questionnaire, offenders are placed into classification categories. Then, with the aid of supervision guidelines, and discussions with the offender, an individual case plan is developed and reevaluated periodically. Under the CMC system there are five types of supervision classifications and strategies:[94]

1. *Selective Intervention–Situational (SI–S).* Clients in this category require the least time and present the fewest supervision problems. These offenders usually do not have prior criminal records—the basis of their current offense was some unusual or unexpected situation—and have few if any treatment or social service needs. Supervision strategies, therefore, consist of helping the client deal with the situation that led to their offense.

2. *Selective Intervention–Treatment (SI–T).* Like the SI–S clients, SI–T clients are prosocial, stable, and capable. However, unlike SI–S clients, the SI–T clients manifest a chronic problem, such as substance abuse, violence, sexual deviance, or extreme emotional distress. Consequently, the supervision strategy appropriate for these clients is to refer them to an appropriate treatment provider and monitor that treatment.

3. *Environmental Structure (ES).* Clients can be considered medium to low-risk "regular supervision." These offenders are often the target of manipulation by their peers and are usually impulsive. They frequently need encouragement to overcome poor job skills, lack of proper education, association with criminal peers, and training in impulse control.

4. *Casework/Control.* These types of offenders can be categorized as medium to high risk. They often have chaotic lifestyles—unstable relationships, poor employment record, substance abuse, and frequent moves—and need firm guidance. Strategies for this group include treatment for substance abuse and emotional problems.

5. *Limit Setting (LS).* These offenders are at high risk to commit new crimes because they hold antisocial values and beliefs and are motivated to commit crimes by greed and thrill seeking. Often these clients are committed to a criminal way of life and need close monitoring, strict rule enforcement, and help in developing alternative—and legal—means of satisfying their need for excitement.

The Georgia Department of Rehabilitation adopted a probation classification system, based on the Wisconsin model, with the following goals:

1. To improve the effectiveness of service delivery;
2. To develop a uniform standard for classification on a statewide basis; and
3. To provide a database for budgeting and staff development on a workload rather than on a caseload model.

The methods used by Georgia to implement a differential supervision program are representative of those of many jurisdictions that have attempted to adopt the CMC system. Probation officials complete the risk and needs assessment, and based on the offenders' scores place them into supervision levels. The forms presented in Figures 10.4 and 10.5, used by Georgia probation officers, illustrate how this process works.

Evaluations of CMC System.   Having a classification system on paper is not the same as having one in operation. In many departments, line officers, preferring to circumvent formal classification systems, maintain their own informal, individualized methods. Based on the second author's personal experience and reports of other researchers, there is an uncertain relationship between classification and what actually occurs in the field.[95] Line staff often rationalizes their individual approach by claiming (often with some merit) that large caseloads make it impractical to strictly follow departmental guidelines. The highly personal styles of supervision officers do not lend themselves to the goal of uniform classification standards and the implementation of an objective system of differential supervision. Line officer resistance, however, can be overcome. Criminal justice professional Anthony Walsh, himself a former probation officer, confessed that he was one who complained about filling out forms when the system first came out, but that the CMC system must be seen as more than bureaucratic paper pushing. In fact, once Walsh got used to the system, he realized it was an efficiency-enhancing device that will ultimately save time.[96] In addition, many line officers and probation and parole administrators would agree with Kenneth Lerner, Gary Arling, and Christopher Baird that properly implemented programs of differential supervision can significantly improve case management and the delivery of services.[97]

Prior formal evaluations of the CMC system in community corrections gave generally favorable, though mixed, results.[98] Harris and her colleagues report that four earlier studies all found that CMC subjects did better than non-CMC subjects, although they all used different measures of success.[99] In their evaluation Harris and her colleagues also found that CMC clients had lower rates of revocation than the control group, but when rules violations and arrests were analyzed, the CMC-supervised offenders had higher rates of recidivism. Harris and colleagues interpreted this finding as an indicator that CMC-trained officers had increased sensitivity to offender's needs and motivations, and the officers were, therefore, more sensitive to rules violations leading to revocation.[100]

(text continues on page 332)

FIGURE 10.4 *Probationer Need/Risk Reassessment*

GEORGIA DEPARTMENT OF OFFENDER REHABILITATION
** PROBATIONER NEED/RISK REASSESSMENT **

(P3) CASE NUMBER	PROBATIONER NAME	DATE	CLASSIFIER I.D.	CLASSIFIER NAME
	(Last)			(Last)

** REASSESSMENT QUESTIONS AND RATING SCALES **	SCORE

A. NUMBER OF ADDRESS CHANGES IN LAST 12 MONTHS
[0] None   [+1] One   [+2] Two   [+3] Three or more

B. AGE AT FIRST CONVICTION
[0] 24 or older   [+2] 20 – 23   [+4] 19 or younger

C. NUMBER OF PROBATION/PAROLE REVOCATIONS
[0] None   [+4] One or more

D. NUMBER OF FELONY CONVICTIONS (including present offense)
[0] None   [+1] One   [+2] Two   [+4] Three or more

E. ALCOHOL USAGE/PROBLEMS
[0] No apparent problems   [+2] Moderate problems   [+4] Serious problems

F. DRUG USAGE/PROBLEMS
[0] No apparent problems   [+2] Moderate problems   [+4] Serious problems

G. EMPLOYMENT
[0] Continuous employment since period of last classification; not applicable
[+2] Period of unemployment less than six weeks
[+4] Period of unemployment more than six weeks

H. MARITAL/FAMILY PROBLEMS
[0] None   [+1] Few   [+2] Moderate   [+4] Severe

I. EMOTIONAL PROBLEMS
[0] None   [+1] Few   [+2] Moderate   [+4] Severe

J. SOCIAL AND/OR JOB-RELATED PROBLEMS
[0] None   [+1] Few   [+2] Moderate   [+4] Severe

K. FINANCIAL PROBLEMS
[0] None   [+1] Few   [+2] Moderate   [+4] Severe

L. RESPONSE TO SUPERVISION (circle those which apply, add and place total in box)
[0] Complies with all conditions; no apparent problems
[+2] Does not report as scheduled
[+2] Fails to meet financial conditions of probation
[+2] Has been re-arrested and/or has criminal charges pending

M. P.O.'s IMPRESSIONS OF PROBATIONER'S NEEDS/RISK STATUS
[0] No apparent difficulties, reasonable performance compliance
[+2] Some non-crucial Needs/Risk areas, not directly affecting probation and/or ability to abide by conditions
[+4] Significant level of Needs/Risk with direct, although mild affect on probation and/or community functioning
[+6] Moderate level of Needs/Risk, adversely affecting ability to function in the community and on probation
[+8] High level of Needs/Risk, severely limiting ability to function in the community and on probation

LEVEL OF SUPERVISION		
TOTAL POINTS	LEVEL	CODE
	Administrative	1
00 - 07	Minimum	2
08 - 14	Medium	3
15 - 24	High	4
25 +	Maximum	5

** OVERALL TOTAL

LEVEL OF SUPERVISION

P–3

Source: Georgia Department of Offender Rehabilitation.

FIGURE 10.5   *Supervision Levels in Georgia*

Supervision Levels in Georgia

Administrative Classification

Although there is no standard of supervision required for this classification, probationers who have absconded, who are serving a prison sentence on a new offense and have not been revoked on the present offense, and probationers receiving no direct supervision per court approval, should be classified as Administrative.

Minimum (Nondirect Supervision)

1. (Division minimum requirement). Mail in change of address or employment, monthly payment of fine, restitution, court cost, etc.
2. Monthly mail-in report.
3. Monthly telephone contact with probationer.

Minimum (Direct Supervision)

1. (Division minimum requirement). Monthly telephone contact with probation officer.
2. Quarterly face-to-face contact with probation officer.
3. Monthly telephone contact with probation officer *and* quarterly face-to-face contact with probation officer.

Medium

1. (Division minimum requirement). Monthly telephone contact with probation officer *and* quarterly face-to-face contact with probation officer.
2. Monthly face-to-face contact with probation officer.
3. Monthly face-to-face contact with probation officer and one field contact or collateral contact quarterly.

High

1. (Division minimum requirement). Monthly face-to-face contact with probation officer *and* one field contact or collateral contact quarterly.
2. Monthly face-to-face contact with probation officer *and* monthly field contact or collateral contact (two contacts per month).
3. Two monthly face-to-face contacts with probation officer, monthly field contact, *and* monthly collateral contact. (Four contacts per month).

Maximum

1. (Division minimum requirement). Two monthly face-to-face contacts with probation officer, monthly field contact, *and* monthly collateral contact. (Four contacts per month).
2. Two monthly face-to-face contacts with probation officer *and* two monthly field contacts. (Four contacts per month).
3. Four monthly face-to-face contacts with probation officer, two monthly field contacts, *and* two monthly collateral contacts. (Eight contacts per month).

Regardless, it is clear that administration officials play a crucial role in the implementation of formal differential supervision programs. Todd Clear and Kenneth Gallagher, in their comprehensive study of classification practices, found that many probation managers, in the rush to embrace a seemingly promising strategy, overlook the issue of whether the new system will work in their area. They contend that managers often select an instrument without paying attention to the issue of generalizability, that is, whether the instrument can accurately discriminate among clients as to their likelihood of committing new crimes or their needs. If such mistakes occur, clients classified as "high risk" may not need as much supervision as they are receiving, and "low-risk" clients may be receiving more supervision than required. Besides the potential safety risks and additional costs such misclassifications may bring, there is also the potential that staff will recognize these "mistakes" and begin to distrust the instruments they are using, and perhaps "fudging" the results. As a result, the practice of classifying clients may bear little resemblance to the original system, and any planning or budget gains intended when the system was implemented could be lost.[101] However, notwithstanding the problematic aspects of implementing a differential supervision program, if line staff and administration work together Clear and Gallagher contend, "classification can be an important advance in the effectiveness of probation work," as can be the next type of intermediate sanction we discuss, day reporting centers.

Day Reporting Centers

Originating in England in the early 1970s and then developed in the United States in the mid-1980s, **day reporting centers (DRCs)** are intermediate sanctions that combine a high level of control with the delivery of treatment and other services needed by the offenders served. DRCs are facilities that offenders report to on a daily basis, providing structure for the day, control of behavior, and opportunities for treatment and services.[102] The structure comes from the fact that clients of DRCs are usually required to provide daily hour-by-hour schedules. Control is achieved through the number of contacts required on a daily and weekly basis (often forty or fifty per week); required participation in counseling, educational or training programs; and urinalysis tests for substance abuse. Many DRCs also have curfews, and electronic monitoring may be a feature of the program for some offenders.[103]

Parent and colleagues in a report funded by the National Institute of Justice (NIJ), identified 114 programs in twenty-two states and collected data on fifty-four day reporting centers.[104] Most programs start the offenders off with a high level of contacts, including daily face-to-face meetings at the DRC, phone contacts, and field visits at home or at work. The Hampden County, Massachusetts, DRC, for example, starts each client on a schedule of at least fifty contacts per week.[105] The amount of contacts may decrease with time, but overall the level of supervision at DRCs is greater than for any other intermediate sanction.

DRCs are very flexible and as a result the programs vary tremendously. They are unique because they focus on one location for the program, with usually a team approach to working with clients. Many are "back-end" programs, designed for those coming out of jail or prison. But more and more programs also work with those on probation, and others are alternatives for pretrial detainees.[106] The duration of the programs ranges from forty days to nine months, with the average being five to six months. The programs and services offered in the DRCs also vary widely. These can include any, but usually not all, of the following: job-search assistance, substance abuse education, group or individual counseling, job-placement services, educational programs, substance abuse treatment, life skills training, housing assistance, recreation and leisure programming, day care support, literacy programs, community reentry programs, and community service placement.[107]

The types of clients they serve also vary. Although a goal of DRCs is to reduce the costs of incarceration, the NIJ survey found that most clients were recruited from the ranks of probationers or parolees. Also, almost three-fourths of DRCs admit parole and probation violators, and some are designed to provide services for those with special needs: released prisoners, women with children, the mentally ill, and those with developmental disabilities.[108]

Evaluation of Day Reporting Centers.   There are not many DRC evaluations. Moreover, because DRCs provide such a wide variety of services to a wide variety of clients, it is almost necessary to evaluate each center individually. It is very difficult to generalize to all DRCs. However, because an important goal of most DRCs is to reduce the costs of confinement, we can see if this goal has been achieved. Some studies also look at program completion rates and rearrest rates to get a measure of program effectiveness.

In order to reduce the costs of confinement, DRCs must recruit their clients from those already incarcerated or those who would otherwise become incarcerated. However, as previously noted, the Parent and colleagues NIJ study found that most DRCs recruit their clients from the ranks of probationers and parolees. Although we cannot tell whether these offenders would become incarcerated if not for the DRCs, it seems that at least for a majority of offenders, the DRCs are providing services to clients who otherwise may be under regular supervision. Under this scenario, no cost savings would be realized. However, because almost three-fourths of all DRCs admit probation and parole violators, some cost savings are realized as the average cost of a DRC is $35.04 whereas jail costs are anywhere from $50 to $100 per day.[109]

Program completion rates are not very high. Parent and colleagues found that for most of the fifty-four DRCs studied, half of their clients do not successfully complete the program (the range of termination rates was 14 to 86 percent).[110] Interestingly, termination rates were higher for service-oriented rather than surveillance-oriented programs. This may be because service-oriented programs have more rules which, along with greater expectations of their clients, may actually increase the chances that an offender might fail in the program. The NIJ study also reported that programs with curfews reported fewer terminations.

As pointed out previously, each day reporting center is a bit different from the others. The programs and services offered and the clients served vary from center to center. Because they offer services and supervision in one facility, and offer them to a wide variety of clients, DRCs have established an important niche for themselves in community corrections. If, in addition, each DRC explicitly defines its goals and objectives, it will be better able to measure whether it has achieved these goals. If one of the goals is to reduce prison and jail crowding, and DRCs target released inmates for placement in the program, the future of DRCs in community corrections seems secure.

Two types of intermediate sanctions that have seen increasing use in recent years are community service and restitution. A reason for the growth is that, besides being intermediate sanctions, both are also often used as part of diversion programs (see Chapter Eleven) and they fit in well with the philosophy and goals or restorative justice (discussed later in the chapter).

Community Service

Community service is an alternative sanction whereby an offender is ordered to provide a certain number of hours (often between 40 and 1,000) of free services to the public, usually the city or county government or a charitable organization, as part of his or her sentence. The services may involve picking up litter from roadsides; doing yard maintenance; painting homes or buildings; splitting and stacking fire wood; or working in public or nonprofit agencies, such as libraries, city parks, homeless shelters, food banks, or charitable organizations.

One of the appeals of community service is that it combines both punishment *and* rehabilitation. Those ordered to do community service are receiving consequences for their misdeeds; they must work at prescribed tasks, and their freedom is curtailed until the work is completed. Therefore, it is punitive. They are also engaged in constructive work; they are often interacting with other members of society; they may be learning a skill useful for future occupations; and, as a consequence of all of these factors, their self-esteem may improve. Hence, community service is also seen as rehabilitative. As noted previously, community service can also be used in diversion programs, and it fits in well with the principles of restorative justice (to be discussed shortly).[111]

It is easy to see why community service is so attractive to the public, judges, and criminal justice professionals. The question of whether it is effective is another matter. There is no doubt that community service projects provide thousands of hours of work for communities, nonprofit organizations, churches, and individuals, completing projects that otherwise may not be done. They also save the criminal justice system money when offenders are placed in community service programs rather than correctional facilities. However, there is no evidence that community service programs reduce recidivism, and the hidden costs of community service are sometimes hard to calculate. For example, how do we calculate the costs of failing to complete community service, a failure rate found to be 15 to 50 percent in some programs?[112] What are the costs of sending those who fail to complete their community service hours back to the court for further processing? And, what about those who may commit crimes while doing their community service? How are those costs estimated?

There is no doubt that community service can be an important, cost-effective, and beneficial sanction for some offenders who would otherwise be incarcerated, but whether it can really be "all things to all people"[113] remains to be seen. Another type of intermediate sanction that has wide appeal and is often linked with community service is restitution.

Restitution

Simply defined, **restitution** is the offender paying back the victim for the harm caused by the crime. Restitution can be made by monetary payments, by returning or replacing stolen or damaged property, or by carrying out direct services to the victim.[114] Besides paying for property, the payment can also be for time lost from work, insurance deductibles, or medical expenses. Restitution can be part of a diversion program, in which case it is normally used in theft or damage to property cases; or it can be part of a criminal sentence for more serious property, and even violent, crimes so that victims may receive compensation.

In federal criminal cases, the court's authority to order restitution comes entirely from statutes.[115] Until 1982, restitution could only be imposed as a condition of probation. In 1982, Congress passed the Victim Witness Protection Act giving courts the authority to impose restitution as part of a sentence, not merely as a condition of probation. In 1990, the Supreme Court ruled in *Hughey v. United States* that victim compensation was limited to harm caused as a direct result of the offense of conviction. Since the *Hughey* decision, Congress has continued to extend restitution to the point where, today, restitution is mandatory in most cases.[116] In addition, crime victims' bills of rights have been enacted in all states, with about one-half mandating victim restitution, and thirty-one states have passed victim rights constitutional amendments, at least ten of which require mandatory restitution.[117]

As with community service, restitution is appealing because it combines punishment and rehabilitation. Restitution is retributive because it is a sanction imposed by the court as a direct result of the offense committed. Moreover, the monetary payments are often a burden to offenders, thereby contributing to the punitive aspect of restitution. But it is also rehabilitative. Offenders who complete the required restitution payments should have a sense of accomplishment and enhanced self-image. In order to complete the payments, it is hoped that they also have developed helpful life skills such as good work habits and budgeting. Restitution is also important to victims and victim advocates because it allows for the recovery of at least some of the economic and psychological losses suffered from a crime. In addition, restitution is often a part of a restorative justice process and, as such, may allow offenders to express remorse for their crimes, a potentially important step in their rehabilitation.[118]

As with community service, it is easy to see why restitution has become so appealing in most jurisdictions, but the evidence on effectiveness is mixed. Not all restitution payments are collected, and even when an offender is deemed able to afford the payments yet fails to pay, community corrections officials may avoid revocation if the offender has committed no crime or other violation. Such a failure to pay the restitution or be revoked for not paying contradicts many of the goals and purposes of restitution, including making the offender accountable for his or her actions, showing remorse for the wrongdoing, and paying back the victim for the harm caused. It is also no longer rehabilitative or punitive if the offender does not have to pay. In the few recidivism studies that have been done on restitution programs, the results are mixed. One study found that there was no difference in the probability of returning to prison between a group that paid restitution and another that did not.[119] However, the control group was more likely to be returned to prison for a new crime, whereas the restitution group was more likely to go back for a parole violation. Other studies have shown that restitution programs have somewhat higher failure rates than do regular probation caseloads.[120]

However, we know that there are many benefits that accrue when a restitution program is thorough and working. Victims are more satisfied, offenders benefit, and the community saves money and is probably safer. It is because of this balance between the victim, the offender, and the community that restitution programs have been called "potentially restorative"[121] and are often a part of agreements resulting from a restorative justice program, the subject to which we now turn. This innovation is not only a new program but also involves a paradigm shift regarding how we view our system of justice. Restorative and community justice programs involve a move away from the adversarial and retributive model of justice toward a more "balanced" approach.

Restorative or Community Justice

With the rise of the victim's rights movement in the 1980s, a new paradigm of justice emerged in the 1990s, a balanced approach that calls for involvement by the victim, the offender, and the community in a search for solutions to the crime problem. Because intermediate sanction programs did not fully serve victims in the way that the growing victim's rights movement advocated, many probation and parole departments worked with community members to help develop a new type of response to crime, one that for the first time brought the victim into the justice system as a participating member. This response to crime came to be known as **restorative justice,** or the balanced approach to justice, and later was also called **community justice** by some practitioners.

Although the roots of restorative justice programs come from the traditions of several indigenous peoples and tribes on many continents—the Lakota and

Dakota peoples of North America and the Maori of New Zealand, for example—the researcher Marshall suggests that the first use of the term restorative justice is usually credited to Barnett in 1977.[122] Barnett was referring to principles that resulted from American experiments, both public and private, in the 1970s with mediation between victims and offenders—victim–offender reconciliation programs (VORP)—as restorative in nature. But even before Barnett and these early VORP programs, psychologist Arthur Eglash had, in 1958, and again with Papenek in 1959, raised the possibility that the punishment of criminals could be considered a "creative restitution process" and that the victim, offender, and community all could find "benefit by moving the frame of reference from the harm itself to the process of repairing the harm."[123] The key was the face-to-face encounter between the person harmed and the one doing the harm. Then Schafer in 1965[124] and again in 1970[125] suggested that restitution could be a new paradigm of justice, which could move victim reparation to the forefront of justice practice. Hence, victim–offender mediation programs began, and in those communities where such programs existed, they were a viable sentencing option for judges.

The first formal programs began in Minnesota, Iowa, and Ontario, Canada, from 1970 to 1977.[126] The nascent movement was given momentum in the early 1980s with the rise of the victims' movement, which was given legitimacy, and federal money, with the passage of the federal Victims of Crime Act (VOCA) in 1983 and the establishment of the Office of Victims of Crime (OVC) in the Justice Department. By 1989, there were active VORP programs in at least forty-two jurisdictions in the United States; by 1996 this number had risen to at least 200 programs and Bazemore and Umbreit reported in 2001 at least 320 victim–offender mediation programs in the United States and Canada and more than 700 in Europe.[127]

The movement gained momentum as a result of a speech given by then–attorney general Janet Reno in the spring of 1996. In the speech, Reno stated that she was concerned that many U.S. citizens felt alienated from a justice system that had become too bureaucratic and detached. She outlined her vision of community justice and charged the Office of Justice Programs (OJP) with exploring innovative, community-based programs that would improve the justice system and better serve victims. As a result, the OJP, the National Institute of Justice, the OVC, the Office for Juvenile Justice and Delinquency Prevention, and the Bureau of Justice Assistance worked with the National Institute of Corrections to host a national conversation on restorative justice. More than one hundred practitioners, victims, and researchers from the United States and Canada met for two days to discuss the concept. Then, between June 1997 and January 1998, OJP replicated the national symposia in five locations around the United States. The restorative justice movement was soaring. Because it was primarily a community-based program and was usually an alternative to traditional sentencing, probation and parole departments around the United States worked with community members and other justice professionals in developing many such programs, often facilitating the mediation and providing the space for the meetings to take place. The

American Probation and Parole Association, in fact, includes restorative justice as part of its community justice strategy.[128]

These experiments led to the realization by some practitioners that the needs of victims, the community, and offenders were dependent on each other and that to have any impact on justice all three must be involved. Furthermore, the overloading of many justice agencies—courts, probation and parole offices, and so on—could only be reduced by agencies working in partnership with communities to help prevent crime. Therefore, restorative justice programs recognize the need to employ two or more of the parties to a crime: the victim, the community, and the offender.

However, as with any innovation, changing the traditional justice system to a more restorative system requires changes in practices and principles. There are many practical examples of this change, and we discuss two later in the chapter, but for any of them to be truly restorative in nature, they all must be based on the same principles and values. In 1996 the National Institute of Corrections sponsored a national teleconference on restorative justice. During that conference the participants suggested seven basic principles of restorative justice that can be used to create and evaluate programs embodying this new paradigm.[129] The seven principles are as follows:

- Crime is an offense against human relationships.
- Victims and the community are central to justice processes.
- The first priority of justice processes is to assist victims.
- The second priority is to restore the community, to the degree possible.
- The offender has personal responsibility to victims and to the community for crimes committed.
- The offender will develop improved competency and understanding as a result of the restorative justice experience.
- Stakeholders share responsibilities for restorative justice through partnerships for action.

In 1997 the Mennonite Central Committee published *Fundamental Concepts of Restorative Justice*.[130] Three key ideas were presented as forming the foundation of restorative justice philosophy and programs.

1. Crime is an offense against human relationships. Although the state has certain roles in the system—investigating facts, facilitating system processes, and ensuring safety—the state is not the primary victim. The main victims are those most directly affected by the crime. But there are other victims as well—family members of victims and offenders, witnesses, and other members of the community. A restorative justice process must address the needs of all these victims by maximizing their input and participation. The roles of these various stakeholders will change depending on the situation and their ability and willingness to participate, but a restorative justice system will ensure that their participation is a possibility—

particularly the traditional victims—in order to assign responsibility, restore, heal, and prevent future crimes.

2. Criminal violations create obligations and liabilities. As much as possible, offenders are obliged to make things right and to actively participate in the process. The offender's primary obligation is to the victims, so a restorative justice process gives victims the power to participate in defining those obligations. Offenders are given opportunities to understand the harm they have caused. The offenders then help develop the plans designed to restore the victims and the community, while taking responsibility for their actions. The participation of offenders is voluntary, if possible. However, if offenders do not participate voluntarily, they may be required to accept their participation in the process, although this is less than ideal. The obligations placed on the offender should be geared toward making things right and, although these obligations may be difficult and even painful, they are not intended to be vengeful.

Furthermore, the obligations to the victims (restitution, for example) take precedence over obligations or sanctions to the state (fines, for example). The community also has obligations in the process, obligations to the victims, the offender, and to other community members. The community is obliged to support and help the victims of crime meet their needs. The community is also obliged to support the work involved in integrating offenders back into the community. The community must be involved in defining the obligations of offenders, and the community must make sure there are opportunities for offenders to right their wrongs. Finally, the community is obligated to look after the general welfare of all of its members. As such, the community must take responsibility for the social conditions and the relationships in the community, recognizing that those conditions and relationships might promote both community well being *and* crime. The community, therefore, is obligated to work toward promoting the former and eliminating the latter.

3. Restorative justice seeks to heal and put right the wrongs created by crime. The starting points for justice, in a restorative model, are the needs of the victims. Victim safety is the first priority. Once that safety is achieved, victims' needs for information, validation, restitution, testimony, and support are addressed. The restorative justice process provides the framework to attend to these needs. That framework encourages recovery and healing by maximizing the input and participation of victims. As much as possible, the victims determine their needs and what the outcome of the process will be.

Offenders are also involved in repairing the harm they have caused. The process maximizes participation, dialogue, mutual consent, and exchange of information. Although victims take the lead in determining the terms and conditions of the information exchange, mutual agreement is emphasized; the outcomes are not imposed on anyone. Furthermore, offenders' needs and competencies are considered, with opportunities for remorse, reconciliation, and forgiveness provided. The process also emphasizes the integration of offenders into the community, and offenders are treated respectfully throughout the justice process. Change in behavior is valued over punitive responses. Also, the entire process belongs to the community. Thus, community members are involved in the process and community resources are used to facilitate desired outcomes. Consequently, the process also leads to strengthening the community, which, in turn, helps prevent similar crimes in the future.

Finally, the process is cognizant of intended and unintended consequences of the outcomes, with the goal being fairness in all resolutions. However, this fairness is not achieved through equity of outcomes but by making sure that all parties are heard and their needs addressed. Agreements are monitored to ensure they are kept and that the healing, accountability, and change envisioned by the process are achieved. Discrimination based on race, class, gender, or sexual orientation is not tolerated. Outcomes with deterrence or incapacitation as their goal are discouraged and implemented as a last resort and then only in the least restrictive manner possible while maintaining the goal of restoration.

As can be seen by this brief description of the restorative justice model, a significant paradigm shift is required of all members of the criminal justice system. The new roles in this approach to justice are captured in Table 10.1, which was developed by Gordon Bazemore and revised by Anne Seymour.[131]

It is also clear that parole and probation, and community corrections generally, serve a crucial role in the development of any restorative justice program. Two examples of restorative justice programs follow, the first was a statewide initiative, the second from a county in Oregon.

Minnesota.   In 1992, the state of Minnesota held a statewide conference on restorative justice. As a result of the positive response to that conference, in 1994 the Minnesota Department of Corrections (DOC) created the position of restorative justice planner and the Minnesota DOC Restorative Justice Initiative was passed by the state legislature.[132] The purpose of the initiative is to promote the principals of restorative justice throughout the state. As a result, restorative justice programs have been developed in schools, police agencies, community corrections departments, juvenile facilities, adult institutions, and communities throughout the state (Box 10.2 lists a variety of the programs developed). Examples in parole and probation come from community corrections departments and DOC field services offices that have started victim–offender meeting programs, family group conferencing, a crime repair crew of supervised offenders, an increased emphasis on restitution payments, community panels that meet with offenders, multidisciplinary case management for juveniles, and victim awareness education for probation and parole staff.[133]

Deschutes County, Oregon.   In Deschutes County in central Oregon, justice system officials, local elected officials, and citizens teamed up to develop a community justice system. In this system, "the victim is regarded as the paramount

TABLE 10.1 *Traditional and Restorative Justice Assumptions and Implications for Victims of Crime*

The new roles in the balanced approach of restorative justice, as articulated by Dr. Gordon Bazemore, are included in the second column, and the implications of these roles on victims are summarized in the third column of the following chart:

Traditional[a] Justice	Restorative Justice	Implications for Victims
The criminal justice system controls crime.	Crime control lies primarily in the community.	The community—including victims and their allies—participates in and directly benefits from deterrence.
Offender accountability defined as taking punishment.	Accountability defined as assuming responsibility and taking action to repair harm.	Offenders are held directly accountable to victims.
Crime is an individual act with individual responsibility.	Crime has both individual and social dimensions of responsibility.	Prevention, intervention, and breaking the cycle of violence are important considerations.
Crime is an act against the state, a violation of the law, an abstract idea.	Crime is an act against another person or the community.	The victim is individualized as central to the crime and the criminal justice system process, with the community duly noted as also affected by crimes.
Punishment is effective: **a.** Threat of punishment deters crime. **b.** Punishment changes behavior.	Punishment alone is not effective in changing behavior and is disruptive to community harmony and good relationships.	Punishment is augmented by direct accountability to the victim and to the community, with victims having a strong, consistent voice.
Victims are peripheral to the process.	Victims are central to the process of resolving a crime.	Restorative justice principles are "victim centered."
The offender is defined by deficits.	The offender is defined by his or her capacity to make reparation.	Reparations to the victim and to the community are a priority.
Focus is on establishing blame, on guilt, on past (did he/she do it?).	Focus is on problem solving, on liabilities/obligations, and on the future (what should be done?).	A central goal is to deter future criminal action through conflict resolution, problem solving, and fulfilling obligations to the victim and to the community.
Emphasis is on adversarial relationship.	Emphasis is on dialogue and negotiation.	Victims are active participants in determining appropriate reparations.
Imposition of pain to punish and deter/prevent.	Restitution as a means of restoring both parties; goal of conciliation/restoration.	Restitution holds the offender accountable and is meaningful to both him/her and the victim.

(continued)

TABLE 10.1   *Continued*

Traditional[a] Justice	*Restorative Justice*	*Implications for Victims*
Community is on the sideline, represented abstractly by the state.	Community as facilitator in restorative process.	Just as the community is negatively affected by crime, it is positively affected by restorative justice process.
Response is focused on the offender's past behavior.	Response focused on harmful consequences of the offender's behavior: emphasis on the future.	Crime deterrence in the future focuses on victim and public safety.
Dependence on proxy professionals.	Direct involvement by participants.	Victims and their allies are directly involved in the criminal and juvenile justice and restorative justice processes.

[a]In original publication, called "retributive" justice.

Source: Anne Seymore, "Restorative Justice/Community Justice," Chapter 4 in *1999 National Victim Assistance Academy,* eds. Grace Coleman, Mario Gaboury, Morna Murray, and Anne Seymour, 1999, Washington, DC: Office of Victims of Crime. Retrieved February 6, 2002, from www.ojp.usdoj.gov/ovc/assist/nvaa99/chap4.htm

customer of the justice system. Offenders are held accountable in constructive and meaningful ways, and crime prevention is viewed as a high priority."[134] The district attorney's office has a complete menu of victim services, ranging from when the crime is first reported until the final restitution payment is received. The local circuit court also has a comprehensive assortment of victim services, giving its highest priority to victim–offender mediation. The Department of Community Justice converted several positions formerly reserved for offender counseling to those devoted to victim support and counseling. Although the department still supervises offenders, the supervision now holds the offenders accountable for restoring the victim and paying restitution.

Given that one of the principles of restorative justice is also to restore the community, the Deschutes County Department of Community Justice also has several programs designed to accomplish this goal. For example, the Merchant Accountability Board was formed to help the district attorney's office handle the hundreds of shoplifting, petty theft, and bad checks afflicting retail businesses in the county. Consequently, the merchants developed a program in which one merchant would serve as a stand-in victim for perhaps twelve cases and decide on the amount of restitution. Thus, the case is handled without the cost of prosecution, the stand-in merchant is allowed to emphasize to the offenders how their crimes affect small business in the community, and all the victims (merchants) get their restitution more quickly and efficiently than under the traditional justice system model.[135]

BOX 10.2 • *Sample Restorative Justice Practices in Minnesota*

- **Victim Services** (across much of the state)
- **Community Volunteers—Victim Support,** as victim advocates or supporters working with victims
- **Police Chaplaincy Program and Victim Intervention Program,** for families of homicide, suicide, and accident victims (St. Paul)
- **Community Violence Response Team** (St. Paul)
- **Victim–Offender Meeting Programs** (Summit University/Dispute Resolution Center–St. Paul, Dakota County, Houston County, Brown County, DOC Bemidji District, Mediation Services for Anoka County, Kandiyohi County, Cooperative Solutions [Grand Rapids], DOC in Meeker County, plus individual volunteer mediators providing services to communities around the state)
- **Victim Offender Dialog** in cases of severe violence (Minnesota Department of Corrections, University of Minnesota Center for Restorative Justice and Mediation)
- **Victim–Offender Conferencing,** including large and small group conferencing (Washington County, Kandiyohi County)
- **Family Group Conferencing** is being done in collaboration by schools, human services, churches, community programs, law enforcement, courts and probation, including Black Indian Hispanic and Asian Women in Action, St. Paul Youth Service Bureau, Cooperative Solutions (Austin), Woodbury Police, Carver County Sheriff, Anoka Police, Duluth Police with Arrowhead Juvenile Center, Houston County Mediation and Victim Services, Arrowhead Community Corrections, and Stearns, Martin, Waseca, Winona, Jackson, Dakota, Sibley, Carver, LeSueur, Scott, Goodhue, Faribault, Redwood, and Hennepin Counties
- **Family Group Conferencing** for inmate disputes (Shakopee Women's Prison)
- **Community Conferencing** with adult "livability crime" offenders (Central City Neighborhoods Partnership–Minneapolis)
- **Community Conferencing** for transition/aftercare/reintegration for juveniles leaving correctional facilities (Minnesota Correctional Facility–Red Wing)
- **Circle Sentencing/Peacemaking Circles** (Mille Lacs Band of Ojibway with Mille Lacs County District Court, North Minneapolis, South St. Paul, Milaca and Princeton, Dakota County, Washington County)
- **Child Protection Healing Circles** (Hennepin County Children and Family Services–North Minneapolis)
- **Circles of Success for At Risk Students** (Rum River Educational Cooperative)
- **Community Panels for Offenders:** diversion (Forest Lake Youth Service Bureau, Powderhorn Park–South Minneapolis); probation (DOC Bemidji District Powderhorn Park–South Minneapolis)
- **Crime Repair Crew**—supervised offender community service crews repairing damage of criminal behavior (Dakota County)
- **Community Service on Projects Out in the Community**—Sentencing to Service work crews of jail inmates, prison inmates building low-income housing, and individual placements of offenders (many counties in Minnesota)
- **Community Service Projects** done by inmates in institutions (Minnesota Correctional Facility–Shakopee, Minnesota Correctional Facility–Lino Lakes)
- **Pre-Sentence Investigation Process** which focuses on Restorative Justice and the Balanced Approach (DOC Field Services statewide, Dodge/Fillmore/Olmsted Community Corrections, Anoka County)
- **Victim Restoration Unit within Community Corrections** to prioritize activities related to victims (Dakota County)

(continued)

BOX 10.2 • *Continued*

- **Beat Probation Offices in Neighborhoods** (Hennepin County, Dakota County, Ramsey County)
- **Coordinating Council**—multiagency, cross-disciplinary case management for youth, involving the family (Faribault County)
- **Victim Impact Panels**—MADD (Anoka, Blue Earth, Crow Wing, Dakota, Freeborn, Goodhue, Hennepin, Itasca, Kandiyohi, Ottertail, Ramsey, Rice, Scott, St. Louis, Stearns, Waseca, and Washington Counties)
- **Victim–Offender Driving Impact Panels**—Minnesotans for Safe Driving (Hennepin and Scott)
- **Video for Youth on Impaired and Distracted Driving**—Minnesotans for Safe Driving
- **Video of Youth Victims of Drunk Driving Panel** and youth speakers trained to go out to community groups to talk about their experiences (MADD)
- **Cognitive Skills Programs for Offenders,** with an emphasis on taking responsibility (Dakota County, Ramsey County, DOC Albert Lea District, Arrowhead Juvenile Center, Dodge/Fillmore/Olmsted Community Corrections, Shakopee Women's Prison, Minnesota Correctional Facilities for Juveniles)
- **Victim Empathy Classes for Adult and Juvenile Offenders** (Shakopee Women's Prison, Lino Lakes Prison, Dakota County)
- **Use of Revenue Recapture** to increase restitution collection for victims (increasing numbers of counties)
- **"Restorative Measures"** book, by the Minnesota Department of Children, Families and Learning, used by schools
- **Peer Mediation Programs in Schools** (many schools around the state)
- **Community Dialog and Forums** around shared values, community concerns and conflicts (Woodbury, St. Louis Park, Washington County)
- **Community and Neighborhood Mediation Programs**
- **Corrections Advisory Boards** which include victim and community representation
- **Juvenile Repay Fund** which makes restitution payments to victims after their juvenile offenders earn the money by doing community service work (Dakota, Brown, Ramsey, and Kandiyohi Counties)
- **Prison and Jail Ministry Programs** (state prisons and jails)
- **Community Volunteers** working with inmates in prisons, jails, and back in the community (AMICUS and other programs)
- **Prison and Jail Treatment Programs** which emphasize taking responsibility and understanding the multiple impacts of the harmful behavior on others
- **Inmate Involvement in Developing Prevention Programs** for youth (Minnesota Correctional Facility–Lino Lakes, Minnesota Correctional Facility–Shakopee)
- **Increased Parent Involvement in Juvenile Cases** (family group conferencing, circle processes, Forest Lake Youth Service Bureau family community service)
- **Corrections Involvement in Prevention Efforts** (fire prevention video, mentoring and athletic games with at-risk youth)
- **Teen Courts** (Mayor's Commission against Drugs, Roseville/Falcon Heights/Lauderdale/Little Canada)

Practices in the Development Process
- **Circle Sentencing/Peacemaking Circles** in urban St. Paul (Summit University Neighborhood)
- **Family Group Conferencing or Peacemaking Circles** for transition/aftercare/reintegration for juveniles and adults leaving correctional facilities (St. Croix Camp for Girls, Arrowhead Juvenile Center, Sauk Centre, Minnesota Correctional Facility–Shakopee)

BOX 10.2 • *Continued*

- **Information System for Restitution** which reminds offender monthly, a requirement that offender write letter to victim with explanation if restitution payment will be late (Dakota County)
- **Community Involvement in Designating the Community Service** of offenders who committed crimes in that community
- **Rituals for Reintegration into the Community** when an ex-offender has earned back community respect (St. Paul)

Source: Minnesota Department of Corrections/Restorative Justice Initiative. December 1998.

The Department of Community Justice supervises all community service work in a way that helps restore the community and victims. Working with several nonprofit groups, the department has supervised offenders in their completion of several worthwhile projects, such as the construction of a child abuse center, building a seventy-unit transitional housing shelter, helping to construct a community park, and working with Habitat for Humanity to build a house for a homeless family. These kinds of projects benefit the community and help offenders connect and identify with their communities in a way that might prevent them from committing crimes in the future.

Although these programs are important elements to the county's community justice approach, efforts and programs to prevent crime are also integral to the model. For example, Deschutes County worked with the Oregon Youth Authority to develop a block grant system whereby the county houses its nondangerous juvenile offenders, those who would otherwise be placed in state institutions, in local facilities. These local facilities are paid for through the block grant, and any additional savings are put back into the county in the form of crime prevention programs. The savings have been as much as several hundred thousand dollars a year and are managed by a County Commission on Children and Families.[136] It is a classic example of a win–win situation: Money once used for youth correctional institutions is now being used for crime prevention in the community, further decreasing the need for youth correctional institutions.

Evaluations of Restorative Justice Programs

Although there are several different types of restorative justice programs, most are relatively new and have not been subjected to empirical test. The exceptions to this are victim–offender mediation (VOM) programs and family group conferencing. According to Mark Umbreit there have been forty empirical studies of victim–offender mediation programs in Canada, England, and the United States.[137] The largest of these studies looked at 3,142 juvenile cases referred to programs in four U.S. cities over a two-year period. In these cases, 95 percent of the mediation sessions resulted in a successful, negotiated restitution agreement between the victim and offender. Crime victims who went through the mediation program were more likely to be satisfied with the justice system response to their case than were victims who went through the traditional court process (79 to 57 percent). Victims were also significantly less fearful of being revictimized, and 81 percent of offenders successfully completed their restitution versus only 58 percent of similar offenders who did not participate in VOM. Also, offenders who participated in VOM committed fewer and less serious crimes compared to similar offenders who did not meet with their victims (18 to 27 percent).

There have been eight studies completed evaluating the effect of family group conferencing on youthful offenders. Umbreit reports the largest study was completed in New Zealand evaluating the effect of a law requiring the extensive use of family group conferencing. As a result of the act, passed in 1989, a great deal fewer young offenders appeared in court and were convicted than before the act was passed—10,000 to 20,000 before the act was passed compared to 2,587 in 1990. Moreover, 50 percent fewer youth were committed to correctional institutions (262 in 1988 versus 112 in 1990). Umbreit also reports on a study of Indianapolis youth by McGarrell and his colleagues that found a 25 percent decline in recidivism for the first-time offenders studied.[138]

Challenges of Innovation

Because most probation and parole innovations are of comparatively recent origin, their long-range effectiveness is uncertain. Many of the evaluations previously cited do indicate they work and that realistic program goals can be realized. However, even though the innovations generally have achieved cost savings, acceptable levels of community risk, and improved case management, it is less clear whether they have succeeded in reducing recidivism. Early reports, conducted by the agencies involved, which claim the new programs have dramatically reduced recidivism, must be considered in light of the tendency for statistics producers to focus on data favorable to organizational expectations.[139] The observations of J. Banks, a Georgia Institute of Technology researcher, about his state's ISP can be usefully applied to all of the recent innovations: "Can they divert? Yes they can. Are they cost effective compared to prison? Yes they are. But if you ask me if they can rehabilitate people from a life of crime, that's another matter."[140]

Although the initially positive results of program innovations are encouraging, such programs have dramatically challenged the capabilities of probation and parole personnel. The most urgent challenges are (1) to avoid net widening, (2) to sustain program momentum, and (3) to resist making overly optimistic claims of effectiveness.

1. Regarding net widening, many of these new programs target nonviolent, low-risk offenders who were least likely to be incarcerated anyway. As judges and parole boards become more familiar with these programs, they may have a tendency to use them for defendants who normally would have been granted regu-

lar probation or parole with routine supervision. In this manner, programs originally intended to divert from incarceration instead "widen the net" of social control and, therefore, do not measurably reduce the total number of incarcerated
inmates. Some judges, in order to impose more restrictive supervision conditions,
may be tempted to use the new programs as add-ons to regular sentences. This is
a misuse of these programs: If the programs are truly alternatives to jail, this is appropriate; if people who otherwise would be on probation are entering them, the
programs are being improperly used.

A subtle form of net widening in the operations of ISP, home confinement,
and shock incarceration programs applies to some programs.[141] Oftentimes, when
a new program is established, low-risk, prison-bound offenders are allowed "a
chance" to make it in the new program. However, when one of these offenders
fails in the new program, there is a temptation to respond with a harsher sentence
than would have been the case originally. This is so because the offender is now a
double failure: He or she has committed the original offense and also failed when
given the opportunity to make it in the new program. The criminal justice system
must respond, and often that response is harsher than the original sentence.

2. The second challenge to innovative programs is that, in order for the new
programs to be truly innovative and not merely panaceas, program originators
must sustain initial momentum and retain employee enthusiasm. If this can be accomplished, the programs will become established practices rather than experimental projects. Todd Clear and Vincent O'Leary indicated, "real change means
that line officers perform their work in ways that are consistent with the goals of
change." They concluded that meaningful change can only be achieved by closely
monitoring program efforts because "[l]ocating and exposing a criminal justice (or
community supervision) problem is relatively easy, doing something about it in
the day-to-day operational context is substantially more difficult."[142]

To sustain the programs, it is essential that probation and parole departments adapt to the goals and values of the new programs. A traditional nine-to-
five work schedule, for example, may not be compatible with around-the-clock
monitoring mandated by many of the new programs. Furthermore, there was initially some question whether probation and parole staff, trained for the most part
in the social sciences, could be comfortable with the strict monitoring required by
many intermediate sanction programs. Many using the programs decided it was
necessary to undertake new hiring policies in order to recruit workers in tune with
current surveillance goals. These hiring practices could understandably lead to
some dissention and rivalry with the more senior staff. In addition, some of the
surveillance-oriented hires may have some difficulty with the even newer restorative justice programs that often require new sensitivities to victims *and* offenders.

3. The third challenge facing probation and parole administrators is perhaps the
most difficult: to moderate their program goals and restrain their claims of success.
In order to convince the public, legislators, judges, and parole boards that new programs should be funded, probation and parole agencies may be overselling their

capabilities. Virtually all of the intermediate sanction programs are designed to provide rigorous surveillance and close supervision that, in practice, is often impossible to deliver. Talking tough may gain probation and parole a temporary boost in public confidence; however, if agencies cannot follow through, the ensuing disillusionment ultimately will hinder their missions. This is especially true in situations where claims of reducing offender recidivism cannot be empirically demonstrated. These warnings should not be construed as arguments against the development of innovative programs. The authors agree with Joan Petersilia, Todd Clear, and others that the programs described in this chapter represent the future of U.S. corrections. For this very reason, a cautious approach is in the best interest of all concerned. Joan Petersilia has some insightful advice for those facing the challenges of program innovation: ". . . jurisdictions must have realistic expectations about what they can accomplish, they must tailor programs to fit the offenders they will treat, and they must understand the role that local context and adoption strategies must play. The pressure is on now to try such programs . . . [the] overcrowding crisis has, ironically, created a 'window of opportunity'" for new and innovative programs.[143]

Petersilia goes on to argue, however, that agencies should not charge headlong into these new programs because there may be unforeseen problems or unintended consequences that may lead to the conclusions that the new programs should not be continued. What must be avoided, Petersilia argues, is the opportunity to try something new without first giving the new program an opportunity to succeed. Instead, "a cautious approach" is suggested to innovation, an approach that avoids the problems connected to correctional programs of the past that failed to communicate their goals or show they made progress toward achieving their goals. Short of such information, the new community-based programs were easy targets for budget cuts, leaving prisons as the principal way to deal with offenders, thereby aggravating the present policy dilemma.[144]

Therefore, for any innovative programs to succeed, agencies and the criminal justice system in general must show the new programs ". . . are safe, hold offenders accountable, and cost less than prison." Otherwise, "the public" and policy makers will continue to view institutions as the best answer to the crime problem, leading to ever greater prison populations and the increased costs associated with them. Obviously, whichever way we go has important ramifications for social services, education, health care, and even the economy and society generally.

Summary

Many probation and parole departments have developed new programs incorporating intensive supervision, house arrest, and shock incarceration. The programs are designed as intermediate sanctions—more stringent than traditional probation but less restrictive than long periods of incarceration. They feature intrusive supervision with frequent offender contact, small caseloads of selected participants who are being diverted from jails or prisons, and substantial cost savings when compared with incarceration. In addition, a sizable number of probation and parole departments have embraced the ideas of differential supervision where offenders are supervised to a degree that is commensurate with their risk and needs. Others have opened day reporting centers to keep daily tabs on some offenders, and a significant and growing number of jurisdictions have started restorative justice programs of some type. Taken together, these new programs have energized the field and have partially restored public, legislative, and judicial confidence in probation and parole.

Intensive supervision programs, emphasizing reporting requirements, community service, participation in treatment programs, and the collection of supervision fees, are in place in all fifty states. In Georgia, offenders are put into the program by judges at sentencing; in other states, candidates apply only after they have started serving a prison sentence; whereas in still others, offenders are placed into the program after being granted probation. Some programs, however, use all three methods in selecting candidates for intensive supervision. The prototypical ISP uses the principles of effective supervision developed by Andrews, Gendreau, and their colleagues and appears to hold much promise.

Home confinement programs restrict offenders to their homes during certain hours. Many of these programs have incorporated electronic devices to monitor compliance with home curfews. The increasing use of electronic surveillance has raised unresolved philosophical, ethical, legal, and practical issues.

Shock incarceration programs, which offer a military boot camp experience followed by probation, continue to be popular. These programs give young, first-time (as adults) offenders the opportunity to avoid the negative effects of long-time incarceration by participating in a regimen (for about three months) of physical training and rigid discipline. Also, many community corrections departments have objectively structured their supervision methods by implementing programs of differential supervision. The development of an objective risk and needs scale (based in most instances on a Wisconsin Model) was the impetus for more accurate supervision classification.

Day reporting centers are "one-stop shops" where offenders report on a daily basis, providing structure for the day, control of behavior, and opportunities for treatment and services. There is no one model for day reporting centers; each is tailored to the needs and resources of the specific community in which it is located and the offender population it is serving. Among other services, the centers provide substance abuse or mental health treatment; and help with job searches, life skills, educational programs, reentry programs, or any other treatment or program deemed necessary—as long as the needed resources are available in the community.

Community service is an alternative sanction requiring an offender to provide free services to the community for a certain number of hours. The services can be for individuals (such as yard maintenance for the elderly), for private, nonprofit organizations or groups (such as helping build a homeless shelter), or for government agencies (such as cleaning up a city park). Restitution involves an offender paying back the victim or victims for the harm caused by the crime. The actual restitution can be money, returning or replacing stolen or damaged property, or the completion of some service directly for the victim.

Restorative justice programs are victim-centered responses to crime that allow those most directly affected by crime to have a direct say in the community response to the harm caused by the crime. Restorative justice programs offer support and assistance to crime victims, work toward restoring the emotional and material losses incurred by victims, hold offenders accountable for their crimes, provide opportunities for problem solving among the major players involved in a crime, offer offenders opportunities to reintegrate into the community, and strengthen public safety through building the community.

Most preliminary reports indicate the new programs are working, at least to some extent: Cost savings have been achieved, community risk has not been seriously jeopardized, offenders are being diverted from lengthy incarceration, victim's needs are being met, and case management has been improved. However, the programs have seriously challenged community corrections administrators to sustain initial momentum, to restructure department procedures, to maintain line staff commitment, and all the while avoiding setting unrealistic program goals or widening the net of social control. Rather than proceeding with unbridled optimism, the authors and other researchers have suggested that probation and parole planners adopt a cautious and measured approach to innovation.

Key People and Terms

Boot camps (322)
Client Management Classification (CMC) (327)
Community justice (336)
Community service (334)
Curfew (311)
Day reporting centers (DRCs) (332)
Differential supervision (327)
Electronic monitoring (314)
Home confinement (311)

Home detention (311)
House arrest (311)
Intensive supervision programs (305)
Intermediate sanctions (304)
Net widening (308)
Restitution (335)
Restorative justice (336)
Shock incarceration (322)

Key Legal Case

Hughey v. United States

Questions for Discussion and Review

1. What is intensive supervision probation? How does it differ from regular probation?

2. Discuss the effectiveness of intensive supervision probation programs, including the prototypical ISP.

3. Discuss the three levels of home confinement. Compare home confinement with and without electronic monitoring (EM).

4. Discuss the various types of electronic monitoring devices. What kinds of offenders are

most suitable to these devices? Explain your answer.

5. What are some unresolved philosophical, moral, practical, and ethical issues regarding electronic monitoring?

6. What is shock incarceration? How effective is it in achieving the goals of those who devise these programs?

7. Discuss differential supervision and its impact on probation and parole.

8. What are day reporting centers? How effective are they in achieving their goals?

9. Discuss the principles of restorative justice. How does restorative justice differ from traditional justice?

10. What challenges does a parole and probation administrator face when trying to create innovative programs?

Relevant Internet Sites

American Probation and Parole Association, information on intermediate sanctions and restorative justice: www.appa-net.org

National Criminal Justice Reference Service, including corrections publications: http://virlib.ncjrs.org/Corrections.asp

Georgia Department of Corrections, providing information on intermediate sanctions in Georgia: www.dcor.state.ga.us

BI Incorporated, which develops, sells, services, and administers electronic monitoring equipment: www.bi.com/Technology

National Institute of Corrections, including many publication web pages on intermediate sanctions: www.nicic.org

International Centre for Justice and Reconciliation, a large selection of restorative justice information and materials: www.restorativejustice.org

Restorative Justice on-line notebook: www.ojp.usdoj.gov/nij/rest-just/index.htm

EXERCISE • *Programming Decisions*

By Ruth Taylor

Several different programs were discussed in this chapter. It is often the case that more than one program is necessary or helpful for the same offender or ex-offender. The programs chosen might mean the difference between a successful and unsuccessful term of parole. Read the following case and decide what programs are appropriate for Donald. Justify and explain your decisions on the basis of what is best for Donald and for community safety.

Donald is a fifty-four-year-old, African American male who was released from prison after serving eight years for three counts of robbery I. He used a knife to rob a convenience store and was apprehended not far from the site of the crime. There was an order from another county to transfer Donald to that county so he could serve thirty days in jail for an assault IV against a public safety officer. After release from the state institution, Donald completed the thirty days in that county's jail.

(continued)

EXERCISE • *Continued*

This was Donald's fifth time in prison; he has an extensive criminal history spanning thirty-five years. Donald was first arrested at age nineteen for larceny, which earned him probation. His later offenses included multiple counts of assault, robbery, burglary, ex-convict in possession of a weapon, forgery, resisting arrest, and attempted murder. Donald has never successfully completed community supervision because of numerous violations for new criminal activity. While he was incarcerated, he was segregated in the intensive management unit, the specialized unit designed for inmates who were deemed a threat to the safe and orderly operation of the institution.

After his jail time, Donald was released to the county in which he committed his most recent offense. He proposed an address with his daughter but this was denied because she declined to let him stay there. He had no immediate resources to help him secure his own residence. Thus, he reported to his parole office requesting subsidy housing in a downtown hotel. The rooms were full, so he was given a bed at a local homeless shelter.

Donald was in pretty good physical health. He was in need of an eye exam but he required no immediate medications or services. His parole order conditions required a mental health evaluation and anger management counseling. He reported no previous mental health diagnosis or concerns, although he made mention of occasional bouts of minor depressional episodes. He denied that he needed any services.

Prior to his most recent incarceration, Donald had worked sporadically but had never held a job for more than two months. He had no employment skills or training and lacked an employment history of any sort. He had a GED but he reported an inability to write very well.

Donald lacked any significant social support in the community. His daughter, the one family member in the area, did not want anything to do with him. He had a lot of old acquaintances and he verbalized a desire to associate with them now that he was released. He had no apparent prosocial activities and reported no hobbies.

Donald denied any addiction issues, although a review of his file reveals a number of offenses that involved alcohol, including assaults against his then-girlfriend, who filed a restraining order against him. He had never been referred to treatment.

Notes

1. Sheldon Glueck, "The Significance and Promise of Probation," in *Probation and Criminal Justice*, ed. Sheldon Glueck (New York: Macmillan, 1933).

2. James Byrne. "Bending Granite: The Implementation of Intensive Probation Supervision in Massachusetts," Annual Meeting of the American Society of Criminology, San Diego (November, 1985).

3. Gerald J. Bayens, Michael W. Manske, and John Ortiz Smykla, "The Attitudes of Criminal Justice Workgroups toward Intensive Supervised Probation," *American Journal of Criminal Justice* 22 (1998): 189–206.

4. Belinda McCarthy, "Introduction," in *Intermediate Punishments: Intensive Supervision, Home Confinement and Electronic Surveillance*, ed. Belinda McCarthy (Monsey, NY: Criminal Justice Press, 1987) 1.

5. Joan Petersilia, *Expanding Options for Criminal Sentencing* (Santa Monica, CA: Rand Corporation, 1987) 5.

6. Quoted in Petersilia 5.

7. Joan M. Petersilia and Susan Turner, "An Evaluation of Intensive Supervision in California," *Journal of Law and Criminology* 82 (1991): 610–658.

8. John Rosecrance, "Probation Supervision: Mission Impossible," *Federal Probation* 50 (March, 1986): 27–28.

9. John Conrad, "News of the Future," *Federal Probation* 50 (June, 1986): 84.

10. Edward Latessa, "The Cost Effectiveness of Intensive Supervision," *Federal Probation* 50 (June, 1986): 71.

11. Petersilia 12.

12. Billie S. Erwin, "Turning Up the Heat on Probationers in Georgia," *Federal Probation* 50 (June, 1986): 17–24.

13. Petersilia 11; Paul Gendreau, Mario Paparozzi, Tracy Little, and Murray Goddard, "Does Punishing Smarter Work? An Assessment of the New Generation of Alternative Sanctions in Probation," *Forum* 5, 1 (1993). Retrieved May 2, 2002, from www.csc-scc.gc.ca/text/pblct/forum/e053j.shtml

14. Billie S. Erwin and Lawrence A. Bennett, "New Dimensions in Probation: Georgia's Experience with Intensive Supervision Probation (IPS)," *Research in Brief* (Washington, DC: National Institute of Justice, January, 1987).

15. Gendreau et al. 3.

16. Joan M. Petersilia and Susan Turner, "An Evaluation of Intensive Supervision in California," *Journal of Law and Criminology* 82 (1991): 610–658.

17. Michael Tonry, "Stated and Latent Features of ISP," *Crime and Delinquency* 36 (1990): 174–190.

18. Andrew Von Hirsch, Michael Wasik, and J. Greene, "Punishment in the Community and the Principles of Just Desert," *Rutgers Law Journal* 29 (1989): 595–618.

19. Gendreau et al. 3–4.

20. Elizabeth P. Deschenes, Susan Turner, and Joan Petersilia, "A Dual Experiment in Intensive Community Supervision: Minnesota's Prison Diversion and Enhanced Supervised Release Programs," *Prison Journal* 75 (1995): 330–356.

21. Todd R. Clear and P. L. Hardyman, "The New Intensive Supervision Movement," *Crime and Delinquency* 36 (1990): 42–60.

22. Billie S. Erwin, *Evaluation of Intensive Probation Supervision in Georgia* (Atlanta: Georgia Department of Corrections, July, 1987).

23. Michael Tonry, "Evaluating Intermediate Sanction Programs," in *Community Corrections: Probation, Parole and Intermediate Sanctions*, ed. Joan Petersilia (New York: Oxford University Press, 1998) 84.

24. Gendreau et al. 5.

25. F. S. Pearson, "Evaluation of New Jersey's Intensive Supervision Program," *Crime and Delinquency* 34 (1987): 437–448.

26. James Byrne and L. Kelly, "Restructuring Probation as an Intermediate Sanction: An Evaluation of the Massachusetts Intensive Probation Supervision Program, *Final Report to the National Institute of Justice, Research Program on the Punishment and Control of Offenders* (Washington DC: National Institute of Justice, 1989).

27. Petersilia and Turner.

28. Cited in Gendreau et al.

29. D. Andrews, L. Zinger, R. D. Hoge, J. Bonta, P. Gendreau, and F. T. Cullen, "Does Correctional Treatment Work? A Clinically Relevant and Psychologically Informed Meta-Analysis," *Criminology* 28 (1990): 369–404.

30. Gendreau et al.

31. A. Jolin and B. Stipak, "Drug Treatment and Electronically Monitored Home Confinement: An Evaluation of a Community-Based Sentencing Option," *Crime and Delinquency* 38 (1992): 158–170; Frank S. Pearson, "Evaluation of New Jersey's Intensive Supervision Program," *Crime and Delinquency* 34 (1988): 437–448.

32. Petersilia and Turner 8.

33. Andrews et al.; P. Gendreau and D. Andrews, "Tertiary Prevention: What the Meta-Analyses of the Offender Treatment Literature Tell Us about 'What Works'," *Canadian Journal of Criminology* 32 (1990): 173–184; P. Gendreau, "The Principles of Effective Intervention with Offenders," in *Choosing Correctional Options That Work*, ed. A. T. Harland (Thousand Oaks, CA: Sage, 1996) 117–130.

34. Edward Latessa, Lawrence Travis, Betsy Fulton, and Amy Stichman, *Evaluating the Prototypical ISP* (Washington, DC: National Institute of Justice, 1998).

35. For a more detailed description of the prototypical ISP, see B. Fulton, S. Stone, and P. Gendreau, *Restructuring Intensive Supervision Programs: Applying "What Works"* (Lexington, KY: American Probation and Parole Association, 1994); or B. Fulton, P. Gendreau, and M. Paparozzi, "APPA's Prototypical Intensive Supervision Program: ISP as It Was Meant to Be," *Perspectives* 19, 2 (1996): 25–41.

36. Latessa et al. 7–8.

37. Joan Petersilia and Susan Turner, *Evaluating Intensive Supervised Probation/Parole: Results of a Nationwide Experiment* (Washington, DC: National Institute of Justice, 1993) 5.

38. Byrne and Kelly.

39. D. Andrews and J. Bonta, *The Psychology of Criminal Conduct* (Cincinnati, OH: Anderson, 1994).

40. Richard Enos, John E. Holman, and Marnie E. Carroll, *Alternative Sentencing: Electronically Monitored Correctional Supervision*, 2nd ed. (Bristol, IN: Wyndham Hall, 1999).

41. Tonry, "Evaluating Intermediate Sanction Programs" 79–96.

42. "A Report on Community Control, Radio Frequency (RF) Monitoring and Global Positioning Satellite (GPS) Monitoring," August 2002, Florida Department of Corrections. Retrieved December 22, 2003, from www.dc.state.fl.us/pub/gpsrf/2002/index.html

43. "Overview of Community Corrections," *2001–2002 Annual Report,* 2003, Florida Department of Corrections. Retrieved December 22, 2003, from www.dc.state.fl.us/pub/annual/0102/stats/stat_cs.html

44. Quoted in Petersilia 37.

45. Lori Nolting and Paula Tully Bryant, "House Arrest: A Homemade Alternative to Prison," *Correctional Compass,* January, 2000. Retrieved May 29, 2002, from www.dc.fl.us/pub/compass/0001/page09.html

46. Nolting and Bryant 2.

47. Marcus Nieto, "Community Correction Punishments: An Alternative to Incarceration for Nonviolent Offenders," May, 1996, California Research Bureau, Sacramento, CA. Retrieved May 29, 2002, from www.library.ca.gov/CRB/96/08/

48. Nieto 5.

49. Ralph Schwitzgebel, "Electronic Innovation in Behavioral Sciences: A Call to Responsibility," *American Psychologist* 22 (1967): 364–370.

50. Ann H. Crowe, Linda Sydney, Pat Bancroft, and Beverly Lawrence, *Offender Supervision with Electronic Technology* (Lexington, KY: Council of State Governments, 2002).

51. M. Renzema, "Home Confinement Programs: Development, Implementation, and Impact," in *Smart Sentencing: The Emergence of Intermediate Sanctions,* eds. J. M. Byrne, A. J. Lurigio, and J. Petersilia (Newbury Park: Sage, 1992).

52. Tonry, "Evaluating Intermediate Sanction Programs" 79–96.

53. Kathleen Maguire and Ann L. Pastore, eds., *Sourcebook of Criminal Justice Statistics* (Washington, DC: Bureau of Justice Statistics, 1999).

54. Cited in Annesley K. Schmidt and Christine E. Curtis, "Electronic Monitors," *Intermediate Punishments,* ed. Belinda R. McCarthy (Monsey, NY: Criminal Justice Press, 1987).

55. J. Robert Lilly, "Home Incarceration in Kentucky: An Empirical Analysis," Annual Meeting of the American Society of Criminology, San Diego, CA (November, 1985).

56. J. Robert Lilly, Richard A. Ball, and Jennifer Wright, "Home Incarceration with Electronic Monitoring in Kenton County, Kentucky: An Evaluation," *Intermediate Punishments: Intensive Supervision, Home Confinement and Electronic Surveillance,* ed. Belinda McCarthy (Monsey, NY: Criminal Justice Press, 1987) 189–203.

57. Lilly et al. 189–203.

58. Lilly et al. 192.

59. J. Robert Lilly, Richard A. Ball, G. David Curry, and John McMullen, "Electronic Monitoring of the Drunk Driver: A Seven Year Study of the Home Confinement Alternative," *Crime and Delinquency* 39 (1993): 462–484.

60. "The Region Slumlord moves in, Begins Serving Time" *Los Angeles Times* (July 14, 1987): 2.

61. Don Terry, "Brooklyn Landlord Is Freed Eight Days Early," *New York Times* (February 20, 1988): 30, 1.

62. "Overview of Community Corrections," *2000–2001 Annual Report,* 2002, Florida Department of Corrections. Retrieved May 29, 2002, from www.dc.state.fl.us/pub/annual/0001/stat_cs2.html

63. "Overview of Community Corrections," 2002 1.

64. Florida Department of Corrections, personal correspondence, March 16, 1988.

65. "Overview of Community Corrections," 2002 3.

66. *Corrections Digest* 19 (February 24, 1988): 8.

67. Rolando V. del Carmen and Joseph Vaughn, "Legal Issues in the Use of Electronic Surveillance in Probation," *Federal Probation* 50 (June, 1986): 60–69.

68. Joan Petersilia, *House Arrest* (Washington, DC: National Institute of Justice, Crime File Study Guide, 1988) 3.

69. Enos et al.

70. Enos et al. 210.

71. Enos et al. 211.

72. Joan Petersilia, *Reforming Probation and Parole* (Lanham, MD: American Correctional Association, 2002) 71.

73. Enos et al. 212.

74. Enos et al. 212.

75. John Braithwaite, *Crime, Shame, and Reintegration.* (New York: Cambridge University Press, 1989).

76. Enos et al. 213.

77. Charles Friel and Joseph Vaughn, "A Consumer's Guide to the Electronic Monitoring of Probationers," *Federal Probation* 50 (September, 1986): 5.

78. Annesley K. Schmidt, "Electronic Monitors," *Federal Probation* 50 (1986): 58.

79. G. F. Vito and H. E. Allen, "Shock Probation in Ohio: A Comparison of Outcomes," *International*

Journal of Offender Therapy and Comparative Criminology 25 (1981): 70–76.

80. P. Cromwell, G. Killinger, H. Kerper, and C. Walker, *Probation and Parole in the Criminal Justice System* (St. Paul, MN: West, 1987) 70.

81. Gennaro Vito, "Developments in Shock Probation," *Federal Probation* 48 (1984): 27.

82. Vito 27.

83. Quoted in Petersilia, *Expanding Options* 63.

84. Camille B. Camp and George M. Camp, *The 2000 Corrections Yearbook: Adult Corrections* (Middletown, CT: Criminal Justice Institute, 2000) 120.

85. Doris Layton MacKenzie, "NIJ Sponsored Studies Ask: Does Shock Incarceration Work?" *Corrections Compendium* 18 (1993): 5–12.

86. Dennis E. Mack, "High Impact Incarceration Program: Rikers Boot Camp." *American Jails* 6 (1992): 63–65.

87. Doris Layton MacKenzie, Robert Brame, David McDowall, and Claire Souryal. "Boot Camp Prisons and Recidivism in Eight States," *Criminology* 33 (1995): 327–357.

88. Dale G. Parent, "Boot Camps and Prison Crowding," *Correctional Boot Camps: A Tough Intermediate Sanction,* eds. Doris L. MacKenzie and Eugene E. Hebert (Washington, DC: U.S. Department of Justice, 1996) 263.

89. Doris Layton MacKenzie and James W. Shaw, "Inmate Adjustment and Change during Shock Incarceration: The Impact of Correctional Boot Camp Programs." *Justice Quarterly* 7 (1990): 125–150.

90. Doris Layton MacKenzie and Claire Souryal "Inmates' Attitude Change during Incarceration: A Comparison of Boot Camp with Traditional Prison," *Justice Quarterly* 12 (1995): 325–354.

91. S. Christopher Baird, Richard Heinz, and Brian Bemus, "The Wisconsin Case Classification/Staff Development," *Classification: American Correctional Association Monograph* (College Park, MD: American Correctional Association, 1982) 36.

92. Patricia M. Harris, Raymond Gingerich, and Tiffany A. Whittaker "The 'Effectiveness' of Differential Supervision," Annual Meetings of the American Society of Criminology, San Francisco, CA (November 14–18, 2000).

93. Quoted in Joan M. Petersilia, *The Influence of Criminal Justice Research* (Santa Monica, CA: The Rand Corporation, 1987) 75.

94. Harris et al.

95. For a full discussion of this issue, see John Rosecrance, "Probation Supervision: Mission Impossible," *Federal Probation* 50 (March, 1986): 25–31.

96. Anthony Walsh, *Understanding, Assessing and Counseling the Criminal Justice Client* (Monterey, CA: Brooks/Cole, 1988) 75–76.

97. Kenneth Lerner, Gary Arling, and S. Christopher Baird, "Client Management Classification Strategies for Case Supervision," *Crime and Delinquency* 32 (1986): 254–271.

98. Harris et al.

99. Lerner, Arling, and Baird; M. Eisenberg and G. Markley "Something Works in Community Supervision," *Federal Probation* 51 (1987): 28–32; R. F. McManus, D. I. Stagg, and R. C. McDuffie, "CMC as an Effective Supervision Tool: The South Carolina Perspective," *Perspectives* (1988): 30–34; K. Leininger, "Effectiveness of Client Management Classification." Florida Department of Corrections. Unpublished manuscript (1998).

100. Harris 22.

101. Todd Clear and Kenneth Gallagher, "Probation and Parole Supervision: A Review of Current Classification Practices," *Crime and Delinquency* 31 (1985): 423–444.

102. Enos et al.

103. Tonry, "Evaluating Intermediate Sanction Programs" 79–96; Belinda R. McCarthy, Bernard J. McCarthy, Jr., and Mathew C. Leone, *Community-Based Corrections* (Belmont, CA: Wadsworth, 2001).

104. Dale G. Parent, Jim Byrne, Vered Tsarfaty, Laura Valade, and Julie Esselman, *Day Reporting Centers* (Washington, DC: National Institute of Justice 1995).

105. Jack McDevitt and Robyn Miliano, "Day Reporting Centers: An Innovative Concept in Intermediate Sanctions," in *Smart Sentencing: The Emergence of Intermediate Sanctions*, eds. James M. Byrne, Arthur J. Lurigio, and Joan Petersilia (Newbury Park, CA: Sage 1992) 152–165.

106. Tonry, "Evaluating Intermediate Sanction Programs."

107. McDevitt and Miliano; and Parent et al.

108. Parent et al.

109. Parent et al.

110. Parent et al.

111. Daniel W. Van Ness, *Restorative Justice around the World*, 2000, Vienna, Austria: United Nations Crime Congress: Ancillary Meeting. Retrieved February 10, 2004, from www.acpf.org/WC8th/WC8th/RestractiveJusticeAroundTheWorld.html

112. David C. Anderson, *Sensible Justice: Alternatives to Prison* (New York: New Press, 1998) 33–34.

113. McCarthy et al. 228.

114. Van Ness 5.

115. Catharine M. Goodwin, "Looking at the Law," *Federal Probation* 62, 2 (1998): 95.

116. Goodwin 95.

117. Morna Murray, "Restitution" Chapter 5, Section 2 in *1999 National Victim Assistance Academy,* eds. Grace Coleman, Mario Gaboury, Morna Murray, and Anne Seymour, 1999, Washington, DC: Office of Victims of Crime. Retrieved February, 14, 2002, from www.ojp.usdoj.gov/ovc/assist/nvaa99/chap5–2.htm

118. Kenneth Jensen and Stephen Gibbons, "Shame and Religion as Factors in the Rehabilitation of Serious Offenders," *Religion, the Community, and the Rehabilitation of Criminal Offenders,* eds. Thomas P. O'Connor and Nathaniel J. Pallone (Binghamton, NY: Haworth Press, 2002).

119. Paul F. Cromwell, Rolando V. del Carmen, and Leanne F. Alarid, *Community-Based Corrections,* 5th ed. (Belmont, CA: Wadsworth, 2002) 291.

120. Todd R. Clear and Harry R. Dammer, *The Offender in the Community,* 2nd ed. (Belmont, CA: Wadsworth, 2003) 215.

121. Van Ness 5.

122. T. Marshall, *Restorative Justice: An Overview* (St. Paul, MN: Center for Restorative Justice and Mediation, 1998).

123. John R. Gehm, "Victim–Offender Mediation Programs: An Exploration of Practice and Theoretical Frameworks," *Western Criminology Review* 1 (1998). Retrieved February 6, 2002, from http://wcr.sonoma.edu/v1n1/gehm.html

124. Stephen Schafer, "The Correctional Rejuvenation of Restitution to the Victim in Crime," in *Interdisciplinary Problems in Criminology,* eds. Walter C. Reckless and C. L. Newman (Columbus: Ohio State University, 1965) 159–168.

125. Stephen Schafer, "Restitution to Victims of Crime—An Old Correctional Aim Modernized," *Minnesota Law Review* 50 (1970): 243–265.

126. Gehm; Howard Zehr, *Changing Lenses* (Scottdale, PA: Herald Press, 1995).

127. Gordon Bazemore and Mark Umbreit, *A Comparison of Four Restorative Conferencing Models* (Washington, DC: Office of Juvenile Justice and Delinquency Prevention 2001).

128. American Probation and Parole Association, "Community Justice," 2002, Lexington, KY: American Probation and Parole Association. Retrieved July 3, 2002, from www.appa-net.org/about%20appa/communityjustice_1.htm

129. Anne Seymour, "Restorative Justice/Community Justice," Chapter 4 in *1999 National Victim Assistance Academy,* eds. Grace Coleman, Mario Gaboury, Morna Murray, and Anne Seymour, 1999, Washington, DC: Office of Victims of Crime. Retrieved February 6, 2002, from www.ojp.usdoj.gov/ovc/assist/nvaa99/chap4.htm

130. Howard Zehr and H. Mika, *Fundamental Concepts of Restorative Justice* (Harrisonburg, VA: Mennonite Central Committee 1997) cited in Seymour.

131. Seymour.

132. Kay Pranis, "The Minnesota Restorative Justice Initiative: A Model Experience," *The Crime Victims Report,* (May/June, 1997). Retrieved June 25, 2002, from www.ojp.usdoj.gov/nij/rest-just/ch1/mnrjmodel.html

133. Pranis.

134. Dennis Maloney, "Justice and the Community," *Oregon's Future* 1 (1998): 17.

135. Maloney 18.

136. Maloney.

137. Mark S. Umbreit, "The Impact of Restorative Justice: What We Are Learning from Research," Center for Restorative Justice and Peacemaking, University of Minnesota, St. Paul, MN. Unpublished fact sheet, 2000.

138. Umbreit.

139. Richard McCleary, Andrew Gordon, David McDowall, and Michael Maltz, "How a Regression Artifact Can Make Any Delinquency Intervention Program Look Effective," *Evaluation Studies Review Annual Vol. 4,* ed. Lynn Sechrest (Beverly Hills, CA: Sage, 1981).

140. Quoted in Stephen Gettinger, "Intensive Supervision: Can It Rehabilitate Probation," in *Annual Editions: Criminal Justice* (Guilford, CT: Dushkin Publishing, 1985) 218.

141. Petersilia, *Expanding Options* 87.

142. Clear and O'Leary 8.

143. Petersilia, *Expanding Options* 94–95.

144. Petersilia, *Expanding Options* 95.

11

Pretrial Release, Diversion, Special Programs, and Halfway Houses

The Variety of Community Corrections

Besides probation and parole, community corrections include the variety of non-institutional correctional programs for arrestees, defendants, or offenders. These programs include pretrial release services; diversion programs; programs for offenders with special needs, such as sex offenders, the mentally ill, and those who abuse drugs or alcohol; and halfway houses. Although there is a great deal of overlap between and among these programs and types of offenders—for example diversion programs for drug abusers, or the developmentally delayed who are convicted of a sex offense—we discuss them as separate entities in this chapter, making note when appropriate of the possibility of co-occurrence. This chapter, therefore, reviews important aspects of each of these parts of community corrections, indicating their place within community corrections and the larger criminal justice system. We begin with pretrial release.

Pretrial Release

Pretrial release, or pretrial services, if fully implemented, can perform very important and vital functions in the early stages of processing cases in the criminal justice system. Deciding whether an arrestee should be held in jail or released back into the community and, if released, released under what conditions, can not only save money for unnecessary jail costs but it can also keep defendants free and able to participate in their community and family lives and make the criminal justice system more just. There are two important functions of pretrial release programs.

They are (1) to gather and present information about recent arrestees and about release options available to judicial officers that will then be used to determine whether a person should be released and, if so, under what conditions; and (2) to supervise those released from custody during the period before trial, ensuring they comply with their release conditions and that they appear in court when required.[1]

When both of these functions are achieved, jurisdictions can minimize uncalled for pretrial detention, decrease jail crowding, improve public safety, and make it more likely that released defendants appear in court. Pretrial release programs can also make the justice system more fair and equitable by reducing discrimination based on wealth and socioeconomic status, focusing instead on the risk of flight or danger to the community. Pretrial release has, therefore, become a crucial component of the criminal justice system, although it is a component that, in its latest form, has only been in existence since the 1960s.

Historical Background

Pretrial release services stem from practices that are hundreds of years old, going back to medieval England where those accused of crimes were held in local jails until a traveling magistrate arrived in their communities. This would often take months, leaving the detainees to spend their time in unsanitary dungeons.[2] The local sheriffs were not happy about keeping these defendants in their custody, so they frequently turned them over to a friend, relative, or employer, who would be legally liable for making sure the defendant appeared in court. If the defendant failed to appear in court, the third party could be imprisoned or made to pay a fine to the sheriff.

This practice of releasing the defendant before trial with a personal or financial guarantee became known as **bail.** As is often true today, the practice of bail was misused from the beginning, with many sheriffs releasing all those who could make bail and jailing the rest. Then, in 1275 this misuse was addressed by establishing certain offenses as bailable and others as not bailable.[3] After a time, the authority to set bail was taken away from sheriffs and placed with magistrates. In 1689 the English Bill of Rights prohibited the setting of excessive bail, a provision included in the U.S. Constitution's Eighth Amendment.

As the population in the United States grew and became more diverse, the posting of bond became more commercialized. Bail bondsmen were willing to assume the financial responsibility for defendants in return for a percentage of the bail (paid by the defendant). This practice obviously weakened, and in some cases eliminated, the importance of personal ties to the community. The practice of commercial bonding also had its problems. Numerous studies during the 1920s documented several of these problems:

1. Persons without money had virtually no chance to gain pretrial release and were often held in unsafe jails for long periods of time.

2. There were no standards for setting bail and discrimination was common.
3. Usually less than 5 percent of the defendants who were released failed to appear for court appearances.
4. Those detained before trial were more likely to be indicted, convicted, and receive prison sentences than those released before trial. Yet, one-third of the defendants detained before trial were never convicted.
5. Bail bondsmen were often problematic, discriminating against some clients and sometimes posting bond without the funds to cover it.[4]

These findings were confirmed over the years, but it was not until the 1960s that something was done to improve the system.

Manhattan Bail Project

In 1960, retired engineer and philanthropist **Louis Schweitzer** and **Herb Sturz,** a magazine editor, founded the Vera Foundation after recognizing that the system of bailing clients before trial was unjust: an accused was able to gain release only if she or he had enough money to post bail. The Vera Foundation was founded with the goal of making the system more equitable. Schweitzer and Sturz, working with a small staff and with leaders of New York's criminal justice system, investigated the problem, came up with a solution, and rigorously tested it. The experiment was called the **Manhattan Bail Project,** and it demonstrated that those too poor to make bail but with housing arrangements, family ties, and employment could safely be released before trial.[5] The legislation that followed, including the Federal Bail Reform Act of 1966, allowed judges to consider these types of factors, rather than only the seriousness of the charge, when setting conditions of release and to use conditions other than a money bond to allow an accused to be released before trial.

Because of the success of the Manhattan Bail Project, the number of pretrial release programs grew rapidly. Throughout the 1960s and 1970s more than 200 pretrial release programs were developed. With jail crowding increasing as a problem in the 1980s, a "second generation" of pretrial services came into existence, focusing on trying to identify defendants unable to make bail but who would be acceptable risks for release either on their own recognizance or under supervision. These new programs were not so much rooted in concerns about equal justice as they were with keeping jail populations in check.[6] Today there are more than 300 programs in rural, suburban, and urban jurisdictions, with a growing number of them administered by probation departments. According to a survey conducted by the National Pretrial Services Resource Center in 2001, of the pretrial programs started in the 1980s, 27 percent were in probation departments, 36 percent in courts, and 16 percent were programs located in jails. However, 34 percent of programs started since 1990 are in probation departments, 24 percent are in courts, and 27 percent are in jails.[7]

Program Operations

The foundation of pretrial services programs is providing valid and reliable information to the courts about newly arrested defendants and available supervisory options. At minimum, pretrial program agents should provide the courts with the following:

- The identity of the defendant, including date of birth and gender;
- The defendant's community ties, including residence, employment, and family status;
- The defendant's physical and mental health, including substance use or abuse;
- The defendant's criminal record, including juvenile arrests and adjudications; and
- The defendant's record of compliance with earlier release conditions, including record of appearing for court on time.[8]

The defendants are the most important source of information and should be interviewed as soon as possible after arrest. Other sources of information include the pretrial program's own records, other criminal justice agency records, motor vehicle departments, the defendant's family members, and the defendant's employer. All information should be verified or, if not, be labeled as unverified in the report to the court.[9] An example of an interview form used in Kentucky can be seen in Figure 11.1.

Pretrial program agents generally use the information they collect to make a recommendation or identify options to a court official who then makes the "release or detention" decision. This process of risk assessment is obviously a crucial step in the decision-making process and, if the defendant is released, in supervising him or her to ensure appearance in court. When a defendant does miss a court date, programs attempt to contact him or her immediately to resolve the problem.

Pretrial service agents can do some things to help ensure compliance with the conditions of release and make sure the defendant appears in court, thereby contributing to public safety. For example, agents can make sure released defendants comply with the conditions of release, including curfews, orders restraining defendants from contacting possible victims or witnesses, home confinement (including the use of electronic monitors), and drug and alcohol testing. Program staff can also provide direct "intensive" supervision of released defendants and can collaborate with police, day reporting centers, and other agencies and community organizations to monitor compliance.[10]

Although there are more than 300 pretrial service agencies in jurisdictions throughout the United States, many courts continue to make release decisions without access to the kinds of information pretrial programs usually provide. Also, even those jurisdictions with well-established pretrial programs have challenges to be dealt with in the near future. Much remains to be done for pretrial

FIGURE 11.1 *Kentucky Defendant Interview Form*

```
AOC-PT-21
Rev. 9-94    AKA: _____    Social Security Number: _____

NAME: _____ DOB. ___/___/___ Age: ___ Sex ___ Race: ___
         Last        First      Middle/Maiden

         DATE OF ARREST: _____ CHARGE: _____
         COURT: _____  _____
VERIFIED COURT DATE: _____    _____
Yes  No
```

		PRESENT ADDRESS: _____

PRESENT ADDRESS: _____
                  Street/Apt. No.   City   State   Zip Code

LENGTH OF RESIDENCE: Present Yrs. ___ Mos. ___ Area: Yrs. ___ Mos. ___ Phone: ( ) _____
                     □ Own □ Rent □ Other _____

ALTERNATE/PRIOR
RESIDENCE: _____
            Street/Apt. No.   City   State   Zip Code
With Whom: _____ Phone: ( ) _____ Lgth. Of Res.: Yrs. ___ Mos. ___

LIVES WITH: □ Alone □ Spouse □ Parents □ Grandparents □ Children □ Brother/Sister □ Other Relatives □ Other ____
MARITAL STATUS: □ Single □ Married □ Divorced □ Widowed □ Common Law □ Separated No. of Children: ____
SPOUSE'S   SPOUSE'S SOURCE
NAME: _____   OF INCOME: _____
FAMILY IN AREA Name: _____   Relationship: _____
                Address: _____ Phone: ( ) _____

□ EMPLOYED □ UNEMPLOYED   How Long Yrs. _____ Mos. _____
□ Full-time □ Part-time □ Seasonal □ Welfare □ Unemployment □ Disability □ Retirement □ Other ____
EMPLOYER: _____   Job Position: _____
EMPLOYER'S ADDRESS: _____
                    Street   City   State   Zip Code
         Phone: ( ) _____ Can Contact: □ Yes □ No Who _____
PRIOR/OTHER SOURCE
OF INCOME   Source: _____   Job Position: _____
            Address: _____
            Phone: ( ) _____ Length of Employment _____
ATTENDS SCHOOL □ Yes □ No   School: _____
                                   Address: _____
GED or High School Degree: □ Yes □ No   Can Contact □ Yes □ No Phone: ( ) _____

PRIOR ARREST: □ Yes □ None If yes, Where _____
PENDING CHARGES □ Yes □ No How Released: _____ Next Court Date: _____
        Where: _____   Charges: _____
ON PROBATION/PAROLE: □ Yes □ No   Probation/Parole Officer's Name: _____
Charges: _____   Address: _____
                                   Phone ( ) _____
DRIVER'S LICENSE NUMBER: _____ □ Kentucky □ None □ Other _____
```

| IN COURT | Name | Address | Relationship | Phone |
|---|---|---|---|---|
| | 1. | | | |
| | 2. | | | |
| | 3. | | | |
| | 4. | | | |

```
AOI: Yes □  No □                    Case Number: _____

Court Dates: 2. _____ 3. _____ 4. _____ 5. _____ 6. _____

Are the current charges domestic related?  Yes □  No □    Addendum  Yes □  No □
```

ELIGIBLE INELIGIBLE	COURTS INITIAL DECISION/ JUDGE Date/Time	24 Hour Review: Yes No Courts Decision	HOW RELEASED:
_____ Points			

(continued)
```

FIGURE 11.1   *Continued*

A.2 Warning and Points Scoring Form

This interview form will used by the Judge or Trial Commissioner to set bail. It will also be used for personal identification, future bond reviews, service of warrants, and sentencing if found guilty. The judge may allow your attorney or probation/parole officer to review the information. Except for these situations, any information you provide will be confidential and not released without your written consent or court order. You do not have to say anything, and can stop answering questions at any time. Signing this form means you want to be interviewed.

DECLINED INTERVIEW OR REFUSED TO SIGN AFTER BEING WARNED: _____

                                                                S/Defendant

Witnessed By: _____   Witnessed By: _____
Date and Time: _____   Interviewer: _____
                                             Date and Time: _____

*Circle only one number for each
category of criteria except Miscellaneous
and Previous Criminal Record*

RESIDENCE
+5   Has been a resident of the Commonwealth for more than one year.
+3   Has been a resident of the Commonwealth for less than one year but more than three months.

PERSONAL TIES
+4   Lives with spouse, grandparents, children, parents, and/or guardian.
+3   Lives with other relatives.
+2   Lives with non-related roommates.

ECONOMIC TIES (Double length of employment of part-time)
+5   Has held present job for more than one year OR is a full-time student.
+4   Has held present job for less than one year but more than three months.
+3   Is dependent on spouse, parents, other relatives, or legal guardian, unemployment, disability, retirement, or welfare compensation.
+2   Has held present job for less than three months.

MISCELLANEOUS
+3   Owns property in the Commonwealth.
+1   Has a telephone.
+1   Expects someone at arraignment.

PREVIOUS CRIMINAL RECORD (+)
+3   No convictions on record (excluding traffic violations) in last two years.

(A) _____TOTAL POSITIVE POINTS

PREVIOUS CRIMINAL RECORD (-) (FTA must be verified by court records).
-3   AWOL on record (current military personnel only).
-5   Probated or paroled after felony conviction in last two years.
-5   FTA on traffic citation in last two years.
-10   FTA on misdemeanor charge in last five years.
-15   FTA on felony charge at any time.
-15   Violation Conditional Release while case is pending and active.

(B) _____ TOTAL NEGATIVE POINTS
(C) _____ TOTAL ADDENDUM POINTS

_____ TOTAL PRETRIAL RELEASE POINTS
("A" minus "B" minus "C")

COMMENTS:

RECORD: (Please check the appropriate box)

	CLEAR	ATTACHED
COURTNET		
DOT		
NCIC		
KSP Manual File		
LINK-DV		
OTHER		

services programs in order for them to fully contribute to the criminal justice system, such as

- Bringing pretrial services to jurisdictions currently without them;
- Including juveniles charged as adults in pretrial services;
- Using new technology to improve the quality and effectiveness of pretrial services;
- Developing systems that delegate release authority and improve relationships between releasing authorities and pretrial services; and
- Researching the effectiveness of pretrial services and educating and training pretrial officers at the national, state, and local levels.[11]

Pretrial release programs provide a vital service to the criminal justice system and to the communities in which they operate. By providing courts with valid and reliable information on which to base release decisions, pretrial services help alleviate jail crowding; help improve the quality of justice in communities; make the streets safer; and keep defendants who belong in the community, in the community. In this sense, pretrial services are a type of diversion program, moving qualified defendants out of the criminal justice system before they become too immersed in it. We now move to other, specific forms of diversion programs.

Diversion Programs

Discretion is an important part of all criminal justice decision making. Victims or bystanders may decide to report an offense or not; police may decide to make an arrest, or not; they might ignore a minor offense completely; they might send an alleged offender home or refer him or her to a human service agency; they might send the person off with a warning. A prosecutor may seek formal charges against a defendant, seek civil action against him or her, arrange for an informal remedy such as paying restitution, refer him or her to a treatment program in return for deferring prosecution, or drop the charges completely.

Many of these examples could be considered diversion, which occurs whenever a criminal justice agent uses **discretion** to cease formal criminal justice processing, thereby *diverting* defendants out of the criminal justice system. In many cases, alternative means of treating offenders are also employed. Thus, the term **diversion** often refers to *formal* or *organized* efforts to process offenders *out* of the traditional criminal justice system. These programs almost always occur in the community and can occur anytime after a crime is discovered and before adjudication. The important point is that formal processing of the individual stops—before arrest, before charges are filed, or before trial.[12]

Diversion may be used by police, by prosecutors, or by judges. It may or may not involve agencies other than those in the criminal justice system. Furthermore, there are many different purposes for diversion.[13] These include a decision to mitigate the harshness of some penalties, such as those for minor drug possession; diversion may also be used for some minor, perhaps first-time, offenders to help them avoid the stigma of a criminal or delinquent label while still holding the possibility of conviction and jail over their heads; diversion may also be a means to get some types of defendants into treatment—alcoholics, drug users, the mentally ill, or minor offenders with anger management problems; for defendants who otherwise might not be prosecuted at all (because of heavy caseloads, for example), diversion may also be considered an intermediate sanction, falling in between total dismissal of all charges and conviction and sentencing.

Clearly, diversion involves some intervention into the life of the accused, although usually not as dramatic as a formal criminal justice response. These interventions range from warnings and reprimands to problem-solving mechanisms, such as mediation or arbitration, to supervision by a professional either within or outside the criminal justice system and often involving participation in some sort of therapy, treatment, or educational program.[14] Diversion programs are also used for both adults and juveniles, and are almost exclusively used for minor, often misdemeanant, offenders. In many states diversion is limited to statutorily specified offenses, with specific conditions for completion. This is often particularly true for adults who qualify for diversion. For example, many states have passed laws mandating drug treatment diversion for nonviolent drug offenders, with California's Proposition 36 receiving the most attention.[15] In other states adult diversion may be limited to those convicted of possession of small quantities of drugs, driving under the influence of intoxicants, and domestic violence, with appropriate treatment mandated following acceptance in the program. Defendants arrested for one of these offenses are evaluated for inclusion in a diversion program and, if accepted, criminal proceedings are suspended. The divertee, usually under the supervision of a case manager or probation officer, then must begin a treatment program, for example substance abuse or anger management treatment. On successful completion of the program, the case against the defendant is dismissed and there will be no record of conviction. Oftentimes, if the person fails to complete the treatment program, formal criminal justice processing will resume. Descriptions of two contemporary diversion programs follow.

Program Operations

Merrimack County, New Hampshire, Adult Diversion Program.[16]   Begun in 1992, the Merrimack County Adult Diversion Program was first part of the county attorney's office but was later moved to the Department of Corrections (DOC). Staffing for the program includes a director, programs coordinator, receptionist, a DOC employee serving as the program's substance abuse counselor, and a contracted social worker who assesses potential diversion clients. The program also has an advisory board that helps establish policy and reviews client participation.

Program participants must be at least seventeen years old, charged with nonviolent offenses, with no history of violent criminal behavior, and be willing to participate in the program. Participants do not have to plead guilty to participate in the program. Program placement occurs in three steps:

1. The agency making the arrest decides whether an arrestee is eligible, using a Diversion Offender Profile. Those identified as eligible are referred to the Merrimack County attorney.
2. The county attorney discusses the referral with the arresting agency to decide if it is a strong case and whether diversion is appropriate. If charges are filed and diversion seems to fit, charging is completed, the case is placed on a suspended calendar, and the defendant is referred to the diversion program for a final assessment.
3. The final assessment is conducted, including an interview with the defendant, an evaluation for substance abuse, and a social work evaluation.

The Diversion Offender Profile was developed by Merrimack County criminal justice officials. The profile eliminates for consideration in the diversion program people with any of the following characteristics:

- Those charged with violent, sex-related, or drug-trafficking offenses;
- Those with previous convictions resulting in incarceration for more than seven days;
- Those who have already participated in diversion;
- Those charged with crimes that represent major threats to society or require general deterrents;
- Those charged with crimes whose convictions "would justify" a prison sentence; and
- Those with prior person, property, or drug-related convictions.

It takes an average of 138 days to complete the diversion program assessment. The substance abuse assessment includes a drug abuse test and an alcohol screening test. The results of these tests determine placement in one of three supervision levels:

- Level 1 is for those assessed as not having substance abuse related disorders. Clients falling into this level of supervision must attend educational and informational workshops on substance abuse.
- Level 2 is for those assessed as having substance abuse problems. These clients also attend the substance abuse workshops but in addition are required to attend ninety-minute group sessions. These clients also must submit to regular substance abuse testing.
- Level 3 is for those assessed as requiring inpatient treatment. Once they successfully complete their treatment program, these clients move to Level 2.

The social work assessment tests a defendant's mental, emotional, and behavioral conditions. This assessment is conducted by a licensed social worker and focuses on a defendant's self-perception, problems contributing to negative behavior, and past and present mental and emotional problems and treatment.

The final decision to accept or reject a defendant is made by the program director and program coordinator. If accepted into the program, the defendant and his or her attorney then meet with the program director or designated staff member to review the program. A written diversion contract is presented to the defendant, outlining the defendant's responsibilities and conditions of supervision. After reviewing the contract, it is signed by the program director, the defendant, his or her counsel, and the county attorney. There are four mandatory conditions of supervision:

- Six hundred hours of community service.
- A tour of the New Hampshire State Prison for Men in Concord.
- Restitution payments if ordered by the county attorney.
- Ten hours of substance abuse classes to be completed within six months of program acceptance.

There are also specific diversion program conditions under the life skills component, which consist of educational classes and two-hour workshops. Clients must complete a total of thirty hours of these classes and workshops. The specific content of these classes and workshops is determined in consultation with the program coordinator and the client. Possible topics include conflict resolution, stress management, domestic violence, job search skills, parenting skills, wellness, communication skills, and AIDS/sexually transmitted diseases.

A quasi-experimental evaluation of the Merrimack County Adult Diversion Program conducted by the Pretrial Services Resource Center (PSRC) in Washington, DC, found "a marked difference in recidivism rates between persons successfully completing diversion and other similar defendants not participating in or having been terminated from diversion."[17] Although the findings were "tempered by the limitations of the research design and the data sample" the PSRC felt confident enough in their results to make the following conclusions about diversion in Merrimack County:

- A well-defined subgroup exists in Merrimack County that is suitable for diversion placement.
- The diversion program has established itself as an effective and needed component in the county's continuum of sanctions to address and deter criminal behavior.
- The diversion program operates in compliance with nationally recognized diversion standards.
- The diversion program is in a good position to apply services that may help reduce future recidivism.[18]

Polk County, Oregon, Victim Offender Reconciliation Program for Juveniles.[19]
Polk County, Oregon's, Victim Offender Reconciliation Program (VORP) is a
private, nonprofit organization offering a range of mediation services, including
victim offender mediation for adults and juveniles, parent teen mediation, neighbor-
to-neighbor mediation, school mediation, and landlord/tenant mediation. Polk
County VORP is one of the oldest such programs in Oregon, first organized in
1984. The mission of Polk County VORP ". . . is to provide an opportunity for victims and offenders, family members, and neighbors to be reconciled through
peaceful dialogue and negotiated settlements."[20] A full-time director and two
part-time staff run the VORP office. At least twenty volunteers, trained in basic
mediation and VORP, also serve the center. Volunteers are assigned cases, carry
out case development, conduct premeetings with the offender and the victim,
schedule the mediation, and serve as mediators. Staff also carry a VORP mediation caseload and engage in community education, training, public relations, and
other types of mediation.

All juvenile VORP cases are referred to the program via the juvenile justice
system. Most of the referrals are from the Polk County Juvenile Department although local police departments and an alternative community diversion program called Sanction Courts occasionally refer cases. Most cases are referred to
VORP before the case is adjudicated and the youth are kept on informal supervision by the Juvenile Department until the final VORP report is received. A few
adjudicated cases are referred by a judge, depending on victim willingness,
mostly to determine restitution. Youth referred to the program must admit responsibility for the offense, but otherwise criteria for referral are minimal—Polk
County VORP will look at any problem, dispute, or situation; determine whether
it is appropriate for mediation; and, if so, work cooperatively to achieve a mediated solution.

In 1999, 75.1 percent of the referrals were for misdemeanors and 24.9 percent
for felonies. Referrals were for such offenses as assault, burglary, criminal mischief, curfew violation, harassment, menacing, reckless endangering, theft, tres-
passing, unauthorized use of a motor vehicle, and unauthorized use of a weapon.
Sixty-seven percent of the referrals were for property offenses, 28 percent were for
offenses against persons, and the rest were for "other" offenses.

After a case has been referred to VORP by the Juvenile Department, the department sends a letter to both the offender's family and the victim notifying them
of the referral. VORP staff then assigns the case to a mediator who then tries to contact both parties within one week of referral. The practice is to meet face to face with
the offender and his or her family first. After the mediation process is explained,
the youth is asked to share his or her account of the incident and suggest possible
solutions. The parents are then asked for their input. If, after this meeting, the youth
agrees to mediation and the mediator deems it appropriate, a meeting is then
scheduled with the victim. This meeting is very similar to the first, with mediation
being explained and the victim relating his or her side of the story, including an accounting of losses incurred. This meeting is also important to determine what the

victim needs to feel safe when meeting with the offender who harmed her or him. A time and date for mediation is then agreed on.

The mediators generally convene the sessions around a table. Sitting around the table are the offender and a parent or parents, the victim, the victim's parents if the victim is also a juvenile, and the mediator. Lawyers are excluded from these meetings. Cases involving more than one offender or several victims may be handled in one large session, often involving comediators.

Introductions are made, a confidentiality agreement, which must be signed, is reviewed, as is the process. The offender is usually invited to first give an account of the incident, and then the victim shares his or her story and asks questions. The mediator generally remains quiet at this stage, allowing the conversation to flow naturally between the two parties.

Mediators make it clear, however, that the session is not for "fact finding." What the offender can learn from the process—what choices were available, what the consequences of the actions were, and what can be done in the future—are more important than the "facts." Once this conversation seems to have run its course, the mediator moves the session to how to make things right. There are no set rules or agendas for this phase of the process. Both victim and offender may suggest possible solutions and means for repairing the harm that has occurred. Although monetary restitution is frequently an outcome, it is not usually the goal. Rather, the contract that comes from the session often deals more with the youth's future. For example, if monetary restitution is a part of the solution, the group will explore ways the youth may earn the money to pay it, including community service programs run by the county allowing the youth to receive money that can be sent directly to the victim. The Juvenile Department can arrange the actual community service but it is often created by the participants in the mediation session.

Other parts of the contract may include completing an education or training program, providing some specific services to the victim, or staying in touch with the victim via correspondence concerning the progress of the youth's life. The mediator writes down the components of the agreement or contract and both parties sign it. Four copies of the contract are made: one for the victim, one for the offender, one for the VORP office, and one for the Juvenile Department.

The VORP staff monitors compliance with each contract and collects restitution to pay to victims. The responsibility for compliance is left with the youth; however, if a payment is late, staff will call the youth to find out the reason and may contact the victim to negotiate adjusted payments if there are extenuating circumstances. One hundred and nine cases were mediated in 2000, and 108 of these were resolved successfully. That is 99.1 percent of all mediations, 44.8 percent of referrals. One case was mediated and not resolved. In many of the resolved cases, no contract was necessary because the victim was satisfied with an apology. Ninety-seven percent of the contracts that were negotiated were successfully completed. Polk County VORP offenders paid $1,266.93 in restitution in 1999 and performed sixty-two hours of community service negotiated in mediation. This may not seem like a lot but in a rural county with a population of 60,000, 109 juvenile cases resolved outside of the court can make a big difference.

After the mediation, participants made positive statements concerning the process. For example, one offender parent said, "The preparation was splendid. They ran us through how it was gonna go. Did a good job asking probing questions." An offender stated, "Victims have a right to see who was in their stuff," whereas a victim stated, "VORP is really good for the small things. It alleviates court cost and saves taxpayers money." Another victim, who represented a store, stated, "Over the fifteen years I've been involved, that was the only way we were ever getting any money back. Circuit court might make them pay, city court doesn't. It's more cost effective for us to seek the money through mediation than through a civil process."

Even though programs such as those described are very successful, that does not mean that diversion programs are without problems or critics. Some of these criticisms are discussed next.

Criticisms of Diversion

Probably the most frequently heard criticism of diversion programs is that they widen the net of criminal and juvenile justice. That is, offenders who otherwise would have their charges dismissed, or even be outright ignored by the juvenile or criminal justice system, are being "captured" in the net of diversion programs, simply because the programs are available. In this sense, formal diversion programs are not really diverting offenders out of the system because the programs are a part of the bigger system of justice. And not only are diversion programs keeping people in the system but also they often do so in the absence of due process, requiring participants to admit guilt before trial in order to participate in the program (see the preceding example on Polk County VORP).

A second criticism is that, in this era of being "tough on crime," many citizens are reluctant to accept diversion programs because they are too "soft"; that is, they do not punish offenders enough or hold them accountable for their actions. Mothers against Drunk Driving, for example, has a goal of enacting tougher, more comprehensive sanctions against high-risk drivers,[21] and most diversion programs would not fit into that category.

Diversion programs also may detract from traditional probation, parole, and community corrections programming. By funneling money to diversion programs, funds for more traditional programs may not be available and those in need of traditional probation and parole supervision may not receive it, or they may receive only a watered-down version of it. The other side of this coin is that budget cuts may reduce the effectiveness of diversion programs by either removing staff altogether or reassigning them to the formal justice system. Some cases may not be considered for placement in diversion programs at all, and, therefore, they may be dismissed or closed with no sanction or consequence.

Regardless of these criticisms, informal and formal diversion programs are here to stay. They are a useful response to a variety of offenses and types of offenders. As noted previously, they are also often used for defendants with special needs, such as those with substance abuse, mental illness, or developmental disabilities. These are the clients with special needs to whom we now turn, as well as another type of client who usually is not considered eligible for diversion but who nonetheless requires some special attention and often unique methods of supervision, the sex offender.

Offenders with Special Needs

Many clients in the criminal justice system have problems or issues that call for specific techniques, treatment, training, or empathy by the professionals working with the clients. These offenders with special needs include those with mental disorders, those who are developmentally delayed, sex offenders, and substance abusers. Although two or more of these issues may occur in the same person, we treat them individually here, recognizing that co-occurring problems are frequent and create additional problems for supervision.

Offenders Who Are Mentally Ill

The link between crime and mental illness is often taken for granted by citizens and criminal justice professionals. People who are mentally ill sometimes commit crimes; for many of them, the most appropriate response to such behavior is through the mental health professions and their affiliated agencies. However, with the closing of many mental health institutions throughout the United States, and the cutting of funds for community-based mental health programs, the criminal justice system has been taking on an increasing load regarding this population of offenders, not by choice, but because there is no other socially acceptable alternative available. In a special report published by the Bureau of Justice Statistics (BJS), Paula Ditton reported that an estimated 283,800 offenders who were mentally ill were in U.S. prisons and jails at midyear 1998. Furthermore, Ditton reported that BJS surveys revealed that 16 percent of state prison inmates, 7 percent of federal inmates, and 16 percent of those in local jails reported either a mental condition or an overnight stay in a mental hospital and that about 16 percent, or about 547,800 probationers, said they had had a mental condition or stayed overnight in a mental hospital at some point in their lives.[22]

Because most inmates eventually get out of prison or jail and move to a community setting with some sort of supervision, the total number of offenders being supervised in the community with mental health problems may approach 750,000 in the near future. According to the BJS study, offenders who are mentally ill have characteristics that are somewhat different than the "normal" offender population (see Figure 11.2). For example, they are more likely to be female, white, and middle aged. Nearly 22 percent of females on probation were identified as mentally ill; nearly 20 percent of white offenders on probation and more than 21 percent of probationers ages forty-five to fifty-four were identified as mentally ill.

FIGURE 11.2 *Inmates and Probationers Identified as Mentally Ill, by Gender, Race/Hispanic Origin, and Age*

Offender Characteristic	State Inmates	Federal Inmates	Jail Inmates	Probationers
Gender				
Male	15.8 %	7.0 %	15.6 %	14.7 %
Female	23.6	12.5	22.7	21.7
Race/Hispanic origin				
White[a]	22.6%	11.8 %	21.7%	19.6 %
Black[a]	13.5	5.6	13.7	10.4
Hispanic	11.0	4.1	11.1	9.0
Age				
24 or younger	14.4 %	6.6%	13.3 %	13.8 %
25–34	14.8	5.9	15.7	13.8
35–44	18.4	7.5	19.3	19.8
45–54	19.7	10.3	22.7	21.1
55 or older	15.6	8.9	20.4	16.0

[a]Excludes Hispanics.

Source: Paula M. Ditton, *Mental Health and Treatment of Inmates and Probationers* (Washington, DC: Bureau of Justice Statistics, July, 1999).

Offenders who are mentally ill were also more likely than other offenders to have committed violent crimes (see Figure 11.3). Twenty-eight percent of mentally ill probationers compared to 18 percent of other probationers had committed violent offenses. These offenders are also slightly more likely to be on probation for a property offense than other probationers (30.4 percent versus 28.5 percent), but they are less likely to be on probation for a drug or public-order offense than regular probationers (16.1 percent versus 20.7 percent and 24.7 percent versus 31.6 percent respectively).

Inmates who are mentally ill in state and federal prisons and those in jails also reported longer criminal histories, and among repeat offenders, the mentally ill were again more likely to report violent offenses (see Figure 11.4). Although probationers had shorter criminal histories, more than 29 percent of the mentally ill were violent recidivists, compared to 17 percent of other probationers (see Figure 11.5).

Homelessness and unemployment were also more prevalent among the mentally ill than other inmates and probationers. During the year before their arrest, 30 percent of inmates who are mentally ill were in jail, and 20 percent of those in state or federal prison reported having lived on the street or in a shelter. This can be compared to 17 percent of other inmates in jails, and about 9 percent of state

(text continues on page 373)

FIGURE 11.3 *Most Serious Current Offense of Inmates and Probationers, by Mental Health Status*

Most Serious Offense	State Prison		Federal Prison		Local Jail		Probation	
	Mentally Ill Inmates	Other Inmates	Mentally Ill Inmates	Other Inmates	Mentally Ill Inmates	Other Inmates	Mentally Ill Probationers	Other Probationers
All offenses	100.0%	100.0%	100.0%	100.0%	100.0%	100.0%	100.0%	100.0%
Violent offenses	52.9%	46.1%	33.1%	13.3%	29.9%	25.6%	28.4%	18.4%
Murder[a]	13.2	11.4	1.9	1.4	3.5	2.7	0.5	0.9
Sexual assault	12.4	7.9	1.9	0.7	5.2	2.8	6.8	4.1
Robbery	13.0	14.4	20.8	9.1	4.7	6.9	2.0	1.4
Assault	10.9	9.0	3.8	1.1	14.4	11.0	14.0	10.5
Property offenses	24.4%	21.5%	8.7%	6.7%	31.3%	26.0%	30.4%	28.5%
Burglary	12.1	10.5	1.0	0.3	9.1	7.4	6.4	4.3
Larceny/theft	4.6	4.1	1.3	0.4	8.4	7.9	5.3	8.8
Fraud	3.1	2.6	5.0	4.9	5.2	4.4	11.7	9.2
Drug offenses	12.8%	22.2%	40.4%	64.4%	15.2%	23.3%	16.1%	20.7%
Possession	5.7	9.4	3.9	11.9	7.3	12.3	7.2	11.0
Trafficking	6.6	12.2	35.7	46.6	7.0	9.6	6.7	9.2
Public-order offenses	9.9%	9.8%	17.0%	14.6%	23.2%	24.6%	24.7%	31.6%

Note: Detail does not sum to total because of excluded offense categories.

[a]Includes nonnegligent manslaughter.

Source: Paula M. Ditton, *Mental Health and Treatment of Inmates and Probationers* (Washington, DC: Bureau of Justice Statistics, July, 1999).

FIGURE 11.4 *Criminal History of Inmates, by Mental Health Status*

	State Prison		Federal Prison		Local Jail	
	Mentally Ill Inmates	*Other Inmates*	*Mentally Ill Inmates*	*Other Inmates*	*Mentally Ill Inmates*	*Other Inmates*
Criminal history						
None	18.8%	21.2%	24.3%	38.8%	21.0%	28.4%
Priors	81.2	78.8	75.7	61.2	79.0	71.6
Violent recidivists	53.4	44.9	43.7	21.6	46.0	31.6
Other recidivists	27.8	33.8	32.0	39.6	33.0	40.0
Number of prior probation/ incarceration sentences						
0	18.8%	21.2%	24.3%	38.8%	21.0%	28.4%
1	15.5	19.4	14.0	18.2	14.7	17.9
2	13.8	17.0	12.9	14.7	10.1	11.5
3 to 5	26.3	25.5	23.6	18.9	23.5	19.7
6 to 10	15.6	11.6	15.4	7.3	17.6	14.6
11 or more	10.0	5.3	9.7	2.2	13.2	7.8

Source: Paula M. Ditton, *Mental Health and Treatment of Inmates and Probationers* (Washington, DC: Bureau of Justice Statistics, July, 1999).

FIGURE 11.5 *Criminal History of Mentally Ill and Other Probationers*

	Probationers	
Criminal History	*Mentally Ill*	*Other*
None	43.4%	54.1%
Priors	56.6	45.9
Violent recidivists	29.1	17.1
Other recidivists	27.6	28.8

Source: Paula M. Ditton, *Mental Health and Treatment of Inmates and Probationers* (Washington, DC: Bureau of Justice Statistics, July, 1999).

prison inmates and 3 percent of federal inmates reporting a period of homelessness during the year prior to their arrest (see Figure 11.6).

Offenders who are mentally ill also often have a more difficult time relating to others and interacting socially. Their characteristic styles of interacting are such traits as "assertiveness, defiance, hostility, aggression, and adversarial or

FIGURE 11.6   *Homelessness, Employment, and Sources of Income of Inmates, by Mental Health Status*

	State Prison		Federal Prison		Local Jail	
	Mentally Ill Inmates	*Other Inmates*	*Mentally Ill Inmates*	*Other Inmates*	*Mentally Ill Inmates*	*Other Inmates*
Homeless						
In year before arrest	20.1%	8.8%	18.6%	3.2%	30.3%	17.3%
At time of arrest	3.9	1.2	3.9	0.3	6.9	2.9
Employed in month before arrest						
Yes	61.2%	69.6%	62.3%	72.5%	52.9%	66.6%
No	38.8	30.4	37.7	27.5	47.1	33.4
Sources of income[a]						
Wages	56.7%	65.6%	54.0%	66.4%	62.9%	77.1%
Family/friends	22.0	17.7	20.1	12.3	19.7	15.4
Illegal sources	23.4	27.0	22.5	28.8	19.4	14.4
Welfare	15.4	7.8	13.7	3.9	21.9	12.3
Pension[b]	17.3	4.1	16.5	3.7	18.4	4.9
Compensation payments	3.1	1.9	4.7	1.8	3.0	2.1

[a]Detail sums to more than 100% because offenders may have reported more than one source of income. For prisoners detail includes any income received in the month prior to arrest. For jail inmates, detail includes any income received in the year prior to arrest.

[b]Includes supplemental security income, social security, or other pension.

Source: Paula M. Ditton, *Mental Health and Treatment of Inmates and Probationers* (Washington, DC: Bureau of Justice Statistics, July, 1999).

antiauthority attitudes. . . ."[23] For some offenders, the symptoms of the illness itself will make the supervision difficult: hallucinations, delusions, paranoia, and depression all make difficult challenges for the PO–client relationship.

Supervision Issues.   With these facts in mind, there are many supervision issues relatively unique to clients who are mentally ill. First, they are more likely to be white, female, and more violent than the stereotypical probation and parole client, who is more often minority, male, and convicted of a property offense. The needs of clients who are mentally ill are often more extreme than those of the stereotypical client in the community. Housing, independent living, vocational needs, employment, communicating with their POs, treatment needs, and medical needs are some of the issues. Simply understanding court orders and making it to court-appointed meetings can be a challenge for the client who is acutely mentally ill. Moreover, probation and parole agents often receive little, if any, training in managing people with serious psychiatric disorders or in managing the special needs and requirements of clients who are mentally ill. Resources needed to meet the many needs of clients with mental illness are often lacking and difficult to access.[24] Comprehensive programs are needed that address the special needs of probationers and parolees who are mentally ill. These programs should include combinations of the following:

1. Mental health programs, either provided by a community mental health agency, the probation department, or jointly.
2. Cross-training of probation officers in mental health issues, and of mental health staff in corrections issues. In order to effectively supervise clients who are mentally ill in the community, probation staff and mental health providers need to understand what they each do.
3. Special supervision practices, which may include more frequent monitoring of these clients, more flexibility in sanctions, specialized caseloads, and relapse prevention efforts spearheaded by the probation or parole officer.
4. Systems integration strategies, such as community planning boards, information exchange, and interagency memoranda of understanding. It is important that these groups include not only community corrections and mental health professionals but also other services, such as housing, health care, alcohol and drug treatment, entitlement assistance, and education and vocational training programs.[25]

The criminal justice system must continue to address the problems and needs of offenders and clients who are mentally ill. With probably 300,000 offenders who are mentally ill now incarcerated in our prisons and jails, and perhaps 600,000 supervised on probation, it is an issue that is not going to go away. Only with proper planning, sufficient funds, and coordination among the various agencies involved will the needs of these clients, and the safety of the communities, be met. This is also true of the next group of offenders with special needs we discuss, those with developmental disabilities.

Offenders with Developmental Disabilities

A group of offenders with many problems similar to offenders who are mentally ill are those with developmental disabilities (DD), commonly called mental retardation (MR). This is particularly true because up to 60 percent of persons with developmental disabilities also manifest severe behavioral disorders or psychiatric illness.[26] Like mental illness, developmental disabilities are many and complex. The American Association on Mental Retardation defines mental retardation as

characterized by significantly subaverage intellectual functioning, existing concurrently with related limitation in two or more of the following applicable adaptive skill areas: communication, self-care, home living, social skills, community use, self-direction, health and safety, functional academics, leisure and work.[27]

Joan Petersilia provided the following definition:

Generally speaking, a person with developmental disabilities is anyone who has a mental impairment that manifested itself before the person attained age twenty-two, is likely to continue indefinitely, and results in substantial functional limitations in three or more major life activities (e.g., self-care, language, learning, mobility, capacity for independent living). The major categories of developmental disabilities are autism, cerebral palsy, epilepsy, and mental retardation. Such persons are also referred to as "mentally retarded," "intellectually handicapped," "developmentally delayed," or "severely learning disabled." They are estimated to make up 3 to 5 percent of the U.S. population.[28]

A 1999 Department of Justice Report stated that 3 percent of offenders in prison or on probation are considered mentally retarded or significantly developmentally delayed.[29] Multiplying this by the number of prisoners and those on probation and parole, it is estimated that there are approximately 60,000 adults who are developmentally disabled in prisons and jails in the United States, 120,000 on probation, and 22,500 on parole.[30]

Petersilia, in another work, also described the issues and problems these clients pose in a correctional setting, stating that they often have

a childlike quality of thinking, coupled with slowness in learning new material. MR persons have little long-term perspective and little ability to think in a causal way to understand the consequences of their actions. They are usually followers, easily manipulated, and often used by others with more intelligence and/or experience.[31]

MR/DD offenders also have a high rate of aggressive behavior compared to the general population, and incarcerated offenders who are mentally retarded commit more violent and nonviolent offenses than the general prison population.[32] Evidence also indicates that persons with MR/DD have limited decision-making skills; have an increased rate of medical disorders, including genetic diseases, nutritional disorders, and cardiovascular disease; experience increased morbidity and mortality than the general population; and manifest deficits in independent living skills and in social skills.[33]

The problems and challenges posed for probation and parole officers by clients manifesting these problems are obvious. All of the problems experienced by "normal" offenders—finding housing, getting jobs or training, developing normal social lives—are made worse when the symptoms just described are added. Simply understanding what a job interview is and how to dress appropriately for it is beyond the capacity of some MR/DD clients. Yet there are very few programs in the United States that specifically deal with these offenders. South Carolina has the Habilitation Unit for Developmentally Disabled offenders that prepares MR/DD offenders for release from prison and includes a 90-day follow-up program. Boston's MassCAPP program and the Mentally Retarded Offenders Program in Lancaster County (Pennsylvania) are two other programs of note. Texas, in 1987, was the first, and remains one of the few, states to create a state agency charged with coordinating the policies and services for offenders with special needs, the Texas Council on Offenders with Mental Impairments (TCOMI).[34] In 2000–2001, TCOMI's funding was designed for the following:

> *Goal:* To provide a comprehensive continuity-of-care system for offenders with special needs through collaboration and coordination.
>
> *Objective:* To divert offenders with special needs into treatment alternatives.
>
> *Strategy:* To provide projects that coordinate multiagency efforts for offenders with special needs through case management and treatment services.[35]

TCOMI funds and operates community-based programs in sixteen Texas communities. These community-based programs serve offenders who are mentally ill or mentally retarded who need intensive treatment. These services may include case management, psychiatric assessment and support, medication, residential substance abuse treatment, and continuity of care through collaboration and coordination. TCOMI programs divert identified offenders in the preindictment phase and refer them to treatment, if applicable. If an offender is already adjudicated or incarcerated, these programs assist in transitional planning. They may contract for services through mental health or mental retardation centers in the communities. Because most of these offenders are indigent, the TCOMI programs assist the clients with the Social Security Administration, and help them obtain Supplemental Security Income (SSI) or Medicaid. TCOMI reports a 63 percent reduction in arrest rates for offenders participating in their programs for twelve months.[36]

As can be seen, many of the needs of MR/DD clients are very similar to those who are mentally ill: Housing, independent living, vocational and educational, employment, communicating with their POs, and medical needs are some of the issues of similarity. As with mental illness, probation and parole officers usually receive minimal training in managing people who are developmentally delayed or their special needs and requirements. And resources required to meet the many needs are often scarce. These similarities are why Texas has combined the agency charged with serving this population of offenders into one agency. Other states may wish to follow Texas's lead on this. Regardless, it is imperative that community corrections agencies across the United States continue to address, or in some cases begin to address, the problems and needs of MR/DD clients. This is probably most likely to be successful through a collaborative effort involving community corrections, medical and social service agencies, and other members and organizations in communities.

A group of clients whose needs and supervision issues are typically being met by most jurisdictions are sex offenders, a group of special needs offenders to whom we now turn.

Sex Offenders

Probably more than any other type of offender, sex offenders on probation or parole are a cause of concern, consternation, and even protest. This is particularly true of child molesters or pedophiles because of the trauma created in their victims and the probable community outrage following the release of a convicted pedophile into the community. Sex offenders are also considered one of the most difficult populations to supervise in the community. This is so for a variety of reasons: There are several types of sex offenses and types of sex offenders, each potentially requiring some unique conditions or techniques of supervision; the consequences of reoffense are very serious; unlike other types of offenders, factors such as compliance, a prosocial lifestyle, and employment may not indicate a reduced probability to reoffend[37]; and because most victims knew their assailants as family members or "friends," reintegration into a home or community is often more difficult than it is for other types of offenders.

Sex offenses include any sexual act prohibited by law. This includes forcible rape (including acquaintance rape), child sexual molestation, voyeurism, exhibitionism, and prostitution. In 1997, there were about 234,000 convicted sex offenders under the care, custody, or control of corrections agencies on any given day. By 1998, this figure had grown to approximately 265,000.[38] About 60 percent of these, or approximately 140,000 in 1997, were being supervised in the community[39] (see Figure 11.7).

About 234,000 convicted sex offenders are under the care, custody, or control of corrections agencies on an average day. Nearly 60% are under conditional supervision in the community.

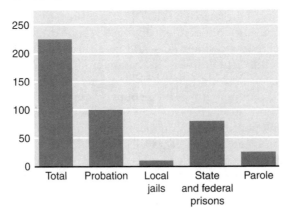

FIGURE 11.7 *Convicted Sex Offenders under Correctional Supervision*

Source: Lawrence A. Greenfeld, *Sex Offenses and Offenders* (Washington, DC Bureau of Justice Statistics, 1997).

Additionally, most of those incarcerated will be released to a community, probably under the supervision of a parole officer. Research, clinical practice, and supervision experience by probation and parole officers tell us that sex offenders in the community should be managed and supervised differently from other types of offenders.[40] The following are several characteristics of typical sex offenders, although not all sex offenders share all of these characteristics and the absence of one of these characteristics does not mean someone is not a sex offender.

- Sex crimes flourish in secrecy. Sex offenders have secretive and manipulative lifestyles, and many of their sexual assaults are so well planned that they appear to occur without forethought. The skills used to manipulate victims have also been employed to manipulate criminal justice officials.
- Many sex offenders are otherwise highly functioning people who use their social skills to commit their crimes.
- Sex offenders typically have developed complicated and persistent psychological and social systems to assist them in denying and minimizing the harm they inflict on others, and often they are very accomplished at presenting to others a facade designed to hide the truth about themselves.
- Many sex offenders commit a wide range and large number of sexually deviant acts during their lives and show a continued propensity to reoffend. In a study of 561 compulsive adult subjects, rapists reported a lifetime average of 7 incidents and exhibitionists more than 500. In this sample of 561 voluntary subjects, about 54 percent reported having at least two paraphilias (sexual deviations); 20 percent participated in deviant behavior without regard to victim gender; and 23.3 percent reported offending against both family and nonfamily victims.[41]

It is easy to see that this population of offenders poses a challenge to anyone supervising them in the community. Because of the tremendous harm that offenses would cause potential victims, and because of the possibility of intense and angry community response to reoffenses, the supervision of sex offenders in the community is a serious issue for probation and parole agencies and communities throughout the United States. The primary goal of managing sex offenders in the community is the prevention of future victimization. To that end, the Center for Sex Offender Management argues that a comprehensive approach to sex offender management is necessary, an approach that includes several key elements:

Collaboration. Collaboration among those agencies and individuals charged with initiating and implementing effective supervision and treatment practices is essential to managing sex offenders safely in the community. Given the secrecy, manipulation, and deception that characterize sex offending behavior, there also must be a clear set of operating norms for all involved to minimize the ability of offenders to circumvent the goals of supervision.

Victim-centered approach. Because a primary goal of supervision is the protection of victims and the prevention of future victimization, supervision agencies should work closely with victim advocacy organizations to ensure that their policies do not retraumatize victims of sexual assault, or inadvertently jeopardize the safety of others. Although supervision agencies have traditionally been offender focused in their work, the most comprehensive and responsible approaches to the community management of sex offenders are those that focus on the needs and safety of both past and potential victims of sexual assault. In this regard, concern for the protection of the victim and the community guide policy development, program implementation, and the actions and approaches of supervision agents and other practitioners who are either working with victims of sexual assault or supervising perpetrators.

Sex offender specific treatment. Mandated specialized treatment as part of probation or parole conditions is an integral component of effective community supervision. The notion that sex offenders should be involved in treatment in no way suggests that they be allowed to escape responsibility for their own actions—or that they should be "coddled." The offense-specific treatment that research has shown to be most effective holds offenders accountable, is victim centered, and is limited in its confidentiality. It is based on the notion that if an offender can be taught to manage successfully his or her propensity to sexually abuse, he or she becomes less of a risk to past and potential victims.

Clear and consistent policies. Clear and consistent policies at all levels (state, local, and agency) are crucial components of community supervision. Clear policy defines how cases will be investigated, prosecuted, and adjudicated. It also defines the method of community supervision, the roles various agencies play in the supervision process, and the response to indications of risk of relapse. Consensus-built policy establishes the goals of the system and helps jurisdictions to identify clearly what role each agency will play in managing these cases.[42]

By using these methods, many jurisdictions have achieved a level of success supervising sex offenders. Several studies, for example, have presented optimistic results concerning the effectiveness of treatment programs that are empirically based, offense specific, and comprehensive.[43] A meta-analysis of treatment outcome studies published in 1995 found there was an 8 percent reduction in recidivism rates for offenders who participated in treatment, a small but significant result. Research by Hanson and Bussiere demonstrated that sex offenders who fail to complete treatment programs are at an increased risk for both sexual and general recidivism.[44]

However, it is clear that more needs to be done. The United States has come a long way in the past thirty years in dealing with sex offenses and offenders, and community corrections has played a crucial role in those changes. However, we cannot hope to eliminate this crime that has roots in the structure of our society by treating one individual at a time. By treating and controlling only those who are caught and convicted, we will miss many, perhaps most, offenders. But by continuing to evaluate the effectiveness of the models of supervision, modifying them according to what works, and keeping community and public safety in the forefront of concerns, supervising sex offenders will continue to improve, and hence so will the safety of our communities.

The final group of offenders with special needs we discuss, those with substance abuse problems, also pose some unique challenges for community corrections, including the fact that all of the previously addressed types of offenders with special needs may also be involved in abusing substances.

Substance Abusing Offenders

The connection between substance abuse and crime has long been made; therefore, it is not surprising that a large number of offenders under the supervision of correctional agencies have abused drugs or alcohol. A profile of prison inmates conducted by the BJS reported that nearly 75 percent of the nation's prison inmates had used drugs. More than 50 percent reported that they had used drugs in the month before committing their offense of conviction and that they were under the influence of drugs or alcohol when they committed those offenses.[45] Because most prison inmates will eventually be released to the community, this statistic suggests that of the 753,141 offenders on parole in 2002,[46] maybe 564,000 of them have used drugs at some time. Also drug use among jail inmates is nearly twice the rate of drug use in the general population, and in another BJS study three out of four jail inmates admitted using drugs at some time in their lives and nearly one-third of the property offenders reported that they were under the influence of drugs when they committed their offenses.[47]

It is also not surprising that many offenders on probation are involved in drugs. For example, in 1992 more than one-third of felons convicted of drug possession and one-fourth convicted of drug trafficking were sentenced to probation. In a 1995 study of probation caseloads, 70 percent of probationers reported that they had used drugs at some time; one-third said that they had used drugs in the month before their arrests, and 14 percent reported that they were on drugs when they committed their offenses.[48]

Clearly, dealing with clients with substance abuse problems is important to community corrections. But it is not simply a matter of intensively supervising them, or drug testing them, or putting them in a treatment program that becomes available. Substance abuse is a complex social problem. There are many substances that are abused, and each may have a different affect on the abuser and call for a different approach in supervision. Also, besides differences in ethnicity, age, gender, educational level, status, and class, those who use and abuse substances also exhibit various personality traits (self-concepts, attitudes, values, motives) and deficiencies (such as impulsivity, depression, low self-esteem, anxiety, low frustration tolerance, sociopathy, and psychopathy).[49] Such variety calls for flexibility and balance when supervising substance abusing clients, a balance between the law enforcement and social worker roles (see Chapters Five and Nine) and the flexibility to know when to assume which role.

To effectively deal with substance abusing clients (keep recidivism rates low), POs must walk the tightrope between law enforcement and treatment. Many addict clients may require the strict "law enforcement" approach to supervision that will set limits on their behaviors and compels them, if necessary, to seek treatment if they continue to use or abuse substances.[50] However, there is a great deal of research evidence that shows that drug treatment is an effective and cost-effective strategy for controlling substance use and abuse, even among those who have been coerced into treatment and those who fail to complete treatment.[51] But because of the variety of problems and deficits apparent with substance abusing clients who find themselves enmeshed in the criminal justice system, the treatment programs and services available to community corrections should be varied, including urinalysis, detoxification, educational and vocational training, traditional counseling, HIV education, life skills training, psychiatric and psychotherapy treatment, relapse prevention programs, and self-help groups.[52]

Unfortunately, this variety of services and treatment modalities are not available in all communities, and many (if not most) substance abusing clients must take what is available, often having to wait a long time to get it. One model designed to link the law enforcement, sanction approach with the treatment approach is the federally funded Treatment Accountability for Safer Communities program.

Treatment Accountability for Safer Communities.[53]   Created by the federal government in 1972, Treatment Accountability for Safer Communities (TASC) is a program designed to break the addiction–crime cycle of nonviolent, drug-involved offenders. TASC links criminal justice sanctions with the therapeutic interventions of treatment programs. TASC moves offenders through the criminal justice process and into drug treatment; it also monitors clients in addition to providing probation, parole, or any other type of criminal justice supervision. TASC is a comprehensive case management system, facilitating unique interactions among the criminal justice system, treatment service providers, and the offender. The TASC model includes four distinct activities:

- *Identification* of drug-involved offenders to determine their appropriateness for referral by the criminal justice system into the TASC case management system.
- *Assessment* of the offender's drug and alcohol treatment needs.
- *Referral* of the offender to the appropriate drug treatment placement.
- *Continuous case management* of the offender, through reporting protocols, urine monitoring, and ancillary requirements, to ensure compliance with criminal justice orders and the drug treatment regimen.

The TASC model has the ability to provide case management and treatment at any point in the criminal justice process—from pretrial, through the courts, jail programs, probation, intermediate sanctions, to reintegration of the offender into the community. TASC programs work to ensure that offenders receive the appropriate type and level of treatment, that they regularly attend treatment, that treatment satisfactorily progresses, and that the treatment provided is effective.

The TASC model can be applied in urban, rural, and suburban jurisdictions and can be applied to the unique requirements of special populations. There are ten organizational and operational elements critical to the model. These elements provide the foundation and structure that link TASC to the criminal justice and drug treatment systems.

TASC Organizational Elements
- A broad base of support from the criminal justice system, with a formal system for effective communication.
- A broad base of support from the treatment community, with a formal system for effective communication.
- An independent TASC unit, with a designated administrator.
- Staff training, as outlined in TASC policies and procedures.
- A system of data collection for program management and evaluation.

TASC Operational Elements
- Explicit and agreed-on eligibility criteria.
- Screening procedures for the early identification of eligible offenders.
- Documented procedures for assessment and referral.
- Documented policies, procedures, and technology for drug testing.
- Procedures for offender monitoring with established success and failure criteria and procedures for regular reporting to the criminal justice referral source.

The TASC model of case management and accountability has been adapted in many areas of the criminal justice system, including drug courts, juvenile justice, welfare-to-work programs, and family courts. The assessment, referral, case management, and monitoring of these adaptations all follow the basic functions of TASC.

Recognizing the need for distinct systems of cooperation in order to achieve the goals of accessing services such as substance abuse treatment, the TASC model can still meet the referring system's goals of reintegration, employment, child safety, or diversion. TASC has enjoyed more than thirty years of effective interventions throughout the United States by maintaining its core identity while adapting to multiple system needs.[54]

One traditional way to deal with special needs offenders discussed in this section, as well as some minor offenders, those recently released from prison, and others, is through halfway houses. Some clients spend time in halfway houses while on probation; others live in these facilities after release from prison. Regardless, halfway houses represent an important aspect of community corrections, rich in history and variety.

Halfway Houses

One traditional way to treat drug and alcohol offenders, mentally ill offenders, some minor offenders, and those recently released from prison is in halfway houses. **Halfway houses** are relatively small (often five to twenty-five beds) community residential facilities, often with a treatment component, designed to accommodate offenders who need more structured settings than traditional probation and parole provide. There are two primary purposes for these facilities, often called "halfway-in" and "halfway-out" houses. The halfway-in house often has a punitive or treatment component and is used directly by the courts as a sentencing option for those in need of treatment or more control and structure than regular probation or intensive supervision probation can provide, and as a sanction for some probation or parole violators. Offenders are usually confined to the halfway house facility, unless they are employed or attending an educational or training program. For these types of houses, the goal is not so much community integration as it is treatment or sanctioning.[55]

The halfway-out house provides reintegration and transitional services for offenders released from prison. These types of houses usually are less structured, encourage their clients to reestablish family and community ties, and may provide services designed to help with the reintegration process (such as employment services and independent living skills) as well as provide or refer clients to relevant treatment providers.[56] It was these types of houses from which the halfway house movement developed.

History of Halfway Houses

The idea of halfway houses can be traced to the early 1800s in England, Ireland, and the United States. In the United States, the first proposals for halfway houses occurred in 1817 in both Pennsylvania and Massachusetts.[57] In Pennsylvania, the proposal followed a serious riot in a prison where a commission was assigned to look into the problems with the prison system. In Massachusetts, a state commission acknowledged the hardships confronting released prisoners, particularly regarding social stigma and employment, and recommended what today we would call halfway houses. However, no such houses were established until a group of Quaker women, including Abby Hopper Gibbons, founded the Women's Prison Association (WPA) in New York City in 1845. In June of that year the WPA opened the Isaac T. Hopper House, named for the founder of the Prison Association of New York and father of Abby Hopper Gibbons. The house helped discharged female prisoners back into society and thus was the first halfway house in the world.[58] Both the Hopper House and the WPA remain active to this day (see the next section).

The next stage in the history of halfway houses was when the Temporary Asylum for Discharged Female Prisoners (TADFP) was incorporated on April 30, 1864, "to provide shelter, instruction, and employment for such women as have been discharged from the Correction Institutions of the State, and who, with a desire to reform, have no home but the abode of vice and misery." Located in Dedham, Massachusetts, the asylum came into existence largely through the efforts of Hannah Balch Chickering, a "self-appointed visitor, librarian, and chaplain" to women at the Dedham jail. Mrs. Chickering was convinced of the "imperative need" to prepare inmates for their return to society while they served their sentences. Clients at the asylum were taught "all branches of domestic service and needlework" and the basic elements of a "common school education," and arrangements were made to find employment for the inmates after leaving the asylum. Initially, the asylum was supported by voluntary contributions, the earnings of the inmates, and a small appropriation by the state; legacies later created an endowment. In 1910 the charter was amended to change the name to the Dedham Temporary Home for Women and Children, and the function to another form of social service: the convalescent care of women and children. About this time the home also became known as Chickering House, in memory of its founder. In 1943 the charter was further amended to include care for men. In 1946 funding from the Greater Boston Community Federation was suspended and Chickering House closed. Income on the endowment continues to provide convalescent aid to established charitable agencies and hospital social service departments.[59]

In the late 1890s, the American Prison Association (now the American Correctional Association) opposed opening a halfway house in New York arguing that such a facility would continue the stigma of prison and create a "permanent class of undesirable citizens."[60] In 1896, however, Maud Booth, cofounder of Volunteers of America, spoke at New York's Sing Sing Prison. Following that speaking engagement, five inmates came forward, determined to reform their lives. These five prisoners were the beginning of the Volunteer Prison League, which was formed on Christmas Eve, 1896. Their motto was "Look Up and Hope." Within a year after her speech at Sing Sing, the Volunteer Prison League was organized in seven more state prisons, including San Quentin, and the roll book contained more than 1,200 names. By 1923, more than 100,000 men had been enrolled in forty-six state and federal prisons. Of those Volunteer Prison League members who were released, nearly 80 percent never returned to prison life.

Borrowing on the group motto, Maud Booth was instrumental in setting up the first halfway house in New York City, known as Hope Hall. Soon there were Hope Halls in several cities throughout the United States, including Chicago, San Francisco, and New Orleans. On their release from prison, ex-convicts could go to one of the Hope Halls, which provided them with a place to stay free of charge. In addition to providing housing, Hope Halls assisted released prisoners in securing jobs. Maud Booth even hired several of these men to work in her private home and in the offices of the Volunteers of America, which continues to provide such services to ex-offenders today.[61]

Largely as a result of the Great Depression and some changes in parole requirements, the halfway house movement suffered a major setback during the 1930s through the early 1950s.[62] By the mid to late 1950s and into the 1960s, however, the movement had again gained momentum to the point where the International Halfway House Association was formed in 1964. Renamed the International

Association of Residential and Community Alternatives in 1989, and known today as the International Community Corrections Association, the organization now represents more than 250 private agencies operating more than 1,500 residential and community alternative programs throughout the world, offering a variety of services including community corrections centers, educational and vocational services, drug testing and treatment, tutoring, residential outreach, and aftercare.[63] This is reflective of the growing diversity of halfway houses generally, moving beyond residences for released prisoners to include diversion programs, probationary placements, a treatment facility for alcohol or substance abusers, a mental health facility, a residence for pretrial detainees, and a facility for other persons or groups in need such as the homeless or victims of domestic violence.

As can be seen, halfway houses comprise a wide variety of organizational and programmatic functions. They can be halfway-in or halfway-out houses. They can be owned and controlled by private groups or foundations or by a branch of the government. Many facilities are very small, but some are relatively large. Some are gender specific; others are coed. Some are age specific; others welcome a broad range of residents. Some are punitive in orientation; others are treatment oriented. Some are designed for very short stays; others allow for indefinite habitation. Some serve specific populations, such as drug-involved offenders or born-again Christians; others serve anyone who comes in the door. It is very difficult to stereotype and categorize the halfway house. Following are a few specific program examples that try to capture some of the variability and promise of halfway houses in the United States.

Program Examples

***Hopper Home Alternative to Incarceration.*[64]**   The Hopper Home Alternative to Incarceration (ATI) Program is a residential, community-based program for women who, without the program, would be incarcerated for several years in New York state prisons. As noted previously, the Hopper Home ATI Program was created by the Women's Prison Association to meet the needs of women involved in the criminal justice system and addresses both criminal justice and human service needs. The home is a transitional residence and an intensive day, evening, and weekend reporting program. Hopper Home is a safe, clean, drug-free sixteen-bed residence with twenty-four-hour supervision for women who meet the following eligibility requirements:

- Eighteen years of age or older
- At risk of incarceration or detention
- Facing a minimum of four months of actual jail time
- Not charged with arson
- Violent charges are assessed on an individual basis
- Substance abusers must be detoxed and able to attend a day treatment program

- Acceptable by other ATI programs and in need of dual supervision
- Are pregnant up to their third trimester

All residents have a case planner who assesses their needs and makes appropriate referrals. Women in this program must obey all Hopper Home's rules and regularly report to court and referral agencies. Clients also participate in a range of activities, including intensive case management; scheduled group meetings and workshops on the premises; and a mandatory structured day program involving HIV prevention, parent support groups, domestic violence education, and independent life skills training.

Center on Juvenile and Criminal Justice Supportive Living Program.[65]   The Supportive Living Program (SLP) was started in 1992 as part of the Center on Juvenile and Criminal Justice Bay Area Parole Services Network to reduce the number of California state parolees returning to prison on parole violations. SLP provides drug and alcohol treatment services for sixteen clients housed in two San Francisco residences for up to 180 days. Case managers meet with new clients and develop individualized treatment plans addressing their specific social and psychological needs. Case managers use an addiction severity tool to assess treatment needs. Case plans are culturally specific and usually include education, vocational training, employment, family reunification, mental health programs, postrelease housing, and life skills training.

For substance abuse treatment, SLP uses social model recovery principles, focusing on experiential learning and building self-reliance among clients who are often overinstitutionalized. Residents are encouraged to secure outside employment and to use resources available in the community. SLP clients participate in weekly group and individual counseling sessions. Group sessions focus on relapse prevention, building support for ongoing recovery, anger management, life skills, employment readiness, and tools for getting off parole and staying out of a criminal lifestyle. Staff members are selected on the basis of clinical training and on experience-based knowledge of substance abuse and its dangers. This approach facilitates the development of trust and support among staff and residents.

Since its inception, "SLP graduates have consistently shown higher rates of employment and lower rates of recidivism. The successes of SLP have led many programs across the country to use it as a model."[66]

Sponsors, Inc.[67]   Sponsors, Inc., is a private, nonprofit, tax-exempt agency incorporated in 1973 in Eugene, Oregon. The mission of the agency is to help ex-offenders released from Oregon correctional facilities in their transition back to the community. Sponsors, Inc., has thirty-seven beds, thirty-one for men at two facilities and six for women at one facility. Clients are referred in several ways. The county parole and probation office refers people when their release plans reveal that an offender does not have a place to stay, or the place he or she has chosen is not acceptable. Another referral source is word of mouth among offenders and prerelease counseling conducted by Sponsors, Inc., staff at state correctional institutions. A third referral source is the county jail. Inmates serving one year or less, or some probation or parole violators, are referred to the facilities by jail personnel. Finally, some participants are walk-ins—those who are involved in the criminal justice system but find themselves homeless.

Sponsors' clients are mostly indigent, repeat offenders and those without stable support systems in the community. Most clients are between twenty-five and forty-five years of age and have been incarcerated an average of three or four times. Among the males, about one-third are sex offenders (although the types of crimes run the entire spectrum of criminal behavior), one-fifth are veterans, and about 3 percent have a diagnosed disability. Approximately 75 percent have an alcohol or drug problem. The only crime categorically excluded from the program is arson, although exceptions have been made for this in the past as well. Slightly more than 67 percent of Sponsors' clients have finished high school (36 percent obtained the GED).

Sponsors, Inc., has a staff and board who are personally experienced in the issues affecting the people they serve. For example, as of 1999, three staff members were actively involved in recovery programs, and five were both involved in recovery programs and were ex-offenders. Staff members also possess diverse skills, have formal educations, and hold responsible positions in the community.

On entering the program, participants and their case managers develop transition plans. The plans include all aspects of their release plans developed for them in the correctional institutions, any requirements placed on them by their probation or parole officers, and program requirements. If treatment is mandated, signed releases of information are required in order to monitor attendance. Program requirements always include full-time employment (except for the disabled) or full-time enrollment in an accredited educational program. Once employment is attained, clients must put at least 50 percent of their take-home pay in a restricted bank account managed by Sponsors, Inc.

Residents have a 10:00 P.M. curfew the first week in the program and later a 10:00 P.M. curfew Sunday through Thursday. Once employed or in school, the curfew is completely dropped but the client must spend four nights a week on site and must check in with his or her case manager at least four times per week.

The program has a mandatory drug-testing program. Residents must also agree to abstain from alcohol use and stay out of bars and taverns, regardless of whether this is a release condition. If any drug or alcohol use is detected, clients may be terminated from the program, placed on a curfew, or given other sanctions. Their parole officers, in consultation with the case manager, determine whether a revocation hearing or some other sanction is applied.

Successful residents have an average stay of about sixty days for males, ninety days for females. Unsuccessful participants stay an average of twenty-five days. For Sponsors, Inc., residents are considered successful if, when they complete the program and leave the facility, they

- Are employed full time or enrolled in an accredited educational program;
- Have abstained from the use of nonprescription controlled substances and alcohol as verified by drug testing and Breathalyzers;

- Are in compliance with all release requirements (verified by parole officers); and
- Have acquired permanent, stable housing, verified by a rental agreement or other reliable source.

Sixty-five percent of those who enter Sponsors, Inc., meet all of these criteria when they leave the program and are, therefore, considered successful.

Summary

There are many aspects to community corrections besides parole and probation. These include pretrial release services, diversion programs, programs for offenders with special needs, and halfway houses. Pretrial release services have a long history and serve an important role in the criminal justice system. These programs gather and present information about those arrested to judicial officers who then decide whether an arrestee should be released and under what conditions. Pretrial release programs also supervise those released from custody before trial to make sure they appear in court when required. Pretrial release services also make the system more fair and just because they often make it possible for those who cannot afford bail to be released on their own recognizance or under supervision.

Diversion occurs whenever an agent of the criminal justice system uses discretion to end formal criminal justice processing. Diversion can be informal discretionary acts, or formal and organized programs engaged in by police, prosecutors, judges, or other criminal justice officials. Diversion can include warnings and reprimands, mediation, supervision of various sorts, and often require some sort of treatment or therapy. Many states now are mandating that minor drug offenders be diverted into drug treatment programs rather than being sent to jail or prison. Criticisms of diversion include net widening, a lack of due process guarantees, being too soft on crime, and taking away funding from traditional community corrections programs.

Offenders with special needs also are addressed in this chapter. These include offenders who are mentally ill, offenders with developmental disabilities, sex offenders, and offenders with substance abuse problems. Each of these types of offenders presents problems of supervision in the community, problems that are sometimes unique to that type of offender, and sometimes shared by one or more of the other offenders with special needs. In addition, some of these conditions may co-occur in certain offenders, further complicating the supervision process.

One traditional way of dealing with offenders with special needs, as well as some minor offenders, those recently released from prison, and others, is in halfway houses. Halfway houses are community residential facilities that either sanction or treat those who are halfway in the criminal justice system, or provide transitional services for those recently released from prison, or halfway out. Halfway houses serve a wide variety of clients and serve many purposes, both in and out of the criminal justice system. They occupy an important niche in community corrections, one that needs to be recognized and further developed.

Key People and Terms

Bail (358)
Discretion (363)
Diversion (363)
Halfway houses (384)

Manhattan Bail Project (359)
Pretrial release (357)
Louis Schweitzer (359)
Herb Sturz (359)

Questions for Discussion and Review

1. What are the functions of pretrial release? What purposes does pretrial release serve for the criminal justice system?

2. What are some problems with using bail as a system of pretrial release?

3. Describe the Manhattan Bail Project and its impact on pretrial release programs.

4. What is diversion? Who uses diversion and under what circumstances? What are some examples of diversion programs?

5. What are some unique characteristics of offenders who are mentally ill? Why is this population often difficult to supervise?

6. What makes MR/DD clients particularly challenging to supervise?

7. What are some characteristics of typical sex offenders? Describe a comprehensive approach to sex offender management.

8. Discuss the connection between drugs and crime. What are the challenges to supervising this population in the community?

9. What are the types of halfway houses and what are their purposes? Give some examples of halfway house programs.

Relevant Internet Sites

Pretrial Services Resource Center, an independent, nonprofit clearinghouse for information and technical assistance on pretrial issues: www.pretrial.org

Texas Council on Offenders with Mental Impairments, a coordinating body for issues involving offenders with mental illnesses and mental retardation: www.tdcj.state.tx.us/tcomi/tcomi-home.htm

Center for Sex Offender Management, organization whose goal is to enhance public safety by preventing further victimization through improving the management of adult and juvenile sex offenders in the community: www.csom.org

National TASC (Treatment Accountability for Safer Communities), a membership organization representing individuals and programs dedicated to the professional delivery of treatment and case management services to substance abusing populations: www.nationaltasc.org

International Association of Residential and Community Alternatives, formerly the International Halfway House Association: www.iccaweb.org

EXERCISE • *Dual-Diagnosed Client*

By Toni Dragt

Offenders with special needs pose several unique and challenging problems for community supervision. Moreover, many probation and parole clients have been diagnosed with more than one of the traits discussed in this chapter, making their supervision even more complex. Read the following case and, given the numerous elements involved, decide what you would recommend regarding the numerous probation violations. Is revocation of probation appropriate? Should other avenues for treatment be pursued before beginning revocation procedures? How does the mental illness involved affect your decision making? Should a decision concerning child custody be pursued or delayed?

Jane was placed on probation for two years, including six months of jail time, for possession of methamphetamines. She has been dual-diagnosed with Borderline Personality Disorder and an addiction to alcohol. She also has a history of self-harm by cutting herself. As a condition of her probation, Jane was mandated to attend outpatient treatment, regular Alcoholics Anonymous meetings, and abstain from using alcohol or drugs—other than her prescribed psychotropic medications. Jane has temporarily lost custody of her three-and-one-half-year-old son, although she has permission for supervised visits. Therefore, the court also ordered her to attend, and complete, a series of parenting classes. You have been assigned as Jane's probation officer. After about four months of relatively incident free supervision following her release from jail, you receive a call from Jane's social worker from the state Division of Services to Children and Families. He tells you that Jane was just admitted to a local hospital after she attempted suicide by cutting herself. Her blood alcohol level at the time of admittance was .21, more than twice the legal limit. The social worker also tells you that Jane has not followed through with her outpatient treatment, has stopped attending the parenting classes, and has missed the last two scheduled supervised visitations with her son. What do you do?

Notes

1. Barry Mahoney, Bruce D. Beaudin, John A. Carver, III, Daniel B. Ryan, and Richard B. Hoffman, *Pretrial Services Programs: Responsibilities and Potential* (Washington DC: National Institute of Justice, 2001).

2. Belinda Rodgers McCarthy, Bernard J. McCarthy, Jr., and Mathew C. Leone, *Community-Based Corrections*, 4th ed. (Belmont, CA: Wadsworth/Thomson, 2001) 41.

3. McCarthy et al. 42.

4. McCarthy et al. 42.

5. Vera Institute of Justice, "Mission and Origins," May, 2003, New York: Vera Institute of Justice. Retrieved August 25, 2003, from www.vera.org/about/about_2.asp

6. Mahoney et al. 14.

7. John Clark and D. Alan Henry, *Pretrial Services Programming at the Start of the Twenty-first Century: A Survey of Pretrial Services Programs*, undated, Pretrial Services Resource Center. Retrieved August 21, 2003, from www.pretrial.org/surveyresults.html

8. Mahoney et al. 1.

9 Mahoney et al. 1.

10. Mahoney el al. 2.

11. Mahoney et al. 57

12. Marilyn D. McShane and Wesley Krause, *Community Corrections* (New York: Macmillan, 1993) 17.

13. John O. Smykla, *Community-Based Corrections: Principles and Practices* (New York: Macmillan, 1981) 59.

14. Smykla 60.

15. Health Policy Tracking Service, "Drug Courts and Diversion Programs," April, 2003, Denver, CO: National Conference of State Legislatures. Retrieved August 22, 2003, from www.ncsl.org/programs/health/drugcourts.htm

16. Justice Research and Statistics Association, *Creating a New Criminal Justice System for the Twenty-First Century: Findings and Results from State and Local Program Evaluations* (Washington, DC: Office of Justice Programs, 2000) 27–37.

17. Justice Research and Statistics Association 35.

18. Justice Research and Statistics Association 36–37.

19. Mark S. Umbreit, Robert B. Coates, and Betty Vos, "Juvenile Victim Offender Mediation in Six Oregon Counties," July, 2001, Salem, OR: Oregon Dispute Resolution Commission. Retrieved August 26, 2003, from www.odrc.state.or.us/pdfs/vom_fnlrpt.pdf

20. Umbreit, et al. C-33

21. Mothers against Drunk Driving, *Annual Report 2001–2002*, undated, Irving, TX: MADD. Retrieved August 27, 2003, from www.madd.org/docs/2002_annual_report.pdf

22. Paula M. Ditton, *Mental Health and Treatment of Inmates and Probationers* (Washington, DC: Bureau of Justice Statistics, July, 1999).

23. R. Blackburn, "Criminality and the Interpersonal Circle in Mentally Disordered Offenders," *Criminal Justice and Behavior* 25 (1998): 156.

24. Bonita M. Veysey, "Mentally Ill Offenders in the Community: Challenges for the Future," in *Mentally Ill Offenders in the Community* (Longmont CO: National Institute of Corrections, 1995).

25. Veysey 5–9.

26. P. W. Davidson, N. N. Cain, J. E. Sloane-Reeves, A. Van Speybroeck, J. Segel, J. Gutkin, L. Quijano et al., "Characteristics of Community-Based Individuals with Mental Retardation and Aggressive Behavior Disorders," *American Journal on Mental Retardation* 98 (1994): 704.

27. American Association on Mental Retardation, *Mental Retardation: Definition, Classification, and Systems of Support*, 9th ed. (Washington, DC: American Association on Mental Retardation, 1992).

28. Joan Petersilia, "Invisible Victims: Violence against Persons with Developmental Disabilities," *Human Rights* 27 (2000): 9.

29. Travis County Community Supervision and Corrections Department, *Criminal Justice Plan, 2004–2005*, May, 2003, Austin TX: Community Supervision and Corrections Department. Retrieved September 5, 2003, from www.co.travis.tx.us/cjp

30. Lauren E. Glaze, *Probation and Parole in the United States, 2002* (Washington, DC: Bureau of Justice Statistics, 2003).

31. Joan Petersilia, "Justice for All? Offenders with Mental Retardation and the California Correctional System," *Prison Journal* 77 (1997): 358.

32. "Exploratory Assessment of Services Received and Perceived to Be Needed By High-Need Offenders in the State of Oregon" (Monmouth, OR: Department of Criminal Justice, Western Oregon University, 1999): 10.

33. "Exploratory Assessment of Services" 10–11.

34. Dee Kifowit, "TCOMI: The Pioneer," *Texas Supervision* 3,2 (2000).

35. Kifowit 1.

36. E. Anne Brockett and Estella Guillen, "Community Justice for the Mentally Impaired," *Texas Supervision* 3,2 (2000) 1.

37. Wisconsin Department of Corrections Sex Offender Registry Program, "Sex Offender Supervision and Rules," undated, Madison, WI: Wisconsin Department of Corrections. Retrieved September 10, 2003, from http://offender.doc.state.wi.us/public/proginfo/rules.jsp

38. Center for Sex Offender Management, "Myths and Facts about Sex Offenders," August, 2000, Silver Spring, MD: Center for Sex Offender Management. Retrieved September 10, 2003, from www.csom.org/pubs/mythsfacts.pdf

39. Lawrence A. Greenfeld, *Sex Offenses and Offenders* (Washington, DC: Bureau of Justice Statistics, 1997).

40. Kim English, Suzanne Pullen, and Linda Jones, *Managing Adult Sex Offenders in the Community—A Containment Approach* (Washington, DC: National Institute of Justice, 1997) 2.

41. English et al. 2.

42. Center for Sex Offender Management, "Community Supervision of the Sex Offender: An Overview of Current and Promising Practices," January 2000, Silver Spring, MD: Center for Sex Offender Management. Retrieved September 11, 2003, from www.csom.org/pubs/supervision2.pdf

43. Center for Sex Offender Management, "Myths and Facts about Sex Offenders" 6.

44. Center for Sex Offender Management, "Myths and Facts about Sex Offenders" 6.

45. Arthur J. Lurigio and James A. Swartz, "The Nexus between Drugs and Crime: Theory, Research, and Practice," *Federal Probation* 63,3 (1999): 68.

46. Glaze 1.

47. Lurigio and Swartz 68.

48. Lurigio and Swartz 68.

49. Sam Torres and Robert M. Latta, "Selecting the Substance Abuse Specialist," *Federal Probation* 64,1 (2000): 48.

50. Torres and Latta 49.

51. Lurigio and Swartz 70.

52. Lurigio and Swartz 70–71.

53. Bureau of Justice Assistance, *Treatment Accountability for Safer Communities* (Washington, DC: Bureau of Justice Assistance, 1995).

54. National TASC, *The TASC Model Core Benefits and Functions*, 2003, Alexandria, VA: National TASC. Retrieved September 13, 2003, from www.national tasc.org/corefunc.htm

55. Jody Klein-Saffron, "Electronic Monitoring versus Halfway Houses: A Study of Federal Offenders," *Alternatives to Incarceration* (1995) 24–25; and Smykla 159.

56. Klein-Saffron 25.

57. McCarthy et al. 245; Smykla 157–158.

58. The Women's Prison Association and Home, *The Founding Years*, 1999, New York: Women's Prison Association. Retrieved September 15, 2003, from www.correctionhistory.org/html/chronicl/wpa/html/wpaone2.htm

59. *Dedham Temporary Home for Women and Children*, April, 1990, Arthur and Elizabeth Schlesinger Library on the History of Women in America, Cambridge, MA: Radcliffe College. Retrieved September 15, 2003, from www.radcliffe.edu/schles/libcolls/mssarch/findaids/Dedham.html

60. Smylka 158.

61. "Ballington and Maud Ballington Booth," *The Extra Mile*, undated, Washington, DC: Points of Light Foundation. Retrieved September 16, 2003, from www.extramile.us/honorees/booth.html

62. Smykla 158.

63. "ICCA Information," *International Community Corrections Association*, 1998, La Crosse, WI: ICCA. Retrieved September 16, 2003, from www.iccaweb.org/

64. "Hopper Home," *Women's Prison Association and Home, Inc.*, 2000, New York: Women's Prison Association and Home. Retrieved September 16, 2003, from www.wpaonline.org/WEBSITE/HHAIP.htm

65. "Supportive Living Program," *Center on Juvenile and Criminal Justice*, 2003, San Francisco: Center on Juvenile and Criminal Justice. Retrieved September 17, 2003, from www.cjcj.org/programs/supportive_living.php

66. "Supportive Living Program" 1.

67. Ron Chase, "A Case Study in Transition for Ex-Offenders: Sponsors, Inc.," *Southern Illinois University Law Journal* 23 (1999): 511–515.

Part IV

New Perspectives

12

Probation and Parole in the Twenty-First Century

The Past Is Prologue

Corrections is currently in the midst of a crisis. Prison crowding dominates correctional events and negatively impacts the entire system. Our correctional institutions evoke images of places where desperate individuals "packed together like sardines" are forced to live in "zoolike conditions." Hurried prison construction cannot keep pace with demand for bed space. Local jails, themselves overcrowded, can no longer hold inmates until prison cells are available. Jailers are demanding (sometimes in court suits) that state officials take convicted felons off their hands. And still the prisoners keep coming, put there by judicial decisions or legislative or public mandates that reflect a "get-tough" or "truth-in-sentencing" philosophy. There is agreement that something must be done and that prison alternatives have to be developed.

In most cases, that "something" is an alternative involving probation, parole, and community corrections. However they are currently being packaged, community corrections programs still mitigate the harshness of incarceration and will continue to do so in the twenty-first century. Before discussing the future, a brief historical review will show that mitigation has been a theme of probation and parole since their inception. In addition, the current "reforms" of probation and parole, like those of the past, often have unintended consequences that subvert original goals. The problematic aspects of watching over offenders faced by today's officers were shared by their historical counterparts.

The historical forerunners of probation (benefit of clergy, judicial reprieve, and recognizance) and parole (banishment and transportation) were developed to mitigate prevailing sentences. English magistrates and prison wardens used them to avoid imposing unusually long sentences that were the norm at that time. In the United States, probation and parole were institutionalized as formal responses to the "evils" of imprisonment. Reformers in the early nineteenth and twentieth centuries advanced them as cornerstones in a comprehensive program of correctional rehabilitation. Parole and probation were "sold" to judicial, legislative, and correctional leaders not only as alternatives to prison but also as vehicles for "correcting" offenders. Whereas prisons mainly turned out hardened criminals, it was agreed that probation and parole could produce law-abiding citizens, and at a fraction of the cost of incarceration.

Large-scale probation and parole programs were launched with optimism characteristic of reform movements. However, implementation proved a difficult task and the day-to-day practices of probation and parole often bore little resemblance to the initial program goals. In some jurisdictions, the rhetoric of rehabilitation masked the reality of programs whose purpose was social control. Although the initial enthusiasm was gradually tempered, probation and parole departments, by the middle of the twentieth century, had become accepted bureaucratic entities. The incorporation of a medical model into the field temporarily gave practitioners additional legitimacy. When rehabilitation was devalued and eventually abandoned in the 1970s, probation and parole were left without a dominant rationale, other than being an instrument of mitigation. As such, they were vulnerable to public questioning and criticism for allowing criminals to circumvent deserved punishment.

The public had become suspicious of probation and parole and other community corrections programs, equating them with a "slap on the wrist" that seemed to embolden rather than deter offenders. In some corners, community corrections were seen as part of the problem and not the solution to criminal activity. Efforts to curtail community corrections, however, were short lived because of massive prison crowding. The alternative to placing defendants on probation or granting inmates parole was to release offenders into the community without any supervision. This was not a palatable solution for either judges or parole boards. At least probation and parole were something, and, as such, they were seized on as readily available alternatives.

Probation and parole administrators and advocates, not wanting their services categorized as merely expedient alternatives, responded by adding offender control as the centerpiece of a reform program. Monitoring and close supervision replaced counseling and treatment as the dominant themes of current probation and parole agencies. These new programs of intrusive supervision are being touted as harsh punishments, almost as tough as prison. In much the same manner as the reformers of the 1920s promised that rehabilitation would correct offenders, today's reformers are promising that carefully controlled correctional clients can be coerced into compliance with societal laws. Although this development has received a favorable response from a punishment-oriented public, there may be unintended consequences unfavorable to reform goals. For example, criminal justice professor Philip Harris believes that it is not clear that any lasting gains will result from the attempt to shape alternatives to prison in the same form as imprisonment. In fact, such tactics, Harris argues, may lead to the further legitimization of the principles that make imprisonment distasteful. Thus, ". . . reformers are reduced to what is undoubtedly a futile, but nonetheless damaging effort to try to 'outprison' imprisonment by constructing alternatives that are generally painful, intimidating and incapacitative."[1]

There is one facet of probation and parole work, however, that has not changed appreciably since John Augustus and Alexander MaConochie developed these services. Relationships between clients and line officers are characterized by wariness and distrust. The peculiar nature of accepting help from a person who can also damage is not easily resolved. Although the PO's dilemma of whether to provide surveillance or assistance has been widely reported (see Chapter Five), clients' problems with the acceptance of probation and parole staff at face value have received less consideration. Through their access to courts or parole boards, POs have the power to negatively impact the lives of their clients. Correctional clients assume that if they step out of line their officers, no matter how friendly, will take coercive action.

The high caseloads POs must carry, leading to a lack of time to develop the needed relationship, is at the core of the problem. However, the inability to develop an honest relationship between officers and their offender clients is further complicated by the different social worlds they inhabit. Their perspectives on reality and purpose are often widely divergent. No matter how well meaning, sensitive, or skilled the probation and parole staff become, there will always be a degree of superficiality in their relationships with clients. POs in the twenty-first century, regardless of their training or expertise, will be faced with clients who do not really trust them. Besides reform movements to repackage probation and parole (in line with the public demand for more punitive approaches) and the continuing presence of wary clients, other important trends and developments will shape probation and parole throughout the twenty-first century.

The Twenty-First Century

Following is a list of those trends deemed particularly influential on probation and parole in the twenty-first century. There will be

1. An increasing number of clients
2. Continuing budgetary problems
3. A more involved public
4. A refinement of intensive supervision programs
5. An increase in electronic monitoring and shock incarceration programs
6. A need for independent research
7. More support for rehabilitation
8. Conflicting program goals

More Clients

There will be a continued glut of probation and parole clients with no end in sight. Although the near double-digit growth of the 1980s and 1990s appear to be over, probation and parole are still growing about 3 percent per year. If this trend continues, by the year 2010 there will be approximately 5 million adults on probation and 950,000 on parole. In the meantime, the prison population will swell perhaps to more than 2.5 million (these are conservative estimates and will likely be exceeded, perhaps dramatically). Punitive sentencing philosophies may show signs of moderating by 2010, but there will be so many defendants in the criminal court pipeline that any slowdown in correctional clients will barely be noticeable. Even though private firms will take a small percentage of those placed on probation and parole, most of these clients will be assigned to governmental agencies.

There is a growing resistance to privatization, and entrepreneurs will be discouraged by the small profit margins in providing long-term community supervision. Two areas that will experience an increasing private-sector presence are the operation of electronic monitoring programs and the compiling of PSI reports. However, these developments will not detract appreciably from the responsibilities of traditional agencies. Although an increasing number of private firms will operate monitoring devices, their function, in most cases, will be to inform probation or parole officers of curfew violations and not take full responsibility for cases. Most private PSIs will be submitted by the defense in addition to those done by court officers. Private PSI reports raise the issues of objectivity and fairness (because they are contracted by the defense) and, therefore, will never be relied on as primary presentence reports.

The presence of private PSIs will serve to improve the overall quality of presentence reports. In cases where private PSIs are submitted, court officers will be especially careful to compile accurate information and to present it in an objective manner. Hopefully, such efforts will carry over into cases that do not involve private competition. Most of the current prison alternatives, such as community service, restitution and victim compensation, intensive supervision, halfway houses, house arrest, and prerelease centers, are connected with or monitored by probation and parole agencies. This trend will continue, in large part because of the issue of oversight. Probation and parole are seen as the logical agencies to monitor compliance with program objectives. In this manner, most new programs are, or eventually will be, "add-ons" to existing probation and parole programs.

There is continuing support for probation and parole from judges, correctional officials, and clients. In one survey of judicial attitudes toward sentencing, judges showed strong support for probation and were "vehement" in their opposition to flat sentences that preclude the possibility of parole. One judge, in a comment that is representative, indicated that without parole, there "would be a return to the Devil's Island mentality for all sentenced prisoners."[2] Correctional officials (such as jailers or prison wardens) remain staunch advocates of probation and parole. They recognize that without the front-end (probation) and backdoor (parole) safety valves, prison and jail populations would be uncontrollable. The majority of states are currently facing unprecedented fiscal crises, and prison growth is often a major contributor. In order to ameliorate these crises, by 2003 several states took steps to reduce their prison populations by implementing sentencing reforms (abolishing mandatory sentences), commuting sentences, and closing prisons.[3] Such changes inevitably include an increased use of probation and parole, or, more likely, some combination of both, because jurisdictions are reluctant to eliminate all forms of supervision for the released or convicted offenders.

Correctional clients invariably are strong supporters of probation and parole. They would rather be supervised in the community, however intrusive, than be supervised behind bars. It is safe to say that correctional clients will rarely turn down an opportunity to be placed on probation and parole, although there is some evidence that some would rather go to jail than be placed on intensive supervision.[4] Public and legislative support for probation has been grudgingly won over by the punitive programs being emphasized and by pragmatic cost considerations. Probation and parole are qualitatively cheaper than incarceration. Even high-cost programs, such as intensive supervision and electronic monitoring (which can run up to $7,000 per year for each participant), are far less expensive than the cost of keeping an offender in prison ($20,000 to $25,000 per year) or the construction of new prisons ($60,000 to $100,000 per cell). Ironically, even though probation and parole can generate such savings, they themselves are faced with severe budgetary problems.

Budget Blues

Today's probation and parole administrators are in the unenviable position of being responsive to increased demands for their services and to public demand for less government spending. Nowhere is this dilemma more apparent than in California, and this problem has been in existence for quite some time. In the years preceding the passage of Proposition 13 in 1978 (which severely restricts the ability of counties to collect property taxes), probation departments, on the average, lost 30 percent of their officers, whereas the number of probationers increased by 15 percent. During this period of retrenchment, the amount of money spent on each probationer decreased almost 25 percent.[5] This occurred at the same time more serious offenders were being placed on probation. Much of the savings from probation was funneled into prison budgets (at the expense of parole). These problems have all increased in recent years with the huge budget deficits experienced by California in 2003 (estimated to be $38 billion).

The budgetary woes of probation and parole are not limited to California. After conducting a nationwide study of fiscal spending on corrections, Timothy Fitzharris concluded: "Probation agencies have had greater budgetary problems than any other part of the justice system."[6] Politicians throughout the United States, when facing budgetary crunches, have been unwilling to cut back on fire, police, or health and instead have often trimmed the budgets of probation and parole. When dealing with actual cutbacks or funding freezes, probation and parole agencies have had no alternative but to increase the size of caseloads. Average probation and parole caseloads in most areas range from 150 to 250. Even though some additional funding has become available for special programs (that promise to divert from prison or jail), most probation and parole agencies remain in dire financial straits. There seems to be no relief from this financial straitjacket of inadequate funding and increased caseloads in the foreseeable future. Because probation and parole agencies typically lack political clout, they remain vulnerable to the budget cutter's red pencil. Although all this makes for unpleasant managerial decisions, it could prove a blessing in disguise.

Budget difficulties may force probation and parole agencies into making long overdue changes in operations. One area of particular importance involves differential supervision and case management (see Chapter Ten). With the number of clients increasing dramatically, it becomes vital to allocate the supervision officer's time in an effective manner. Every caseload has its share of paper men and women—those who do not need any supervision.

Robert Cushman, former president of the American Justice Institute, clearly states this case: "It is common knowledge to most practitioners that many probationers and parolees need no help and may do better just being left alone."[7] This observation is quite correct and would suggest that agencies identify their paper cases and terminate supervision, or if that is not possible, place them in caseloads where no contact is required (often called case bank or administrative caseloads). It is logical to assume that fully 25 percent of all probation and parole cases require no supervision and could be handled in this manner. Such action would free up the officer's time to better concentrate on cases requiring personal attention. All too often clients, whose needs and risk of reoffending are negligible, are kept on caseloads that require regular contact and frequent case entries.

Moreover, we have known this for quite some time as much the same conclusion was reported in 1975 by Lawrence Bennett and Max Ziegler. In a largely overlooked national research project, they clearly demonstrated that continuing to keep well-adjusted parolees on supervision for more than one year was unnecessary. This is so because those completing their first year on parole with little difficulty tended to have a nine out of ten chance of satisfactorily completing the second and third years of parole also without serious difficulty. Bennett and Ziegler concluded that ". . . if paroling authorities would adopt a policy of discharge at the end of one year of arrest-free parole, a considerable amount of resources could be available for reallocation in areas of the criminal justice system where there has been a chronic need for money and manpower."[8]

Many jurisdictions have heeded such advice in the years since this was written, limiting the length of parole or postprison supervision. But perhaps more can be done. Policies that encourage wholesale early termination will have to overcome line officer unwillingness to give up their easy cases, and the traditional opposition of judges and parole boards to losing jurisdiction over offenders. However, the crush of new cases may force such action. Already there are signs that many departments, faced with budget problems, have implemented programs designed to improve case management and allocation of resources.

The best known of these programs is Case Management Classification (CMC) discussed in Chapter Ten. According to its advocates, CMC has significantly improved the delivery of supervision services (while making some minor impact on recidivism) in more than one hundred jurisdictions, representing 25 percent of probation and parole agencies throughout the United States.[9] The trend toward improving case management through differential supervision classification is arguably one of the most positive developments in probation and parole. Tighter agency budgets will fuel continued expansion and refinement of this concept in the twenty-first century, as well as an increase in public involvement.

Public Involvement

The public will become more involved in probation and parole throughout the twenty-first century. Although correctional officials have long maintained that a more informed citizenry would be supportive of probation and parole, an increasing public presence will not necessarily achieve that end. Unfortunately, much of the public involvement will result from unpleasant incidents. Legal suits against probation and parole personnel may continue to escalate. In addition, communities will attempt to banish probationers and parolees from their midst.

The trend toward more litigation will result from court rulings favorable to plaintiffs who claim they have been injured by the acts of correctional officials. Litigation insurance and indemnification will become important issues for all personnel in the field. Individual officers will more carefully examine their potential liability before taking controversial actions. Such considerations could lead to overcautious inaction or excessive concern with justifying one's actions. As the public and attorneys become aware of litigation possibilities, the actions of probation and parole personnel will be the subject of continued scrutiny. However, in these instances, the goal is not to suggest improvement but to expose actions that can be brought to court. Supreme Court decisions and other legal rulings cannot be predicted precisely, but the trend is definitely leaning toward more litigation and increased liability. Probation and parole officers and agencies are increasingly aware that they can be sued.

In the future there will be more incidents in which community leaders severely oppose the release of notorious offenders into their neighborhoods. Probationers and parolees who have committed heinous crimes will increasingly be identified and hounded out of town by irate citizens. The case of convicted rapist Larry Singleton was the catalyst for a number of such vigilant actions. Singleton was first released on parole after serving eight years for the kidnap, rape, and attempted murder (he hacked off the victim's forearms and left her to die) of a teenage hitchhiker.[10] When parole officers were unable to find a town that would accept him, Singleton lived in a trailer on the grounds of San Quentin Prison. Parole officials at the time admitted they could not guarantee his safety in any other setting. When Singleton was nearing parole release, communities where he supposedly wanted to reside rejected the idea and formed committees to keep him out.

The publicity surrounding the Singleton case was dramatic. Throughout the United States, local communities are questioning the presence of convicted murderers, rapists, and pedophiles in their neighborhoods and are seeking avenues to expel them as well as developing plans to keep out notorious criminals in the future. In several states, bills have been introduced to bar the release of paroled prisoners to the counties in which they had most recently lived. Even though the legality of such actions may be questionable, it seems clear that the public is determined to be heard on this matter. No longer can the release of offenders into the community be assured. The negative affect of notorious cases that are featured in the media will set back the cause of community corrections. Instead of working to integrate offenders, many communities will concentrate on trying to expel them.

However, not all the news is bad. For example, some community corrections departments are establishing tax exempt 501(c) 3 nonprofit organizations so community members may make charitable contributions to favored programs. Furthermore, with the continuing importance and rise of restorative and community justice programs throughout the United States, more and more citizens will become involved in probation and parole, and criminal justice generally. The guiding principles behind restorative and community justice programs all directly or indirectly lead to more public involvement (see Chapter Ten). Restorative justice programs start with the idea that crime is an offense against human relationships and, therefore, the programs must ensure the participation of all affected parties. Offenders are required to participate in restorative justice programs; they must work with others to make things right. And finally, restorative justice programs seek to heal the victims of crime and put right the wrongs created by crime. This is an inclusive, participatory process that maximizes participation and communication. It is clear that this entire process involves the community in ways the current justice system often does not. Although we have a long way to go in the paradigm shift required to a fully restorative justice system, and in fact we may never fully get there, the many jurisdictions that have embraced and implemented these programs during the past twenty years, and the continuing movement in this direction, suggests that it is a movement that will continue to grow and will continue to get the public more involved. This is not necessarily the case for intensive supervision programs.

Refining Intensive Supervision

Even though intensive supervision programs currently are very popular and will continue to be so for the next several years, they will soon be less emphasized by probation and parole departments. Intensive supervision programs will continue to function as small specialized units, but not as major agency undertakings, focusing instead on those offenders who will benefit most from these programs. The refinement of intensive supervision programs comes from (1) their failure to significantly reduce recidivism and (2) the inability of line officers to maintain supervision standards.

Whereas early recidivism figures from Georgia and other programs were promising, most researchers now agree that intensive supervision programs have about the same, or even somewhat higher, recidivism rates as traditional probation (see Chapter Ten). Even the prototypical ISP, developed by Latessa and his colleagues and reviewed in Chapter Ten, did not reduce recidivism. In their effort to sell intensive supervision, many departments have promised to reduce recidivism. Because this is unlikely to occur to any significant degree, the ensuing disappointment will restrict the growth of ISPs.

The advocates of ISP often talk of rigorous supervision standards that require frequent face-to-face contacts (for example, five times per week) between officer and offender. In actual practice, such contacts are not occurring.[11] Probation and parole officers simply do not have the time to see all their clients (even with reduced caseloads) on a frequent basis. Moreover, after a few weeks of supervision there is not much to say and the quality of their contacts deteriorates considerably. The levels of intrusiveness required by many ISPs are unrealistic and in some situations counterproductive—the higher recidivism rates are very much tied to increased supervision leading to more technical violations. John Rosecrance was involved in experimental intensive supervision programs and found, as did his colleagues, that in many cases a supervising officer had to back off from overcontacting offenders, regardless of official policies, and further that long-term surveillance of seemingly compliant offenders invariably is relaxed. John Whitehead and Edward Latessa demonstrated that ISP officers follow similar tactics.[12] In actual practice, the levels of supervision intensity and service delivery are generally far lower than those advertised by program organizers. When this becomes known, the legitimacy of such programs will be questioned. However, probation and parole agencies have an alternative device, one that will not grow weary of meaningless interactions, knock off early, or be unavailable at odd hours. This device will be electronic.

Electronic Surveillance and Shock Incarceration

Electronic surveillance and shock incarceration programs have become established programs in most probation and parole agencies. The expansion of electronic monitoring resulted from improved technology, public acceptance of its surveillance component, and increasing middle-class participation. Shock incarceration will be given a boost by widely held perceptions that prison life should be harder and that inmates be more productive.

Dick Joranby, public defender in Florida's Palm Beach County, the location of the first project to test electronic monitoring, commented that the program is "transforming the future of corrections" because "anytime we can find an alternative to incarceration we win."[13] The makers of electronic devices are continually improving their technical capabilities, and now have most of the computer glitches corrected. They have developed amazing and perhaps frightening monitoring capabilities, such as Global Positioning Systems, which make constant surveillance a reality. Prison systems also will adopt some electronic devices in order to control unruly inmates.

Even though civil libertarians will continue to question electronic monitoring as an unwarranted, unethical, and illegal intrusion on individual privacy, their criticism could be largely overlooked in the rush to institute more electronic programs. The allure of twenty-four-hour monitoring will continue to find a receptive audience among a crime-weary public. They will be convinced easily that around-the-clock surveillance can better guarantee compliance with tough community release provisions. The anticipated failure of intensive supervision officers to keep up with required personal contacts will highlight the need for more vigilant procedures (such as those promised by electronic monitoring). As electronic monitoring increases, so too will be the problem of violation. Obviously, not all violations of the 150-feet rule (from your home) will warrant revocation, but precisely how much leeway the offender is given and how much discretion is accorded the supervision officer are thorny problems with no easy answer.

Some of the most ardent supporters of electronic monitoring are middle-class offenders who much prefer electronic surveillance at home (no matter how intrusive) to incarceration in jail. With the increasing passage of so called slammer laws (mandating a certain period of incarceration on conviction), middle-class offenders who traditionally paid fines or were placed on straight probation will have to spend some time in jail. This is especially true for drunken driving offenders who, in most states, now serve some time in custody. Middle-class defendants are often prime candidates for electronic surveillance because they may have low recidivism rates, and they can pay the necessary service fees. In this manner, electronic program organizers can demonstrate a system that diverts offenders from jail, demonstrates low recidivism rates, pays for itself, and whose participants eagerly volunteer. Much the same way that an influx of drug-offending college students into the criminal justice system in the 1960s stimulated the development of diversion programs, so too will today's middle-class offenders, seeking to be diverted from mandatory jail sentences, increase the implementation of electronic monitoring programs.

In a 1987 public opinion study, the Edna McConnel Clark Foundation concluded that most Americans feel that prisons are too soft and that inmates should be forced to do hard physical labor.[14] More recently, these attitudes have changed somewhat, particularly for nonviolent offenders. Three polls released in 2002 confirm a change in public opinion away from punitive punishment and toward an approach that balances punishment and treatment.[15] Many Americans believe that military training for young offenders will help prepare them for adult life by instilling the discipline to resist the temptations of criminality. They are now beginning to believe, and research results confirm this, that a combination of military discipline *and* treatment is more effective than the discipline alone. Such balanced shock incarceration programs have tapped a rich vein of public support that is not likely to be withdrawn. Funding for such programs (that usually involve probation and parole after incarceration) seems assured. Shock incarceration will continue to occupy an established niche in twenty-first-century probation and parole. Although electronic monitoring and shock incarceration are widely supported, there is still a question as to how effective they are in the field. Research is needed to clarify their actual impact on offender behavior.

Need for Research

After analyzing criminal justice for more than two years, the 1967 president's crime commission report found a "shocking lack of empirical data." The commission concluded: "The greatest need is the need to know."[16] Notwithstanding some important research developments, such as the founding of the National Institute of Justice to serve as a coordinator for criminal justice studies, the "need to know" remains a major concern and will be so for the foreseeable future. The new intermediate sanctions (house arrest, intensive supervision and shock incarceration, etc.) need to be carefully and continually evaluated. It can be assumed that not all these approaches will work equally well with all offenders. Probation and parole agencies need to know not only what works but also with whom it works best. Joan Petersilia, while conducting a National Institute of Justice project, indicated the "central issue for justice research is that of identifying offender subgroups for whom one type of treatment or sanction is more appropriate than another."[17] Although there is consensus that research is needed and appropriate, there are some barriers to its effective use. For one, many program developers are searching for a panacea, not for an objective appraisal, and for another, the world of academic research is far different from that of the street-level officer.

In order to keep new probation and parole programs funded and operating, organizers must demonstrate some positive findings, preferably a reduction in recidivism. They often do not have the leisure of conducting comprehensive research over long periods of time; they must justify program expenditures to skeptical lawmakers. In this climate of accountability, it is not unreasonable to accentuate immediate positive findings and to ignore possible long-term difficulties. Additionally, it is hard to explain that subgroups of offenders each react differently to the programs. Consequently, there is a tendency to claim that a single approach is effective for all or most offenders.

Such panaceas, by offering the possibility that things will improve, serve to energize correctional programs and stimulate enthusiastic support. Independent researchers, with no vested interest in a successful outcome, often must burst the bubble of highly acclaimed programs. Todd Clear, in a National Institute of Justice article, observed "The concept of the interaction effect—that types of treatment are effective for some types of offenders and not for others, and that no treatment is effective for everybody—is one of the most widely documented concepts in the field of correctional rehabilitation."[18] This is a message that many administrators do not want to receive or to make public. Because researchers are often the bearers of bad or confusing tidings, they are not fully supported by many practitioners.

Research efforts, no matter how well done or authenticated, rarely make it down to the officer level. Most POs do not read academic journals, where research activities are typically published, and generally dismiss the efforts of researchers as being irrelevant to their everyday activities. Even though forward-looking administrators support research, it is difficult for the results of that research to be meaningfully implemented, but there have been some notable exceptions. For example, findings from the Vera Institute of Justice's Manhattan Bail Project were influential in the development of release on own recognizance (ROR) programs; research into parole recidivism by Donald Gottfredson and others was eventually incorporated into the salient factor score that is routinely used to make release decisions; research by the Wisconsin Department of Corrections developed a risk and needs scale that is used by many probation and parole departments; and the work of Gendreau and his colleagues has led to some important developments in what constitutes effective interventions. Notwithstanding the significance of these, line officers remain unaffected by the vast majority of research efforts. Much of this can be explained by the different perspectives of practitioners and academics.

Jack Davis, a line officer and a Ph.D. with extensive research experience, graphically describes the different worlds occupied by working probation officers and academic researchers:[19]

- In the academic world, the emphasis is on empirical evidence, and no attempt is made to judge whether actions and decisions are right or wrong.
- In the working world of probation, actions or decisions are judged as right or wrong.
- Academics simply report on their research findings, and if they evaluate certain programs, the emphasis is on objective data, facts, and norms.
- In probation offices, the emphasis is on subjective meanings of right or wrong.
- In the academic world, standards of "good" and "bad" conform to objective criteria. The term *good* is applied universally to something that is factually correct and conforms to theory and empirical research.
- In the practical world of probation, standards of "good" and "bad" are subjective and can vary from office to office, although very often probation officers emphasize the same standards.
- Academics are interested in trends and generalizations, and they probably think much of probation work is trivial.
- Probation officers believe that their work is essential for the maintenance of the system.

Davis continues by stating that the academic world would most likely say that it takes little skill to write a two-page report or to do the job of a PO, and that many probation reports would not conform to academic standards because they are subjective, full of value judgments, and do not conform to knowledge in criminal justice. However, ". . . in the practical world of probation, this is the crux of our happiness or misery at work."

Ultimately, the world of probation is not academically oriented. The immediate goals of probation are observance of guidelines in manuals, obeying orders, listening to supervisors and higher officials even though they may disagree, and processing cases on time. In the final analysis, the goal of the PO is to handle the offender, and Davis argues that it would be a major task to reorganize the practical world of probation to the world of academia. In fact, they are two different worlds and it is probably neither necessary nor desirable to combine them. That is, no one can prove for certain that the world of academia will better serve the practical world of probation. For example, it may be dysfunctional to the goals of probation to tell a new probationer that he or she is being punished as well as being rehabilitated. Alternatively, it may be dysfunctional to ask probation officers to handle excessive caseloads because researchers have found that such caseloads do not affect outcomes. Davis concludes with the statement that he believes ". . . that academics will have to stay in their world and practitioners in their world at this time."[20]

Although it may be possible for some academic researchers to bridge the gap between college campus and probation office, in most cases research efforts will not have much impact on field operations. This is unfortunate and hopefully more departments will see the need for staff involvement in all levels of research and program implementation. However, it remains very difficult for the worlds of academia and corrections to meaningfully interact. The readers of this book, as the future members of probation and parole staffs, can change this by bringing the classroom to the field and vice versa. Both perspectives are vitally important and need to be shared. One of the areas, noted previously, where research has made a difference is that of treatment or rehabilitation.

The Comeback of Rehabilitation

Several times in this book the demise of rehabilitation has been proclaimed. However, to paraphrase the words of Mark Twain, reports of its death may be premature. Not all academicians or practitioners have completely abandoned the concept that offenders can be rehabilitated and that it should be the job of probation and parole officers to do it. Some, after a temporary flirtation with a justice model (which stresses evenhandedness in sentencing but downplays the possibility of rehabilitation), have surfaced again as advocates of rehabilitation. Several probation departments are bucking the trend toward implementing punitive supervision regimens and instead are offering programs that service rather than monitor. Most of these programs offer or require treatment for certain types of offenders, usually sex, or alcohol or drug, offenders. In fact, strong evidence of the return of rehabilitation is found in California where, in November 2000, voters passed Proposition 36. This proposition, implemented in July 2001, requires that nonviolent drug offenders be placed in drug treatment and rehabilitation programs, rather than being incarcerated. These offenders are placed on formal probation and are supervised at home, work, or in treatment by probation officers. Although the current movement toward rehabilitation may remain tentative, it will continue to gain considerable momentum and may rival the control model for philosophical and practical dominance.

In 1982, Francis Cullen and Karen Gilbert chronicled the problematic aspects of following punishment-oriented doctrines and asked criminal justice researchers and practitioners to "reaffirm rehabilitation."[21] Although at the time their work was hailed as an important contribution, it did not bring about the desired result because most agencies proceeded to implement control models. There are indications, however, that some in the field are willing to stand up for rehabilitation. In 1987, Paul Gendreau and Robert Ross, in a comprehensive review of the current offender rehabilitation literature, discovered that a surprising number of assistance-oriented programs were being undertaken. They indicated that although a "criminal justice virus of negativitis" had infected many of their academic colleagues, rehabilitation efforts were succeeding in a variety of probation and parole settings, and further that "the principles underlying effective rehabilitation generalize across too many intervention strategies and offender samples to be dismissed as trivial."[22] Gendreau and Ross believe that rehabilitation advocates should speak out and forcefully present their case to government and private funding agencies, and if this is done in an appropriate manner, their agenda will be seriously considered. This work was, of course, followed up by the groundbreaking work by Andrews, Gendreau, and their colleagues that led to the development of the "principles of effective intervention."[23]

The probation department in Montgomery County (Dayton, Ohio) is one of those agencies that has heard the rehabilitation message and is convinced. They are unabashedly providing a wide range of assistance programs to their clients. Probation administrators are convinced that rehabilitation should be an important goal of supervision. Toward that end, they offer an impressive array of services, designed to meet the probationers' needs. Montgomery County has allocated a good portion of their staff to providing specialized services, such as drug counseling, job placement, and mental health treatment for offenders. In addition they operate a twenty-four-hour emergency service unit and an intensive supervision branch that emphasizes assistance and community brokering rather than surveillance and control. They also maintain an inventory of community resources and support the development of local outreach services to offenders.[24]

The Montgomery County probation officials are active in professional organizations, such as the American Correctional Association, and are willing spokespersons for the rehabilitation concept. They will find an increasingly responsive audience who eventually will come to praise rehabilitation rather than to bury it. Such a possibility was suggested by a panel of researchers led by Susan Martin in 1981 when they argued that the promise of rehabilitation is so convincing that every effort should be made to try to realize that promise before it is discarded. In short, Martin and colleagues believed that U.S. society cannot avoid the problem of how to deal with criminal offenders, that we must avoid simplistic solutions and instead ". . . systematically develop, implement, test and evaluate a variety of intervention programs in the search for a more humane and effective correctional policy."[25]

In 2000, Francis Cullen and Paul Gendreau also made an argument for rehabilitation, one based on the idea that there is no evidence that punitive correctional programs either produce positive gains for offenders (e.g., institutional adjustment, development of human capital) or reduce recidivism. Rather, our "best bet" to reduce recidivism and improve the lives and behaviors of those who move through the correctional system is to "involve them in rehabilitation programs that have therapeutic integrity." Moreover, Cullen and Gendreau argued that this is not simply a matter of "doing good" for offenders, but it is a matter of public safety as well. That is, rehabilitating offenders may be an essential method of reducing recidivism and avoiding further victimizing citizens. Failing to practice treatment approaches that are known to be effective is the same as abandoning those who otherwise would be victimized.[26]

Even though a large percentage of the public continues to advocate for long prison sentences, this number has gone down in recent years and a high percentage also supports rehabilitating offenders.[27] In fact, three public opinion polls released in 2002 found considerable public sentiment that rehabilitation, through the use of probation, parole, and other community alternatives, should be a major correctional goal.[28] These contradictory trends—support for punishment and for rehabilitation—will complicate the occupational lives of future probation and parole officers.

Conflicting Goals

As probation and parole agencies move through the next decades, they will be buffeted by conflicting goals and competing ideologies. Although correctional leaders continue to call for an unambiguous mission with definitive responsibilities, the nature of probation and parole work makes such an achievement unlikely. Attempting to change human behavior, by whatever means, is a complex endeavor, not easily subsumed into one all-purpose modality. The parameters of surveillance and treatment, reintegration and intrusiveness, inevitably blur during the supervision process. The PO's dilemma (whether to emphasize control or assistance) and the discretionary use of authority are issues with no pat answers. Furthermore, POs are going to face complex situations that cannot be resolved by following guidelines, however precisely prescribed.

If the anticipated rebirth of rehabilitation occurs, there will be conflicting philosophies vying for dominance. The advocates of offender control, firmly believing in the "rightness" of their position, will not easily relinquish their current influence. Probation and parole will become the battleground on which rehabilitation and punishment philosophies are pitted. At times there may well be disputes within departments over whether to stress assistance or control. During the mid-1970s John Rosecrance witnessed a similar unsettling process when rehabilitation was being abandoned for more punitive approaches. These competing philosophical models will be influenced by public and legislative trends that cannot be fully anticipated, except that they probably will not be definitive or easily identified at the time.

Some of the conflict and ambiguity could be avoided if probation and parole were fully accepted as a process of mitigation. However, correctional professionals are unwilling to accept the possibility that probation and parole are essentially a nonsanction, in the words of the first probation officer John Augustus: "a side of mercy in opposition to strict, untempered legality."[29] Your authors agree with Richard Gray that probation and parole at their root are "getting off" and further, only ". . . when probation [and parole] is understood as the systematic extension, supervision, and evaluation of an essentially unwarranted opportunity for self improvement, will the much vaunted law enforcement/social work dichotomy be finally laid to rest in a conceptual framework broad enough to provide both necessary parts of the task."[30]

Although probation and parole work is confusing, contradictory, and beset with organizational problems typical of bureaucratic employment, it is also rewarding and self-fulfilling. Individual POs and administrators can make a real difference in the lives of their clients. Twenty-first-century officers will be sustained by witnessing the positive changes that often occur in their clients, changes that they helped bring about. Although there is a PO's dilemma, there is also a PO's reward—clients who often, despite great odds, "make it."

In summary we are optimistic about the future of community corrections. Although there is trouble and contention in the field, there is also firm determination that things can be improved, that problems can be addressed. Many jurisdictions continue to exhibit vitality and enthusiasm, belying the notion that probation and parole agencies have been rendered impotent by financial, philosophical, and organizational difficulty. For all their problems, they remain vital components in the criminal justice system. Returning to the Sheldon Glueck analogy, probation and parole are alive and well, and with proper care they may yet bloom.

Questions for Discussion and Review

1. In what ways can probation and parole be seen as the mitigation of punishment?

2. List and briefly discuss the eight trends that will be particularly relevant to probation and parole in the upcoming years?

3. What are the promises and what are the pitfalls awaiting probation and parole in the next five years? Ten? Twenty?

Relevant Internet Sites

California Probation Services Task Force, a group assigned to assess programs, services, organizational structures, and funding related to probation services: www2.courtinfo.ca. gov/probation/index.htm

Center for Juvenile and Criminal Justice, a private nonprofit organization whose mission is to reduce the reliance on incarceration as a solution to social problems: www.cjcj.org/about/index.php

Open Society Institute's Criminal Justice Initiative, an organization whose goal is to promote sensible and fair criminal justice policies and practices, and to redirect resources away from prisons and toward effective crime prevention and rehabilitation programs: www.soros.org/crime

Notes

1. Quoted in Alan Harland and Philip Harris, "Developing and Implementing Alternatives to Incarceration: A Problem of Planned Change in Criminal Justice," *University of Illinois Law Review* (1984): 347.

2. Alexander Smith, Harriet Pollack, and E. Warren Benton, "Sentencing Problems: A Pragmatic View," *Federal Probation* 51 (September, 1987): 70.

3. Justice Policy Institute, "States Reduce Incarceration, Change Sentencing Laws to Address Fiscal Crises." Retrieved January 7, 2003, from <www.justicepolicy.org/cutting2/ntlstatespending.pdf>

4. Joan Petersilia and Elizabeth Piper Deschenes, "Perceptions of Punishment: Inmates and Staff Rank the Severity of Prison versus Intermediate Sanctions," *The Prison Journal* 74 (1994): 306–328.

5. Joan Petersilia, Susan Turner, James Kahan, and Joyce Peterson, *Granting Felons Probation: Public Risks and Alternatives* (Santa Monica: Rand Corporation, 1985) 9.

6. Quoted in Petersilia et al. 9.

7. Robert Cushman, "Probation in the 1980's: A Public Administration Viewpoint," in *Probation and Justice: Reconsideration of Mission*, eds. Patrick McAnany, Doug Thomson, and David Fogel (Cambridge, MA: Oelgeschlager, Gunn and Hain, 1984) 332

8. Lawrence Bennett and Max Ziegler, "Early Discharge: A Suggested Approach to Increased Efficiency in Parole," *Federal Probation* 39 (September, 1975): 30.

9. Patricia M. Harris, Raymond Gingerich, and Tiffany A. Whittaker, "The 'Effectiveness' of Differential Supervision," American Society of Criminology Annual Meetings, San Francisco, CA (November 14–18, 2000).

10. "Singleton Case Spurs Reform in California Parole Law," *Corrections Digest* 10 (June, 1987): 9.

11. Edward Latessa, "The Effectiveness of Intensive Supervision with High Risk Probationers," in *Intermediate Punishments: Intensive Supervision, Home Confinement and Electronic Surveillance*, ed. Belinda McCarthy (Monsey, NY: Willow Tree Press, 1987) 109.

12. Latessa; also see John Whitehead and Charles Lindquist, "Intensive Supervision: Office Perspective," in *Intermediate Punishments: Intensive Supervision Home Confinement and Electronic Surveillance*, ed. Belinda McCarthy (Monsey, NY: Willow Tree Press, 1987).

13. Dee Reid, "High-Tech House Arrest," *Technology Review* 13 (July, 1986): 13–14.

14. John Doble, "The Public Agenda Foundation," *Crime and Punishment: The Public View* (New York: Edna McConnel Clark Foundation, 1987) 34.

15. Justice Policy Institute 2.

16. President's Commission on Law Enforcement and Criminal Justice, *The Challenge of Crime in a Free Society* (Washington, DC: U.S. Government Printing Office, 1967) 273.

17. Joan Petersilia, *The Influence of Criminal Justice Research* (Santa Monica: Rand Corporation, 1987) 4.

18. Todd Clear, "Statistical Prediction in Corrections," *Research in Corrections* 1 (March, 1988): 25.

19. Jack Davis, "Academic and Practical Aspects of Probation: A Comparison," *Federal Probation* 47 (December, 1983): 10.

20. Davis 10.

21. Francis Cullen and Karen Gilbert, *Reaffirming Rehabilitation* (Cincinnati, OH: Anderson, 1982).

22. Paul Gendreau and Robert Ross, "Revivification of Rehabilitation: Evidence from the 1980s," *Justice Quarterly* 4 (September, 1987): 395.

23. D. Andrews, L. Zinger, R. D. Hoge, J. Bonta, P. Gendreau, and F. T. Cullen, "Does Correctional Treatment Work? A Clinically Relevant and Psychologically Informed Meta-Analysis," *Criminology* 28 (1990): 369–404.

24. Bruce Gibson, personal correspondence to John Rosecrance, 1987.

25. Susan Martin, Lee Sechrest, and Robin Redner, *Rehabilitation of Criminal Offenders: Directions for Research* (Washington, DC: National Academy of Sciences, 1981) 10.

26. Francis T. Cullen and Paul Gendreau, "Assessing Correctional Rehabilitation: Policy, Practice, and Prospects," *Criminal Justice 2000 Vol. 3*, ed. Julie

Horney (Washington, DC: National Institute of Justice, 2000): 109–175.

27. Justice Policy Institute 3.

28. Justice Policy Institute 3.

29. Quoted in Richard Gray, "Probation: An Exploration in Meaning," *Federal Probation* 50 (December, 1986): 28.

30. Gray 30.

Glossary

bail Money or surety provided by a defendant or others to guarantee a defendant's appearance in court for prosecution. Generally, dangerous defendants or those considered a flight risk are not eligible for bail.

banishment Medieval penal practice whereby convicted criminals were permanently "cast out" of their communities or villages, thereby escaping execution.

benefit of clergy A privilege granted clerics, nuns, and priests allowing them to have their criminal cases transferred from secular to ecclesiastic or bishops courts where the penalties were far less severe.

boot camps A type of shock incarceration where young, first-time offenders are placed into a rigid military-type facility designed to instill discipline, respect for authority, and self esteem; usually followed by conditional release in the community.

brokerage system The model of probation supervision involving identifying the needs of clients and referring them to the appropriate service agency in the community.

bureaucracy A type of organization based on formal rules and discipline, where authority is hierarchical and positions within the organization depend on technical expertise.

burnout A syndrome of emotional exhaustion and cynicism that occurs frequently among individuals who do "people work" of some kind.

Case Management Classification (CMC) A system of differential supervision whereby, through a risk and needs assessment, the system attempts to identify the proper level of supervision for probationers or parolees.

casework Probation or parole supervision model based on the idea of providing services that help probationers and parolees live productive, crime-free lives.

chronos Series of chronological entries logging and reporting each contact a PO has with an offender.

civil disabilities The rights lost as a result of criminal (usually felony) conviction. These may include the right to vote, to hold public office, and to be employed in certain occupations.

Client Management Classification (CMC) The differential supervision model developed by the state of Wisconsin and used by more than one hundred jurisdictions throughout the United States.

community service An alternative sanction whereby an offender is ordered to provide a certain number of hours (often between 40 and 1,000) of free services to the public, usually the city or county government or a charitable organization, as part of his or her sentence.

consolidated parole board Parole release decision-making body that is an agency within a state's department of corrections. Staff personnel and working guidelines are provided by the department of corrections.

curfew A type of home confinement that obliges the client to remain in his or her residence during a specific time period, often at night.

dangerous men An informal classification by parole officers of parolees who cannot be effectively controlled and who are, therefore, a threat to cause trouble.

day reporting centers (DRCs) Facilities that offenders report to on a daily basis, providing structure for the day, control of behavior, and opportunities for treatment and services.

deal case The type of sentence recommendation made by a PSI writer involving cases where a plea bargain was made.

determinate sentencing A sentencing structure whereby the court sentences an offender to a fixed amount of time, or within a narrow range of time, to be served in incarceration or in the community. The amount of time served is set by statute and must be served, minus any good time or meritorious good time earned.

differential supervision A type of intermediate sanction that uses a risk/needs assessment tool to classify probation and parole clients into appropriate supervision categories, from low risk to high risk.

discretion The authority of criminal justice officials to make decisions based on their judgment rather than established rules or laws.

discretionary parole The parole of an inmate from prison at the discretion of a parole board after the inmate has served a minimum of time in prison. The specific amount of time is generally set at sentencing and is statutorily mandated.

discretionary release Conditional release of an inmate by a parole board based on statutory or administrative eligibility.

diversion Formal or organized efforts to process offenders out of the traditional criminal justice system. Diversion programs almost always occur in the community and can occur anytime after a crime is discovered and before adjudication.

diversion case The type of sentence recommendation made by a PSI writer involving cases where the defendant is referred to diversion.

electronic monitoring A type of intermediate sanction that uses telemetry technology to monitor an offender's presence in a particular place where he or she is required to remain. Electronic monitoring is used in conjunction with intensive supervision and home confinement.

field contacts Probation or parole officer visits to a client's home or place of employment.

good time Number of days deducted from a sentence (per days or months served) for good behavior in prison (e.g., for every thirty days of good behavior, an inmate's sentence is reduced five days). The amount of good time is usually set by the legislature, but many still also allow the institution to grant good time.)

guided group interaction The counseling technique for offenders based on the assumption that a group can influence an individual's behavior and thinking, and by proper manipulation of this influence, offenders can be led to prosocial behavior. A leader guides and directs conversations among group members and puts guided group interaction into motion.

halfway houses Relatively small (often five to twenty-five beds) community residential facilities, often with a treatment component, designed to accommodate offenders who need more struc-

tured settings than traditional probation and parole provide.

heavy-duty case A label assigned to PSI cases indicating that the defendant will receive more severe penalties (jail or prison) in the recommendation because the offense, the offender, or the circumstances of the offense are deemed particularly serious.

home confinement A term used for three types of intermediate sanctions involving offenders confined to their homes under various conditions, including curfews, house arrest, and home detention.

home detention A type of home confinement in which offenders serve their sentences in their own homes, with or without electronic monitoring. Offenders normally have curfews and may not leave their residences except for employment, treatment, educational, or other approved purposes.

house arrest A type of home confinement where an offender is incarcerated in his or her home and where, with few exceptions—such as a medical emergency—the offender must remain in his or her residence day and night.

independent parole board Parole release decision-making body that is a separate department, with its own staff and command structure, from a state's department of corrections.

indeterminate sentence A method of sentencing that links the probability of committing new offenses with an offender's prison release date. Length of punishment is not based solely on the past offense but is determined, in large part, by an assessment of the offender's future behavior. Policies of indeterminate sentencing seek to ensure that, within limits, defendants will remain in custody only as long as they remain a danger to others.

individualized justice A rehabilitative penal philosophy that emphasizes the offender, not the offense.

initial interview The crucial first meeting between a PO and his or her client when the supervision plan, reporting schedule, and parole or probation conditions are discussed.

intensive supervision programs (ISP) A probation or parole program where the officer-to-offender ratio is low, frequent contacts with the PO are required, strict reporting requirements are enforced, and other conditions, such as regular drug tests and electronic monitoring, may be required.

intermediate sanctions Sanctions that exist along a continuum of criminal penalties somewhere between probation and incarceration. Examples of intermediate sanctions include community service, day fines, house arrest, and electronic monitoring.

Interstate Compact Agreement An agreement between states to transfer parolees or probationers from the supervision of one state to another.

Irish Plan Penal practice developed in Ireland by Sir Walter Crofton in 1854. The plan involved stages of institutional control, from solitary labor to release under supervision, with the higher levels earned by good conduct, hard work, and the accumulation of marks.

joint case The type of sentencing recommendation made by a PSI writer involving cases where the defendant is denied probation and the investigator recommends an appropriate prison sentence.

judicial reprieve Temporarily halting the execution or imposition of sentencing, allowing a defendant time to apply for a pardon or fulfill other obligations or tasks.

leadership A continuous process toward organizational prosperity, generating an environment that encourages creativity so that organizational goals and objectives are achieved in a cooperative and coordinated way.

lightweight case A label assigned to PSI cases indicating that the defendant will be accorded some leniency in the recommendation because the offense was minor, the offender had no prior criminal record, or the offense was relatively innocuous.

mandatory release The compulsory, conditional release of inmates from prison after serving their determinate sentence minus any good time or meritorious good time earned. The remainder of their original sentence is served under parole supervision.

Manhattan Bail Project Experiment that demonstrated that those too poor to make bail but with housing arrangements, family ties, and employment could safely be released before trial.

mark system In Maconochie's penal system, a system of credit for good behavior and hard work. Inmates could earn ten or more marks per day, use them to buy food and supplies, and save them to earn their early release—for each ten marks saved, a convict's prison term was shortened by one day.

max out The release of inmates from prison after they have served their maximum sentenced term.

medical model The approach to corrections that assumes the offender is physically, mentally, or socially "sick." Crime, therefore, is a symptom of a criminal's illness and a cry for help, requiring early and correct diagnosis followed by therapeutic intervention (treatment).

meritorious good time Number of days deducted from a sentence, beyond those allowed for good time, which inmates can earn by participating in various programs such as vocational training, work details, counseling, medical experiments, or educational classes.

mitigation Reduction of damages or of punishment.

paper men An informal classification by parole officers of parolees who are easy to control; those whom POs do not have to worry about but who remain, "on paper," on their caseloads.

parole A conditional release from a correctional institution prior to the completion of a sentence under the supervision of a parole agency to serve the remainder of a sentence in the community.

parole order The official document containing the conditions of parole, granting an inmate release from a correctional institution.

passive officer A probation and parole officer characterized by a low commitment to both control and assistance.

presentence investigation (PSI) An investigation of a criminal defendant to reveal factors relevant to sentencing, and pertaining to the background of the defendant and the nature of the crime committed.

presentence report A report prepared by a court's probation officer, after a person has been convicted of an offense, summarizing for the court the background information needed to determine the appropriate sentence.

pretrial release The official release of an accused person from criminal justice custody, for all or part of the time before or during prosecution, on the condition that he or she appear in court when required.

probation A sentence usually not involving confinement that places a convicted offender under the supervision, with conditions, of a probation officer or agent.

probation case with some jail time The type of sentencing recommendation made by a PSI writer involving cases where the defendant is recommended for probation with some jail time.

probation officer's dilemma The often mutually exclusive requirements of the probation officers job: to maintain surveillance over clients while at the same time helping (or treating) them.

protective officer A probation and parole officer characterized by a high commitment to both control and assistance.

punitive officer A probation and parole officer characterized by a high commitment to control and a low commitment to assistance.

reality therapy The counseling technique introduced by William Glasser, who argued that those who seek psychotherapy suffer from the inability to fulfill their basic needs: to be loved and to be respected. The therapist's role is to convince clients they must fulfill their needs in appropriate manners by helping them to acknowledge responsibility for their actions. Having accomplished this, clients can fulfill their needs within the framework of reality, the here and now.

recidivism The repetition of or return to criminality by previously convicted offenders, including re-arrest, reconviction, and reincarceration.

recognizance An early English and colonial American practice whereby a bond for the peace or for good behavior was placed by an offender, requiring the offender to comply with conditions set by the court and to appear in court at a later date to decide if the conditions of the bond had been met. If they were not met, the bond was forfeited to the king or to the court.

reentry The transition of inmates from prison to the community.

restitution An alternative sanction whereby the offender pays back the victim for the harm caused by the crime. Restitution can be made by monetary payments, by returning or replacing stolen or damaged property, or by carrying out direct services to the victim.

restorative justice A paradigm of justice that calls for involvement by the victim, the offender, and the community in a search for solutions to the crime problem, seeking to repair the harm done by the crime, and restore the offender to the community; also called *community justice* by some practitioners.

revocation The termination of probation or parole for cause, usually resulting in (re)incarceration.

Rule 32(c) Rule in the Federal Rules of Criminal Procedure, adopted by the Supreme Court, specifying that the probation department submit a presentence report in every case, unless the court directed otherwise.

salient factor score Scoring device developed and used by the U.S. Parole Commission to assess an applicant's probable success on parole.

sentencing guidelines Sentencing forms, usually designed as a matrix or grid containing crimes on one axis and criminal histories on the other, which guide a judge in determining sentence length. In most jurisdictions, the sentence given must fall within the range of months found at the intersection of crime and criminal history, unless mitigating or aggravating factors exist.

shock incarceration/boot camp Programs modeled after military basic training, intended to "shock" offenders into changing their behaviors by exposing them to regimented lifestyles, requiring extensive physical exertion and mental discipline. The focus is on learning accountability and responsibility.

straight probation case The type of sentencing recommendation made by a PSI writer involving cases where the defendant is recommended for probation only.

street-level bureaucrats Public service workers who interact directly with citizens in the course of their jobs and who have substantial discretion in the execution of their work.

supervision plan The plan developed by a parole officer that specifies what parolees should do to overcome problems (unemployment, alcoholism, drug abuse, or marital) that might interfere with law-abiding reintegration into the community.

systems analysis The review of the functional elements within the system in order to evaluate the effectiveness of the overall system.

theory X The belief by managers that assumes workers have an inherent dislike for work and will avoid exerting themselves when they can. Because humans dislike work, they must be coerced, controlled, or threatened with punishment to be motivated.

theory Y The belief by managers that assumes that work is as natural as play for most people and that workers will exert effort toward goals as long as they feel a commitment toward those objectives. Because humans can enjoy work, the average person can accept responsibility, and a model of authority based on coercion and fear is replaced with one based on collaboration and reason.

ticket-of-leave A precursor to parole, used first in Australia and later in Ireland, consisting of a license or permit giving a convict a conditional pardon, based on good behavior and hard work in prison, releasing the convict to live and work in the community, subject to continued good behavior and revocable if misconduct occurred.

tolling probation The temporary suspension of probation brought about because defendants are unavailable for court appearances (usually because of absconding). The probation is reinstated when the defendant appears in, or is brought to, court.

transactional analysis (TA) The counseling technique developed by Eric Berne as an understandable, sophisticated theory about people's thinking, feelings, and behavior, describing what happens when people interact. TA acknowledges the importance of early childhood development as the "script" that influences later behavior. Counselors help clients analyze their transactions with others so they can be aware of their ego state—child, adult, or parent. When clients can relate their behavior to a particular ego state, they can take action to alter the state and change their behavior.

transportation English practice, begun in 1597, involving the forced exile of convicted criminals who worked as galley hands on ships and later were sent to faraway lands or colonies as indentured servants.

truth-in-sentencing Federal legislation requiring that Part I violent offenders (those convicted of murder, nonnegligent manslaughter, rape, robbery, or aggravated assault) must serve not less than 85 percent of their sentence in prison before becoming eligible for release and in order for states to be eligible for an incentive grant program established in the 1994 Federal Crime Act.

typing the defendant The process occurring early in the sentencing recommendation process whereby presentence writers place defendants into categories or types of possible sentence recommendations based on the defendant's current offense and prior criminal record.

welfare officer A probation and parole officer characterized by a low commitment to control and a high commitment to assistance.

whistle-blowing Revealing wrongdoing within an organization to the public or to those in positions of authority.

Index